FOURTH EDITION

COMPARING THEORIES OF CHILD DEVELOPMENT

FOURTH EDITION

COMPARING
THEORIES OF
CHILD DEVELOPMENT

R. MURRAY THOMAS
UNIVERSITY OF CALIFORNIA, SANTA BARBARA
EMERITUS

BROOKS/COLE PUBLISHING COMPANY

I(T)P™ An International Thomson Publishing Company

Pacific Grove • Albany • Bonn • Boston • Cincinnati • Detroit • London • Madrid • Melbourne
Mexico City • New York • Paris • San Francisco • Singapore • Tokyo • Toronto • Washington

Sponsoring Editor: Jim Brace-Thompson
Marketing Team: Gay Meixel and Romy Fineroff
Editorial Assistant: Dorothy Kormos
Production Editor: Penelope Sky
Manuscript Editor: Catherine Cambron
Permissions Editor: May Clark
Interior Design: Vernon T. Boes

Interior Illustration: Nancy Warner and John Foster
Cover Design: Cheryl Carrington
Cover Photo: Sandra Eisner/Photonica
Art Editor: Kathy Joneson
Cover Printing: Phoenix Color Corporation
Printing and Binding: Quebecor/Fairfield

For more information, contact:

BROOKS/COLE PUBLISHING COMPANY
511 Forest Lodge Road
Pacific Grove, CA 93950
USA

International Thomson Publishing Europe
Berkshire House 168-173
High Holborn
London WC1V 7AA
England

Thomas Nelson Australia
102 Dodds Street
South Melbourne, 3205
Victoria, Australia

Nelson Canada
1120 Birchmount Road
Scarborough, Ontario
Canada M1K 5G4

International Thomson Editores
Campos Eliseos 385, Piso 7
Col. Polanco
11560 México D. F. México

International Thomson Publishing GmbH
Königswinterer Strasse 418
53227 Bonn
Germany

International Thomson Publishing Asia
221 Henderson Road
#05-10 Henderson Building
Singapore 0315

International Thomson Publishing Japan
Hirakawacho Kyowa Building, 3F
2-2-1 Hirakawacho
Chiyoda-ku, Tokyo 102
Japan

Printed in the United States of America

10   9   8   7   6   5   4   3   2   1

Library of Congress Cataloging-in-Publication Data

Thomas, R. Murray (Robert Murray)
    Comparing theories of child development / R. Murray Thomas. —4th
ed.
      p.   cm.
    Includes bibliographical references and indexes.
    ISBN 0-534-33903-4
    1. Child psychology. 2. Child development. I. Title.
BF721.T456 1995
155.4'01—dc20

95-15016
CIP

To Shirley

Contents

PART ONE

Standards of Comparison   1

Ways of analyzing likenesses and differences among theories

CHAPTER ONE

Theories, Models, Paradigms, and Such   3

The Difference Your Choice of Theory Can Make   5
The Word *Theory* and Other Terms   12
Good Theory, Bad Theory   16
Conclusion   26
For Further Reading   26

CHAPTER TWO

The Contents of Child Development Theories 28

Content Characteristics   28
Conclusion   47
For Further Reading   48

PART TWO

Sources of Theories   49

A search for the wellsprings of child development theories

CHAPTER THREE

Cultural Origins of Scientific Theories   53

Refining Descriptive Data   53

Introducing Alternative Perspectives 56
Systematizing Information 59
Refining Definitions 65
Improving Quantification 66
Extending Commonsense Insights 68
Replacing Dubious Explanations 69
Interpreting Puzzling Observations 69
Avoiding Troublesome Issues 70
Responding to Existing Theories 71
For Further Reading 71

CHAPTER FOUR

COMMONSENSE ATTRIBUTION THEORY 73

The Causes of Human Action 74
Talk about Children: Grist for Commonsense Psychology's Mill 75
Applying an Attribution Theory 76
The Development of People's Commonsense Theory 83
Implications of the Theory for the Treatment of Children 84
Children's Interpretations of Their Own Behavior 84
Privilege and Responsibility 85
Practical Applications 87
Naive Psychology: An Assessment 88
For Further Reading 93

PERSPECTIVE A

Distinguishing Normal from Abnormal Development 95

PART THREE

THE PSYCHOANALYTIC TRADITION 103

A search for developmental causes and cures of neuroses

CHAPTER FIVE

SIGMUND FREUD'S PSYCHOANALYSIS 105

Levels of Consciousness 106

The Psychic Apparatus   108
The Psychosexual Stages of Development   113
Two Facets of Development   120
Anna Freud's Psychoanalysis of Children   126
Practical Applications   128
Freudian Theory: An Assessment   129
For Further Reading   134

C H A P T E R   S I x

ERIKSON'S VARIATION ON FREUD'S THEME   136

Ego Identity and the Healthy Personality   136
The Epigenetic Principle   137
The Grid of Psychosocial Stages   138
Practical Applications   151
Erikson's Version of Psychoanalysis: An Assessment   151
For Further Reading   153

P E R S P E C T I V E   B

Identifying States of Consciousness   155

PART FOUR

BEHAVIORISM AND
SOCIAL LEARNING MODELS   167

*A search for the way principles of learning and social
contexts explain development*

C H A P T E R   S E V E N

SKINNER'S OPERANT CONDITIONING   171

The Nature of Operant Conditioning   171
Conditioned Reinforcement and Chaining   175
The Scope of Skinner's Theory   177
Heredity versus Environment   178
The Stages of Child Rearing   180
Bijou and Baer's Additions to Radical Behaviorism   184
Enhanced Behaviorism   187
Practical Applications   190

Skinner's Operant Conditioning: An Assessment   191
For Further Reading   194

CHAPTER EIGHT

SOCIAL LEARNING THEORY AND CONTEXTUALISM   196

Bandura's Conception of Social Learning or Social Cognition   196
Practical Applications of Bandura's Model   207
Bandura's Social Learning Theory: An Assessment   208
Rotter's Social Learning Views   210
The Nature of Contextualism   212
For Further Reading   219

PERSPECTIVE C

Judging the Appropriateness
of Research Models   221

PART FIVE

THE GROWTH OF THOUGHT AND LANGUAGE   229

*A search for patterns of development in children's
cognitive and verbal skills and for the mechanisms
that bring these patterns about*

CHAPTER NINE

PIAGET'S COGNITIVE DEVELOPMENT THEORY   231

Piaget's Clinical Method   231
Piaget's Conception of Knowledge   233
The Mechanisms of Development   236
Levels and Stages of Development   240
Four Concepts: A Closer Look   252
Educational Applications of the Theory   258
Piaget's Theory: An Assessment   264
For Further Reading   269

CHAPTER TEN

VYGOTSKY AND THE SOVIET TRADITION   270

Key Influences on Vygotsky's Theory   271

The Development of Thought and Language   278
Key Generalizations about Development   286
Central Concerns in Soviet Developmental Theory: 1920s–1980s   288
Practical Applications   289
Vygotsky's Theory: An Assessment   291
For Further Reading   293

P E R S P E C T I V E D

Estimating the Future of Stage Theories   **295**

PART SIX

COMPUTER ANALOGUES AND THE SELF   **311**

*A search for the way children gain skill in processing
information and for how a child's innermost self develops*

C H A P T E R   E L E V E N

INFORMATION-PROCESSING THEORIES   **313**

Classical Components of the Information-Processing System   314
Modes of Investigation   323
Modifications of Classical Theory   324
Information Processing and Development   332
Practical Applications   337
Information-Processing Theories: An Assessment   338
For Further Reading   341

C H A P T E R   T W E L V E

CONCEPTIONS OF THE SELF:
HUMANISTIC AND OTHERWISE   **342**

Defining the Self   342
The Humanistic Persuasion   343
Humanistic Theory: An Assessment   356
Other Conceptions of the Self   361
For Further Reading   366

PERSPECTIVE E
Speaking of Cause   367

PART SEVEN

ENVIRONMENTS, GENETIC PLANS,
AND THE BIOLOGICAL CHILD   375
*A search for patterns of environmental influence
and for the biological sources of development*

CHAPTER THIRTEEN
ECOLOGICAL PSYCHOLOGY   379
Backgrounds of Ecological Psychology   380
Bronfenbrenner's Ecological Theory   382
Practical Applications   389
Ecological Theory: An Assessment   390
For Further Reading   393

CHAPTER FOURTEEN
ETHOLOGY AND SOCIOBIOLOGY   394
A Foundation of Neo-Darwinism   395
Ethology's Place in the Study of Children   396
Relevant Propositions from Ethology   397
Fruitful Research Methods   404
Practical Applications and Research Challenges   407
Ethological Theory: An Assessment   408
For Further Reading   411

CHAPTER FIFTEEN
A BIO-ELECTROCHEMICAL MODEL   413
Level 1: The Unitary Child   415
Level 2: The Organic Child   418
Level 3: The Cellular Child   422
Level 4: The Molecular Child   426
Level 5: The Elemental/Atomic Child   429
Level 6: The Subatomic-Particle Child   432

The Bio-Electrochemical Model: An Assessment   433
For Further Reading   437

P E R S P E C T I V E F

Charting Trends of the Times

439

PART EIGHT

THEORY CENTERED IN VALUES: MORAL DEVELOPMENT

457

A search for the ways children's and youths' moral reasoning and moral behavior evolve

C H A P T E R S I X T E E N

KOHLBERG'S MODEL OF MORAL DEVELOPMENT

461

The Theory's Focus   462
Kohlberg's Research Methods   463
The Levels and Stages of Moral Growth   464
The Interaction of Nature and Nurture   466
The Three Characteristics of Stages   469
Practical Applications: Fashioning a Program of Moral Education   471
Kohlberg's Theory: An Assessment   473
For Further Reading   476

C H A P T E R S E V E N T E E N

AN INTEGRATED THEORY OF MORAL DEVELOPMENT

477

Problems with Existing Theories   477
Foundational Definitions and Assumptions   478
Prinicipal Features of the Model   478
Foundational Components   480
The Nature of Long-Term Memory   481
The Nature of Environments   488
Working Memory   491

Stages of Moral Development   492
An Integrated Moral Development Theory: An Assessment   493

PERSPECTIVE G

Depicting Theories in the Guise of Metaphors   497

REFERENCES   501
NAME INDEX   521
SUBJECT INDEX   528

PREFACE

As I suggested in the first three editions of this book, child development experts are dissatisfied people. They are not content with existing explanations of how a child grows up, so they search for better interpretations. For guidance, they set up goals that may be either stated or implied. The primary purpose of this book is to identify these goals and to describe the findings of more than two dozen theorists. A secondary purpose is to inspect a series of child development issues that bridge a variety of theories. Because its range is so broad, *Comparing Theories of Child Development, Fourth Edition* is suitable for use in many different courses, from introductory to graduate levels.

Like the earlier versions, this book serves the same purpose in the world of theories that a three-week guided tour of Europe has in the world of travel. I do not pretend to give a detailed, in-depth account of any one territory. Instead, I propose to (1) suggest profitable ways to compare theories (Chapters One, Two, and Three); (2) describe key aspects of various representative theories (Chapters Four through Seventeen); and (3) analyze a series of topics related to many theories (Perspectives A through G). The fourteen chapters that describe individual theories are organized by a seven-part structure, each part reflecting one or more of the theorist's key goals in improving our understanding of development.

The most obvious innovation is the addition of two new chapters, "Cultural Origins of Scientific Theories" (Chapter Three) and "A Bio-Electrochemical Model" (Chapter Fifteen). To make room for this material, chapters on Gesell and Havighurst have been dropped; the main thrust of their work is now described in Chapter Three. To further improve the present edition, I have expanded the criteria for judging the goodness of a theory, updated information about research related to many of the theories, and made minor additions to most of the chapters that treat specific theoretical positions.

There are many more interesting developmental theories than a single volume can accommodate. My choices reflect the following criteria:

1. *Has the theory been popular?* Have many people subscribed to it or at least been acquainted with it?
2. *Has the theory been influential?* Has it affected people's treatment of children or influenced the beliefs of other theorists?
3. *Is the theory representative of a class or family of theories?* Theories often fall into groups, with numerous similarities and differences among mem-

bers. I have chosen only a few variants (in some cases only one) to represent each class. I have been influenced not only by the representativeness of a theory but also by my own tastes, and thus I've included certain examples that I feel are more interesting than others.

Acknowledgments

A note of appreciation is due to my students and colleagues at the University of California, Santa Barbara. They have always been helpful in offering comments that have forced me to improve the clarity and accuracy of what I say and write. I also wish to thank the following reviewers: Jeanette R. Drews, University of Utah; Alice Honig, Syracuse University; Charles Nelson, University of Minnesota—Minneapolis; and Noreen Webber, Nova University.

In addition, I would like to express my gratitude to those who read earlier versions of the book and provided valuable suggestions for improving it: Armin Arndt, Eastern Washington University; Andrew Collins, University of Minnesota; Bernard S. Gorman; Michael Green, University of North Carolina, Charlotte; Billie Housego, University of British Columbia; Jane Ledingham, University of Ottawa; James Moran, Virginia Polytechnic Institute; Ronald Mullis, North Dakota State University; Richard Newman, State University of New York at Stony Brook; Samuel Snyder, North Carolina State University at Raleigh; Judy Todd and Eleanor Willemson, Santa Clara University; and Alastair Younger, University of Ottawa.

Finally, I appreciate the wisdom and diligence shown by members of the Brooks/Cole staff.

R. Murray Thomas

FOURTH EDITION

COMPARING THEORIES OF CHILD DEVELOPMENT

PART ONE

STANDARDS OF COMPARISON

*Ways of analyzing likenesses
and differences among theories*

Because this book compares theories of child development, it is reasonable to ask at the outset, compares theories against what standards? Or, compares them along what dimensions? The two chapters comprising Part One are designed to answer these questions.

Chapter One defines the way such terms as *facts, theory,* and *model* are used throughout the book. It also describes a variety of standards or criteria that people often use to distinguish "good theory" from "bad theory."

Chapter Two looks at theories in a different way. It reviews a range of topics or questions on which a child development theory may focus. These questions are intended as guides to identifying the contents of a theory—that is, as guides to the substantive focus of the theory.

Part One, then, suggests viewpoints from which the theories surveyed in Chapters Three through Seventeen can be analyzed at an introductory or basic level.

CHAPTER ONE

THEORIES, MODELS, PARADIGMS, AND SUCH

Many people—parents, teachers, college students—often say, "I don't want a lot of theorizing. I want to know what children are really like. It's the facts of child development I'm interested in."

For such people, "theorizing" means speculating about children in the quiet of a study, producing a kind of armchair philosophy that has little or nothing to do with the way children grow up in the real world. "Facts," they feel, are practical and useful. Facts show how children really develop and why they behave as they do. For these people a book on child development theories is of no value.

This kind of distinction between "fact" and "theory" is not the one intended in this book. I see the relationship between the two in a different way. I consider facts or data to be either discrete observations and measurements of children and their actions, or summaries of such observations and measurements. Here are three typical examples of discrete observations:

A first-grade teacher poured all of the water from a bowl into a tall drinking glass, then asked six-year-old Anne if the amount of water now in the glass was the same as the amount that had been in the bowl. Anne said there was now more in the glass.

The parents of thirteen-year-old Martin were upset because, they said, the boy acted "like a sissy." Martin did not like to play with other boys. He wore fancy rings and bracelets. His mother found him in her bedroom putting rouge on his lips and darkening his eyelids with her eye shadow. His father said, "Marty even walks like a girl."

One Friday afternoon in autumn, eighteen-year-old Jim was forced to stay after school to retake a test he had failed in chemistry class. As a result, he was late for practice with the high-school football team on which he played defensive tackle. That same afternoon Jim's sixteen-year-old sister, Kristen, was late for an after-school session of the school's prizewinning concert orchestra because she had been delayed by her duties as secretary of the Academic Honor Society. In the orchestra, Kristen was the leading violinist. Meanwhile, Jim's and Kristen's ten-year-old sister, Penny, was home recovering from a lung in-fection associated with the cystic fibrosis she had suffered throughout her life. Penny's mother used this opportunity to help Penny clear up her confusion about the meaning of negative numbers and "*x* is the unknown," which were topics in Penny's fifth-grade class's study of pre-algebra mathematics.

Facts or data can also be in the form of summaries of observations or measurements: the average height of twelve-year-old girls, a list of the reactions of five-year-olds when they first enter kindergarten, the percentage of sixteen-year-olds who have smoked marijuana.

If these are facts, then what is theory? There is no easy, definitive answer to this question; many different meanings for theory are found in writings on philosophy and science. For the purposes of this book, however, I have simplified matters by adopting one definition broad enough to encompass all the different authors included here: theory is *an explanation of how the facts fit together.* More precisely, theorizing about child development means the act of proposing (1) which facts are most important for understanding children and (2) what sorts of relationships among the facts are most significant for producing this understanding. Theory is what makes sense out of facts. Theory gives facts their meaning. Without theory, facts remain a clutter of disorganized specks on the canvas, unconnected spots that form no picture of how and why children grow up as they do.

Two important types of relationships typically found within theories are the *structural* and the *causal*. A view of structural relationships is provided by a theory's scheme for assigning facts to particular categories or classes so that the facts can conveniently be compared and contrasted. Such classification systems are often referred to as *taxonomies, typologies,* or *organizing schemes.* Perhaps the simplest and most familiar way of classifying children's development is by age periods—the prenatal stage (embryonic and fetal phases), the neonatal stage, infancy, childhood (early, middle, and late phases), and adolescence (early, middle, and late phases). Another traditional way to categorize children has been in terms of their tested mental abilities. Test scores result in each child's being assigned to one of an ascending series of levels—mentally retarded (idiot, imbecile, moron), below normal (or slow learner), normal, above normal, and gifted (or genius). Although most psychologists probably regard this particular mental-ability structure as outmoded—an unduly simplistic way to describe children's intellectual skills—the system's categories still appear to be widely used. As later chapters demonstrate, a variety of other classification schemes appear as significant features of the theories that are discussed.

Although structural schemes are useful for delineating ways in which children are alike and different, such schemes do nothing to explain why children develop as they do. Explanation is provided by a theory's version of causal relationships that are reflected in *if-then* and *unless-then* statements and descriptions of cause and effect.

> "If an expectant mother contracts rubella (German measles) during the first three months of pregnancy, then there is a 50 percent chance that the child she bears will suffer brain, ear, eye, or heart abnormalities."

"Unless children are rewarded for displaying generosity, they will not become generous."

"One cause of juvenile delinquency is parents' neglecting their children."

As explained in Chapter Two, the most common way theorists describe their propositions about cause is in terms of heredity and environment. Hereditary causes are assumed to be factors deriving from biological inheritance. Environmental causes are assumed to be influences on development that derive from the child's physical and social surroundings.

In summary, then, a book on theories of child development can serve as a practical guide to understanding children, for it describes the patterning of different beliefs about what children are like and how they should be treated.

THE DIFFERENCE YOUR CHOICE OF THEORY CAN MAKE

A theory of child development can be likened to a lens through which we view children and their growth. The theory filters out certain facts and gives a particular pattern to those it lets in. To illustrate the way such filtering operates, let's briefly consider how the stories of Anne, Martin, Jim, Kristen, and Penny presented in the preceding section might be interpreted from the viewpoints of four theories presented later. These interpretations are simplified, since you have not yet had a chance to inspect any of the theories in detail, but still illustrate the point that the theory chosen for interpreting facts about children determines the meaning assigned to those facts. When you have read further, you will recognize the complexities that the cases of our five illustrative children would involve if interpreted more completely.

The theorists whose lenses we will peer through are Piaget, Freud, Bandura, and proponents of a bio-electrochemical vision of development.

A Piagetian Viewpoint

For more than fifty years a Swiss child psychologist, Jean Piaget, collected facts about how children of different ages solved reasoning problems, expressed their dreams, made moral judgments, and carried out other mental activities. He proposed that a child's modes of thought form a series of stages of intellectual growth common to all children in all cultures. We might reasonably suggest, then, that Piagetians would interpret the cases of our five youngsters in terms of these stages.

For instance, we would expect an advocate of Piaget's theory to explain that Anne thought there was more water in the tall glass than in the shallow bowl because she had not yet reached the stage at which children understand conservation of volume. By *conservation* we mean that Anne does not yet recognize that the quantity of water remains the same (is conserved) even though the height and width of the two containers differ.

When we turn to Martin's effeminate behavior, we are on less secure ground in speculating about what a Piagetian would conclude, because Piaget focused little if any attention on matters of socially unconventional behavior. Piaget was more concerned with the thought processes of the typical or average child than with personal and social behavior that differed from a particular society's norms for sex-appropriate actions. However, Piaget did give a good deal of attention to children's moral judgments—what children considered right and wrong and how they supported such decisions. His studies led him to propose that such development involves two domains, the *heteronomous* and the *autonomous*. People operating from a heteronomous perspective accord unilateral respect for authorities (parents, teachers, the clergy, the police) and for the rules they prescribe. People operating from an autonomous perspective base their moral judgments on mutual regard among peers or equals and respect for the rules that guide their interaction. Whereas heteronomous morality requires obedience to authority and to rules produced by authority, autonomous morality is based on reciprocity and equality among peers. Piaget suggested that development in reasoning tended to progress from heteronomous morality to autonomous morality. Applying this perspective to the case of Martin, we might speculate that Martin has entered a stage of autonomous morality in which he considers other males who embrace his preferences in personal adornment to be his equals. These recently adopted peers, rather than his parents, provide the standards of moral behavior on which Martin can defend his behavior.

Next, consider Jim, the football player who was obliged to take a make-up test in chemistry. Among Piaget's mental-development stages, the most advanced level is that of formal operations, a period that most children begin to enter in early adolescence. This is the time when the young become properly equipped to grasp abstract concepts and hypothetical proposals. Although most adolescents reach the formal-operations period, not all achieve the same quality of formal-operations thought. Some become far more skilled than others at abstract reasoning. Thus, from a Piagetian viewpoint, Jim's difficulty in chemistry class might result from a limited command of formal operations—that is, from Jim's restricted ability to master such concepts as catalysts and compounds, monochlorides and molecular weights, vinyl polymers and valences. In contrast, Jim's sixteen-year-old sister, Kristen, appears well advanced in formal-operations thought, if her position in the Academic Honor Society is a good indicator of scholastic excellence.

Piagetian theory also has something to say about the younger sister's confusion over pre-algebra mathematics. At age ten, Penny seems near the end of the concrete-operations stage of Piaget's mental-growth hierarchy. During this concrete-operations period children can be expected to have trouble with such abstract notions as negative numbers and "x is the unknown." Penny is barely on the brink of entering the formal-operations period. To understand abstract concepts, she needs extra help, including concrete visual examples (such as a weather thermometer to illustrate negative numbers). Even with this help she is still likely to have difficulty applying the new concepts to situations other than ones she has been directly taught, because her skill of generalizing from one setting to another is not as highly developed as it will be when she is fully within the formal-operations period.

Let's turn now to a second theorist's perceptions of the same five cases.

A Freudian Viewpoint

Toward the end of the nineteenth century and the beginning of the twentieth, Sigmund Freud devised a theory of child development based on childhood recollections of adults he treated for neuroses in his Vienna, Austria, psychiatric practice. Freud, like Piaget, proposed that children develop through a series of stages. However, instead of concerning himself with children's reasoning skills, Freud focused on *psychosexual* development. He identified steps in personality growth as influenced by children's ways of satisfying sexual drives from one period of childhood to another.

For example, Freud theorized that between the ages of three and five, the typical child views the opposite-sex parent as a desirable love object that he or she wants to possess exclusively. In essence, the boy yearns to possess his mother, and the girl her father. However, the child recognizes that she or he has been bested in this competition by the same-sex parent. In other words, the boy's father has been the victor in the contest for the mother's sexual attention, and the girl's mother has been the victor in the competition for the father's love. To resolve this problem of yearning for the opposite-sex parent, the typical child in Freud's system seeks to acquire the characteristics of the victor. This means that the boy identifies with his father and seeks to adopt his father's traits, the traits of masculinity. In like fashion, the girl identifies with her mother and tries to behave in those feminine ways that apparently have made her mother successfully attractive. This process of identification, then, explains from a Freudian viewpoint why the typical boy develops characteristics that his society considers masculine and the typical girl develops characteristics considered feminine.

However, Freudians point out that sometimes the process of resolving the parental love conflict goes awry. The boy may not identify with his father's traits. Instead, he identifies with his mother's characteristics, or perhaps some other twist occurs in the normal process. Consequently the boy adopts feminine characteristics. From a Freudian perspective, we could reasonably assume that such a twist occurred in Martin's case. The boy apparently did not achieve a proper resolution of the conflict he faced in middle childhood, so that in early adolescence he is displaying sexually inappropriate behavior. To find out how this actually happened, Freudians would wish to gather information from the boy's unconscious mind— information collected by means of dream interpretation and by analyzing the free-flowing thoughts that Martin expresses while he is in a relaxed condition.

We can speculate that Freudians also would see Anne's reactions from a psychosexual viewpoint. Freudians—or at least some Freudians—would interpret Anne's reactions to the bowl and the tall glass in terms of sexual symbols. The meaning of the bowl-and-glass incident, they might say, lies in the unconscious portion of the girl's mind and relates to Anne's concerns about her own drives and the ways they are being satisfied or frustrated. In Freud's view, containers such as bowls and glasses symbolize female sex organs, whereas protruding, projectile-like objects symbolize the male. But exactly how such symbolization might fit into Anne's personality structure in the bowl-and-glass experiment would likely be unclear to psychoanalysts until they collected more information about the girl's feelings and thought processes. This information, intended to reveal the child's unconscious motives, might be gathered through the analyst's listening to Anne's comments while she played with dolls or recounted her fantasies.

According to Freudian theory, when an adolescent is prevented from directly expressing the sexual drive through copulation with a partner of the opposite sex, the resulting pent-up sexual energy may be expended in a substitute activity. This process of relieving sexual pressure through socially acceptable channels is *sublimation*. Thus, from a psychoanalytic perspective, Kristen's enthusiasm for the violin and Jim's for football might represent sublimation. Furthermore, Jim's dedication to such a violent sport as football could be viewed as an expression of the competition between the *life instinct* and the *death instinct*, which in Freudian theory are the basic forces motivating all human behavior.

A psychoanalytic view of Penny might hold that the child's attentive, nurturing mother serves as an influential model of what Penny would like to become. Thus, through a process of psychological identification, Penny is gradually adopting her mother's personality traits, especially those that the child's father has found most appealing.

A Social Learning Viewpoint

The popular version of social learning theory espoused by Albert Bandura offers a further vantage point from which to interpret development. Bandura is an American psychologist who has long pursued his academic career at Stanford University. Three precepts of his theoretical position are as follows:

1. Most of what children learn as they grow up is acquired from imitating what they see and hear other people do and say. In other words, most of a child's learning occurs in social situations rather than in isolation.
2. Children copy the behavior of people whose actions bring results that children value and wish to have for themselves.
3. The learnings that become a child's habitual ways of acting are those that are reinforced with rewards. Learnings that are not reinforced are dropped.

Although Bandura's theory is considerably more complex than these propositions suggest, the three should suffice for illustrating how the facts about our five young people can be analyzed from a social learning perspective.

We can account for Anne's reaction to the bowl and drinking glass demonstration by estimating that she gave the same answer she had heard other children give, and she believed those children had been commended for that response.

In the case of Martin, we would speculate that he had enjoyed the way women—and perhaps certain men—adorned themselves, gestured, and walked. Their actions just happened to be modes of behavior regarded as feminine in present-day Western culture. Because Martin admired what he had seen, he began modeling his lifestyle on that of his idols in the hope that he himself would thus become as appealing. Over the past few decades, increasing visibility of gay men and lesbians has made it easier for Martin to adopt a lifestyle that his parents find objectionable.

As for Jim, social learning theorists would not necessarily assume that he did poorly in chemistry because he lacked the necessary mental ability. Instead, they would pay more attention to his apparent motives. Jim likely recognized that football stars were held in higher esteem by his schoolmates than were students who excelled in chemistry. As a result, he concentrated on mastering the skills of a defensive tackle rather than on memorizing the contents of the chemistry text.

Because all children are required to attend school and engage in academic tasks, Kristen may have begun her study of school subjects mainly as an obligation. Then, as she performed well in the role of student, she would have been praised by her parents and teachers and admired by her classmates. These verbal rewards would be supplemented by other types of reinforcement—gifts from her parents, high grades on report cards, election to the Academic Honor Society. The accumulation of such symbols of approval would fuel Kristen's desire to pursue academic excellence with ever-increasing vigor. Her interest in the violin probably began when she delighted in the performance of violinists she saw television or in school concerts. She hoped to emulate these musical achievements by adding skill as a violinist to her other accomplishments.

The chance that Penny will succeed with her mathematics assignment is increased if her mother follows this pattern of instruction: she should (1) demonstrate by simple steps how each problem is solved (modeling the desired behavior); (2) have Penny try each step (gradualism); (3) compliment Penny for each part she performs correctly (positive reinforcement); (4) demonstrate once again any parts that were not performed correctly (remodeling the desired behavior); and (5) commend Penny when she performs those parts correctly (positive reinforcement).

A Bio-Electrochemical Viewpoint

Bio-electrochemical theory depicts the child as an organism—a living machine—that develops and acts by means of electrical and chemical exchanges within the body as well as electrochemical transactions between the body and the surrounding environment. Such analysis of development can take place at different levels of detail, from the broad organic level (heart, lungs, brain), through the cellular and molecular, to the minute elemental or atomic (oxygen, hydrogen, chlorine). Although it is far beyond the scope of this chapter to attempt an extensive biochemical analysis of our five young people, we can offer several examples to show how such an outlook differs from the other theoretical positions we have discussed in its view of development.

To explain Anne's faulty analysis of the bowl-and-glass experiment, we would propose that the patterning of linkages among her brain cells did not equip her to solve the perceptual puzzle she faced. She misjudged the capacity of the two water containers because she could not apply the principle of compensation. She failed to recognize that the quantity of poured water remained the same because the bowl's greater diameter compensated for its restricted height, while the drinking glass's greater height compensated for its restricted diameter. However, as time passes and the network of Anne's brain-cell linkages grows additionally complex, we can expect her interpretations of such phenomena to become increasingly logical. This growth in reasoning skill results from the interaction of two causal factors. First, a genetically controlled timing system that resides in the DNA (deoxyribonucleic acid) of all the body cells establishes the basic rate at which the network of brain cells matures and becomes ready for processing various kinds of stimuli. Second, daily experiences with physical and social surroundings determine which patterns of interconnections develop among the cells. As Anne's experiences accumulate, each item of knowledge and skill that she acquires becomes imprinted in her nervous system as a particular configuration of cell linkages.

Now for the case of Martin: One biochemical interpretation of his behavior would suggest that the combination of genes he inherited from his parents has caused his glandular system to excrete an inordinate proportion of the female sex hormone, estrogen, thereby predisposing Martin to adopt effeminate mannerisms. Or, as another option, instead of a malfunction in the clustering of genes, Martin's glandular system may have been turned awry by some other event that produced the same outcome, an oversupply of estrogen and a penchant for feminine ways. Or perhaps a minuscule cell cluster at the base of Martin's brain (the third interstitial nucleus of the anterior hypothalamus, or INAH3) is the size of the INAH3 in homosexual males whose brains have been analyzed. In gay males, that cluster is smaller (more the size of those cells in heterosexual women) than in heterosexual males. The INAH3 might be the root of Martin's sexual orientation. Simon LeVay, the scientist who announced the INAH3 differences, explained:

> Since I looked at adult brains, we don't know if the differences I found were there at birth or if they appeared later. Although most psychiatrists now agree that sexual orientation is a stable attribute of human personality, my work doesn't address whether it's established before birth. The differences I found could have developed after a person was born—a sort of "use it or lose it" phenomenon—though I doubt it. (LeVay in Nimmons, 1994, p. 66)

Next consider Jim. As a defensive tackle, he is a heavily muscled youth with a high level of energy. His physical condition has been determined by three forces. First, the pattern of genes derived from his parents has established the basic plan for his body structure and the pace at which that structure matures. Next, his diet provides the nutrients that fuel his activities and rebuild his body parts. Finally, his exercise regimen of lifting weights, stretching, and running fosters the muscle strength, agility, and stamina required for succeeding in such a strenuous sport as football. We might further assume that Jim's coach has warned him to avoid tobacco and alcohol and to resist the temptation to ingest anabolic steroid drugs that could help build muscle and bone but also could seriously endanger his health.

Kristen's position as the high-school orchestra's premier violinist implies that her genetic endowment has equipped her with an acute innate sensitivity to differences in musical pitch. An instrument such as the piano merely requires that the performer strike the right key in order to produce the correct tone. In contrast, with most stringed instruments, the musician must press her finger at precise points along each string in order to sound notes that are accurately in tune. This means that if Kristen is to perform well on the violin, she must have a sufficiently keen sense of pitch to match her finger positions to proper tones. Although training in pitch discrimination can effect a modest measure of improvement in this skill, the basic talent must originate from the individual's genetic inheritance.

The cystic fibrosis from which Penny suffers is a genetic disorder that renders its victims highly susceptible to lung infections. The disease also damages a person's ability to absorb fats and certain other nutrients from food. Researchers have identified a defective recessive gene as the cause of the malady. The flawed gene appears to impair the function of glands in the lining of the bronchial tubes, causing excessive amounts of a thick mucus that contributes to chronic lung infections. The gene also distorts normal functions of the pancreas and of sweat glands. Obviously, Penny's mother and father were both carriers of the pernicious gene, since the symptoms of cystic fibrosis appear only in people who have received a pair of them. The incidence of cystic fibrosis among whites is 1 per 2,000 live births. In contrast, among nonwhites, such as black Africans, the disease is quite rare, afflicting perhaps only 1 person in 90,000. When cystic fibrosis was first identified in the 1930s, prior to the advent of effective antibiotics, nearly all sufferers died in childhood. However, since 1975 the outlook for children like Penny has dramatically improved. With proper antibiotic treatment, she has at least a 70-percent chance of living into adulthood, although she will never enjoy perfect health (Clayman, 1989, p. 328). As genetic research advances, there is hope that the rapidly growing field of genetic engineering will soon equip scientists to re-pair or replace errant genes while the embryo is in the womb, thereby thwart-ing the development of such diseases as cystic fibrosis before the child is even born.

Before leaving our quartet of illustrative theories, I should state explicitly that the interpretations I have offered of the data about the five young people are not the only ones that might be drawn from the four theoretical positions. Other interpreters might find other implications in the data. Thus the conclusions that were presented are not definitive; they are simply examples of meanings that logically could be offered from the four perspectives. The brief glimpse I have given of each theory is just enough to suggest how data can assume quite different meanings when different theories are used for organizing the facts. A more complete examination of each theory is found in later chapters.

THE WORD *THEORY* AND OTHER TERMS

So far in our discussion I have used the word *theory* almost exclusively in referring to authors' schemes for organizing data. However, in the literature on child development a variety of terms are used—a problem for newcomers to child development theory. How do such words as *theory, model, paradigm, analogue,* and *metatheory* relate to one another? Solving this problem would be simple if all writers intended the same meaning for a given term, but they do not. One writer will use *theory* and *model* as synonyms; another will not. Before we move further into the analysis of theories, we need to inspect a number of these terms to see how they are used by different authors.

Of the many words we might consider, I have selected thirteen of the most common to discuss. The first six are used almost synonymously by many writers; they are *theory, model, paradigm, analogue, structure,* and *system.* The seventh is *metatheory,* a term of recent popularity that appears to have spawned a brood of related *meta* words. The last six are typically used for identifying kinds of statements made within a theory; these are *assumption, axiom, postulate, hypothesis, principle,* and *law.*

When we read about theories of child development, we must be alert to the meaning the writer explicitly or implicitly assigns to the word *theory.* As noted earlier, for the purposes of this book a theory is any statement describing (1) which facts are most important for understanding children and (2) what sorts of relationships among facts are most significant for producing this understanding. Other writers place more restrictions on the term. For example, *theory* can be defined as "a set of statements, including (a) general laws and principles that serve as axioms, (b) other laws, or theorems, that are deducible from the axioms, and (c) definitions of concepts" (Reese & Overton, 1970, p. 117). B. F. Skinner, whose views of development are depicted in Chapter Seven, occasionally denied that his explanation of behavior qualified as theory; and if a very restricted definition of the term is applied, he would appear to be correct in his denial. However, in the broad sense of the word that I have adopted in these pages, Skinner's explanation does indeed qualify as theory (Skinner, 1950).

The word *model* has become increasingly popular in recent decades as a label for theoretical proposals. However, the term has caused some confusion because one writer will use it in a broad sense while another will limit its meaning. In its broad sense, *model* can mean any tentative ideational plan of relationships among variables. At this general level, a model can be a worldview (Kuhn, 1962) or a world hypothesis (Pepper, 1942) that suggests something about the basic nature of people or of reality. For example, some child development theories are founded on a machine model in contrast to others founded on a dynamic organism model. That is, one camp of theorists pictures the growing child as a machine that reacts to things done to it by the environment: the child's behavior is primarily a product of the way the environment manipulates it. The other group pictures the child as an active, seeking organism who determines his or her own behavior by internally motivated desires. In a more limited sense writers have used the word *model* to mean, for example, an exclusively mathematical or graphic representation of the way something operates (Suppes, 1969, pp. 10–17). We therefore should try to decide which of these meanings a writer about child development intends. In the following chapters I will use *model* in the same broad sense as I am using *theory*—as any scheme intended to describe relationships among variables or facts of child development.

Another common term in child development literature is *paradigm*. Some people use *paradigm* to mean only a very general model (Kuhn, 1962)—an overall viewpoint or description of relationships about reality. Others use it to mean either a broad, general picture or as a more specific, more precise description of relationships among variables. In this sense, they equate *paradigm* with *model* and use the terms interchangeably. Again, it is well to determine the way an author intends the term to be used.

Theorists use the term *analogy* or *analogue* when comparing an aspect of growth to something else in order to help explain that aspect of growth. For instance, theorists may say that the mind of the growing child is like a computer, consisting of a finite amount of storage space for ideas and a system for retrieving the ideas when they are needed. Or theorists may liken a highly mobile two-year-old to an inquisitive puppy that noses into everything without any notion of danger or responsibility. Analogies are thus kinds of models, in the sense of one thing representing qualities of something else. In this book, *analogy* or *analogue* will refer to a comparison between child development in a general sense and some other object or system; for example, an analogy would liken stages of growth to steps on a ladder the child ascends as the years pass.

The words *structure* and *system* are considered together, for they commonly carry the same meaning. Each identifies the elements that comprise something and describes the way these elements are interrelated. Therefore, a theorist's entire complex of beliefs and their interconnections can be called a system. Likewise, one segment of an overall complex of beliefs can be singled out as a separate entity with its own constituent parts and be called a system or subsystem by itself. So we can speak of Piaget's complete set of ideas about child development as his system or theoretical structure, or we can pick one segment of this complex—such as Piaget's explanation of children's play—and view it as a subsystem with its own inner workings (Hall & Lindzey, 1970, pp. 317–318).

Beginning in the 1970s, a host of new *meta* words sprang up in the human development literature: *metatheory, metamemory, metacognition, meta-analysis, metalearning, metaperception, metaprinciples,* and more. This rash of neologisms has caused some confusion, since authors often fail to explain how they intend such terms. Furthermore, although there is some consistency of usage, not all authors use a given *meta* word with the same meaning. In contemporary human development literature the prefix *meta* is most often intended to mean "an analysis of" or "knowledge about" the subject to which the prefix is attached. Thus *metacognition* is knowledge about cognition, or thinking about thinking. In like manner, *metamemory* is an awareness of how memory operates, and *metalearning* is the analysis of how learning occurs. Following this same pattern, *metatheory* becomes the analysis of what *theory* is about, how *theory* is developed or used. As a result, what we are doing throughout this book, and especially in these first two chapters, is *metatheory.*

Although most *meta* terms in child development literature seem to mean "knowledge about" some process, sometimes they are not intended that way. Not long ago I asked an author what he meant by *metatheory* in one of his recent articles. Did he mean "an analysis of" theory? Or was *metatheory* in this instance an overarching, umbrella theory that encompassed more specific subtheories, as some writers use the term? The author responded that he meant neither of those alternatives. Instead, on this occasion he used the word to mean a precursor of true theory—a set of preliminary speculations that would not as yet qualify as tightly knit theory. So, because the meanings for *meta* terms have not been standardized, it is well to study a theorist's *meta* words with some care to estimate which meaning she or he is seeking to convey.

Next we turn to six words that refer to types of statements that may be included in a theory: *assumption, axiom, postulate, hypothesis, principle,* and *law.* Again, not all writers assign identical meanings to these terms. Here, we will look at the most widely accepted meaning of each.

One useful way to approach the six terms is to think of their roles in a series of four phases a theorist may go through in creating and refining a model of child development (see Table 1.1). First, the theorist accepts certain concepts as true without testing them. These self-evident beliefs are frequently called *assumptions, axioms,* or *postulates.* An axiom or postulate is a formal statement of the convic-

TABLE 1.1
Terms and phases in theory building

	Phase 1	Phase 2	Phase 3	Phase 4
	Foundation convictions	Model descriptions	Logical deductions	Conclusions
Products of the phase:	axioms postulates assumptions	structure system	hypotheses	principles laws
The theorist's behavior:	accepts certain beliefs as self-evident	defines the parts of the model and their interrelations	suggests relationships or outcomes that reasonably might be expected if the model accurately represents the aspect of development it is supposed to describe	draws generalizations from evidence collected to test or estimate the accuracy of the model

Note: Although the process of theory building can thus be described as four sequential steps or phases, in practice a theorist frequently may not move systematically through the sequence. More often than not, theorists appear to shuttle back and forth among the phases, revising here and altering there, to produce a scheme they believe provides a convincing interpretation of the facts.

tion on which the theorist's model will be founded. In contrast, an assumption is either informally stated by the theorist or is not stated at all. Sometimes theorists are unaware that they are making certain assumptions until critics point them out.

After establishing a foundation of assumptions and postulates, the theorist erects the superstructure of the model. Typically the model (or at least certain aspects of it) is proposed in only a tentative form because the author is not sure that it represents an accurate picture of the way children develop. The author is saying, in effect, that it seems likely that children grow up this way and for these reasons, but the author is not entirely sure. So to answer questions that are still puzzling about the theory's validity, the theorist composes some *if-then* statements that derive logically from the model. These yet-to-be-proven statements are usually called *hypotheses.*

One popular way to state a hypothesis is in an if-then form. For example, in Chapter Three we mention a developmental-task theory advocated by American psychologist Robert J. Havighurst. The theory proposes that as children grow up, every few years they meet a new set of physical-growth and social-psychological problems they must solve—in other words, tasks they must carry out. The theory further contends that if children do not successfully solve a problem at one age level, they will have difficulty carrying out their developmental tasks at higher age levels in the future. From this general proposal, we can create hypotheses to test the validity of Havighurst's notion.

As one illustration, we can take the area of emotional development called "giving and receiving affection." Within this area, the preadolescent child is said to face the task of "learning to give as much love as one receives." In early adolescence, the emotional-development task the child is to accomplish is that of "accepting oneself as a worthwhile person, really worthy of love." So we now have a pair of sequential tasks in hand and are thereby able to offer the following hypothesis:

> If, by the end of late childhood, a girl has not learned to give as much love as she receives, then in early adolescence she will not accept herself as a worthwhile person, really worthy of love.

As soon as we define the key terms in this statement (such as *late childhood, as much love, early adolescence, accept herself,* and *worthwhile person*), we are ready to set up an experiment or make observations of adolescents that will test the validity of the hypothesis. In effect, we observe children to decide whether this statement—one aspect of the theory—is true in real life.

A hypothesis or tentative estimate of the real state of affairs is not always in the form of an if-then statement. It can be a simple declarative sentence that only implies the if-then condition. For example, we could rephrase our hypothesis to read:

> A girl who has not learned to give as much love as she receives by the time she reaches the end of late childhood will not accept herself as a worthwhile person, really worthy of love, during her adolescent years.

Or, as another option, the hypothesis can be phrased as a question:

> Will a girl who has not learned by the end of late childhood to give as much love as she receives be able to accept herself as a worthwhile person, really worthy of love, when she is an early adolescent?

Whatever the form in which a hypothetical relationship is cast, its status in theory building is the same. It functions as a reasonable but unproven idea whose validity needs to be examined.

When investigators have collected enough evidence to convince themselves that a hypothesized relationship is valid, they may then draw a generalization about it that they call a "principle." Thus I am using the term *principle* to mean a generalization that is accepted as true—not because it seems self-evident but because it is supported by what the theorists believe are sound data. Or if they regard the empirical data and logic behind it as irrefutable, they can accord the generalization a higher status and term it a *law* or a *law of nature.*

Finally, on the topic of terminology, it is useful to make a distinction between evidence and proof. Perhaps our most basic motive for comparing theories is to discover which of them is "true" or, at least, which parts of them are "valid." We might say that we are seeking proof of the theories. In this search I find it helpful to define the terms *evidence* and *proof* in the following way:

> *Evidence* is a public thing. It consists of the arguments, the logic, the patterns of reasoning, and the facts that bear upon what it treats. This book is intended to present evidence about the theories it includes.

> *Proof,* in contrast, is a personal, private thing. It is a conviction that something is true.

Distinguishing between these two concepts is important, as is illustrated by the arguments that arise over whether a generalization should be labeled an assumption, a hypothesis, or a principle. These arguments seem to arise because those who are disagreeing either (1) have different kinds of evidence at hand or (2) are convinced by different kinds or amounts of evidence. The sort of evidence one person accepts as proof of a theory may not be the same sort that another accepts. A generalization about child growth that I accept as a proven principle or law may be one that you still consider a hypothesis.

GOOD THEORY, BAD THEORY

Typically when we compare theories we are interested not only in learning how they are alike or different but also in judging whether one is better than another. To make this judgment, we need to decide what our standards of "goodness" will be. Everyone does not use the same standards for appraisal. Therefore let's review some of the more common standards people use in differentiating good theory from bad.

We will consider fourteen popular standards of judgment. These are not necessarily ones you *should* adopt as your own; rather they are ones you *might* adopt if they seem convincing and if they fit into your own set of values. Further, you will likely discover that they are not all of equal importance to you. You may wish to revise certain ones, eliminate others, and add a few of your own. In this way you will devise your own standards for judging child development theories.

At the beginning of this chapter the term *theory* was defined in a very broad manner, as a description of (1) which facts are most important for understanding children and (2) what sorts of relationships among facts are most significant for producing this understanding. Some people use *theory* in a more restricted way, often by adding the sort of criteria described by the fourteen standards that follow. For instance, some people are unwilling to call a collection of ideas a theory unless the collection both is internally consistent in structure and clearly provides for the generation of testable hypotheses. However, we will use these standards not to decide what should be called a theory but to decide how worthwhile or how "good" a theory is.

STANDARD 1:   A theory is better if it accurately reflects the facts of the real world of children.

Some theorists are criticized for producing a model of development that does not accurately represent children. We will consider three reasons why a theory may not match the facts of child development.

First, a theorist may draw conclusions from a study of only a few children, then improperly apply these conclusions to many children—the error of generalizing beyond the data. This criticism does not apply to the common practice of studying a representative sample of children and then extending the resulting conclusions to the larger population of children accurately reflected by the sample. Indeed, such sampling is involved in virtually all research on development. But it is an error to apply conclusions about a small group to a larger population when there is good reason to believe that the conditions of the two groups are significantly different. For instance, Arnold Gesell (Chapter Three) has been criticized for improperly generalizing conclusions from a study of children who came to his clinic at Yale University. He apparently assumed that the group of children he observed and measured were accurate representatives of nearly all other children. But there is a serious question about whether his conclusions correctly describe child growth in other cultural settings.

Likewise, in the eighteenth century, Jean-Jacques Rousseau wrote at length about the nature of children, founding his beliefs on three sorts of evidence: (1) his experience as a tutor for several sons of aristocratic European families, (2) some casual observations of French peasant children, and (3) hearsay impressions of the personalities of "noble savages" in primitive cultures. Rousseau's critics have questioned whether his descriptions of child development, based on such limited data, actually matched the experience of all the children to whom he applied his conclusions.

Second, a theory may not describe children accurately because a researcher who studies one facet of child growth may not be satisfied to limit conclusions to that facet. Instead, in an effort to discover general principles of growth that explain all sorts of behavior, the researcher applies the conclusions to explain other aspects of child growth as well. For example, he or she may measure trends in children's physical growth and then seek to apply the pattern of increases and plateaus in physical growth to other areas of development, such as social or emotional or mental development. But principles governing one aspect of development may not be the same as those governing another, so risk may be involved in generalizing in this way.

The third cause of conflict between theory and fact may arise from the researcher's faulty memory or inaccurate observation of children. Probably none of us can help being influenced by memories of our own childhood or by our casual impressions of children we have seen and talked with. Unless we are careful to use controlled observing, testing, and measuring of children, we risk allowing distorted observations from the past or from casual impressions to influence the schemes we devise for explaining development.

STANDARD 2:   A theory is better if it is stated in a way that makes it clearly understandable to anyone who is reasonably competent (in other words, anyone who has a suitable command of language, mathematics, and logical analysis).

Anyone with reasonable competence should be able to understand (1) what facets or events in the real world each part of the theory refers to, (2) the meaning of terms used in the model, (3) the key assumptions on which the model is founded, and (4) how the explanations and predictions are logically derived from the definitions and assumptions.

This standard may appear simple and straightforward, but in practice it can be quite controversial. If we find that a theory lacks clarity, is it the theorist's fault for being obscure or confused, or is it our own fault for lacking the competence needed to understand the theorist? We usually have a higher regard for a theory whose elements we can readily comprehend.

STANDARD 3:   A theory is better if it not only explains why past events occurred but also accurately predicts future events. Furthermore, it is better if it enables us to make accurate predictions about the specific behaviors of a particular child rather than only speculations about general growth patterns for a group of children.

People who seek to understand children are usually interested in both the past and the future. They look to the past to learn what forces in a child's life caused the child to be the way she or he is today. They look to the future to estimate what the child will probably be like in coming years.

Many theories are better suited to explaining the past than to foretelling the future. And of those that say something of the future, most are better able to predict general characteristics of a typical child or of children in general than to predict the specific development characteristics of a particular child. However, those interested in child development—researchers, parents, teachers, physicians—

more highly value a theory that produces specific predictions about a given child than one that foretells only general growth directions or yields only estimates of how the average child will turn out. It is my own belief that a social learning theorist (Chapter Eight) is better prepared to make predictions about a specific child's verbal development than are people who base their judgment solely on Havighurst's developmental-task theory (Chapter Three).

STANDARD 4:   A theory is better if it offers practical guidance in solving daily problems of child rearing to people responsible for the welfare of children— parents, teachers, camp counselors, pediatricians, clinical psychologists, juvenile court judges, and so on.

Many people consider this standard, which is a practical extension of standard 3, to be the most important one, for they are interested in theory only to the extent that it improves their own skills in understanding and treating the children they meet daily. In contrast, some theorists, and readers of theory, are not particularly concerned with translating ideas into advice on child rearing. Rather, they are searching for basic principles of human growth and behavior; whether these principles will enable people to treat children with greater skill is an entirely incidental question.

STANDARD 5:   A theory is better if it is internally consistent.

The essence of a theory is its structure—its elements and the way they interact. Theorists choose different ways to display this framework of their beliefs. For example, although all theorists explain their models of development verbally, some supplement their verbal descriptions with mathematical symbols that permit the theory's components to be manipulated according to rules of logic. By quantifying the components, a theorist hopes to gain precision in analyzing and predicting child growth and behavior. Piaget is an example of a theorist who has sought to enhance the clarity of his verbal explanations with such symbols (Piaget, 1950).

Another way to supplement verbal description is through diagrams. For example, if a theory involves two main dimensions that interact (such as the relationship between chronological age and mental growth), then the relationship can be displayed as a simple graph, with age on one axis and mental growth on the other. More complex diagrammatic versions of theories appear in Chapters Four, Five, Six, Eleven, Thirteen, and Seventeen.

Whatever the mode of presentation, however—words, mathematical symbols, or diagrams—the system should be internally consistent. A person seeking to understand the system should not have to disregard one segment of a model in order to comprehend another. The parts should all fit together logically.

STANDARD 6:   A theory is better if it is *economical*—founded on as few unproven assumptions as possible and requiring the simplest possible mechanisms to explain all the phenomena it encompasses.

This criterion is often referred to as the *law of parsimony, Occam's razor,* or *Morgan's canon*—the last in recognition of a biologist, Lloyd Morgan, who proposed that if two explanations of a phenomenon fit the facts equally well, it is better in the long run to choose the simpler of the explanations. Note that the purpose of this standard is not to discourage theorists from formulating complex explanations of complex events—indeed, simpler explanations can prove to be inaccurate. Instead it is intended to reduce the establishment of theories with elaborate hypothesized internal mechanisms not well supported by evidence. Frequently the more complicated the theory, the more difficult it is to test, and proponents are left to support it with argument and emotion.

STANDARD 7:   A theory is better if it is falsifiable or disconfirmable.

In scientific circles a theory is generally conceived to be an estimate of the truth rather than a definite statement of the truth. Researchers must test the validity of hypotheses derived from the theory in order to determine to what extent the theory does indeed explain the facts satisfactorily. If a theory's hypotheses can be tested to determine whether they are true, then the reverse should also obtain—it should be possible to test that a hypothesis is false. Many scientists feel that the validity of a theory should not only be confirmable through logic and the presentation of data, but should also be falsifiable or disconfirmable.

Some theories of child development, however, do not appear to display this characteristic of falsifiability; that is, we cannot conceive of a research result that such a theory is unprepared to answer. The theory is built to explain the negative outcome of an experiment as well as the positive outcome.

The following example illustrates the problem of falsifiability. Imagine that we create a theory of social development in which diet is the prime determinant of a child's social adjustment. We contend that a proper combination of B vitamins is particularly important. The proper combination produces a child who is socially constructive and amiable. The improper combination produces a child who is resentful and commits antisocial acts. Our hypothesis, in this form, becomes falsifiable when we have specified the proper and the improper B-vitamin combinations. Now we can create experiments to determine whether this aspect of the theory is valid or not. But let us add another element to our theory. We will call it the *counterpoise factor* and propose that when it is present, the B-vitamin combinations work in just the opposite way we would normally expect. By adding this factor, we have rendered our theory nonfalsifiable. If someone tries to test our theory and discovers that many children who eat the improper B-vitamin combination are socially well adjusted, we explain that in those children the counterpoise factor has been operating. Thus the theory is nonfalsifiable—it is always "correct."

Addressing this matter of falsifiability, Jaan Valsiner contends:

> Theories are hierarchically organized systems of propositions about reality where every single proposition is related to others and follows from some more general assumption that the theory constructor has accepted. Such systems are

more likely to be adequate if they are constructed by a scientist who knows the empirical phenomenology well—in this sense many aspects of theories grow out of the author's intuitive integration of the empirical knowledge with the abstract bases of the theory. Explicit testing of the theory in the research process involves only some aspects of the theory that the constructor considers important. Depending on the theory constructor's psychological tolerance for failure, different scientists react to the disconfirmation of the selected aspects of the theory in variable ways. . . . Some may accept the disconfirmation and reject the theory. The believers in the absolute truthfulness of the data in their role as "final judges" might react in this way. Others may refuse to accept the disconfirming empirical evidence. (1987, pp. 143–144)

Many researchers are uncomfortable with a theory that is nonfalsifiable, so they include standard 7 among the criteria they apply for judging the worth of theories. Among the models reviewed in this book, those of Freud and humanistic psychologists might be considered the least falsifiable.

STANDARD 8:   A theory is better if the evidence supporting it is convincing.

This is the *strength-of-evidence* characteristic. It concerns how much confidence people place in a proposed model as a result of the sources, types, and amounts of evidence offered in support of the model.

The issue of support is complicated by the fact that not everyone agrees about which sources are most trustworthy. Some people are convinced if the evidence derives from a particular authority. That authority may be a respected publication—the Christian Bible, the Islamic Koran, an encyclopedia, a scientific journal, a popular periodical, a scholarly book. In other cases the authority is a distinguished person—scientist, philosopher, medical doctor, political dignitary, Nobel Prize recipient, religious leader, television personality, or representative of a government agency.

Preferences for types of evidence also vary. For some people, the authority's testimonial is sufficient confirmation of a theory's worth. Others are persuaded by records of individual childhood case studies, such as those compiled by Freud in his psychiatric practice. Whereas some readers are satisfied with narrative accounts of child growth, others require statistical analyses, complete with information on the numbers of children studied and on how likely it is that those children accurately represent the population about whom generalizations are being drawn. Some people are content to learn only the results of research studies, whereas others demand details about the research methods used so they can decide how much faith to place in the results.

As for the quantity of evidence, it seems obvious that the more information submitted in support of a theory, the more willing people are to accept it. Hence, the advocates of a theory seek to substantiate their position with as much documentation as possible. The longer the list of favorable references, the better.

In summary, people are most likely to accept theories buttressed by large amounts of the types of evidence they prefer, provided by sources they regard highly.

STANDARD 9:   A theory is better if it is able to accommodate new data.

Here the issue is a model's *adaptability*. There seem to be three principal reactions that a theory's proponents may adopt when new data appear to challenge some aspect of their theory. The first two reactions—reinterpretation and revision—involve accepting and accommodating the data. The third reaction—rejection—involves repudiating the data as either irrelevant or inaccurate, so that the theory is left intact.

Reinterpretation involves explaining how data that seem incompatible with the theory can actually fit into it quite nicely, so that what at first looks like a problem turns out to be no more than a misunderstanding. Reinterpretation can be illustrated with the Freudian model. Psychoanalytic theory includes the concept of *free-floating anxiety*—a persistent feeling of dread and distress that does not result from any apparent threat in the individual's life. Freudians explain that the anxiety is the result of repressed painful psychological conflicts, such as a youth's deep-seated guilt resulting from sexual desires for the opposite-sex parent. The theory proposes that such thoughts are so disturbing that the mind automatically drives them into the person's unconscious, where they continue to seethe and express themselves in disguised ways. To dispel the anxiety, the individual must go through psychoanalytic therapy, during which the repressed material is brought into consciousness and relived in an emotionally acceptable fashion. In recent decades, however, the invention of drugs that relieve anxiety has cast doubt on this Freudian explanation. When proponents of psychoanalysis are confronted with information about the efficacy of these drugs, they can still maintain the integrity of their theory by reinterpreting the drugs' ostensible effect. Claiming that the anxiety-reducing medications have not truly resolved the unconscious strife, a proponent of psychoanalysis may explain that the drugs have merely blocked the anxiety, leaving the pent-up psychic energy to rechannel itself through other forms of deviance, such as in headaches or compulsive behavior.

Revision means altering the theory in order to reconcile the conflict between it and the new facts. For example, one traditional strain of behaviorism (Chapter Seven) has held that children acquire only those learnings that are directly reinforced. In other words, children adopt only those behaviors for which they are personally rewarded. However, following the publication of the theory, research conducted to test such a proposal demonstrated that children also learn by seeing other people being rewarded (Bandura, 1977). As a result, behaviorism revisionists have incorporated these newer data by recognizing both vicarious and direct reinforcement as significant influences on learning.

Rejection can be either passive or active. Passive rejection takes the form of stonewalling—steadfastly denying the possibility that the new data might have any bearing at all on the validity of the theory. Active rejection, on the other hand, involves discrediting the data by exposing flaws in the way the facts were gathered, reported, or interpreted. The data, and not the theory, are held to blame.

In summary, assessing a model's adaptability involves judging how reasonable the theory's adherents have been in their manner of reinterpreting, incorporating, or rejecting potentially contradictory evidence.

STANDARD 10:   A theory is better if it provides an unusual view of development.

This *novelty* or *originality* standard concerns to what degree a newly proposed theory differs from existing ones.

All four models described earlier in this chapter have added innovative features to the child development scene. If asked to rank the four in terms of their novelty, I would consider Freud the frontrunner, far outstripping the other three. Not only were the general contours of his model quite out of the ordinary for his day, so were the multitude of details with which he embellished the structure. I would then locate Piaget in second place, with Bandura a slightly distant third. My reasons should become apparent when you read Chapters Five, Eight, and Nine. However, the bio-electrochemical paradigm is something different—an outlier not properly classed with the others. Seeing human development as a series of systematic biochemical changes is nothing new; biochemical explanations have a long history. Therefore, the originality we seek is not found in the general notion of a biochemical perspective. Instead, the novelty resides in the host of minitheories created periodically to explain the quantities of new data about child development continually being generated by the world's scientific community. In sum, we might view Freud's, Piaget's, and Bandura's proposals as "theories in place"—as fairly stable conceptions of how children grow. In contrast, the bio-electrochemical model is more like a moving picture, a shifting panorama whose features are constantly under revision as more facts are discovered and new subtheories are devised to suggest what those facts could mean.

STANDARD 11:   A theory is better if it offers reasonable answers to questions about all conceivable child-development phenomena.

This criterion refers to a system's *comprehensiveness* or, in nomenclature proposed by P. R. Thagard (1978), a system's *consilience.*

It may be many theorist's ultimate dream to devise a model capable of explaining every aspect of development—a model furnishing satisfactory answers to all questions about how and why children grow up as they do. In pursuit of this dream, different authors adopt different strategies. As a way to begin, some seek to discover principles that encompass all facets of development—physical, mental, social, emotional, and more. These overarching conceptions might be called macromodels. By way of illustration, consider the general growth principles posited by Kurt Lewin. He contended that children's development is marked by a common set of changes in all their physical and psychological attributes. In his view, with the passing years children's structures and functions become more differentiated and specialized, the boundaries separating one function from another grow more pronounced and rigid, the organization of functions increases in complexity, and behavior becomes more realistic (Barker, Dembo, & Lewin, 1943, pp. 441–442). Such principles served as the foundation of the scheme he devised for explaining all varieties of development.

In contrast to theorists who start at the macro level are others who work in quite a different manner. They begin by creating what might be called micromodels, designed to explain no more than a single restricted aspect of child growth. For instance, to interpret the development of children's reading ability, researchers have invented models to elucidate each component of reading skill. Thus, separate theories focus on how children recognize printed words, analyze prefixes and suffixes, match the sight of words to their sounds, acquire concepts, identify story themes, draw inferences, and far more.

The advantage of the very general macromodels is that they extend over many facets of development, but their very abstractness causes them to neglect the multitude of variables that differentiate one facet from another. As a consequence, they are relatively useless for explaining or predicting specific aspects of develop- ment with any precision. At the opposite pole from macrotheorists, the creators of microtheories take pains to identify the specific variables that their restricted aspect of development involves. Consequently, their schemes are of greater practical use for explaining and predicting individual children's development than are broad principles of growth. However, microtheories are limited to explaining only that narrow facet of development for which they are designed.

In sum, Lewin's macroprinciples and the reading analysts' micromodels represent extreme opposites in the range of development characteristics embraced by a theory. None of the theories described in Chapters Four through Seventeen belongs at either of these polar positions; all fall somewhere between the two extremes. There may come a day when macromodels and micromodels can be merged and integrated to form a monumental master theory capable of explaining all aspects of development. That day, if it ever arrives, is apparently in the far distant future. Meanwhile, consumers of child development theories must be content with something less.

In view of this discussion, it may prove desirable to recast standard 11 in a slightly more modest and realistic form: a theory is better if it offers reasonable answers to questions about as many aspects of development as can be addressed at a level of specificity that offers practical help in predicting and guiding child growth and behavior.

STANDARD 12:   A theory is better if it stimulates the creation of new research techniques and the discovery of new knowledge.

This can be called the *fertility criterion.* Some theories have been highly fertile— remarkable for the number of new vistas they have opened and the amount of research they have stimulated. As a review of child development journals will attest, a great proportion of published investigations from the 1960s through the 1980s trace their origins to Piaget's writings. Likewise, behaviorism, social learning theory, and information-processing models have been highly effective motivators of research in recent years. In contrast, the work of Havighurst and other develop- mental-task proponents has not generated much of a search for new knowledge.

Among researchers, the fertility factor is often regarded as the most valued function of a theory, because models of development that stimulate many ideas for research will exert the greatest influence toward expanding the world's store of knowledge. Such stimulation can take several forms. Perhaps the simplest form is that which leads to *direct replication studies*—empirical studies on which the original theory was based are repeated by other researchers to determine whether the same empirical outcomes and theoretical conclusions result as those reported by the original theorist. Stimulation also can lead to *hypothesis testing,* where a general principle, which is part of the theory, generates hypotheses that can be tested on actual children to determine more precisely the conditions under which the principle validly applies. A third form of stimulation is *verification studies,* where research is conducted to discover whether some theoretical proposal is borne out in real life. Verification is typically sought when a theorist's notions seem to conflict with common sense or with some other theorist's well-accepted proposal. A fourth form can be dubbed *population applicability* because the purpose of the research is to discover whether an empirical finding or a theoretical conclusion based on one population of children is equally true in other populations, such as among children of different age levels, cultures, or ability levels. A fifth form is *discrepancy resolution,* referring to research designed to resolve, or at least to expose, what seem to be a theory's internal inconsistencies. A sixth form is *extended theorizing*, when a theorist's ideas stimulate another theorist to create proposals that extend beyond those of the original author, with the extended theorizing resulting in new possibilities for empirical studies.

STANDARD 13: A theory is better if it continues to attract attention and enlist adherents over an extended period of time.

This is the attribute of *durability* and *historical significance.* Long-lasting theories are esteemed for having stood the test of time, weathering the vicissitudes of social progress. The conceptions of development that best exemplify such durability are the ones embedded in the world's persisting religious and philosophical traditions—the Judaic-Christian-Islamic line, Hinduism and its derivatives (Buddhism, Jainism, Sikhism), China's Confucianism and Taoism, Shinto in Japan, and the like (Thomas, 1988). Because newer theories of development that can be labeled "scientific" are of such recent origin, too little time has yet passed to test their longevity. In effect, scientific studies of the growing child extend back hardly more than a century. (An estimate of the short-term fate of the theories presented in this book is offered later under Perspective F.)

It is not always easy to judge a theory's historical significance, because vestiges of theoretical proposals can gradually merge into cultural tradition without leaving clear traces of their origin. For example, aspects of theories that have entered the realm of conventional wisdom in recent times, and whose beginnings may soon be forgotten, include Freud's concepts of ego and unconscious motivation, Carl Jung's introversion and extroversion, and Alfred Adler's inferiority complex. Another point to consider in appraising historical significance is that notions from one theory often become building blocks in a subsequent model, making it difficult to determine how the credit for such notions should be distributed among the various authors of an evolving sequence of theories.

STANDARD 14:   A good theory is satisfying. It explains development in a way that we feel makes good sense.

This might be called the standard of *self-affirmation*. It is a sort of catchall that depends not only on the previous standards but also on emotional and intuitive factors that we cannot readily identify. The operation of these factors is reflected in our saying about a theory, "I just can't believe that's true" or "I can't believe that's the whole story," when we do not know exactly what it is we find dissatisfying about it. Or we may consider a theory valid because "it feels right" or "it rings true—it seems to be the way things are."

Among the theories described later in this book, the one type that appears to depend most heavily on self-affirmation factors is humanistic psychology, for it is based on the theorist's belief that the individual's real world is the one she or he personally experiences. The feelings and inner experiences of the child are most important, no matter what sorts of objective factors exist in the world around the child. The development of the child's personally sensed *self* is what interests the humanistic psychologist, and this self is known only through introspection. The advocate of humanistic theory, therefore, can comfortably accept a theory because "it feels right" and "makes intuitive sense" without requiring confirmation from outside, "objective" data. On the other hand, a radical behaviorist, although she might informally say she "feels" her theory is true, does not cite this feeling as validating evidence; instead she is compelled by her theoretical position to produce observational or experimental evidence to support the theory.

In the final analysis, of course, any theory must be convincing to be accepted.

Conclusion

This chapter has presented an initial taste of several quite different theories, and a suggestion of the very different conclusions that can be drawn through interpreting child behavior from each theory's point of view. Some general theoretical terms and meanings that can be assigned to them were identified. Illustrative standards for judging the worth of a theory were proposed. The material in this chapter should serve as useful background for Chapter Two, which suggests a series of questions one can ask about the contents of theories when comparing different models of child development.

FOR FURTHER READING

The following publications are useful sources of information about theoretical terminology, criteria for judging the worth of theories, and illustrative appraisals of theories.

Cirillo, W., and S. Wapner (1986) *Value Presuppositions in Theories of Human Development.* Hillsdale, N.J.: Erlbaum.
Green, M. (1989) *Theories of Human Development: A Comparative Approach.* Englewood Cliffs, N.J.: Prentice-Hall.

Lerner, R. M. (1986) *Concepts and Theories of Human Development* (2nd ed.). New York: Random House.

Lundin, R. W. (1991) *Theories and Systems of Psychology* (4th ed.). Lexington, Mass.: D. C. Heath.

Maier, H. W. (1988) *Three Theories of Child Development* (3rd ed.). Lanham: University Press of America.

Marx, M. H., and H. A. Cronan-Hillix. (1987) *Systems and Theories in Psychology* (4th ed.). New York: McGraw-Hill.

Miller, P. H. (1993) *Theories of Developmental Psychology* (3rd ed.). New York: W. H. Freeman.

Salkind, N. J. (1985) *Theories of Human Development* (2nd ed.). New York: Wiley.

Skinner, B. F. (1972) *Cumulative Record: A Selection of Papers* (3rd ed.). New York: Appleton-Century-Crofts. (See Skinner's questioning the need for theory in the selection in Part II entitled "Are Theories of Learning Necessary?")

Thomas, R. M. (ed.). (1988) *Oriental Theories of Human Development.* New York: Peter Lang.

CHAPTER TWO

THE CONTENTS OF CHILD DEVELOPMENT THEORIES

In comparing theories, we need to consider not only the sorts of criteria described in Chapter One but also the theories' content characteristics. By *content* I mean both the aspects of child development on which theorists focus attention and the key philosophical and methodological convictions that undergird the models they propose.

This chapter introduces a variety of content categories often included in theories. One aim is to alert you to questions that child development theories frequently try to answer, so you can decide which questions are most important from your viewpoint. Another aim is to show that not all theorists seek to answer the same questions or accord the same significance to a given question. This is important to recognize because two theories that at first appear to be in conflict may simply be directed at different aspects of child growth. Two ostensibly conflicting viewpoints might even be satisfactorily combined, as J. Dollard and N. E. Miller sought to do with behaviorist and psychoanalytic theories in their book *Personality and Psychotherapy* (1950).

In this chapter, a number of questions that identify either the content focus of theories or their philosophical and methodological understructure will be presented. The questions are organized into thirteen clusters. The names of the clusters and an overall question that encompasses the subquestions in each are given in the following section.

CONTENT CHARACTERISTICS

1. *Scope or range:* What age levels, aspects of development, and human cultures are the objects of the theory?
2. *Nature and nurture:* How does heredity compare with environment as a contributor to development?
3. *Direction of development:* What sort of maturity or what future condition does the infant grow toward?
4. *Continuous versus stepwise change:* Do children grow by imperceptibly small increments or do they periodically move up from one identifiable stage to another?
5. *Original moral condition:* Is the child born moral, immoral, or amoral?

6. *Personality structure:* What are the key components of human personality, and how are these related to each other?
7. *Motivation and the learning process:* What motivates development, and by what process does a child learn?
8. *Individual differences:* How does the theory account for differences in development among children of the same chronological age?
9. *Desirable versus undesirable, and normal versus abnormal:* How does the theory distinguish desirable from undersirable development and normal from abnormal development?
10. *Philosophical origins and assumptions:* From what philosophical viewpoint has the theory arisen, and on what assumptions is it founded?
11. *Investigative methods:* What methods has the theorist used for gathering, analyzing, and validating ideas, and how have these methods influenced the content and structure of the theory?
12. *Appeal for acceptance:* On what sort of appeal does the theorist depend to convince people of the theory's worth?
13. *Terminology:* What special terms are used in the theory, and how do they relate to similar concepts in other theories?

Before inspecting each of these topics in some detail, we should note three characteristics of this list. First, the topics are not mutually exclusive. They overlap and crisscross. For example, when we discuss Freud's proposed structure for personality development, we necessarily consider as well his growth stages, his idea of the child's original moral condition, and his special terminology. These questions are not separate entities but simply different angles from which to view the integrated body of a theory.

Second, the list itself is not proposed as the one and only correct list of topics for analyzing theories of development. It is just one possible listing, which I have found helpful for directing attention to significant aspects of theories. Other lists, different in content or organized in a different pattern, serve other people just as well.

Third, topics at the beginning of the list are more distinctly developmental than the rest. Within the broad field of psychology, practitioners are traditionally divided into several loosely defined groups: specialists in the clinical treatment of behavior disorders, specialists who compare human behavior with that of animals, specialists in research on learning, and specialists in development. This last group is the one we are concerned with. Developmental psychologists have a dominant interest in questions about how and why people change with the passing of time or the advancement of age. In our list of thirteen topics, items 1 through 5 are most distinctly concerns of developmentalists. Items 6 through 13 are generally of equal or greater interest to practitioners in other psychological groups. Now let's turn to a more detailed explanation of the topics.

1. Scope or range   The term *scope* is used here to identify three aspects of a theory: (a) its *age range*—the way the theory marks the beginning and end of the development period; (b) its *variety of aspects*—the number and kinds of facets stressed or included by the theory; and (c) its *cultural range*—the variety of cultures the theory proposes to describe. To discover how a particular theorist treats these matters, we can be guided by the following set of questions:

1.1 How are the beginning and end of the development period defined? What characteristics, such as age in years, particular changes in behavior, or changes in growth rate, define this period?

Some of the schemes discussed in later chapters are best labeled *theories of human development* since they propose structures and principles describing the entire life span, from conception to death. Others are more accurately called *theories of child development* because they focus exclusively, or primarily, on the first two decades or so of life. In this book we are concerned only with these initial two decades, even if the theory being considered extends its application into adulthood and old age.

Many theories use chronological age as the chief measure of child development periods, with either biological conception or birth marking the lower limit and age eighteen or twenty-one marking the upper limit. Thus the adolescent years are typically included within the span of the term *child development,* although some writers prefer to limit the word *childhood* to the years before puberty—age twelve or fourteen—and *adolescence* to the years between puberty and adulthood.

Other theorists find chronological age an unsatisfactory dimension in analyzing development (Wohlwill, 1976). They use some other characteristic, such as the attainment of adult height or the emergence of specified adult behaviors, as the indicator that childhood is over. Also their boundary lines for stages of growth throughout the childhood period are set by developmental signs other than years since birth.

Some authors focus their theories on the entire range of childhood and adolescent experiences, whereas others attend to only one segment of this range.

1.2 What aspects of growth or behavior does the theory include or emphasize?

Some models concentrate on a narrow range of behavior. For example, Kohlberg's model (Chapter Sixteen) is concerned solely with moral aspects, and humanistic psychologists (Chapter Twelve) focus chiefly on the development of the self. Other theories are much broader in scope. Havighurst's scheme (Chapter Three) involves physical, emotional, moral, cognitive, and social aspects. Gesell's model (Chapter Three) also includes a wide range of behaviors and growth characteristics.

1.3 Does the theory propose to explain child development in all cultures or only in certain ones?

Most theorists want their model to apply to as many children as possible. In effect, they try to produce a universal theory. Their broad-ranging statements imply that they are talking about children in all places and all times. Such theorists include Piaget, Freud, Skinner, and many more. Others state that their proposals are intended to describe development within defined cultural or geographic domains. For example, Havighurst has said that his "tasks of development" are ones faced by mid-twentieth-century North American boys and girls, particularly those from the middle and upper social classes.

These three facets of a theory's scope help delineate the territory the theorist is trying to map out.

2. Nature and nurture   Over the decades the most fundamental concern of child development theorists has been the relationship between heredity and environment. The terminology of the debate has varied from time to time—nature versus nurture, nativism versus cultural relativism, genetics versus social controls, maturation versus learning, innate traits versus acquired characteristics—but the basic issue has been the same: How do inborn factors compare with environmental factors in contributing to a child's development?

As demonstrated throughout most of this book, the question of what causes development is typically cast in terms of heredity and environment, thus implying that the way a child grows up results from only two sources of influence: (1) her inherited nature and (2) the way she is nurtured by parents and others. However, some theorists have proposed other possible causes as well. Before identifying these additional possibilities, we will first inspect the issue of the relationship between nature and nurture, since it remains the central concern of most psychologists, biologists, and sociologists when they argue questions of cause. As the debate has progressed over the years, the focal question has shifted somewhat, moving first from *which one* to *how much,* and then subsequently to *in what manner* (Anastasi, 1958). We will inspect each of these focuses in turn.

Which one? In past centuries philosophers seemed to be answering the question, Which causes developmental changes, a child's heredity or environment? An example from the environmentalist side of the issue is the proposal of British philosopher John Locke (1632–1704) that at birth a child's mind is a void, an unmarked page or *tabula rasa* on which the contents of the mind are sketched by the child's experiences as the child grows up. At the other extreme was Rousseau (1712–1778), who considered the child's inherited "nature" to be the most influential force in determining the child's steps in development.

This controversy can be simply illustrated as positions on either side of a fence (see Table 2.1). Traditionally the people on the heredity side have been divided into

T A B L E 2.1
Heredity or environment: which one?

| | *Hereditarians* | |
Environmentalists	*Preformationists*	*Predeterminists*
The child's experiences are preeminent in determining development.	Environment has no influence.	Environment has little influence.

two groups: the *preformationists* and the *predeterminists.* The distinction between preformationists and predeterminists chiefly concerns how powerful the theorist believes hereditary effects are. Preformationists believe that *all* of an individual's potentials—his or her personality, values, motives, mental abilities, and emotional makeup—exist completely formed within the infant at birth. As the child advances in age, these potentials unfold on a prearranged genetic schedule. Since all signifi-cant elements of development are preformed, the particular environment in which the child grows up has no role in determining development. Predeterminists, however, are not so willing to dismiss the influence of a child's physical and social surroundings. They believe environment has some effect. But since they believe a child's genetic schedule is so important, they belong on the heredity side of the controversy along with the preformationists.

Actually the issue of which one—heredity or environment—determines de-velopment is rather silly, since even rudimentary reasoning makes plain that neither factor can exert influence or even exist without the other. A child's heredity cannot display itself in a condition of nothingness—in a nonenvironment. Nor can a child be spontaneously generated without ancestors, as if springing out of nowhere to be influenced by an environment. Even the most radical environmentalists and here-ditarians of the past recognized the necessary existence of both factors, nature *and* nurture. So the argument actually was not over which one, but rather how much.

How much? During the nineteenth century and through the first half of the twentieth, the nature versus nurture issue centered primarily on the question of how much heredity contributed to development in comparison to environment. Graph-ically the issue can be pictured as a line, with the heredity component above and the environment component below (see Table 2.2). A given theorist's position on the issue can be identified at some point along the line. To illustrate, we cite the fa-mous debate that attracted the attention of American psychologists in the 1920s and 1930s concerning which factor contributed more to a child's intellectual growth, heredity or environment. By statistical methods, B. S. Burks (1928) concluded that heredity deserved 83 percent of the credit for mental ability, and environment only 17. Other investigators (Leahy, 1935; Shuttleworth, 1935) also concluded that heredity played the major role, though the proportions they derived were some-what different. Still other researchers, using a series of studies conducted in the midwestern United States, concluded that the opposite was true—that en-vironment was the stronger factor in determining mental ability (Skeels, 1940;

T A B L E 2.2
Heridity or environment: how much?

	Extreme hereditarians	Moderates	Extreme environmentalists
Percentage of nature's contribution	95%	50%	5%
Percentage of nurture's contribution	5%	50%	95%

Skodak, 1939). This debate has never been settled, and the main reason may well be that the wrong question—or at least an unprofitable question—was being asked.

Investigations based on the issue of how much have led to conflicting conclusions about the same data and to interpretations of questionable usefulness. As a consequence, in recent decades there has been a strong movement among people interested in these matters to recast the key question from *how much* to *how* or *in what manner* the factors interact (Anastasi, 1958).

In what manner do nature and nuture interact? A basic tenet of this modern interactionist approach is that nature and nurture are two different dimensions, each operating 100 percent in its role. Although this approach does not really abandon concern with how much, its more important question by far is, How does the interaction of heredity and environment take place in order to produce the observed development of the child? This question has a variety of answers, each depending on the point of view of the particular theorist being examined. Since the present chapter is intended only to outline issues that theories treat and to pose guide questions for use in comparing theories, a wide array of interpretations of interaction will not be analyzed here. Rather, only two views will be described that illustrate the extent to which ideas about interaction can vary.

According to the first view, heredity defines the boundaries of potential development, and environment determines where, within these boundaries, a child's actual development is realized. "Heredity determines what we can do, and environment what we do do" (Montagu, 1959). Furthermore, it is assumed that the boundaries differ for different characteristics. For certain traits, such as eye color, heredity sets very narrow limits within which environmental forces—such as nutrition—can operate. For other characteristics, such as the cognitive ability to analyze complex abstract relationships, the boundaries set by heredity appear to be wide, allowing considerable room for the operation of such environmental factors as nutrition, instruction, rewards for the child who practices such analysis, and many more.

This interactionist viewpoint also assumes that the potential defined by heredity is manifested differently at different times in the child's life. For example, at puberty, a genetically timed ripening occurs for the primary sex characteristics (maturing ova in girls, maturing sperm in boys, and maturing systems for delivering these cells) and such secondary sex characteristics as changes in body shape. Thus puberty produces different potentials from those available when the child was age two or four or six.

From this interactionist perspective, the question of how much nature contributes as compared to nurture is no longer of prime interest. Instead we now seek to know (1) how wide are the boundaries set by heredity for various aspects of development—physical traits, cognitive abilities, frustration tolerance, and others; (2) what environmental forces influence the way these aspects manifest themselves in the child's structure and behavior; and (3) how this interaction of inherited potential and environmental forces operates at different stages of the child's growth period.

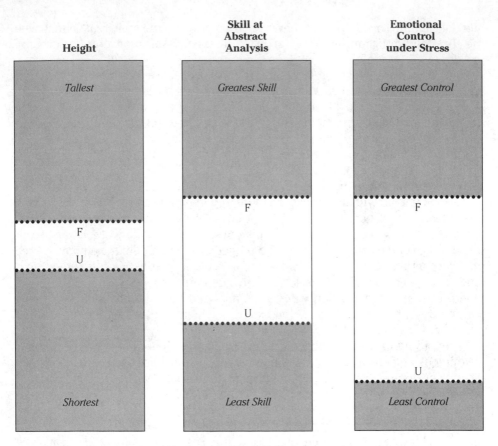

•••• = Hypothesized upper and lower boundaries of inherited potential
F = Development in favorable environment
U = Development in unfavorable environment

FIGURE 2.1
An interactionist viewpoint: in what manner?

Some idea of how the complex interrelations of this model differ from the interrelations of the *which one* and *how much* approaches can be shown in the simplified diagram in Figure 2.1. Three concepts are plotted here:

1. *Genetic influence over different developmental characteristics varies from one characteristic to another.* The three characteristics shown in Figure 2.1 are height, skill at analyzing abstract relationships, and emotional control under stress. The top and bottom of each box represent, respectively, the greatest and least genetic potential that is humanly possible for that characteristic (at a certain age level). The white space in each box represents one hypothetical child's genetic potential for that characteristic.

2. *Heredity establishes boundaries of potential for each characteristic.* In Figure 2.1 the hypothetical upper limit for development—for example, the tallest that child can grow—is the upper dotted line. The lower limit—the shortest height the child can grow to—is the lower dotted line.
3. *Environmental influences determine where within the boundaries a child's development will manifest itself.* The range within which environment can affect development is shown as the white area between the dotted lines in each characteristic. The letter *F* signifies the level of development a child will exhibit if the environmental influences are very favorable (near the upper limit). The letter *U* signifies the level of development exhibited if environmental conditions are very unfavorable (near the lower limit).

Thus in Figure 2.1 we hypothesize that there is more leeway for the influence of environmental factors in determining a child's emotional control than in determining either height or skill at abstract analysis. Whether such a hypothesis is true becomes a matter of empirical investigation.

To complete this first analysis of interaction, it is necessary to explain which environmental factors are most potent in determining how genetic potential is realized and how these forces are interrelated, as well as to describe how the interaction may vary at different stages of the child's development.

This first interactionist approach does not tell us—as older theories that addressed the question *how much* did—what proportion of development is due to heredity and what proportion is due to environment, but it still enables us to differentiate between environmentalists and hereditarians. In terms of Figure 2.1, theorists who picture the area between the inherited potential boundaries as narrow are hereditarians, for they believe the child's genetically designed nature does not permit much manipulation by environmental factors. Theorists who picture the boundaries as widely separated are more environmentalist, for they think environmental influences greatly affect the way development characteristics are manifested.

Let's turn now to the second way of viewing the *in what manner* approach to interaction. Some writers consider interaction in terms of how directly heredity influences development (Anastasi, 1958). To illustrate, let us consider three examples of mental development that range in scale from very direct to very indirect hereditary influence.

At the very direct end of the scale is the case of a child suffering from phenylketonuria. This mental defect results from hereditary metabolic dysfunctions that are not significantly improved by changes made in the child's environment—the affected child will remain mentally defective (Anastasi, 1958, p. 198).

Heredity has a less direct influence on mental development in cases of hereditary blindness or deafness. A blind or deaf child who is raised in an environment designed for children with normal sight and hearing will typically display symptoms of retarded mental growth. Although sight and hearing cannot be restored, changes can be made in the environment to compensate for the handicap. A blind child can be given audio-recordings of books and can be taught to read by the braille method;

the deaf child can be taught sign language and lip reading. These compensatory measures enable mental development to proceed far more normally.

Our third example from the very indirect end of the scale of hereditary influence concerns social stereotypes. We recognize that genetic endowment has much influence in determining a child's skin color, height, weight, facial features, acuity of senses, and so forth. People within a given culture often associate certain intellectual or personality traits with such physical characteristics. In other words, people often hold social stereotypes. If a child's facial features and her movements are usually viewed in her society as typical of sweet, clever girls, then people will often treat this child as though she were sweet and bright. Since the way people treat a child influences the way that child comes to perceive herself, we can conclude that the child's self-concept—her feeling of adequacy—is at least partly the result of social stereotypes associated with inherited physical characteristics. In effect, if the child perceives herself as clever rather than dull, she may be motivated to display higher levels of mental development than if she believed herself dull. Heredity, in this instance, has influenced mental development in a very indirect manner.

As noted earlier, although theorists who adopt one of these interactionist approaches emphasize the *in what manner* or *how* of the interaction between nature and nurture, they have not abandoned the question *how much*. However, they phrase the question in new ways. For instance, when Anastasi (1958, p. 206) proposed that it is best to view nature and nurture in terms of a scale running from direct to indirect, she added that the more indirectly heredity influences a behavior, "the wider will be the range of variation of possible outcomes." In other words, there is not much room for environment to influence those characteristics that most directly depend on genetic factors. Yet environment can very much influence those characteristics that are very indirectly linked to heredity. Thus Anastasi is still posing a *how much* question in terms of the amount of variability possible.

What can we say then about modern theorists' position on the heredity versus environment issue? Today, most theorists consider themselves interactionists in that they think both nature and nurture are indispensable and work together to produce development. However, this does not mean that the debate has ended; theorists continue to disagree on the conditions of the interaction between nature and nurture. Indeed, one of the most incendiary social controversies in North American educational circles in recent years centered on the question of whether the genetic endowment of certain racial groups limits their potential mental ability compared to that of other racial groups (Hebb, 1970; Hirsch, 1970; Jensen, 1969, 1973; Layzer, 1974). Since the issues are complex and far from settled, arguments of this type can be expected to continue in the years ahead.

When we analyze theories of development, we can include such guide questions as the following:

2.1 Can the theorist be identified by such traditional labels as *preformationist, predeterminist, interactionist, hereditarian,* or *environmentalist?*

2.2 Does the theorist see some aspects of development as being more constrained by hereditary boundaries than others? For example: Are the inherited potential boundaries narrower or the heredity connections more direct for skin color than for oral language skills (if, indeed, two such different characteristics can be adequately compared in terms of amounts)?

2.3 Does the theorist see heredity as more constraining for certain growth characteristics at different periods of childhood? For example: Are the inherited potential boundaries for the development of reading ability different at age six than they are at age twelve?

2.4 Does the theorist describe the process by which the interaction of nature and nurture takes place?

In contrast to most present-day theorists, some writers have proposed further sources of influence besides heredity and environment. Examples of such proposals are the conceptions of a respected developmentalist, T. C. Schneirla, and two beliefs common to many of the world's major religious traditions.

Schneirla (1957) suggested that a third force affecting development is the growing organism—the child himself or herself. This influence arises from the manner in which hereditary and environmental factors interact. For example, assume that an infant is born with a genetic structure that predisposes him to a high level of activity. As a result, he sleeps less than most babies. When he is awake he cries for his parents' attention. Although the parents seek to provide the comfort and care their son seems to require, they soon become physically tired and emotionally irritated by his irregular rest habits and demanding activity. Their irritation is reflected in the way they handle the child and in the harshness of their voices when they lose their patience. In their frustration and exhaustion, they increasingly escape by closing the door to the baby's bedroom to "let him cry it out." This treatment serves to heighten, rather than decrease, their son's activity level because the child is stimulated by his emotional distress to make even greater demands on his parents' time and patience. In effect, a cycle of interaction has been established in which the evolving characteristics of the organism—the growing child—become a significant influence—a third force—in determining the way the environment will treat the child. Schneirla concluded, in essence, that "the individual seems to be interactive with itself throughout development, as the processes of each stage open the way for further stimulus-reaction relationships depending on the scope of the intrinsic and extrinsic conditions then prevalent" (1957, p. 86).

We turn now to a pair of additional influences found in concepts of development embedded in many of the world's religions: *human will* and *supernatural intervention.* In the case of will, the assumption is made that a person's life pattern is not determined entirely by genetic and environmental variables but is influenced as well by the individual's free-will choices and by how hard he or she tries to implement such choices. This conception of the importance of will appears in such diverse religions as Christianity, Judaism, Islam, Confucianism, Hinduism, and Shintoism, as well as in much of the commonsense or naive psychology of the general public.

The operation of *supernatural intervention* as a contributor to development is a central element in most if not all religious traditions. Adherents of such traditions believe that a person's developmental fate can be determined to a large degree by the action of destructive supernatural forces (Satan or other evil spirits) and of constructive or salutary powers (God, Allah, cosmic energy, or other beneficent spirits). Sometimes the supernatural powers act on their own volition to influence people's lives. In other cases supernatural intercession is solicited by people through prayers, rituals, and offerings. This type of cause is generally given no place in such modern "scientific theories" as those described in Chapters Three through Seventeen (Thomas, 1985, p. 719). (Nevertheless, proponents of scientific theories may sometimes in their daily lives display a belief in supernatural influence. Particularly in times of danger, as during a child's illness or a threat to the family's safety, even a scientific developmentalist may appeal to a supreme power to intercede).

3. Direction of development   The terms *growth* and *development** both imply change, and identifying the directions of this change has been a central concern of theorists.

A good example of a theory that gives central attention to directions of development is that of Heinz Werner (1961), whom we meet briefly in Perspective D in Part Five, "Estimating the Future of Stage Theories." Werner proposed that one direction of growth was from rigidity to flexibility: whereas an infant displays rigid behaviors suited specifically to given situations and does not readily alter these behaviors to suit new conditions, an adolescent's behaviors are more flexible and adapt readily to changed conditions.

Perhaps the easiest way to discover a theory's directions of development is to ask, How does the child differ from the adult? In Piaget's model, young children are very self-centered, constrained to interpret events solely from their own viewpoint. Normal adults, on the other hand, understand that different people may interpret events from rather different perspectives.

In our search for the directions described or implied in a theory, we can ask:

3.1 What aspects of behavior or growth (for example, physical growth, cognitive development, social skills) are encompassed by a particular principle or statement of direction?

3.2 What interrelationships, if any, exist between the direction of change of one aspect and that of another? For example: Does attainment of physical maturity precede attainment of intellectual maturity? Does the differentiation of behaviors in the young child proceed more rapidly than the integration of various individual actions into smoothly flowing systems of behavior?

4. Continuous versus stepwise change   Usually theories not only define directions of change, they tell whether this change occurs gradually in small increments or dramatically in large periodic steps (steep advances) followed by periods of less apparent change (plateaus). Skinner's behaviorism is an example of a theory that pictures growth as occurring in imperceptibly small increments. In contrast, other theories picture growth as shifting from one major step or stage to

---

Growth is often defined as change in size, *development* as change in the complexity and functions of the individual. However, each term may be defined as change in both size and function. It is in this second, more inclusive manner that the terms are used in this book.

another. Piaget proposed steps and substeps of cognitive development. Freud identified several major psychosexual stages of growth. Havighurst proposed that children at different points in their life are confronted with particular tasks of growing up and that these tasks form a series of stages in development. In effect, the essence of many theories is found in the sorts of stages postulated and in the way the child's movement from one level to the next is viewed. The controversy about these matters among developmentalists has traditionally been known as the *continuity–discontinuity issue.*

Everyone agrees that development from one day to the next is gradual. No one claims that a twelve-year-old girl is a prepuberal child one week and a full-blown adolescent the next. In this sense growth is continuous and occurs in small increments. The real question then is whether, during this process, the child's structure and behavior periodically display symptoms that warrant the label of a new stage of development. Behaviorists such as Skinner answer no to this question; other theorists answer yes. Those who answer yes are then obligated to identify the traits of a stage so that, following their theories, we can recognize a new stage when we see one.

Consequently, in analyzing a theorist's position on the issue of continuity versus discontinuity, we first pose this question:

4.1 Does children's development proceed through a series of small, continuous increments without any dramatic changes or identifiable qualitative plateaus? Or do children develop from one recognizable stage to another?

If the answer to this first query is that children pass through stages, then we can profitably pose several more questions:

4.2 How does the theorist define *stage* or *step* or *period?*

4.3 How many stages are identified in the system, and what are the names and distinguishing characteristics of each stage?

4.4 On what aspects of life or growth do the stages focus? In other words, what dimensions of development do the stages represent? For example: Are these stages of physical growth? Of sexual development? Of socialization? Of moral judgment? Of oral language development?

4.5 Do the aspects or dimensions have the same importance at all times during childhood? For example: Are physical growth stages more prominent in the early years than they are later in childhood?

Since the matter of whether children are growing up "normally" is of interest to many people—parents, teachers, pediatricians, and children themselves—it is also useful to ask what a theory expects of developmental stages. To begin:

4.6 How are the levels or stages related to chronological age?

Of the proposals discussed in later chapters, the most specific in correlating age with growth characteristics is Gesell's (Chapter Three). Gesell described in rather definite terms what the typical two-year-old is like and how his or her characteristics differ from those of the one-year-old and the three-year-old. The stages described by Piaget, Freud, and Havighurst are less closely tied to specific ages than Gesell's, and Maslow's levels of human needs (Chapter Twelve) are even less specifically correlated with chronological age than Piaget's and Freud's stages.

The question of the correlation between age and stage is not the only one pertinent to the task of judging the normality of a child's growth. For example, a number of questions arise about the universality and invariance of stages.

4.7 Are the stages universal—that is, true for all children in all cultures? Or do children in one culture pass through different stages from those in another? Within a culture, is it possible for a child to skip what has been described as a stage, or must everyone move through the stages in a single defined sequence? If a child can skip a stage or proceed by a different path than some of his or her peers, why does this deviation occur?

Many theorists consider the stages they describe to be universal—found among all children in all cultures—and their sequence invariant. *Invariant* means that not only are the stages found in all cultures for which we have reports, but the nature of development is such that no other sequence in the pattern of growth stages is possible. Such writers as Piaget (Chapter Nine), Kohlberg (Chapter Sixteen), and Erik Erikson (Chapter Six) have assumed invariance, although some critics have questioned this position (Phillips & Kelly, 1975). Remember, therefore, not only to inquire about a theorist's position but also to consider whether the evidence or line of reasoning used to support that position is convincing.

Three other sets of questions can be asked about how growth rates, fixation at a stage, and regression to an earlier stage may be treated in a theory.

4.8 Does everyone go through the stages at the same pace? If not, why not?

The terms *retarded, normal, advanced,* and *gifted* have traditionally been used to describe children who are growing at particular rates compared to their age-mates, regardless of whether growth is viewed as continuous or stepwise. Question 4.8 is directed at whether a theory recognizes such phenomena and, if so, how it accounts for them.

Another question related to the rate of passing through stages is this one:

4.9 Can a child display typical characteristics of more than one stage at the same time? If so, why does this occur?

Some theorists (Gesell, Havighurst) make little or no mention of this possibility; others accord it considerable attention (Erikson, Piaget, Kohlberg). An example of the simultaneous presence of multiple stages is found in Piaget's subtheory about children's ideas of causality. When Piaget studied what children believe causes certain physical events in the world, he concluded that a child who accounts for cloud movements by saying elves push the clouds is operating on a lower level of thought than a child who says that air currents (rising hot air, descending cool air) move the clouds. Piaget found, however, that while a child may use fantasy beings (elves) to account for certain physical events, the same child may give naturalistic explanations (air currents) to account for others. In effect, the child is operating on two stage levels at the same time (Piaget, 1930).

4.10 Can a child's progress through the stages become arrested or fixated at a particular stage? If so, what causes the fixation? What can be done to release it and stimulate progress to the next stage?

Theorists account for fixation in several ways. Gesell's system, which can be labeled a predeterminist theory, views arrested development as caused by inadequate genetic endowment. Behaviorists feel it results from inadequate stimulus from the environment. Freud's psychoanalysis views it as seated in either too much satisfaction of needs at the present stage of development or too little satisfaction.

4.11 Can a child return to an earlier stage after entering a more advanced one? If so, what causes this *regression* or *retrogression?* What can be done to help the child recover and move ahead once more?

Regression, like fixation, is of particular interest to therapists, whose task it is to assist children whose development seems to be going awry. The most popular explanation among theorists who recognize the phenomenon of regression is that a child slips back to an earlier stage of development when the adjustment skills developed at the present stage prove inadequate for coping with current problems. However, some theorists contend that there is no such thing as true regression. The child does not really slip back but just gives the appearance of regressing by adopting a segment of behavior from an earlier time.

Our concern with retardation, fixation, regression, and uneven development can also lead logically to another question:

4.12 If a child experiences growth problems at one stage, how may these problems influence success at subsequent levels? And how can we best deal with such problems?

For most theorists, problems that are not adequately resolved at one stage either will prevent the child from moving on to the next or will make it difficult for the child to adjust to subsequent levels. And most feel that therapy or retraining is required to correct or ameliorate the problems and thus enable the child to continue developing. However, not all theories see the issue in this same light. Theories, like Gesell's, that see genetic factors as greatly restricting the range within which environmental factors can affect development, do not usually propose therapy or retraining. For instance, Gesell's model of development contains the concept of alternating "good" and "bad" years or phases of growth. This pattern of alternation is seen as a "natural" one, common to virtually all children. So problems at one level of growth are seen as instances of "going through a bad phase" that will naturally pass with time. Patience rather than therapy is needed to wait out the passing of the phase (Ilg & Ames, 1955, pp. 22–24).

In summary, twelve sets of questions have been proposed to guide our inquiry into the way a theorist handles the issue of continuity versus discontinuity. Although most of the questions are directed at theories that view growth as occurring in steps or stages, a number of them are also useful for understanding nonstage or continuous theories as well. For example, we can ask whether a continuous growth model pictures all children as developing along the same route (4.7) and at the same pace (4.8). We can also ask whether a child can become fixated (4.10) or can regress (4.11) and how growth problems can be ameliorated (4.12).

5. Original moral condition   An issue of greater interest in past centuries than today concerns the child's natural moral mode. Some theorists either state outright or imply that the child at birth, and by natural inclination, is in a particular moral condition: good (moral), bad (immoral), or neutral (amoral). The eighteenth-century writer on child development and social policy Jean-Jacques Rousseau contended that children are innately moral. He felt that if they are to remain good, they need to be protected throughout their growing years from the corruptions of an immoral society (Rousseau, 1773). Fundamentalist Christian doctrine, in contrast, has pictured children as innately immoral, having received the sin of Adam and Eve in their psychic inheritance. Such children need a great deal of strict guidance if they are to be saved from devilish ways (*New England Primer*, 1836; Dunstan, 1961, p. 208). Freudians regard children as innately amoral—that is, without knowledge of right or wrong at birth—but with a capacity to internalize the morals of their social environment so that these values eventually become a part of their personalities, the part Freud labeled the superego. Maslow, as a humanistic psychologist, viewed the child's sense of morals as partly innate and partly learned.

Therefore, in comparing theories, we may wish to ask:

5.1 What is the original or genetically determined condition of the child: moral, immoral, or amoral? Can the newborn be some mixture of the three, depending on which aspect of development is under consideration?

6. Personality structure   Most theories of development assume that the child has a psychological system or a sort of mental machinery, which is known by such terms as *personality, mind, cognitive structure,* or *intervening variables.* Usually this system is assumed to contain elements or functions that interact to determine the child's behavior. Part of the task of understanding development, then, consists of identifying these components and the ways they interact over the first two decades of life. Freud's system includes three key elements: the *id,* the *ego,* and the *superego.* Information-processing theorists often distinguish among such components as the *sense organs, short-term memory,* and *long-term memory.* Piaget distinguished three basic mental operations: *assimilation, accommodation,* and *equilibration.* Thus, in analyzing a theory, we may wish to ask:

6.1 What are the components of personality or of behavior?

6.2 How do the components interact and change as the child grows up?

7. *Motivation and the learning process*   In the field of psychology the topics of motivation and learning are often considered separately. However, *motivation* is typically seen as the impetus for learning, directing the child's attention toward what she or he will seek to learn. Since motivation can be viewed as a beginning step or condition in the learning process, they are discussed together here.

Not all theorists use the same words to identify motivating forces, but the two most popular terms are *need* and *drive*. These terms are like two sides of a coin—two ways of looking at the same phenomenon. The word *need* implies intake—a void seeking to be filled. *Drive* implies output—pent-up energy searching for a place to invest or expend itself. Thus the need for food is the hunger drive, and the need for drink is the thirst drive. Although some theorists favor the term *need* (humanistic psychologists) and others favor *drive* (behaviorists), in each case the intention is to identify a motivating force that energizes behavior.

In some theories little or no attention is given to describing motivating forces (Gesell in Chapter Three, Kohlberg in Chapter Sixteen). In others, motivating forces are at the center of the schemes (Freud in Chapter Five, Maslow in Chapter Twelve).

Furthermore, some theorists conceive of a single general force that activates all behavior. In Freud's early model, he called this general force *libido*, an energy arising in a component of the personality called the *id* but utilized by other components of the personality as well to fuel their functions. Freud originally pictured libidinal energy as dominantly a sexual drive. However, in his later years he suggested that development and behavior are motivated by the interaction of two contrary drives—a life-promoting force (*libido*, from a source termed *eros*) that accounted for constructive events in the personality, and a death-directed force (*thanatos*) that accounted for destructive ones (S. Freud, 1938, pp. 5–6).

Many theories of personality and development either explicitly or implicitly differentiate among levels of needs. For example, a commonly postulated basic need from the field of biology is that of self-preservation. But when we observe behavior, we can propose that this basic need is manifested through a variety of more specific needs, such as those for food, for oxygen, for sexual expression, and for succor (the need to be nursed, supported, and consoled) (Hall & Lindzey, 1970, pp. 174–180).

Theorists, then, differ in the number of motivating forces they identify or imply, as well as in the way they name and organize the proposed drives or needs. Therefore we may wish to include in our guide questions the following:

7.1 Does the theorist identify or imply forces that motivate behavior? If so, what are these forces and what are their characteristics?

Not all theorists who propose the existence of various drives or needs agree as to the potency of each. For instance, Freud described his general force, libidinal energy, as being preeminently sexual. An early colleague of Freud's, Alfred Adler (1870–1937), disagreed that the prepotent human drive was sexual. Although he recognized sex as a significant drive, Adler contended that the truly overriding motive in human development was a *will to power*, a striving for superiority. He wrote that "whatever premises all our philosophers and psychologists dream of—self-preservation, pleasure principle, equalization—all these are but vague representations, attempts to express the great upward drive" (Adler, 1930, p. 398).

Maslow's system (Chapter Twelve) also recognizes differences in the potency of various motivating forces but pictures their operation in a manner different from Freud's or Adler's. Maslow suggested that a person's needs are arranged in a hierarchy, like steps on a ladder, with the lower-step needs requiring fulfillment before the upper-step needs. He relegated such survival needs as those for food, drink, and physical safety to the lower levels of the hierarchy, and drives for creative expression and "self-actualization" to the upper levels.

Not only may theorists claim that some needs are more significant than others throughout life, but they may also propose that certain needs are more potent at one stage of development than at another. For instance, a need for physical protection and nurturance is often considered more important during infancy, whereas a need for sexual expression is considered more demanding following puberty. (See the developmental tasks of Chapter Three.)

From this discussion we can generate another set of guide questions:

7.2 If several motivating forces are identified in the theory, do all of them carry equal power and importance? If not, which are more significant and why? If they differ in potency, do their relative degrees of power change from one growth stage or one age level to another?

Most theorists agree that a child not only is motivated strongly or weakly, but also is motivated toward particular things in the environment. In other words, a motivating force has not only power but also direction. Theorists do not agree, however, about the source or cause of this direction. The question is essentially this:

7.3 Which source—the child's inner needs or the environment's stimuli—is more important in determining where the child directs his or her attention?

Theorists such as Piaget and Freud credit inner needs with the greater power to direct attention, whereas behaviorists consider environmental stimuli to be more powerful. To a substantial degree, this difference of opinion reflects the more basic disagreement about which model each camp of theorists believes best represents human behavior. As we saw in Chapter One, some theories of development are founded on the analogy of the machine, and others are based on the analogy of an organism. A machine reacts to things done to it by outside forces. It is "motivated" by environmental stimuli. An organism contains internal driving forces that seek expression in the environment; it is motivated by inner needs that direct its attention to those things in the environment that will likely fulfill these needs.

I noted earlier that motivation or stimulation is commonly considered to be a beginning step in the learning process. Exactly what steps occur after this stimulation is a matter of dispute among theorists. A behaviorist such as Skinner sketches one picture of the process, Piaget quite a different picture, and social learning proponents still another. Therefore, in analyzing theories, we can suitably ask:

7.4 In this theory, how does motivation fit into the overall picture of the learning process?

7.5 What are the necessary conditions for learning to occur? What elements or mechanisms comprise the learning process, and how do the elements interact?

8. Individual differences   It is obvious that children of a given age level are not all alike. They differ in many ways. Theories of child development also differ in how they treat this matter of variation. Some theorists—Gesell, for example—give little recognition to the issue of differences. They talk almost exclusively about the typical child, passing over the fact that nearly all children deviate to some degree from the average. Other theories, such as behaviorism and contextualism, account more adequately for differences among individuals. Hence, to guide comparisons among theories, we can ask:

8.1 What sorts of individual differences among children are given attention in the theory?

8.2 How does the theory account for such differences? To what extent do the factors that cause differences arise from heredity or from environment, and how do the causal factors operate or develop?

9. Desirable versus undesirable, normal versus abnormal   One of the most common practical questions asked by parents, teachers, and others who deal with children is whether a child's development is normal. Since not everyone defines the term *normal* in the same way, this question can be misleading. In one sense *normal* is used to mean "well adjusted" or "getting along very nicely." In another sense it means that the child's growth is about average for his age, or her behavior is common for her size or grade in school. We encounter problems of communication when these two meanings are mixed. For example, smoking cigarettes is very common among American youths in their upper teens and early twenties, so in this sense smoking is "normal"—that is, typical. But medical evidence suggests that smoking is not desirable, so in the sense of "getting along very nicely," smoking is not normal.

Whereas some theorists specifically differentiate between normal and abnormal growth, others only imply this distinction. They specify normal or desired goals of growth, then simply assume that deviations from the path toward the goals are undesirable.

Because matters of *normal, natural,* and *desirable* development are somewhat complex and are of considerable practical importance for child rearing, Perspective A in Part Two has been dedicated to the topic of "Distinguishing Normal from Abnormal Development."

To guide our efforts in sorting through these matters, we can ask:

9.1 Is normal or natural or desirable development defined, or at least implied? If two or more of these terms appear in the theory, are they used synonymously? If not, how are they differentiated from one another?

9.2 Is abnormal, unnatural, or undesirable development identified? If two or more of these terms appear in the theory, are they used synonymously? If not, how are they differentiated?

9.3 What causes abnormal, unnatural, or undesirable development? What, if anything, can be done to change such development into normal, natural, or desirable growth?

10. Philosophical origins and assumptions   No theory is an entirely new creation. Each has its philosophical progenitors, and our understanding of a theory is usually enhanced by our learning something of this ancestry. Our grasp of Maslow's brand of humanistic psychology (Chapter Twelve) is enriched by our knowing that his proposals, in part, represent his reaction against what he believed were the shortcomings of both psychoanalysis and behaviorism. We can profit from knowing that Erikson's ideas (Chapter Six) are founded primarily on Freud's teachings but have been influenced as well by methodology and concepts from cultural anthropology.

So we add another pair of queries to our list:

10.1 On what philosophical traditions, beliefs, and assumptions is the theory founded?

10.2 Against what beliefs is the theory reacting?

11. Investigative methods   There is something of a chicken-and-egg relationship between a theory and its investigative methods. We never know whether the theory's structure has defined the methods used for gathering data, or whether instead the data-collecting methods have dictated the structure. In any event, models of child development are heavily influenced by the investigative techniques used in producing the data they treat.

For instance, Freud's main method of collecting information was to listen to neurotic adults recall incidents from their childhood and from their current dreams. Clearly the particular recollections this method evoked influenced the nature of the theory he proposed. The charge that his theory gives a gloomy, disturbed view of human development has been raised by critics who blame his choice of neurotic informants as the cause of the ostensibly pessimistic picture he paints of child growth. Likewise, his dependence on self-reports of memories and dreams as his source of data is compatible with his willingness to fashion an imaginary structure of the "mind" from which these memories and dreams are generated. In contrast, Skinner rejected introspective reports as sources of evidence and depended instead on descriptions of child behavior as recorded by an outside observer. This dedication to observable events is compatible with Skinner's unwillingness to speculate about such hypothetical elements as an unseeable "mind" or such mental components as Freud's id, ego, and superego.

Thus, in analyzing theories, we can ask:

11.1 What investigative methods are used by the theorist?

11.2 How have these methods influenced the form and content of the theory?

12. Appeal for acceptance   Typically, theorists want others to believe their proposals. To this end they seek to present the sorts of arguments they feel will appeal to the people they want to accept their scheme. For instance, such fundamentalist Christian theorists as P. A. Captain (1984) appeal to parishioners' faith in the word of God as found in the Bible and on a set of deductions about child rearing that theologians draw from church doctrine. Classical psychoanalysts propose that, in addition to the intuitive good sense their theory makes, a person becomes convinced of its validity by going through the process of psychoanalysis. Experimental psychologists describe their experiments in detail and cast the results in statistical form, with the expectation that anyone who questions the results can carry out the same experiments and see the validity of the conclusions.

Thus different theorists use different approaches in soliciting acceptance of their schemes. Likewise, different consumers of theories consider some sorts of evidence more convincing than others. Whether you find a particular model of development more useful or valid than another depends on how well the theorist's mode of appeal matches the types of evidence you regard as most acceptable. Hence we may ask:

12.1 On what sorts of evidence or on what kind of appeal does the theory depend to convince people of its worth?

13. Terminology   In the following chapters you will find many terms created or adopted by theorists to describe their ideas of personality structure, growth stages, and growth principles. These include *growth gradients, id, epigenetic principle, formal operations, contextualism, chaining, zone of proximal development,* and many more. Often the essence of a theorist's position is contained in the terms used. If you comprehend the terms, you understand the substance of the theorist's beliefs.

If, in our investigation of a theory, we answer the twelve clusters of questions already considered in this chapter, then we will likely have learned the meaning of most or all the key terms in the theory. But in case we have missed any, we can add two final sets of queries:

13.1 Does the theory have a special terminology? If so, what does each term mean?

13.2 Do the terms refer to concepts unique to this theory, or do they identify things for which other theorists have used different words?

CONCLUSION

In this chapter, we have proposed a series of questions that can be asked about the contents and philosophical underpinnings of theories we wish to analyze and compare. This list does not include all the questions that could be asked; it contains ones I feel are of general interest. You may wish to add others that focus on matters of particular importance to you.

In the following chapters separate theories are described. The aim in organizing each chapter has been to answer, as far as space permits, the questions posed in this chapter. However, none of the chapters is designed like a catechism, with a sequential list of answers to these questions. Instead, each chapter is presented in a form intended to give the essence of the theorist's approach in a logical and interesting fashion. In the process, as many of the questions posed in this chapter are answered as is feasible. Some chapters do not treat certain questions because the theorist or theorists did not ask such questions. In other instances a topic plays such a small part in a particular theory that it is not worth discussing in this introductory level volume.

Now, with the perspectives of Chapters One and Two in mind, we move to the theories themselves.

FOR FURTHER READING

You may wish to find additional topics and questions to supplement the list given in this chapter. If so, your most convenient source may be child development textbooks. Chapter titles and topic headings in such books often imply questions the authors believe are important for theorists to answer, so that an inspection of titles and headings can suggest additional guide questions. Furthermore, under such headings you often find concise answers to the questions as seen from various theorists' points of view.

To aid you in this search, the following list of representative sources is suggested:

Bee, H. L. (1989) *The Developing Child.* New York: Harper & Row.
Broughton, J. M. (ed.). (1987) *Critical Theories of Psychological Development.* New York: Plenum.
Cole, M., and S. R. Cole. (1993) *The Development of Children.* New York: Freeman.
Damon, W. (ed.). (1989) *Child Development Today and Tomorrow.* San Francisco: Jossey-Bass.
Fisher, C. B., and R. M. Lerner. (1994) *Applied Developmental Psychology.* New York: McGraw-Hill.
Hetherington, E. M., and R. D. Parke (eds.). (1993) *Contemporary Readings in Child Psychology.* New York: McGraw-Hill.
Jahoda, G. (1993) *Crossroads Between Culture and Mind: Continuities and Change in Theories of Human Nature.* Cambridge, Mass.: Harvard University Press.
Kreppner, K., and R. M. Lerner. (1989) *Family Systems and Life-Span Development.* Hillsdale, N.J.: Erlbaum.
Mussen, P. H. (ed.). (1983) *Handbook of Child Psychology.* New York: Wiley.
Mussen, P. H., J. J. Conger, and J. Kagan. (1990) *Child Development and Personality.* New York: Harper & Row.

SOURCES OF THEORIES

A search for the wellsprings of child development theories

The proposition advanced in Part Two is that scientific theories, such as those described in Chapters Five through Seventeen, are responses to objectionable features either of commonsense notions about development shared within a society or of existing scientific theories. The purpose of Chapter Three is to illustrate this proposition with examples of features regarded as objectionable and of alternative innovations that theorists have introduced. Chapter Four then demonstrates how people's everyday commonsense assertions about children can be analyzed to reveal the underlying theoretical organization of such convictions. First, it is useful to recognize the meanings assigned here to the expressions *commonsense notions* and *scientific theories,* both of which may mean different things to different people.

THE NATURE OF COMMON SENSE

In ancient Greece, Aristotle proposed that there were five external senses—sight, hearing, taste, smell, and touch—plus a common sense, located in the heart, which served as the coordinating center for the other five. Remnants of this belief are still found in our language in such statements as "She learned it by heart." Later philosophers relocated the common sense in the brain. In the present context, the term *common sense* has a different meaning.

For many people, common sense refers to convictions held by a person because the truth of such beliefs is self-evident. If we need no special training or special instruments to arrive at a conclusion about something we see or hear or smell, then we usually say our conclusion is "just common sense." We believe that anyone in his or her "right mind" would come to the same conclusion. This sort of common sense—the recognition of self-evident conclusions—is part of what I intend.

Common sense is also equated with the term *popular opinion,* and this meaning is the other part of the definition that will be relied on here. To some people common sense means an idea that everybody, or nearly everybody, subscribes to, whether the idea is obvious or not. In our culture, for example, the fact that the earth is a sphere is common sense today, though that "fact" is not obvious to the eye. Nor was that "fact" common sense at the time of Columbus.

The phrase "a commonsense view of child development" thus identifies those beliefs shared by a large proportion of society—with many of the beliefs being self-evident conclusions. Such shared convictions are sometimes referred to as *naive psychology.*

THE NATURE OF SCIENTIFIC THEORIES

The term *science* is generally used to identify both a general method of seeking the truth and a body of information compiled by the use of that method. Observations of scientists at work reveal no single specific scientific method. Rather, what scientists hold in common is a set of general precepts or attitudes that guide their efforts.

One of these precepts is that conclusions about human development should be founded on empirical evidence—that is, on evidence derived from the direct study of people's appearance and behavior. Thus, scientific knowledge is not merely common sense; instead, it involves the careful collection of empirical evidence and the logical interpretation of the evidence. Scientific theories are products of that interpretation.

A second precept is that all conclusions are subject to revision as the result of additional empirical evidence and its analysis. Consequently, from a scientific perspective, no answers to questions about development should be regarded as final and definitive. Each answer is assumed to be no more than an approximation of the truth, an approximation that requires further testing and refinement.

What, then, is the connection between common sense and scientific concepts? The connection is quite intimate, since the matters scientists study derive from traditional cultural beliefs. Hence, scientific endeavors can be conceived as activities designed to refine data, introduce alternative perspectives, systematize information, refine definitions, improve quantification, extend commonsense insights, replace dubious explanations, and interpret puzzling observations. These functions are illustrated in Chapter Three.

HEIDER'S VERSION OF NAIVE PSYCHOLOGY

It would be an error to presume that people's commonsense beliefs are no more than random, disparate notions that lack any coherent organization. On the contrary, analyses of naive psychology suggest that a unifying structure links the beliefs in a network of logic—a network seldom apparent to the people who hold those convictions. Everyone appears to subscribe to his or her own informal theory of child development without being clearly aware of the form of that theory. Furthermore, within a cohesive culture one person's conception tends to have much in common with another's.

An American psychologist, Fritz Heider, took on the task of discovering the components of commonsense theory and estimating how those components interact. Heider, in effect, sought to expose the structure underlying the naive psychology reflected in the way many people talk about children. Chapter Four offers an expanded rendition of that structure. The chapter addresses the question, To what causes do people attribute children's growth and behavior? For that reason, the chapter qualifies as a version of *attribution theory.*

Earlier I proposed that commonsense theory consists of beliefs shared by a large proportion of society—with many of these beliefs being self-evident conclusions. Although this definition may at first appear uncomplicated, we will see, when we analyze specific convictions, that people do not all agree on what they believe about children's growth and development. Differences of opinion are especially apparent in large, complex modern societies in which scholars have both the time and desire to speculate and conduct research about the nature of humanity. These thinkers come up with ideas that sometimes conflict with most people's common sense. But as the novel ideas are communicated, many people become convinced of their validity and join this new school of thought. Such splintering of common sense into different camps can be expected to occur more frequently in societies that are blessed (or burdened) not only with the leisure time for speculation but also with highly penetrating mass communication devices— television, radio, newspapers, magazines, and books. Smaller, more isolated and cohesive societies subscribe to a more commonly accepted set of convictions about children than do larger, more disparate ones. Therefore, as we consider one version of commonsense theory, there may be a problem of consensus.

Furthermore, the common sense outlined in Chapter Four applies chiefly to societies that have evolved from European roots. How closely this version represents common sense in traditional African, Asian, Native American, and Pacific Island cultures is only partly known (Thomas, 1988).

Another aspect of naive psychology that deserves attention was described by an American developmental psychologist, A. L. Baldwin (1967, p. 38):

> It is important to realize . . . that naive psychology is not a stated theory but a body of beliefs about human behavior. Only the systematic description of naive psychology gives it the look of a theory.

Thus we are interested not just in the commonsense beliefs themselves but in the systematic way they are analyzed. We may ask, however, whether such everyday beliefs about children deserve a chapter in a book on formal theories. Aren't naive assumptions too ordinary to warrant serious discussion? For at least three reasons, naive psychology does deserve attention.

First, commonsense psychology is the sort that all of us use, either entirely or to a great degree, in dealing with children during the routine of daily living. A study of the structure and content of naive notions of development should help us analyze the strengths and weaknesses of such notions. As a result, we may be able to alter at least some of the least defensible aspects of our commonsense opinions and perhaps substitute more valid ones.

Second, the analysis of common sense can help us understand the nature of more formal theories of development because those theories often include many commonsense assumptions. After we observe the way psychologists such as

Heider analyze naive beliefs, we will be better prepared to recognize the naive-psychology aspects of other theories we study.

Finally, as noted earlier, formal models of development are often theorists' reactions against naive-psychology notions that they believe are in error. Thus, when we recognize the commonsense ideas theorists are reacting against, we are better equipped to understand the formal theories. In effect, naive psychology serves as one foundation on which formal theories are constructed.

V. L. Lee (1988, pp. 17–18, 25) characterized this relationship between common sense (ordinary knowledge) and formal theorizing (scientific knowledge) in the following manner:

> Scientific knowledge is extraordinary knowledge. It is knowledge of phenomena beyond ordinary observation. Probing beyond ordinary observation is part of what we ask and expect of a science. . . . We should expect inquiry to start in what is known and deliberately to surpass it. We want an academic psychology that can provide extraordinary knowledge and that can link its extraordinary knowledge step-by-step to the foundation given in ordinary psychology. . . . Ordinary psychology is constitutive of our experience of conduct and it is not easily set aside.

For these reasons, a chapter on commonsense psychology is of value in a book about theories of development.

FIRST KEY ISSUE:
NORMAL, NATURAL, DESIRABLE DEVELOPMENT

The final segment of each of the following parts of this book is dedicated to a discussion of one key issue, called a "Perspective," in the realm of child development. The issue chosen for Part Two concerns the normality or desirability of development. I selected this topic because so many of the people responsible for the care of the young want to know how to decide whether the development of a child or an adolescent is *normal* or *natural* or *proper* or *desirable*. Should such words be used as synonyms, or is it better to distinguish among them? And if the terms should be differentiated, how is this best accomplished? More specifically, what popular options are available for defining these terms, and what are the advantages and disadvantages of each option? The reasons that this issue fits properly into Part Two should become apparent after you have read Chapter Three.

CHAPTER THREE

CULTURAL ORIGINS
OF SCIENTIFIC THEORIES

The purpose of this chapter is to illustrate ways that scientific investigations and formal theories can be interpreted as responses to unsatisfactory features of traditional commonsense views of child development. Investigators guided by the precepts of science have improved traditional cultural conceptions of development in a variety of ways. They have refined descriptive data, introduced alternative perspectives, systematized information, refined definitions, improved quantification, extended commonsense insights, replaced dubious explanations, and interpreted puzzling observations. We will inspect each of these functions in turn, but also note how dedication to scientific canons has caused theorists to avoid several issues that over the centuries have held a prominent place in cultural conceptions of development. Finally, we will point out how certain scientific theories described in this book represent reactions against several of the other theories.

REFINING DESCRIPTIVE DATA

People's attempts to understand their world begin with observations of how things appear. Only after they can describe appearances do people speculate about how one thing relates to another and what causes things to change. Thus descriptions of appearances serve as a foundation for theorizing about relationships and processes. This order of events—description precedes theorizing—is characteristic of both everyday living and scientific investigation. So it is with theories of child development, which are founded on descriptions of children's physical characteristics and their behavior at different age levels.

Before the late nineteenth century, the observations on which almost everyone based beliefs about child development were rather casual. Even such influential writers as the French social philosopher Jean-Jacques Rousseau (1712–1778) and the German founder of the kindergarten movement, F. W. A. Froebel (1782–1852), were unsystematic in compiling their perceptions of child characteristics. Then, by the late eighteenth century, several European scholars made initial efforts to apply the methods of natural science in collecting and manipulating observations of human growth. Dietrich Tiedemann (1748–1803) is credited with producing the first psychological diary of the growth of a young child. Another German, Friedrich August Carus (1770–1808), attempted to develop a general science of life span psychological development. A Belgian astronomer and statistician, Lambert Adolphe Quételet (1796–1874), proposed sophisticated methods for analyzing multiple influences on human development. And the English author of *On the Origin of Species,* Charles Darwin (1809–1882), in 1877 published a diary of child growth entitled *Biographical Sketch of an Infant,* a work now considered one of the best early efforts at careful observation of human development.

Subsequently, in the United States in 1891, G. Stanley Hall published "The Contents of Children's Minds on Entering School," thereby launching a tradition that dominated child development investigation in the United States during the first half of the twentieth century. This is the tradition of measuring and observing groups of children and then summarizing the results in the form of averages for different age levels. Studies of this type have focused on a wide array of children's characteristics, ranging from measurements of height and weight, through the testing of mental and physical skills, to observations of social relations, sleep habits, and outbursts of anger. The number of such published studies from around the world runs into many thousands. They have been called *normative, descriptive* investigations because they describe the normal—in the sense of average—status of children on specified characteristics at different age levels. The summarized results of these studies typically are labeled *descriptive norms* or *age norms.*

The theorist who best exemplifies the normative-descriptive school of child development is Arnold Gesell, a physician and child psychologist who in the early 1900s studied under Hall at Clark University before setting up a clinic at Yale University to conduct descriptive research on children. Gesell's apparent intention was to chart with as much care and thoroughness as possible children's characteristics at each age level in a great many facets of their lives.

Gesell was born in 1880 in Wisconsin, where he was educated and eventually took a college degree in teaching before earning a Ph.D. in psychology at Clark University in Massachusetts in 1906. In 1911 Gesell was appointed to the Yale faculty as an assistant professor of education. At the same time he established the Clinic of Child Development, which he directed during the next thirty-seven years. While at Yale he earned a doctorate in medicine (1915), and his clinic was attached to the school of medicine. After Gesell's retirement, several of his coworkers set up a private institution near Yale in New Haven, naming it the Gesell Institute of Child Development. Gesell served as a consultant to the clinic from 1950 through 1958. He died in 1961, but the work of his clinic has continued since that time.

Over the decades, Gesell and his colleagues pursued the task of describing the observable changes in child growth and behavior from birth into adolescence. Although their principal concern was with development after birth, the group also conducted studies on prenatal growth stages. The research portion of Gesell's work consisted mainly of studying "fifty or more" children, each brought to the clinic to be examined yearly from infancy through age ten. "Most of these children were of high-average or superior intelligence, and came from [New England] homes of good or high socioeconomic status" (Gesell et al., 1977, p. xiv). These data enabled the group to describe *maturity traits* and developmental steps, called *growth gradients,* for the typical child in ten major areas, with each area defined by the subcategories shown in parentheses in the following list (Gesell et al., 1977, p. 58):

1. *Motor characteristics* (bodily activity, eyes and hands)
2. *Personal hygiene* (eating, sleeping, elimination, bath, dressing, health, somatic complaints, tensional outlets)
3. *Emotional expression* (affective attitudes, assertion, anger, crying, and related behavior)
4. *Fears and dreams*
5. *Self and sex*
6. *Interpersonal relations* (mother-child, father-child, child-child, siblings, family, grandparents, groupings in play, manners)
7. *Play and pastimes* (general interests, reading, music, radio, television, movies)
8. *School life* (adjustment to school, classroom demeanor, reading, writing, arithmetic)
9. *Ethical sense* (blaming and alibiing; responsiveness to direction, punishment, praise, and reason; sense of good and bad, truth, and property)
10. *Philosophic outlook* (time, space, language and thought, death, deity)

An inspection of this list shows that Gesell adopted a multifaceted view of children rather than concentrating on one or two aspects of their growth. The topics cover growth areas of daily concern to parents and teachers, which helps account for the popularity of the numerous books emanating from the Gesell Institute. For example, the 1976 edition of *Your Four Year Old* (Ames & Ilg, 1976) had been reprinted seventeen times by the late 1980s. The volumes are not composed of statistical tables showing the frequency of certain behaviors or the number of children above or below the average at a given level. Instead, Gesell and his staff digested the statistics and turned them into specific statements of what a child is like at a given age. For example, here are typical descriptions of an aspect of behavior—children's fears—for ages five and six, from a volume by two of Gesell's closest coworkers, Frances L. Ilg and Louise B. Ames.

> *5-year-olds:* Not a fearful age. More visual fears than others. Less fear of animals, bad people, bogeymen. Concrete, down-to-earth fears: bodily harm, falling, dogs. The dark. That mother will not return.

> *6-year-olds:* Very fearful. Especially auditory fears: doorbell, telephone, static, ugly voice tones, flushing of toilet, insect and bird noises. Fear of supernatural: ghosts, witches. Fear that someone is hiding under the bed. Fear of the elements: fire, water, thunder, lightning. Fear of sleeping alone in a room or of being only one on a floor of a house. (1955, pp. 172–173)

Gesell and his associates have been lauded for the innovative child-study techniques they introduced from the 1920s into the 1940s, but they have also been criticized for a lack of attention to individual differences among children and for offering unduly simplistic, dogmatic statements about "what most children are like." For instance, Gesell asserted that the even-numbered years of children's development from ages five through sixteen are worse years and the odd-numbered years better years. This practice is reflected in the remarks just quoted about children's fears at ages five and six. Gesell further declared that between ages two and five the better and worse periods of development alternated within each year—a better period starting soon after the child's birthday and a worse one beginning six months later (Ilg & Ames, 1955, p. 22).

Perhaps an even more important criticism is the charge that the Gesell group's reports of "typical development" at each age level have given the incorrect impression that what children *are* like at a given age is consequently what they *should be* like. This is the problem of implying that behavior common at a particular age is normal in the sense of desirable—an issue so often confused in people's minds that it warrants the special attention given it in Perspective A at the close of Part Two.

In summary, one of the most important advances in the field of human development over the past century has been the great emphasis on careful empirical observations and measurements of children. The work of such pioneers as Gesell provided a foundation for a host of subsequent research that has afforded proper recognition to both average growth trends and individual differences among children. Such studies have led to highly refined descriptions of child development and have furnished ample material for the creation of new theories. The aspects of Gesell's work that critics found objectionable, such as his issuing unduly simplistic generalizations, have been rectified by later researchers.

INTRODUCING ALTERNATIVE PERSPECTIVES

Novel conceptions of human development are certainly not the exclusive province of modern-day theorists. Throughout the world and over the centuries, philosophers and religious leaders have suggested innovative explanations of how people develop. Among the most widely recognized proposals have been those submitted by such philosophers and prophets as Plato, Moses, Confucius, Lao-tzu, Siddhartha Gautama (the Buddha), Jesus, the Prophet Muhammad, John Locke, Friedrich Hegel, Karl Marx, and others. Although the creation of alternative modes of explaining the human condition is nothing new, the great rate at which novel notions of development appear is of quite recent vintage. Several factors seem to have contributed to this rapid rise in original explanations. One factor has been the scientific community's suspicion of "ultimate answers," a suspicion founded on the conviction that the theories and facts presently at hand are no more than an approximation of the real truth. Thus, newer, more accurate approximations are welcomed. A second factor is the proliferation throughout the twentieth century of the number of people whose chosen task is the investigation and interpretation of human development. A host of new explanations might well be expected from such a multitude of investigators. Third, the advent of new technologies—computers, videocameras, electron microscopes, and far more—has stimulated the collection of vast amounts of new evidence about development, evidence not adequately explained by existing theories. Questions generated by these floods of data have invited the submission of new styles of interpretation.

In summary, more proposals about why people grow up the way they do have appeared over the past century than at any other time in history. The proposals have taken the form of macrotheories, minitheories, micromodels, hypotheses, and the like.

This idea of innovative perspectives can be illustrated with a developmental-task model devised by a group of American psychologists and educators active in the Progressive Education Association between the 1930s and mid-1950s. A leading member of the group was Robert J. Havighurst (1913–1951), a University of Chicago professor who advocated replacing the term *needs* with the phrase *developmental tasks* because he had "seen so much misunderstanding result from the use of the equivocal term 'needs' as a central concept" (1953, p. 330). He felt that this new phrase better described what children and youths are attempting to do as they grow up. According to Havighurst, the developmental tasks of life are pursuits that

> constitute a healthy and satisfactory growth in our society. They are those things a person must learn if he is to be judged and to judge himself to be a reasonably happy and successful person. A developmental task is a task which arises at or about a certain period in the life of the individual, successful achievement of which leads to his happiness and to success with later tasks, while failure leads to unhappiness in the individual, disapproval by society, and difficulty with later tasks. (1953, p. 2)

What are the tasks at different age levels? How many are there? Havighurst said that the number is somewhat arbitrary. It depends both on the way a person chooses to specify them and also on the particular society the person is talking about. For instance, the task of learning independent locomotion can be seen either as a single complex task composed of subactivities (creeping, walking, trotting, running, hopping, jumping) or as six different small tasks.

Some tasks arise mainly from the biological nature of humans and thus are found in all human societies. Their form is essentially the same in all cultures. Other tasks derive their characteristics from the unique cultural patterns of a given society; these either exist in different forms in different societies or else are found in some cultures but not in others. A task like learning to walk, which depends primarily on genetically determined growth factors, is essentially the same in all societies and arises at about the same time in a child's life. However, the task of selecting and preparing for an occupation is a complex one in highly industrialized societies that are characterized by much specialization and division of labor, whereas in nonindustrialized societies, in which nearly everyone is a farmer or hunter or fisher, the task of choosing a vocation is perhaps simpler and is achieved at a younger age. Furthermore, the tasks of learning to read and write, which are so important in highly literate cultures, do not even exist in preliterate ones.

Consequently, lists of developmental tasks are not the same for all cultures, and the items in these lists are determined to some degree by the personal value systems of the people who prepare them. Havighurst admitted that the description of tasks he produced was "based on American democratic values seen from a middle-class point of view, with some attempt at pointing out the variations for lower-class and upper-class Americans" (1953, p. 26).

Havighurst felt that, in applying the developmental-task approach to children's education, it is most useful to define six to ten tasks at each stage of development. One such application is shown in Table 3.1, which is adapted from a table by Tryon and Lilienthal (1950). The chart contains ten general categories or types of tasks. These categories are listed in the far left column. To find the specific tasks in each category and at each age level, look to the right of the category name.

For example, consider the first category, that of the child's achieving an appropriate pattern of dependence and independence in growth. In the second column from the left, we find two specific tasks the infant faces in this category: (1) establishing oneself as a very dependent being and (2) beginning the establishment of self-awareness. For children at the stage of early adolescence (fifth column), we find one task described in this category: establishing one's independence from adults in all areas of behavior. In a similar manner we can find the specific tasks for each growth stage in any of the ten task categories.

Just as the number of tasks is somewhat arbitrary, so also are the stages through which an individual's development is traced. Tryon and Lilienthal identified five stages from birth to around age 20. Havighurst, however, divided the entire life span into six stages: (1) infancy and early childhood (birth through age 5), (2) middle childhood (ages 6 through 12), (3) adolescence (ages 13 through 17), (4) early adulthood (ages 18 through 30), (5) middle ages (ages 31 through 54), and (6) later maturity (ages 55 and beyond).

Applications of developmental-task theory have been of several kinds. One type has been an effort to improve school curricula and out-of-school programs for children. As curriculum planners have sought to suit schoolwork to pupils' needs, they have assessed how well the subject matter and activities of the current curriculum match the developmental tasks identified for children at different age levels. In this way improvements have been made in parts of the course of study that apparently had not previously contributed toward the achievement of important tasks (Tryon & Lilienthal, 1950). Leaders in charge of extracurricular and out-of-school programs for young people have also used task analysis in selecting activities to be included in their programs.

As a further type of application, authors of child development textbooks in both North America and Europe have described childhood from a developmental-task perspective (see, for example, Bernard, 1970; Hurlock, 1968; Muller, 1969; Travers, 1977). They have assumed that an understanding of the tasks children are attempting to accomplish will help parents and teachers be more patient with such attempts and provide activities that help the young succeed in these endeavors.

Although the developmental-task model has not been a particularly fruitful source of empirical studies over the decades, it still continues to serve as a conceptual framework for a limited number of researchers. For example, A. Palmonari, M. L. Pombeni, and E. Kirchler (1990) studied the influence of peer groups on adolescents' attempts to cope with developmental tasks. D. A. Dangelo (1989) inspected the way changing times affect the roles assigned to adolescent females in literature that concerns adolescents. M. Ittyejerah and A. Samarapungavan (1989) studied the performance of congenitally blind children performing cognitive tasks. T. A. Kindermann (1993), in research on infants, tracked changes in mother-child interactions as infants became more competent in performing developmental tasks. K. M. May and C. R. Logan (1993) examined the relationship between young college students' perceptions of their families and how successfully those students accomplished developmental tasks appropriate to their age.

In this section, we have taken developmental-task theory as an example of an alternative perspective to traditional cultural views of child growth. However, scores of other current theories, including all those described in the following chapters, would serve that purpose equally well.

Systematizing Information

After careful observations and measurements of children have been collected, one way to derive meaning from the resulting conglomeration of facts is to assign each fact to a category in a classification structure. Although commonsense conceptions of development include ways of classifying observations of child growth and behavior, those ways tend to be intuitive rather than consciously devised, and thus they frequently lack clarity and consistency. On the other hand, scientific theories typically provide explicit, logically organized categories that promote systematic comparisons among data. As noted in Chapter One, formal classification schemes are often referred to as *typologies* (with each category dedicated to a particular type of development or behavior) or *taxonomies* (with the term *taxon* and its plural form, *taxa*, referring to the system's categories).

Classification structures can differ from one another in the number and complexity of their categories. An example of a scheme involving only two categories is Piaget's proposal that children's moral judgments can be either *heteronomous* or *autonomous*. Whereas heteronomous morality requires obedience to authority and to authority-produced rules, autonomous morality is based on the child's dedication to the principle of reciprocity and equality among peers. In terms of this dichotomy, a child's moral judgments can be relegated to either the heteronomous or the autonomous grouping. A system providing a larger number of classes is Gesell's arrangement of ten principal types of development, several of which contain between three and eight subtypes. The developmental-task matrix displayed in Table 3.1 is even more complex, with a different set of subclasses for each age level under ten principal tasks.

Classification systems are not always cast in a permanent form but, instead, may evolve as new discoveries suggest more refined categories. A example of an expanding system can be found in the area of developmental disabilities. In Great Britain in 1886, only two statutory types of child disabilities were considered to warrant special attention. Both described people with varieties of mental retardation: idiot and imbecile. By 1913 five more categories had been added: moral imbecile, mentally defective (feebleminded), blind, deaf, epileptic, and physically defective. By 1945 there were twelve classes, some incorporating more than one of

TABLE 3.1

The tasks of five stages of development in ten categories of behavior

	Infancy (birth to 1 or 2)	Early childhood (2–3 to 5, 6, or 7)	Late childhood (5, 6, or 7 to pubescence)	Early adolescence (pubescence to puberty)	Late adolescence (puberty to early maturity)
I Achieving appropriate pattern of dependence and independence	• establishing oneself as very dependent being • beginning to establish self-awareness	• adjusting to less attention; becoming independent physically (while remaining dependent emotionally)	• freeing oneself from primary identification with adults	• beginning to establish independence from adults in all behavior areas	• establishing oneself as an independent individual in an adult manner
II Achieving appropriate pattern of giving and receiving affection	• developing a feeling for affection	• developing ability to give affection • learning to share affection	• learning to give as much love as one receives; forming friendships with peers	• accepting oneself as worthwhile person, worthy of love	• building strong mutual affectional bond with possible marriage partner
III Relating to changing social groups*	• becoming aware of the alive vs. the inanimate, the familiar vs. the unfamiliar • developing rudimentary social interaction	• beginning to develop ability to interact with age-mates • adjusting to family expectations for child as member of the social unit	• clarifying adult world vs. child's world • establishing peer grouping and learning to belong	• behaving according to shifting peer code	• adopting adult-patterned social values by learning new peer code

IV Developing a conscience	• beginning to adjust to expectations of others	• developing ability to take directions, to be obedient in presence of authority • developing ability to be obedient in absence of authority (conscience substitutes for)	• learning more rules; developing true morality	• learning to verbalize contradictions in moral codes, discrepancies between principle and practice; resolving these problems responsibly
V Learning one's psycho-socio-biological sex role		• learning to identify with adult male and female roles	• beginning to identify with same-sex social contemporaries	• strong identification with one's own sex • learning one's role in heterosexual relationships • exploring possibilities for future mate; acquiring "desirability" • choosing an occupation • preparing for future role as responsible citizen
VI Accepting and adjusting to a changing body	• adjusting to adult feeding demands • adjusting to adult cleanliness demands • adjusting to adult attitudes toward genital manipulation	• adjusting to expectations based on improving muscular abilities • developing sex modesty		• reorganizing self-concept in the face of significant bodily changes • accepting one's appearance • learning appropriate outlets for sexual drives

TABLE 3.1
(continued)

	Infancy (birth to 1 or 2)	Early childhood (2–3 to 5, 6, or 7)	Late childhood (5, 6, or 7 to pubescence)	Early adolescence (pubescence to puberty)	Late adolescence (puberty to early maturity)
VII Managing a changing body and learning new motor patterns	• developing physiological equilibrium • developing eye-hand coordination • establishing satisfactory rhythm of rest and activity	• developing large muscle control • learning to coordinate large and small muscles	• improving skill in use of small muscles	• controlling and using "new" body	
VIII Learning to understand and control the physical world	• exploring the physical world	• meeting adult restrictions on exploration and manipulation of expanding environment	• learning more realistic ways of studying and controlling physical world		

IX Developing an appropriate symbol system and conceptual abilities	• developing pre-verbal communication • developing verbal communication • rudimentary concept formation	• learning to use language to exchange ideas or to influence • beginning to understand causal relationships • making finer conceptual distinctions; thinking reflectively	• improving one's use of the symbol system • great elaboration of concept pattern	• using language to express and clarify more complex concepts • moving from the concrete to the abstract; applying general principles to the particular	• reaching one's potential level of reasoning
X Relating oneself to the cosmos		• developing a rudimentary notion of one's place in the cosmos	• developing a scientific approach		• formulating a workable belief and value system

*This table does not deal with the developmental tasks of relating to "secondary" social groups. As the child grows and develops, he or she must relate to groups other than the family and peers—to school, community, nation, world. There are not yet sufficient data to enable us to delineate the specific developmental tasks in this area.

Source: Adapted from Tryon and Lilienthal, 1950, pp. 77–89.

the earlier designations (severely subnormal subsumed both idiot and imbecile), and others being added to extend earlier categories (partially sighted was added to blind, and partially hearing was added to deaf). By 1981 the official types numbered fourteen, with several additional varieties suggested but not officially adopted. The 1981 list was as follows: child with learning difficulties (severe), child with learning difficulties (mild), blind, partially sighted, deaf, partially hearing, epileptic, maladjusted, disruptive, physically handicapped, speech defective, delicate, dyslexic, and autistic. Additional suggested types included neuropathic child, inconsequential child, psychiatrically crippled child, aphasic child, and others (Tomlinson, 1982).

A kind of chicken-and-egg relationship can obtain between collecting facts and classifying them; research can begin either with an existing classification scheme or with the collection of data that provide the basis for a classification system. In the first of these approaches, investigators begin with a typology that defines what they are looking for in their empirical studies. The typology determines what kind of information they seek, the instruments they use, and how they record the information. For example, the 1981 British categories have guided the systematic survey of the percentages of children in the population who display the different kinds of disabilities (Tomlinson, 1982).

In the second approach, data collection precedes the creation of a classification structure. Investigators begin with no more than a very general notion of the kind of development they are seeking to explain—eye-hand coordination, concept formation, physical agility, or speech behavior, for example. Then they observe children in situations that elicit this general sort of behavior, and record what they see and hear. Next, they peruse the records in order to devise meaningful categories into which to cast the data. This process of inductive thought is sometimes called "following the data." To illustrate, in a study of young people's modes of moral reasoning, the investigators described six cases of wrongdoing for 542 youths to judge. The youths' task was to propose the consequences the offenders in the cases should face and to explain why such consequences would be appropriate. The researchers conducted this portion of the study without any preconceptions about how participants' explanations should be categorized. Subsequently the researchers derived categories by inspecting the entire collection of participants' answers and deciding what sorts of classes might reasonably accommodate all the explanations. This analysis produced five major categories, described as (1) moral values, consisting of moral principles and conditions under which the principles should be applied; (2) the intended aims of consequences; (3) causes underlying offenders' misdeeds; (4) the feasibility of applying different consequences; and (5) the kinds of people who would be qualified to impose consequences. A variety of subcategories were defined for each of the five classes. The resulting taxonomy was then used to classify the 542 respondents' opinions (Thomas & Diver-Stamnes, 1993).

Each of the theories described in later chapters of this book is characterized by its unique way of systematizing data. A theory's special mode of classifying observations of children is typically one of its most distinctive and appealing features.

REFINING DEFINITIONS

A common difficulty with commonsense conceptions of development is that the meanings of the terms they employ are often inexact and differ from one person to another. Consider, for example, such words as *ability, backward, careless, cause, crazy, genius, inborn, intelligence, lazy, learning, maturation, mentally disturbed, natural development, smart,* and *stubborn.* Instead of using such vague terms, modern theorists usually try to define their key concepts in ways that convey their exact meanings. Two devices they use are lifelike examples and operational definitions.

Providing lifelike examples involves explaining classification categories by describing events that both the theorist and the reading audience have experienced. This shared experience can be either direct or vicarious. It is direct whenever both the theorist and his or her audience have faced that particular event in their own lives. Both had reading lessons when they attended elementary school, both have talked on the telephone, and both have shopped in stores. However, the experience is only vicarious whenever the theorist delineates an event in such graphic terms that members of the audience can easily imagine it, even though they have never faced the depicted situation in their own lives. Freud made liberal use of vicarious happenings by offering detailed descriptions of neurotic clients he treated in his psychiatric practice. Through this device he sought to convey his meanings for such terms as *conversion hysteria* (a psychological disturbance expressed in the form of a bodily ailment), *rationalization* (a socially acceptable reason offered for an act derived from an ignoble intent), and *unconscious motivation* (people's lack of awareness of why they act as they do). In a similar way, Piaget's books are replete with quotations of children's solutions to problems posed for them, with the quotations helping to clarify Piaget's meanings for such expressions as *egocentric thought* (interpretation of events solely from one's own point of view) and *centration* (recognition of only one dimension of a multidimensional phenomenon).

The phrase *operational definition* means communicating the intent of a term by specifying the operations carried out in assessing or measuring the phenomenon to which the term refers. By way of illustration, consider the word *intelligence.* Defining this term operationally consists of explaining the way intelligence is evaluated, an explanation that usually consists of describing the tests used and the conditions under which they were administered. Psychologists commonly recognize that when mental abilities are measured by different tests, a child may earn a higher score on one test than on another. Because the kinds of items on one test often differ markedly from those on another, different tests assess somewhat different specific mental abilities. Intelligence as measured by the Stanford-Binet Scale (Terman & Merrill, 1960) is not the same as that measured by Guilford's items (1967), by Gardner's approach (1983), or by Piaget's cognitive-reasoning tasks (1950). Researchers who use operational definitions often alert their readers to this fact with some such explanation as the following: "Throughout the following report, the word *intelligence* means the level of a child's performance on the Wechsler Intelligence Scale for Children." Or: "In this book, *intelligence* refers solely to the scores children earn on the Primary Mental Abilities Tests."

Although precision in defining important terms is a typical aim of present-day theorists and of researchers who conduct empirical studies, critical readers do not always agree that the aim has been completely fulfilled. We will meet this issue of clarity of definitions again in discussing theories in later chapters.

IMPROVING QUANTIFICATION

A further unsatisfactory feature of commonsense conceptions of development is their lack of precision in reporting quantities. The numbers of children in a population who display a given trait may be described as *many, few, most, hardly any, lots, some,* or *a majority.* The frequency of a child's arriving late at school may be expressed as *sometimes, often, usually, rarely,* or *occasionally.* Although such inexact designations are of some use, they usually fail to provide the precision needed for a sophisticated understanding of the issue being investigated. Furthermore, it is not uncommon for people to cite extreme amounts whenever the behavior they have observed impresses them as particularly objectionable or praiseworthy: "She never listens to a thing I say" or "He always does what he's told." On these occasions, a more careful study of events might show that the actual quantities were not so extreme.

The same problem of precision arises in commonsense comparisons among individual children or among groups that are differentiated by age, gender, ethnic origin, socioeconomic status, religious affiliation, or some other quality. The purpose of these comparisons is to reveal the degree of similarity between the compared entities with regard to some characteristic—academic achievement, moral reasoning, athletic skills, self-confidence, time of entering puberty, or use of illicit drugs, for example. Commonsense phrases used to describe the extent of similarity include *very much alike, distinctly different, quite the same, almost opposites, nearly identical,* and *somewhat similar.* Again, people who value precision consider such vague expressions insufficient. As a result, throughout the twentieth century and especially in recent years, creators of child development theories have sought to improve the quantitative nature of the evidence on which they base their models. An illustration of this trend is the matter of sampling.

It is common practice for theorists to derive their explanatory principles from the study of a particular group of children and then to suggest that those same principles apply equally well to the larger population of children from which the group was drawn. In other words, a theory based on analyzing the development of the few is presumed to be valid for explaining the development of the many. Consider, then, three instances of sampling procedures from the first half of this century. Gesell's research on fewer than sixty American children led him to draw conclusions about all children everywhere. Piaget's ostensibly universal stages of cognitive development were founded on observations of an undisclosed but apparently quite restricted number of Swiss children. Freud's generalizations about all children's psychosexual stages derived from recollections of childhood reported to him by a limited number of adult neurotics he treated in his role as a therapist in Vienna. The question in each of these instances is whether the sample of subjects who formed the theorist's database was truly representative of the broad population of children to which the theory was then applied. Should not Gesell, Piaget, and Freud have sampled far more children, or at least have confined their generalizations to a population of children whose cultural environments were like those of the subjects they studied? Or would it not have been wiser of them to cast their proposals in a more tentative form, expressing their views as probabilities rather than certainties?

Since those early decades, several circumstances have encouraged theorists to offer more convincing quantification of the evidence undergirding their systems. First, an increasing number of critics have reproved authors for failing to buttress their proposals with convincing quantitative support. Second, new forms of statistical analysis have been introduced. Third, such technological innovations as videotape recorders have rendered observations of children more accurate, and the art of testing children has improved. Finally, the ready availability of computers has made the manipulation and transportation of large amounts of data infinitely more accurate and rapid than was envisioned a few years ago. To illustrate the influence of these trends, consider a recent instance of sampling that stands in contrast to Gesell's, Piaget's, and Freud's early procedures. Over the 1990–1991 school year, a study of reading literacy was conducted with 210,000 children, ages nine and fourteen, attending government schools in thirty-two countries (Elley, 1994). Not only was the sampling of children extensive, so also was the sampling of types of reading materials, which included

> short simple fables, long 1500 word narratives, dense scientific prose, short personal notes, complex graphs, and functional tasks like following directions, interpreting maps, using timetables, and other document-type items. Prodigious efforts were made by the researchers and national representatives to minimize any cultural or linguistic biases, and the statistical machinery of the Rasch model was systematically used . . . both to help identify troublesome [test] items, and to create defensible international scales. (Elley, 1994, p. xxi)

Although the survey report was not presented in the form of a theory, it did contain components of theory as that term was defined in Chapter One. That definition, when applied in the present context, describes theorizing as the act of proposing which facts are most important for understanding children's development of reading literacy, and what sorts of relationships among the facts are most important for producing this understanding. The facts investigated (and thus deemed important) by the research team included such variables as children's socioeconomic status, the availability of reading materials in their homes, the language used at home, the amount of time children watched television, their teachers' instructional methods, the age at which children were introduced to reading, their access to libraries and bookstores, and far more. By means of statistical analyses, the investigators were able to determine the degree to which each of these conditions was associated with reading skill in different nations and in different kinds of schools. The report, in effect, provided the basic ingredients for creating a theory of the development of reading competence founded on a widespread sampling of cultural settings, types of schools, types of home backgrounds, community resources, genders, and kinds of reading materials. The report also contained a multitude of statistical tables to support the generalizations the authors drew about levels of reading skill and the relationship of these levels to influential environmental conditions. In brief, quantification was very extensive and fittingly detailed.

Sometimes a theory is introduced with no more than a modicum of quantitative support. Subsequently, empirical studies are conducted to test, refine, and revise the scheme. Such has been the case with Piaget's cognitive-development model. Over the past several decades, hundreds of investigators throughout the world have founded their research on Piagetian concepts. Their results have verified numerous proposals of Piaget's, while revising other of his ideas in ways that more convincingly explain children's cognitive growth under various environmental conditions. Thus, authors often submit theories that are no more than provisional estimates of "the truth"—estimates that await empirical testing and precise quantification. This practice seems most defensible when the authors openly admit the tentative, yet-to-be-proven nature of their schemes.

In summary, creators of formal theories increasingly support their views with more precise quantitative evidence than that found in traditional cultural descriptions of development.

EXTENDING COMMONSENSE INSIGHTS

Sometimes the role of formal theory is to extend or elaborate commonsense convictions. For example, in many present-day societies, as well as those of the past, a popular belief has been that the most fundamental purpose of human development is to equip people to survive. Typically this purpose has been seen as extending beyond bare survival, so that the aim of development is to foster people's health, longevity, physical comfort, and personal satisfaction. In its commonsense version, belief in a survival motive has sometimes been limited to the individual (self-interest) or to the immediate group (family, clan, tribe). Other versions propose that the survival aim encompasses all of humanity, so development is driven by the need to protect humans as a species. But in recent times, sociobiologists have extended this traditional concept to a more fundamental level. After citing studies of altruistic behavior (individuals' sacrifice of their own welfare for the welfare of others) in various species, such theorists have suggested that the most natural purpose of life is not the survival of the species, since species are eliminated or altered with the passing of time. Rather, the basic aim is the survival of the genes, which are the carriers of life itself (Wilson, 1975, pp. 3–4). (See Chapter Fourteen.)

Sometimes researchers extend commonsense insights by refining popular notions about development. In all literate societies, common sense has recognized that people of the same chronological age do not all learn to read and write equally well. However, in past centuries the extent to which different individuals' literacy skills deviate from the average has been no more than vaguely acknowledged. One major contribution of researchers in recent times has been their precision in describing individual differences in literacy and explaining why such differences occur (Elley, 1994). For instance, studies of reading ability have suggested that the range of reading skill within a typical grade level in school is double the number of that grade. Thus, in a heterogeneous group of fourth graders, the least adept reader will not perform as well as an average first grader (four grades below), while the most talented will read as skillfully as an average eighth grader (four grades above) (Thomas & Thomas, 1965). Similar advances in knowledge of human differences have been achieved in all other aspects of development as well.

REPLACING DUBIOUS EXPLANATIONS

A noteworthy attribute of child development theorists is their willingness to question tradition, to be suspicious of commonsense interpretations, and to challenge explanations that seem at odds with the facts. Consequently, the schemes they create are often intended to replace popular beliefs.

Perhaps the most dramatic instance of a scientific conception's supplanting a traditional cultural view is the case of Charles Darwin's nineteenth-century proposition about human origins. Darwin's detailed observations of hundreds of animal species living in diverse environments led him to conclude that humans had not suddenly been created in their present form a few thousand years ago. Instead, he theorized that humans were the product of an evolutionary process that began many eons ago and that linked together all forms of the earth's animal life in a complex developmental network. Although many religious fundamentalists continue today to hold their particular denomination's doctrinal view of human origins, nearly all members of the international scientific community and a large portion of the informed public subscribe to some form of Darwinism.

It is not unusual for members of certain religious sects to attribute children's disobedience to the operation of evil spirits. Thus, a boy turns delinquent because he is possessed by satanic forces that distort his faculties of judgment and will. To expel the spirits, it may be necessary to "beat the devil out of him." However, modern-day theorists question this interpretation and replace it with other alternatives. Skinner's radical behaviorism (Chapter Seven) would blame the boy's misbehavior on the pattern of rewards and punishments he has experienced following his delinquent acts. Bandura's social learning theory (Chapter Eight) would propose that the boy has modeled his life after the wrong kinds of heroes. Freudians (Chapter Five) could account for the misconduct by surmising that the youngster's psychosexual development has gone awry.

INTERPRETING PUZZLING OBSERVATIONS

In all societies, such phenomena as pregnancy, the advent of puberty, and the growth of reasoning skills have elicited varied explanations. Take pregnancy, for example. Although in most societies the act of sexual intercourse is believed to be the cause of pregnancy, such a conviction is not universal. Among traditional

Trobriand Islanders of the South Pacific, pregnancy is believed to result from one ancestral spirit inserting another ancestral spirit into the mother's womb. This action, they contend, is most readily accomplished if the opening has been enlarged by intercourse, hence explaining why women who have frequent intercourse become pregnant more often than those who do not (Malinowski, 1948, p. 236).

In some cultures environmental conditions at the time a child is conceived are thought to determine certain of the child's characteristics. The Chenchu in the Hyderabad hill country of India believe that a child conceived in the rain will cry a great deal and one conceived in total darkness will be born blind. To prevent such misfortunes, parents refrain from copulating in the rain or in darkness (Oswalt, 1972, p. 149).

Even in advanced industrial societies, members of the general populace may wonder why intercourse on some occasions and between some couples results in pregnancy and on other occasions and between other couples it does not. Present-day science provides answers to this question in the form of theories about the viability of sperm and ova (Lenhoff, 1989), the physiology of the reproductive organs (Seppala & Hamberger, 1991), environmental conditions (Elkington, 1986), the influence of the participants' emotions and of endorphins in their brains (Distler & Beck, 1990), and more.

Avoiding Troublesome Issues

Theorists dedicated to the canons of science not only revise, refine, extend, and replace cultural conceptions of development, but also avoid addressing a number of topics that traditionally have held an important place in popular belief systems. Three such topics concern the nature of the child's soul, the influence of supernatural forces in development, and life after death. For each of these topics there are questions to be answered.

The soul   When does the soul enter the child—before birth or after? What are the functions of the soul? How is *soul* distinguished from *mind*? Are the structure and function of the soul unchanging throughout childhood and adolescence, or does the soul—like the mind and body—develop? Are there good souls and bad souls? If so, what determines whether a soul will be good or bad?

Supernatural intervention   What supernatural forces may intervene in the child's development—a single almighty god with angel emissaries that contend against a satanic force (Judaism, Christianity, Islam), multiple gods with different powers (Hinduism, Buddhism, Jainism), ancestral spirits (Confucianism, Shinto), or other invisible forces that inhabit nearly all objects (animism)? What determines whether the supernatural forces will help or hinder the child's development? Is the influence of such powers limited to particular aspects of development?

Life after death   When children die, is that the final end, or do they continue to exist in some noncorporeal form? In their phantasmic state, where do children go and what determines their destination? During their assignment to the spirit world, do children continue to develop?

Whereas long-standing cultural conceptions of development furnish answers to these queries, theorists operating from a scientific perspective rarely even entertain such questions, because the answers are not amenable to the empirical tests and logic on which scientific inquiry depends. Traditional belief systems rely on faith in the word of an authoritative sage or document that proclaims truth. Since accepting unverified assertions is contrary to the spirit of science, most modern-day theorists simply set aside questions whose answers cannot be assessed empirically. Perhaps some day the invention of ingenious investigative techniques will furnish ways to settle such issues empirically, but clearly that day has not yet arrived.

RESPONDING TO EXISTING THEORIES

Not all theoretical proposals are intended to revise or replace commonsense beliefs. Some are reactions to unsatisfactory features of certain modern-day theories. John Watson introduced behaviorism to replace what he considered to be the unscientific speculations of mentalism (Part Four). Abraham Maslow's humanistic model was devised to correct shortcomings of both psychoanalysis and behaviorism (Chapter Twelve). Robbie Case's cognitive-growth levels were designed to improve on Piaget's stages (Perspective D). Urie Bronfenbrenner proposed an ecological model to clarify patterns of environmental influence that he felt were inadequately recognized by other theorists (Chapter Thirteen).

In addition, the multitude of variants of existing models that continually appear are often intended to alter minor aspects of those models while still supporting the models' basic tenets. Such is the case with Erikson's addenda to psychoanalysis (Chapter Six), with Elkonin's extension of Vygotsky's stages of development (Chapter Ten), and with the numerous refinements of information-processing theory to be found in the professional literature (Chapter Eleven).

FOR FURTHER READING

Ames, L. B., and C. C. Haber. (1990) *Your Eight Year Old.* New York: Dell. This book exemplifies the publications that members of the Gesell Institute have written for each age level to answer parents' child-rearing queries.

Gesell, A., F. L. Ilg, L. B. Ames, and G. E. Bullis. (1977) *The Child from Five to Ten.* New York: Harper & Row. This volume presents the Gesell Institute interpretation of child development. The book includes detailed descriptions of maturity traits and growth gradients.

Hartman, D. (1990) "Jewish Theory of Human Development," in R. M. Thomas (ed.), *The Encyclopedia of Human Development and Education.* Oxford: Pergamon.

Havighurst, R. J. (1953) *Human Development and Education.* New York: Longmans, Green. The most complete analysis of the developmental-task approach available.

Kelley, H. H. (1992) "Common-Sense Psychology and Scientific Psychology," in M. R. Rosenzweig and L. W. Porter (eds.), *Annual Review of Psychology,* Vol. 43. Palo Alto, Calif.: Annual Reviews.

Lin, H. Y. (1990) "Confucian Theory of Human Development," in R. M. Thomas (ed.), *The Encyclopedia of Human Development and Education.* Oxford: Pergamon.

Obeid, R. A. (1990) "Islamic Theory of Human Development," in R. M. Thomas (ed.), *The Encyclopedia of Human Development and Education.* Oxford: Pergamon.

Stevenson, H., H. Azuma, and K. Hakuta (eds.). (1986) *Child Development and Education in Japan.* New York: W. H. Freeman.

Thomas, R. M. (1990) "Christian Theory of Human Development," in R. M. Thomas (ed.), *The Encyclopedia of Human Development and Education.* Oxford: Pergamon.

Thomas, R. M. (1990) "Hindu Theory of Human Development," in R. M. Thomas (ed.), *The Encyclopedia of Human Development and Education.* Oxford: Pergamon.

CHAPTER FOUR

COMMONSENSE ATTRIBUTION THEORY

As explained in the introduction to Part Two, a "commonsense" view of child development identifies those beliefs shared by a large proportion of society, with many of the beliefs being self-evident conclusions. Of course, members of the general public have not assembled their collection of convictions into an organized theory. However, psychologists have managed to infer from people's behavior the major dimensions of this assortment of convictions and have described how the dimensions appear to interact. A version of this inferred belief system is what I am referring to as *commonsense attribution theory*. It "deals with the rules the average individual uses in attempting to infer the causes of observed behavior" (Jones et al., 1971, p. x).

We could adopt any of several ways to construct a commonsense theory of development. We might conduct a poll, asking a sample of people to answer questions about children. We might collect folklore, proverbs, and traditional sorts of advice about child raising, and then search for the pattern of concepts that underlies them. We could observe adults as they interact with children or as they talk about children and then estimate what theory of child nature is implied in such action and talk. We might analyze a society's laws relating to children, on the assumption that laws reflect a common set of beliefs for that society. Or we could use all of these approaches. However, due to space limitations, in this chapter we will use only two: an analysis of typical daily talk and an inspection of a few key laws that relate to children.

For the analysis of talk, our basic guide will be the work of Fritz Heider (1896–1988), as later enhanced by the theorists who followed his lead. Heider was born in Vienna, was raised in Graz (Austria), and after completing doctoral studies in 1920 went to Berlin where he came into direct contact with such Gestalt psychologists as Kurt Lewin (1890–1947). In 1931 Heider accepted an appointment to work with another German Gestaltist,* Kurt Koffka (1886–1941), at Smith

*In the German language, the term *Gestalt* means *configuration*. The term is used in reference to any organized group of items whose patterning gives the group a significance or meaning that is more than simply the sum of the individual items. In the realm of child development, Gestalt theorists adopt a *holistic* or *field* view. They consider the child to be a unified, integrated organism. To the Gestalt theorist, a new stimulus or experience does not merely add a new element to the child's store of actions or knowledge, leaving the previous elements undisturbed; rather, each new experience alters the relationship of many or all the existing elements that have made up the personality to this point, so the patterning of the whole personality is influenced.

College in the United States. After nearly two decades at Smith, Heider moved to the University of Kansas to continue his mission of discovering the underlying framework of the naive psychology that seems to guide the way most of us account for human behavior (Weiner, 1980, p. xv). The principles he derived are described in *The Psychology of Interpersonal Relations* (Heider, 1958). However, because his description focuses primarily on adults and not on children, it is necessary in this chapter to extend his treatment to show how commonsense psychology views a child's developmental changes from one age level to the next. In making this extension, I have depended not only on people's everyday language but also on civil and criminal laws commonly found in modern North American communities.

There is no single version of commonsense theory; this chapter is designed only to suggest some of the main lines of naive theory and to illustrate the way Heider and his followers have identified such lines. The material included here falls far short of reflecting the complexities of various forms of such theory.

The present-day derivative of Heider's naive psychology is called *attribution theory*, meaning a scheme that attempts to explain how and why people attribute human behavior to particular causes. Using the term *attribution* to distinguish this model from others may seem a bit odd, since essentially all theories of human development or personality attribute human thought and action to those factors the theorists regard as the most potent causes. For example, Freudians attribute much of development to the ways the child's inner drives interact with such agents of the environment as parents. Behaviorists attribute development to the way the consequences of a child's present actions will influence the way the child acts in the future. However, even though all theorists "attribute," it is the particular line of theorizing set off by Heider that is typically referred to as attribution theory, so I am using the term *commonsense attribution theory* to identify one model of development built on Heider's work. In preparing the version offered in the following pages, I have combined Heider's proposals with contributions from E. E. Jones and K. E. Davis (1965), H. H. Kelley (1967, 1971, 1972, 1973), and K. G. Shaver (1975). I have also included elements derived from my own observations of the way people talk about children and adolescents.

THE CAUSES OF HUMAN ACTION

The central question that commonsense psychology seeks to answer is, Why do people act as they do? When this question is translated into child development terms it becomes, How and why does the pattern of children's behavior change as they grow up?

Shaver (1975, p. 29) suggested that the motive behind all human effort to estimate causes arises from the need to simplify the "perceptual world by *explaining* the present and past behavior of others and by *predicting* with some degree of accuracy what those people are likely to do in the future." As children grow up, the frequency with which they themselves make causal attributions increases as their attribution scheme (their commonsense theory) becomes more complex and increasingly similar to the basic principles embraced by most adults in their society.

According to Heider and his followers, the way people simplify the problem of explaining their perceptual world is by reducing to a small number the causal factors they believe are part of the individual person and the environment. The behavior of children and adults is then interpreted in terms of how these factors interact. In the version of attribution theory reviewed here, the significant properties of the person are ability, intention, motivation, conscience, emotional dispositions, and an aptitude for empathy (the skill of experiencing life from the viewpoint of other people). The significant properties of the environment are opportunity, task difficulty, environmental coercion, and situation and role prescription. The theory also makes room for the operation of such indeterminate influences as luck and supernatural intervention.

To suggest the flavor of the raw materials from which such a theory is constructed, I have prefaced the analysis of these factors with a fictitious conversation, a typical chat about children that might be overheard in many U.S. neighborhoods. Phrases from this conversation will be used later to illustrate, from the viewpoint of commonsense attribution theory, the convictions about child behavior that underlie people's daily interactions. Examples will also be drawn from phrases often heard in other everyday conversations.

TALK ABOUT CHILDREN:
GRIST FOR COMMONSENSE PSYCHOLOGY'S MILL

Mrs. Campbell and Mr. Young meet in a supermarket.

> *Mr. Young:*   What do you think of the kids' third-grade teacher? I think she's expecting too much of them. My son Freddie says hardly anyone in the class can do the math. Have you seen the problems she gives?
>
> *Mrs. Campbell:*   Yes, Doris brings work home every day. But luckily she seems to get it done all right without my help.
>
> *Mr. Young:*   She must be pretty smart.
>
> *Mrs. Campbell:*   It's not just that. She works hard at it, too. I guess having to compete with her twelve-year-old brother has caused her to try hard. He's good at physical activities but kind of average in school work, so she seems to want to show that she's good with her brain. She tries to get attention that way.
>
> *Mr. Young:*   Oh, yes, your son. I saw in the paper that he's on the football team.
>
> *Mrs. Campbell:*   Well, he's crazy about sports. But getting on the team isn't much of a distinction. Nearly every boy who showed up was put in uniform.
>
> *Mr. Young:*   But isn't he some kind of a star?
>
> *Mrs. Campbell:*   Well, for the first couple of weeks he was the starting quarterback. He's growing up fast—tall and strong for his age, and he throws

the ball well. But then he had a streak of bad luck. He sprained his ankle, and that put him out for over a week. Since then the coach hasn't given him a fair chance to show what he can do. The poor kid's spending every game on the bench.

Mr. Young: That's too bad. But I'm surprised he sticks with it when he isn't allowed to show his stuff.

Mrs. Campbell: Well, he did talk about quitting. He's really trained hard for this team, so sitting on the bench seems such a waste of energy and talent. But when he mentioned quitting to the other kids, they called him chicken, so he decided to stick it out. But he really hates it.

Mr. Young: What a shame. Isn't there something you could do?

Mrs. Campbell: Oh, I can't bring myself to say anything. It's the coach's job to decide who plays and who sits.

Mr. Young: By the way, I see you didn't bring your baby with you.

Mrs. Campbell: No, I left him at home with Doris.

Mr. Young: Really? Aren't you afraid to leave a nine-year-old in charge of such a small baby?

Mrs. Campbell: Oh, no. Doris is very good at it, and she likes it. And she likes the compliments she gets for doing a good job.

Mr. Young: Well, that's brave. I don't think I'd let our daughter Charlene try that, even at fourteen. It's not that Charlene can't do it. It's just that she's always thinking of something else—mostly boys and loud music. Well, I'd better get going. I left Charlene out in the car. She's fiddling with all the gadgets, pretending she's driving. She just can't wait till she's sixteen to get a driver's license. God willing, she'll be less flighty by then so I won't have to be criticizing her all the time about the way she drives. But I guess that goes with being a parent of a teenager.

Mrs. Campbell: I'm through shopping. I'll walk out with you. *(They push their shopping carts out the door and into the parking lot.)*

Mr. Young: Is that your dog in the car?

Mrs. Campbell: Yes, that's Mollie. Watch. She'll sit up and wave her paw when she sees me. She'll want a treat. She knows I always get dog biscuits at the market. Say, isn't one of those paper sacks in your cart getting wet?

Mr. Young: Uh-oh, the milk carton must be leaking. And the sack's coming apart. I'll have to go back and get a plastic bag.

APPLYING AN ATTRIBUTION THEORY

The components of our version of causal-attribution theory are displayed in Figure 4.1. With the conversation between Mrs. Campbell and Mr. Young in mind, we'll inspect each of the components in turn.

The *self*, represented in Figure 4.1 by the box at the left, is the subconscious conception of personality held by a perceiver who seeks to explain the causes of events observed in the environment. In the present case, there are two perceivers, Mrs. Campbell and Mr. Young. We are assuming that they both believe that the listed

The Self: The Perceiver's Dispositional Properties	The Environment
1. Mental ability, comprising 　1.1 intelligence 　1.2 maturation rate 　1.3 experience that produces knowledge of 　　1.3.1 the effects of various actions and 　　1.3.2 the presumed desirability of such effects 2. Physical ability, comprising 　2.1 body build 　2.2 maturation rate 　2.3 exercise and nutrition 3. Intention 4. Motivation 5. Conscience: ought forces 6. Emotional dispositions 7. Empathic attitude	A Types of environments 　A.1 Humans: same dispositional properties as those of the perceiver 　A.2 Higher animal species: modifications of dispositional properties of humans 　A.3 Inanimate objects: devoid of human dispositional properties B Characteristics of environments 　B.1 Opportunities and restrictions 　B.2 Task difficulty 　B.3 Environmental coercion 　B.4 Situation and role prescriptions

Indeterminate and Supernatural Influences

1. Luck, chance
2. Supernatural forces: God, Satan, astrological conditions, and so on

FIGURE 4.1
Framework of a commonsense attribution theory

dispositional properties are the personality traits that chiefly determine how children and adults act under various environmental conditions. In the box at the right, I have distinguished three types of environments: those composed of humans, of higher animal species (such as dolphins, cats, dogs), and of inanimate objects (such as houses, cars, shopping bags). I have identified four characteristics of such environments that people, in their commonsense psychology, often conceive to be causes of events. The box at the bottom is assigned two sorts of forces—luck and supernatural interventions—that people may include in their causal attributions. The elements comprising each of these three sources of cause are defined below.

The Self: The Perceiver's Dispositions

A central concept in Heider's system of analysis is the can-do or personal power aspect of personality. In Heider's analysis of people's conversations, beliefs about personal power are reflected in the terms *can* and *cannot:* "Hardly anyone in the class can do the math." "It's not that Charlene can't do it." Personal power has several components. The most important is *ability*, represented as items 1 and 2 in the self portion of Figure 4.1. Other components that exert a minor influence are *attitudes* (represented in Figure 4.1 as *emotional dispositions*), *social status*, and such *temporary personal conditions* as fatigue.

We begin our analysis with ability. During an average day, a typical teenager uses many specific skills or abilities in performing tasks. However, in commonsense psychology, these abilities are not all discrete and unconnected. Instead, they seem to fall into two categories, mental and physical. It is not uncommon for people to believe that a youth can have one level of ability in the mental realm and another in the physical. For example, it seems reasonable that a twelve-year-old boy might be a fine football player but not much of a scholar and that his nine-year-old sister might be the opposite. But it seems less common for people to see that within either category a youth's subabilities may vary. In short, people seem to think that mental ability is all-encompassing, a unitary skill or aptitude that covers all intellectual task performance. So Mr. Young, on hearing of Doris's skill in mathematics, concludes that Doris must be smart in general. Mrs. Campbell, too, reflects this idea of an all-encompassing mental ability by saying that Doris is "good with her brain." The belief that abilities are divided into physical and mental realms that are each unitary rather than composed of rather discrete subskills is widely accepted, even though the belief is somewhat at odds with present-day theory and empirical evidence (Gardner, 1983; Kail & Pellegrino, 1985; Pellegrino & Varnhagen, 1985).

Consider, next, people's ideas about three factors that contribute to mental ability: intelligence, maturation rate, and experience. The term *intelligence* is typically used to identify a child's inherited potential for being "smart" or "bright." This potential is recognized as maturing over time, with some children's maturation rates being faster than others'. As intellectual potential advances, experience with the world is necessary to equip the child with a storehouse of knowledge, particularly about the effects that different actions will produce and about the presumed desirability of those effects (Shaver, 1975, pp. 45–46).

The factors that make up physical ability parallel the components of mental ability—body build, maturation rate, and the experiential factors of exercise and nutrition. A person's basic body build, in the sense of neuromuscular potential, is usually assumed to be inherited. This potential evolves over time, with the maturation rate for some children differing from that of others ("He's growing up fast—tall and strong for his age"). Experience, in the form of exercise and nutrition, also contributes to physical ability ("He's really trained hard for this team").

As people try to understand and predict their own and others' behavior, they are interested in knowing whether a person's ability is high, medium, or low. It is therefore useful for us to examine three kinds of information on which this judgment is based. This analysis involves presumed relationships between personal power and the environmental factor of *task difficulty*.

The first clue to ability level is the proportion of other people who can perform the task or tasks we have in mind. Specifically, if only a few people can perform the task, then any individual who does so is credited with having high ability. The main cause of success is thought to reside in the individual's personal power, and consequently that individual is accorded respect. But if nearly everyone can perform the task, then we conclude that it was easy, and those people who perform it successfully are not credited with much ability. In fact, the cause of success is not attributed to the person at all but to the environment. We believe the individual succeeded because environmental factors were in his or her favor.

A second important factor in judging ability is a knowledge of the people who have already performed the task. This matter is far more significant for assessing ability in childhood and adolescence than in the adult years because children's physical and mental skills increase noticeably with age, whereas adult skills are thought to be stable until the declining years. So in naive psychology we seek to learn the ages of the people with whom a given child is being compared. It is considered fairest to compare the child with age peers—often age-mates of the same sex. However, it is frequently useful to compare the child with older or younger children as well. A young child who performs as well as an average child several years older is credited with high ability and is labeled gifted, bright, or even genius. An older child who performs no better than an average child several years younger is said to be retarded, deficient, or handicapped.

A third sort of information that tells us about ability level is the amount of effort exerted to perform a task—in other words, a child's strength of motivation. The child who succeeds with ease is credited with greater ability than the one who has to struggle and strain to accomplish the same job.

Temporary conditions, such as fatigue and illness, influence how a person performs on a given occasion, but these conditions do not decrease the true ability attributed to that individual.

To close this brief look at commonsense notions of personal power, note three of the most significant assumptions underlying naive psychology's view of child development:

1. Abilities are considered rather permanent attributes of an individual. They do not change over the short term.
2. Abilities increase, sometimes regularly and sometimes in spurts, over the period of childhood and adolescence. To a great extent, the study of child development is the study of the manner in which abilities increase. A child described as a "problem learner" in school is usually one whose abilities are not increasing at the rate considered desirable.
3. Abilities are determined by both heredity (for example: "His good memory is from his mother's side of the family") and environment ("It was easy for her to learn to read with all those books in her house"). However, the proportion that each of these two sources contributes to various abilities and the manner in which the two interact are not clear.

Consider, now, the next two dispositional properties of the self: *intention* and *motivation*. Not only must children have the personal power to perform, they must also *want* to do it. So ability and effort are both necessary for action.

Intention refers to whether or not a child has purposely chosen to act in a given way. Intention is a crucial factor in commonsense psychology since estimates of whether or not children "meant to do it" determine the esteem or blame they incur. Children whose behavior is interpreted as reflecting good intentions are credited with "good character," whereas those who seem directed by bad inentions get a reputation for "bad character." Although the notion of intention underlies a great quantity of people's judgments of children, usually the term *intention* is not used outright but, instead, is simply implied: "She seems to want to show that she's good with her brain." "He's crazy about sports." "He did talk about quitting." "It's not that Charlene can't do it. It's just that she's always thinking of something else." Children who do something wrong are less likely to be censured if it seems they "didn't mean it." Likewise, when something that children have done turns out well, they receive little or no credit if it appears that it was not on purpose but "just happened" or was "accidental." Because the assignment of credit and blame depends so heavily on apparent intentions, the way people attribute intention to children has a critical influence on child rearing, schooling, law enforcement, counseling, peer relations, and the like. Shaver (1975, pp. 28–29) observed that

> from the psychologist's point of view, to be attributionally valuable, an action must be judged to have originated from an intention. . . . Ultimately, the careful perceiver will rely on his assessment of the circumstances surrounding the action, on his other knowledge of the actor, and on his own past experience as an actor in similar situations to arrive at a choice of an intention behind the action.

The fourth property of self, *motivation,* is used here to mean the amount of effort invested toward carrying out an act. This amount is typically considered to be under the child's intentional control, as reflected in such remarks as "He just doesn't try hard enough" or "When she puts her mind to it, she plugs right along till it's done." Sometimes, however, the fact that children do not accomplish some act is attributed not to their lack of trying, but rather to their limited reservoir of energy: "She was too worn out to finish." Children are credited with having "good character" if they have impressed others with the amount of effort they seem to apply to tasks they face. For instance, the pupil who is thought to have limited ability will often be awarded higher marks in school tasks if he appears to have tried hard. And parents who wish to impress others with their children's good character often insert motivation ascriptions into conversations: "She works hard at it, too" and "He's really trained hard for this team."

The next two properties of self, *conscience* and *emotional dispositions,* influence the intent and motivation that compose the "try-to" aspect of personality.

Conscience is an internalized set of social rules or standards, of do's and don'ts, that Heider called *ought forces* (1958, pp. 218–243). When children violate the rules, they "feel bad." When they abide by the rules, they "feel good" or "feel proud" or "have a clear conscience." Most people believe the contents of conscience are not innate but, instead, are gradually acquired from the environment— from adults, from peers, and from mass communication media over the period of childhood and adolescence ("At his age, he still doesn't know any better" or "She's just now learning to be responsible"). Conscience functions as both a stimulator of action ("If she hadn't helped her injured friend, she would have felt terrible") and an inhibitor ("Oh, I can't bring myself to say anything—it's the coach's job to decide who plays and who sits").

The sixth postulated property, *emotional dispositions,* is a catch-all collection of feelings that influence both the direction of people's intentions and the effort they put into the tasks they attempt. Such dispositions include desires and fears, interests and prejudices, likes and dislikes: "He's crazy about sports." "Doris is very good at it, and she likes it." Shaver (1975, p. 29) has contended that, for purposes of explaining and predicting someone's behavior, identifying a *dispositional attribution* is superior to identifying an intention because "it provides an answer to the question 'Why?' that is a more fully satisfactory explanation, and at the same time is a better estimate of future action."

Finally, the term *empathic attitude* refers to people's ability to see and feel things from the perspective of someone else—what George Mead (1934) referred to as "taking the role of the other." Shaver (1975, p. 23) suggested that "individual differences in perceivers' ability to make interpersonal judgments accurately are probably related to differences in experience, intelligence, and empathic ability."

With the components of the self now described, we next consider the roles of environments in attribution theory.

Environments: Types and Characteristics

The three types of environments listed in Figure 4.1 are identified by the kinds of elements that make them up: humans, higher animal species, and inanimate objects. My reason for distinguishing between the first and third of these should be obvious. The humans who inhabit the social world all possess the traits that compose the self, whereas the objects that make up the physical world have none of those traits. This difference is clearly of great import when people attribute cause. For example, when Mr. Young's grocery sack began to split, he accounted for the cause by speculating that a carton of milk was leaking, but he did not attribute ability, intention, motivation, or emotional dispositions to either the carton or the sack. If we pressed him to explain the cause, he probably would have cited factors in the inanimate world—the effect of moisture on paper as compared to plastic, the damage incurred in the manufacture or transport of milk cartons, and the like. On the other hand, he attributed self properties to his daughter Charlene when he explained why she fiddled with the gadgets in the car.

The second type of environment proposed in Figure 4.1, *higher animal species,* has been included to illustrate the fact that people often ascribe many, if not all, human dispositional properties to higher animal species whose characteristics appear to approximate properties of the human self. Mrs. Campbell was indulging in such anthropomorphic reasoning when she implied that her dog Mollie exhibited intelligence, intention, and emotional dispositions: "She'll want a treat. She knows I always get dog biscuits at the market." We might then propose the following commonsense attribution principle: the farther down that a species is located in the phyla of the animal kingdom, (1) the less likely people will attribute human properties to a member of that species and (2) the more likely characteristics of inanimate objects will be ascribed to that creature. Hence, it is improbable that Mrs. Campbell would speak of garden slugs or paramecia with the same empathic spirit she displayed when talking about Mollie.

Next, let's consider the four environmental charcteristics or functions included in Figure 4.1. First, social and physical environments can either open opportunities (at age sixteen Charlene can get a driver's license) or restrict opportunities ("Since then the coach hasn't given him a fair chance to show what he can do").

Some tasks are more difficult to accomplish than others. Hence, if a child cannot perform a task, or can do so only with great effort, the task can be blamed for being too difficult and the child held faultless. As already noted, people's judgments of the "objective" difficulty level of tasks are typically based on what proportion of children of the same age, size, and sex can succeed with the task. If many can accomplish it, and particularly if they do so with little effort, then the task is considered to be easy; a child succeeding with that task will receive little or no credit for intelligence, physical ability, or for trying hard ("Getting on the team isn't much of a distinction. Nearly every boy who showed up was put in uniform"). On the other hand, a child who fails at tasks that most age-mates accomplish is blamed for low ability, for lack of intent, or for insufficient effort.

The third hypothesized function is *environmental coercion,* meaning pressures (ought forces) exerted by children's social and physical surroundings that impel them to act in approved ways or else prevent them from acting in unacceptable ways ("When he mentioned quitting to the other kids, they called him chicken, so he decided to stick it out"). Environmental coercion has an intimate link to conscience since most people believe that children gradually learn the rules of their society and incorporate these rules into their own personalities as habits and as the contents of conscience. This is the *socialization* process. Parents, teachers, pastors, the police, and others seek to effect such socialization (1) by offering direct instruction and models of behavior, and (2) by imposing consequences (rewards and punishments) that will motivate children to acquire values deemed desirable and to eschew those deemed improper. As examples of consequences, Mrs. Campbell observed that Doris "likes the compliments she gets for doing a good job," and Mr. Young hoped, "I won't have to be criticizing Charlene all the time about the way she drives." Ultimately, a youth is considered to be appropriately socialized—socially mature—when society's do's and don'ts have assumed the form of an internalized moral gyroscope in that individual's personality.

The final pair of environmental characteristics are *situation* and *role prescriptions.* The theory proposes that people often base their estimates of cause on their notion of how situations and social roles affect children's behavior. Situational attributions are reflected in such remarks as "He was very subdued because he was in church" or "She was able to muster unusual strength to carry her friend to safety." People's regard for role prescriptions are reflected in such comments as "It's the coach's job to decide who plays and who sits" and "I guess that goes with being a parent of a teenager" or "Don't expect too much of him since he's still a small child."

Indeterminate and Supernatural Influences

In addition to seeing causes in the self and in the social and physical environment, many people include two further sets of factors in their causal ascriptions. The first is an amorphous category that represents the attributer's puzzlement about what factors are actually responsible for an event. The words *luck, chance,* and *fate* signify a speaker's admission that the cause of an event is inexplicable. Mrs. Campbell was avoiding any self or environmental reasons for her son's injury when she proposed that "a streak of bad luck" had produced his sprained ankle and his subsequent confinement to the bench. As for Doris's math assignments, "luckily she seems to get it done all right without my help."

Sometimes an apparent lack of convincing causes in self properties or in the environment prompts people to locate causes in supernatural forces—God, the devil, evil spirits, astrological configurations, and the like ("God willing, she'll be less flighty by then"). Ascribing cause to such influences has important implications for the ways people attempt to channel children's development. If they believe a self characteristic (lack of intention, insufficient motivation) caused a child to fail at a task, they will often directly enjoin the child to pay attention and exert more effort. Or if they believe the environment has failed to furnish suitable opportunities, they may seek to rearrange the environment so opportunities become available. But if they think God is in control of the child's performance, they probably will pray for help rather than work directly with the child or the environment.

Summary

A commonsense attribution theory is a proposal about the likely structure of reasoning that, at a subconscious level, determines how most people in a society account for why things happen as they do. Key components of this postulated structure, as inferred from the way people talk about affairs of the day, are displayed in Figure 4.1 and defined briefly above. However, an essential element of the theory is missing: a description of the actual way people assign causes on a particular occasion. That is, what is needed is an explanation of which components are involved in a given decision about cause, including an interpretation of the weight or degree of force that various components in the interaction contribute to the decision. (The only segment above that directed any attention to interactions was the description of how people judge ability as it relates to task difficulty.) However, engaging in a detailed analysis of such interactions requires far more space than this chapter allows. Hence this issue of interactions is noted but not pursued. (You may wish to try your hand at performing such analysis by listening to a conversation in which the participants offer estimates of the cause of some child or adolescent behavior and then speculating about which components of Figure 4.1 are likely involved in the causal attributions the participants offer and which components likely exerted the greatest influence on their decisions.)

THE DEVELOPMENT OF PEOPLE'S COMMONSENSE THEORY

We may well ask how the members of a society adopt such a mode of ascribing cause. In response, I would suggest that the contents of commonsense theory are not innate but, instead, are acquired gradually as the infant progresses through childhood and adolescence. The lessons children learn over the years result from their being directly instructed by adults and peers, overhearing adults and peers talk about other people's behavior, and reading books and watching television. The content of such lessons is then corroborated, and perhaps revised, by the child's direct observations of people in action. In short, an individual's subconscious theory evolves in keeping with the rate of the child's neural maturation and the range of the child's experiences with the social and physical world.

Commonsense attributions can vary from one society to another, according to prevailing notions of cause embedded in the society's philosophical foundations. For instance, the naive theory acquired by a typical child in a society with a strong Confucian foundation (China, Korea) or a Shinto foundation (Japan) will more often credit a person's motivation as the cause for success or failure than would be the case in North America and Western Europe, where environmental factors are frequently considered more significant (Munro, 1977; Stevenson, Azuma, & Hakuta, 1986; Thomas, 1988).

IMPLICATIONS OF THE THEORY
FOR THE TREATMENT OF CHILDREN

From naive psychology's factors that account for action, we can draw several implications about child rearing to guide adults' treatment of children. For instance, if we want to help a child complete a task at which she is currently failing, we first need to estimate which of three factors—ability, task difficulty, or effort—is causing the failure. Then we can try to remedy the faulty condition of the identified factor.

If we think the child is striving as well as she is able and that her ability cannot be improved very readily, then we logically should attempt to reduce the difficulty of the task so she can succeed. To reduce the task's difficulty level, we can either do part of the task ourselves or break it down into smaller steps she can manage. However, in many cases we either cannot or do not wish to simplify the task. Then we may concentrate on improving the child's ability through training. In other cases we may conclude that the child's abilities are sufficient, but she either has not focused on the task (direction of motivation) or has not tried hard enough. So we try to convince the child that the task is something she really wants to do. We might try logic, cajoling, promises of rewards, or threats of punishment to motivate her to action (Heider, 1958, p. 123).

If this line of reasoning appears too obvious to be worth analyzing, it is not surprising. It's all common sense.

CHILDREN'S INTERPRETATIONS
OF THEIR OWN BEHAVIOR

So far we have looked only at ways adults use commonsense psychology in explaining children's behavior. But equally important, or perhaps even more impor-tant, is children's use of commonsense psychology as a foundation for their own attitudes and behavior. One child may consistently avoid engaging in new experiences because he has a very low regard for his ability or personal power in relation to virtually all unfamiliar tasks. People perceive him as being "painfully shy" because of his "negative self-concept," his "low level of self-esteem and self-efficacy," or his "general feelings of inferiority." Another child may be willing to try some tasks but unwilling to try others. She may account for this difference by contending that some of the tasks are easy but others are too hard, or else she may attribute the difference to the factor of motivation: "I like to do these things, but those others don't interest me." Still a third child appears to have unflagging confidence in his personal power, so that he eagerly takes on any new task and then attributes any failures to not having tried hard enough the first time (Weiner, 1974).

The importance of understanding a child's system of attributions lies in the observation that people do not behave on the basis of reality but rather act on the basis of their perceptions of reality. That is, they act on their attributions. Thus what stimulates a child to try a task is not the *objective fact* that she can succeed; instead it is her *belief* that she can do it. Hence, from this view of human development, an important measure of a child's or youth's personal maturity is how closely his or her pattern of attributions fits conditions of the real world. This measure is reflected in the question, How accurately can an individual predict the outcome of a task performance when he or she really tries (exerts strong effort) to accomplish the task? The child who predicts more accurately—who correctly estimates the relation of personal power to the difficulty level of tasks—is regarded as the more mature.

PRIVILEGE AND RESPONSIBILITY

Like other theories of development, commonsense theory depicts child growth in terms of stages. The three most general stages are *infancy, childhood,* and *adolescence.* The borders between them are distinguished by relatively sudden physiological and psychological changes. An infant or baby crosses the border into childhood when he becomes "more of a real person" through learning to walk and talk at around a year and a half or two years of age. The child crosses the border into adolescence or teenage status when sexual functions mature and such secondary sex characteristics as voice change, a spurt in height, body hair, and changes in skin texture show up around the ages of twelve to fifteen.

Paralleling these marks of physical maturation are a series of changes in privilege and responsibility that society regards as suitable for the growing child. Consequently one way to analyze directions or stages of development from a commonsense perspective is to do so in terms of the sorts of privileges and responsibilities that are added at different age levels.

The phrase *growth in privileges* here means increased opportunities to engage in a wider variety of activities, particularly activities the child considers desirable. In other words, she can do more things that she would like to do. *Growth in responsibility* means that the child incurs the obligation to carry out, under her own initiative or supervision, additional tasks that society considers proper, constructive, and desirable. In naive psychology, responsibility is composed of what Heider has called *ought forces* (1958, pp. 218–243). These are attitudes shared widely by a community regarding the duties people should fulfill. Such duties are necessary for providing individuals with a stable, predictable social environment in which to live, in the same way that "man can operate in the physical environment only when physical laws hold" (Heider, 1958, p. 229).

As suggested by the folk saying, "With each privilege you incur a responsibility," common sense conceives privilege and responsibility to be the opposite ends of a balance scale. Throughout children's development, their increasing abilities enable them to do more things for themselves, so they gradually are permitted by their society to carry out a greater variety of actions and make more decisions on their own. But as children gain privileges, society—primarily in the form of parents and teachers—adds oughts, or duties. Much of the conflict between children and adults during the first two decades of life comes from (1) children wanting more privileges at an early age and (2) adults seeking to postpone the privileges or to impose responsibilities before children want them.

Since the most commonly agreed upon gauge of developmental level is chronological age, society uses age for defining when children's abilities (and sense of responsibility) are sufficient to permit them to try certain tasks or make certain decisions. Some of these age expectations are in the form of custom, such as the custom in certain Christian churches of having children gain church membership at around age twelve. Other expectations are formalized as laws and regulations. By inspecting these laws, we can see what the common sense of the day considers to be proper steps or stages of development. For example, the stage of early childhood is typically distinguished from later childhood by school entrance laws. In the United States children are both permitted and obligated to attend school around age five or six. Such formal regulations, such as the school's curriculum guidelines, delineate substages within the major steps. For instance, it is common in North American schools to focus kindergarten activities on broadening the children's experience with their physical and social world and less on formally teaching them reading, writing, or arithmetic. But when children enter first grade at age six or so, they are expected to begin reading, writing, and formally analyzing quantitative concepts.

Criminal law reflects the commonsense belief that children before puberty are not yet reasonable or responsible beings, and even after puberty they are not considered to be entirely reasonable. The California penal code states that children under age fourteen are not capable of committing actual crimes unless there is "clear proof that at the time of committing the act charged against them, they knew its wrongfulness." So the excuse that "she didn't know what she was doing" is sufficient for not prosecuting a child as a "reasonable" adult would be prosecuted. Between ages fourteen and seventeen, youths are still considered only partially responsible beings, so that when they commit unlawful acts they are labeled delinquents rather than criminals and are processed through special juvenile courts. Furthermore, many states prohibit the public press from publishing the names of youths under age eighteen who are involved in crimes, in the belief that prior to eighteen an adolescent is still not fully responsible and does not deserve public blame and shame.

The number of laws, both civil and criminal, that use age eighteen as the cut off point for various privileges and responsibilities suggests that common sense today defines the period of childhood and adolescence as extending from birth through age seventeen, even though in North American society many youths are still not economically independent of their parents by age eighteen. There is a general expectation, or hope, that all youths will graduate from high school, and this usually occurs around age eighteen. In recent years the legal voting age was lowered from twenty-one to eighteen. One result of this was to make the voting age more closely coincide with the age at which boys acquire the privilege or obligation to fight and die for their country (age seventeen—voluntary enlistment; age eighteen— registering for conscription).

In effect, laws and customs reflect common notions of steps in development, with each step representing a point at which abilities and children's acceptance of ought forces are sufficient for them to be accorded new privileges and responsibili- ties. However, reaching the designated age for taking a step is not a guarantee that a privilege or responsibility will actually be provided. Other measures of develop- ment are also used. Before a child is considered ready for first grade, for example, he is tested or observed to determine whether he has the abilities needed to succeed at typical first-grade tasks. And Mr. Young's daughter, Charlene, is not guaranteed a driver's license at age sixteen. The girl's driving skill and knowledge of traffic laws will also be tested, and she will be denied a license until she has proven her skill. On the other hand, privileges are sometimes given before the minimum age level is reached. An adolescent who is slightly underage but who can prove her driving skill and a compelling need to drive (such as to provide the family income) may be given a driver's license before age sixteen. In sum, age is the main criterion of developmental sufficiency in commonsense psychology, but other criteria are also used to accommodate individual differences in children's ability.

Thus commonsense psychology proposes (1) generalizations that describe the average child and (2) minor amendments that describe children who deviate from the average. These conclusions that form a society's naive view of development are found in the customs, regulations, and laws that apply to life in the home, in the school, and in the wider community.

PRACTICAL APPLICATIONS

When the word *practical* is defined as "something firmly tied to the realities of daily living," then commonsense attribution theory by its very nature is indeed practical since it represents the framework of assumptions that underlie the way people in everyday life account for how and why children develop as they do. Furthermore, when *practical* is defined as "something useful in the solution of daily problems," commonsense theory again qualifies as practical for it explains the system of reasoning people employ as they interpret children's behavior. For example, if we know from commonsense theory about the interaction that most people assume exists among ability, task difficulty, and trying hard, we are better prepared to understand the structure of parents' reasoning as we hear them explain why their child is or is not developing satisfactorily.

Another practical function of commonsense theory is its potential usefulness in revealing to us the structure of our own unstated assumptions about children's growth. As a consequence of such self-revelation, we may newly recognize that certain of our underlying beliefs, when carefully analyzed, prove to be contradictory or perhaps inconsistent with research evidence. Armed with this increased awareness, we may be able to devise a more logical version of attribution theory, a version that properly fits with our personal system of values and the available facts about children's growth.

NAIVE PSYCHOLOGY: AN ASSESSMENT

This appraisal of commonsense theory is based on the fourteen evaluation standards introduced in Chapter One. My estimates of how well naive theory meets the standards are represented as marks on the following fourteen scales; then my explanations for the ratings are given. Your value system or your weighing of evidence may differ from mine, so you may well arrive at a different pattern of marks.

The logic behind my ratings may be easier to follow if we begin with item 5, the degree of internal consistency in the theory. There is necessarily considerable consistency among the beliefs supporting people's treatment of children. Otherwise child rearing would be far more chaotic than it is. However, as Heider pointed out, one can also criticize naive theory and its sources of data for "the many contradictions that are to be found in this body of material, such as antithetical proverbs or contradictions in a person's interpretation of even simple events" (1958, p. 5). Which is the proper guide to child raising: "A little love and kindness goes a long way" or "Spare the rod and spoil the child"? How does a teacher reconcile the contradictions in his observation that "she really doesn't have the ability to do it, but she tries so hard that she is able to overachieve"? In judging item 5, then, the substantial consistencies in naive theory are balanced against what seem to be a substantial number of contradictions, and the theory is rated in the upper portion of the "moderately well" segment.

There are at least two ways of looking at item 2, regarding the clarity of naive theory. First, naive psychology is not some scientist's creation. It is the set of assumptions upon which people base their treatment of children. So a first way of viewing the issue of clarity in item 2 is reflected in the question, Are the assumptions about children that make up common sense clearly understood and agreed upon within a given society? I believe the answer to this is that the contents of commonsense psychology are only moderately clear. People in a society have different assumptions about what makes sense in terms of child development. Even within a given person's set of assumptions there are contradictions, as illustrated above. However, there is considerable clarity about many aspects of naive

NAIVE THEORY

How well do I think the theory meets the standards?

Standards	Very well	Moderately well	Very poorly
1. Reflects the real world of children	X		
2. Is clearly understandable		X	
3. Explains the past and predicts the future		X	
4. Guides child rearing	X		
5. Is internally consistent	X		
6. Is economical		X	
7. Is falsifiable		X	
8. Is supported by convincing evidence	X		
9. Adapts to new data		X	
10. Is novel	a		X
11. Is comprehensive	X		
12. Stimulates new discoveries	X		
13. Is durable	X	a	
14. Is self-satisfying		X	

psychology. If there were not, we would have far more conflict in our society than we do.

A second way to look at the clarity issue is illustrated by the question, Have psychologists who analyze naive theory clearly described all of its characteristics? Heider made a good start toward clarifying the structure of commonsense views, writers such as A. L. Baldwin (1967) extended Heider's general system to focus it more distinctly on childhood, and a large body of literature has grown up over the past few decades to expand attribution theory still further (Worchel & Cooper, 1979). However, much of the contemporary literature focuses on adults rather than on children so that many aspects of children's use of naive psychology remain to be investigated.

Therefore from both points of view—from people's understanding and agreeing upon the nature of commonsense beliefs and from psychologists' descriptions of the underlying structure—I have estimated that naive theory is only moderately clear.

Now to item 1: Does naive theory accurately describe the real world of child-hood and adolescence? I believe that to a great extent it does. As Heider observed, "The ordinary person has a great and profound understanding of himself and of other people which, though unformulated or only vaguely conceived, enables him to interact with others in more or less adaptive ways. . . . Intuitive knowledge may be remarkably penetrating and can go a long way toward the understanding of human behavior" (1958, p. 2). However, there are, at the same time, some notably unrealistic aspects to commonsense views. One of the most obvious is the tendency for people to attribute happenings in a child's development or behavior to a single cause. A careful analysis of events illustrates that any event results from multiple causes, with some causes exerting more influence than others. Past arguments about whether nature or nurture caused a particular development exemplify this commonsense tendency to attribute a happening to a single cause. Baldwin wrote that "in many ways this feature of naive theory is its most insidious error and creeps most easily into attempts to develop a better, more scientific theory of human behavior" (1967, p. 75).

Numerous other aspects of naive theory bring into question its accuracy in describing children. For example, studies in recent decades of intellectual abilities have furnished a mass of evidence that contradicts the commonsense notion that the level of ability in one subarea of mental life will be the same in all other subareas. As a consequence, psychologists have moved increasingly away from a single general intelligence test that yields one overall intelligence quotient and have moved instead toward the use of multiple-factor tests that yield separate scores for each of several types of mental skills (Gardner, 1983; Harris & Harris, 1971). Likewise, studies of children's reading readiness contradict the belief that the time when all children are ready to begin reading is when they enter first grade (Durkin, 1976).

Thus, balancing the strengths of naive theory against its weaknesses in terms of describing children realistically, I rated the theory in the upper portion of the "moderately well" segment.

Related to a realistic view of children are item 3 (explains the past, predicts the future) and item 4 (guides child-rearing practices). Since naive theory is better prepared to explain past events than to predict future ones, it cannot achieve a top rating for its ability to guide child rearing. As Baldwin pointed out, the theory's weakness in predicting the future behavior of children rests to a great extent on two of its prominent characteristics. First, it does not specify all of the conditions or causes that interact to bring about an event or an aspect of development. For this reason, if the cause it does identify is not the most powerful of those actually operating, then the prediction will be in error.

Second, naive theory assumes that the child has a *free will.* The issue of free will is an old one in philosophy, one that has never been resolved satisfactorily. The concept of free will is usually discussed in connection with the contrasting or contrary concept of *determinism,* which has long been a basic tenet of the physical sciences or what is known as the *scientific method.* Determinism is a belief that everything that happens has been absolutely set or established by preceding conditions and could not have turned out any other way. In effect, if you know all the causal factors, you can make an exact, error-free prediction of what will happen. In contrast, the concept of free will holds that determinism may be true for strictly physical phenomena, such as thunderstorms and the growth of violets, but events that involve human decisions are influenced as well by the individual's freedom to make a choice. In effect, in human events a knowledge of preceding conditions or causal factors enables us to estimate likely outcomes, but we still must consider the individual's free will. The issue of determinism versus free will is a complex one. Here I simply point out that the idea of free will poses problems for naive theory when the theory is used as the basis for predicting future child behavior. No matter how much is known about causal conditions in a child's life, if the child has freedom of choice, errorless predictions of future development or behavior are not possible. When we treat a child a given way, we never know for sure how the child will interpret our actions and choose to respond.

Therefore, even though naive theory contains a lot of folk truths that, over the generations, have enabled people to guide children's development with some measure of success, it also has shortcomings that limit the accuracy of its predictions and child-guidance suggestions. Hence I rate naive theory in the moderate range for items 3 and 4.

Item 6 was difficult to mark because in some ways naive theory is too economical—that is, it makes what appear to be simplistic assumptions about aspects of development that seem to require more complex explanations. You may recall from Chapter One that Morgan's canon states: A theory is better if it is economical in the sense that it is founded on as few unproven assumptions as possible and requires rather simple mechanisms to explain all the phenomena encompassed by the theory. Naive theory violates this standard by failing in some ways to provide the simple mechanisms and in other ways to explain all the phenomena. In failing to fulfill the attribute of simplicity, naive theory may be too complex—for example, it still accepts certain assumptions about the divisions of the mind held over from faculty psychology. In failing to fulfill the attribute of explaining all the phenomena, naive theory may be too simple or simplistic.

Let us consider this charge of oversimplification in more detail. Baldwin (1967, pp. 64–70) illustrated this problem with examples focusing on matters of perception and intentional action. He pointed out that the assumption is made in naive psychology that everyone perceives things in the same way. In other words, the child's perceptual equipment is like a television camera, recording sight and sound "the way they really are." And everyone's camera records events in the same way. (This assumption underlies the practice in courts of having witnesses describe what they perceived so the judge and jury can determine what "really" happened.) But today a growing body of research suggests that perception is far more complex than naive theory would suppose. In effect, naive theory neglects the complexities of the phenomenon and proposes an overly simple picture of what apparently occurs.

Baldwin claimed that, in like manner, common sense fails to explain adequately the relationship between a person's intention and his actions. This objection leads us to the traditional philosophical issue of *teleology*. In a teleological explanation, the main cause of an event is found in the future rather than in the past or present. Instead of specifying the past and present conditions that have caused a young child to speak a few words, the teleological approach identifies some future purpose or outcome that has "caused" the speech behavior. For example, a child learns to speak because she now will be able to communicate her wants more adequately. Or, adolescents seek sexual mates out of a need to reproduce and thus preserve the human species for the future. Although this line of logic may at first appear reasonable, it is not in keeping with basic rules traditionally followed in the natural sciences. In the natural sciences, a cause does not appear in the future—that is, a cause does not appear before its effect. Thus, for people who want child development theory to adhere to the tenets of biological and physical sciences, the teleological aspects of naive theory are an embarrassment, just as are the beliefs in free will and single causal factors.

There are, of course, theorists who say that human behavior follows different laws (at least to some degree) from those governing nonhuman events. For these theorists, including the humanistic psychologists (Chapter Twelve), teleological causation and free will are not objectionable features of commonsense psychology.

In terms of its economy of explanation, then, naive theory oversimplifies certain aspects of development, thus violating part of item 6, and I have rated it only "moderately well."

As for item 7, falsifiability, parts of the theory are testable or disconfirmable, and other parts are not. Although many research studies conducted over the past century on child development represent successful efforts to test the validity of commonsense views, some important aspects of the theory have not as yet appeared testable or falsifiable. These aspects have depended for their confirmation on personal opinion or faith. Two examples of such aspects are the concepts of free will and teleological causation. Balancing these positive and negative factors against each other, I rated item 7 in the "moderately well" range of the scale.

Apparently most people believe there is a substantial amount of evidence undergirding their beliefs (item 8), with evidence in the form of what others have told them (their relatives, educators, pastors, law enforcement personnel, and the like) and what their own observations have suggested. If they did not have faith in these sources of evidence, they would likely abandon such beliefs. However, it also happens that when people feel that their child-rearing methods "aren't working out," they then may seek to learn "what the experts have to say" or "what research can tell us." Hence, I have marked item 8 between the "very well" and "moderately well" positions.

In the case of adaptability (item 9), I have estimated that commonsense theory deserves a "moderately well" rating. This estimate is based on the observation that long-held convictions about why children grow up the way they do are often resistant to data that would suggest those ideas are in error. On the other hand, if enough evidence is forthcoming from apparently reputable sources, common sense may change. An example is the debate over breast feeding versus bottle feeding. In the early decades of this century, the advertised nutritive virtues of bottle feeding—along with its convenience—persuaded a good many mothers to cease suckling their infants. However, in recent years, nutritionists' reports of the superiority of breast milk have convinced numbers of new mothers to adopt breast feeding (Grams, 1988). A second instance is the change in public attitude toward the use of tobacco. In the more distant past, adolescents who took up smoking cigarettes were often viewed as "just growing up." Most people seemed to consider smoking quite normal, and those who disapproved of smoking tended to view it as hardly more than a costly, somewhat irritating habit that is probably hard on the lungs. But not until recently has smoking been considered a serious threat to the health of both the smokers themselves and people in their vicinity. As a result, strong measures are being applied to curtail the use of tobacco (Kirsch, 1987). Today, naive theory appears to be adapting to the accumulation of evidence about the damaging effects of smoking on development.

I rated the novelty of naive theory in two ways. Commonsense beliefs are certainly nothing new. Instead, they have evolved gradually over the centuries. For this reason, I have placed the large X in the "very poorly" region. On the other hand, Heider and subsequent attribution theorists have demonstrated considerable ingenuity in the ways they have analyzed cultural beliefs. In recognition of their originality, I have added a small a (for *attribution*) in the "very well" region.

High marks are earned by naive theory for its comprehensiveness, fertility, and durability. The theory is very comprehensive in that it encompasses all aspects of development: physical, mental, social, emotional. It is also fertile, in that hosts of new theories and new research have resulted from observers' dissatisfaction with commonsense answers (Chapter Three). People's commonsense beliefs are also highly durable, many of them lasting over the centuries in much the same form. Thus, for durability I have placed a large X in the "very well" region. However, I have also placed a small a in the upper reaches of the "moderately well" sector to indicate that I believe the form of attribution theory proposed by psychologists will change somewhat over the years as analysts discover new ways to describe the structure of commonsense beliefs.

Finally, naive theory is, overall, moderately self-satisfying (item 14). Although much of my own treatment of children is based on commonsense notions, in many ways this common sense fails to answer my child development questions adequately and I am left discontented with naive theory. This discontent serves as a sufficient stimulus for learning what more formal theories, such as the ones in the following chapters, offer.

FOR FURTHER READING

Heider, F. (1958) *The Psychology of Interpersonal Relations.* New York: Wiley. Heider described what he conceives to be the theoretical framework on which people's commonsense psychology is founded.

Heider, F. (1983) *The Life of a Psychologist: An Autobiography.* Lawrence, Kan.: University of Kansas Press. The author described the geographical and intellectual routes he traveled to arrive at attribution theory.

Shaver, K. G. (1975) *An Introduction to Attribution Processes.* Cambridge, Mass.: Winthrop.

Distinguishing Normal from Abnormal Development

How can decisions be made about whether development is normal, natural, proper, or desirable?

The question of what kinds of growth and behavior are normal at each stage of childhood and adolescence is obviously of great concern to people who daily engage in the care and guidance of the young. Not only is the question of great interest, but it is also one of considerable confusion, partly because such words as *normal* and *natural*—and their opposites, *abnormal* and *unnatural*—are not assigned the same meanings by everyone. Even greater confusion results when people who use the terms have not decided for themselves precisely what they intend. Consequently, students of child development can profit from both (1) recognizing the varied meanings that such words can carry and (2) deciding precisely what criteria they themselves wish to apply in clarifying their use of the terms. These two matters are the focus of this perspective.

DIVERSE MEANINGS OF NORMAL, NATURAL, AND DESIRABLE

In the realm of child development, there are two common uses of the word *normal:* to describe (1) statistical similarity or frequency and (2) desirability or acceptability. The first refers to how much a child's condition is like the condition of others of the same category. Typical categories are ones defined by such characteristics as age, sex, grade in school, ethnic background, birth order, socioeconomic status, and the like. The second use of *normal*—that of desirability or acceptability—refers to how closely a child's condition matches the value system of the person making the judgment about normality. In this second sense, *normal* means *approved, admirable, satisfactory, proper, acceptable,* and the like. It is possible for a child to be normal in the first sense and abnormal in the second, or vice versa. An eight-year-old with an intelligence quotient of 150 could be judged statistically abnormal, but normal (or supranormal) in terms of desirability. A sixteen-year-old could be judged statistically normal in the use of marijuana (in a community in which 70 percent of the age group has used the drug) but abnormal in the sense of desirable behavior.

There are also alternative uses of *natural.* One is the degree of statistical similarity to others of the same category. The other is the likelihood that development will progress satisfactorily without special intervention. Consider, first, the statistical usage. If some characteristic of a child is found very frequently in the group of which the child is a member (age group, ethnic group, intelligence-level category, or some other), then the child's development is judged to be statistically natural, meaning "what is most likely to be expected." This meaning is implied in such remarks as: "She's growing up quite naturally," or "It's just natural to pass through a phase like that." Gesell's growth gradients and Havighurst's developmental tasks would qualify as indicators of such natural development. Whatever is common at an age level is *natural.*

Consider, now, the second use of *natural,* which is the course of development that can be expected if the influences on the child's life continue in the usual pattern. In other words, if no special intervention or treatment is instituted to alter the child's life, such-and-such outcomes will probably result. For example, if the teenager's wisdom teeth are not extracted now, the other teeth will naturally become jammed together, causing both an improper bite and an unpleasant appearance. If the seven-year-old's parents continue to praise her for the friendly way she greets visitors, she will naturally develop a pleasing social manner.

However, child-rearing difficulties can occur if people fail to distinguish between the foregoing two meanings of *natural.* Problems arise whenever people interpret "statistically natural" as always implying "the way things *should* be." This is the error of confusing "is" with "ought," an error illustrated in the tendency of Gesell and his colleagues to interpret normative descriptions at different age levels as natural, thus requiring no special intervention to alter the course of development. The remedy for such an error lies in recognizing that statistically common or natural events need to be inspected carefully in order to determine how desirable they are in relation to the values held by the person making the judgment. In some instances, development should not be allowed to continue in its present, or natural, course. Instead, steps should be taken to intervene. However, in other instances, even though the present growth characteristic is not the most desirable, experience demonstrates that no special intervention at this time would likely correct the condition, so it is best to "let nature take its course."

The two most common situations in which nonintervention with unsatisfactory development is warranted are those in which (1) particular internal maturation changes are necessary before the desired development can occur and (2) changes in the environment that will remedy the present unsatisfactory condition are bound to appear without special intervention. Consider, for example, the vestiges of "baby talk," or indistinct enunciation, that often remain in the speech of four- or five-year-olds. Studies of children's speech patterns at successive age levels have shown that articulation deviations from "standard" speech usually disappear during the early years of elementary school without specific remedial measures. As H. Winitz (1969, p. 60) noted, the great majority of children naturally arrive at producing nearly all sounds correctly by eight years of age. This *natural correction* apparently results from a combination of factors, including the advancing internal maturation of the child's auditory-perception mechanism, which equips the child to detect differences between his or her enunciation and that of other people, and the increasingly mature speech of the child's age-mates, which serves as a model the child chooses to emulate, particularly if age-mates and school personnel voice their disapproval of "baby talk." From such observations as this, we can derive a rule of thumb for deciding when to let nature take its course:

(1) If the genetically timed internal maturation of the child's nervous system and musculature (necessary for a desired type of behavior) has not yet occurred, then it is appropriate to await such maturation rather than to adopt special efforts to produce the behavior ahead of its maturational schedule. Pressuring children to perform at levels beyond their present maturational capacity may not only be futile, but it may damage children's sense of worth and self-confidence. (2) If changes that typically can be expected to occur in a child's environment are ones that will probably correct an existing undesired characteristic, then it is unnecessary at the present time to adopt remedial measures to alter that characteristic.

The reciprocal of this prescript can then serve as a guide to when intervention is advisable for changing the "natural" course of events:

Even though a particular characteristic of a child's present development is *natural* (in the sense of frequent or common among other children at this stage of life), special efforts to alter that charcteristic are warranted if (1) the characteristic is judged to be unsatisfactory, (2) the child's maturational capacity is sufficient to achieve the desired improvement, and (3) it is unlikely that factors in the child's environment will "naturally" change in ways that will remedy the objectionable characteristic.

DECISIONS ABOUT NORMAL OR NATURAL AS SIMILAR OR FREQUENT

A question that can now be asked is what kinds of evidence a person needs to decide whether a child's development is *normal* or *natural* in the statistical sense of *similar* or *frequent*. I would propose three kinds.

The first is a description of where children are spread along a particular dimension (such as weight by age, smoking habits by gender and age, child abuse by gender, or English-language fluency by ethnic designation). The description is most helpful when it is in the form of a distribution showing the percentage of children at different points along the dimension. The distribution can be equally helpful if it is summarized in the form of the group's average (mean or median) and extent of variability (standard deviation or distance between percentiles 20 and 80). Or, when information is offered in dichotomous or trichotomous form (yes–no or often–sometimes–never), the results are typically in the form of percentages of people in each subcategory.

The second kind of evidence needed is a description of where our particular child or adolescent stands in relation to the group, such as how the child's height, weight, or score on an oral English-language test compares to the group's status or *norms.* These first two types of evidence are objective, in the sense that anybody making the decision would arrive at the same conclusion.

The third type consists of the line of reasoning that establishes the cutoff point on the distribution that distinguishes normal from abnormal (or natural from unnatural) or that stipulates degrees of normality *(very normal, somewhat normal, slightly abnormal, very abnormal)*. This is not an objective judgment. Instead, it is a decision reflecting the values held by the person making the appraisal. Hence it calls for support in the form of a rationale explaining the values on which the decision is founded. A convincing rationale is what I find missing in the writings of such people as Gesell and his colleagues who work in a normative-descriptive mode.

DECISIONS ABOUT *NORMAL* AS *DESIRABLE* OR *ACCEPTABLE*

Establishing criteria that define *normal* (or *natural*) as *desirable*—or at least as *acceptable*—is a subjective act that can differ greatly from one person to another. The source of the criteria is the set of values held by the definer, and therefore the criteria require clarification (1) of the elements that go into the definition and (2) of the proper sources of evidence for making a decision about the normality of a given child's growth. Apparently many people base their judgments of such normality on vague, intuitive impressions instead of specific, rational standards (with *rational* meaning *under conscious cognitive control*). I believe it is important for teachers, parents, counselors, and pediatricians not to be satisfied with amorphous, subconscious conceptions of such normality but to clearly identify what they believe constitutes desirable or acceptable development.

One way to begin explicating the components of such a conception is to offer a general definition of *normal,* then to explain the line of logic supporting the components. The following general definition illustrates this process:

> Children are developing normally (properly, desirably, satisfactorily) when: (1) they feel that they are fulfilling their own needs at least moderately well, (2) their behavior does not unduly encroach on other people's rights and opportunities, (3) they fulfill those responsibilities typically held as reasonable for people of their ability (physical and mental) within their particular social environment, and (4) their personal characteristics do not cause other people to treat them in ways which harm them physically, psychologically, or socially or which deny them opportunities [equal to the opportunities enjoyed by their peers] to pursue their ambitions. (Thomas, 1990, p. 50)

This definition is the one to which I subscribe. I thus become obligated to explain the values on which I base the four components. My rationale, then, is as follows.

1. Fulfilling One's Own Needs

This first criterion derives from two convictions: (1) that each child has physical and psychological needs that, when satisfied, bring feelings of joy and contentment and that, when frustrated, bring feelings of misery and distress; and (2) that the child deserves to have these needs met as promptly and as thoroughly as conditions permit. The term *conditions,* in this case, refers to the way children's needs and abilities interact with environmental factors. It is clear that infants, with their very limited abilities, must depend almost entirely on other people to satisfy needs. But as time passes, and children's internal maturation combines with experience to foster rapid growth in abilities, they depend less and less on the services of others for need satisfaction.

It is apparent that the goal of prompt need fulfillment can never be perfectly achieved, because two or more competing needs can arise simultaneously or, as is so often the case, the environment does not permit immediate satisfaction. In early childhood, mother may be doing the laundry at the moment the toddler seeks solace. In later childhood, the girl scout may be far from a doctor when she suffers a sprained ankle during a hike in the mountains. In adolescence, the teenage girl and boy may find their sexual urges rising as they sit next to each other in the school library. Thus the goal of immediate need satisfaction can, at best, only be approximated, but I still hold it as an ideal to pursue. I believe that children who unduly suffer unmet needs are not developing properly.

2–3. Respecting Others' Rights and Bearing One's Own Responsibilities

In contrast to the introspective nature of the first criterion, the second and third standards represent perceptions from society's viewpoint. The rationale supporting these two standards holds that no one, except the rare hermit, lives alone. Instead, people live in interdependent groups, sharing common territories and dividing up the tasks of daily living, cooperating, and competing. Under these conditions, if the greatest good is to result for the greatest number, individuals cannot be concerned exclusively with indulging their own desires without regard for others. It thus becomes a matter of enlightened self-interest for people to recognize that, in the long run, their own needs will be best satisfied if they permit others to exercise the same rights that they themselves enjoy. Furthermore, their own needs will be best met if they, and all other members of the society, bear a fair share of the responsibility to perform the tasks that make the society operate efficiently. Criteria 2 and 3, in effect, represent the social aspect of satisfactory development. From the viewpoint of the group, individuals who fail to abide by society's customs are not developing properly.

4. The Importance of Societal Attitudes and Socioeconomic Opportunities

Frequently children's failure to achieve optimal development is caused by their being treated in prejudicial ways by others. Restrictions are placed on their opportunities to reach their desired potential. The fault, in many instances, lies in other people's basing their judgments of a child or youth on normative impressions or stereotypes. This can occur when a general conclusion about an easily identified group—Catholics, Jews, blacks, Irish, Latin Americans, adolescents, overweight children, the homeless—is applied to every member of the group in equal measure. In other words, individuals who bear the group label are not judged on their own characteristics but are branded with a generalization about "those kinds of people." As a result, opportunities for individuals can be restricted. Parents can determine their children's playmates and can influence which boys their adolescent daughter dates. Teachers and club leaders can decide which children will work together and how privileges, praise, and blame are meted out. Employers establish who gets a job and who is assigned to which tasks. Finally, children and teenagers themselves play a highly significant role in deciding which groups their age peers will be allowed to join. In short, failure of a child to develop in the most desirable way can be due to prejudicial attitudes of people in the environment who control opportunities for growth, self-expression, and need fulfillment.

SOURCES OF INFORMATION ABOUT DESIRABLE DEVELOPMENT

My purpose in proposing the foregoing criteria has not been to suggest that my definition is the only right one. A review of theories in this book will reveal other definitions reflecting somewhat different values. My intention, then, is to illustrate the process of stating a definition and defending it with a line of reasoning.

A definition at such a level of specificity can also serve as a guide to the types of information a person will need for answering questions like these: Is this child developing properly? Am I expecting too much of that teenager? Do I really have anything to worry about? Should I be trying some special intervention or should I just let nature take its course?

Some of the needed information may be in the form of summary statements about groups—information about children and youths at different age levels as provided by researchers working in the normative-descriptive modes of Gesell and Havighurst. For example, in applying four standards suggested above, it can be helpful to have normative information about (1) needs and developmental tasks that are especially prominent at different age levels (first criterion), (2) the typical abilities of children at successive ages and the accompanying rights and responsibilities that society holds for those age stages (second and third criteria), and (3) stereotypical attitudes held within the society about ethnic, religious, gender, and age groups (the fourth criterion). Such normative information provides a useful starting point—a set of probabilities—which then need to be verified and refined by information about the particular child whose development we are seeking to evaluate. In other words, normative data provide a rough guess about what factors may influence the development of a child during a given age period. What is next required is precise information about this specific child. Such information can be gathered through observing and interviewing the child, questioning people who know the child, and administering tests that can reveal something of the child's physical skills, cognitive abilities, views of social relationships, emotional responses, and perceptions of self.

In summary, then, I have suggested that normative-descriptive studies of children at different age levels are useful for showing where a given child or adolescent stands in relation to age-mates. However, knowing that a child is close to the group average or is distant from the average does not tell if that child's development is *proper* or *satisfactory* or even *acceptable*. Judgments about the desirability of a given child's growth depend on the particular values that underlie the judge's standards of appropriate development.

PART THREE

THE PSYCHOANALYTIC
TRADITION

A search for developmental causes and cures of neuroses

From the viewpoint of the general public, the most unsettling theory of child development proposed during the past century has been Sigmund Freud's psychoanalysis. In the late 1800s and throughout the 1900s, many people were shocked by Freud's contention that sexual motives—with sex interpreted in a broad sense—underlie much if not all human behavior. More shocking still is the notion of infantile sexuality. To the lay public and medical profession of the late 1800s and early 1900s, the idea that little children have sensuous thoughts that are important determinants of their personal and social adjustment was clearly a distortion of the truth by a dirty-minded neurotic (S. Freud, 1917, pp. 323–325, 1938, p. 9; Hartmann, 1959, p. 11).

Not as morally shocking but no less disturbing personally was Freud's suggestion that much of the time we do not consciously know why we act the way we do. Instead of behaving as rational beings, we are driven and manipulated by primitive urges and by traumas from our past that reside in what Freud called our *unconscious mind.* In the sixteenth century, Copernicus had already insulted humanity by suggesting that the earth is not the center of the universe. Darwin had carried the insult further by proposing that humans are descendants of lower forms of life and therefore not the divine, unique beings that they had led themselves to believe. Now Freud pushed insult another step by contending that one's conscious mind was neither master of one's fate nor captain of one's soul; instead, each person was a victim of unconscious drives.

However, over the years since Freud first put forth his theory, it has gained a substantial following of believers. His work, and the revisions of it by later generations, now represents a major branch of psychology. Indeed, many of his key ideas have nearly achieved the status of common sense. For these reasons, the psychoanalytic tradition deserves a prominent place in a survey of theories of child development.

Chapter Five presents central concepts of the theory as Freud himself devised them. The chapter ends with a brief description of contributions subsequently made by Freud's third daughter, Anna, specifically concerning the portion of the overall theory that deals with childhood.

Chapter Six illustrates a major extension of psychoanalysis by a disciple of Freud, Erik Erikson. Of the various revised versions of psychoanalysis fashioned during the twentieth century, Erikson's has been the most significant for the field of child development, particularly for the years of adolescence.

At the end of Part Three, Perspective B ("Identifying States of Consciousness") treats the question of different levels of consciousness, a matter of vital concern in Freudian theory.

CHAPTER FIVE

SIGMUND FREUD'S PSYCHOANALYSIS

Often we will best understand how a theorist arrived at a model of development if we recognize the sequence of experiences that were instrumental in guiding the direction of his theorizing. Since this seems particularly true in the case of psychoanalysis, let's begin the account of Freud's model by looking briefly at the medical puzzles that stimulated him to speculate about the nature of children and the forces that determine their development.

Sigmund Freud (1856–1939) was an Austrian neurologist who, early in his career of private medical practice in Vienna, encountered some very perplexing cases. Patients came to him with a variety of ailments, such as paralysis of the hand or aches or blurred vision, which could not be explained by traditional physiological knowledge. Although the patients' symptoms suggested that nerve tissue had been damaged, examination showed the nervous system to be intact.

How could people suffer such ailments without any organic impairment of the nervous system? While Freud was pondering this problem, he learned about the work that Jean Charcot was conducting on hypnotism in Paris. Charcot had shown that under a hypnotic spell people could be told that they would have one or another bodily symptom after they awakened from the hypnotic state, but would not remember the cause of this symptom. They would not recall that they had received a suggestion under hypnosis. And, indeed, after coming out of hypnosis, they did exhibit the suggested symptoms, such as paralysis of a leg, numbness of the skin, or deafness. Charcot, in addition, was able to use hypnosis to relieve people of certain symptoms. Under hypnosis, patients were told that they no longer suffered the ailment that had brought them to the clinic. Upon awakening, at least some of these patients had lost the symptom of which they had complained (S. Freud, 1910, p. 21).

Freud's interest in Charcot's experiments was so great that he spent the year 1885–1886 in Paris studying the methods and effects of hypnosis. At the same time, he asked questions that might explain these curious phenomena: What relation might there be between the strange cases Freud faced in his medical practice and the cases Charcot exhibited in his clinic? How must human personality be structured and how must mind be related to body in order to cause such things to occur (S. Freud, 1910, pp. 16–22)?

To answer these queries, Freud, over the next several decades, developed his psychoanalytic theory of personality. Included in the theory is a conception of child development that has exerted significant influence over a number of areas of child psychology today—child psychiatry, counseling children and adolescents, nursery school teaching methods, and research in child development. Certain concepts from Freudian theory have now been generally accepted by psychologists, educators, and social workers, and even by those who reject most of psychoanalytic theory. In effect, Freud's views have had a decided influence on people concerned with raising children.

Psychoanalytic theory in its entirety is quite complex. Not only does it have many ramifications, but adherents of psychoanalysis often disagree with one another on important issues. Freud himself altered the theory in major ways on several occasions. For these reasons, the following discussion presents only a simplified sketch of the theory's main elements.

The early part of the chapter comprises descriptions of (1) levels of consciousness, (2) the apparatus of mental life, (3) psychosexual stages of child development, and (4) the development of consciousness and ego strength. Following these are (5) a brief review of some contributions to psychoanalytic theory and practice by Anna Freud, (6) practical applications, and (7) an assessment of the theory.

LEVELS OF CONSCIOUSNESS

Early in the process of formulating his theory, Freud proposed that each person has an *unconscious* aspect of mind in addition to the conscious aspect of which the individual is aware. By the *unconscious* Freud meant a sort of mental receptacle for ideas, a receptacle from which the individual cannot recall ideas at will. These ideas, of which we are unaware, influence our actions just as much as if they were conscious. In effect, much of what we do arises from unconscious motivation (S. Freud, 1923, p. 4).

The concept of an unconscious state of mind was not entirely new in the field of philosophy. An occasional theorist over the centuries had postulated such an aspect. However, it was Freud who elaborated the concept and assigned it a central role in behavior.

By proposing the unconscious, Freud was able to account for otherwise unexplainable disorders suffered by his patients. He hypothesized that a person who faces a distressing, unsolved problem in daily life will find the problem psychologically painful. So the individual's personality, to escape this pain of unresolved conflicts, automatically resolves the problem by pushing the distressing thoughts out of consciousness. The patient actively "forgets" the matter. But Freud believed that such forgotten material does not leave the mind. Instead, it is only relegated to an unconscious condition—in other words, it is "repressed"—in order to keep the sufferer unaware of its existence and, consequently, enable the person to feel more at peace. But the problem, now unconscious, continues to agitate, and it expresses itself in devious ways. One mode of expression can be a bodily ailment, such as a headache or paralysis of some part of the body. So it was that Freud concluded that the strange symptoms displayed by his patients were caused by unresolved mental conflicts that seethed insistently in their unconscious minds. Not only were these bodily disorders, which he called *conversion hysteria symp-*

toms, the consequence of repressed mental conflicts but so, Freud believed, was the entire array of neurotic symptoms, an array including phobias, obsessions, compulsions, and anxieties.

To alleviate such symptoms—in effect, to cure the neuroses—Freud proposed that the repressed conflict, which had originated in a problem of development earlier in the patient's life, had to be brought into consciousness. The patient had to recognize the origin of the difficulties and verbally relive the original conflict situation, but this time work out the conflict in a constructive, emotionally satisfying manner and thus be cured of the neuroses.

In order to make his therapeutic scheme work, Freud had to devise a process for uncovering the unconscious conflicts and presenting them so that patients would accept the conflicts as true and deserving of serious attention. Early in his career Freud tried different means for uncovering unconscious conflicts. He began with hypnosis but, as he later reported, "I soon came to dislike hypnosis, for it was a temperamental and . . . mystical ally" (S. Freud, 1910, p. 22). Hence he gave it up in favor of free association and dream interpretation.

The process of *free association* consists of encouraging the patient to relax, usually on a couch, and to describe free-flowing thoughts without editing them. The analyst listens to hours of such narration in order to locate underlying themes of conflict that are hints or symbols of hidden problems. By using the process of relaxed, free association, the therapist is assuming that "the repressed wishful impulse . . . is on the look-out for an opportunity of being activated, and when that happens it succeeds in sending into consciousness a disguised and unrecogniz-able substitute for what had been repressed" (S. Freud, 1910, p. 27). It is the analyst's task to unmask the significant elements of the patient's narration and reveal them for what they really are in the individual's past development.

In a like manner, Freud used *dream interpretation* as a window, albeit murky and distorted, for viewing the contents of the unconscious. He believed that during sleep, a censor force, which seeks to prevent unconscious conflicts from entering consciousness, is not as alert as during waking life. So dreams, in Freud's scheme, are products of the person's trying to satisfy wishes and solve problems during sleep. The dream serves as an audiovisual symbol of unconscious urges pressing for expression into consciousness. The analyst is skilled in interpreting dreams in a way that reveals the nature and source of the patient's unconscious conflicts (S. Freud, 1900).

The significance of Freud's reliance on free association and dream interpreta-tion is twofold. First, both techniques were tools crucial to the conduct of his system of therapy. Second, and more important for our present purposes, they served almost exclusively as the sources of data about childhood on which he erected his model of development. Rather than spending his time directly observing children in the process of their development, Freud spent endless hours listening to adult neurotics produce memories of childhood. On these memories, extracted from free associations and dreams, he built his picture of sexual growth.

In addition to introducing a view of the mind as consisting of both conscious and unconscious aspects, Freud also distinguished two levels of unconsciousness. One level, he said, contains those ideas that are not in consciousness at the moment, that are latent. We can recall them, "bring them to mind," if we choose, even though it may take a bit of effort. This first level Freud labeled the *precon-scious*. The second level contains the truly repressed ideas, those held down purposely by the personality's resistance forces because allowing them to enter consciousness would be too painful for the conscious personality to face. This second level, deeper and less accessible than the preconscious, is the *true* or prototype unconscious in the Freudian scheme. In a sense, then, the preconscious is a shadow zone between the open, bright conscious and the closed, dark uncon-scious (S. Freud, 1923, pp. 4–5). A person has thoughts or ideas at each of these levels.

THE PSYCHIC APPARATUS

The levels of consciousness serve as a sort of three-tiered arena in which a person's psychic life takes place. Within the psychical arena, the three main functionaries that compete and cooperate to produce this performance were conceived by Freud to be the *id*, the *ego*, and the *superego*. In the course of a child's development, these three do not appear simultaneously. The id comes first—it is already present at birth. The ego develops out of the growing infant's efforts to satisfy needs through transactions with the environment. Some years later the superego develops as an internal representative of the rules and values of the environment.

The way the development of the id, ego, and superego becomes intertwined with stages of the child's psychosexual growth is rather complex. In order to make this development easier to grasp, I will divide the explanation into two parts. The first, which comprises this section on the psychic apparatus, treats the nature and functions of the id, ego, and superego. The second, in the next section, describes their relation to the psychosexual growth stages that Freud proposed.

As a preface to these matters, we need to recognize that all behavior, physical and psychological, needs energy to activate it. In psychoanalytic theory the sources of all energy are the instincts, with *instinct* defined as an inborn factor that gives force and direction to psychological activities. For at least three decades Freud experimented with various conceptions of instincts. Then in 1920 he settled on a basic pair of motivating forces—the *life* and *death* instincts—which he thought vied for expression and supremacy in directing psychic behavior throughout a person's life span. The influence of the life instinct is reflected in constructive acts, in acts of love and altruism. The influence of the death instinct is displayed in destructive acts, in hate and in aggression. Freud applied the word *libido* to the psychic energy deriving from the life instinct, but he coined no parallel term for the energy emitting from the death instinct (S. Freud, 1920).

From the viewpoint of the instincts, the process of living consists of a continual competition between the opposing life and death forces—love against hate, life preservation against self-destruction. Often a mode of behaving represents a fusion of the two, as when aggression against a threatening enemy (motivated by the death instinct) preserves one's life and promotes one's welfare (which is the objective of the life instinct). Although throughout childhood and well into adult life the evidences of the life instinct appear to be the more prominent, the ultimate victory obviously goes to the opposing force, when, at life's close, the organism loses all animation and returns to the passive inorganic state that is the ultimate aim of the death instinct.

Now that we have the pair of basic instinctual energy sources in mind, we turn to the psychic apparatus through which the forces are invested or expended. In psychoanalytic theory, the personality of the newborn consists of a single operating component called the *id*. It is at the unconscious level and "contains everything that is inherited, that is present at birth, that is laid down in the constitution—above all, therefore, the instincts" (S. Freud, 1938, p. 2). It is within this id that libido builds up as a sort of pressure, searching for expression. Seen another way, libidinal energy arising from the id assumes the form of *needs* that demand fulfillment. The expenditure or release of libido is experienced by the infant as pleasure. The blocking of libidinal release is experienced as pain. So the id operates on the *pleasure principle,* which says, "Get as much pleasure as possible as soon as possible without regard for anyone else or anything else in the world." In its converse form the principle becomes "Avoid as much pain as possible."

Hence psychoanalysis pictures the newborn baby as all id, seeking only to satisfy its needs for food, for drink, for warmth, for elimination of body wastes, for freedom from skin irritants, and for affection—affection in the sense of being cuddled by its mother or mother substitute. The newborn's awareness of its condition and of the world is ostensibly very fuzzy. Freudians suppose that a baby does not distinguish among objects in its environment, nor does it recognize a difference between itself and other people or things. The newborn is aware only of discomfort or pain, which signals unfulfilled needs that require attention. The only observable methods the infant has for reacting to these pain or tension signals are crying, mouthing, and randomly moving its arms and legs.

But as time passes and the infant's experience with the world increases, more precise awareness of the environment begins to develop. The earliest level of awareness results in the *primary process,* which is the baby's act of creating in its memory an image of an object that will fulfill a need. For example, when the newborn feels hunger pangs, he automatically cries until someone feeds him. The food reduces the tension of hunger, and the baby experiences pleasure. As days pass, this cycle of hunger, feeding, and tension reduction is played over and over, so that gradually the taste, smell, feel, and sight of the food and of the feeder (usually the mother) are stored as images in the baby's memory. As a result, the infant, by means of the primary process, can now imagine those things that will bring a particular variety of satisfaction or a particular mode of expending libidinal energy.

It is important to recognize that the primary process is a rather chaotic, irrational mode of thought that does not distinguish between reasonable and unreasonable need-fulfilling images. The concern of the id and its primary process thinking is to gain satisfaction, regardless of whether or not the method of satisfaction is practical or will be tolerated by the environment. What the personality next requires, then, is a component that recognizes the nature of the environment as well as the demands of the id and can, therefore, provide realistic methods of investing energy. This second component of the psychic apparatus is called the *ego.* Freud postulated that the ego arises from, or separates out of, the id and is fueled by libidinal energy from the id. In effect, the id's primary process develops images of things that fulfill needs, but the image is only an initial, incomplete step toward satisfaction. Another agent, the ego, is required to bring the dream into reality. Freud explained that "the ego is that part of the id which has been modified by the direct influence of the external world through the medium" of conscious perception (S. Freud, 1923, p. 15). Furthermore, he proposed:

> It is to this ego that consciousness is attached; the ego controls the . . . discharge of excitations into the external world; it is the mental agency which supervises all its own constituent processes, and which goes to sleep at night, though even then it exercises the censorship on dreams. (1923, p. 7)

Hence the ego serves as a decision maker that tries to negotiate a satisfactory solution to the conflicting demands that come on the one side from the id (which says, "I want") and on the other side from the environment or "real world" (which says, "You'll get it with a minimum of cost or pain only under these conditions"). Whereas the id works on the pleasure principle, the ego operates on the *reality principle,* which can be stated as follows: "Recognize the conditions and demands of the real world and then seek methods of fulfilling the id's needs that are acceptable in such a world."

To play its role of negotiator, the ego is constantly assessing the kinds and strengths of needs arising from the id and at the same time assessing the conditions of the environment. From this assessment, the ego attempts to devise behaviors that represent the best compromise between the id and the outside world. Or, as is sometimes the case, the ego must negotiate a compromise among several demands coming simultaneously from the id, such as the demands of hunger and fatigue arising at the same moment.

We noted that the id, by means of the primary process, associates certain objects with need fulfillment. These associations are stored as memory images. It is now up to the ego to turn the images into reality. This problem-solving act is called the *secondary process.* The individual's skills of perceiving, remembering, analyzing, and taking action develop from this constant interaction among (1) the id's needs, (2) the maturing bodily organs, such as eyes and ears, and (3) the ego's increasing awareness of the complexities of the world.

The Superego's Role

Our next concern is with the third component of the psychic apparatus, the *superego.* Early in a child's life the rules of the world—the rules of *do* and *don't*—are enforced by the environment. The infant, in Freud's system, has no inborn inner voice telling her what is right and what is wrong. In effect, the child is born neither moral nor immoral, but *amoral.* She has no knowledge of good or bad. Her morality is simply that of getting pleasure (as demanded by the id) in a manner that will avoid punishment or pain (a manner arranged by the ego). The very young child, therefore, does not automatically feel bad or guilty or ashamed when she transgresses one of society's expectations. She feels bad only when the consequences of her behavior are either the withholding of rewards or the application of punishment. It is usually the child's parents who produce her good and bad feelings by manipulating the system of rewards and punishments she will experience.

Although children are not born with knowledge of what is good and what is evil, they are born with a capacity for two things: (1) to develop internal values and (2) to feel good (pleased and proud) when they abide by these values and to feel bad (sad, ashamed, and guilty) when transgressing them. Over the years of childhood and adolescence this capacity acquires contents in the form of moral values the child adopts from the environment. It is this third component of the growing personality that Freud labeled *superego.* How and why the superego appears and grows are matters intimately involved in the psychosexual stages of development and will be discussed in connection with them. For the present we will restrict our attention to the role the superego plays in the mental life of the older child and adolescent.

Just as Freud pictured the ego as developing out of the id, so he saw the superego arising from the ego (S. Freud, 1923, pp. 18–29). He explained:

> This new psychical agency continues to carry on the functions which have hitherto been performed by the people in the external world: It observes the ego, gives it orders, judges it and threatens it with punishments, exactly like the parents whose place it has taken. (1938, p. 62)

Freud conceived of the superego as having two aspects, the *conscience* and the *ego ideal.* The conscience represents the "should nots" of the child's world, the things for which he has been punished. The ego ideal represents the "shoulds," the positive moral values the child has been taught. Whereas very young children must be punished for transgressions and rewarded for good behavior by their parents, maturing children gradually do not need outside sanctions. Their superego plays the punishing and rewarding roles for them. For disobeying the values they have now accepted as their own, maturing children's conscience punishes them with guilt, shame, and fear. For abiding by their moral values, their ego ideal rewards them with feelings of self-righteousness, self-praise, and pride.

With the addition of the superego to the id and ego, the apparatus of the mind is complete. The behavior of older children and adolescents is thus a result of the way the ego has negotiated a settlement among three conflicting sources of demands: (1) the id, which insists on immediate fulfillment of wishes, (2) the environment, which sets conditions under which wishes can be satisfied without punishment, and (3) the superego, which presses youths to live up to a set of moral values they have incorporated from their parents and from other significant people in their world.

Mechanisms of Defense

As the ego develops over the years, it evolves techniques or habits for accommodating the conflicting demands made on it. A strong, mature ego uses direct means to accomplish this. It frankly admits the nature of instinctual demands, environmental forces, and the superego's commands. Then it proposes forthright, reasoned ways to effect a solution that satisfies each source of demand to an acceptable degree. But an ego that is weak, still childish and immature, slips into using more devious techniques of adjustment, techniques that Freud called *defense mechanisms.* The ego, in effect, seeks to fool itself and others concerning the state of affairs it faces, for it feels inadequate to solve the conflict among the demands that confront it.

The most significant defense technique, *repression,* has already been described. It is the automatic, nonconscious process of pushing distressing matters out of consciousness and into the unconscious. Although repression clears the conscious mind of worries, the repressed material continues to foment distress in the unconscious and to produce the sorts of neurotic symptoms that Freud met in his medical practice.

A second mechanism is *sublimation,* the substitution of a culturally higher, socially more acceptable mode of expressing sexual or aggressive energy. Such altruistic acts as caring for children or aiding the sick, or such artistic endeavors as writing poetry or performing a ballet, are viewed by Freudians as substitutes for direct sexual behavior.

A third defense technique is *regression,* which consists of returning to an earlier, more primitive mode of adjusting to problems. A person may turn to this device when facing a new or distressing situation. As a simple example, a twelve-year-old girl feels frustrated when her mother criticizes her in public, so the girl begins sucking her thumb or the corner of her handkerchief as she did when she sought solace as an infant.

A mechanism that has been readily adopted into commonsense understanding is that of *projection.* When children sense within their own personality a motive of which they are ashamed or which they fear, they may not admit its existence consciously to themselves, but instead may constantly see this motive in other people, attributing to others those unacceptable acts and feelings that their own id urges them to express. Thus the child who harbors hate in her own unconscious will accuse others of hating her, claiming at the same time that she herself bears no malice. Likewise, a person who is repressing strong sexual desires of which he is ashamed will assume that others are trying to seduce or assault him sexually.

The device called *reaction formation* has been particularly useful to psychoanalysts, for it enables them to explain behavior that would otherwise appear to refute typical predictions that derive from the theory. Reaction formation consists of a child's adopting behavior that is just the opposite of an instinctual urge. For instance, a child may act compulsively clean, avoiding dirt and frequently washing her hands and changing her clothes. The direct interpretation of such behavior is that the child desires to be clean—cleanliness is her basic need. But Freudians would suspect something different. Since in their theory the basic drives involve such sensuous pleasure as sexual stimulation and bowel and urinary functions, they would propose that the child is not motivated by a basic cleanliness need. Instead, she really wants to become soiled, to mess around in dirt and feces, but she has been punished by her parents for expressing such desires so now she feels her basic urges are wicked. To control them, she represses the original desires and in her conscious life adopts the opposite sort of behavior as a desperate means of mastering the urges of which she is ashamed. In short, her behavior represents a reaction against her instinctual drives.

Three more defense mechanisms can be briefly described. *Compensation* is a device by which children seek to overcome a personal or environmental barrier by substituting success in some other realm of life than the one in which they suffer the weakness. *Rationalization* consists of giving a socially acceptable reason for a behavior that actually was motivated by a less honorable reason. *Escape* is leaving the scene of a distressing experience. The escape can be either physical, such as a girl's running away from home, or psychological, such as a youth's retreating into daydreams in school when the lesson is confusing.

These defense mechanisms, which are only some of those identified by Freud and his followers, illustrate the kinds of strategies the ego employs to satisfy, as well as possible, the conflicting demands made on it.

Now that we have identified the main components of the psyche and their functions, we can look at the psychosexual growth stages involved in the development of these components.

The Psychosexual Stages of Development

To account for the sorts of dreams and memories of childhood that his patients described, Freud produced a model of child development that featured a series of growth stages. The current neuroses of his patients, he thought, were the result of inadequate solutions to the problems the individual had faced as a child at one or more of these stages. He labeled these growth steps *psychosexual phases* because he believed the development of the personality—the *psyche*—was critically influenced by the manner in which the child learned to expend sex energy (libido) from one period of life to the next. In other words, Freud proposed that the most significant emotional experiences during childhood and adolescence are those associated with expending libido in relation to a series of particularly sensitive zones of the body on which children's attention focuses at different points of development. These *erogenous zones*, in chronological sequence, are the mouth, the anus, and the genital organs. At the time a particular zone is the chief focus for the release of libido, the child not only derives sensuous (sexual, in a broad meaning of the term) pleasure from use of the zone, but the child's relationships with other people are heavily influenced by the way they respond to the child's attention to the zone. In essence, Freud proposed that the personal-social relationships children develop—their feelings about themselves and others, and their ways of treating themselves and others—are founded in the experiences the children have at each psychosexual stage. Personality problems that arise as children seek to work their way through a stage may go unresolved, be repressed by the frantic ego, and continue to agitate within the unconscious and cause neuroses for years afterwards.

Although the number of developmental periods identified between birth and adulthood may vary slightly from one psychoanalytic theorist to another, all of them cite at least five major stages: oral (ages 0–1), anal (ages 2–3), infantile-genital (ages 3–4 or so), latency (ages 4 or 5 to puberty), mature-genital (from midteens to adulthood). We will examine these stages and the substages involved in several of them.

Birth: The Traumatic Beginning

Birth is not a stage of growth, but it is a highly significant event in psychoanalytic theory because it is regarded as the first great shock of the child's life. In the Freudian view, the newborn is overwhelmed with stimulation from the environment into which he or she emerges from the womb. The reaction is intense fear, for the undeveloped ego has no means to cope adequately with such a flood of stimuli. The birth trauma, then, is the prototype of all subsequent fear-producing situations children will meet as they grow to old age. When later in life they are confronted by extreme stimuli—either extreme instinctual demands or extreme pressures from the environment—and their existing ego techniques are ineffective for mastering the stimuli, the original fear occasioned by the birth trauma will be reactivated, and they will revert to infantile behavior. Consequently, according to Freudian theory, an easier birth, involving less shock upon entering the world, can be expected to build less fear into the unconscious of the growing child, who may then be able to face frustrating experiences later in life with greater emotional control.

Stage 1: The Oral Period (Ages 0–1)

The psychoanalytic model of the child pictures the newborn not as a passive slab of damp clay on which environmental experiences will engrave a personality structure but as a dynamic energy system pressing to expend its energy. Or more precisely, the id of the neonate is seeking to invest libidinal energy in images of objects that will satisfy the instinctual needs and bring the pleasure of release. This act of investment (the primary process of the id) is called *cathexis*. When the id channels energy into an image of an object, it is said to be *cathecting* that object.

Following birth, the natural initial object for cathexis is the mother's breast or a suitable substitute because it is through the mouth that newborns must now obtain life-sustaining nourishment. Newborns must also use their mouth and nose for breathing. The nerve endings in the lips and mouth are particularly sensitive and offer the infant special pleasure. Freud wrote:

> The baby's obstinate persistence in sucking gives evidence at an early stage of a need for satisfaction which, though it originates from and is instigated by the taking of nourishment, nevertheless strives to obtain pleasure independently of nourishment and for that reason may and should be termed *sexual.* (1938, p. 11)

The adequacy with which children satisfy the need for food, drink, and breath gives them their first impressions of the world and of their relation to it. Not only are their personalities influenced by how soon and how completely the pent-up libidinal energy is released, but the atmosphere associated with how these needs for release are either met or neglected affects them also. If their mothers hold them affectionately and soothingly during the feeding process, children will pass through the oral period in a happier, more confident state than if they are never cuddled and if distressing sounds and sights bombard them while feeding.

In addition to taking the food and drink, infants use the oral zone to investigate the parts of the world they can reach. They examine most objects by putting the objects to their lips or into their mouths. Freud suggested that the basic reason children mouth objects is that they wish to *incorporate* the objects and thus to control and master them.

The infant's personality, being mostly pleasure-seeking id, begins to distinguish *me* from *not me* (evidence of a growing ego) by regarding pleasure-giving objects as *self* and non-pleasure-giving objects as *non-self.*

Some psychoanalysts divide the oral period into two substages, the early or *receptive stage* and the late or *biting stage.*

The receptive stage covers the first few months of life, when erotic pleasure is derived from sucking, swallowing, and mouthing. At this time infants are rather passive and play an extremely dependent role. If their feeding and other dependency needs are not adequately met or if great conflict is associated with those needs a residue of unfulfillment and conflict is repressed into the unconscious to reveal itself in subsequent years, often as neurotic overdependency or a compulsive habit of trying to "take in" other people and objects. In essence, Freudian theory sees the experience children have with satisfying instinctual drives at a particular psychosexual stage as forming a model for attitudes or relationships that may be carried over to later life.

The biting stage occurs during the latter portion of infancy when teeth are erupting and gums are harder. The dominant zone of gratification is still the mouth, but at this point the act of touching things with the lips or of swallowing is not as satisfying as biting or chewing. As infants' perceptual skills mature, they begin to recognize the features of outside objects more clearly. The infant now recognizes that one object, such as mother, can have both pleasure-giving and pain-giving functions. Mother gratifies hunger when the baby cries. But mother also has to carry out other activities in her life, so she cannot satisfy the baby's demands immediately all the time, and the baby finds this postponement painful.

As a result, infants develop their first *ambivalent* feelings. They both love and hate the same object. Freudian theory proposes that children's early ambivalent feelings and sadistic tendencies are expressed in biting—biting mother's breast, people's fingers, toys, and the like. If progress through this stage is incomplete, so that the infant experiences insufficient satisfaction of biting needs and has inadequate opportunities to express ambivalence without unduly painful repercussions, then a residue of conflict remains in the unconscious to disturb the individual in later life. If children's progress through the latter oral stage is arrested—that is, if they become *fixated* at this point in psychosexual growth—then they may evidence such fixation as an adult through a pattern of "biting" criticism of others or by frequently "chewing out" people around him.

This phenomenon of fixation can occur at any of the psychosexual stages. Freudians hold that fixation—carrying into later life those modes of libidinal gratification suited to an earlier stage—can be the result of either too little or too much satisfaction at the stage in question. If the child's attempts at libidinal investment in an erogenous zone are frustrated, so there remains pent-up energy and inadequate satisfaction, then fixation may occur in the form of a constant seeking to gain the satisfaction in symbolic ways in subsequent years. In contrast, if so much satisfaction with a given erogenous zone is experienced so that the child does not wish to abandon this pleasure by moving ahead to mature forms of libidinal expression, then fixation may again be the result. At each psychosexual stage, children progress most satisfactorily if they gain enough pleasure to move ahead without dragging along a residue of unfulfilled needs, yet do not gain so much satisfaction that they are unwilling to advance.

Stage 2: The Anal Period (Ages 2–3)

During the second and third years of life, much of the attention of child and parents typically focuses on establishing proper control of the bowels. This time of life is usually called the anal period, because the prime concern is with expelling and retaining feces. However, it is sometimes referred to as the *anal-urethral period,* because control of urinary functions is also involved. Thus the dominant zones of gratification or libido investment become the anal cavity, the sphincter muscles of the lower bowel, and the muscles of the urinary system.

The shift of the child's attention to the anal area does not mean that the expression of instinctual energy via the oral zone has stopped. It means, rather, that anal activities usually become of major concern for both child and parent. In response to questions about the sequence of the oral, anal, and genital stages, Freud wrote:

> It would be a mistake to suppose that these three phases succeed one another in a clear-cut fashion. One may appear in addition to another; they may overlap one another, may be present along side of one another. (1938, p. 12)

In the anal period, much of children's important contact with adults and much of the emotion adults express toward them are related to toilet training. Like the oral stage, the anal period can be divided into two subperiods, the first concerned with pleasure in expelling feces and urine, and the second with retaining these materials.

During the *expulsion stage,* children meet their first serious experience with an external barrier (parents' coercion to have the child control the bowels) to an instinctual cathexis (wishing to defecate). If the child is to accomplish bowel and bladder control, the ego must apply resistance to the child's urge to eliminate at the moment she feels the need. Thus the ego must borrow libido from the id to energize the resistance. Such a use of libidinal force by the ego—or at a later stage, by the superego—is called *countercathexis* or *anticathexis.* In short, the cathexis or energy investment of the id in the pleasurable release of defecation must be countered by an opposing cathexis of the ego if the child is to meet the parents' demands for cleanliness and thus retain their love.

This is a crucial time for the child to learn to earn love, praise, and approval. If the period is not handled properly by parents—if they harshly impose cleanliness standards before the child is physiologically prepared to control the bowels and bladder, for example—then the child's personality will retain vestiges of fear, guilt, and defiance. The repressed conflict may produce an adult who is compulsively regular and clean or, in contrast, one who is bitter and, in a symbolic sense, voids and urinates on others in social interaction. The frequent use of the words *crap, shit,* and *bullshit* among adults is said to reflect a measure of fixation at the anal stage.

In the second half of the anal period, children have learned to *retain* feces and urine at will. They now gain sensuous satisfaction by holding in—that is, by keeping the product they value. Freudians suggest that the child's idea of things having value comes from this period, and inadequate passage through the stage may show up later in life in acts of hoarding and collecting things.

Stage 3: The Infantile-Genital Period (Ages 3–4 or so)

The boy's penis and the girl's clitoris and vulva become the key objects of erotic pleasure during the third major psychosexual period. It, too, can be divided into two phases.

During the first phase, called the *phallic stage,* the child discovers that fondling the genitals, titillation, and masturbation (but without orgasm) give erotic pleasure. The child next associates fondling the genitals with a love object with whom he or she wishes to have some sort of sexual relations. For the boy, Freud wrote:

> The object that has been found turns out to be almost identical with the first object of the oral pleasure-instinct, which was reached by attachment (to the nutritional instinct). Though it is not actually the mother's breast, at least it is the mother. We call the mother the first *love*-object. (1917, p. 329)

While the boy is viewing his mother as the desired object, he is at the same time recognizing that he cannot have her all to himself, for his father is the successful competitor for her affections. The resulting psychological conflict—wanting to possess mother but prevented from doing so by the powerful father—has been labeled the *Oedipus complex* or *Oedipus conflict.* The girl is in the opposite situation, wanting her father as her love partner but being defeated in this contest by her mother. The resulting conflict for the girl has been called the *Electra complex,* but both the boy's and girl's problems are usually subsumed under the Oedipus label.

During this period the child experiences strong ambivalent feelings, seeking the parent of the opposite sex as a lover, but at the same time both fearing and loving the parent of the same sex. An adequate resolution of the Oedipus situation occurs when the child rejects the sexual feelings toward the taboo object, the opposite-sex parent, and, at the same time, identifies with the parent of the same sex. By identifying with the same-sex parent, the child both assuages feelings of fear of reprisal and incorporates the traits of the same-sex parent, the traits that made that parent win the love of the other. In effect, the boy identifies with his father and seeks to adopt his father's characteristics. The girl does the same with her mother. This is the way Freudian theory accounts for the development of masculine and feminine characteristics that fit the mode of the society into which the child is raised.

It is during this process of solving the Oedipus conflict by repressing sexual desires and adopting parental characteristics that the superego evolves. To control what they now consider their dangerous sexual urges, children incorporate parental values into their personalities. These values, in the form of a superego that separates out of the ego, enable children to reward and punish themselves and thus control their own behavior in the absence of outside authority figures.

If the Oedipus conflict is not adequately resolved through repression of sexual impulses and identification with the like-sex parent, remnants of the conflict remain in the unconscious to distort the personality of the adolescent and adult. For instance, homosexuality sometimes has been explained as the child's identifying with the other-sex parent and thus modeling his or her subsequent living habits and sexual tastes after the opposite-sex parent rather than the same-sex one.

The resolution of the Oedipus complex leads into the second portion of the infantile-genital stage, called the *latency period.* Since this time of latent eroticism is so different in its manifestations from the early infantile-genital stage, I treat it as a major period by itself.

Stage 4: The Latency Period
(from Ages 4 or 5 to Puberty at Ages 11–13)

During this period, the dominant zone of gratification is still the genital area, but this is usually not displayed in the child's behavior, for both the boy and girl are repressing expressions of sex in order to solve the Oedipus conflict. The child has cathected or adopted both the gratifying and punishing parts of the parents and thus considers talk and displays of sex to be "nasty." The boy stops masturbating because he is afraid of being punished by having his penis cut off, and the girl stops because she is afraid of losing parental love. According to Freud (1938, p. 10), the child falls "victim to *infantile amnesia*" and "forgets" (by use of repression) the sex urges and activities of the first five years of life.

Throughout the years of latency the child's interests in working and playing primarily with children of his or her own sex is a manifestation of efforts to control sexual thoughts. This period has sometimes been called the *gang age,* because children seldom voluntarily form groups that include the opposite sex. Because of this same-sex tendency in social relationships, the period is also referred to as the *homosexual phase,* although the homosexual relationships often do not involve any overt sexual acts. Indeed, the rejection of "sex" that the child so strongly evidences at this time in order to control Oedipal tendencies can preclude even thinking about physical displays that might be construed as sexual, whether the object of these displays is a same-sex or opposite-sex peer. In effect, the superego serves as a strong, moralistic internal representative of parental, and thus societal, rules. Playing by the rules both in games and in other daily activities becomes a matter of great importance to children in this phase of growth.

Solving the Oedipus conflict and working through the latency phase successfully is a difficult, stressful task, and often children fail to complete it successfully. Some become fixated at this stage, so that in adult life they never feel comfortable around the opposite sex, and they may avoid sexual relations with the opposite sex or else perform sexual activities in an emotionally detached or aggressive manner.

Stage 5: The Mature-Genital Period (from Ages 14–16 to 18 or 21)

The maturing of sexual functions at puberty and beyond is signaled in girls by menstruation and such secondary bodily changes as the rounding of the breasts and the growth of underarm and pubic hair. The parallel maturation in boys is shown by growth of the genital organs, the appearance of sperm cells, nocturnal emissions of semen (often accompanied by erotic dreams), lowering of the voice pitch, and the growth of underarm, facial, and pubic hair.

The primary zone of erotic pleasure or libidinal cathexis is still the penis in the boy and the clitoral area in the girl, but now the gratification involves sexual orgasm. Whereas during the latent period the child was interested primarily in peers of the same sex, now the attention turns to the opposite sex. In mature sexuality the dominant erotic activity becomes copulation with a partner of the opposite sex. To make the transition from the rejection of sex at the latency phase to the wholehearted pursuit of heterosexual activity is typically a psychologically demanding challenge, particularly in societies that have erected moral barriers against intercourse between unmarried people, especially between adolescents. And such was the case in the late-nineteenth-century Viennese society from which Freud drew so many of his patients on whose psychoanalytic histories he erected his theory.

The process of working through the problems of this transition successfully not only enables the youth to gratify sexual instincts in a mature fashion but also gives her or him a less egocentric, more objective perspective of the world in general. The superego has been well formed, with its appropriate conscience and ego ideal. The ego operates on the reality principle, having developed direct modes of solving life's problems and not depending unduly on defense mechanisms.

However, it is during this final stage of psychosexual development that society's rules about the conditions under which sexual intercourse is permissible often press youths to adopt sublimation as a defense mechanism. That is, the adolescent abstains from copulation and substitutes instead artistic or philanthropic activities to express sexual drives indirectly. The substitute may be writing poetry, reading literature, singing or playing a musical instrument, caring for children, aiding the handicapped, engaging in sports, or the like. (The question of whether such sublimation actually does satisfy sexual urges is an unsettled issue, still debated among psychoanalysts and among psychiatrists of other persuasions.)

The Stages and Therapy

Freud's concept of stages is the key to the practice of psychoanalysis as a method of aiding both children and adults who suffer neuroses, with *neuroses* meaning psychic disorders that are distressing but do not cause the person to view the world in a seriously distorted way, as is the case in psychoses. The task of the therapist is to use free association and dream interpretation to search back through the patient's psychosexual history to locate the stage at which unresolved conflicts were repressed. Through analysis, the therapist hopes to reveal to the patient the original causes of the repressed problem and, by consciously reviewing the original conflicts, to help the patient recognize them for what they are and to integrate this new understanding into the personality. In short, the conflict is dug up and relived both intellectually and emotionally. When this process is complete, the neurotic symptoms that brought the patient to the psychoanalyst are expected to disappear. Thus psychoanalysts do not attempt to change neurotic symptoms directly—which they believe is folly—but, rather, to find the repressed conflict that is causing the symptom. They believe that when the conflict is resolved and psychologically integrated, the symptoms will evaporate. Treating a symptom directly, they say, does not solve the problem but at best only causes the patient to substitute a different symptom for the one that has been treated. The underlying cause, they insist, must be found and relived realistically. (As we will see in Part Four, behaviorists believe quite the opposite.)

TWO FACETS OF DEVELOPMENT

Now that the main features of Freud's model have been described, we will consider two aspects of it in more detail. The discussion will illustrate something of the complexity of Freud's speculation about development and also show how these aspects—the development of consciousness and of ego strength—fit into the overall framework.

The Development of Consciousness

In Freud's system, the conscious aspect of mental life does not burst forth in its mature, ultimate state at the time of birth or during infancy. Instead, both consciousness and the preconscious develop over the years as the personality is influenced by increasing internal maturation and by everwidening experiences with the world. This development is perhaps best explained in terms of the relationship that evolves among the levels of awareness (conscious, preconscious, unconscious) and the apparatus of mental life (id, ego, superego).

One of the major challenges Freud faced over the last two or three decades of his life was that of describing clearly the way levels of consciousness interacted with the id, ego, and superego as the child grew up. As he admitted, his attempts at solving this riddle met with only partial success because of the difficulty of penetrating such tangled and clouded territories as the preconscious and unconscious. "And the profound obscurity of the background of our ignorance is scarcely illuminated by a few glimmers of insight" (S. Freud, 1938, p. 20). Nevertheless, he did depict something of what he saw with the aid of such glimmers, and Figure 5.1 attempts to diagram this. (For Freud's sketches of the adult mind, see 1923, p. 14; 1933, p. 111.)

The diagrams, based on Freud's opinions about the course of personality development in the Western industrialized society he knew best, sketch the anatomy of the mind at three age levels—one month, three years, and twelve years.

Shortly after birth the mind of the newborn in Freud's system is nearly all unconscious, with the unconscious dominated by the instinctual urges arising from the core of the id. Indeed, throughout life the commanding functionary in the unconscious is the id, operating on the pleasure principle without regard for the rules of the outside world. At this beginning stage of life the ego, as arbitrator between instinctual demands and the realities of the outside world, is as yet very small and weak. Only a tiny part of the ego can properly be called conscious, for the young infant has but an embryonic, vague awareness of its existence.

When we identify the ego as the operative of the personality that takes action in the real world to expend instinctual energy from the id, then it is reasonable to assume that the predominant portion of the ego shortly after birth must be preconscious and/or unconscious. This assumption is based on the observation that most—or perhaps all—behavior of the newborn is performed without conscious intent. The neonate does not have to decide to make the heart beat, the lungs breathe, the lips suck, the eyelids close under strong light, or the arms and legs

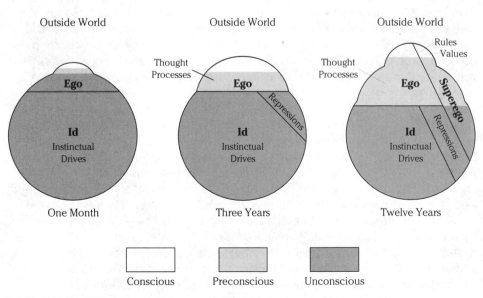

FIGURE 5.1
Developmental trends in the structure of the mind

wiggle. All these actions take place automatically. But as time passes, the internal maturation of the neural system and sensations from the outside world press the infant to become increasingly aware of what possible actions may fulfill needs arising from the unconscious sources. The child also becomes more skilled in choosing from among these possibilities those acts that are likely to bring the greatest satisfaction at the least expense in terms of pain. In short, the reality principle on which the ego operates begins to guide more of the infant's behavior.

By age three, the child's transactions with the world have improved the clarity of consciousness and greatly expanded the area of the preconscious. At this point we can identify more precisely the characteristics of the conscious and the preconscious and describe their interactions.

The conscious—sometimes called the *system perceptual conscious*—is what the individual is attending to at the moment. It is what we are presently aware of seeing, hearing, feeling, or thinking about. The conscious is the outermost surface of the mental apparatus, the part in immediate contact with the outside world. The conscious is the nucleus of the ego (S. Freud, 1923, pp. 9, 18).

The images or ideas on which our attention is focused at the moment are limited in number and scope. We cannot keep many things in consciousness at one time. Rather, the images are like a sequence of individual pictures; each appears momentarily, then shifts in form or passes by to make way for the next. This notion of the kaleidoscopic nature of the conscious is reflected in the phrase *stream of consciousness.* However, once the images pass, they are not gone forever. Either we can purposely bring them to mind again by recalling them to the stage of consciousness, or else they may intrude from without (as sense impressions on the eyes and ears from sources in the environment) or extrude from within (as thoughts and feelings that rise into our awareness from we know not where). However, whether from an outside or an inside source, these things that catch our attention must have one characteristic: they must be *perceptible.* They must assume a recognizable form as an image or a verbal symbol or word construction. In other words, amorphous, raw sensations from one's unconscious cannot be perceived until they are cast either as *mental images* (pictorial or auditory forms as in dreams) or as *verbal symbols* or *word presentations* (words, phrases, and sentences that have been attached to sensations recorded from the outside world).

Functions of the preconscious   With this logic in mind, let us consider the reasons that Freud postulated the existence of a *preconscious* as an intermediary between the conscious and the unconscious. Freud envisioned the unconscious (chiefly the domain of the id) as the receptacle for instinctual energy, for ill-defined needs and urges. But he also needed a receptacle for material that was not in the mind at the moment but that could be recalled at will. So, as the storage area for memory traces of conscious perceptions from the past, for material not at the moment "conscious" but available to be retrieved if desired, he created the preconscious. Whereas the unconscious was pictured mainly as the operating arena for the id, the preconscious was described as basically under control of the ego.

In addition to being the storage area for retrievable memory traces, the preconscious was pictured as the processing chamber in which the ego receives amorphous urges from the id and recasts them into the image or verbal form required for their perception by the conscious ego. Recall that before the conscious ego can find ways to satisfy inner needs through trafficking in the real world, the needs must be put into perceptible shape. Freud proposed that this act of translating was performed by preconscious molding procedures that "we may—roughly and inexactly—sum up under the name of thought-processes" (S. Freud, 1923, pp. 9–10). It seems likely that what he meant by *thought-processes* are those mental acts known as analyzing, synthesizing, denoting, identifying, evaluating, and such.

In speaking of things arising from the unconscious and seeking expression, Freud distinguished between the route taken by ideas and the route taken by feelings. While ideas need to be processed by the preconscious, clothed by it in the recognizable raiment of familiar images or word presentations before they can appear in consciousness, feelings do not. Rather, they are emitted directly into consciousness from the unconscious (S. Freud, 1923, pp. 12–13).

Having identified the conscious and preconscious roles performed by the ego, we can now understand more clearly the differences between the mental maps for the one-month-old and three-year-old in Figure 5.1. The neonate's preconscious barely, if at all, exists, and the conscious is very limited in scope and clarity. But by age three the conscious is more extensive and acute, and the preconscious is far larger, in the sense of containing rapidly increasing numbers of memory traces drawn from experiences in the world. Furthermore, the preconscious has acquired certain of its contents—particularly its thought processes—from the unconscious. As the hypothetical twelve-year-old mind also illustrates, this trend of the preconscious becoming more complex over the years continues throughout the period of child and adolescent development. Greater internal maturation of the neural system interacts with more and more experiences in the outside world to produce more memory traces and more sophisticated thought processes.

The dynamics of repression   A comparison of the diagrams of the one-month-old and three-year-old minds also shows that the ego has now added something of its own to the unconscious. This something consists of psychologically painful thoughts that have been repressed into an unconscious condition by the ego because it found them too unbearable to maintain in consciousness or preconsciousness but did not know how to eliminate or solve them in a satisfactory conscious manner. We assume that these repressed materials at age three are seated in anxieties that arose during the oral and anal stages (from birth through about ages two to three) from conflicts with the parents. For example, in Freud's view parents' unreasonable and often harsh demands for bowel and bladder control when the child is not yet ready for such control can cause the child to feel inadequate and to fear the loss of parental love. Since the child's weak ego cannot solve the conflict on the conscious level, the ego frantically relegates the painful events to the unconscious. And, as the diagram of the twelve-year-old mind suggests, we can assume that the amount of repressed material will increase by that age due to the psychic conflicts experienced during the Oedipal period around ages three to five and thereafter.

In summary, then, throughout the early years of life, the child's conscious grows in clarity, and the ego builds up a supply center of recallable memories from past perceptions, memories deposited in an expanding preconscious. At the same time, particularly painful problems that the immature ego is ill prepared to master are pushed out of consciousness to be actively held in the unconscious by means of energy borrowed from the id. The supply of psychic energy available for conducting conscious and preconscious affairs is thus depleted by this diverting of energy for purposes of repression. Furthermore, as noted earlier, such repressed problems are really postponed rather than solved, for they continue to seethe and to express themselves out of the unconscious in deviant ways, such as neuroses.

The third diagram, the hypothetical twelve-year-old mind, also shows the new functionary, the superego, which has grown out of the ego during the Oedipal period of middle childhood. Freud proposed that the superego starts developing around age three, or perhaps slightly earlier, in which case a sliver of its influence could have been included in the diagram of the three-year-old mind. The superego at the conscious and preconscious levels appears as the set of conscious values or rules of living that guide the older child's behavior even when parents, teachers, and police are not present. But the existence in the adolescent's psyche of free-floating anxiety and of vague feelings of guilt and shame that are not attached to any particular event suggests that the superego has an unconscious aspect as well. In effect, the older child or adolescent can "feel bad" without knowing why. This means, in Freud's scheme, that the youth has incorporated into his or her personality certain parental expectations that he or she does not consciously recognize. Apparently these expectations or standards are ones associated with traumatic early experiences that have since been repressed.

Thus, as children grow up, the relationships among levels of consciousness and the psychic operatives (id, ego, and superego) shift so that children gain increasing control over their fate. At the same time, they are victimized by repressions that sap their psychic energy, divert their attention from reasonable conscious action, and cause distressing, illogical thoughts and behavior.

Developing Ego Strength

Closely tied to the processes I have just described is the matter of developing a strong ego. Although Freud did not describe ego strength in exactly the terms used here, it seems reasonable to assume, from all he wrote about the ego, that the following definition faithfully reflects his opinion: a strong ego is one that has at its command sufficient adjustment techniques to (1) fulfill the id's instinctual needs without neglecting or unduly postponing any need and, at the same time, (2) satisfy the expectations imposed on the individual by both (a) the physical and social environments and (b) the individual's superego.

A weak ego, in contrast, is one that lacks sufficient conscious methods of expending instinctual energy that are acceptable to the environment and superego. A weak ego, faced by conflicting demands that it cannot consciously satisfy, reverts to its emergency technique of repression. Consequently, the weaker a person's ego, the more repressions we can expect to accumulate in the unconscious to plague her or him—unless, of course, some outside agent, such as a parent or other caretaker, intervenes to reduce the number of demands pressed upon the ego from the environment. It is in this matter of intervention that Freud's concept of ego strength bears important implications for child-raising practices.

The newborn's ego is very weak. It has only a few, simplistic methods for arbitrating the conflict between id demands and environmental requirements. Children require far greater neural maturation and experience with the world to develop the broad array of sophisticated adjustment methods that mark the strong ego. If neonates are to survive and avoid storing up a dangerous cargo of repressions to bear through life, they require a lot of outside help from parents and others. Although there is nothing these outside agents can do to control the instinctual drives arising from the id, they can do something about the environment. Their aid in reducing the weak ego's burden of decisions can take two general forms. First, parents can provide infants with certain things that they cannot obtain by themselves, such as food and warmth. Parents can also furnish, in gradual steps, opportunities for children to exercise their bodies and perceptual systems so that they learn to comprehend and act on their world in increasingly effective ways. Second, parents can protect infants from intense stimuli that could overwhelm their perceptual capacities, stimuli that frighten infants because they cannot understand or control them. Examples of such stimuli are loud noises, flashes of light, loss of support so the child suddenly drops, angry arguments and fights, and the like. But perhaps even more important is the parental role of protecting young children from societal expectations that are beyond children's capacity to fulfill. It was in relation to this role that Freud particularly criticized European child-rearing practices of his day. He felt that since nothing could be done to lessen the instinctual-drive demands on the weak ego, it was necessary for society to permit these drives freer direct expression in the early years of life instead of strictly censoring such expression.

> From a biological standpoint the ego comes to grief over the task of mastering the excitations of the early sexual period, at a time when its immaturity makes it incompetent to do so. It is in this lagging of ego development behind libidinal development that we see the essential precondition of neurosis; and we cannot escape the conclusion that neuroses could be avoided if the childish ego were spared this task—if, that is to say, the child's sexual life were allowed free play, as happens among many primitive peoples. (S. Freud, 1938, p. 57)

While Freud proposed that fewer repressions and subsequent neuroses would develop if sexual urges (including sucking and biting in the oral stage and bowel and urinary activities in the anal stage) were allowed "free play," he proposed as well that civilization as we know it would not have developed under such free-expression conditions. He believed that the early "damming up" of the sexual instinct forced the growing child and subsequently the adult to redirect at least a portion of this energy into other channels through the adjustment technique of sublimation. This redirecting or sublimating process, he felt, caused many of the developments of our culture, since diverted libido was put to the task of fueling inventions, art works, literary creations, social service, and the like (S. Freud, 1938, p. 58). So in this sense, the variegated culture that we enjoy has been paid for, at least partially, by repressions by a weak ego early in life.

What, then, does all this mean for parents and other caretakers who wish to guide child growth in ways that promote the development of a strong ego and keep at a minimum repressions that will cause distressing neurotic symptoms? The answer, from a psychoanalytic viewpoint, consists of five principles. Both actual parents and surrogate parents should do the following:

1. Recognize the nature of instinctual urges and accept the desirability of permitting expression of the urges.
2. Recognize the normal psychosexual stages of development and the sorts of conflicts the child faces at each stage.
3. Provide at each developmental stage enough opportunities for the child to satisfy instinctual drives within an atmosphere of understanding, but not furnish so much satisfaction that the child becomes fixated at that point and is unwilling to move ahead to the next stage.
4. Furnish plenty of nurture and protection to the infant in the early years so that the child's weak ego is not overwhelmed by the physical environment and societal standards.
5. As time passes, provide increasing amounts of guidance (teaching) in problem solving so that the ego develops an ever-expanding repertoire of conscious adjustment techniques to fill all kinds of instinctual demands under all sorts of environmental conditions.

In summary, the theory Freud devised to explain the origins of adult neuroses yielded, as a by-product, a number of general principles for guiding the normal personality development of children at all stages of the growth process, including the development of a strong ego.

Now that we have considered key elements of Freud's model of child development, we will look briefly at the sorts of contributions his daughter Anna made to his work.

ANNA FREUD'S PSYCHOANALYSIS OF CHILDREN

Sigmund Freud's model of child development was not constructed from direct observations of children. It was fashioned from the free associations and dreams of the neurotic adults he treated. However, Freud's daughter Anna (1895–1982) spent a major part of her adult life as a psychoanalyst working directly with children. She was a rather strict adherent of her father's theory, but she found it desirable to clarify and embellish certain aspects of it on the basis of her experience treating childhood neuroses. Her additions to Freudian theory were not published as a single, comprehensive treatise, but appeared instead as occasional articles and speeches over a period of forty years, from the 1920s to the mid-1960s. These scattered works have since been brought together in five volumes as *The Writings of Anna Freud* (1974).

The kinds of contributions she made can be illustrated with three examples. These concern (1) the psychoanalytic treatment of a child while his or her superego is still being formed, (2) the value of direct observations of children, and (3) implications of psychoanalysis for raising the normal child.

Status of the Superego

Like her father, Anna Freud explained that many adult neuroses result from an overly punitive superego. It is the task of the psychoanalyst to help the patient reorganize the contents of the superego so they fit reality more adequately and do not pose unreasonable standards to which the individual is forced to aspire. In the adult neurotic, this rebuilding task is long and painful, for the superego has, since the time of early adolescence, become a powerful component of the personality, highly resistant to alterations. But in the older child or early adolescent, the superego is yet in the process of formation. The child is still in a state of transition between (1) receiving orders or values from her or his parents or parent figures and (2) receiving orders from the evolving superego, which has not yet separated from either the ego or its external sources (parents, peers, teachers).

Adult psychoanalysis need involve only the patient and the analyst. However, in Anna Freud's opinion, childhood neuroses are best treated by the analyst working both with the child and with such important agents of his environment as parents and teachers. By changing parents' expectations for, and treatment of, the child, the analyst hopes to influence the contents of the as-yet-dependent superego and cure the neurosis with greater speed than would be possible in an adult, whose overly demanding superego has already solidified. Thus the analyst who works with children manipulates the environment in addition to re-forming the relationships within the child's personality among the id, ego, and superego (A. Freud, 1974, vol. I, pp. 57–58).

Direct Observations of Children

In adult psychoanalysis, the source of the therapist's information is almost exclusively the patient's talk about herself. However, children are not as adept at explaining, upon command, their past history, worries, and fantasies. Thus Anna Freud recommended that in child analysis dream interpretation should be supplemented with information provided by the child's family and by the therapist's observations of the child's actions. By noting patterns of feeding, sleep, illness, play, and the like, the analyst can select aspects of behavior that, according to psychoanalytic theory, grew out of the earlier oral, anal, and infantile-genital periods. Therefore in child analysis certain types of observations can serve as substitutes for the free-association data on which the analysis of adults' psychological problems is usually founded (A. Freud, 1974, vol. V, pp. 95–101).

Psychoanalysis and Child-Rearing Practices

In 1956 Anna Freud stated, "While we are unable to alter the innate givens of a human being, we may be in the position to relieve some of the external pressures which interact with them" (1974, vol. V, pp. 265–266). She believed that psychoanalytic theory could make a major contribution toward the relief of such external pressures by helping parents gain "insight into the potential harm done to young children during the critical years of their development by the manner in which their needs, drives, wishes, and emotional dependencies are met" (1974, vol. V, p. 266). She then explained that the types of help psychoanalysis had already provided included (1) the sexual enlightenment of children; (2) recognition of the role of conflict, conscience, and anxiety in the development of the child, a recognition that resulted in parents' limiting their authority over the child; (3) freedom for the child to express aggression; (4) recognition of the importance of the mother-infant relationship; and (5) an understanding of the mother's role as an auxiliary ego for the growing child.

In summary, Anna Freud extended psychoanalytic theory by adding to it a variety of conclusions she extracted from her direct observations of, and therapy sessions with, children at several stages of their development.

PRACTICAL APPLICATIONS

Freudian theory has been applied to the treatment of children in at least three major ways: in general child-rearing practices, in schooling at the early childhood level, and in modes of therapy.

Over the past few decades, psychoanalytic suggestions have exerted substantial influence on the child-rearing views of "concerned and well-read" adults, especially in Europe and America. These suggestions have focused on children's emotional needs, particularly in the areas of sex and aggression, and on such concepts as unconscious motivation. For instance, from the Freudian proposals about the oral stage comes the recommendation that infants be given plenty of opportunities to be cuddled and to satisfy their sucking needs, especially at feeding times. From beliefs about the anal phase comes the recommendation that toilet training should not be attempted too early, nor should it be enforced in a punitive fashion. Furthermore, toilet training should not be accompanied by distressing emotional outbursts from parents or even by half-disguised expressions of disgust, which the child interprets as threats of the withdrawal of parents' love if the child does not perform how, when, and where the parents desire. There are also suggestions about how adults can best react to children's sexual curiosity during the years of childhood and adolescence. And from Freud's proposals about unconscious motivation, parents have increasingly come to expect that children may not be aware of the true reasons they act as they do because the stimuli for the acts may be repressed intentions. Thus, when children are asked to explain why they have acted in a given manner, the reasons they offer may simply be rationalizations—that is, socially acceptable explanations for behavior that actually derives from ignoble motives.

In the realm of formal education, nursery school and kindergarten practice in particular has been influenced by Freudian beliefs about sexual curiosity, nontraumatic toilet training, the symbolic meaning of children's play with water and such messy substances as mud and finger paints, children's needs for such physical contact as hugging and stroking, their inquisitiveness about the usually hidden body parts of the opposite sex, and the importance of teachers as role models with whom the child may identify.

Techniques of psychotherapy for disturbed children have also been strongly affected by psychoanalytic theory. In order to understand the dynamics of interaction among members of the child's family, therapists provide dolls that can represent family members and then interpret in psychoanalytic terms the child's dramatic play with the dolls. In other cases the child is asked to draw a picture of his or her family and to talk about the relationships among the members and how he or she feels about them. Furthermore, children's use of such play materials as punching bags and wet clay has been interpreted as revealing the sources of a disturbed child's shame, hate, distrust, or fear. Use of such materials has also been judged of cathartic value, relieving in socially acceptable ways the child's pent-up distress.

FREUDIAN THEORY: AN ASSESSMENT

My assessment of psychoanalytic theory in terms of the fourteen appraisal standards is given on the accompanying rating scale. My explanation for these ratings begins with the items I rated the highest and then moves to those I rated lower.

There can be little doubt that Freudian theory deserves high marks for originality and for its success in stimulating new discoveries. Freud's notions were so novel (item 10) that they amazed academicians and shocked the general public throughout Europe and the Americas. As for fertility (item 12), the theory has been the basis for hundreds of clinical studies focusing on children's development, usually in the form of personality deviations. It has also motivated investigators to launch new journals dedicated entirely to psychoanalytic topics (*Psychoanalytic Study of the Child, Contemporary Psychoanalysis, International Journal of Psycho-Analysis,* and more). Authors have written scores of books that offer extensions or revisions of the theory. Especially during the decades of its greatest popularity (the 1940s into the early 1960s), the Freudian model furnished numerous ideas for investigations by experimental psychologists, including such prominent behaviorists as J. Dollard and N. E. Miller (1950), and R. Sears, L. Rau, and R. Alpert (1965).* Even though enthusiasm for psychoanalytic theory among psychologists has dampened since the scheme's heyday, there still continues to be lively interest in the theory, an interest that has stimulated a regular output of clinical and experimental in-

---

*For summaries of experimental studies, see Frenkel-Brunswik (1954), Hilgard (1952), Holt (1989), and Kris (1947).

FREUDIAN THEORY

How well do I think the theory meets the standards?

Standards	Very well	Moderately well	Very poorly
1. Reflects the real world of children		X	
2. Is clearly understandable		X	
3. Explains the past and predicts the future	specificity X	accuracy ?	
4. Guides child rearing	X		
5. Is internally consistent		X	
6. Is economical		X	
7. Is falsifiable			X
8. Is supported by convincing evidence		X	
9. Adapts to new data			X
10. Is novel	X		
11. Is comprehensive		X	
12. Stimulates new discoveries	X		
13. Is durable		X	
14. Is self-satisfying		X	

vestigations, new interpretations, and debate. More than 450 books featuring Freudian topics were published from 1984 to 1994. For the seven-year period from 1983 to 1990, *Psychological Abstracts* cites 4,567 journal articles on psychoanalysis, with 45 of them on child psychoanalysis and 18 more on child development issues. Over the years 1990 to 1994, standard lists of magazine and journal articles have included more than 700 entries focusing on Freud and his proposals, with most of the articles written in English, French, German, or Spanish.

The rather high rating on item 4 is my estimate of the substantial influence psychoanalytic suggestions have exerted on the child-rearing views as summarized above under practical applications. Frequently, specific beliefs about child raising derived from Freudian theory appear as topics in both professional and popular publications and in the mass media (Emde, 1992; Nagel, 1994). However, although psychoanalytic theory offers guidance for handling children's emotional growth, it offers little or no help for directing children's academic (cognitive) development or physical growth, except in cases of physical ailments suspected of having a psychological origin. The rating on item 4, therefore, is a balance between Freudian suggestions about emotional development and the lack of suggestions about cognitive and physical growth. The somewhat narrow focus on the way psychosexual and social relations affect children's emotional lives also caused me to rate the theory's comprehensiveness on the lower edge of the "moderately well" region (item 11).

As for the theory's clarity (item 2), I estimate that it deserves a mark slightly above the middle of the scale. Freudians explain the system's main components rather clearly, I feel, at least in general. And Freud's practice of illustrating these components with examples from cases of people undergoing psychoanalysis helps communicate what he intends. But when we move beyond the basic outline of the theory's structure, many puzzles appear, calling for greater clarification. As one illustration of confusion, E. Nagel complained that the Freudian

> sometimes describes the main theoretical components of the mental apparatus as "units of functions," and suggests that unconscious drives are like dispositions. But he also declares that these components possess energies and conflict with one another—though without explaining in what sense functions can be charged with energies or dispositions can be engaged in conflicts. (1959, p. 46)

In short, when we inspect the psychoanalytic model of child development in detail, we find it can profit from a good deal of additional clarification.

The issue of clarity is also related to item 1 (reflects real world of children), which I have rated slightly below the center. I believe that in Freud's favor are his (1) bringing to public view the importance and commonality of sexual interests in childhood and adolescence, (2) identifying defense mechanisms children develop, (3) describing children's ambivalent feelings—hate combined with love—toward parents and others close to them, and similar proposals. Observations of children's behavior would appear to substantiate these findings as phenomena in real children's lives (Hilgard, 1952).

But balanced against such items, which are confirmable by direct observation or assessment, is a large portion of Freudian theory that has not been substantiated in such an open or public manner. Some critics have been particularly blunt in their charges that psychoanalysts have failed to conduct the investigations that will convincingly test the theory's proposals. M. Scriven wrote:

> As a set of hypotheses it was a great achievement 50 years ago; as no more than a set of hypotheses it is a great disgrace today. . . . It is in fact the most sophisticated form of metaphysics ever to enjoy support as a scientific theory. (1959, pp. 226–227)

Part of the difficulty with Freud's model as an accurate reflector of real children's development lies in the source of data on which he founded his theory. He did not directly observe, test, or measure children during their years of growth, as did many other theorists. Actually, there were at least four somewhat slippery steps between his data and the growing child. His process of collecting data during therapy sessions with neurotic adults involved (step 1) the analyst's *interpreting* from his viewpoint or through his "lens" (step 2) ostensibly *symbolic* material derived from (step 3) reported *dreams* and *memories* of neurotics about (step 4) *ostensible experiences* from their childhood one or more decades earlier. In view of this mode of gathering information, the theory's data base might be a distortion of typical children's actions, thoughts, and emotions during each phase of growing up. I am skeptical about how well it represents real children's development, and I share the opinion of those critics who ask that the Freudian model be supported more adequately with publicly verifiable facts. For this reason, I have ranked it rather low on item 8 (convincing evidence). Although Freud's interpretation of adult cases in his psychiatric practice is ingenious and interesting (and, indeed, the interpretations might be right), I still do not regard that type of evidence as the most direct kind on which to found a theory of child development.

Probably the main reason psychoanalytic theory has been difficult either to verify or to refute is not that its adherents are stubbornly defensive or are inept researchers (though in some instances they may be), but that many of its key elements, including the unconscious, repression, reaction formation, and symbolism, seem to render it nonfalsifiable. These elements have caused critics to harbor "the suspicion that Freudian theory can always be so manipulated that it escapes refutation no matter what the well-established facts may be" (Nagel, 1959, p. 44). Since I share this suspicion, I have rated psychoanalysis at the bottom on item 7 (falsifiability) and near the bottom on its ability to adapt to new data (item 9). With such devices as repression, reaction formation, symbols, and a complex unconscious mind in their tool kit, Freudians have been inclined to rationalize away those data that seem at odds with their theory rather than altering the theory to accommodate the data in some logical fashion.

Imagine that we wish to check the validity of the concept of the Oedipus conflict, and will do so by interviewing adolescents about the sexual ideas they had during their earlier childhood years. If the adolescents' answers corroborate the notion that the father–daughter, mother–son "family romance" is widespread, we might consider these answers as evidence supporting the Oedipus-complex concept. But let us say that we get just the opposite results from our interviews. The adolescents, seeking to be as truthful as possible, rarely have any memories of Oedipal strivings. Can we then interpret this as evidence against the notion of a universal Oedipus conflict? Freudians would say no. They would contend, instead, that the negative responses show that the earlier sexual urges have been repressed into the unconscious, so the adolescents' denial of such thoughts is proof of both the Oedipus complex and of the defense mechanism of repression. Under these conditions, there is no way to test the validity of the Oedipus concept through the retrospective interview that Freudians use as the source of evidence about how children develop.

The concept of reaction formation poses the same problem for assessing the theory. Reaction formation is the defense mechanism that occurs when people are driven by an urge or wish (id) that conflicts with their moral values (superego), and to solve the conflict they (ego) repress the urge and behave as if their motives were just the opposite. A child's overt sex play is seen as direct evidence of the proposed libidinal energy. But the opposite behavior—puritanical avoidance of sex—is interpreted as an expression of exactly the same libidinal or sexual energy but expressed through the mechanism of *reaction formation.* Likewise, both the child who habitually fights (displaying direct aggression) and the one who is the habitual pacifist (showing reaction formation) are seen as driven by the same aggressive urge (death instinct). Once more, an appraiser of the theory is at a loss in deciding how to handle a model that derives identical conclusions from diametrically opposed data.

The role of symbols in Freud's scheme presents other puzzles. Freud proposed that a person's ego, in cooperation with the superego, censors repressed material that seeks to arise from the unconscious into consciousness. But he also said that repressed wishes can sneak past the censor in disguise—that is, in symbolic form. For instance, I noted in Chapter One that Freud considered any elongated, projectile-shaped object that appeared in a dream to be a symbol of the male penis. An open, containerlike object symbolized the female vagina (Freud, 1900). In a similar fashion, Freud interpreted many other images from dreams as symbols, rather than as direct descriptions, of events in people's daily lives. So Freudians, with this notion of symbolism in their analytic armory, can interpret all sorts of thoughts that people express as support for their theory.

So, Freud's model of child development and personality structure may be correct, but the game of verification is unmanageable if it must be played with the elastic ground rules permitted by the inclusion of such concepts as the above. The fairly low mark given for item 5 (internal consistency) is also primarily a result of these considerations.

On item 6, whether the theory is economical, I have marked Freud's theory near the middle. While some aspects of his model appear to be direct, economical ways to explain the phenomena on which he focuses, others appear to me unduly complex. There should be simpler ways to account for the phenomena in question. For instance, there should be less confusing and simpler ways to account for fixations than to claim that they are caused by both over- and undersatisfaction of needs at a given psychosexual stage. Furthermore, there should be simpler ways to account for the prepuberal child's personal-social behavior than the Oedipus complex that Freud proposed. This is not to say Freud is wrong, but the same phenomena can be attributed to simpler sets of factors.

I view the durability of psychoanalytic theory (item 13) in three ways. First is the longevity of those elements of the theory that have entered the realm of common sense—unconscious motivation, childhood sexuality, adjustment mechanisms, and the like. These, I believe, will last a long time. Second is the significance of psychoanalysis as an event in the history of psychology. Freud's scheme probably will hold a prominent place in future accounts of how theories evolve. Third is the importance of Freudian theory in its entirety as the principal perspective from which to interpret children's development. In light of the way most developmentalists in recent years have abandoned psychoanalysis as the main model in which to place their confidence, I would give the theory as a whole low marks on long-term popularity. By combining these three assessments I arrived at the "moderately well" rating for psychoanalysis on item 13.

The difficulty experienced in giving a reasonable rating on item 3 (explains the past and predicts the future) is reflected by the two marks on the line. The mark for specificity is at the high end of the scale, principally because Freudian explanations of what psychosexual events occurred earlier in an individual's life, and why they occurred, are quite specific. Psychoanalysis emphasizes the past history of development as uncovered through free association and dream interpretation. But psychoanalytic predictions of the future are usually sketched in a more general way, often in terms of possible deviant development that might occur if the child's needs during upcoming psychosexual stages are not dealt with wisely by the adults who most affect the child's life. In consideration of the theory's very specific explanations of the past and more general predictions of the future, I have given it relatively high marks for *specificity*.

However, *accuracy* of explanation and prediction is quite a different matter. For the sorts of reasons given in the discussion of falsifiability, I am skeptical about the validity of explanations founded on the theory. On the basis of this skepticism, I have used a question mark as a rating in the lower range of item 3. The theory needs better validation.

Finally we come to the self-satisfying quality of Freud's model (item 14). In the case of psychoanalytic theory, this standard is of particular importance because Freud's proposals have depended so heavily on personal affirmation for their acceptance. By *personal affirmation* I mean the "feeling" that psychoanalytic theory does indeed describe the way one's personality evolves and functions. Or as S. Hook noted (1959, p. 213), some Freudians' response to criticism has been that "psychoanalysis may be unscientific, but it is true." And to some degree I must admit to sharing such a feeling. Despite the shortcomings of Freudian theory when judged against common scientific criteria like the foregoing standards, much of the theory makes a kind of existential sense to me. I believe in the unconscious, in repression, in our use of defense mechanisms, and in many other concepts the theory includes. But I remain skeptical about still other aspects of the model. For these reasons, I have rated it in the middle of the scale for item 14.

FOR FURTHER READING

The first two books are paperbacks offering concise, simplified, and accurate accounts of psychoanalytic theory.

Hall, C. S. (1954) *A Primer of Freudian Psychology.* New York: World. This is a systematic description of psychoanalysis as a theory of personality development. Hall has based his account on material drawn from a variety of Freud's writings.
Stafford-Clark, D (1967). *What Freud Really Said.* London: Penguin. A description of the evolution of Freud's ideas, including summaries of several of his most significant publications.

The next items are translations of Freud's own writings. The first of these is a seventy-five-page summary of psychoanalytic theory written near the close of his career. The second is a thirty-volume edition of his complete works, useful for its detail and for the picture it offers of Freud's revisions over a period of nearly five decades. The third is an autobiographical portrait of Freud during the last ten years of his life.

Freud, S. (1938) *An Outline of Psychoanalysis.* London: Hogarth, 1973.
Freud, S. (1964) *The Standard Edition of the Complete Psychological Works of Sigmund Freud.* James Strachey, translator and editor. London: Hogarth. In thirty volumes.

Freud, S. (1992) *The Diary of Sigmund Freud 1929–1939: A Record of the Final Decade.* New York: Scribner's.

The most complete source of Anna Freud's works is the following collection:

Freud, A. (1974) *The Writings of Anna Freud.* New York: International Universities Press. In five volumes.

Recent assessments of Freudian tradition are found in the following:

Anthony, E. J. (1986) "The Contributions of Child Psychoanalysis to Psychoanalysis." *Psychoanalytic Study of the Child,* Vol. 41, pp. 61–87. A summary of Anna and Sigmund Freud's views about such contributions.

Bowie, M. (1994) *Psychoanalysis and the Future of Theory.* Cambridge, Mass.: Blackwell.

Crews, F. (1993) "The Unknown Freud." *New York Review of Books,* Vol. 48, No. 19, pp. 55–66.

Fisher, S. (1985) *The Scientific Credibility of Freud's Theories and Therapy.* New York: Columbia University Press.

Holt, R. F. (1989) *Freud Revisited: A Fresh Look at Psychoanalytic Theory.* New York: Guilford.

Stephansky, P. E. (1986) *Freud, Appraisals and Reappraisals.* Hillsdale, N.J.: Analytic Press.

CHAPTER SIX

ERIKSON'S VARIATION ON FREUD'S THEME

Erik Homburger Erikson (1902–1994) was a German-born psychoanalyst whose self-imposed mission was to extend and refine Freud's notions of personality development, with particular attention to child development.

Three of the most significant features of Erikson's refinement have been his proposals regarding

1. The development of the *healthy personality*, in contrast to Freud's emphasis on the growth and cure of neurotic behavior.
2. The process of socializing the child into a particular culture by passage through a series of innately determined *psychosocial stages* that parallel Freud's psychosexual stages.
3. The individual's task of achieving *ego identity* by means of solving specified identity crises at each psychosocial stage of growth.

Erikson's professional career began in Vienna, where he graduated from the Vienna Psychoanalytic Institute before coming to the United States in 1933. He entered clinical practice in the United States, became a citizen in 1939, and over a period of four decades made significant contributions to the literature on psychoanalysis, personality theory, educational practice, and social anthropology.

Much of Freud's theory—the existence and nature of the unconscious, the tripartite composition of the mind (id, ego, superego), psychosexual stages, and more—was accepted by Erikson as valid. Since he accepted these concepts, Erikson wrote relatively little about them. Instead, he centered his work on those facets of psychoanalytic theory he believed required extension and, to some degree, revision. In discussing Erikson's contributions, I concentrate on the key additions he proposed, not on his entire system of beliefs. These additions are (1) the nature of a healthy personality and of ego identity, (2) the epigenetic principle, and (3) stages of psychosocial growth and the identity crises. Finally, there is an assessment of Erikson's ideas from the viewpoint of someone who works with children and is interested in theory construction.

EGO IDENTITY AND THE HEALTHY PERSONALITY

Erikson agreed with those critics of Freud who claimed that Freud had focused only on neurotic personalities and, in consequence, had neglected to define the nature of healthy personalities or to trace their pattern of development. Erikson sought to right this imbalance, and he began by identifying the characteristics of the healthy personality. These characteristics would be the goals and signs of desirable human development.

One statement of such characteristics that Erikson found suitable was that of Marie Jahoda, an American psychologist who believed that a healthy personality *actively masters* the environment, shows a certain *unity of personality,* and is able to *perceive* the world and self *correctly* (Erikson, 1968, p. 92). The newborn child displays none of these characteristics. The healthiest adult personality displays them all. Thus, in Erikson's view, "childhood is defined by [the characteristics'] initial absence and by their gradual development in complex steps of increasing differentiation" (1968, p. 92).

Phrased in a different way, growing up is a process of achieving *ego identity.* In Erikson's system, ego identity has two aspects. The first or inner-focused aspect is the person's recognition of his or her own unified "selfsameness and continuity in time" (Erikson, 1959, p. 23). It is knowing and accepting oneself. The second or outer-focused aspect is the individual's recognition of and identification with the ideals and essential pattern of his or her culture; it includes sharing "some kind of essential character with others" (Erikson, 1968, p. 104). People who have attained ego identity have a clear picture and an acceptance of both their inner essence and the group culture in which they live.

Since, in Erikson's view, human development consists of moving from nonego identity to ego identity, his picture of the developmental process features a description of "conflicts, inner and outer, which the vital personality weathers, re-emerging from each crisis with an increased sense of inner unity, with an increase of good judgment, and an increase in the capacity 'to do well' according to his own standards and to the standards of those who are significant to him" (Erikson, 1968, p. 92).

THE EPIGENETIC PRINCIPLE

Studies of the development of the human organism while it is still in the mother's womb have suggested that it develops from a single fertilized cell and follows the same general stages as all human organisms, until, after about nine months, a highly complex, multicellular baby with many differentiated but coordinated parts is born. The entire pattern of development, it is believed, is governed by a genetic structure common to all humans. In other words, the genes establish a construction plan and timetable for the development of each part.

Studies of physical development after birth suggest that the genetic plan does not stop with birth. Rather, the sequence of development of such skills as crawling and walking and such characteristics as adolescent breast growth in girls and facial hair in boys has been established by the genetic plan. These characteristics arise at a particular time in life according to a preestablished time schedule that is little affected by environmental influences.

The term *epigenetic principle* has been given to this belief that everything that grows is governed by a preset construction plan: "Out of this ground plan the parts arise, each part having its time of special ascendency, until all parts have arisen to form a functioning whole" (Erikson, 1968, p. 92).

Many people have accepted the principle as a guide to understanding physical growth. But Erikson extended the principle to social and psychological growth as well, proposing that personality appears to develop also according to steps "predetermined in the human organism's readiness to be driven toward, to be aware of, and to interact with a widening radius of significant individuals and institutions" (1968, p. 93). He recognized that this interaction would be somewhat different from one culture to another since the different cultures in which children grow up can vary in many significant ways. However, he held that personality growth follows a sequence of "inner laws" that set the potentialities for the kinds of significant interactions the child will achieve with the people and institutions she does meet in her particular culture.

In short, Erikson proposed that it is the nature of the human species to pass through an identifiable series of psychosocial stages as the individual grows up, stages determined genetically, regardless of the culture in which the growth occurs. The social environment, however, does have a significant effect on the nature of the crises arising at each stage and on the success with which the child and adolescent will master the stage.

THE GRID OF PSYCHOSOCIAL STAGES

Erikson accepted Freud's set of psychosexual stages as a basically valid description of the key concerns of personality development from infancy to adulthood. However, Erikson felt that the Freudian formulation was incomplete in at least four respects.

First, he thought Freud gave too little recognition to children's socialization, particularly to the various patterns of behavior that different cultures consider desirable—patterns children need to adopt or adapt if they are to be given the approval of the group within which they grow up.

Second, Erikson believed there are stages of development after adolescence that Freud failed to recognize. Thus Erikson defined more clearly four additional levels from puberty and beyond.

Third, Erikson believed the interaction of the individual with his or her social environment produces a series of eight major *psychosocial crises* the individual must work through in order to achieve eventual ego identity and psychological health. Since Freud had not defined crises in a clear fashion, Erikson did so.*

Finally, Erikson believed that the concepts of development could be better understood if they were cast in the form of a grid or matrix; such a grid had not been employed by Freud. Erikson produced a number of grids to clarify the interaction and correlation among various aspects of development. One of these "worksheets," as he called them, is produced in an adapted form as Table 6.1.

*Note that Erikson's version of Freudian stages in Table 6.1 and Table 6.2 adds one stage to those described in Chapter Five. That is, Erikson inserted *puberty and adolescence* between Freud's *latency* and *mature genitality* stages, and he moved *mature genitality* from the later teen years into the twenties.

TABLE 6.1
A psychosocial development worksheet

Stage Number	Column A psychosocial crisis	Column B radius of significant relations	Column C psychosocial modalities	Column D Freud's psycho-sexual stages	Column E approximate ages in years
I	trust versus mistrust	maternal person	to get to give in return	oral-respiratory, sensory-kinesthetic (incorporative modes)	0–1
II	autonomy versus shame, doubt	parental persons	to hold on to let go	anal-urethral, muscular (retentive-eliminative)	2–3
III	initiative versus guilt	basic family	to make (going after) to "make like" (playing)	infantile-genital, locomotor (intrusive, inclusive)	3–6
IV	industry versus inferiority	"neighborhood" and school	to make things (completing) to make things together	latency	7–12 or so
V	identity and repudiation versus identity diffusion	peer groups and out-groups; models of leadership	to be oneself (or not to be) to share being oneself	puberty and adolescence	12–18 or so
VI	intimacy and solidarity versus isolation	partners in friendship, sex, competition, cooperation	to lose and find oneself in another	mature genitality	the 20s
VII	generativity versus self-absorption	divided labor and shared household	to make be to take care of		late 20s to 50s
VIII	integrity versus despair	"humankind" "my kind"	to be, through having been to face not being		50s and beyond

Based on Erikson, 1959, p. 166.

Among Erikson's most significant additions to child development theory is his proposal that an individual undergoes eight psychosocial crises during development. These are listed in column A of Table 6.1. Each crisis or stage is phrased as a struggle between two opposite or conflicting personality characteristics. The trait of *trust* vies for dominance over *mistrust* in the infant's personality. At the next stage, the trait of *autonomy* struggles for ascendancy over *shame* and *doubt*. Six subsequent crises mark the next six stages of psychosocial growth to full ego identity or psychological maturity in the adult.

Although these conflicting traits or tendencies are cast in the form of absolutes, such as "absolute trust" versus "absolute mistrust," in reality they form graduated scales in the personality. Complete trust appears at one end of the scale line and complete mistrust at the other. Between these extremes are gradations that the individual may attain. In reality, no one reaches either extreme. Each personality represents some mixture of self-trust and mistrust, as well as some combination of trusting and mistrusting other people and the world in general. Consequently one way of describing the configuration of a given child's or adolescent's personality within Erikson's system would be to identify where, along each of these scale lines, the individual stands at any particular time.

Before we consider each of the stages in more detail, let's examine the other columns in Table 6.1 so the relationship between this material and the psychosocial crises is clear.

Column B of Table 6.1 lists the expanding circle of significant people with whom the growing child interacts. The particular crisis the child or adolescent faces at a given stage is worked out through interaction with the people or the social setting identified in column B as appropriate to the crisis.

Column C suggests those acts on which the growing child's attention concentrates at each crisis stage, and column D indicates which psychosexual step correlates with each act. Thus, during Freud's oral stage of earliest infancy, the baby concentrates on the acts (psychosocial modalities) of getting and giving in return. At the psychosexual stage of puberty, stage V, the young person concentrates on the acts of being oneself and sharing being oneself.

Keeping this worksheet in mind, we will consider in more detail the nature of Erikson's eight successive psychosocial crises or phases (Erikson, 1959, pp. 65–98).

Basic Trust versus Basic Mistrust

Erikson proposed that a sense of *trust*—being able to predict and depend upon one's own behavior and the behavior of others—is derived primarily from the experiences of the first year of life. In other words, a child's fundamental attitude about the dependability of the world is built chiefly on the relationship established as an infant during the oral or incorporative stage when feeding and mouthing objects are of prime importance. The most important person in the infant's life at this juncture is the mother or mother substitute. The particular point on the trust–mistrust scale that the child ultimately reaches will depend to a great extent on the quality of his or her relationship to the maternal figure during this first year out of the womb. If the infant's need for food, for exercising the lips and gums and the sucking mechanism, is frequently frustrated, the infant will begin life more toward the mistrust end of the scale. If the quality of affectional relationships at this time is poor, with the mother emotionally rejecting the baby while tending to its physical needs, the sense of trust will be damaged. This sets a poor foundation for the trust–mistrust ratio on which the child is to build the rest of his or her life.

As to how permanent the damage done at this early stage will be, Erikson said that the manner in which this first crisis, like the succeeding ones, is settled at the crisis period is not necessarily unalterable for the rest of the person's life. Damage to the sense of trust that occurs by an unsatisfactory infant-mother relationship during the first year of life can be repaired somewhat in later years by the child's enjoying a particularly trustworthy social environment. However, the damage will not be completely undone by later positive experiences. In like manner, an infant who establishes a secure attitude of trust during the first year may have this attitude shaken in later years by experience with undependable people who are significant to him. But he will still retain a measure of self-trust and feel a trust of others founded on his success in passing through the trust–mistrust crisis of infancy. This principle of the permanence of influences during a crisis period is valid as well for the other crises faced at subsequent stages of growth.

Autonomy versus Shame and Doubt

In parallel with Freud's psychosexual anal stage during the second year of life, Erikson proposed a second psychosocial crisis. This second stage is influenced by the child's maturing muscle system, with an increased ability to expel or retain things, particularly bodily wastes. Evacuating the bowels and bladder not only causes children to feel good but gives them a growing sense of power through control over the evacuation system.

In Erikson's opinion, children's new sense of power is the basis for their developing a sense of autonomy, of being able to do things for themselves. At the same time they run the risk of trying too much too soon and thereby attracting the censure of those around them. Thus during this period children require a delicate balance between (1) parental firmness that lets children know that they have a trustworthy world that will prevent them from overstepping the bounds, and (2) parental flexibility and patience that allows children gradually to gain bowel and bladder control at a pace commensurate with their understanding and the conscious control of their sphincter muscles. If outer control is too rigid or too early, demanding they control bowel and bladder before they are able, children will be faced with "a double rebellion and a double defeat" (Erikson, 1959, p. 68). They are powerless to manage their bowels and powerless to control their parents' actions. So they either seek satisfaction by regressing to oral activities—thumb-sucking, whining, and demanding attention—or fake progression by becoming hostile and willful. They may pretend that they have achieved control by rejecting others' aid, even though really lacking the ability to be so independent.

Erikson proposed that parents who impose strict bowel training on the two-year-old may influence the child to become an overcompulsive adult who is stingy and meticulous with love, energy, time, and money. This overcompulsive behavior is accompanied by a lasting sense of doubt and shame. In contrast, firm but gradual and kindly bowel training can aid the child in developing a sense of *self-control without loss of self-esteem* and produce an adult with a strong but socially acceptable sense of autonomy (Erikson, 1959, p. 68).

Initiative versus Guilt

During the fourth and fifth years of life, children gain more skill in using language, in moving about, and in handling things. As a result, the child's imagination expands to encompass "so many things that he cannot avoid frightening himself with what he has dreamed and thought up. Nevertheless, out of all this he must emerge with a sense of *unbroken initiative* as a basis for a high and yet realistic sense of ambition and independence" (Erikson, 1959, p. 75).

This is the time of the Oedipus conflict, when the conscience develops and serves as a control on initiative. Fear of sexual impulses toward the opposite-sex parent causes feelings of guilt. In order to navigate through this period successfully, the child needs the guidance of parents and teachers who understand the trials the child is facing. Through such understanding, the important adults in the child's life can alleviate the hatred and guilt the child may feel. This permits the "peaceful cultivation of initiative, a truly free sense of enterprise" (Erikson, 1959, p. 82). The child's mental and physical skills, unfettered by overbearing guilt, permit him or her to go after life in a self-confident way.

Industry versus Inferiority

Throughout the Freudian latency period, in the years before puberty, children want to get busy with activities worth their attention and to pursue these activities with their peers. In Erikson's opinion, children during the elementary school years need and enjoy hours of make-believe games and play, but they become dissatisfied with too much of this and want to do something worthwhile. They want to earn recognition by producing something, to gain the satisfaction of completing work by perseverance.

If adults pose tasks for children that they can accomplish and that they recognize as interesting and worthy, and if the adults furnish the guidance needed for completing the tasks, then children have a better chance to come through the latency period with a sound sense of industry. However, if the child has not solved the Oedipal conflict or if family life has not prepared him or her well for school life, the period can produce just the opposite—a sense of inadequacy and inferiority. Feelings of inferiority may also occur if the things the child has already learned to do well are considered insignificant by the teacher and classmates. Furthermore, in

Erikson's opinion, the child may have potential abilities that, if not evoked and nurtured during latency, may "develop late or never" (1959, p. 87).

Identity versus Identity Diffusion

Of all the growth stages, the one on which Erikson focused the greatest attention in his writing is the period of adolescence, particularly the onset of adolescence. During the early teens, with the arrival of puberty, the body grows rapidly and changes in curious ways. These changes are disturbing to both girls and boys. Their social roles take on new form, and the views they held of themselves in childhood no longer fit their new appearance and their new feelings for the opposite sex. In addition, adults and peers adopt new expectations for them as they move from childhood into youth. The confusion this creates for the incipient adolescent has been labeled the *identity crisis* by Erikson.

During this period the results of earlier years' experiences should lead to a successful integration of the individual's basic drives with her or his physical and intellectual endowment and opportunities in life. In effect, the child's development over the first dozen or so years should now synthesize to give a sense of *ego identity* or self-definition.

> The sense of ego identity, then, is the accrued confidence that one's ability to maintain inner sameness and continuity is matched by the sameness and continuity of one's meaning for others. Thus, self-esteem . . . grows to be a conviction that one is learning effective steps toward a tangible future, that one is developing a defined personality within a social reality which one understands. (Erikson, 1959, p. 89)

Furthermore, young adolescents should gain an increasing strength of purpose and understanding of reality as they recognize that their own way of dealing with life—their way of mastering reality—is a proper variant of the ways in which other people successfully deal with their lives.

The great danger of this period has been termed either *role confusion* or *identity diffusion* by Erikson (1963, p. 261; 1959, p. 92). In this situation, youths do not know who they are to themselves or to others. As a defense against a sense of identity diffusion, adolescents may overidentify with heroes or cliques and with crowds and causes; they can temporarily lose their own individuality. They help one another during these years of confusion and of unclear occupational direction by clustering together, by stereotyping themselves in their clothes and speech, in their ideals, and in their idols and enemies. They are frequently intolerant of others outside their clique. In search of self, they often come into conflict with parents, siblings, and others close to them while refighting "many of the battles of earlier years, even though to do so they must artificially appoint perfectly well-meaning people to play the roles of adversaries" (Erikson, 1963, p. 261).

Youths who solve the problems of the adolescent years come through with a strong sense of their own individuality and a recognition that they are acceptable to their society. Those who fail to work their way through the identity crisis continue to display in later life such marks of immaturity as intolerance, clannishness, cruel treatment of people who are "different," blind identification or loyalty to heroes and idols, and the like.

Three Adult Stages

With his description of the adolescent identity crisis, Erikson carried the narrative of psychosocial development through the second decade of life. However, unlike Freud, he did not stop at this point in describing personality growth. Rather, he added three more stages, depicting key conflicts faced by adults in their early, middle, and later years. Since our chief concern in this book is with growth through the teenage years, I will not dwell on the three adult stages but will simply mention the nature of the crises faced at those levels.

The transition from adolescence to adulthood is accompanied by the crisis of *intimacy and distantiation versus self-absorption.* Or, phrased another way, it is a crisis of intimacy and solidarity versus isolation. In Erikson's view, the youth who emerges from adolescence with a reasonable sense of his or her own identity is then prepared to establish a nonexploitative intimacy, sexually and intellectually, with a companion of the opposite sex. The youth whose identity is secure is also prepared to defend his or her rights and individuality against attackers. This ability to defend oneself is termed *distantiation* by Erikson. In his words, distantiation is the readiness to "repudiate, to isolate, and if necessary to destroy those forces and people whose essence seems dangerous to one's own" (1959, p. 95). Youths who fail at this stage are unable to establish intimate relations with a companion, so they retreat into self-absorption.

During the second adult stage, the psychosocial conflict involves *generativity versus stagnation* (or generativity versus self-absorption). Sexual partners who find true genitality (capacity for orgasmic potency with a love partner of the opposite sex) wish to combine their personalities in producing and caring for offspring, a condition that Erikson labeled *generativity.* Such partners are not simply absorbed in their own welfare.

In later years of adulthood the crisis involves *integrity versus despair and disgust.* The older person who achieves integrity is one who accepts his own life cycle and "is ready to defend the dignity of his own life style against all physical and economic threats" (Erikson, 1959, p. 98).

These, then, are the eight stages of development as conceived by Erikson in his theory of psychosocial periods. After he introduced this scheme in 1959, he periodically embellished it with additional propositions. For instance, in *Insight and Responsibility* (Erikson, 1964) he expanded his picture of positive ego development by describing a series of human *virtues,* which he identified as "qualities of strength."

> I . . . speak of Hope, Will, Purpose, and Competence as the rudiments of virtue developed in childhood; of Fidelity as the adolescent virtue; and of Love, Care, and Wisdom as the central virtues of adulthood. (Erikson, 1964, pp. 113, 115)

These virtues, he said, are an expression of the integration of the psychosexual and psychosocial growth schedules. Each virtue has its particular time of arousal and emphasis in the hierarchy of epigenetic growth stages. For example, Erikson postulated that the virtue of *hope* arises during early infancy, that of *will* around ages two and three, and that of *purpose* in the preschool years of age three to six. Furthermore, each virtue builds upon those that have developed before it. "Will cannot be trained until hope is secure, nor can love become reciprocal until fidelity has proven reliable" (Erikson, 1964, p. 115). The meanings assigned to these virtues by Erikson and their relationship to the psychosexual and psychosocial stages are displayed in Table 6.2.

Roles of heredity and environment   When a theorist suggests that such traits as hope, fidelity, and wisdom trace their essential development to specified age periods that are universal for all children, two questions arise about the theorist's beliefs concerning the roles of heredity and environment. First, does the theorist mean that all children inherit a time-schedule mechanism that preordains the sequence in which character traits evolve and the time when each trait becomes of primary developmental import? Second, does the theorist mean that the actual form each trait assumes is inherited, and that, consequently, the child's social environment has little or no effect on the nature of the hope, fidelity, and wisdom that the child will display in her personality?

In response to these queries, Erikson would say yes to the first and no to the second. Yes, he did mean that the epigenetic principle establishes the sequence and the general time when particular psychosexual and psychosocial concerns appear in center stage, demanding primary attention. But no, the form that a given trait assumes is not determined by the child's genetic nature. Instead, the way a psychosocial concern is resolved and the way the personality characteristics that the child or youth comes to display are formed depend on the way she or he interacts with the social institutions of the particular culture. So although Erikson postulated that the crucial time for the development of hope arises during infancy for all people, he said that the degree of hope or optimism the individual child achieves is determined by the way that child is treated during the first year of life. And such treatment varies greatly from one society to another and from one family to another. In effect, Erikson accorded a very prominent role to the culture as an influence on the form that psychosocial traits assume as children grow up.

Toys and reasons   The importance of social institutions in the sculpturing of the child's personality was also emphasized in another, more recent extension of Erikson's theory described in *Toys and Reasons* (Erikson, 1977). The general subject of Erikson's attention in this book is human play, with the term *play* used in a very broad sense. According to Erikson, children are engaging in their play when they use imagination to devise mental models of their place in their expanding world. These models are visions designed by children to make sense out of their feelings and skills in relation to the array of puzzling stimuli that impinge on them from without. At each stage of development, such play or the creation of such

TABLE 6.2
Stages in the development of virtues

Stage Number	Column A Freud's psychosexual stages	Column B Erikson's psychosocial crises	Column C Erikson's virtues or qualities of strength	Column D approximate ages in years
I	oral-respiratory	trust versus mistrust	*hope:* the enduring belief that fervent wishes can be fulfilled despite "the dark urges and rages which mark the beginning of existence"	0–1
II	anal-urethral	autonomy versus shame, doubt	*will:* the constant determination to exercise both free choice and self-restraint, despite the shame and doubt experienced during infancy	2–3
III	infantile-genital	initiative versus guilt	*purpose:* the "courage to envisage and pursue valued goals uninhibited by the defeat of infantile fantasies, by guilt and by the foiling fear of punishment"	3–6
IV	latency	industry versus inferiority	*competence:* the free use of skill and intelligence in completing tasks, "unimpaired by infantile inferiority"	7–12 or so
V	puberty and adolescence	identity and repudiation versus identity diffusion	*fidelity:* sustaining freely pledged loyalties despite contradictions in value systems	12–18 or so
VI	mature genitality	intimacy and solidarity versus isolation	*love:* "mutuality of devotion forever subduing the antagonisms inherent in divided function"	the 20s
VII		generativity versus self-absorption	*care:* concern for obligations "generated by love, necessity, or accident"	late 20s to 50s
VIII		integrity versus despair	*wisdom:* "detached concern with life itself, in the face of death itself"	50s and beyond

Based on Erikson, 1964, pp. 115–134.

visions functions as a tool to help the individual solve the psychosocial conflict on which she or he is focusing at that stage.

Three aspects of Erikson's conception of play are of particular note. First, play in this sense is not an activity limited to the period of childhood, but rather is pursued throughout the entire life span. Nor are these imaginative, playful acts simply pastimes—something nonserious to do when we are not engaged in the work of life. Instead, such acts, during either working time or leisure time, are marks of the lifelong "human propensity to create model situations in which aspects of the past are re-lived, the present represented and renewed, and the future anticipated" (Erikson, 1977, p. 44). Therefore the child is playing when he builds a structure of blocks or dramatizes with dolls an encounter in the life of a family, but the physicist is also playing when she fashions a model of the universe, and the army general is playing when devising a battle strategy and conducting war according to the "rules of the game."

Second, although the psychological purpose of play is to enable the individual to organize and master his or her own existence, play cannot fulfill this purpose if conducted only in a solitary setting. There is an essential social quality to much if not all play. In Erikson's view, individuals' imaginative models or mental pictures of themselves in their world need to be shared with and affirmed by others. Growing children do not achieve identity or self-concept in isolation but through the interplay of their imaginative creations with those of significant people in their environments. For the preschooler, this interplay can be the child's producing a visual construction with toys and blocks in the presence of an understanding observer. In spontaneous dramatic play with peers, the child has his or her model situation affirmed and clarified by other children participating in the drama in a way that makes sense to them all—they have produced a shared vision of their world. The games of school-age children are also microcosms—miniature, imagined worlds with defined roles, goals, boundaries of time and space, and rules that define the right way to do things. So also are the games of adults, whether in the form of sporting events and parlor pastimes or in the form of maneuvers in national politics and war (Erikson, 1977, pp. 53–64).

Third, within any society, as time passes, the dominant shared visions or worldviews assume rather permanent form. Each individual or each generation does not create entirely new ones. The dominant models become traditional and ritualized, and people who share these ways of viewing themselves within their world become convinced that theirs are the right ways or best ways. To perpetuate such models, the institutions of the society—the family, church, school, social club, mass communication media, judiciary, business organizations, and government—teach the viewpoints and rituals to the young. In this way one group of people perpetuates a culture or pattern of rituals and worldviews that differs from the patterns perpetuated by other groups.

Whereas the biologically inherited genes differentiate the human species from such other species as chimpanzees and hummingbirds, it is the set of socializing institutions within a given culture that causes differences between the people in that society and the people in another society. These resulting groups of people, each marked by the attitudinal and ritual signs of its own culture, are what Erikson called *pseudo-species:*

> By pseudo-speciation, then, we mean a sense of irreversible difference between one's own and other "kinds," which can attach itself to evolved major differences among human populations or, indeed, to smaller and smaller differences which have come to loom large. In the form of man's "in"-group loyalties, such a specific sense of being elect—as a tribe or nation, creed, class, or ideology—can contribute to the highest achievements in citizenship, courage, and workmanship and can, in fact, weld together in new loyalties (*civis Romanus,* Christian love) previously inimical entities. In the form of new "out"-group enmities, on the other hand, it can express itself most variably—in mortal hatred as well as in phobic avoidance, or in sheer clannishness. (Erikson, 1977, pp. 76–77)

Of the various aspects of play, as Erikson used the term, the one facet on which he centered particular attention in *Toys and Reasons* is that of *ritualization.* He fitted various forms of ritualization into his stages of the life cycle, tracing each form from its beginnings in childhood and adolescence to its form in the adult world. Erikson's chart of the ontogeny of ritualization is shown in Table 6.3. As the chart suggests, the evolution of ritualization according to the epigenetic schedule proceeds as follows.

The earliest beginning of ritual in infancy was labeled *mutuality of recognition* by Erikson, for the first social interaction in the infant's life involves the infant's needs being cared for by parents, particularly by the mother. By means of the child-care ritual—the mother's touch, her smile, the name she gives the child—a mutual mode of recognizing each other and of affirming their identities and relationship develops. This initial ritual serves as the foundation for subsequent rituals of mutual recognition and bonding that will mark later stages of life: the relationship between teacher and pupil, club or gang leader and group member, chieftain and warrior, political figure and citizen, God and believer. Erikson proposed that people are born with the need for such "regular and mutual affirmation and certification" and that its absence can radically harm an infant (Erikson, 1977, p. 88). He called this aspect of ritualization the *numinous,* for it represents reassurance for the individual through familiarity and mutuality in relation to an object or personage of devotion. Among the institutions of adult society, that of organized religion most obviously represents the numinous:

> The believer, by appropriate gestures, confesses his dependence and his childlike faith and seeks, by appropriate offerings, to secure the privilege of being lifted up to the very bosom of the divine which, indeed, may be seen to graciously respond, with the faint smile of an inclined face. (Erikson, 1977, pp. 89–90)

This first aspect of ritualization, the numinous, develops throughout life and combines with subsequently developed rituals to form the complex that makes up the cultural patterns the child's personality acquires.

The second aspect, arising at age two or three in relation to the toilet-training stage, is that of discriminating good from bad. From these early years the rituals involved with making judgments develop until they reach their most formal version

TABLE 6.3
Stages in the development of ritualization

Infancy age 0–1	Early childhood age 2–3	Play age age 3–6	School age age 6–12	Adolescence age 12–18	Elements in adult rituals	Principal societal institutions in adult life*
mutuality of recognition					numinous	church, family
	discrimination of good and bad				judicious	court of law
		dramatic elaboration			dramatic	stage, movies, television, literature
			rules of performance		formal	school, craft training agency, licensing agency for vocations
				solidarity of conviction	ideological	political group, church, military
					generational sanction	marriage, guardianship, professional training and licensing agencies (for teachers, physicians, clergy, etc.)

Based on Erikson, 1977, pp. 85–114.
*The institutions in adult life are partly quoted directly from Erikson and partly the present author's extrapolations from the general tenor of Erikson's analyses.

in the procedures of judicial courts. Hence Erikson applied the word *judicious* to this second sequence of imaginative models of a culture.

The third sort of ritualization is seated in the dramatic play of the preschool years, ages three through six, when the child's new sense of guilt at the time of the Oedipus conflict motivates the child to seek a resolution of the conflict through imagined dramas. For example, in his clinical experience with children, Erikson observed them use toys as elements in creating a narrative with a plot that includes conflicts that are finally resolved. These are the elements—plot, conflict, resolution—that make up the sophisticated adult versions of ritualization performed on the stage, in motion pictures, and on radio and television. Effective drama is a vision of reality condensed in space and time and experienced by the audience as "unbearably personal and yet miraculously shared" (Erikson, 1977, p. 102).

A fourth element of ritualization, emphasized during the elementary school years (ages six to twelve), is that of *methodological performance.* During this stage, children are assigned a series of tasks that prepare them to master the skills and work habits that will enable them to participate in the economic and technological life of the society, be it agricultural, industrial, commercial, or literary. This stage is the beginning of the child's learning to gain satisfaction through competently performing the formal tasks of the society. This "work role which we begin to envisage for ourselves at the end of childhood is, under favorable conditions, the most reassuring role of all, just because it confirms us in skills and permits us to recognize ourselves in visible works" (Erikson, 1977, p. 106).

A fifth element that enters at the time of adolescence is the adoption by the growing youth of a set of convictions that tie together in a coherent manner (1) the psychosocial identity he or she has achieved up to this point and (2) the structure and expectations of the adult culture. Erikson identified two varieties of ritual prominent during these years. First are the *spontaneous "rites"* by which adolescents ritualize relations with their peers and mark their subculture as distinct from childhood and adulthood. Second are the *formal rites,* such as school graduation and joining the church, which represent the passage into, and adoption of, adult status and values. The solidifying of convictions during adolescence leads to the development of the mature ideologies of adult life.

The final stage in the evolution of ritualization is *generational sanction,* because as the youth achieves adult status he or she is officially authorized, through such rituals as marriage and guardianship, to take on the teaching, productive, and curative roles for a new generation of children. Whereas the child and adolescent are the objects of rituals supervised by adults, the new adult now becomes the ritualizer for the young. The evolution of ritualization for the growing years is now complete.

Erikson's unflagging desire to enrich the psychoanalytic model prompted him at the end of the eighth decade of his own life to publish yet another view of growth, this time a retrospective account from the vantage point of old age, an unraveling of the stages of development from the final phase of life back to birth (Erikson, 1982). In this work he reiterated his confidence in psychoanalytic inquiry as the most profitable method for depicting how human personality develops.

PRACTICAL APPLICATIONS

In the main, the applications described in Chapter Five for Freudian theory are the same as those for Erikson's extension of psychoanalysis. Like Freud's model, Erikson's variation has guided general child rearing, influenced early childhood education, and generated techniques of therapy for disturbed children. In particular, Erikson's description of an adolescent identity crisis has influenced parents' treatment of adolescents and has encouraged school personnel to help students master the crisis by means of life-adjustment courses and study units on self-understanding in social studies and literature classes (Tyler, 1986). A *Psychosocial Stage Inventory* founded on Erikson's model has been used in research on the adjustment of children and youths in various societies (Gray, Ispa, & Thornburg, 1986; Rosenthal, Moore, & Taylor, 1983; Sandor & Rosenthal, 1986). Techniques of therapy for disturbed and learning-disabled adolescents have also been affected by Erikson's attention to youths' struggle for identity (Pickar & Turi, 1986; M. Rose, 1986).

ERIKSON'S VERSION OF PSYCHOANALYSIS: AN ASSESSMENT

Since Erikson's theory is an extension of the psychoanalytic model and is in essential agreement with it, the evaluation of Freudian theory at the end of Chapter Five is also applicable to Erikson's theory in most respects. Therefore, rather than repeat the assessment from Chapter Five, I will confine my appraisal in the following paragraphs to ways in which Erikson's views and contributions differ from Freud's. But before identifying differences, I should note that the work of both men has continued to occupy a very prominent place in the teaching of psychology in recent years. An inspection of fourteen popular child development textbooks showed that the authors most frequently mentioned were Piaget, Skinner, and Erikson (Hogan & Vahey, 1984). A survey of the author indexes in twenty-four introductory psychology texts found that the five names cited most often, in descending order, were Freud, Piaget, Skinner, Bandura, and Erikson (Knapp, 1985).

As for Erikson's particular contributions, he has been acclaimed for his detailed definitions of psychosocial stages and the proposed identity crisis of adolescence, and has been credited as well with significant contributions to psychoanalytic research methodology. Among the complaints critics have launched against Freud is the charge that he was anthropologically naive. By this they mean that he based his theory on a very narrow range of personalities, assuming that the themes of neurotic behavior and thought he found in his patients were an accurate reflection of the modes found in the rest of humanity. In effect, critics have questioned how accurately the patients met in a late-nineteenth-century Viennese psychiatric practice, who were mainly women of upper-middle-class Jewish society, represent people in general. Erikson, in contrast, drew the cases on which he based his speculations from a far wider geographical sampling than Freud. Erikson was a psychoanalyst in Europe, but he also participated in intensive studies of cases at the Harvard Psychological Clinic, of infants suffering neuroses at the Yale University Department of Psychiatry, of normal adolescents in northern California, of Sioux and Yurok Indians, and of numerous other Americans. Furthermore, he focused more attention on normal development than did Freud, particularly the normal development of the healthy self or ego in personal and social relations.

Erikson also furthered the development of *psychohistory,* which is the analysis of the psychological development of individuals by the use of what they have written and said and by reports of their actions. Perhaps the most notable of his analyses of world figures have been those of Martin Luther (1958) and Gandhi (1969). His purpose in these endeavors was to identify significant relationships between the life histories of great leaders and "the historical moment of their emergence" (Erikson, 1975, p. 10). In particular, he concentrated on "the powers of recovery inherent in the young ego" (Erikson, 1958, p. 8).

This same concern for the influence of the broad social setting on personality development caused Erikson to seek ways for elucidating and verifying impressions derived from the psychoanalytic interview. He saw sociological and anthropological research techniques as serving to help clinicians recognize the importance of the social environment in which their data are obtained.

> Clinical evidence, finally, will be decisively clarified, but not changed in nature, by a sharpened awareness (such as now emanates from sociological studies) of the psychotherapist's as well as the patient's position in society and history. (Erikson, 1964, p. 80)

As for its stimulation value, Erikson's model continues to attract the interest of empirical investigators and theorists alike. The sorts of studies that his work has inspired others to pursue in recent times include comparative concepts of the *self* (Tuttman, 1988); conceiving of the *self* in terms of successive ego growth rings related to Eriksonian development stages (Hamachek, 1985); the social adjustment of Australian adolescents from varied ethnic backgrounds (Rosenthal, Moore, & Taylor, 1983); a validation of Erikson's model among South African blacks and whites (Ochse & Plug, 1986); late-adolescent identity as related to self-esteem (Dusek, Carter, & Levy, 1986); identity and intimacy crises (Sandor & Rosenthal, 1986); an expanded formulation of Erikson's view of ego formation (Cole & Levine, 1987); a reconceptualization of Erikson's development cycles (Logan, 1986); and an extended account of intimacy in Erikson's theory (Franz & White, 1985).

All of the foregoing points I would put on the credit side of the assessment ledger. On the debit side I find the same basic problems of scientific validation described in the assessment of Freud's theory. For example, not everyone has found the evidence cited in support of Erikson's proposed psychosocial crises to be convincing. Some of the difficulties with the evidence are reflected in the following questions: Isn't the major evidence in favor of Erikson's scheme mainly in the form of his interpretation of selected, illustrative clinical cases—cases of individuals in therapy, of such figures as Luther and Hitler, and of such groups as Sioux Indians? And couldn't another theorist find as convincing a variety of illustrations as these to suggest that psychosocial crises come in quite a different order than that suggested by Erikson? For example, why is the crisis of autonomy versus shame necessarily set in the second year of life? Couldn't we easily find behaviors at other ages that could reasonably be interpreted as symptoms of an autonomy crisis, behavior such as the striving for independence that appears to mark the years of adolescence?

In conclusion, Erikson's writings about development have generated much discussion in psychological circles and have attracted the admiration of many readers who have found his insights true in their own experience. But many of his proposals, like Freud's, must be accepted on faith, faith in the theorist's interpretive skills and in his authority rather than on experimental and observational evidence that would more clearly compel readers to arrive at the same conclusions. Of course, this charge can be made against many other theories of development as well.

FOR FURTHER READING

The two books by Erikson that most directly describe his overall theory of development are the following:

(1963) *Childhood and Society,* 2d ed. New York: Norton.
(1968) *Identity: Youth and Crisis.* New York: Norton.

Volumes illustrating the manner in which Erikson embellishes his basic theory with further proposals are these:

(1977) *Toys and Reasons.* New York: Norton.
(1982) *The Life Cycle Completed.* New York: Norton.

For a biographical study of the theorist, see:

Coles, R. (1970) *Erik H. Erikson: The Growth of His Work.* New York: Little, Brown.

Identifying States of Consciousness

Of what significance for human behavior are states of consciousness, how can one state be distinguished from another, and how do nonconscious mental functions develop during the first two decades of life?

Over the past century the topic "states of consciousness" or "levels of consciousness" has intermittently been in favor and out of favor with theorists. When in favor, the matter has inspired assorted proposals about the nature and development of consciousness states. To illustrate how the issue has been addressed in various theories, the following perspective (1) reviews diverse conceptions of conscious and nonconscious mental operations, (2) considers problems of identifying nonconscious states, and (3) suggests how nonconscious aspects of mind may develop throughout childhood and adolescence.

VARIED CONCEPTIONS OF CONSCIOUSNESS STATES

One convenient way to describe beliefs about consciousness is by differentiating among three categories of theories: (1) ones that deny the existence of *nonconscious* or *unconscious* psychological processes; (2) ones that do not address the consciousness issue but, nevertheless, permit inferences about the possible existence of multiple states; and (3) ones that directly propose a system of states or levels and identify their characteristics.

The Absence of Nonconscious Mental Activity

An initial problem in this debate is how best to define the term *conscious*. Among popular choices are the following:

> *Dictionary definitions,* such as (a) *awareness*—which means "recognizing one's own existence, sensations, feelings, thoughts, and surroundings or (b) having one's mental processes fully active" (Flexner & Hauck, 1987, p. 432).

> *Philosophers' and psychologists' proposals,* such as these: (a) *attention* is the "criterion of consciousness" so that consciousness and attention become nearly synonymous (Boring, 1963, p. 231); or (b) the term *conscious* refers to

people's conceptual thought—and because concepts assume the form of words, *conscious mental activity* is that variety of thought that people can express in words (Dreikurs, 1950, p. 50).

An advantage of the dictionary definitions and the one offered by Boring is that, while their looseness may beg for greater precision, they still convey a sense of truth that people can verify in daily experience—equating *conscious* with the act of "paying attention" seems to make intuitive sense. An advantage of Dreikurs's proposal *(conscious = concepts = words)* is that his definition provides a neatly measurable distinction between conscious and nonconscious cognition—any psychological event that can be expressed in words is conscious, and any that cannot be put in words is unconscious. But critics could charge that this meaning is too narrow, since it excludes cognitions or intuitions that people "are aware of" but cannot readily explain.

My aim in mentioning alternative notions of *conscious* is not to catalog all intended meanings nor to judge one as better than another for all purposes. Rather my intent is only to point out that people who speak of *conscious* or *consciousness* do not all agree on what these terms mean, so it is useful to discover what a given theorist presumes when talking about such matters.

Consider, now, theorists who have contended that mental life is entirely conscious so there can be no such thing as unconscious mental operations. Psychology had taken the form of philosophical speculation until, in the latter 1800s, it assumed the character of an empirical science in the laboratories of Wilhelm Wundt (1832–1920) in Germany in 1879 and of E. B. Titchener (1867–1927) in the United States in 1895. In the opinion of these pioneers, the human mind is able to observe all of its own inner workings. Hence the approach to understanding mental functions should consist of a type of introspection by which trained observers attempt to analyze their own percepts, memories, and thoughts and to describe these phenomena in terms of elementary sensations, images, and feelings. This version of psychological science became known as *structuralism,* since the investigators' purpose was to identify the structures of the mind. Structuralism provided no place for nonconscious psychic activities.

The denial of nonconscious mental events was carried even further when John B. Watson's (1878–1959) revolutionary article "Psychology as a Behaviorist Views It" (1913) launched the behaviorism movement that would dominate much of psychological activity over the next half century, particularly in the United States. Watson rejected any such concepts as *mind* and *thought.* Psychology, he said, was strictly the science of observable behavior, so there could be no *intellect* or *mentality.* People's supposed *mental activity* was no more than silent speech, as evidenced by barely perceptible movements of the speech organs when people were ostensibly "thinking." Thus Watson's extreme behaviorism not only eliminated the possibility of unconscious mental events but of conscious ones as well. R. S. Woodworth, president of the American Psychological Association in 1914, is credited with observing that psychology had "lost its soul" when structuralist theorists divorced psychology from religious philosophy; now, thanks to Watson, psychology had "lost its mind" (Roback, 1964).

Inferred States of Consciousness

Information-processing theory illustrates a model of development that typically does not allude to matters of consciousness but, nevertheless, permits speculation about states of consciousness implied by the theory's structure. As we will see in Chapter Eleven, information-processing models portray mental activity as a procedure that involves (1) receiving stimuli from the environment, (2) transmitting and storing coded messages in the neural system, and ultimately (3) activating muscles to produce observed behavior. Each of these phases can be analyzed into constituent substages, some of them conscious, but others unconscious in that they operate without the individual's intent or awareness. For example, in such a stimulus receptor as the eye or ear, a crude filtering action takes place that identifies certain gross characteristics of a stimulus. The person experiencing the stimulus does not intend to perform such filtering nor is even aware that it is occurring. The performance is automatic, and in that sense is unconscious. In like manner, a variety of other functions of the information-processing system are equally unintentional, automatic, and unrecognized. As J. F. Kihlstrom explained:

> Certainly a good deal of mental activity is unconscious in the strict sense of being inaccessible to phenomenal awareness under any circumstances. In conversational speech, for example, the listener is aware of the meanings of the words uttered by the speaker but not of the phonological and linguistic principles by which the meaning of the speaker's utterance is decoded. Although we have conscious access to the products of these mental processes—in that we are aware of the meaning of the utterance . . . and can communicate this knowledge to others—we have no conscious access to their operations. . . . One thing is now clear: consciousness is not to be identified with any particular perceptual-cognitive functions such as discriminative response to stimulation, perception, memory, or the higher mental processes involved in judgment or problem-solving. All of these functions can take place outside of phenomenal awareness. (1987, pp. 1447, 1450)

Just as information-processing theory can thus be analyzed to reveal its implied levels of consciousness, so also can other models of development that do not directly describe consciousness states. Such is true of Piaget's scheme, Soviet theories, humanistic proposals, and more.

Outright Claims for States or Levels of Consciousness

Although Freud can be credited with popularizing "the unconscious," it is clear that he neither invented nor first discovered the notion of unconscious mental actions. For centuries philosophers had speculated about such matters. And at the time Freud's career began, an active dialogue about the unconscious was already being conducted among scholars in both Europe and America, as suggested by L. L. Whyte's (1960) list of more than forty authors who preceded Freud in writing about the unconscious mind.

Over the years the most common way of categorizing states of consciousness has been to divide mental events into two types, *conscious* and *unconscious.* Earlier

I pointed out the lack of agreement about the meaning of *conscious*. But that lack is far exceeded by differences of opinion regarding the term *unconscious*. Furthermore, some authors, not content with the bipartite conscious/unconscious division, have embellished their theories with additional components. Freud imposed a *preconscious* between the conscious and unconscious, and Carl Jung postulated a *racial unconscious* undergirding each individual's personal unconscious (Jung, 1953).

It is apparent that such differences of opinion are nothing new. H. Ellenberger noted in his *The Discovery of the Unconscious* (1970) that European thinkers by 1900 had already ascribed four separate functions to the unconscious mind. And R. C. Fuller (1986) listed these as

> (1) the conservative function of recording memories and registering perceptions which often escape conscious attention; (2) the dissolutive function, as evidenced by hypnotic behaviors and the multiple or split personalities of schizophrenic patients; (3) the creative function of innovative or inspirational thinking; and (4) the mythopoetic function of fabricating inner romances, fantasies, or dreams which give psychic life a kind of autonomous reality apart from events that transpire in the physical universe. (p. 4)

Psychologist D. B. Klein (1977, pp. 171–178) sought to dispel some of the confusion about nonconscious processes by describing additional ways authors have used the term *unconscious*. The last pair of the following six ways are associated with Jung and Freud, the two theorists best known for making unconscious processes an intimate part of their models of development.

1. *Ignorance.* When we are aware of our desires (such as wanting to sleep or wanting something sweet to eat) but fail to recognize the precise metabolic conditions that stimulate these desires, we are said to be "unconscious of" or "ignorant of" the physiological causes of our desires.

2. *Inattention.* Perceptual distraction may cause people to be "unconscious of" what is going on around them. For example, a mother shouts to her ten-year-old son as he plays tag with friends, but the boy fails to answer because he is concentrating so intently on the game that he remains oblivious of his mother's call. Or, during a class discussion, a high school teacher asks for a girl's opinion, but the girl is unable to respond because she was distracted by her own thoughts when the teacher posed his question.

3. *Subliminal stimulation.* The obverse of inattention is people's unconscious reception of stimuli of which they are unaware. Even though they are not aware of attending to a stimulus, such as a word flashed for an instant on a television screen, they are nevertheless affected by it. This notion of subliminal influences requires the assumption that there is a threshold or borderline—called the *limen*—between conscious and unconscious levels of stimulus perception. According to Klein, "In the area of sales promotion these modes of stimulation have been regarded as 'hidden persuaders.' Whether they ought to be classified as subconscious rather than unconscious influences is a moot point. As subthreshold modes of stimulation they may be classified as subconscious, but as influences eluding awareness they might be classified as being unconscious" (1977, p. 172).

4. *Conditioning.* A phenomenon related to subliminal stimulation is classical conditioning. For instance, a two-year-old girl has burst into tears when, on each of three occasions, she has been knocked to the ground by a neighbor's barking dog. A week later, as her parents watch an evening television drama, the child begins to cry as she hears a dog bark on the TV program. As interpreted from the viewpoint of conditioning, the child's being knocked to the ground (unconditioned stimulus) produced her original fright and weeping (unconditioned response). And because barking accompanied each attack, any barking she now hears (conditioned stimulus) is sufficient to set off the weeping (conditioned response). Since the child did not consciously intend to associate barking with weeping, the automatic establishment of such an association qualifies as an unconscious mental event.

5. *Jung's collective unconscious.* Carl Jung (1875–1961), a compatriot of Freud until they parted company in 1912, proposed that all humans inherit residual psychic impressions that derive from

> the experiences of remote ancestors in coping with recurrent situations of crucial biological significance. These would be experiences directly related to survival in the history of the human race and thus have to do with themes of universal appeal. The resulting racial memory or collective unconscious is presumed to render mankind sensitive to thoughts of spirits, gods, storms, motherhood, birth, mother earth, monsters, sunshine, and whatever else may have impressed preliterate man as a force for good or evil. (Klein, 1977, p. 175)

According to Jung, this phylogenetic unconscious provides a foundation of inclinations—referred to as *archetypes*—for how to think and act, with the inclinations then fashioned into behavior by the individual's own direct experiences with the world.

6. *Freud's states or levels of consciousness.* Throughout this perspective I have referred to *states* and *levels.* I have done so—following Freud's lead—because these words are convenient categories for directing our discussion and not because everyone who has written about such matters has pictured consciousness in terms of states or levels.

Freud's voluminous written works spanned more than sixty years (from age twenty-one to eighty-two), so it is hardly surprising that he occasionally changed his opinion about such an elusive topic as the unconscious. In delineating the architecture of the mind, he spoke sometimes of levels, with the preconscious deeper than the conscious, and the unconscious deeper yet. At other times he spoke of states: "We must be prepared . . . to assume the existence in us not only of a second consciousness, but of a third, fourth, perhaps of an unlimited number of states of consciousness, all unknown to us and to one another" (1915b, p. 170). Periodically he used a spatial analogy, comparing the unconscious to a "large anteroom, in which the various mental excitations are crowding upon one another," then picturing consciousness as a smaller reception room adjacent to the anteroom (Klein, 1977, p. 177). On still other occasions Freud avoided speaking of levels, states, or places and referred instead to mental "systems" and to "psychical acts which lack consciousness" (S. Freud, 1915b, p. 170).

But more important than his metaphors and labels are the characteristics Freud assigned to various states of consciousness. I believe that identifying such charac-

TABLE B.1
Attributes of Freudian states of consciousness

Conscious	Preconscious	Unconscious
Type of psychic function		
secondary process—the reality principle	pleasure principle translated into reality principle	primary process—the pleasure principle
complex, rational thought that recognizes demands of surrounding environment	complex, rational thought that recognizes demands of surrounding environment	complex thought unchecked by logical contradiction, causal association, or knowledge of outside world
Use of psychic energy		
expends energy	expends energy	generates and expends energy
Types of psychic contents		
acknowledged sensations, perceptions, and decisions; emotions and feelings	adjustment mechanisms, recallable memories, all readily available items of information at individual's disposal	instinctual drives, wish impulses, repressed sexual memories, other repressed memories, and items still unidentified; no emotions
a portion of the superego	censor guarding the gate between the unconscious and conscious	
	a portion of the superego	
Storage capacity for psychic contents		
very small	moderately large	very large, perhaps infinite
Sense of time		
sense of past, present, future	sense of past, present, future	no sense of time
Values		
positive and negative attitudes, doubts, personal convictions	attitudes, doubts, personal convictions	no negative attitudes, no doubts, no personal convictions

Abstracted from Archard (1984, p. 25), S. Freud (1915b), and Klein (1977, pp. 186–189).

teristics is best performed in terms of the most prominent version of his model of the mind—the tripartite structure of conscious, preconscious, and unconscious described in Chapter Five. The attributes of mind are displayed in Table B.1.

Thus the past century has witnessed a considerable ebb and flow in the debate over types and levels of consciousness. That debate not only continues today but is bound to endure into the future. These issues will likely never be settled because of the difficulties encountered in trying to pin down such evasive entities as *preconscious* and *unconscious* in order to comprehend them. This problem of how to identify *nonconscious* events is our next concern.

IDENTIFYING AND COMPREHENDING NONCONSCIOUS STATES

Because alleged nonconscious functions are, by definition, beyond the realm of direct inspection, the task of judging the validity of different theorists' views of the preconscious, subconscious, or unconscious becomes most elusive. Since such functions cannot be witnessed immediately, their existence must be inferred. This leads to the question, From what kinds of evidence do theorists draw their inferences about the nature of nonconscious mental events?

An examination of our earlier list of nonconscious functions suggests that theorists may base their inferences on three sources of evidence: (1) people's acting without conscious intent and then being unable to identify the source of their actions, (2) people's failure to respond to stimuli, and (3) presumed symbolic behavior. The first two may be employed by proponents of nearly any variety of theory, except for extreme behaviorism. The third is particularly associated with such theories as Jung's and Freud's.

1. A lack of conscious intent may be revealed when people are asked "Why did you do that?" and they answer, "I guess I did it without thinking," or "I didn't even realize I did it," or "I suppose it's kind of automatic." This sort of evidence is used to support inferences about unconscious mental functions underlying conditioned responses, certain creative endeavors, subliminal stimulation, hypnotic behavior and multiple personalities, and acts practiced to a level of automaticity, as observed in a skilled typist, pianist, chauffeur, or athlete.

2. Failure to respond to stimuli, in the sense of inattentiveness, can be interpreted as evidence of a hypothetical, unconscious mental filtering system that blocks all stimuli from consciousness except for the single stimulus on which the individual is concentrating at the moment. Some authors have proposed that a malfunction of such a filtering mechanism accounts for some children's having difficulty attending to academic tasks in school because they are so easily distracted by irrelevant sights and sounds around them. In other words, a faulty filter allows too many stimuli to invade consciousness, thereby destroying the child's concentration on an assigned task (Thomas, 1989c, p. 188).

3. The phrase "presumed symbolic behavior" refers to the proposal that contents of the unconscious cannot reveal themselves to the conscious mind in their original form but, instead, must disguise their true nature. In other words, thoughts that arise in consciousness may not be what their appearance suggests but, rather, can be symbols of something different. In Jung's analytic theory, the items in consciousness can be representatives or embodiments of vague predispositions (related to pain, birth, death, sun, darkness, power, women, men, sex, magic, and the like) inherited from ancient ancestors and now residing deep in a racial unconscious. In Freud's psychoanalytic theory, items in consciousness can symbolize distressing, and now repressed, memories of sexual events from the past that are too threatening to the individual's conscious sense of well-being to be admitted into consciousness in their true form. The only opportunity for the psychic energy of

such repressed material to expend itself occurs when the unacceptable memories mask their actual identity in symbolic garb, thereby rendering themselves acceptable to consciousness. Evidence that items in consciousness are actually camouflaged material from the unconscious has been sought in a host of phenomena— dreams, slips of the tongue, perceptual mistakes, bodily ailments, posture and movements, responses to projective devices (ink-blot tests, word-association tests, unfinished sentences), artistic productions, and the like.

Perhaps the greatest danger in using presumed symbolic behavior as a window to the unconscious lies in the fact that the interpreter of symbols is "only human" and not an objective, omniscient evaluator. Might not the Jungian analyst or Freudian psychoanalyst be projecting his or her own unconscious contents onto the client's behavior when interpreting that behavior as symbolic?

In summary, then, theorists' conceptions of the nature of nonconscious mental activities represent inferences that do not yield readily to empirical verification. This difficulty caused Fuller (1986, p. 5) to contend that "inasmuch as 'facts' about the unconscious cannot be ascertained empirically, theories which purport to explain men's and women's depths have almost entirely been shaped by philosophical and cultural factors." To illustrate this point, he cited the cool reception psychoanalytic theory received in the United States during the early decades of the twentieth century, and he proposed that "the ideological incompatibility between Freud's tragic view of life and the optimistic bent of the American mind was sufficient to account for the reluctance of academic psychologists to give psychoanalysis a more serious reading. . . . American psychology is the creation of a cultural tradition which esteems vigor and flexibility; it consequently resists trammeling the self with a complex inner structure" (pp. 124–125).

Even among Americans who did embrace psychoanalysis, there was a tendency to revise those aspects of Freud's theory that appeared to deny the mind's positive, progressive, and creative powers. Such revisionism caused Freud to observe that the popular view of psychoanalysis in the United States "is no evidence of a friendly attitude toward the subject or a particularly broad dissemination of, or profound understanding of its teachings" (Oberndorf in Fuller, 1986, p. 120).

In discussing other theories, Fuller cited additional support for his proposition that the philosophical preferences of a society affect the image of the unconscious espoused by theorists in that society. For instance, he observed that in the rise of humanistic psychology during the 1960s (Chapter Twelve) the movement's American trendsetters envisioned an unconscious core of personality whose power "gives the individual an innate potential for self-enhancement (i.e., successful adaptation to the physical and social environments) and self-transcendence (i.e., adaptation to some supranatural environment)." This notion that the "unconscious is the aesthetic medium through which the individual can align himself with an immanent life force" is a conviction Fuller traced back to the writings of the colonial theologian Jonathan Edwards (1703–1758), the philosopher-poet Ralph Waldo Emerson (1803–1882), and the psychologist-philosopher William James (1842–1910) (Fuller, 1986, p. 155).

If Fuller's proposal is correct, then we can expect new theories of the future to reflect their authors' cultural settings in their inferences about unconscious mental activities.

How Nonconscious Functions Develop

My final task here is to speculate about how, from the viewpoint of different theories, nonconscious mental operations emerge during the first two decades of life. I have chosen information processing and psychoanalysis as the two theories to use for briefly illustrating a way of estimating which of a theory's unconscious contents and functions are innate and which are acquired. *Innate characteristics* are considered to be of two types: (1) those that are fully operative at birth and (2) those that arise at some point during childhood according to a genetic time schedule *(internal maturation). Acquired characteristics* are the unconscious aspects of personality derived from the child's transactions with the environment.

An Information-Processing Example

In the simplified version of information-processing theory depicted in Figure B.1, cognitive functions assume the following pattern: (a) goals rise in long-term memory; (b) sensory receptors (mainly eyes and ears) search the environment for stimuli pertinent to the goals; (c) as the stimuli impinge on the receptors, gross features of the stimuli are identified (feature detection and pattern recognition) and sent as coded messages to (d) short-term working memory, where the configuration of the stimuli is compared to analogous coded images stored in long-term memory, so that an interpretation can be constructed regarding what the received stimuli mean. The product of this interpretation can then (e) be stored in long-term memory and/or (f) lead to immediate overt action in the environment. The contents of long-term memory fall into two categories: *declarative knowledge* and *procedural knowledge.* Memories in the form of declarative knowledge are of two sorts. First is *episodic knowledge,* meaning knowledge of specific objects (people, places) and events (a birthday party, graduation from elementary school) that the child experienced in the past. Second is *semantic knowledge,* comprising abstract conceptions not limited to any particular time or place (judging distances, recalling names, catching a ball, estimating people's moods). In contrast to declarative knowledge, procedural knowledge consists of that "repertoire of skills, rules, and strategies that operate on declarative knowledge in the course of perception, memory, thought, and action" (Kihlstrom, 1987, p. 1446).

   With this model of the mind before us, we are prepared to speculate about the sources of its unconscious aspects during childhood and adolescence. For the purpose of this exercise, *conscious* is defined as "any knowledge we can bring into awareness and, preferably, describe in some manner." *Unconscious,* as the obverse, refers to any knowledge or function that we cannot bring to awareness. Thus all declarative knowledge has the potential for being conscious, in that the individual can become aware of it under the right circumstances (goals from

The Person

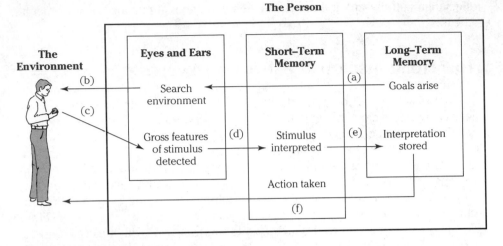

FIGURE B.1
A simplified version of information processing

long-term memory link with stimuli from the environment to energize declarative contents into consciousness). However, "procedural knowledge is not available to introspection under any circumstances. Thus, procedural knowledge appears to be unconscious in the strict sense of the term. We are aware of the goals and conditions of procedures, and the products of their execution, but not of the operations themselves" (Kihlstrom, 1987, p. 1446).

Now to the question of how and when, during the first two decades of life, unconscious knowledge develops. To begin, theorist J. A. Fodor (1983) suggested that the mind contains an array of innate modules governing basic domains of mental functions, such as language, visual perception, and muscular coordination. These modules are genetically "hardwired" into the nervous system and do their work outside of conscious awareness and voluntary control. However, the modules are not entirely operational at birth. Instead, they gradually realize their potential as the child's neural system matures and the child engages in an expanding variety of encounters with the environment. For example, the evolution of language usage in childhood has been traced across cultures, revealing similar stages of language acquisition among all children, regardless of the particular vernacular used in their environment—Chinese, English, Spanish, Malay, Urdu, or some other (Drum, 1990). This evidence is cited to support the notion that inherited propensities that underlie such mental procedures are universal (characteristic of the entire human species), unconscious, and evolve by gradual stages. Furthermore, the pace at which one type of innate function matures can differ from the pace of another, so that a trait such as depth perception will be achieved sooner than will the use of complex language structures.

Distinctive from innate mental functions are those cognitive procedures acquired through experience. For instance, in the case of learning a skill, such as tying a shoelace, the activity is initially conscious as the child intently concentrates on each step of the process. But the act eventually becomes automatic, rendered unconscious by virtue of practice. The number of such skills increases at an accelerating rate as children grow older and their internal neural maturation combines with experience to extend the child's ability to manage more and more aspects of the environment. We might then offer this proposition: the point in a child's development that a particular cognitive function will be acquired and transposed into the form of an unconscious habit is governed by (1) the present maturational level of the neural system, (2) the state of that part of the child's experiential history necessary for learning the skill, (3) an opportunity for encountering the skill, (4) the child's level of motivation for gaining the skill, and (5) sufficient practice to make the skill automatic. The first two events provide the *essential readiness* for acquiring the skill. Not until they are in place can the remaining three steps occur, which may be immediately after readiness is sufficient, or it can be years later or perhaps never.

Such a line of reasoning as the above illustrates how, from the perspective of one version of information processing, inferences can be drawn about the way unconscious mental contents are acquired during childhood.

A Psychoanalytic Example

Consider the attributes listed under the Freudian unconscious in Table B.1. From among them, I would estimate that three are fully operative at birth—the energy-generating function (instinctual drives), the wish impulses, and the primary process (pleasure principle)—because all three are necessary for launching and sustaining development. Other than these, the rest of the personality attributes in Table B.1 are no more than potentials at the time of birth. Freud maintained that the original state of the personality is entirely unconscious and that the preconscious and conscious levels gradually arise out of this primary state as a result of the maturing of the nervous system and the child's interactions with the world.

As the months and years advance, the child's progressive neural maturation combines with environmental experiences to determine when a variety of the acquired aspects of personality appear. For example, although Freud rarely spoke directly about intelligence, he did state that a sufficient (though unspecified) level of intellectual development is necessary before defense mechanisms can be acquired. He wrote that repression, as an ego-defense function of the preconscious, is not "present from the very beginning, and it cannot occur until a sharp distinction has been established between what is conscious and what is unconscious: the essence of repression lies simply in turning something away, and keeping it at a distance, from the conscious" (1915a, p. 147). He believed that other adjustment mechanisms, such as denial and reaction formation, did not require the same level of cognitive complexity as repression and thus could be learned at a somewhat younger (though unspecified) age (Klein, 1977, p. 148).

As soon as repression is operative, memories of unacceptable desires and behavior (chiefly of a sexual nature) accumulate in the unconscious. The quantity of repressions and their potency depends chiefly on the wisdom of those in charge of raising the child. According to psychoanalytic theory, the more demanding and punitive child-rearing practices are, the greater the number and the potency of repressions. Which events will be repressed is determined by the ego operating at the preconscious level. And this decision is governed to a great extent by the composition of that specific child's superego, which imposes standards of right and wrong that are not innate but are acquired, particularly at the time of the Oedipus conflict, around ages three to five.

CONCLUSION

During much of the twentieth century, formal concern with nonconscious mental processes was found almost exclusively in psychoanalysis and in its onetime bedfellows, the theories of Jung and Alfred Adler. However, as the cognitive psychology movement has gained ascendance over behaviorism, psychoanalysis, and humanistic psychology during the final quarter of the century, there appears to be a growing interest in identifying and understanding varied states of consciousness within the proliferating cognitive psychology paradigms. As developmental theorists move into the twenty-first century, this interest seems bound to grow.

BEHAVIORISM AND SOCIAL LEARNING MODELS

A search for the way principles of learning and social contexts explain development

Some psychologists have been very uneasy about theories that propose *mental elements,* such as thoughts, attitudes, soul, ego, needs, or the preconscious. These psychologists are also troubled about hypothetical *mental functions*: repression, epigenesis, reasoning, dispositions, and the like. The problem, they say, is that they are not convinced that these supposed elements and functions really exist, or at least not in the form that various speculators have proposed. It is clear that no one has ever seen or directly measured such things as mind or the unconscious. Another problem is that one theorist who writes about mentality or personality often posits very different elements and functions than do other theorists. And if mind is unavailable for inspection, how do we know which theorist is right?

It was this sort of doubting that motivated John B. Watson (1878–1959) to publish his article "Psychology as a Behaviorist Views It" (1913) and thereby launch the *behaviorism* movement in psychology. Watson and his followers felt that it is both misleading and unprofitable to study some cogitator's fantasies about what the structure of a person's mind or unconscious might be like. They proposed, instead, that it is much more objective and scientific to observe the way people act under different environmental conditions. The observations can then be organized, analyzed, and stated as principles that are intended to explain the behavior. In short, proponents of this point of view claim that the proper business of psychology is to identify the observable conditions that influence the behavior of humans and nonhuman organisms.

Since the time of Watson's early advocacy of behaviorism, the movement has attracted many followers and has spawned numerous subgroups. Behaviorism dominated experimental psychology, particularly in the United States, from the 1920s until well into the 1960s. And though far less popular today, the movement still continues to be an influential force. In Part Four we consider several varieties of behaviorism as they apply to child development. Chapter Seven focuses primarily on B. F. Skinner's operant conditioning and on Sidney Bijou and Donald Baer's application of this approach to child development. The chapter also illustrates some variants advocated in recent years by neobehaviorists (*liberal* behaviorists) who have sought to bring the movement into closer proximity with the data of present-day cognitive psychology.

A derivative of behaviorism that rose to prominence in the 1960s and 1970s is *social learning theory,* which includes a present-day version called *contextualism.*

167

In contrast to Watsonian behaviorism, social learning theory does recognize cognitive activity, even while emphasizing the analysis of overt behavior. Precepts and investigative methods of social learning theory and contextualism are traced in Chapter Eight.

But before starting our detailed inspection of these matters, it is useful to recognize that there is considerable confusion about how to characterize conceptual schemes referred to as *behaviorism*. For example, some writers have distinguished between S-R and S-O-R behaviorists (Woodworth, 1929). The S-R designation has been applied to psychologists who focus on observable stimuli (S) and on a person's subsequent response (R), without suggesting what might be happening inside the person between the S and the R. Both Watson and Skinner have often been identified as S-R theorists. In contrast, the S-O-R symbol designates psychologists who are willing to speculate about what occurs within the organism (O) that transposes a stimulus into a response. Different theorists refer to the O function in different ways. Some call it *intervening variables,* some call it *thinking* or *cognitive activity,* and others call it *information processing*. It is possible to assign social learning theorists, contextualists, and certain types of neobehaviorists to the S-O-R camp.

However, objections have been raised about the validity of both the S-R and S-O-R formulas. One complaint is that: "Stimulus-response psychologies lead us to expect that given a stimulus, we might predict the response, and that given a response, we might retrodict the stimulus. . . . This formulation treats acts and feelings as mechanical responses to stimuli, and it treats persons as robots or penny-in-the-slot machines" (Lee, 1988, pp. 151–152). So, according to this observation, children should not be pictured simply as response machines that act only when stimulated by environmental forces. Rather children should be seen as initiators of their own behavior, ones who draw on stimuli from the environment (E). In that event, it might be more reasonable to posit a relationship of $O \rightarrow E \rightarrow O \rightarrow R$. Or, as another possibility, the interaction of O and E to produce R might be pictured as $O \leftrightarrow E = R$. In effect, these conflicting proposals indicate that there is a large measure of disagreement among psychologists about such matters.

A second source of confusion is the abundance of adjectives attached to the word *behaviorism* to distinguish one version from another. As early as the 1920s, A. A. Roback, an early student of behaviorism, identified ten classes and seventeen subclasses of behaviorism that he divided into four general groupings:

> structural behaviorism (focusing on the mechanics of organisms), functional behaviorism (focusing on the relationship between an organism and its environment), psychobehaviorism (allowing consciousness and introspection a role in psychology along with behaviorism), and nominal behaviorism (encompassing theorists such as McDougall who called themselves behaviorists but whose theories included little of Watson's original behavioristic platform). (Logue, 1985, p. 177)

In recent times, different conceptions of behaviorism have borne such varied designations as *original, classical, standard, strict, extreme, methodological, metaphysical, modified, radical, liberal, operant, eclectic, social, paradigmatic, purposive, cognitive, sane, subjective, true*, and *interbehaviorist* (Lee, 1988, p. 81; Logue, 1985, pp. 176–177). Not only is there a multiplicity of such terms, but one author frequently invests a given term with meanings different from those employed by another. Consequently, when reading the professional literature, we do well to inspect with care the details of each author's writings about behaviorism to determine exactly what he or she intends.

The reason Skinner's version of behaviorism is featured in Chapter Seven is that he is the best-known behaviorist of the past half century. He created operant behaviorism and "has more fully and more explicitly explored the implications of a contingency-oriented psychology than any other psychologist" (Lee, 1988, p. 79). And A. C. Catania and S. Harnad (1988, p. 3) state that: "Of all contemporary psychologists, B. F. Skinner is perhaps the most honored and the most maligned, the most widely recognized and the most misrepresented, the most cited and the most misunderstood."

Part Four closes with a perspective that addresses the question, What research methods are associated with different theories, and what are the strengths and limitations of such methods? In answer, the perspective proposes how different theorists' research methods can be influenced by considerations of control, reality, precision, reproducibility, significance, and feasibility.

CHAPTER SEVEN

SKINNER'S OPERANT CONDITIONING

By the time his career ended in 1990, no American research psychologist was better known than Burrhus Frederic Skinner (1904–1990). The public fame of this Harvard professor resulted from his skillful and often controversial application of his learning theory to the solution of practical educational, personal adjustment, and social problems. In the mid-1950s he refined and popularized such learning devices as teaching machines and programmed textbooks (Skinner, 1972). In the late 1960s the behavior modification approach to therapy for disturbed people drew heavily on Skinnerian doctrine. In the 1970s his book *Beyond Freedom and Dignity* (1971) recommended a plan for social control through operant conditioning that he contended would produce an increasingly peaceful, orderly, cooperative, and efficient society. His theory also has clear implications for the field of child development.

In this chapter I trace the outlines of Skinner's system and describe the principal ways the system can be applied to the understanding of child growth and behavior. Later in the chapter I discuss the work of Sidney W. Bijou and Donald M. Baer, who have been leaders among child psychologists in applying Skinnerian concepts to the analysis of child development. Finally, I note some newer departures to illustrate a variety of behaviorist perspectives that have appeared in recent times.

THE NATURE OF OPERANT CONDITIONING

The seeds of Skinner's behaviorism can be traced back to Pavlov's dog. In the early twentieth century the Russian physiologist Ivan Petrovich Pavlov (1849–1936) demonstrated what has become known as *classical conditioning.* He placed meat powder (called an *unconditioned stimulus*) on a dog's tongue, which caused the dog to automatically salivate (called the *unconditioned response*). Then, on a series of subsequent occasions (called *trials*) Pavlov sounded a bell at the same time he gave the food (the meat powder) to the dog. When the food was accompanied by the bell enough times, he found that he could withhold the food and the bell's sound itself would cause the dog to salivate. The bell was now the *conditioned stimulus* that brought about the *conditioned response* of salivating. Classical conditioning, then—which often is called *respondent conditioning*—consists of substituting a new stimulus for an old one by presenting the two at the same time, or nearly the same time, then dropping the old stimulus and allowing the new one to bring about the original response. Pavlov's work inaugurated the era of *S-R* or *stimulus-response* psychology.

American behaviorists adopted the S-R concept as the appropriate model for explaining human behavior without having to speculate about what was possibly going on inside an organism's central nervous system. It was no longer necessary to imagine such things as mind or soul to account for the way people acted. By observing what sorts of stimuli elicited what sorts of responses, psychologists could explain what makes people behave as they do.

One problem that early behaviorists met was that they often could not identify accurately what stimulus was bringing about the responses they observed. Hence they were forced to assume the operation of stimuli they actually could not locate. In the 1930s Skinner suggested a solution to this common problem. He proposed that there was not one kind of conditioning but two. One was the classical S-R relationship demonstrated by Pavlov. The other, and by far the more frequent in human behavior, Skinner labeled *operant* or *instrumental conditioning.* Instead of the behavior being drawn out or elicited by a stimulus, the behavior (response) was simply *emitted* or expressed without any observable stimulus evoking it.

For example, a pigeon in a cage just naturally does pigeon-like things—walking about and pecking. A baby in a cradle just makes natural baby movements—wiggling its arms and legs in a random way. In Skinner's opinion, it is not important to identify the stimulus that started the pecking and the arm and leg movements. Rather, if we are to understand why behavior occurs, it is far more important to inspect the *consequences* of these movements, for the consequences are what come to control actions. The term *consequences* here refers to whether the pigeon's or infant's movements bring satisfaction to the organism. If the pigeon is hungry and happens to peck a plastic lever that drops food pellets into the cage, then this consequence of the food's satisfying the hunger drive may strengthen the tendency for the pigeon to peck the lever again the next time it is hungry and is in the same cage. After the pigeon has had enough trials at this task, it gradually will become more efficient; that is, it will gradually eliminate the previous random walking and pecking at other things and will peck the lever directly when hungry. So we say the pigeon has *learned* lever pecking, and this learning has been caused or controlled by the consequences of fulfilling the hunger need.

It was Skinner's contention that all or nearly all behavior is a result of either respondent (classical) or operant conditioning, with by far the larger part of human behavior being operant as the child increases in age. If the consequences are rewarding, the actions will more likely be repeated the next time the individual is in a similar situation. If the consequences are either painful or simply useless, the actions will less likely be repeated in the future. Rewarding consequences strengthen tendencies to act; nonrewarding consequences weaken tendencies to act the same way again, so eventually the nonrewarding acts will be dropped or *extinguished* entirely.

This is the general idea of classical (respondent) and operant conditioning. However, in this introduction the theory has been oversimplified, and I have used terms that Skinner and his followers would find imprecise and perhaps misleading. For instance, Skinnerians do not approve of such terms as *hunger need* if such terms require that we assume something inside a person that we cannot observe. They also object to such words as *reward* when its use assumes a feeling state that cannot readily be identified and that is considered to be the cause of some sort of behavior. However, I used these terms, just as Skinner himself used them, because they are familiar and explain the issues more easily than if I had started off with only behaviorist definitions. However, at this point I will begin using more standard behaviorist wording in order to delineate the key features of Skinnerian theory.

To begin, I should point out that Skinner on occasion denied that he had constructed a theory (Skinner, 1972, pp. 69–71). He claimed to be more of an empiricist, collecting observable facts of behavior and summarizing them in terms of principles. He proposed that he simply told it as it is. However, in the broad way that *theory* was defined in Chapter One, his formulations do indeed qualify as theory, as his other writings would also attest (Skinner, 1974, pp. 18–20).

He created the concept of *operant* or *instrumental* conditioning to focus prime attention on the importance of consequences in controlling the acts that immediately preceded them. In other words, the act is the operator (operant) or instrument that brings about the consequence.

Types of Consequences

What most people think of as a reward is called a *reinforcer* by behaviorists. A consequence is a *positive reinforcer* if it causes the act to increase in the future when a similar situation arises. For example, if a hungry infant is fed right after he happens to hit a rattle in his crib, the tendency for him to hit the rattle next time he is hungry is increased. This means that feeding has positively reinforced rattle hitting. Likewise, if an affection-hungry school girl picks papers up from around her desk and thus is given a hug by her teacher and told, "You're a great helper, Jenny," then the tendency for Jenny to pick up papers in the future is strengthened. The hug and kind words have positively reinforced the act of tidying up.

Sometimes a child's acts stop an unpleasant condition. For instance, the second-grade teacher is screaming at the children to get into their seats and keep quiet. The unpleasant screaming stops as soon as the children are all in their seats. So the act of sitting down has been instrumental in stopping the unpleasant harangue. The pleasant state of quiet is, for the children, a *negative reinforcer* for sitting down. In effect, a consequence of an action is called a negative reinforcer if the action has caused some unpleasant (*aversive*, in behaviorist terms) condition to stop. Next time the teacher starts ranting at the class, the children can be expected to sit down more promptly because sitting down produced the happy state of quiet the first time.

That is, both positive and negative reinforcement are rewarding. Both increase the likelihood that the child will repeat the same act in similar future circumstances. It is positive reinforcement if it starts a pleasant consequence. It is negative reinforcement if it stops an unpleasant consequence, such as noise or criticism.

A third sort of consequence is *punishment*. Consequences are called punishing or aversive if they reduce the tendency for the child to behave the same way in the future. Punishment, as any parent or teacher knows, is supposed to discourage acts of the same sort on later occasions. Punishment can involve either imposing something unpleasant (spanking, requiring extra homework) or removing something pleasant (taking away privileges).

But punishment is not the only way to eliminate undesired acts. Another way is simply not to reinforce the acts. If a child crosses his eyes in school to get attention but no one pays any attention to this antic, the eye crossing can be expected to stop for it has failed to achieve the desired consequences. In brief, *extinction* of the behavior occurs.

Studies by some behaviorists in the past have caused them to conclude that punishment only temporarily suppresses the expression of undesired behaviors; it does not eliminate or extinguish them. These investigators have claimed that when the punishing agent is not present, the undesired behaviors occur again. However, other analyses of the influence of punishment have caused some learning theorists to disagree that punishment is merely a temporary suppressor. They have concluded instead that punishment can be as effective as nonreinforcement in extinguishing undesired acts (Hilgard & Bower, 1975, pp. 223–225).

The foregoing elements, then, represent the basic framework of operant conditioning. If consequences of acts are reinforcing, then the acts will be learned and will appear again when the child is in similar situations. These reinforced actions become habits and form a pattern of behavior that might be called the child's style of life or personality. Consequences that are unrewarding—either punishing or simply nonreinforcing—result in behaviors being dropped from the child's repertoire of actions.

Skinner's Notion of Learning

In the discussion so far I have used the word *learning* to refer to a child's coming to the point of habitually showing a particular behavior when in a given situation. However, there is really a more precise way to view learning from the standpoint of operant conditioning. You may recall that in the operant type of conditioning, the focus is not on how we get the child to display a behavior in the first place but on what happens to that behavior as the result of the consequences that follow it. From this perspective, learning is not seen as the process of the child's first displaying the behavior but rather as the process of her displaying it consistently—that is, of her responding at a high rate of frequency when in similar stimulus situations. For example, if a nine-year-old girl comes home from playing with neighborhood friends only one time in ten when her mother calls, "Time to come in, Karin," then we would say that Karin has not learned very well to come when called. Her rate of response is only 10 percent. We do not mean Karin is ignorant of how to return home when her mother calls; her occasional correct response shows that the excepted behavior is in her repertoire. But in saying she has not learned very well, we mean she does not respond consistently in this stimulus situation. However, her mother can increase Karin's rate of responding (help her better learn to come when called) by manipulating the consequences. Or, in behaviorist terms, she can rearrange the *reinforcement schedule* to increase her daughter's tendency to come when summoned.

Skinner made particularly useful contributions to the analysis of the effect on behavior of different kinds of reinforcement schedules. For example, the effects on performance differ when *continuous reinforcement* (rewarding every time the desired act occurs) is used rather than *intermittent reinforcement* (rewarding only certain times the act occurs). Furthermore, different schedules of intermittent reinforcement yield different results. A *fixed-ratio* schedule (such as rewarding every third or every fifth response) has a different effect from a *fixed-interval* schedule (rewarding a response after every two minutes or every five minutes). These sorts of schedules, combined with a variety of others, can produce an array of different behavior results (Hilgard & Bower, 1975, pp. 216–217). For example, when an eight-year-old pupil is in the early stages of learning to raise his hand to speak in class rather than to shout out his opinion, he can profitably be rewarded on each occasion that he raises his hand. But after the habit has been well established, intermittent reward will probably serve to maintain the habit against extinction better than continuous reinforcement.

We can summarize Skinner's viewpoint by saying that from his behaviorist perspective child development is a process of the growing individual's learning increasingly complex and refined ways of acting as a result of the consequences that have followed the behavior she or he has attempted. The role of parents and teachers is therefore twofold: (1) to get children to try desirable acts and (2) to arrange consequences of children's acts so that desirable behavior is reinforced and undesirable behavior is extinguished through nonreinforcement or punishment.

CONDITIONED REINFORCEMENT AND CHAINING

One charge frequently aimed at the operant-conditioning model is that the theory is oversimplified. While critics admit that operant conditioning might account for certain simple acts, they claim it cannot explain complex skills or creative thinking. However, Skinner proposed several mechanisms that he believed readily account for any sort of behavior that people exhibit, whether the actions are—as nonbehaviorists might say—mental or physical.

The first mechanism is described in the principle of *conditioned reinforcement*: a consequence (called a *stimulus*) that is not originally a reinforcing one can become reinforcing through repeated association with a consequence that is already reinforcing (Keller & Schoenfeld, 1950, p. 232). In other words, if a mother comes to feed her infant son each time he is hungry, and the consequence of the feeding is that it satisfies the infant's hunger, then after enough repetitions of this act the appearance of mother herself—even without food—becomes reinforcing or satisfying. Mother now has the power of being a reinforcer. She has become a *conditioned* or a *secondary* reinforcer. Her appearance and the associated acts that accompanied the original feeding—her smiling and saying, "What a good boy"— can now be used to reinforce or teach other behaviors. For instance, when the growing infant happens to say "mah" during his babblings, the mother's smile and her comment, "What a smart boy—now say Mama," serve to reinforce the utterance of "mah." Consequently, the chance of the child's uttering "mah" again in the mother's presence is increased.

Not only does a growing child soon build up a significant store of conditioned reinforcements that can serve as rewards for actions, but many of these secondary reinforcers become generalized to other actions. That is, the reinforcer not only strengthens its original act but, by being associated with many actions, comes to strengthen any with which it is connected. For adolescents, money is a strong generalized reinforcer and can be used to strengthen or reward all sorts of behavior. For both younger and older children, such phrases as "good girl" and "that's the way to do it" become generalized reinforcers, attached to many behaviors.

F. S. Keller and W. N. Schoenfeld summarized in the following way the two principles that govern these examples:

> Once established, a secondary reinforcement is independent and nonspecific; it not only will strengthen the same response which produced the original reinforcement, but will also condition a new and unrelated response. Moreover, it will do so even in the presence of a different motive.
>
> Through generalization, many stimuli besides the one correlated with reinforcement acquire reinforcing value—positive or negative. (1950, p. 260)

Two other conditioning functions that help explain complex behavior are shaping and chaining. *Shaping* consists of first reinforcing any gross approximation that the child achieves of a desired refined act. Then, after the gross form of the behavior has been well established, it can be shaped by gradual steps into the ultimate refined form by requiring better and better approximations before reinforcement is provided. For instance, in teaching a child to bat a ball, we first offer praise for her swinging the bat, whether or not she hits the ball. As her swing improves, we no longer praise just any swing, but only those that hit the ball. When she can hit the ball nearly every time, we limit our praise to her hitting the ball into the field in front of her, and we do not praise foul balls that bounce to the side or to the rear. This process of gradually placing more precise limits on the kinds of acts that are reinforced continues, enabling the child to shape her batting skill until she can hit the ball in more precise directions and to specified distances. In a similar fashion, shaping helps expand and refine children's verbal behavior as their utterances are altered by the positive and negative reactions of people with whom they interact.

Chaining enables a person to hook together a sequence of small, individual conditioned acts to compose a complex skill. The process of chaining begins at the final end of the chain rather than at the beginning. Each preceding link of the chain is hooked on by associating it with the link that has already been established through reinforcement. For instance, consider the complex skill known as "having good table manners." We start with a child who yearns for both food and parental approval. Over a sequence of days the child is permitted to eat and is told, "That's fine" and "You're doing a good job" when he uses a fork rather than his fingers for lifting small pieces of meat to his mouth. When the pattern of using the fork is established, we add a new requirement. The child must use a knife and fork to cut large pieces of meat into smaller pieces before he is permitted to eat or is com-plimented for his actions. When he has learned these two links—eating with the fork after cutting up the pieces—we impose a new requirement, that of tucking a napkin into his shirt before he cuts up the meat, picks up pieces with the fork, eats, and is complimented. By such a process an extended set of habits or conditioned links can be formed into a complicated skill.

In summary, the simple mechanism of reinforcement not only accounts for specific simple acts, but the processes of secondary reinforcement, stimulus generalization, shaping (response discrimination), and chaining can account for all sorts of complex activities, in the opinion of behaviorists. And, they say, it is not necessary for us to fashion these processes consciously; they occur as natural behavior in everyone.

THE SCOPE OF SKINNER'S THEORY

In at least three important ways, Skinner's theory can be called broad in scope. First, it is not limited to any cultural setting; it purports to explain development in all societies. Second, its principles apply to all age levels, from the prenatal period to death. Third, it claims to explain all varieties of behavior—physical, mental, social, emotional. Although the first two claims have not attracted much criticism, the third has been the center of an extended debate, so it warrants close attention.

As noted earlier, behaviorism was originally a reaction against *mentalism*. It was a reaction against the notion that human action was caused by ideas or feelings that arose in an unobservable place called *mind* or *soul*. Furthermore, behaviorism was a reaction against mentalists' research methods, which consisted largely of introspection, of a philosopher pondering about the nature of his own thoughts and emotions and then proposing elements or functions of the mind that he thought produced or controlled the thoughts and emotions.

Early behaviorists like Watson and Max Meyer claimed that if psychology is truly to become a science, it must focus solely on objective, publicly witnessed information. Such things as thoughts, mind, and feelings should have no place in this proposed science of human behavior. However, critics of behaviorism said that it is nonsense to deny the existence of such obvious phenomena as thoughts and feelings simply because these things are not directly seen by people outside the skin of the person who is doing the thinking and feeling. In sum, over the past half century behaviorists, including Skinner, have been charged with proposing a simplistic, mindless psychology. But Skinner, while admitting the charges are valid criticisms of early behaviorists, denied that they applied to him. In order to distin-guish himself from the others, he created two labels: (1) *methodological behavior-ism* to identify those who would ignore the existence of thoughts and feelings and

(2) *radical behaviorism* to identify his own position, which recognizes thoughts and feelings as normal "covert acts" and accepts introspection as a legitimate mode of inquiry (Skinner, 1974, pp. 13–18).

According to Skinner, the sin of mentalism—as practiced by Freud, Piaget, and many others—was to focus exclusively on mental events. This focus distracted their attention away from an analysis of the external environment's consequences that are the elements, he said, that really account for why people act as they do. But in censuring the mentalists, Skinner did not uncritically embrace the methodological-behaviorist position of Watson and, more recently, of J. R. Kantor. Rather, Skinner criticized methodological behaviorism for committing the opposite error:

> By dealing exclusively with external antecedent events, it turned away from self-observation and self-knowledge. Radical behaviorism restores some kind of balance. It does not insist upon truth by agreement and can therefore consider events taking place in the private world within the skin. It does not call these events unobservable, and it does not dismiss them as subjective. It simply questions the nature of the object observed and the reliability of the observations. (1974, pp. 16–17)

So Skinner accepted thoughts and feelings, but he believed that people's techniques for investigating them are not well developed or very trustworthy. Consequently, he judged it best to depend heavily on an analysis of environmental conditions and people's observable reactions in order to understand a person's genetic and environmental history. He found it of no explanatory help to create such words as *mind* or *consciousness* to account for a person's inner life. He contended (1974, p. 17) that "what is felt or introspectively observed is not some nonphysical world of consciousness, mind, or mental life but the observer's own body." In other words, Skinner did not divide the person into the traditional opposing aspects of physical and mental. He considered the individual to be an integrated unit. Some actions are observed by people outside the individual's skin (overt behavior) while other actions, which are internal, are observed only by the individual through introspection (covert behavior).

HEREDITY VERSUS ENVIRONMENT

Behaviorists traditionally have been criticized for underestimating the role of heredity in development. However, Skinner reacted to such criticism by again distinguishing between the viewpoint of methodological behaviorists and his own. Several decades ago, Watson claimed he could take any healthy infant and raise it to become whatever he chose: doctor, lawyer, artist, beggar, thief. However, Skinner (1974, p. 221) dismissed this claim by calling it a "careless remark" and proposed instead what he considered a more balanced view of the relative contributions of genetic endowment and environmental influences.

To understand Skinner's own position, we should first recognize that he believed the basic drive behind all behavior, human as well as nonhuman, is to survive. All actions are designed to promote the survival of both the individual and the species. Humans, like other species, inherit biological potentials that serve in some ways to enhance and in other ways to limit the chance of surviving in different environments. The potentials that a person inherits have been determined over past eons of time by the survival of the fittest, Darwin's natural selection. People with those traits that promoted survival lived on to produce offspring with these same high-survival characteristics. People lacking such traits died early, so their strains were not reproduced.

For purposes of analysis, it is useful to divide inherited characteristics into two types, although in actual practice the two merge into each other. The first type is well suited to stable environments, and the second to variable, unpredictable environments. That is, some environmental conditions—conditions of climate or the nature of predators and diseases, for example—are relatively permanent over time. In these environments that are stable over a period of centuries, a species can directly inherit traits that arm it for survival—traits like a heavy, white fur coat to match the arctic snow color and instincts or reflexes that give ample warning of approaching predators. But frequently, environmental conditions cannot be directly predicted. Conditions change from year to year, even from day to day. In such settings it is not helpful to inherit a specific, limited reflex or instinct. Rather, it is better to inherit the ability to change behavior on the basis of the environment's reaction. In other words, a species can inherit learning capacity, the ability to profit from the consequences of behavior. This is the second sort of inheritance, which Skinner considered the most important thing humans derive from their genetic endowment. Humans' high level of intelligence or adaptability results from an unusually sensitive genetic potential for operant conditioning.

When Skinner was pressed to tell exactly which behaviors or personality traits he believed people inherit and which he thought they learn, he refrained from identifying specific items, for he claimed that not enough research has been completed to give clear answers. But he stated that many of the things that other theorists, such as Gesell and Freud, attributed to heredity are actually learned through conditioning. Skinner concluded that

> genetic causes sometimes become a kind of dumping ground: any aspect of behavior which at the moment escapes analysis in terms of contingencies of reinforcement is likely to be assigned to genetic endowment, and we are likely to accept the explanation because we are so accustomed to going no further than a stage of the organism. (1974, p. 44)

Skinner, then, would not place himself at either extreme in the nature–nurture controversy. And he rejected the methodological behaviorists' contention that human personality is completely malleable, ready to be formed into whatever pattern the controllers of reinforcement desire. In his novel about a utopian community, *Walden Two* (1948), Skinner described a society in which all children have a highly similar environment until age ten since they are all raised together in communal centers over the first decade of their lives rather than in individual families. Yet even with this common environment, the children living in Walden Two displayed a range of intelligence "almost as great as in the population at large. This seems to be true of other abilities and skills as well" (Skinner, 1948, p. 104). In effect, Skinner proposed that genetic endowment accounts for a significant amount of the variation among children. He was not a thoroughgoing environmentalist. Nevertheless, he appeared to assign a more important role to environmental forces than do the other theorists studied so far in this book.

THE STAGES OF CHILD REARING

In several previous chapters we have seen that theories of development are some-times divided into *stage* and *nonstage* models. A stage model typically pictures the growth of the child as a series of distinct steps or phases. At around a particular age, the child changes noticeably from being one sort of person into being another sort. Then, for some time, the child retains the characteristics of this second sort until once more she or he makes a noticeable change and reaches a new level or phase of growth.

Contrasting with this conception of sudden change from one phase to another is the nonstage model that pictures growth as a very gradual process. Changes occur in minuscule amounts. It is true that in both stage and nonstage theories the child at age six will be obviously different from the way she looked and acted at age three. But to nonstage theorists she has not arrived at six by any sudden leaps or insights. Instead, age six is just an accumulation of very slight alterations since age three.

Generally, stage theories have been proposed by investigators who say heredity plays the greater role in development, whereas nonstage models have been devised by those who give more credit to the environment. This linking of stages with hereditarians and gradual growth with environmentalists is not a logical necessity. Gradual growth could reasonably be attributed to a genetic time schedule, and stages might be accounted for by sudden major changes in environmental forces. However, the observed linking has been the dominant trend, and Skinner's theory fits the pattern by being a nonstage model.

Skinner saw development as a continuous, incremental sequence of specific conditioned acts. It is not that he was unable to conceive of behavior being studied in terms of age or the passage of time, "as in the development of a child's verbal behavior or his problem-solving strategies or in the sequence of stages through which a person passes on his way from infancy to maturity" (Skinner, 1972, pp. 567–573). But he felt that (1) it is more accurate to view the developmental steps as very small ones, and (2) it is unprofitable to focus only on *what* happens at a particular stage and to ignore the question *why* it occurs. In other words, he was critical not only of picturing growth as major jumps followed by lengthy plateaus, but also of the developmentalists', or what he referred to as *structuralists'*, failing to explain why these changes come about, other than to state that the cause is an assumed internal maturation whose timing follows a genetic clock. Skinner's interest was in the management or control of development, not in just describing what it looks like when it takes place.

So in his writings he made almost no point of describing the characteristics of children at different age levels. Despite this, he did give some prominent attention to stages, though his stages were *phases of the environmental treatment of the child,* treatment designed to produce optimal development. In short, he prescribed ways to treat children at different age levels to promote their happiness and well-being. To explain what these prescriptions were, I draw upon two of Skinner's publications, which were issued in the middle of his academic career. The first is an article from a 1945 *Ladies Home Journal* describing an air-conditioned, sanitary box in which he and his wife raised their infant daughter (Skinner, 1972, pp. 567–573). The second is the novel *Walden Two* (Skinner, 1948), and particularly the series of chapters detailing child-care methods in the utopian community. I will use child rearing in Walden Two as the focus of the discussion.

Ideal Child Rearing

In the psychologist's ideal child-rearing system, boys and girls are not raised by their individual families but are brought up in communal care centers till they reach puberty. At around age thirteen, adolescents, individually or in pairs, set up their own living quarters in the apartment complex that houses the adults in the mythical rural American town called Walden Two.

The first two decades of life in Walden Two are divided into five child-raising stages: (1) a lower-nursery stage for infants from birth to age 1, (2) an upper-nursery stage for those ages 1 and 2, (3) a middle-childhood phase for ages 3–6, (4) later childhood for ages 7–13, and (5) adolescence after age 13.

The basic philosophy during this entire two-decade span is that it is important to fulfill children's needs as quickly and as completely as possible in their earliest years. Then, very gradually, the demands and annoyances of normal life are introduced at a scientifically controlled rate that ensures that children can master them without acquiring negative feelings. This system of *behavioral engineering* or controlled operant conditioning is designed to encourage "the productive and strengthening emotions—love and joy. . . . But sorrow and hate—and the high-voltage excitements of anger, fear, and rage—are out of proportion with the needs of modern life, and they're wasteful and dangerous." In Walden Two such emotions, along with jealousy and envy, which "breed unhappiness," are almost unknown (Skinner, 1948, p. 83).

This pattern of providing an initially easy environment that becomes more and more difficult as children acquire the ability to adjust is intended to yield the reward of "escape from the petty emotions which eat the heart out of the unprepared." Children raised in Walden Two not only get the satisfaction of pleasant social relations, they also become far more efficient workers "because they can stick to a job without suffering the aches and pains which soon beset most of us. They get new horizons, for they are spared the emotions characteristic of frustration and failure" (Skinner, 1948, pp. 90–91).

This is the general strategy of child rearing. During the first five years after birth adults see that no important need goes unsatisfied, so the child begins life practically free of anxiety and frustration. But eventually, through the mastery of gradually increasing frustrations, youths in Walden Two experience "the heartache and the thousand natural shocks that flesh is heir to" (Skinner, 1948, p. 93).

With this overall plan in mind, let us now consider some of the ways Walden Two's adults engineer the environment to produce such admirable results.

Birth to age one   Infants in Walden Two do not stay at home with their mothers but are collected together in the "lower nursery," each baby in an air-conditioned, enclosed crib like the "baby box" in which the Skinners raised their second daughter for the first year of her life. The purpose of the box is to furnish the infant with a healthful climate, free from the confinement of clothes and blankets and from dust and germs. The baby, clad only in a diaper, lies or sits or crawls about on an easily cleaned plastic mattress, plays with rattles and toys hung from the ceiling of the box, and gazes at the passersby through the large glass window that forms one side of the enclosed crib. The walls of the box are insulated from noise and temperature changes. A shade lowered over the window when the baby is asleep prevents light from disturbing the infant's naps.

After Skinner's own daughter, Deborah, had been in such a box for eleven months, he reported that because of the box's filtered air:

> The baby's eyes, ears, and nostrils remain fresh and clean. A weekly bath is enough, provided the face and diaper region are frequently washed. . . . She has always enjoyed deep and extended sleep, and her feeding and eliminative habits have been extraordinarily regular. . . . Although there have been colds in the family, . . . the baby has completely escaped. She has never had a diaper rash. . . .
>
> One of the commonest objections [of friends] was that we were going to raise a "softie" who would be unprepared for the real world. But instead of becoming hypersensitive, our baby has acquired a surprisingly serene tolerance for annoyances. She is not bothered by the clothes she wears at playtime, she is not frightened by loud or sudden noises, she is not frustrated by toys out of reach. . . . A tolerance for any annoyance can be built up by administering it in controlled dosages, rather than in the usual accidental way. Certainly there is no reason to annoy the child throughout the whole of its infancy, merely to prepare it for later childhood. (Skinner, 1972, pp. 570–572)

In Walden Two the parents come each day or so to see the baby, to take it from the box and play with it a while. But this personal attention and display of affection are offered not only by the parents but also by the men and women who are in charge of the nursery. The purpose of sharing the responsibility for infants is to enable a child to imitate numerous desirable models who combine to form "a sort of essential happy adult. He can avoid the idiosyncrasies of a single parent" (Skinner, 1948, p. 119).

Ages one and two   When children are around one year old in Walden Two, they move from their individual cubicles in the lower nursery to the upper nursery. This advanced nursery is composed of several small playrooms furnished with child-size equipment, a dressing room with a locker for each child, and small air-conditioned sleeping rooms. Clad only in diapers, children sleep on easily cleaned plastic mattresses. At playtime they are either naked or in training pants.

Child-raising practices continue to be guided by the principles followed in the lower nursery. Children's needs are met as soon and as completely as possible, with the result that the young child still knows nothing of frustration, anxiety, or fear. This does not mean, however, that the child has no experiences that might bring about frustration. It means, instead, that the behavioral engineers who schedule the child-raising program introduce potentially discouraging experiences "as carefully as we introduce any other emotional situation beginning at about six months" (Skinner, 1948, p. 100). For example, some of the toys children are given are designed to build perseverance.

The personnel of the nursery is balanced between men and women so as to "eliminate all the Freudian problems which arise from the asymmetrical relation to the female parent" (Skinner, 1948, p. 120).

Ages three to six, middle childhood   From the standpoint of sleeping accommodations, this period is divided into two segments. At ages three and four each child is given responsibility for her own cot in a dormitory, and she is introduced to wearing regular clothing. At ages five and six children move into a complex of alcoves, each furnished like a regular room and holding three or four children with their beds and personal belongings. They are expected to gradually assume increased responsibility for the upkeep of their quarters. A careful schedule of conditioning in ethical behavior is conducted so that the foundations of ethical conduct are virtually complete by age six.

Ages seven to thirteen, later childhood   At age seven children move from the alcoves into a complex of small rooms, each room designed for two children. At frequent intervals roommates are changed so children learn to live with different sorts of age-mates. They no longer eat in a dining room for children but use the adults' cafeteria.

It is impossible to distinguish formal from informal education in Walden Two since children are being taught by designed conditioning schedules wherever they are—in their living quarters, on the playground, and in the community's workshops, laboratories, studios, reading rooms, and fields. Early in their lives, children are given work to do, so they come to have a personal stake in contributing to the community.

Walden Two's behavioral engineers claim that their education system is far superior to that of the typical town because teachers do not waste time duplicating home training or changing the cultural and intellectual habits that children might have acquired outside of school.

From the child's first months after birth, the community depends on his natural curiosity and natural needs to motivate him to learn. The behavioral engineers appeal to humans' "drive to control the environment. . . . We don't need to motivate by creating spurious needs. . . . Promising paradise or threatening hellfire is, we assumed, generally admitted to be unproductive" (Skinner, 1948, pp. 87, 101–102).

The education system has no grade levels since "everyone knows that talents and abilities don't develop at the same rate in different children" (Skinner, 1948, p. 97). Pupils are encouraged to progress as rapidly as they like in any field, and they are not expected to waste time in a classroom being bored by activities they have outgrown. No subjects like English or social studies or science are taught. Rather, children are taught techniques of learning and thinking. Then they are provided chances to learn geography, literature, the sciences, and the like by themselves, based on the firm foundation they have received in ways of thinking: logic, statistics, scientific method, psychology, and mathematics. Children who do not appear to have an aptitude for learning a particular skill or type of knowledge are not required to do so. In other words, Walden Two's educators do not "waste time teaching the unteachable" (Skinner, 1948, p. 97).

Age thirteen and beyond, adolescence   As the child passes puberty and becomes sexually potent, Walden Two does not require that he or she postpone mature forms of sexual gratification until age twenty or older. Instead, the adolescent finds "an immediate and satisfying expression of his natural impulses . . . very different from the secrecy and shame which most of us recall in connection with sex at some time or other" (Skinner, 1948, p. 111). When teenagers fall in love, they become engaged, at which time they consult the Manager of Marriages. He examines their interests, school records, and health status. If there are major discrepancies between the couple in intellectual abilities or temperament, they are advised not to marry or, at least, to postpone marriage for a while. But those who do seem well matched are encouraged to marry and begin having children when they are still age fifteen or sixteen. This early satisfaction of sexual needs, combined with young people's early and gradual introduction to the world of work, makes the period of adolescence "brief and painless."

As for their living accommodations, the young teenagers move, at least temporarily, into rooms in the adult apartment complex, where they usually live in pairs. At the time of marriage, or whenever else he or she chooses, the individual can participate in building a larger room for himself or herself or can refurbish an existing room that has become available.

In effect, during the latter teens the youth gradually achieves adult status without the extended period of stress that adolescence in American society has ostensibly involved.

BIJOU AND BAER'S ADDITIONS TO RADICAL BEHAVIORISM

Perhaps the best known of the child development theorists adhering closely to a Skinnerian behaviorist viewpoint have been Sidney W. Bijou and Donald M. Baer. A significant contribution of these two authors has been their adopting three developmental periods suggested by J. R. Kantor (1959) and their illustrating in detail how traditional behaviorism can account for the changes observed in children at each level of growth. The labels attached to the three successive stages have been *universal, basic,* and *societal.*

The *universal stage,* which extends from the prenatal months until symbolic behavior or language becomes prominent at around age two, derives its name from the fact that the growth of infants in all societies is much alike during these first years. Although the infant interacts with the environment and thus is influenced by the consequences of his or her actions, the greater determinant of behavior at this time is the child's maturing biological nature. So environmental stimuli play a very limited role in controlling the infant's "simple but self-preserving respondents" and in guiding the development of other behaviors related to "maintaining the biological necessities of life" (Bijou & Baer, 1965, pp. 2–3). The causes of similarities among children in all societies at this stage are primarily the basic biological similarities of the human species, which are the focus of attention in infancy. But, in addition, the social and physical environments are much the same from one culture to another, "not only because of the similarity in limitations imposed by extreme biological immaturity but also because of the extensive uniformity in infant-caring practices" (Bijou & Baer, 1965, p. 179).

The *basic* or second stage of development covers the years between about age two and ages five or six. By now the child's biological development is sufficiently stable to meet her basic needs, so she is more effective in interacting with the environment and can devote more energy to developing psychological behaviors. The patterns of action acquired during these preschool years depend heavily on the sort of social environment the child's family provides, although part of the child's characteristics are still determined by her biological structure, which results from her genetic inheritance.

During the basic stage, the personality structure is formed through the kinds of opportunities and contingencies the child's parents and other family members habitually provide. In these years the child's basic discriminations and forms of behavior are acquired.

The *societal* or third stage development begins around the time the child enters the primary grades and continues throughout the years of schooling. During this period, a myriad of influences from this culture serve to alter and expand the basic pattern of action or personality structure that was fabricated through biological inheritance and the nurturing practices of his family.

In sum, Bijou and Baer demonstrated how respondent and operant conditioning principles can account for the similarities and differences among children at three successive stages of growth.

Responses to Criticism

In addition to applying radical behaviorism to the interpretation of stages of development, Bijou responded to critics who charge that behaviorism as a learning theory can neither account for child development in general nor explain the causes behind development. He also answered those who claim that radical behaviorism views the child as only a passive organism and that practical applications of conditioning can harm children.

In reply to the first of these criticisms, Bijou stated that while the radical behaviorism model is yet incomplete and therefore is still "on the way to becoming a mature theory," it is nevertheless a "comprehensive approach, including all the essential components of a system" (Bijou, 1979, p. 4). Specifically, modern behaviorism

1. Is founded on a clearly stated philosophy "that the subject matter of psychology is the continuous interaction between a behaving organism and physical and social events that can be observed objectively. . . . Therefore, reductionism, or the analysis of psychological interactions in terms of biological, physical, or chemical processes, is rejected totally" (Bijou, 1979, p. 4).
2. Is a *general* theory whose basic tenets account for (a) the strengthening or weakening of relationships between the child and her environment, (b) changes in abilities and skills, (c) a child's pattern of remembering and forgetting, (d) the transfer of learning from one situation to another, and (e) motivation, emotion, and conflict.
3. Has an established research methodology.
4. Has a precise method for translating basic research into practical applications.

Critics have also claimed that radical behaviorism does not adequately explain the causes underlying children's actions because it fails to identify the events of the past that have contributed to the child's present personality. In reply, Bijou contended that behaviorists are not oblivious to the child's developmental history. However, what is important about this history is not the past events themselves but rather the way such events have shaped the child's skills and attitudes that exist today. Since behaviorists believe that looking to the past cannot inform them accurately of what residue past events have left in the child's present life, they choose instead to observe the child systematically today in order to determine what the present-day consequences are of the child's "interactional history; that is, we learn what the specific events in his or her functional environment mean to him or her" (Bijou, 1979, pp. 5–6).

A further charge frequently leveled at behaviorists is that they view children as passive objects manipulated by environmental forces, objects that "must be stimulated. Hence . . . the person is not seen as playing an active, contributory role in his or her own development" (R. M. Lerner, 1976, p. 279). Bijou wrote that this criticism may be true of Watson's original methodological behaviorism but not of radical behaviorism. The modern behaviorist believes that in every interaction with the environment, children contribute their own responses and internal stimuli, which have been determined by their genetic structure and personal history. Furthermore, as children develop, they respond increasingly to stimuli and environmental factors they themselves have produced, so that they are engaging in active self-management. But this does not mean children's behavior is directed toward some inherent goal, such as the goal of self-actualization in humanistic theory (Chapter Twelve) or of formal operational thought in Piaget's model of cognitive development (Chapter Nine) (Bijou, 1979, pp. 7–8).

Behavior Management

In recent years one of the most popular applications of behaviorism has been in the use of operant conditioning for *behavior management* or *behavior modification.* Such conditioning has been employed by parents for socializing their children, by teachers seeking to control pupils' classroom behavior, and by therapists attempting to alter clients' undesirable habits and phobias. However, objections have been raised in a number of quarters on the grounds that these practices are manipulative, violate human rights, and often harm those who are the objects of the conditioning. Bijou replied that the principles involved are certainly not inhumane but, rather, are simply the normal ones underlying all behavior, human and nonhuman alike. Therefore utilizing the principles consciously and systematically is not an act of malice or exploitation but is just good sense, for it increases the efficiency in the behavior management that parents, teachers, and therapists all normally attempt. As for potential harm that may result, Bijou stated that "this is true for the practical application of any scientific finding when the applier is not adequately trained to the task" (Bijou, 1979, p. 9).

Finally, critics have claimed that behaviorism is useful for analyzing only the simplest stimulus-response learning but fails to account for the complexities of children's language development, problem solving, and creativity. Bijou answered that radical behaviorism is yet a new science, still incomplete, but one that displays great potential for explaining all of these phenomena in terms of observable interactions of children with their environment.

ENHANCED BEHAVIORISM

Although the proportion of psychologists in the behaviorism camp has dwindled since the 1950s, the people currently allied with the movement include a goodly number of spirited innovators dedicated to refining and extending the theory. Their contributions may be in book form or in such behaviorist-oriented journals as *Behaviorism* (started in 1972) and *Journal of Experimental Analysis of Behavior,* as well as in less parochial periodicals, such as *The Journal of Mind and Behavior* and *American Psychologist.* The following three examples illustrate something of the range of topics represented by these contributions.

Multiple-Term Contingencies

In her book *Beyond Behaviorism,* V. L. Lee (1988, pp. 61–62) explained that

> a contingency is an if-then relation between behavior and an end result. . . . If you exceed the speed limit, your chance of getting a ticket increases; if you talk, you hear your own voice; . . . [so] the behavior is required if the end result is to occur. A causal relation is at the heart of the contingency, in the sense that the behavior makes a difference. It produces something that *would not* otherwise occur or prevents something that *would* otherwise occur. . . . Radical behaviorism, the

philosophy of operant psychology, assumes that many acts are shaped and maintained by contingencies of which we are not aware. It assumes that the contingencies of which we are aware constitute only a subset of the total number of contingencies.

Lee portrays every *action* in life as an if-then contingency (*behavior* → *consequence* or *means* → *end*), thereby making such contingencies the basic units of operant behaviorism and, for that matter, of all psychology as a science. "A psychology of action . . . [implies] that in conducting our lives we pursue ends and vary the means to those ends, whether consciously or not" (1988, p. 151). From such a perspective, an individual's complete psychological life is comprised of the entire collection of contingencies found in that person's repertoire of behavior. Child development becomes the process of children accumulating an ever-growing assemblage of actions—that is, of *means* → *end* units.

One of the criticisms of behaviorism has been that it has oversimplified the analysis of people's activity by drawing so much of its evidence from laboratory experiments with nonhuman subjects—white rats, pigeons, and the like. When the generalizations about contingencies derived in such settings are then applied to predicting human behavior, the predictions have often proven faulty. In diagnosing these problem cases, certain behaviorists have proposed that the difficulty lies in the limited number of terms included in the contingency statement. For example, a two-term contingency statement includes only a description of (1) the behavior and (2) the consequence. A two-term statement usually works for certain kinds of events: "If you brush your teeth with peppermint toothpaste, you get a peppermint taste" (Lee, 1988, p. 61). But even in such a simple example as this, the two-term contingency statement fails if there is something wrong with your taste buds. As a solution, M. Sidman (1986) joined others in proposing that multiple-term contingencies need to be adopted to account more accurately for many kinds of behavior. A three-term contingency could be a statement that includes one environmental condition, a behavior, and a consequence: "If a police car is driving behind your car when you exceed the speed limit, your chance of getting a ticket increases." A four-term contingency could consist of a behavior, two environmental conditions, and an outcome: "If you vigorously exercise when the atmospheric temperature is over 100 degrees and the humidity is over 90 percent, your chances of suffering heat prostration are increased." Such a statement can be turned into a five-term contingency if such a personal characteristic as age is added to the formula: "People over age 70 are more likely than people under age 40 to suffer heat prostration if they exercise vigorously when the temperature is over 100 and the humidity over 90."

Clearly this notion that events result from a combination of causal factors is hardly new. A belief in multiple causation is implied every time someone describes such a factor as atmospheric temperature as "a necessary but not sufficient cause." In like manner, a child's being raised in a poor neighborhood cannot be considered the single cause of membership in a youth gang but, rather, only one of a number of contributing conditions. So the point of mentioning multiple-term contingencies here is not to suggest that it is a novel concept. My purpose is to illustrate the way some behaviorists have responded to the criticism that they have been simplistic in depicting causal relations. By applying the concept of multiple-term contingencies, they are able to add precision to explanations of why different people act as they do in different situations.

Egoistic and Altruistic Acts and Character Traits

John B. Watson would have considered the study of such constructs as *character traits* to be far outside the realm of true psychology. Yet the study of unviewable traits is not unusual within the ranks of present-day behaviorists. For instance, in the journal *Behaviorism,* E. Sober (1989) offered a philosophical analysis of *egoism* and *altruism* as motivators of human behavior. Sober first granted that some people's characters are more egoistic (self-serving) and other people's more altruistic (other-serving), but then he concluded that no one's behavior toward others is driven solely by a single trait—egoism or altruism. Instead, any act—whether judged egoistic or altruistic—is governed by a combination of the individual's preferences, especially by the extent to which, in each particular situation, self-interest and others' interests are mutually supporting or are in conflict. (*Mutual support* means that an action simultaneously promotes one's own welfare and that of others; *conflict* means that an action sacrifices either one's own needs or the needs of others.) Under mutual support conditions, we cannot judge whether an individual's character is egoistic or altruistic, since the same act fulfills the needs of both the actor and the recipients. So it is only under conflict conditions that we can judge whether a person's character is more egoistic or altruistic. In effect, not every situation provides the opportunity to decide whether the actor has a more or less altruistic character. "Indeed, it is a possibility not to be dismissed lightly that altruists seldom act altruistically. This is not to say that they act selfishly. Rather, the point is that altruists may seldom find themselves in . . . choice situations" that require them to sacrifice their own welfare for the good of others (Sober, 1989, p. 101).

And like Sober, a variety of other behaviorists of various stripes have been including cognitivist concepts in their analyses of people's actions.

Compatible Perspectives

When behaviorists and cognitive psychologists have written about each other, they have typically adopted a pugilistic approach, bashing members of the opposite camp with charges of engaging in specious logic, failing to make accurate predictions, or practicing unsound methods of data collection and analysis. Although such bouts still take place in the professional literature (L. Miller, 1988; Moore, 1990; Skinner, 1984, 1985; Stemmer, 1989), an increasing number of articles recognize virtue in both behaviorist and cognitivist positions. This attitude of tolerance is exemplified in R. Schnaitier's (1987) claim that mental models do not represent alternatives to behaviorist explanations but, rather, fill a different and complementary explanatory niche to that of behaviorism. His point is that behaviorism and cognitivism do not address the same thing. The object of behaviorism, he contended, is to establish the relation between behavior and the context of its occurrence. In contrast, the object of cognitivism is to establish the design of the internal machinery through which functioning organisms are capable of behaving in context.

In somewhat the same manner, M. Mishkin and T. Appenzeller (1987) reconciled the putative differences between behaviorist and cognitivist interpretations of habits, learning, and behavior by suggesting that learning may be built on two quite different systems—one of them the source of noncognitive habits (behaviorism) and the other the source of cognitive memory (mentalism).

In a different vein, R. A. Kleinginna and A. M. Kleinginna (1988) concluded from their historical review of experimental psychology that experimenters operating from behaviorist, functionalist, and cognitive perspectives have been broadening their areas of study and recognizing commonalities rather than differences among their theoretical positions and research findings.

The question of commonalities has led to an animated debate over the suggestion that present-day cognitive psychology is not a new paradigm but merely a disguised version of behaviorism (Chaplin, 1987; Martindale, 1987). Academicians also continue to argue over A. C. Catania's proposal of a *synthetic behaviorism* that combines the language and practice of behaviorists and cognitivists in a manner intended to resolve long-standing differences (Paniagua, 1986).

In short, the practice of modern-day behaviorism includes a growing diversity of attempts to achieve a rapprochement with the cognitive models that have come to dominate the field of child development in recent decades.

PRACTICAL APPLICATIONS

Behaviorism in all its modern varieties has yielded a substantial body of practical implications for child raising, education, and therapy.

Skinner's model served as the foundation for the programmed textbooks and teaching machines that achieved their greatest popularity in the late 1950s and early 1960s. Skinnner advocated the preparation of *linear learning programs* consisting of logically ordered small steps of information presented to learners, who are required to respond at each step (filling in an answer in an incomplete sentence). Learners then receive immediate feedback about how accurate their answers—and thereby their learning—are at that point. It was Skinner's intention to have the steps arranged so gradually and logically that learners would be correct nearly every time they answered, with the resultant reinforcement (feedback) strengthening the permanence of each stimulus-response learning bond. Principles from this early model of programmed instruction are observed today in many of the *learning packages* being developed for the microcomputers that are playing a rapidly expanding role in classroom and home instruction. In addition, the international *mastery-learning* instructional movement draws on Skinnerian principles for portions of its methodology (Block & Anderson, 1975; Keller & Sherman, 1974).

In the mid-1980s, Skinner rebuked educators for what he labeled "the shame of

American education." He argued that students could learn twice as much as they currently learned with the same amount of time and effort. He proposed that such a goal could be achieved if (1) the aims of education were clarified, (2) each student was permitted to advance at his or her own pace, and (3) the problem of motivation was solved with programmed instructional materials. In Skinner's opinion, much of the fault for the schools' instructional inefficiency lay in the cognitive psychology which, he contended, was taught in the nation's teacher-preparation institutions. He would replace cognitive theory with operant-conditioning technology, thereby equipping teachers to provide more efficient instruction (Skinner, 1984).

Skinner's theory also contributed in a major way to the behavior modification techniques described in Chapter Eight, with the effectiveness of such procedures being demonstrated by a growing quantity of empirical research (Kazdin, 1981, pp. 34–57). For example, findings in studies of preschool, elementary school, and special-class pupils "have indicated that when a teacher pays any kind of attention to unruly conduct, such behavior tends to increase (reinforcement); when she directs her attention to desirable personal-social behavior (reinforcement) and totally ignores undesirable behavior, that behavior tends to decrease (extinction)" (Bijou, 1985).

Behaviorism's practical applications in education and therapy have achieved international scope with the establishment of such organizations as the Association for the Advancement of Behavior Therapy and the International Association of Behavior Analysis. Behavioral courses and service programs have been introduced in such diverse nations as the United States, Britain, Brazil, West Germany, Peru, Australia, Colombia, and New Zealand.

As a final item of practical application, I should note that people who have heard of Skinner's baby box often ask, "Whatever happened to the infant daughter who spent the first months of her life in an Air-Crib?" To satisfy such curiosity, M. Forbes and F. Block (1990, p. 247) report that when Deborah Skinner grew to adulthood, she became a "successful artist, married to a political scientist. . . . Skinner's older daughter, Julie, who was not raised in an Air-Crib, . . . graduated from Radcliffe and later received a doctorate in psychology . . . , [then became] a professor of educational psychology at Indiana University and married a sociologist. Julie raised both her daughters in Air-Cribs."

SKINNER'S OPERANT CONDITIONING: AN ASSESSMENT

I feel that Skinner deserves high scores on six of the criteria proposed in Chapter One.

Skinner's model is clearly described (item 2), enjoying the advantage over mentalist theories of not including in its elements such nonobservable, internal items as ego or conscience, items whose characteristics are difficult to depict to other people.

As attested by *Walden Two* and the programmed learning and behavior modification programs that educators and therapists have adopted in recent years, Skinner's theory offers very detailed guidance for child-rearing practices (item 4).

SKINNER'S THEORY

How well do I think the theory meets the standards?

Standards	Very well	Moderately well	Very poorly
1. Reflects the real world of children		X	
2. Is clearly understandable	X		
3. Explains the past and predicts the future		X	
4. Guides child rearing	X		
5. Is internally consistent	X		
6. Is economical		X	
7. Is falsifiable	X		
8. Is supported by convincing evidence		X	
9. Adapts to new data		NB	Sk
10. Is novel	W	Sk	
11. Is comprehensive		X	
12. Stimulates new discoveries	X		
13. Is durable			X
14. Is self-satisfying		X	

Since the Skinnerian model is founded on empirical studies of overt behavior, and the mechanisms that account for behavior are rather simple, the theory has the qualities of internal consistency (item 5) and falsifiability (item 7). It has also led to a great deal of research and practical application (item 12). It has helped lead to the extensions of behaviorism found in this chapter and Chapter Eight and to the applications mentioned earlier in the realms of programmed instruction and behavior modification practices.

However, strong criticisms have been raised about the theory's being overly simple, unrealistically economical (item 6). This ostensible oversimplification has caused critics to question how adequately the theory reflects the real world of children (item 1) and how well it explains the past and predicts the future (item 3). In particular, Skinner has been charged with extending conclusions derived from animal experiments—primarily with pigeons and rats—to humans, without accounting properly for differences of intellectual quality among the species. For example, Noam Chomsky (1967), as a leader in the field of psycholinguistics, argued that Skinner has been imprecise in analyzing such commonsense terms as *want, like,* and *plan* into operant-conditioning elements. Furthermore, Chomsky assailed Skinner's assumption that children simply repeat the words or phrases they hear—that is, repeat the ones that have brought reinforcement. Chomsky claimed that children formulate for themselves, through unseen mental processes, a deeper grammar that undergirds the meaning of the surface appearance of their sentences. This deep grammar structure enables children to recognize the equivalent meanings of utterances that are dissimilar in their surface structure (*The girl ate the cake* or *The cake was eaten by the girl* or *The cake was gone, for the girl had eaten it*).

Widespread dissatisfaction has also been expressed over Skinner's explanation of creativity. Many psychologists who admit that reinforcement, nonreinforcement, and punishment can affect whether a person retains or drops a given behavior also feel that Skinner avoided the problem of how the behavior got started in the first place. Where does a new or unique behavior come from? Is it proper just to call the pigeon's marching and pecking about the cage *random behavior* without accounting for why the pigeon marches and pecks rather than skates and coughs? How does a brilliant symphony or novel or scientific theory arise? Any psychologist who gives more credit to unobservable thinking behavior—to cognitive activity—can claim that Skinner's few principles of conditioning fail to offer an adequate explanation of innovative or creative acts.

In addition to the foregoing technical objections to radical behaviorism, other critics have, on humane or religious grounds, reacted against Skinner's views. Such criticism is based on a feeling that "it just doesn't seem right" that life operates on the basis of Skinnerian principles. D. B. Stevick, speaking from a Christian perspective, concluded about *Walden Two*:

> Behavioral engineering rules out the risk and the achievement of freedom, love, self-giving, commitment, self-discipline, loyalty, memory, creativity, and hope. The significance of politics, the integrity of art, the warmth and support of human intimacy—all are lost. . . . The most precious thing about man is his humanity. Walden Two commends its deliberate abandonment. (1968, p. 28)

In response to such a charge, Skinner would probably reply that, like it or not, radical behaviorism simply describes the truth about why people act as they do.

On comprehensiveness (item 11), I have placed Skinner's model at the "moderately well" position by balancing (1) radical behaviorism's laudable ability to account for all types of learned behavior against (2) its lack of attention to the biological aspects of development—that is, to the child's growing larger and physiologically more complex with the passing years.

In judging the novelty of behaviorism (item 10), I have included two appraisals. The *W* at the "very well" location is intended to reflect the innovative quality of behaviorism when Watson first introduced the model early in this century. Just as Freud's theory came as a shock to both the scientific community and the general public of his day, so also Watson's notion jarred everyone who had been accustomed to considering such things as *mind* and *thinking* as important realities. Such beliefs were denounced by Watson as delusions. By the time Skinner entered the lists somewhat before midcentury, the early tenets of behaviorism were already familiar to psychologists and to much of the informed public. And though Skinner's contributions were not so unique as Watson's, Skinner (*Sk*) still can be credited with creating novel variants of Watson's ideas and with supporting those variants with evidence from carefully conducted experiments (item 8). However, in regard to the experiments, I believe critics have been correct in complaining that so much of Skinner's supporting data derived from studies of pigeons, rats, and other nonhuman subjects, with insufficient regard for significant differences between people and critters.

I have assigned radical behaviorism two ratings for its adaptability (item 9). The *Sk*, located rather low on the scale, is designed to reflect Skinner's tendency to ignore or to dismiss with cavalier gesture any data that cast doubt on his model. He seemed disinclined to review his convictions in light of new evidence. In contrast, the *NB* placed higher on the scale refers to neobehaviorists' willingness to alter radical behaviorism in ways that render the theory more compatible with research in the realm of cognitive psychology. This judgment is in keeping with Michael J. Mahoney's (1989, p. 1374) suggestion that

> radical or orthodox behaviorism may have lost much of its hold on scientific psychology in large part because of its dogmatic objectivism and scientistic intolerance, an intolerance that has become increasingly more evident as that hold has dissipated. . . . However, I hasten to add that this assertion applies only to orthodox (radical) behaviorism and not to the more common liberal versions of behavior therapy or to the varieties of . . . behaviorism that encourage creativity and innovation in experimental methods and conceptual models.

The rather low rating on durability (item 13) represents the declining popularity of Skinner's theory. Certain aspects of his model (such as the influence of consequences that follow a behavior and the importance of reinforcement schedules) have won a lasting place in general psychology. However, the theory's pristine form now seems somewhat behind the times.

Although I think there is substantial truth in the criticisms leveled at Skinner's model, I also believe the theory has significant virtues. As a result, in terms of its overall self-satisfying quality (item 14), I have rated radical behaviorism at the "moderately well" position.

FOR FURTHER READING

Amsel, A. (1989) *Behaviorism, Neobehaviorism, and Cognitivism in Learning Theory: Historical and Contemporary Perspectives.* Hillsdale, N.J.: Erlbaum.

Bjork, D. W. (1993) *B. F. Skinner: A Life.* New York: Basic Books.

Buckley, K. W. (1989) *Mechanical Man: John Broadus Watson and the Beginning of Behaviorism.* New York: Guilford.

Modgil, S., and C. Modgil. (1987) *B. F. Skinner: Consensus and Controversy.* New York: Falmer.

Skinner, B. F. (1972) *Cumulative Record: A Selection of Papers,* 3d ed. New York: Appleton-Century-Crofts. This book includes representative articles from various stages of Skinner's early career.

Skinner, B. F. (1974) *About Behaviorism.* New York: Knopf. This is a highly readable overview of radical behaviorism.

Skinner, B. F. (1987) *Upon Further Reflection.* Englewood Cliffs, N.J.: Prentice-Hall. In this selection of fourteen succinctly written papers published between 1981 and 1987, Skinner sought to clarify issues that he felt his critics misunderstood or misinterpreted from his previous writings. The articles reflect three aspects of Skinner's professional life—those of the philosopher of science, the experimentalist, and the utopian visionary.

For Bijou and Baer's views, see:

Bijou, S. W., and D. M. Baer. (1961) *Child Development: Vol. I. A Systematic and Empirical View.* New York: Appleton-Century-Crofts. This book presents the authors' overall theoretical scheme.

Bijou, S. W., and D. M. Baer. (1965) *Child Development: II: Universal State of Infancy.* New York: Appleton-Century-Crofts. This volume presents the authors' conception of the first stage of development.

Bijou, S. W. (1976) *Child Development: The Basic Stage of Early Childhood.* Englewood Cliffs, N.J.: Prentice-Hall. This book is a detailed account of the second stage of development.

Chapter Eight

Social Learning Theory and Contextualism

The reason social learning theory is paired with behaviorism in Part Four is that each of them assigns a key role to environmental consequences—especially to reinforcement—in determining the personality characteristics people acquire. Behaviorism can thus be considered at least a partial progenitor of social learning models. The comparisons between the social learning perspective and Skinner's operant behaviorism offered in the following pages are intended to highlight likenesses and differences between the two. The psychologist most often mentioned for contributions to social learning theory is Albert Bandura. Hence his version of the model is featured in the following description, as supplemented by reference to the work of Julian B. Rotter, another pioneer in the field.

The word *contextualism* in relation to human development theories rose in popularity in the late 1970s and throughout the 1980s. R. M. Lerner (1986, p. 26) explained that:

> In contextualism, developmental changes occur as a consequence of reciprocal (bi-directional) relations between the active organism and the active context. Just as the context changes the individual, the individual changes the context. As such, by acting to change a source of their own development—by being both products and producers of their contexts—individuals affect their own development.

Some writers see contextualism as a derivative of social learning theory or of some other established model, such as Roger W. Barker's ecological psychology (Chapter Thirteen) or K. F. Riegel's dialectical theory (1975). In contrast, others regard social learning theory as only one variant of an overarching metatheoretical contextualism viewpoint (Zimmerman, 1983). In any event, the term *social learning theory* predates *contextualism* in popular use, so I address the two in that order in the following presentation. It is also useful to recognize that another term applied to these sorts of theories has been *social cognition,* meaning the way people think about social relationships.

Bandura's Conception of Social Learning or Social Cognition

Social learning theory gets its name from the emphasis it places on social variables as determinants of behavior and personality. It proposes to remedy an overdependence of earlier behaviorism on principles derived mostly from studies of animal learning and of human learning in one-person experiments. Social learning theorists attempt to correct this earlier bias by basing many of their principles on studies of the interaction of two or more people.

The social learning movement has sought to offer both (1) a balanced synthesis of mentalism (known today as *cognitive psychology*) and the principles of behavior modification and (2) an analysis of social influences on human development. In the mid-1970s, E. R. Hilgard and G. H. Bower (1975, p. 599) called this movement "a selective distillation of what is probably a 'consensus' position of moderation on many issues of importance to any theory of learning and behavior modification."

Although Albert Bandura (born 1925), a Stanford University psychologist, shares many basic convictions with behaviorists, he disagrees with traditional S-R theorists on the role of imitation in personality development. Among the areas in which Bandura's position differs from that of such radical behaviorists as Skinner, four are of particular importance: (1) the way a child acquires a new behavior that the child has never attempted before (a phenomenon Skinnerians have difficulty explaining), (2) the key steps involved in the process of learning from models, (3) the way that consequences (reinforcement, punishment) influence future actions, and (4) the development of complex behaviors.

The Origin of New Behavior

According to a commonly held S-R view, a child learns such things as language by first babbling a variety of sounds and then having certain of these sounds rewarded by people around her because the sounds approximate words they use. When the child happens to say *dah* or *ee* or *kee,* she is rewarded with smiles and caresses since the sounds have been uttered in the presence of *daddy, eating,* and *kitty.* When such events occur on several occasions, the sounds become conditioned to the objects they represent in the language of that particular culture. Although such a lucky coincidence between sounds and objects might account for children acquiring some simple words, Bandura and other social learning advocates find it inconceivable that this fortuitous process produces the thousands of words and the complex syntax and grammar that the child has mastered by the time she enters school.

In contrast, social learning theorists propose that most of a child's learning comes from his actively *imitating* or *modeling* what he sees and hears other people say and do. Bandura used the word *modeling*—along with such terms as *observational learning* and *vicarious learning*—to mean that the child adds to his repertoire of actions by seeing or hearing someone else perform the behavior rather than by overtly carrying out the behavior himself (Bandura, 1969, pp. 118–120). So in the social learning theorists' opinion, children's new actions are not simply spontaneous and random hit-or-miss behaviors, with the hits being learned because they are reinforced. Instead, children seek to reproduce what they observe. In some cases this is *one-trial learning.* The first attempt is perfect. In other cases, the first attempt only approximates the desired action, and so requires *shaping* through more refined attempts before children achieve a level of behavior considered satisfactory by the reinforcing agents in their environment.

Some theorists agree with the importance of imitation but feel that the process operates only when children's attempts are directly reinforced as they reproduce an observed action. However, Bandura and other social learning investigators have produced evidence to support the belief that children also learn when the reinforcement is only vicarious. When six-year-old James observes six-year-old Henry being rewarded for saying "please" in order to get something he wants from the teacher, James learns to say "please" in similar circumstances.

People who have spent much time around children are not likely to consider this idea that children imitate others to be a discovery of cosmic dimensions. It seems to be pretty much common sense. Parents, teachers, coaches, and police commonly use principles of modeling to instruct children in how to add a new learning to their array of skills and knowledge. This sort of instruction is reflected in such phrases as "Try it this way," or "Let me show you," or "I'll tell you how to do it," or "Just read the directions." But more controversial and less obvious than these aspects of imitation is the role of *incidental learning*.

The issue of incidental learning has long been a topic of debate among learning theorists. The question at the center of the debate is this: Can people learn something they see or hear if this thing does not fulfill a need they are currently seeking to satisfy or if they are not rewarded for learning it? Many theorists say the answer is no. They claim that a person learns only those things that meet a need he or she is currently seeking to satisfy. Other things in the environment that are not pertinent to fulfilling the present need are passed by and not learned. And many theorists claim that reinforcement or reward is required for learning. Without reinforcement, either direct or vicarious, the child does not acquire a new skill or knowledge. (See the summary of latent-learning studies in Hilgard & Bower, 1975, pp. 134–136.)

However, Bandura and other social learning advocates conducted experiments that suggest that the answer to the incidental-learning question is yes, at least in some cases. Children who are not seeking to satisfy any apparent need and who are not rewarded by a current happening may actually learn from the experience, storing in memory the results of their incidental observation for use at some later, appropriate time. According to Bandura, the error made by psychologists who do not admit to such incidental learning has been their confusing learning with performance. Since children who were not reinforced for a given act in experiments did not perform the act, it was assumed that without reinforcement, vicarious or direct, there had been no learning. But Bandura's evidence has supported the belief that people do not overtly display many things they have learned from a model if these things do not appear to yield sufficient rewards in the situation at hand. In other words, social learning theorists assume that for a given life situation, each of us has a series of possible reactions we might display. We have several answers we might give to the question being posed. However, in this multiple-choice situation, all answers are not equally plausible. Some seem better than others, and those better answers are the only ones we exhibit publicly, so other people do not realize that we have learned additional possible answers as well.

Bandura, then, contends that children do not just happen to hit on a new sort of behavior that is then reinforced; instead children acquire new behaviors by observing models in their environment. But what about children's *creating* novel behaviors that they have not seen before? How does this come about? Again, radical behaviorists seem to consider such novel acts accidental or built up in some way from small links of behaviors already carried out. But the social learning theorist of Bandura's persuasion accounts for novel acts by concluding that

> when exposed to diverse models, observers rarely pattern their behavior exclusively after a single source, nor do they adopt all the attributes even of preferred models. Rather, observers combine aspects of various models into new amalgams that differ from the individual sources. . . . Different observers adopt different combinations of characteristics. (Bandura, 1977, p. 48)

So from the social learning viewpoint, novel behavior results from children's combining different segments of various behaviors they have observed in other people, with the observation including both direct witnessing of events and such indirect modes of securing examples as reading or hearing about ideas and actions.

The Process of Learning from Models

How observational learning takes place is far from completely understood. However, some of the conditions that influence it have been identified. According to Bandura, the main reason children learn from seeing or hearing a model is that the information they thereby acquire help them decide how the observed behavior might help or hinder them in fulfilling their needs on some future occasion. This information is stored in the memory in symbolic form, as images or as verbal symbols, for future reference.

This process of learning from models consists of five main functions: (1) paying *attention,* (2) *coding* for memory, (3) *retaining* in memory, and (4) *carrying out motor actions;* and all four of these steps require (5) *motivation* (Bandura, 1977, pp. 22–29).

First, when children observe a model, they must *attend to the pertinent clues* in the stimulus situation and ignore the aspects of the model and the environment that are incidental and don't affect the performance they seek to learn. Children's failure to perform the behavior properly later, especially if the behavior has been complex, is often due to their misdirecting their attention at the time the model was observed. Teachers frequently try to prevent this error by eliminating as many of the irrelevant stimuli from the setting as possible and by verbally directing children's attention to those aspects of the model's performance that are the most important.

A second requirement for imitative learning is that children accurately record in memory a *visual image* or *semantic code* for the act they have witnessed. Without an adequate coding system, children fail to store what they have seen or heard. There are obvious developmental trends in the ability to profit from models. Older children learn more readily from witnessing others' performances than do younger children. This superiority of older children is due in large part to their more advanced ability to use symbols. Bandura pointed out (1977, p. 30) that infants' use of modeling is confined mainly to instantaneous imitation. Very young children imitate the adult's gesture or word immediately instead of reproducing it after a period of time. But as children grow up and have more experience in associating words or images with objects and events, they can store these symbols in order to recall and reproduce the events after increasingly extended periods of time. In effect, the development of language and of schemes for coding observations enhances children's ability to profit from models. Not only must the observations be coded for memory (the input portion), but the codes must be suitable for transforming the perceptions into overt actions (the output portion). Otherwise the child ends up with useless knowledge, symbols that have been stored but cannot be retrieved in a form that leads to action.

A third factor influencing whether the knowledge will be available when needed is that of *memory permanence.* Although the operation of memory is still poorly understood by psychologists, one thing is clear—memories fade or disappear with time. Therefore much that children learn from observing models is forgotten, so that such learning is no longer available when children need it to solve some problem in life (Bandura, 1969, p. 202). Such memory-aiding techniques as rehearsal (review or practice) and attaching multiple codes to an event (associating a variety of interlinked words or images with the event) serve to keep the stored information at a level that makes it readily retrieved when needed.

A fourth factor influencing the success of learning from models is that of *reproducing* the observed motor activities accurately. It is not enough that observers get the *idea* of the actions to perform or that they code and store the idea adequately, it is also necessary for them to get the motor behavior, the muscular *feel* of the behavior. They usually cannot do this perfectly on the first trial. Thus they need a number of trials in which they approximate the behavior and then receive feedback from this experience to correct the deviations from the ideal that their earlier attempts have involved. It should be apparent that developmental trends in learning efficiency are partially a result of older children's greater muscular strength and control in comparison to that of younger children. Even if younger children could attend properly to the cues of the observed performance and could encode the observations mentally as images or verbal symbols, younger children still would not perform the modeled activities as well because their muscular development is not as advanced as older children's.

The fifth requirement in the process of learning from models is that the learner be *motivated* to carry through the several steps of the process. In the behaviorist tradition, this motivational function has been embedded in the crucial role of the *consequences of behavior.* Since the interpretation that Bandura and other present-day social learning theorists place on the function of consequences differs from that of radical behaviorists like Skinner, we need to pay special attention to this aspect of the learning process.

The Role of Consequences

According to Skinner's theory of operant conditioning, in a given stimulus situation people have a series of likely responses they might give. Which response will actually be given depends upon the comparative strengths of the competing responses in an individual's repertoire of responses. In addition, the strength of a potential response depends on how often that response has been reinforced in the past when the individual has been in a similar situation—that is, when facing what he or she considers a similar problem. In the opinion of radical behaviorists, this strengthening of response tendencies through reinforcement is automatic. When people's actions are reinforced or rewarded, it is not necessary for them consciously to tell themselves, "That worked out well, so I'll try it again in the future." Instead, the strengthening of the response simply comes about without the need for individuals to assess the effect of their behavior. Furthermore, the typical adherent of operant conditioning believes that in order for this automatic strengthening to be most effective, the consequence (reinforcement or reward) must occur as soon as possible after the act so that the two become intimately connected or "conditioned."

However, Bandura disagreed with this interpretation of how consequences influence subsequent behavior.

> Although the issue is not yet completely resolved, there is little evidence that reinforcers function as automatic shapers of human conduct. . . . A vast amount of evidence lends validity to the view that reinforcement serves principally as an informative and motivational operation rather than as a mechanical response strengthener. (Bandura, 1977, p. 21)

By *informative* Bandura means that the consequences, rewarding or punishing, tell the child under what circumstances it would seem wise to try a particular behavior in the future. In other words, the consequences improve the child's prediction of whether a given act will likely lead to pleasant or unpleasant outcomes on a later occasion. Bandura does not believe, as radical behaviorists do, that a consequence exerts its influence in reverse chronology, strengthening the behavior that preceded the rewarding consequence. Rather, he contends that the consequence exerts its influence into the future by giving children information about what effects they can expect if they later act that same way in a similar stimulus circumstance. By adopting such an interpretation, Bandura feels that he places himself in a better position to account for children's learning from models than are the radical behaviorists who propose that consequences automatically reinforce the preceding actions that the individual carried out. That is, Bandura points out that children can learn from observing others as well as from behaving themselves, since watching others can give children the same information they get from their own behavior consequences if they attend to the significant elements of the observed action.

When Bandura speaks of the *motivational* role of consequences, he means that children will more likely try to learn modeled behavior if they value the consequences the behavior seems to produce. If a pupil yearns for the teacher's approval and observes that the teacher gives such approval to children who spell well, then she is motivated to pay attention to the week's spelling words and to rehearse them so they are well stored in memory.

In summary, then, Bandura does not believe that consequences reinforce responses automatically and strengthen the response that immediately preceded the consequences. Instead, he sees consequences as *regulators* of future behavior—they regulate by means of giving the individual information about likely future consequences and by motivating her to act in one way rather than another in order to obtain the results she seeks.

Complex Behaviors

Not only do Bandura's ideas about modeling differ from those of radical or method-ological behaviorists, but his beliefs about how complex behaviors are acquired differ as well. Contrary to more traditional behaviorists, he does not believe a child develops complex behaviors by first imitating one small element of the observed pattern and then gradually building up the entire pattern through a step-by-step accrual of successive elements. Rather, he wrote:

> Patterns of behaviors are typically acquired in large segments or in their entirety rather than through a slow, gradual process based on differential reinforcement. Following demonstrations by a model, or (though to a lesser extent) following verbal descriptions of desired behavior, the learner generally reproduces more or less the entire response pattern, even though he may perform no overt response, and consequently receive no reinforcement, throughout the demonstration period. (Bandura & Walters, 1963, p. 106)

However, once the new behavior has been comprehended through observa-tion, the likelihood that it will be displayed in the child's personality is governed chiefly by schedules of reinforcement and punishment.

A final aspect of imitation learning that is important in Bandura's system is *the nature of the models.* Experimental studies support the commonsense notion of hero worship in the following ways: (1) Children are more likely to model their own behavior after the actions of people they regard as prestigious than after actions of people who are not highly regarded. (2) Children are more likely to adopt behavior patterns from models of their own sex than from the opposite sex. (3) Models who receive rewards, such as money, fame, high socioeconomic status, are more often copied than ones who do not. (4) People who are punished for their behavior tend not to be imitated. (5) Children are more influenced by models they perceive to be similar to themselves, such as in age or social status, than by models they see as being quite different from themselves (Bandura & Walters, 1963, pp. 10–11, 50, 84, 94–100).

In summary, Bandura views imitation as a major device in children's social development, for through the observation of models, children add new options to their repertoire of possible behaviors. Furthermore, models help children decide under what circumstances they can most profitably put these new options into practice.

From Bandura's social learning perspective, we can conceive of child develop-ment as a process (1) of children's gradually expanding their repertoire of answers or possible actions by means of both observing others and trying the actions themselves, and (2) of children's using information from the observed con-sequences to guide future decisions about what response will be most appropriate to fulfill needs and attain rewards. Like Skinner, Bandura does not separate development into a series of stages, but he considers the process of cognitive and social growth to be one of gradual accrual of an ever-widening array of response possibilities for increasingly differentiated stimulus situations.

With Bandura's views of the importance of observational learning in mind, let us turn to a currently popular application of social learning theory in the treatment of deviant behavior.

Normality and Deviance

In putting his model of development to practical use, Bandura centered attention on psychotherapy and the correction of antisocial behavior. His technique of treating deviance does not take the form of curing mental disorders or of alleviating the underlying causes of mental disease, as has been the case in traditional psychiatric practice. Instead, he has rejected the medical concept of deviance, the concept that the person exhibiting the undesired behavior is sick and that this mental condition must be treated to make him well. In place of this belief about curing illness, Bandura advocates what has been termed *behavior modification,* because he is convinced that an act that "is harmful to the individual or departs widely from accepted social and ethical norms" is not symptomatic of some disease but is simply "a way that the individual has learned to cope with environmental and self-imposed demands. Treatment then becomes mainly a problem in social learning rather than one in the medical domain" (Bandura, 1969, p. 10).

In keeping with this viewpoint, Bandura would treat a child who displays undesirable social behavior by manipulating the consequences of the child's acts so that the child finds it more rewarding to adopt more acceptable behavior than to continue in the currently unacceptable pattern. By extrapolating principles from Bandura's discussion, the process of carrying out behavior modification can be summarized in four basic steps:

1. Identify the specific behavior you wish to have the child substitute for the presently unacceptable behavior.
2. Arrange for the child to try out this new, desirable behavior. There are several ways this can be done: simply wait for it to occur spontaneously, provide a model, verbally explain what the desired behavior is, shape it through gradual approximations, or use several of these techniques.
3. Determine what sorts of consequences will be strongly reinforcing or rewarding to the child and what sorts will be punishing.
4. Manipulate consequences so that the desired behavior, when it appears, will yield greater reinforcement than does the undesirable behavior. In other words, arrange a schedule of reinforcement and/or punishment that will make it profitable for the child to give up the old behavior in favor of the new.

Although this process is easy to outline, it is often difficult to carry out in practice. However, such behavior modification is conceived by social learning theorists to be the most effective means possible of correcting a child's deviant acts.

Critics of behavior modification have charged that it is a naive, superficial approach to psychotherapy or personality improvement. They claim that seeking directly to change the child's overt actions fails to get at the underlying cause. Such criticism is based on the view that overt behaviors, such as thumb sucking, temper tantrums, or stealing, are just surface symptoms of an underlying disorder buried deep in the personality, probably in the unconscious. Bandura, in reacting to such charges, says that both psychodynamic and social learning theorists are seeking underlying causes. However, the two camps differ in where they believe these causes lie.

Psychoanalysts propose that the causes are repressed conflicts left over in the unconscious from the child's failing to solve the conflicts faced during earlier psychosexual stages of development. Therefore the therapist digs into the patient's psyche to identify which events in the past produced the conflicts, and then seeks to help the patient consciously relive these events and put them into a mentally healthy perspective. Such analysis, say the psychodynamic therapists, frees the patient from symptoms of deviance, and the personality disorder is cured.

In contrast to this psychodynamic view, social learning therapists hunt for "underlying causes" in the child's present environment. For the social learning theorist, the term *cause* refers to the satisfying consequences that the child's deviant behavior continues to bring. The child's regrettable behavior persists because it pays off or because he or she does not know any other way to behave that will bring more satisfactory consequences. The task of the therapist, then, becomes that of carrying out the four steps of behavior modification.

In both psychodynamic and social learning theories it is possible to "simply treat the symptom" without getting at the "real cause." However, the meaning of this phrase is quite different under the two theories. With the typical psychodynamic approach, "simply treating the symptom" usually means punishing or rewarding a child so she will stop sucking her thumb in school, or he will stop stealing objects from classmates' desks. Or it could mean giving the child a posthypnotic suggestion to avoid thumb-sucking or stealing. However, in the psychodynamic view, such treatment only suppresses the particular symptom on which the treatment has focused. And because the underlying causes—repressed conflicts—have not been touched, other symptoms will arise.

In social learning theory "simply treating the symptom" is a phrase interpreted to mean that the therapist has been too narrow in her or his perception of the number of different situations in which a child's deviant response is used. For instance, a ten-year-old boy throws temper tantrums at home, around the neighborhood, in the classroom, and on the playground when things do not go his way. According to social learning theorists as well as other behaviorists, this pattern of action is maintained because people ultimately yield to the boy's demands in order to "avoid all that fuss." To solve the problem, the teacher may seek to eliminate the tantrums in class (1) by not reinforcing them, (2) by helping the boy observe models who use such techniques as reasoning or discussion instead of tantrums to get their way, and (3) by rewarding the boy's attempts to use these more mature techniques. However, while the undesirable behavior may be reduced in school, it may persist at home, around the neighborhood, and on the playground because the consequences in these out-of-class settings have not been altered. Critics of the behaviorists' reinforcement and punishment approach may charge that the classroom treatment of the problem was just getting at the symptoms but not the cause. But the social learning theorist can reply that if the consequences in all four environments—classroom, home, neighborhood, and playground—were altered, the tantrums would disappear entirely, and the problem would be cured.

However, another difficulty may arise to cause Freudians and their psychodynamic colleagues to continue to criticize the behaviorists' approach. It is possible that the tantrums will disappear in all settings, but the new behavior that is substituted may also be deviant. For example, the boy, when he fails to get his way by tantrums, may withdraw from the classroom group and sit brooding. The psychodynamic therapist can now claim that this is simply *symptom substitution,* that one sort of deviance has replaced another because the real unconscious cause was not unearthed and resolved. The social learning therapist will disagree and will likely say that for any given stimulus situation the ten-year-old has learned a hierarchy of possible responses. The most powerful of these, at the top of his hierarchy of appropriateness, has been the temper tantrum. If the consequences are altered so such behavior does not pay off for the child, then he can be expected to turn to the next most promising option in his strata of habits. By *promising* I mean that response that he estimates will bring the most satisfying results in such stimulus situations. Often this second most likely response is also considered undesirable by the important people in his life. So if withdrawal and brooding is the second choice among his options, the social behavior problem is not solved. He is still labeled a problem child.

According to social learning theorists, this is not a problem of symptom substitution, however; it is a problem of the child's having a response hierarchy whose most promising options (that is, promising in the boy's estimation) are all undesirable ones for the society in which he lives. Therapy does not consist of hunting for an unconscious cause. Rather, it consists of helping the boy learn a new, socially approved behavior that is so rewarding that it takes priority over all of the undesirable responses in his repertoire of likely reactions to frustration, both in school and out (Bandura, 1969, pp. 48–52).

As implied, Bandura subscribes to a *reference-group* interpretation of normality and deviance. A child is normal or abnormal only in terms of how her behavior compares to the behavior of other members of a designated group. This reference group might be Catholics, American ten-year-olds, upper-class children, Central Elementary School fifth graders, or any other group. It should be apparent that a child might be considered normal when compared to one group but deviant when compared to another. Hence, when the question of normality arises, it is important to identify the reference group to be used in answering the question.

This matter of reference groups is important not only for determining normality or deviance in a child's development but also for understanding why attempts at behavior modification may fail. Consider a junior high school girl who steals money and equipment from her classmates and from the teacher. School authorities consider this behavior undesirable, so they seek to change it by altering its consequences. They punish the girl by keeping her after school, and they offer her special privileges if she will go for a period of one month without stealing anything. But she continues to steal, and this puzzles the teacher and principal, for it is apparently contrary to social learning principles. But, in the eyes of the social learning theorist, they have simply failed to realize that the girl is still being reinforced for stealing. She persists in her deviant act because she continues to be rewarded by her own preferred reference group, by her gang of delinquent peers whose approval she values more than that of school authorities. Consequently, deviant behavior cannot be understood or altered without our recognizing that various groups' norms are often in conflict with each other and that the rewards dispensed by one group are more influential than those dispensed by another because the child values the first group more. This means that we need to identify which reference groups or individuals serve as the most valued ones in the child's life.

Finally, social learning theory discourages the application of such traditional psychiatric labels as *neurosis* and *psychopathic personality* to children exhibiting antisocial behavior. These children are not considered diseased or mentally deranged. The cause of their deviance, whether it appears to be harmful to themselves or to be contrary to social norms, is not to be found by use of special medical terms or principles. Instead, social learning theorists contend that "a single set of social learning principles can account for the development of both prosocial and deviant behavior and for modifications of behavior toward greater conformity or greater deviation" (Bandura & Walters, 1963, p. 221). Thus treatment of the child consists of altering the consequences the environment provides for the undesired behavior. It does not consist of searching in the depths of the child's psyche for psychosexual or psychosocial conflicts.

Conscience and Self-Control

In social learning theory a child's conscience or moral values are not inborn. Infants arrive in the world amoral. Then, by the same modeling and conditioning principles that produce all of their other beliefs, they gradually acquire values and a capacity for self-control and self-direction. In other words, one's character is learned, not inherited.

Investigations cited by Bandura support his contention that the development of self-control or conscience is heavily influenced by the models children observe and by patterns of direct reinforcement that they encounter, such as disciplinary measures used by parents and teachers. The degree to which a child will resist temptations has been most readily affected in experimental situations by how immediately the model in the situation is rewarded or punished. The characteristics of the model also influence how likely it is that the child will adopt the modeled self-control or lack of it, with the greatest influence exerted by models who are capable, successful, and prestigious.

The timing of reward and punishment is also important. Bandura suggests that many parents mold a child's conscience—meaning his guilt feelings or self-punishing tendencies—more successfully by withholding privileges than by applying aversive stimuli such as a spanking or isolation. He believes that the frequent superiority of withholding or withdrawing positive reinforcers over applying aversive measures is to a great extent the result of timing. Typically, the parent withholds the reinforcer until the child expresses guilt or some self-punishment response. Then the privilege or desired object is restored to the child. But "parents on most occasions administer aversive stimuli some time after a deviation has occurred and fail to make its termination contingent on the child's expressing self-punitive responses" (Bandura & Walters, 1963, p. 221). As a result of the postponed punishment and the indefiniteness of the time to remove the punishment, the child is less likely to adopt the self-control standards the parent desires. Studies have also suggested that the withholding of privileges serves most effectively to develop the child's self-control if the agents who withhold the rewards and subsequently reinstate them are warm, affectionate people rather than unaffectionate people or people who hold a grudge (Bandura & Walters, 1963, pp. 197–199).

Over the years, Bandura has continued to explore additional tributaries of mainstream social learning theory or, as he came to label his system by the 1980s, of mainstream *social cognitive theory* (Bandura, 1986). For example, he extensively investigated how people's behavior is influenced by their sense of power and ability—that is, by their sense of *self-efficacy*. According to Bandura, self-efficacy beliefs regulate people's social functioning through four major processes: cognition, emotion, motivation, and selection. Cognitive processes involve people analyzing their own behavior in relation to (1) their own personal standards and (2) feedback from their surroundings on how well they have been able to cope with their social environment. These analyses (cognition) are then joined by the individuals' feelings about their experiences (emotion) to influence the activities they attempt (selection) and to determine how strongly they try to succeed (motivation) at those activities (Bandura, 1990c). Bandura has applied his conceptions of self-regulation and self-efficacy to a wide range of practical situations, including athletic performance (1990c), control of AIDS (acquired immune deficiency syndrome) infection (1990a), memory enhancement (1989), moral behavior (1990b, 1991), and organizational efficiency (Bandura & Jourden, 1991).

PRACTICAL APPLICATIONS OF BANDURA'S MODEL

I have already described basic steps in the behavior modification process as practiced today in many schools and clinics. And the sorts of educational applications described in Chapter Seven for radical behaviorism apply as well to ones deriving from Bandura's theory. But the practical use of Bandura's proposal and similar social learning schemes goes well beyond applications of operant conditioning. For instance, the following studies represent only a handful of more than two hundred reported in *Psychological Abstracts* for the years 1983–1994:

1. The treatment of adolescents' problems of acquired immune deficiency syndrome (AIDS) (Flora & Thoresen, 1988), delinquency (Hawkins & Weis, 1985), pregnancy (Hagenhoff et al., 1987), learning disabilities (Gresham & Elliott, 1989),

bulimia (Love et al., 1985), cigarette smoking (Krohn et al., 1985), marijuana use (Akers & Cochran, 1985), alcohol use (Brook & Brook, 1985), and drunk driving (DiBlasio, 1988).

2. The analysis of Dutch children's health-related behavioral intentions (de Vries, Dijkstra, & Kuhlman, 1988), children's aggression in Zapotec Indian communities (Fry, 1988), aggressive behavior in German schools (Petermann, 1987), ways to combat American children's use of illicit drugs (Bush & Iannotti, 1985), middle-childhood social skills in Jerusalem (S. R. Rose, 1987), the development of North American children's prosocial skills (Batson et al., 1987), sex role identification among Soviet preschoolers (Kolominskly & Meltsas, 1985), and the switch from homosexuality to heterosexuality among boys in the Sambia tribe of Papua New Guinea (J. D. Baldwin & Baldwin, 1989).

BANDURA'S SOCIAL LEARNING THEORY: AN ASSESSMENT

Like Skinner's presentation of operant behaviorism, I find Bandura's description of social learning theory easy to understand, internally consistent, and falsifiable (items 2, 5, and 7). Furthermore, as the list of applications just given suggests, Bandura's theory has stimulated a large quantity of empirical studies and thus deserves high marks for its fertility (item 12).

Compared to Skinner's radical behaviorism, social learning theories are not as subject to the charge of devaluing mental activity. And unlike Skinner, social learning theorists have accorded a prominent place to the function of imitation in personality development. They have also conducted their research on people, particularly on children, rather than on animals, thus avoiding the criticism directed at Skinner that he has drawn simplistic conclusions about human development by founding many of his principles on conditioning experiments with pigeons and rats. For all of these reasons. I would rate social learning theorists higher than Skinner on how well they explain the past and predict the future (item 3) and reflect the real world of children (item 1).

I would also give social learning theory a higher rating on economy of explanation (item 6) because Bandura's version appears to suffer less from the criticism of being overparsimonious than does Skinner's behaviorism.

Bandura's model also furnishes clear directions on how to use it to improve child rearing (item 4). Indeed, practical applicability is a characteristic of theories that Bandura has particularly valued. He proposed that a psychological theory should be judged not only by its power to explain and predict behavior, but also by its ability to enhance human functioning. His model, he contended, is strong in this regard, offering specific prescriptions for how to equip people with competencies, self-regulatory skills, and a resilient sense of self-efficacy that promotes psychological well-being and accomplishment (Bandura, 1990c).

Despite the model's array of strengths, parents and teachers who seek information about what children are like at different age levels receive no aid from social cognitive theory, since it describes how children learn, rather than what they are like at different stages of their lives (items 1 and 4). In addition, developmentalists

BANDURA'S SOCIAL COGNITIVE THEORY

How well do I think the theory meets the standards?

Standards	Very well	Moderately well	Very poorly
1. Reflects the real world of children		X	
2. Is clearly understandable	X		
3. Explains the past and predicts the future		X	
4. Guides child rearing		X	
5. Is internally consistent	X		
6. Is economical		X	
7. Is falsifiable	X		
8. Is supported by convincing evidence		X	
9. Adapts to new data		X	
10. Is novel			X
11. Is comprehensive			X
12. Stimulates new discoveries	X		
13. Is durable		X	
14. Is self-satisfying		X	

who see a child's genetic endowment and the influence of internal maturation as prime factors behind child growth may also find fault with social learning theorists' apparent slighting of hereditary influences on development (item 11).

As indicated by the high mark on item 8, I think Bandura and his fellow advocates of a social learning perspective have gone to commendable lengths to furnish convincing empirical support for their proposals.

In respect to novelty (item 10), I would place Bandura's scheme in the "moderately well" category. His proposal that children copy other people's actions and that reward and punishment serve to alter behavior can easily be considered part of naive psychology rather than as remarkable discoveries. On the other hand, I believe Bandura deserves credit for his innovative refinements in the ways imitation and consequences are conceived and are applied in child rearing.

At present, social learning models appear to be enduring quite well (item 13) under whatever flags they fly: *contextualism, social cognition, social ecology,* and the like. Although the social learning perspective has not satisfactorily answered all the questions about development posed by other theorists, parents, and teachers, it has come perhaps the closest of any theory to describing how children acquire the learned, rather than the inherited, aspects of their personalities. An appraisal offered by Hilgard and Bower in the mid-1970s seems equally appropriate today:

> Social learning theory provides the best integrative summary of what modern learning theory has to contribute to solutions of practical problems. It also provides a compatible framework within which to place information-processing theories of language comprehension, memory, imagery, and problem solving. . . . For such reasons, social learning theory would appear to be the "consensus" theoretical framework within which much of learning research (especially on humans) will evolve in the next decade. (1975, p. 605)

In regard to its overall self-satisfying quality (item 14), I would rate social learning theory higher than Skinner's behaviorism.

ROTTER'S SOCIAL LEARNING VIEWS

Julian B. Rotter is an American psychologist whose book *Social Learning and Clinical Psychology* (1954) outlined a view of personality development that drew on concepts from such diverse sources as Alfred Adler's "individual psychology," Kurt Lewin's field theory, and the works of behaviorists Edward L. Thorndike, E. C. Tolman, and Clark Hull (Rotter, 1982, pp. 1–2).

Adler was a Viennese psychiatrist who worked closely with Sigmund Freud until they parted ways in 1912 over key theoretical disagreements. In particular, Adler deposed the sexual drive as the central motivating force behind human behavior and substituted in its place the belief that a deep-seated feeling of inferiority constantly stimulates the child to seek security and a sense of significance. Furthermore, as Rudolph Dreikurs explained:

> The leading idea of the Individual Psychology of Alfred Adler is found in his recognition of the importance of human society, not only for the development of the individual character, but also for the orientation of every single action and emotion in the life of a human being. (1950, p. 1)

Lewin, a German psychologist who emigrated to the United States to teach at the University of Iowa and the Massachusetts Institute of Technology, focused attention on the way a multitude of environmental and biological factors in an individual's life combine to form a field of influence that determines the person's thought and action at any particular moment.

Thorndike was a Columbia University professor who proposed a series of "psychological laws" that govern how learning takes place. Tolman, a University of California psychologist, devised a theory of learning that pictured children's behavior as always goal-directed—as always designed to achieve an objective. Furthermore, in Tolman's opinion, children's experience with the world enables them to create cognitive maps of reality so that most important products of the learning process are the mental maps that guide an individual's future pursuit of goals. Hull was a Yale University professor who offered a precise way of determining how consequences affect behavior during the learning process.

Rotter drew from the foregoing ideas in formulating his own theory. Although his scheme has been less popular than Bandura's, it still continues to exert a minor influence on studies of development and psychotherapy (Burke, 1983; Love et al., 1985). Something of the flavor of Rotter's model can be suggested by his ideas about reinforcement, needs, and expectancies.

The most basic building block in Rotter's theory is the concept of reinforcement as derived from Thorndike's "law of effect," which describes the influence that consequences of a behavior will exert on future behavior in similar circumstances.

A second foundational precept relates to needs. Rotter proposes that the infant is first motivated to action by physiological needs: hunger, thirst, warmth, release of bodily wastes, and others. As the satisfaction of these basic needs becomes associated (through classical conditioning) with such caretakers as parents, the infant develops *learned needs* called *psychological needs* or *acquired goals*. These include goals of pleasing others, of engaging in amicable social relations, of adopting others' characteristics and values, and the like. As the child's social interactions accumulate, psychological needs become powerful motivators on their own, no longer dependent on their physiological antecedents. And because the child's psychological needs are generated out of the particular social interactions in which that child engages, psychological needs can differ from one culture to another, one family to another, and one child to another (Rotter, 1982, pp. 58–61).

Reinforcement creates within children's personalities a series of *expectancies* about what kinds of future behaviors will likely result in rewards and in punishments. Children's experiences thus help define for them the degree to which their intentional actions will produce the outcomes they desire. If they can accurately predict how their actions will influence results, their belief that they are in control of their fate is strengthened (the expectancy that they have internal control of reinforcement). However, if their experience suggests that they cannot govern the outcome by the way they act, then they attribute the control of their fate to external factors (luck, chance, others' power). The extensive psychological literature on *locus of control* over the past two decades is founded on such an expectancies conception of development.

In summary, human development from Rotter's perspective consists of the child's gradually acquiring goals (psychological needs), skills, and expectancies that depend on the experiences (behaviors and their reinforcement consequences) provided by that child's particular social environment. The child's personality at any given time is composed of these goals, skills, and expectancies.

The way Rotter's model guides such practical activities as psychotherapy is reflected in the following proposals:

> The problem of psychotherapy is seen as a learning situation in which the function of the therapist is to help the patient accomplish planned changes in his observable behavior and thinking. Since patients come into therapy with many different motives [acquired goals], different values placed on particular kinds of reinforce-

ments, different expectancies for possible sources of gratification, different limits on skill, and different higher level learning skills, conditions for optimal learning will likewise vary considerably from patient to patient. . . . Consequently, there is no special technique which can be applied to all cases, and differences in therapists must eventually be systematically related to patient differences to obtain maximally efficient results. (Rotter, 1982, pp. 256–257)

With the principal characteristics of two social learning theories now sketched, we next consider what kinds of models can properly be subsumed under the rubric *contextualism.*

THE NATURE OF CONTEXTUALISM

The core concept of the recent contextualism movement is really nothing new. It is the assumption that human development is a process of interaction between (1) the child as a psychobiological organism and (2) the child's sociophysical environment. Hence the virtue of contextualism is to be found in the presumed sophisticated, balanced view of person and context transactions that the movement espouses rather than in any novelty of the basic idea itself. Bandura (1978, p. 344) certainly reflected a contextualist perspective in saying that "psychological functioning involves a continuous reciprocal interaction between behavioral, cognitive, and environmental influences." B. J. Zimmerman's (1983) overview of contextualism paradigms features Bandura's version of social learning theory as a prime example of a contextualist approach. And Rotter's (1982, p. 5) theory likewise qualifies as contextualist when he contended that "the unit of investigation for the study of personality is the interaction of the individual and his or her meaningful environment."

The term *contextualism,* in effect, does not identify any specific model of development but, rather, represents a point of view that can be exemplified by diverse models. Two additional theories that can conveniently be sheltered under the contextualism umbrella are ones proposed by Klaus Riegel and Jaan Valsiner. Their models' principal features are sketched briefly in the following pages to illustrate ways that contextualist theories may be alike and ways they may differ from each other.

Riegel's Dialectical Theory

The concept *dialectic,* as proposed by the German philosopher Georg Wilhelm Friedrich Hegel (1770–1831), refers to an interpretive method in which an assertable proposition (the *thesis*) is necessarily opposed by a second equally reasonable but apparently contradictory proposition (the *antithesis*), with their mutual contradiction subsequently resolved at a higher level of truth by a third proposition (the *synthesis*). Consider this simple application of Hegelian dialectic to the study of child development. Imagine that a researcher spends several hours with each of ten three-year-olds, trying to teach them how to read a page of a beginner's storybook. None of the ten succeeds with the task, thereby leading the investigator to propose that "three-year-olds are not intellectually mature enough to learn to read" *(thesis)*. However, when a friend asks to have her three-year-old daughter try the task, the girl, after a good deal of effort, haltingly reads the page. This leads to an observation that conflicts with the thesis: "A three-year-old did learn to read" *(antithesis)*. To reconcile this pair of contradictory conclusions, the researcher revises the original propositions to form the following synthesis: "Most three-year-olds are not mature enough intellectually to learn to read (at least by the method I used), but a few can learn to read; apparently one reason for this is that chronological age is only a rough correlate (a surrogate variable) of children's evolving reading aptitude, meaning that an estimate of a child's reading readiness cannot accurately be based just on chronological age." Hegel considered this thesis-antithesis-synthesis pattern to be the perpetual law of thought.

In a dramatic political and economic adaptation of Hegel's formula, the German social activist Karl Marx (1818–1883) applied the dialectic scheme to explain societal evolution. In Marx's *dialectical materialism,* he proposed that the production and consumption of the world's products (materials) under capitalism resulted in a dialectic conflict between owners of industry and their workers, a conflict that could be resolved only by socialist revolution.

Recently, Klaus F. Riegel applied Hegel's general dialectical formula to explain the process of human development (1972, 1975, 1976, 1979). To begin, Riegel proposed that the events in children's lives that contribute to development are best studied along four dimensions labeled the *inner-biological,* the *individual-psychological,* the *cultural-sociological,* and the *outer-physical.*

> A dialectic interpretation of development is based on the recognition that the interactions among these progressions of events are not always coordinated and synchronized. Whenever these interactions are out of step or contradictory, a conflict or crisis is said to exist. In a dialectic conception it is the discordance and tension of these contradictory interactions [Hegel's thesis/antithesis] that become the source of new development, more specifically, of leaps in development. Through the development of coordinating and integrative actions and thoughts, synchrony will be established and thereby, progress achieved [Hegel's synthesis]. Yet even as synchrony is attained, new discrepancies emerge and, in doing so, produce a continuous flux of contradictions and developmental change. (Riegel, 1976, p. 350)

Riegel suggested that dialectical discordances can occur within one dimension or between two or more. For example, along the inner-biological progression, an eleven-year-old girl can experience her first menstruation period, the menarche, and at the same time may contract tonsillitis. Hence, there is a conflict between two aspects of the inner-biological dimension in that she must adjust to two distressing biological events, with the infected tonsils adding to the discomfort of the menarche and further disturbing her physiological harmony. In addition, the menarche is an event inconsistent with girl's existing self-concept, so that inner-biological change precipitates disorder in her individual-psychological self. At the same time, the attitudes of her society (cultural-sociological) toward the menarche also can affect her in ways she has not yet experienced, therein requiring revisions in her customary social conduct (such as using sanitary pads and perhaps avoiding other girls when in the school lavatory). Thus, disturbance has occurred across three dimensions as a result of the original inner-biological change. The girl now faces the developmental task of working out a suitable synthesis of the discordant elements. So in Riegel's system the process of growing up is composed of changes in one dimension that produce conflicts in other dimensions, necessitating a new synthesis of the four dimensions if development is to proceed satisfactorily.

By placing the thesis-antithesis-synthesis formula at the center of his theory, Riegel laid the foundation for criticizing an aspect of Piaget's theory of cognitive growth.

> The concepts of conflicts and contradictions ought to receive at least as much attention as the stabilizing concepts [in Piagetian theory] of solutions and agreements. Instead of directing all our attention toward the question of how problems are solved and answers are given, at least equal emphasis should be devoted to the issue of how problems are created and questions are raised. (Riegel, 1976, pp. 349–350)

Riegel also admonished traditional psychologists for emphasizing fixed entities in development—traits, capacities, abilities, skills, and underlying motivating drives. He contended that the emphasis instead should be on children's concrete interactions during activities of daily life within which dialectic operations continually take place. "A dialectic theory of development regards the individual as being in a continuous process of change brought about through the successive interactions of concrete events over time" (Riegel, 1976, p. 394).

Such a conviction bears important implications for research methodology. For example, Riegel cited people's everyday dialogues as prime examples of short-term dialectic exchanges that contribute to increments of development. In successful dialogues, each participant expresses a view of the topic, listens to the other's reply, then responds to the reply, and so on. The resulting chain of exchanges can represent an orderly linkage of questions, answers, contradictions, and subsequent syntheses to form a pattern of ideas not recognized by either speaker prior to their meeting. A step in intellectual development has taken place. Group discussions and interactive social games can perform the same function. Therefore, in regard to investigative goals and methods, Riegel chided linguists and psychologists for concentrating their analyses on formal descriptions or idealized systems of language and on the elements of such systems (words, morphemes, letters, phonemes). In his opinion, progress would be better served if researchers stressed the social aspects of language, especially the communication and the construction of meaning that occur in dialogues (Riegel, 1976, p. 376).

Riegel also identified research procedures devised in recent years to trace longer-term dialectical interactions. For instance, studies of cohorts of children growing up during different eras have shown that differences in social environments between one era and another can be more significant causes of certain child attributes than are the maturational factors cited in the past as determinants of children's characteristics (Riegel, 1976, p. 362). In effect, Riegel pointed out the need for revised research methods if investigations are to be conducted within his dialectical, contextualist paradigm.

In assessing Riegel's dialectical model, I will offer two observations. First, I think his scheme does indeed exemplify contextualism since it pictures the process of development as progressing through interactions among four dimensions, with the cultural-sociological and the outer-physical dimensions assuming strong roles in the process. Furthermore, Riegel advocated research methods that depend on real-life contexts—*in situ* environments—for generating data.

But, as a second observation, I question the practical usefulness of his quartet of dimensions. Although the four appear to offer a logical way to categorize aspects of development, they do not seem as helpful as a number of other analytical schemes (such as analyzing development in terms of interactions among genetic, developmental-history, and present-environment forces). One difficulty with Riegel's model is the problem of distinguishing clearly which dimension is being represented by a particular event or influence in the child's life. For instance, in our illustration of the girl entering puberty, we can ask whether her contracting tonsillitis qualifies as a sociological-cultural event (she was exposed to the germs in a social setting), as an outer-physical event (the setting in which she was infected), or as an inner-biological event (antibodies in her bloodstream combat the streptococcus bacteria). In other words, while it is easy enough to create illustrations that demonstrate the idea of the four dimensions and their interactions (as with our eleven-year-old), investigating specific people's lives in order to distinguish among the dimensions and to chart their transactions is quite a different matter. Getting agreement among investigators about how to analyze individual cases in a profitable way would seem to be most difficult.

To conclude, in its present state of development, the dialectical model's imprecision stands as a barrier to the theory's usefulness in guiding child rearing and in equipping evaluators to judge the theory's internal consistency, falsifiability, and fertility. A search of the journal literature in psychology through the mid-1990s indicates that Riegel's theory has stimulated little or no empirical research or practical applications. Thus, up till now, Riegel's scheme has served more adequately for pointing out shortcomings of other theories—such as Piaget's—than for charting programs of research or of educational and child-raising practices.

Valsiner's Cultural–Historical Theory

The reason Jaan Valsiner's theory belongs under the contextualist banner is that it is "built up within the individual-socioecological frame of reference, whereas the majority of psychological theories are constructed from the perspective of the inter-individual reference system" (1987, p. 230). Valsiner does not focus on internal traits of the child (abilities, attitudes, cognitive styles). Instead, he concentrates on interactions between the child and the environment that produce those ostensibly enduring traits. And instead of emphasizing an imagined stable order of development, he stresses the dynamic, shifting aspects of growth processes. Furthermore, rather than centering attention on likenesses between children and on the uniformity within a given child, he argues that the general rule in development— both from one child to another and within the same child—is "variability of behavior and thinking" (1987, p. 230). Therefore changes in each child's unique environments interact with changes in the child, so that generalizations or "laws of development" that are intended to apply to an entire group of children (five-year-old girls, seventh-grade boys) are of little value because "every individual developing child is an organism interrelated with his environment, and is thus lawful in himself" (Valsiner, 1987, p. 230).

In Valsiner's comments about how closely his views match other people's perspectives, he contended that the foregoing assumptions on which his theory is founded are contrary to the beliefs of laypersons and of "the majority of child psychologists (who have followed the laypersons' common sense)" (1987, p. 230). Consequently, he would anticipate that most people might consider his scheme both radical and unreasonable.

At the core of his theory is the proposal (1) that children's range of experience is defined by the environments they inhabit minute by minute and day by day and (2) that the nature of these environments is to a great extent controlled by children's caregivers—parents, siblings, babysitters, teachers, and the like. Children's psychophysical development is governed principally by what they learn in such settings and by how their health and physical well-being are influenced by their surroundings. And because the succession of environments traversed by one child is so different from that experienced by another, there will be marked dissimilarities in the two children's development. A girl growing up on a Chinese junk in Hong Kong harbor becomes a very different person from the girl raised in an affluent San Francisco suburb. The environments faced by a Hindu boy in a mountain village of Bali are dramatically different from those encountered by a black boy in a South African mining town. Valsiner's attention to such contrasts accounts for his stressing variability over similarity among children in their development.

Although the complexities of Valsiner's model cannot be detailed in the brief treatment given here, his concept of three *zones* can be described to reflect the theory's dominant tack. First is the *zone of free movement* (ZFM). This zone represents the set of items available to influence a child's actions in a particular environmental setting at a given time. The term *items* in this context refers to the areas of the environment, objects (including humans) in that setting, and ways the child can interact with those objects. According to Valsiner (1987, pp. 231–232), "the structure of ZFM is dynamic; given the change in goals or conditions, the boundaries of ZFM are constantly being reorganized. That reorganization may be initiated by either the child or caregivers, or by all of them at the same time."

The kinds of experiences a ZFM provides for a child are limited by the caregivers, who fence off those realms of action they consider unsuitable for the young one's development. Parents can prohibit children from playing with certain companions and can monitor the television programs children see and the books they read. For historical reasons, societies can differ from each other in how liberally they define the ZFM that children are permitted. For instance, a greater diversity of ZFM options is available in Britain's present-day multicultural society than in Saudi Arabia's highly cohesive Muslim culture.

Valsiner's second zone concept is the *zone of promoted action* (ZPA), which represents those modes of action that caregivers encourage or demand within the zone of free movement. Cultures and individual families vary in how restrictively they delineate what constitutes proper or acceptable action in the successive contexts a child moves through day after day. The most controllable situation of parent-child interaction occurs when the zone of free action is very narrow (permitting the child to act in only one way) and coterminous with the zone of promoted action. The decision-making role of parents is much simplified in such a society, since they merely need to urge their children to act in that single permissible way.

A very different child development situation results when the zone of free movement is extremely broad, and the zone of promoted action is very narrow—in fact, almost imperceptible. Under such conditions, both the culture and the particular parents allow children great freedom for developing themselves. Many options for action are available to the child in a given context, with little or no guidance offered by caregivers regarding which option might yield the most desirable long-term results. The rationale behind such parental behavior often derives from the conviction that children grow up the best if they follow their "natural bent": "When left to their own devices, children know what's good for them." In other cases, the young are permitted great freedom of choice simply out of parental neglect; caregivers are distracted by their own interests and pay little or no attention to child-raising responsibilities.

The last of Valsiner's three zones stems from L. S. Vygotsky's theory (Chapter Ten). It is the *zone of proximal development* (ZPD), defined as "the set of actions that the child can perform when helped by another person, but which are not yet available to the child in his individual acting" (Valsiner, 1987, p. 233). In other words, by working together with a caregiver, children are able to carry out activities that are just beyond their own independent abilities.

In Valsiner's opinion, postulating the three zones and analyzing permutations of their interactions enables one to derive insightful interpretations of a variety of child development phenomena—permissive parenting, abusive parenting, methods of instruction, goal setting, rules of behavior, stages of development, and more.

The historical-cultural factors that are assigned a central role in Valsiner's scheme operate at several levels. At the broadest level, people within a given society share in common influential *physical settings* (buildings, mountains, oceans, deserts), *items of material culture* (houses, tents, autos, camels, books, television receivers), *customs* (eating habits, modes of greeting, education, religious ceremonies), *bodies of knowledge* (scientific, social, religious, artistic), and *values* (moral, monetary, aesthetic). The patterning of these cultural elements in a given society is a product of the society's particular historical evolution. And the way that Valsiner's zones of free movement, of promoted action, and of proximal development are delineated for child-raising purposes is governed to a great extent by the particular society's shared cultural characteristics. The society in general, therefore, designates certain right and wrong ways to rear the young.

Just as the cultural traits of a society are rooted in that society's history, so also are the cultural characteristics of parents and teachers rooted in the history of their own upbringing within such a society. "The setting of goals by people who organize child/environment relationships is canalized by their cultural background" (Valsiner, 1987, p. 1143). Yet these personal histories include not only cultural factors common to nearly everyone but also additional factors (or variants of common factors) somewhat unique to their individual families, schools, churches, and companions. The caregiver's developmental history (as constructed from the general culture and subgroup or family culture) influences the way he or she defines the three context zones featured in Valsiner's model.

Finally, the growing child is daily accumulating a history that affects what that child can become in the years ahead. In other words, at any point in the child's development, the accumulation of past experiences in the form of stored knowledge, skills, and attitudes helps define (1) the child's perception of the three context zones and (2) the manner in which the child will react to the way caregivers manage the zones.

Now consider the matter of research from Valsiner's perspective. It is apparent that his theory places demands on the investigator that cannot be met by many of developmental psychology's traditional instruments and methods, such as ability and achievement tests, laboratory experiments, and statistical treatments of group data. Such techniques are hardly appropriate for tracing the developmental effects on a particular child of environments that are in a periodic state of flux. Consequently, the researcher who seeks to comprehend child-environment transactions from the viewpoint of Valsiner's contextualism is like a portrait painter whose model refuses to sit still, whose background scenery is apt to change without warning, and who finds uninvited newcomers intruding onto the set. Therefore more suitable investigative methods for contextual analysis are those of (1) observing caregivers and children in their daily interactions (with such observations recorded on videotape or audiotape), (2) interviewing caregivers and children about how they have interacted during past encounters, and (3) interviewing people and searching historical accounts for information about the society's customs that affect caregiver-child transactions. Detailed examples of such approaches have been included in Valsiner's recent works (1987, 1988a).

In assessing Valsiner's theory, I note that its scope is limited to clarifying only those aspects of development strongly affected by the way caregivers structure children's surroundings. However, as Valsiner points out, such a limitation still leaves a great range of phenomena to which the theory can apply, since so much of children's behavior is influenced by the contexts in which it occurs and the form of those contexts is strongly affected by cultural tradition (Valsiner, 1987, pp. 236–237).

In regard to the realistic quality of the model, I find that it convincingly reflects the actual world of children. It is also easily comprehended, is internally consistent, and appears economical. Although the theory offers no direct guidance for child rearing, it does provide a way caregivers can analyze the zones (freedom of movement, promoted action, proximal development) that caregivers create to form the environments within which children develop. In regard to its analytical potential, the theory is better prepared to explain the past than to predict the future, since the configurations of the environments that a child will later encounter are usually highly complex and not readily discerned ahead of time. This quality of partial indeterminacy of future environments causes Valsiner to describe his scheme as an open system, one whose end products cannot be forecast with much accuracy. In regard to its fertility, the model is of such recent vintage that its potential for stimulating empirical studies cannot yet be judged. Overall, I believe Valsiner's contextualist theory satisfactorily performs the function for which it was intended— that of providing a perspective for interpreting how children's environments are arranged by caregivers who themselves are products of a particular society's cultural history.

As a closing note, I should mention that Valsiner's developmental psychology is a telling example of his own contextual background. During the 1970s he completed his higher education at Tartu University in the Soviet republic of Estonia. In 1980 he left his homeland to spend six months in Western Europe at Justus Liebig University in Germany, then immigrated to the United States, first accepting an appointment in developmental studies at the University of Minnesota, then transferring to the University of North Carolina (1987, pp. ix–x). His contextualist model of development displays elements linked to theorists who have worked in each of these locations. For example, his scheme is strongly imbued with the traditional Soviet concern for ways cultural-historical factors influence develop- ment within social contexts. He has also drawn on Kurt Lewin's notions about how the child's *psychological field* changes from one event in life to another so that

> the developing child and his caregivers are viewed as being engaged in constant negotiation and renegotiation processes involving different "boundaries" in their relationships with one another and the environment at large. The boundary con- ditions define (and redefine) the structured nature of the child-environment rela- tionships, which (following Vygotsky's key idea of internalization of external experience) is gradually carried over from the realm of child's (externally con- strained) actions on the environment into his internally constrained thinking, feeling, and programming of actions. (Valsiner, 1987, p. 231)

In addition, Valsiner's theory stresses the child's very active engagement in the process of growing up, a stress that he credits to the American James Mark Baldwin (1861–1934), the Swiss Jean Piaget (1896–1980), and the Russian Lev Vygotsky (1896–1934).

In closing, I would suggest that when you meet ecological theory in Chapter Thirteen you will recognize that Valsiner's contextualist model could fit into that chapter as reasonably as it has in this one.

FOR FURTHER READING

Bandura, A. (1969) *Principles of Behavior Modification.* New York: Holt, Rinehart & Winston.

Bandura, A. (1977) *Social Learning Theory.* Englewood Cliffs, N.J.: Prentice-Hall.

Bandura, A. (1986) *Social Foundations of Thought and Action: A Social Cognitive Theory.* Englewood Cliffs, N.J.: Prentice-Hall.

Riegel, K. F. (1979) *Foundations of Dialectical Psychology.* New York: Academic Press.

Rotter, J. B. (1982) *The Development and Application of Social Learning Theory.* New York: Praeger.

Valsiner, J. (1987) *Culture and the Development of Children's Action.* Chicester, England: Wiley.

Judging the Appropriateness of Research Methods

What research methods are associated with different theories, and what are the strengths and limitations of such methods?

The aim of this perspective is (1) to identify symbiotic relationships between theory and research methodology and (2) to illustrate significant characteristics of research methods that affect how adequately any particular theory explains child development.

INTERDEPENDENCE OF THEORY AND RESEARCH METHODS

A symbiotic relationship obtains between a theory and the investigative techniques used both to generate and to validate the theory. For instance, Heider's commonsense attribution model was initially founded on ordinary people's comments about why folks act the way they do in everyday life. Then, after Heider created his model for analyzing such comments, hypotheses derived from the theory could be tested by means of additional observations of commonsense situations so as to validate, refine, and extend the scheme.

In contrast, Skinner's theory originated in experiments with animals in laboratory settings, experiments designed to reveal how manipulating animals' environments influenced the habits they acquired. From his observations, Skinner concluded that animals' behavior could be explained and predicted in terms of the kinds of consequences that followed their actions. And because his pigeons and rats were unable to communicate verbally, the experimenter could not depend on testimonials from his subjects about their thinking processes. Nor, indeed, did Skinner consider testimonials or introspection necessary because he was satisfied that his analyses of the connection between actions and their consequences explained the causes of behavior very nicely. When he then applied his theory to people, he assumed that (1) the basic principles of learning in animals fit humans as well and (2) the investigative methods he had developed with animals were, with certain revisions, also proper to use with people.

Humanistic psychologists, in a spirit quite the opposite of Skinnerian behaviorists, have created their notions of development from people's expressions about how they feel about themselves, about other people, and about their hopes for the future. As a result, humanists pay as much attention—or even more—to individuals' revelations about their private thoughts and feelings as to the individuals' overt actions.

In effect, the kinds of original data or observations from which a theory is created strongly affect the focus and scope of the theory. In turn, the model the theorist builds from such data will tend to delineate the methods of investigation to be used for testing, refining, and extending the theory.

Strengths and Limitations of Popular Research Methods

It is important to recognize that the self-serving reciprocity between theory and method can lead to incomplete or distorted interpretations of child development. It is likewise important to realize that no investigative method is perfect in itself. Each displays strengths and limitations that influence the adequacy of any theory to which that method is closely bound. The nature of such limitations can be demonstrated by considering where different research methods are typically located along dimensions of *control, reality, precision, reproducibility, significance,* and *feasibility.*

Control

The dimension labeled *control* refers to how well a researcher can assess or measure the variables that are involved in human development. A basic assumption underlying this dimension is that changes in child growth are the result of a variety of factors, not just one. Hence an important challenge investigators face is that of identifying which factors are involved and how to measure the amount of influence that each factor exerts on development.

A high level of control is achieved when the researcher conducts an experiment in which all but one causal factor are held constant, or else the remaining factors cancel each other out so that only one factor is allowed to vary. Sometimes two or three factors are permitted to vary, and then the researcher uses multivariate statistics to judge the amount of influence each factor has exerted on development. For instance, a popular way to attempt control in heredity–environment studies is to use pairs of monozygotic twins (twins born from the same fertilized ovum), so that their genetic inheritance is ostensibly identical. That is, genetic inheritance is assumed to be constant and environments are allowed to vary (some twins have been raised together in the same family, while others have been separated and grow up in different families). Conclusions are then drawn about the relative influence of heredity and environment on selected aspects of development: personality traits, cognitive ability, physical agility, and the like.

Another common approach to control involves placing children in a laboratory situation in which some environmental factors are held constant while others are varied systematically. The ones that are varied are often called *treatments*. For example, imagine that we wish to study how well children can learn different techniques for memorizing vocabulary words in a foreign language. The techniques will be rehearsal (say the words over and over), association (link new words to other words already in memory), and visual imaging (picture the words' graphic form). We also want to know how such a skill is influenced by age. To conduct our experiment, we decide to use children from three age groups—ages four, six, and eight—so we can estimate how memory ability changes with the passing years. Within each age group, an equal number of children will be randomly assigned to each of the three treatments: rehearsal, association, and visual imaging. By ensuring that the assignment of children is random, we are attempting to rule out the influence of extraneous variables—ones other than age and type of treatment—that might influence the final results. With a reasonably large number of children in each treatment group (perhaps a hundred or more), we feel rather safe in assuming that, because our assignments of children to the three treatments are random, such factors as level of intelligence, previous experience with a foreign language, and study habits are distributed about the same in one group as in the others. Consequently, these extraneous variables will not be the cause of one group succeeding better than another on the final memory scores.

Behaviorists have been particularly dedicated to controlled experiments. And when pigeons or white rats are used as subjects of research on development, even greater control can be wielded over the variables than is true when children are the subjects. Both the heredity and environment of animals can be manipulated with a good deal of precision, so the researcher can feel quite confident that the results derived from the studies reflect the influence of the one or two factors that were permitted to change.

At the opposite end of the control scale from laboratory experiments are the methods used by contextualists (Chapter Eight), ecologists (Chapter Thirteen), and ethologists (Chapter Fourteen), who typically study children in their natural settings. Such researchers may immerse themselves in the daily life of the people they are studying, thus becoming *participant-observers* who seek to disturb normal events as little as possible. Since they cannot actively control variables, the investigators carefully record events over an extended period of time in an effort to estimate which variables have been most influential in effecting the observed outcomes.

Because laboratory researchers' control techniques are designed to rule out or equalize extraneous variables, advocates of this approach tend to assume that "other things being equal, this one variable is the cause of the developmental change." In response, ecologists and ethologists are apt to reply, "But that's the point—other things are never *equal;* other things must be taken into account." In short, critics of traditional laboratory studies charge that experimental control is bought at the expense of facets of life that are significant for understanding child development. And this brings us to the reality dimension.

Reality

The reality criterion concerns how well the research methods reflect the way development actually occurs under natural conditions. The term *natural* in this context means the way children develop without special intervention, such as without the researcher's applying "unnatural" controls.

The danger of ignoring reality is what interested P. Mounoud when he wrote,

If we look critically at the experimental situations which have been devised over the past few decades, we will notice that they present extreme simplifications and impoverishments of reality. Striving to be more experimental, they turn out to be more and more fragmentary. This does not imply any opposition on my part to strict experimental approaches, but we should be conscious of their limitations as well as of their advantages. Above all, it is necessary to place studies of specific problems within broader contexts. (1986, pp. 41–42)

A. L. Brown voiced the same complaint when she observed that attitudes toward research methods in child development have changed in recent times:

Initial forays [in experimental developmental psychology] were . . . adapted from animal laboratories. . . . But children were notoriously unreliable accomplices; the variability in their data suggested perversity rather than compliance. . . . The best situation in which to study very early memory development is in a natural context in which the child is likely to understand the task and be motivated to perform it. Young children's performance on laboratory tasks is often markedly inferior to their performance in a game setting. . . . Mental acts occur in living contexts, and . . . the minimum unit of analysis must be the operations performed by an individual in context. (1979, pp. 248–250)

In a similar vein, critics of Freud have questioned how well psychoanalytic theory reflects reality when its picture of child development is founded on neurotic patients' recollections of their childhood as revealed in dreams and free-association remarks that are interpreted symbolically by a dedicated adherent of the theory.

Thus the conundrum posed for researchers is this: How can we get high levels of both control and reality? No one yet appears to have solved this puzzle, so that any particular investigative method represents some compromise between control and reality. Researchers continue to hunt for ways to wed the pair more compatibly.

Precision

Linked to both control and reality is the matter of *precision,* meaning how accurately aspects of development can be assessed, compared, and contrasted. The battle of precision frequently is waged with an arsenal of such words as *quantitative* versus *qualitative, statistical* versus *narrative, sampling error, critical ratio, interrater reliability, time sampling, scaling, error of measurement,* and more.

One debate among proponents of different theories concerns the desirability of quantitative versus qualitative research methods. Quantitative methods emphasize changes in *amounts* as children develop—in the numbers of words three-year-olds know, in the number of mathematics problems high school sophomores answer correctly, in the percentage of six-year-olds who can read a simple book, and the like. Qualitative methods, on the other hand, emphasize changes in *focus, structure,* or *complexity* as children grow up—in how children perceive the opposite sex before and after puberty, how well they grasp the concept of *fair play,* how adequately they understand other people's points of view, and such.

Strong advocates of precision typically like to have research results cast in numerical form. The more specific the numbers, the better. Reporting "63 percent" is better than reporting "most" or "the majority"—and "63.07 percent" is better yet. Research techniques that yield quantitative results are more often associated with such theoretical schemes as behaviorism and social learning theory than with humanistic psychology and psychoanalysis. It is difficult for a humanist to see how a child's self-concept and dreams of the future can meaningfully be cast in numerical form. Likewise, a psychoanalytic interpretation of the images of racing cars and tunnels in a teenager's dream does not easily lend itself to quantification. From the perspective of humanists and psychoanalysts, precision is obtained by careful observation, detailed recording, and clear descriptions of events—not by numbers.

Often a theory's investigative methods focus on both qualitative and quantitative changes. Piaget, whose early publications contained reports that were almost exclusively qualitative, later added quantification in response to critics' complaints that he had failed to report the proportion of children at different age levels who displayed various modes of thinking. While researchers on both sides of the quantitative–qualitative fence continue to argue for the superiority of their approach, in my mind there is little need to pit one camp against the other. Both quantitative and qualitative reports are needed. Each serves a valuable function in the explanation of child development. The issue, then, becomes one of determining what combination of the two furnishes the clearest picture of how and why children grow up as they do.

Reproducibility

Since theories of development are expected to apply to all children (or at least to all children within a particular culture or type), the evidence on which a theory is founded should be *reproducible*. For example, if a theorist studies one child and concludes that a particular combination of vitamins accounts for the child's improvement in problem-solving skill, then we should be able to reproduce this phenomenon with other children. Feeding the same mixture of vitamins to others and then assessing for improvement in problem solving enables us to discover whether the theorist's proposal applies to all children and thus is a general rule of child development rather than something unique to a single child. Experimental methods commonly used by behaviorists (Chapter Seven), certain social learning theorists (Chapter Eight), Piaget (Chapter Nine), Vygotsky (Chapter Ten), and information-processing advocates (Chapter Eleven) result in high ratings on the reproducibility criterion. But such is often not the case with humanistic (Chapter Twelve), ecological (Chapter Thirteen), and ethological (Chapter Fourteen) theorists. For humanists, the difficulty of reproducing a postulated relationship arises from their emphasis on the uniqueness of each individual's personality and from their dependence on a research methodology of introspection and self-report whose results vary from one person to the next. Contextualists, ecologists, and ethologists may consider it impossible to reproduce a significant event in a child's life if they believe that no combination of environmental and hereditary factors ever completely occurs the same way twice. Thus the best they can do is draw their estimates of theoretical relationships from reoccurrences of natural events that only approximate the original occurrence on which they based their proposals.

Hence the problem of reproducibility is closely linked to matters of control and reality. The more factors that are controlled, the easier it should be to reproduce a posited relationship between cause and effect. At the same time, the more that factors are controlled, the more the research method may distort the natural conditions of daily life.

Significance

The question of *significance* is at stake when people respond to a research outcome with "Who cares?" or "So what?" or "What makes you think the results of this study are significant?" K. P. Hillner, from the vantage point of a humanist, had this issue in mind when he complained,

> Even though methodology merely is a means to a certain end in every system of psychology, traditional behavioristic experimental psychology tends to lose sight of this fact and treats methodology as an end in itself. A specific research problem is chosen because it is amenable to a well-accepted/documented experimental technique, not because it is relevant for unraveling [human] nature or serves as a significant contribution to the psychological literature. One could never accuse a humanist of being guilty of confusing means with ends: The sole criterion of the humanist in choosing research projects is meaningfulness. A given study is undertaken because it is psychologically relevant and pertains to the human issues and concerns, as defined by the humanistic psychologist. For the humanist, the degree of objectivity or validity afforded by a given research technique is purely a secondary matter. (1984, pp. 259–260)

It is often said that the most crucial step in conducting research is that of framing the question the research is to answer. This initial research question, in effect, determines how significant the results of the investigation can be. Hillner's claim, then, is that behaviorists too often have been guided by the question, "What can I learn about child development by using well-established experimental techniques?" rather than by such a query as "What do I most need to learn about child development in order to enhance children's growth and happiness?" Behaviorists, certain social learning theorists, and information-processing advocates reply to such a charge with two counterarguments. First, they deny that the questions they ask are unimportant for explaining development. Second, they contend that investigative techniques that depend heavily on people's naive opinions and introspection and that fail to control for a host of variables are unlikely to produce believable answers for even the "most significant" questions. Thus the issue of significance is connected to matters of control, reality, precision, and reproducibility.

It is apparent that different people value different types of information about development and thus assign different levels of significance to different research methods. Parents who are concerned with daily child-rearing decisions (as in behavior modification) will assign greater significance to research methods that yield answers to immediate child-raising questions than they will to methods (psychoanalytic) that answer questions about factors in a child's distant past that may have influenced early personality development.

But no matter what questions researchers designate as most significant, their efforts to apply investigative methods that furnish convincing answers to their questions are usually restricted by considerations of feasibility.

Feasibility

The *feasibility* dimension concerns the practicality of an investigative method. Frequently researchers first conceive of a study as if ideal conditions existed. Then, as they inspect the circumstances they must face in actually carrying out the study, they retreat from the ideal to the practical by revising their project to accommodate for the constraints imposed by their real-life situation. Four of the most common constraints are those of time, funds, complexity, and the welfare of the children expected to participate in the research.

Consider the matter of time in cases of longitudinal versus cross-sectional research. In longitudinal research, an investigator traces the growth of the same group of children over a period of several years. Such an approach not only provides data about children at successive age levels but also permits the investigator to identify particular patterns of development of individual children in the group. However, researchers are often unable or unwilling to dedicate eight or ten or more years to a single study, especially when they run the risk of not being able to locate all of the original members of the group as the years pass and families move away. Furthermore, a large percentage of the people conducting developmental studies are graduate students doing research for their master's or doctoral degree. Rarely can they afford the time required for conducting longitudinal investigations. Hence they substitute a cross-sectional design by simultaneously studying children of different age groups, perhaps comparing children aged three, six, nine, and twelve in order to draw inferences about developmental changes. However, cross-sectional studies can furnish information only about how groups differ *on the average*. Such studies cannot tell how individual children change over the years, nor can they tell whether today's three-year-old group would actually score the same as today's twelve-year-old group if the three-year-olds could be tested nine years in the future.

Time is also a constraint when an investigator needs schoolchildren as subjects. School personnel and parents are usually unwilling to jeopardize pupils' progress with their schoolwork by their spending many hours in a child development experiment. A further time limitation relates to children's attention span. Young children cannot tolerate lengthy experimental sessions without tiring and becoming bored.

Limitations on funds are a further important restriction on research methods. Financial demands mount with each increase in the equipment needed, the time and personnel required, the number of children to be studied, the distances to be traveled, the complexity of data analysis, and more.

Complexity, as a third form of constraint, refers to how complicated the research design, the data gathering, and the data analysis will be. Very often the methodology that theoretically should yield the most valuable results is far too intricate and convoluted to be implemented in the real world, so the initial ideal plan must be replaced by a simpler one when the research is actually carried out.

A fourth restriction has become more apparent in recent years in the United States and in similar nations where government agencies have become increasingly sensitive to protecting the welfare of the children who are the subjects of research. Typically, regulations for guarding the rights of children obligate researchers to furnish evidence that the investigation they are about to launch will keep the children's identities anonymous, will not damage the children physically or psychologically, and will yield information sufficiently valuable to society to warrant any bother or distress that the subjects might experience. In the main, these regulations represent quite sensible protective measures. However, in some cases regulations have been imposed by pressure groups for political rather than humanitarian reasons and are so restrictive that they rule out the possibility of conducting studies that are both (1) of marked value for understanding child development and (2) very unlikely to jeopardize children's welfare (Strazicich, 1988). In short, regulations—whether reasonable or unreasonable—significantly influence the research methods that can feasibly be adopted.

Conclusion

In summarizing, I would emphasize that understanding why any theory of development has assumed its particular form requires an appreciation of the interdependence among (1) the research methods and data on which the theory was originally built, (2) the subsequent investigative methods that derive from the key questions generated by the theory, and (3) how the theory's research methodology has been influenced by considerations of control, reality, precision, reproducibility, significance, and feasibility.

PART FIVE

THE GROWTH OF THOUGHT AND LANGUAGE

A search for patterns of development in children's cognitive and verbal skills and for the mechanisms that bring these patterns about

The two chapters in Part Five treat a pair of cognitive development theories that have attracted a host of adherents over the past several decades. The theories are (1) Jean Piaget's psychology of the child and (2) development models of the former Soviet Union, particularly as guided by Lev Semenovich Vygotsky. The title of this part—"The Growth of Thought and Language"—is not meant to suggest that other theories described in this volume have ignored mental development or verbal communication. Rather, the title simply highlights the emphasis placed in the Piagetian and Soviet models on the growth of children's cognitive and verbal abilities.

Jean Piaget (1896–1980) was a Swiss who has often been acclaimed as the most influential researcher in the field of child development in the twentieth century. He gained this distinction for proposing a novel model of children's mental development, a model founded on a great quantity of ingenious research on children from the time of birth into adolescence. Beginning in 1921 and continuing for nearly sixty years, he published hundreds of journal articles and books on all sorts of questions related to children's thought processes: how dreams and play evolve, how symbols develop, how moral judgment grows, how perceptions change, how intelligence improves, how numbers are conceived, how physical events occur, and many more. The diverse topics on which Piaget wrote are all connected to his basic model of intellectual growth. The view of Piaget offered in Chapter Nine focuses on the most fundamental elements of that model.

The second theoretical persuasion examined (Chapter Ten) is one that dominated developmental psychology in the Soviet Union for more than six decades. The Soviet perspective has been included for two main reasons. First, it illustrates a development theory that, out of political necessity, conformed to the tenets of the Marxist sociopolitical philosophy on which the Soviet state was founded. Second, Soviet developmentalists displayed noteworthy inventiveness in research methodology and analysis while producing a great quantity of empirical studies on childhood and adolescence.

In terms of chronology, the two chapters make a fitting pair, since Piaget and Vygotsky pursued their initial investigations of child development and contructed their basic systems during the same decade, the 1920s. However, their subsequent careers were markedly different. Vygotsky died in 1934, and his works were sup-pressed until years later, when their release to the world led to the high status they enjoy today. In contrast, Piaget was able to continue his investigations from the 1920s until his death in 1980, a sixty-year career that made him the most famous child development theorist of all time.

Both Piaget's and Vygotsky's systems qualify as stage theories by virtue of their picturing the child as passing from one distinctive phase of cognitive and language development into another. However, some critics have doubted the validity of the stages they proposed, and others have even questioned the whole idea of stages. To delineate key facets of this debate, Perspective D, at the end of Part Five, focuses on the likely future of stage theories.

CHAPTER NINE

PIAGET'S COGNITIVE DEVELOPMENT THEORY

Jean Piaget (1896–1980) was a precocious boy who, in his teens, had already developed an intense interest in biology, particularly in the biological bases of knowledge. By age twenty-one he had earned a doctorate at the university in his hometown of Neuchatel, Switzerland, and had published more than two dozen professional papers on biological studies, most of them concerning mollusks. This early specialization in biology had a lasting influence on his conceptions of the development of the mind.

Upon finishing his doctorate, he shifted his attention to psychology, which he studied in Swiss psychological clinics and at the Sorbonne in Paris. While in Paris (1919–1921), Piaget worked on standardizing tests of children's abilities in the laboratory school of the French expert on intelligence measurement, Alfred Binet. During this time Piaget was not as interested in whether children got the test items correct as he was in the thinking processes that led children to produce the answers they gave, especially the incorrect answers. This interest established the focus of his research during the rest of his career.

Although Piaget is commonly referred to as a child psychologist, the research task he set for himself was that of a *genetic epistemologist*. This means that the central question guiding his investigations was not, What are children like? but, How does knowledge develop in humans? Or more precisely, How does the relationship between the *knower* and the *known* change with the passing of time? So the term *genetic* (meaning the genesis of the mode of development) *epistemology* (the theory of knowledge) does indeed describe the field of his endeavors. Children of different age levels just happened to be the instruments by which his investigations in this field were carried out.

In the following review of Piaget's work, we will consider (1) his methods of research, (2) his conception of knowledge, (3) his conception of the process by which children's knowledge grows, (4) his definition of the stages of intellectual growth, (5) four of his key concepts, (6) the practical applications of his theory in education, (7) research challenges, and, finally, (8) an assessment of his theory.

PIAGET'S CLINICAL METHOD

While working at Binet's test-construction laboratory, Piaget devised the basic technique of studying children that would become the mainstay of his methodology during the next fifty years. His approach, known as a *clinical method,* involved a researcher posing problems for children and then observing how the children went about finding a solution. For children who had not yet reached puberty, the problems usually involved objects the child could see and manipulate, such as two lumps of clay that could be formed into different shapes or two glasses of water of different sizes. By the time the child could use language at age three or four, the experimenter asked questions about solutions to the problems being posed. During the adolescent years, children were more often given verbal problems and asked how they arrived at their solution.

Unlike some other experimenters, Piaget did not limit himself to asking each child a preconceived set of questions. Rather, after beginning an interview with a standard question or two, he felt free to create, on the spot, additional questions designed to probe the thought processes that produced the child's initial answer. Piaget defended this deviation from a single, standard set of questions by explaining that all children do not interpret a given question in the same way. Thus the experimenter probes the child's understanding and may then cast the problem in a different form to help ensure that the problem situation is the same for each child, even though the wording of it may not be identical each time (Phillips, 1975, pp. 4–5).

A typical interview is illustrated in the following passage in which eight-year-old Per is being questioned about some flowers—primulas and other varieties—that the woman interviewer placed before the child. The interviewer's purpose was to discover how Per classifies objects into a general set (flowers) and into subsets within the general set (primulas, violets, tulips). At the point we enter the discussion, Per has already devised three levels of classes: yellow primulas, primulas, and flowers (adapted from Inhelder & Piaget, 1964, p. 107).

Interviewer: Can one put a primula in the box of flowers (without changing the label)?
Per: Yes, a primula is also a flower.
Interviewer: Can I put one of these flowers (a tulip) in the box of primulas?
Per: Yes, it's a flower like the primula.

When the experimenter does so, Per changes her mind and puts it back with the other flowers.

Interviewer: Can one make a bigger bunch with all the flowers or with all the primulas?
Per: It's the same thing, primulas are flowers, aren't they?
Interviewer: Suppose I pick all the primulas, will there be any flowers left?
Per: Oh, yes, there will still be violets, tulips, and other flowers.
Interviewer: Well, suppose I pick all the flowers, will there be any primulas left?
Per: No, primulas are flowers, you're picking them too.
Interviewer: Are there more flowers or more primulas?
Per: The same number, primulas are flowers.
Interviewer: Count the primulas.
Per: Four.

Interviewer: And the flowers?
Per: Seven.
Interviewer: Are they the same number?
Per (astonished): The flowers are more.

In effect, then, Piaget's research methodology consisted of his first observing children's reactions to their surroundings. Then, on the basis of these observations, he composed hypotheses about the sorts of biological and mental structures that underlie their reactions. Finally, he cast the hypotheses in the form of problems or questions that he posed to children in order to reveal their thinking processes and thus test the hypotheses. Over the years he produced many problem situations that were subsequently used by researchers in many parts of the world to investigate matters that Piaget studied, as well as other aspects of development.

PIAGET'S CONCEPTION OF KNOWLEDGE

A useful step toward understanding Piaget's theory is to learn how he defined *knowledge* because his conception differs from most popular beliefs. We can perhaps best see this difference by beginning with a review of four commonsense ideas about knowledge and how it is acquired.

First, common sense holds that knowledge is a body of information or beliefs a person has acquired, either through instruction or through direct experience with the world. This idea of a collection of information is reflected in such everyday phrases as "She's a storehouse of knowledge" and "I wish I had all his knowledge."

Second, it is also a commonsense conviction that a person's knowledge is a fairly faithful representation of what the person has been taught or has witnessed. It is assumed that if two people, both with good eyesight, observe an event from the same vantage point, their knowledge of the event will be essentially identical. The great dependence on witnesses in court cases is founded on this conviction.

Third, common sense indicates that our storehouse of knowledge is increased as we add item upon item from our daily experiences. That is, we take in bits of information and pile them onto the proper heap in the storehouse, with each heap related to a different aspect of life.

Fourth, common sense tells us that whenever we need to recall an item of knowledge from the storehouse of memory, the item can be recovered in essentially the same condition as it was when first acquired. Of course, some details of the item may now be a bit vague, but if we can recall the item at all, it will be basically in its original form.

How did Piaget's views differ from such commonsense notions? To begin, he did not agree that knowledge is a body of acquired information or a state of possessing such information. Instead, he conceived of knowledge as a *process*. To *know* something means to *act* on that thing, with the action being either physical or mental or both. The two-year-old child's knowledge of a ball consists of his picking it up, pressing it with his fingers, tossing it, and observing it bounce away. As children grow up, they gain more experience with such direct, physical knowing, and they mature internally so that they are increasingly freed from having to carry out direct physical behavior in order to know something. They become able to produce mental images and *symbols* (words, mathematical figures) that represent objects and relationships. Hence the older child's knowledge increasingly becomes mental activity. She "thinks about" things by carrying out *interiorized actions* on symbolic objects (Piaget, Apostel, & Mandelbrot, 1957, pp. 44–45). So to Piaget, knowledge was a process or repertoire of actions rather than an inventory of stored information.

Piaget also disagreed with the commonsense idea of *perception,* that is—with the way objects or events are recorded in the child's mind. In Piaget's opinion, the child does not take in a picture of objective reality. Instead, as the child perceives or takes in the world, the picture is biased by the condition of the child's perceptual mechanism. If we adopt the analogy of viewing the world through glass, then in the Piagetian model the child does not record events through a clear window. Rather, he views events through a colored lens that is given its present focus and tint by both (1) the child's past experiences and (2) his current stage of internal maturation. The way that two children know (act on) the same object will not be identical, for the lens of one will have a somewhat different focus and tint than the other's.

But if knowledge is a process of acting on percepts rather than a collection of information, then what is *memory* and how does it operate? Piaget agreed that the results of a person's past actions can be stored as memories to be retrieved when needed. He also agreed that the quantity of memories increases with maturation and experience. But he did not believe that the act of remembering is simply a matter of summoning images of past events from memory and placing them in the showcase of consciousness so that, like museum pieces, they can be viewed in their passive, original condition. Rather, retrieving stored vestiges of the past, which he labeled *active memory,* is "interiorized recitation" or "a reconstitution of the past" (Piaget, 1946, pp. 5, 261). Remembering is a reenacting of the original process of knowing. However, it cannot simply be a repetition of the original knowing because the child's mind has subsequently been altered by additional experiences and further internal maturation. So the interiorized recitation or rehearsal of the stored event is, as it were, now performed on a somewhat altered mental stage according to revised stage directions.

To summarize, in Piaget's system, knowledge is a process of acting—physically and/or mentally—on objects, images, and symbols that the child's perceptual lens has cast into patterns that are somewhat familiar to her or him. The objects are found in the world of direct experience, while the images and symbols can be derived not only from the "real world" but from memory as well.

One way to conceive of mental growth or the development of intelligence is to picture it as a constant effort on the part of the child to expand and refine her knowledge, her repertoire of mental actions. Or, in different terms, "All knowledge is continually in a course of development and of passing from a state of lesser knowledge to one which is more complete and effective" (Piaget, 1972, p. 5).

This idea that a child's knowledge improves with age is hardly a noteworthy discovery. Everyone knows that already. But what everyone does not know is the

TABLE 9.1
Growth in sample aspects of knowledge: Infancy to adolescence

From infancy	Through early and middle childhood	To adolescence
Egocentrism versus objectivity: not distinguishing between self and the environment	partially distinguishing between self and the environment	clearly differentiating self from objects of the environment
Object permanence (conservation): not recognizing (not constructing) the permanence of objects whose location is changed	recognizing (constructing) object permanence when location is changed, but failing to recognize (to construct) which characteristics of objects are unchanged (or are conserved) when objects are transformed	recognizing (constructing) which aspects of objects are unchanged (are conserved) when the objects are transformed
Symbolic functioning: not recognizing (not constructing) that one thing can represent something else	recognizing (constructing) symbolization through such acts of imitation as gesture, play, drawing, and oral echoing	recognizing (constructing) complex written and spoken symbols and signs
Internalization of action: adapting to the environment solely by physical acts	beginning to act internally on objects (manipulate them mentally) while observing them	accomplishing faster, more complete adaptation by internally (mentally) manipulating objects of the environment, their classifications, and their relationships
Classes and relationships: not recognizing (not constructing) classifications of objects or relationships among objects	recognizing (constructing) classes and relationships among objects that are directly touched, seen, or heard	not only recognizing (constructing) classifications of and relationships among objects directly perceived but also (1) of imagined objects and events and (2) of classification and relationship systems themselves

specific way knowledge changes, at what times it changes, and for what likely reasons. These are the things Piaget provided. Table 9.1 illustrates five categories of behavior he treated. In the description, I am using the verbs *recognizing* and *constructing* as synonyms, believing that the more passive *recognizing* is the familiar way people refer to such mental behavior but that *constructing* more accurately reflects Piaget's conception of knowledge as a process of active production on the child's part.

These, then, are some of the directions of intellectual development that Piaget's theory depicts and explains (Piaget & Inhelder, 1969). Our next task is to identify the mechanisms that, in Piaget's opinion, bring about these kinds of development.

THE MECHANISMS OF DEVELOPMENT

The purpose of all behavior or all thought, according to Piaget's system, is to enable the organism—the child—to adapt to the environment in ever more satisfactory ways. Piaget called the techniques of adaptation *schemes* or, in older translations of his writings from the original French, *schemas* or *schemata*. A scheme or technique of adjustment can be biological or mental or both. In Piaget's words: "A scheme is the structure or organization of actions as they are transferred or generalized by repetition in similar or analogous circumstances" (Piaget & Inhelder, 1969, p. 4).

The *grasping* movement of the infant's hand is such a scheme, a physical organization of actions that the infant can generalize to grasp a bottle, a rattle, or the edge of the crib. On the intellectual level, an adolescent's concept of a *series* is also a scheme, a mental organization of actions. The adolescent can apply it in constructing a series of numbers, arranging a series of sweaters according to shades of color, or arranging a series of peers by height or attractiveness.

A scheme can be very simple, such as the action pattern involved by a child's sucking a thumb. Or it can be complex, comprising physical and mental subschemes, as in the chain of acts required for starting a car and driving it down the street or in the mental chain needed for solving quadratic equations.

Schemes always include accompanying feeling tones. When Piaget talked of *affective schemes,* he did not mean schemes distinct from mental structures but "simply the affective aspect of schemes which are otherwise also intellectual" (Piaget, 1963, p. 207).

The newborn's schemes are very limited in number, consisting of reflex action patterns—sucking, crying out, sneezing, flexing limbs, and the like. But as the days pass, other sensorimotor actions build out of these beginnings. Then, still within the first year of life, identifiable intellectual schemes evolve and over the following years multiply enormously. Thus, when we conceptualize child development in terms of schemes, we should picture it as the child's acquiring ever greater quantities of schemes that become interlinked in ever more sophisticated patterns.

How does this process of evolving schemes come about? To understand the process, we needed to learn the meanings Piaget assigned to the words *assimilation* and *accommodation.* To help explain these matters, I would liken schemes to musical themes or tunes, for tunes are organizations of sounds just as schemes are organizations of sensorimotor and mental actions.

The Function of Assimilation

At every point in their lives, children's adaptation to the environment in order to satisfy their needs is accomplished by means of schemes. Children's repertoire of schemes at any given time is like a collection of melodies they already know. When they face the problem of satisfying needs, they inspect the environment to perceive how its apparent structure seems to fit schemes currently in their armory. It's as if children listen to the sounds coming from their surroundings to determine whether they match, or nearly match, a tune they know. When they find what they consider a good match, they have achieved their adaptation. When the infant in the crib drops her doll onto the floor, she inspects the scene to decide whether the conditions of her problem match any scheme or strategy in her repertoire of solutions. A twelve-year-old boy assigned to draw a map of the route from home to school must likewise search his available action structures to find ones appropriate to the task. A high school student listening to her English teacher lecture about the plot structure in *Hamlet* must incorporate the ideas from the lecture into suitable schemes already in her mind if she is to comprehend, or mentally construct, the meanings intended by the teacher.

This process of matching environmental stimuli to existing mental patterns is not simply a matter of ingesting objective reality from the world. Rather, the child reshapes the events of the world somewhat to fit the pattern of his or her existing schemes. It's as if the child hears several tones, and decides that they sound enough like a familiar melody to indeed be that melody.

Piaget applied the label *assimilation* to this process of taking in or understanding events of the world by matching the perceived features of those events to one's existing schemes. As Piaget put it, "To assimilate an object to a schema means conferring to that object one or several meanings" (Piaget, Jonckheere, & Mandelbrot, 1958, p. 59).

The Function of Accommodation

However, often the perceived structure of events does not readily fit the child's available schemes, even with some perceptual bending or shaping of that structure. When this occurs, one of two consequences can be expected. The first is that the event is not assimilated at all. It is ignored or passed by, like a person's rejecting several sounds as meaningless noise instead of recognizing them as a familiar tune. The encounter with the environment simply does not register on the child. Such is the case when a father tries to teach his young son to draw with proper visual perspective but finally concludes, "He can't do it at all. He just doesn't catch on."

The second possible consequence of a poor match between the perceived environment and available schemes is not outright rejection but dissatisfaction and continued efforts to achieve a match.

> New objects which present themselves to consciousness do not have their own qualities which can be isolated . . . they are vague, nebulous, because unassimilable, and thus they create a discomfort from which there emerges sooner or later a new differentiation of the schemas of assimilation. (Piaget, 1963, p. 141)

So it is that schemes, under pressures from perceived realities of the environment, are altered in form or multiplied to accommodate for the lack of an adequate match. In effect, a tune from the child's existing store of melodies is revised to become a variation of the original theme, a variation that better fits the sounds of the world. Piaget used the term *accommodation* to identify this process of altering existing schemes to permit the assimilation of events that otherwise would be incomprehensible.

Since no new event is perfectly identical with those past events that were used in the formation of schemes, there is always some degree of mismatch of schemes with new events. But this mismatch is remedied for by the balancing counterplay between assimilation and accommodation, which are two of the basic innate acts Piaget called *functional invariants*. Assimilation reshapes the environmental input to fit existing schemes, whereas accommodation revises or adds to the schemes to readjust for environmental features that cannot conveniently be ignored or distorted.

Just as adaptation to the world is achieved by the functions of assimilation and accommodation, so within the child's biological-mental self a process of *organization* operates to ensure that all schemes are properly interrelated, properly adjusted to each other to form an integrated person.

> It is sufficiently well known that every intellectual operation is always related to all the others and that its own elements are controlled by the same law. Every schema is thus coordinated with all the other schemata and itself constitutes a totality with differentiated parts. Every act of intelligence presupposes a system of mutual implications and interconnected meanings. (Piaget, 1963, p. 7)

Therefore a child's development, according to Piagetian theory, seems somewhat like a progressively complex symphony. Its multiple melodies are the schemes formed from the balanced counterpoint of assimilation against accommodation. And the interweaving of themes produces a coordinated whole.

All these matters can be summarized in three quotations from Piaget:

> The filtering or modification of the input is called *assimilation;* the modification of internal schemas to fit reality is called *accommodation.* (Piaget & Inhelder, 1969, p. 6)
>   Adaptation is an equilibrium between assimilation and accommodation. (Piaget, 1963, p. 6)
>   The "accord of thought with things" (adaptation) and the "accord of thought with itself" (organization) express this dual functional invariant of adaptation and organization. These two aspects of thought are indissociable: It is by adapting to things that thought organizes itself and it is by organizing itself that it structures things. (Piaget, 1963, p. 8)

Four Causal Factors

We next face the question of what factors or forces determine how this adaptation-organization system will operate in a given child's development. What causes a child to acquire her particular schemes and at what times in her growing up? How does environment as compared to heredity influence the kinds and rate of scheme formation?

In responding to such questions, Piaget proposed four underlying causal factors: (1) heredity (internal maturation), (2) physical experience with the world of objects, (3) social transmission (education), and (4) equilibrium.

1. Heredity   In the continuing debate among developmentalists over the roles of nature and nurture, Piaget has been classified by most writers as an inter-actionist, and certainly he considered himself so. He did not accord either hered-ity or environment greater power in determining development. Instead, he saw each playing a distinct and necessary part to complement the part of the other.

What role did Piaget see nature playing? He said that not only does heredity provide the newborn with the initial equipment to cope with problems she or he will meet in the world, but heredity also establishes a time schedule for new develop-ment possibilities to open up at periodic points throughout the child's growing years. This is the internal-maturation factor in heredity. It functions rather like a legislative body, which from time to time passes a new act of *enabling* legislation. Each such act, or maturational change, creates possibilities for new schemes to be created that could not have been generated earlier, but this action neither requires nor guarantees that the potential schemes will materialize. The extent to which the potentialities are actually realized is determined by the sorts of experiences the child has with his or her environment. So internal maturation is a necessary but not sufficient condition for development to proceed.

Much of the practical use of Piaget's findings for educators and parents lies in his identification of approximate age levels at which the maturation needed for developing particular schemes or intellectual operations occurs. If suitable matura-tion has not yet taken place, it is futile to try to teach the child a particular skill. The probable reason the father failed to teach his young son proper visual perspective was that the maturation necessary for developing the required schemes had not yet occurred.

Piaget (1973, p. 27) viewed as folly the efforts of some psychologists to dissociate the effect of heredity from that of the heredity–environment amalgam in seeking to decide which of the two is more important for development: "If a maturation effect intervenes everywhere, it remains dissociable from the effects of the exercise of learning or of experience."

2. Physical experience   It is essential to recognize that Piaget, unlike most theorists, separated the child's trafficking with the environment into two varieties: (a) direct and generally unguided experience with objects in the world, called *physical experience*; and (b) the guided transmission of knowledge—that is, education in a broad sense, called *social transmission.* We will consider direct experience first, for it is the type on which Piaget has focused the greater part of his attention.

In this case, the child directly manipulates, observes, listens to, and smells objects to see what occurs when they are acted upon. From such investigations the child generates a logic or knowledge of the properties of things and how they work. Piaget stressed that it is not observation of the passive objects themselves that develops the child's logic or intelligence, but the set of conclusions the child draws from those actions that bring about events and influence objects. So simply seeing a feather or brick or lump of clay is not enough for intellectual development to take place. Such development depends on the *experience* derived when physically or mentally participating in such events as the following:

> A chicken feather and a metal bolt are simultaneously dropped from the same height.
> A brick is put into a bucket full of water, and a pine block the size of the brick is put into a second bucket of water.
> Three lumps of clay are rolled into shapes: the first into a ball, the second into a sausage, the third into a long snake.
> The child tries to cut a board—first with scissors, next with a knife, and then with a saw.

These sorts of experiences contribute to the aspect of intellectual development that Piaget (1973, p. 2) called *spontaneous* or *psychological:* "the development of the intelligence itself—what the child learns by himself, what none can teach him and he must discover alone."

Although physical experience with the action of objects is essential to mental growth, by itself it is, like maturation, insufficient to bring about development.

3. Social transmission   This is education in a broad sense: the transmission of knowledge to the child from without. Like the first two factors, this one is important but is insufficient by itself to effect mental growth, for it depends upon both maturation and direct experience to prepare the schemes that permit assimilation of what parents, the school, and the general social milieu seek to teach the child. This factor contributes what Piaget called the *psychosocial* aspect of cognitive development (1973, p. 2).

4. Equilibrium   This last force is the one that maintains a balance among the other three, fitting the maturational, direct experience, and social transmission influences together harmoniously. Piaget (1973, p. 29) felt the need for such a factor because "a whole play of regulation and of compensation is required to result in a coherence."

In summary, then, the sorts of knowledge the child acquires in terms of mental schemes, and the time at which they are acquired, depend upon such factors as maturation, physical experience, social transmission, and equilibrium. These factors regulate the stages of cognitive growth through which, in Piaget's system, all children normally develop. It is to this series of levels or stages that we now turn.

LEVELS AND STAGES OF DEVELOPMENT

As noted in Chapter Two, one of the traditional issues in the field of child development is whether growth proceeds continuously—by imperceptibly small increments—or advances by stages. And if a theorist proposes that it does indeed move by stages, then what criteria does she or he apply in identifying a stage?

Piaget, like apparently all developmentalists, recognized that from day to day, growth is continuous, with no major leaps ahead from one day to the next and no extended plateaus of dormancy in growth. At the same time, when he viewed the entire span of the growth years, Piaget was able to distinguish breaks in the process. These breaks suggested to him that the child has at each such point completed one phase of development and become engaged in a further one.

To say that Piaget proposed *a* series of developmental stages would be over-simplifying his work. Actually, he identified a number of different series, each related to a different aspect of personality or mental life. For example, one series concerns steps in understanding physical causality (1930), another the steps in imitation and play (1951), still another in the conception of moral principles and justice (1948), and others in understanding number (1952), space (Piaget & Inhelder, 1956), and movement (Piaget, 1969). But underlying these and other specific series of stages there appears to be a basic set that provides the frame-work for overall sensorimotor-intellectual development. Let's look at this under-lying set.

There is some confusion in the writings of Piaget and his followers about how many major stages, and their constituent substages, best reflect the growth process. Some authors picture three major levels, others four, and some even five. In the following discussion I have cast the scheme into one of its most familiar forms, with four major levels or periods, each divided into subperiods designated as stages. In this fourfold division, the levels are called (1) the sensorimotor period, (2) the preoperational thought period, (3) the concrete operations period, and (4) the formal operations period. As we trace the child's progress through the stages, we will see him or her grow from being (a) an entirely self-centered infant with no realistic knowledge of his or her environment to become (b) an adolescent who employs logic and language with facility to intellectually manipulate the environ-ment and thus comprehend, ever more realistically, how the world functions.

Although age designations are attached to each of the four periods in the following discussion, they should be regarded as only approximations, as rough averages, for, as Piaget pointed out:

> They are not stages which can be given a constant chronological date. On the contrary, the ages can vary from one society to another. . . . But there is a constant order of succession . . . that is, in order to reach a certain stage, previous steps must be taken. The prestructures . . . which make for further advance must be con-structed.
>
> Thus we reach a hierarchy of (mental) structures which are built in a certain order of integration and . . . appear at senescence to disintegrate in the reverse order. (1973, pp. 10–11)

Level 1: The Sensorimotor Period (Birth to Age Two)

During the first two years, infants are unable to verbalize very well any thoughts they may have, so it is necessary to estimate their intellectual growth by the manner in which they sense (see, hear, feel, taste, smell) their environment and by the manner in which they subsequently act upon it (motor behavior). Piaget's observations of children in this age period enabled him to distinguish six stages through which they develop (Piaget & Inhelder, 1969, pp. 4–12).

The first stage (birth to one month) features infants' adapting to their environment by means of their inherited, ready-to-operate, unlearned *reflexes.* It is by reflex activity that the baby sucks, cries, breathes, coughs, urinates, defecates, and makes gross bodily movements.

The second stage (one to four months) is marked by infants' gradually acquiring adaptive actions as the result of experience. During the first stage there was no distinction between the functions of assimilation and accommodation. But during the second, assimilation and accommodation can be distinguished as infants start to alter their sensorimotor action patterns (their schemes) on the basis of the responses of their environment. "For instance, when the child systematically sucks his thumb, no longer due to chance contacts but through coordination between hand and mouth, this may be called acquired accommodation" (Piaget, 1963, p. 48).

During this second stage the child engages in a great deal of repetitive activity, such as grasping and letting go of something over and over again. These actions, labeled *primary circular reactions,* were interpreted by Piaget as evidence that learning new associations or acquiring knowledge is not accomplished by the environment's imposing them on the child's mind. Rather, as noted in our earlier discussion of Piaget's concept of knowledge, intellectual development even during the sensorimotor period involves understandings "discovered and even created in the course of the child's own searchings" (Piaget, 1963, p. 55). So the repetitious activity of the infant is purposive, designed either to preserve or rediscover an act or skill. In other words, it functions as practice.

The third stage (four to eight months) marks the beginning of the infant's distinguishing between self and outside objects. It also marks the start of intentional acts, of consciously acting to attain a goal. The intention, however, is of a transitional type. The child does not foresee a goal, then attempt an act designed to achieve the goal. That sort of "true" intention comes at the fourth stage. But during the third stage the child will repeat an act that he or she happens to have performed with satisfaction. The primary circular reactions of the second stage were not movements designed to produce a particular result in the environment; they were simply self-centered acts showing no apparent awareness of an environment. However, at this third stage, the repetitive behavior that occurs—the *secondary circular reactions*—suggests a beginning awareness of the environment, for the acts seem directed toward reproducing a result that, by chance, has just been effected. For example, when an infant happens to hit a rattle hanging within reach in her crib, she may enjoy the sound. Then by gradually moving her hands and occasionally hitting the rattle, she begins to distinguish between her hand, the rattle, and other objects, so she comes purposely to grasp or hit the rattle directly and not by chance.

The fourth stage (eight to twelve months) signifies the emergence of clear acts of intelligence. At this stage, infants anticipate people and objects. They search for objects that are out of sight, thus showing that objects have now attained a quality of permanence for them. Prior to this time, if a toy was moved from one location to another, the infant apparently felt that it had dissolved into the nothingness around him or her and that a new toy had appeared from the nothingness at the second location, even though the toy had been shifted from the first spot to the second within the baby's presence. Along with this initial step in recognizing qualities of permanence of objects, the infant also begins to comprehend cause and effect, that certain acts will bring about predicted results. Consequently, the infant can conceive of an end result ahead of time, then fashion an act to bring the result about. The child's behavior now can be called truly intentional and thus qualifies as the beginning of *practical intelligence*, which consists of envisioning goals or desired ends and then employing existing schemes as means for achieving the ends (Piaget & Inhelder, 1969, pp. 10–11).

The fifth stage (twelve to eighteen months) involves the child in *tertiary circular reactions.* Recall that primary circular reactions (one to four months) were events repeated over and over simply to preserve them, a kind of practice. Secondary circular reactions (four to eight months) were the purposive repetition of acts the infant found satisfying the first time, and so chose to repeat again and again, even in new settings—a kind of application of known means to new situations. In contrast, tertiary reactions are not exact repetitions of the original act. Rather, they consist of reproducing the original event in modified form—a kind of variation on the original theme. The one-year-old, according to Piaget (1963, p. 266), tries, "through a sort of experimentation, to find out in which respect the object or the event is new. In other words, he will not only submit to but even provoke new results instead of being satisfied merely to reproduce them once they have been revealed fortuitously."

Prior to the fifth period, acts of intelligence involved only an application of existing schemes to new situations—that is, assimilating new events into already acquired schemes by attending only to the features of the object or event that were similar to existing schemes. But now, in the fifth period, children pay greater heed to the ways the new object or event differs from their present mental constructs, and they employ the process of accommodation to differentiate existing schemes and construct more suitable new ones. So tertiary circular reactions involve "reproductory assimilation with differentiated and intentional accommodation" (Piaget, 1950, p. 104).

The sort of "discovery of new means through active experimentation" (Piaget, 1963, p. 267) that marks this fifth stage was illustrated by Piaget with the case of a child who, sitting on the floor, seeks a toy that is out of reach. During his grasping, he pulls the edge of the small rug on which the toy lies, an act that is either an accident or a substitute for getting the toy. When he notices how his tug on the rug made the toy move toward him, he then intentionally pulls the rug as the instrument for obtaining the object (Piaget & Inhelder, 1969, p. 11).

Object relations   Up to this point in our discussion of mental growth stages, I have implied but not addressed directly one of the most important dimensions of development in Piaget's system. It is that of *object relations,* meaning the way children conceive of themselves in relation to the objects of the world as well as the way they see the objects' relationships to one another. In the beginning, the infant's universe is centered entirely on his or her own body and actions. There are no objects, but only a world of what Piaget called "unsubstantial tableaux" that vaguely appear and then dissolve, never to reappear, or else come back in some altered form (Piaget & Inhelder, 1969, p. 14). Nor is there a single space and time within which sensations of sight, sound, touch, temperature, taste, and smell are coordinated. Being lifted into mother's arms and fed is, in Piaget's estimation, sensed by the baby as separate impressions of postural change, pressures on various parts of the body, the touch of the lips to the nipple, voice sounds, shifting light patterns, and the ingesting of milk—none of which has any connection with the others. When infants' mental organization of the universe is so unstructured, they do not—indeed could not—conceive of cause and effect relationships among objects. Even during the advance of infancy, as they begin to differentiate objects from themselves and invest them with some permanence in time and space, infants' conception of cause remains egocentric: nothing happens in the world except as a result of their own wishes and actions. But by gradual steps over the coming years they recognize more accurately objective causality in the world.

In summary, an important perspective from which to view child development is that of object relations. Among researchers, Piaget is particularly noted for his contributions in tracing developmental changes in children's conceptions of the permanence of objects, the objects' positions in space and time, and causal relations among them. In our continuing discussion of mental stages, this should become readily apparent.

At the sixth and final stage (eighteen to twenty-four months) of the sensori-motor period, the child no longer has to experiment with objects themselves to solve problems, but can represent them mentally and can cognitively combine and manipulate them. In effect, the child is now mentally inventive. For example, a child at this stage sees a toy outside his playpen out of reach. He also sees a stick within arm's reach. He decides that he can use the stick as a tool for pulling the toy to the playpen, and he then uses the stick for this purpose. Prior to the sixth stage he might have gotten the toy if the stick had already been in his hand and he had groped for some time and happened to touch the toy. But he would not have preplanned the act by mentally combining the stick and the toy's distance before picking the stick up. Attainment of this new inventiveness makes intelligence now "capable of entering the framework of language to be transformed, with the aid of the social group, into reflective intelligence" (Piaget, 1963, p. 356).

Level 2: The Preoperational Thought Period (about Age Two to Age Seven)

In our review of this level of preoperational thought, we need to understand what Piaget meant by *operations*. Such understanding will make clear what sort of "operational thought" this level 2 thinking precedes—that is, what sort it prepares the child to perform at a later level of growth.

Operations, in Piaget's system, are ways of manipulating objects in relation to each other, such as arranging them in a series according to size or putting them in classes according to color. If the objects are actually before us, like actual colored blocks or ponies, the manipulations we perform on them, either by physically moving them or by observing how we might move them, are called *concrete operations*. We will meet these operations when we come to the third major period of development, which follows the preoperational level. When concrete operations are transposed into verbal propositions about the relationships that exist or might exist among objects, and these propositions are mentally manipulated, the intellectual actions are called *formal operations* (Piaget, 1969, p. 206). These we will meet at the fourth level of intellectual growth.

An operation, however, is not just any manipulation of objects. Indeed, as the term *preoperational thought* indicates, the mental activities of most children under age seven do not yet qualify as operational. To be classified as operations, actions must be internalizable, reversible, and coordinated into systems that have laws that apply to the entire system and not just to the single operation itself. As Piaget explained, operations

> are actions, since they are carried out on objects before being performed on symbols. They are internalizable, since they can also be carried out in thought without losing their original character of actions. They are reversible as against simple actions which are irreversible. . . . Finally, since operations do not exist in isolation, they are connected in the form of structured wholes. (1972, p. 8)

The characteristics of operations should become clear when we review the third and fourth periods of intellectual growth, for then we will discuss in some detail illustrations of children displaying operational thinking. For the present we will review the preoperational thought period knowing that it leads to children's performing concrete and formal operations.

This preoperational period can be divided into two stages. The first extends from age two to about four and is characterized by egocentric use of language and heavy dependence on perception in problem solving. The second lasts from about age five to around seven and is marked by more social or communicative speech and greater dependence on intuitive thinking rather than just on perception.

Before inspecting these two stages in detail, we need to be aware of the great importance Piaget attributed to language in the development of intelligence during this period. Language, he said, performs three roles: (1) it enables the child to communicate with other people, thus opening the opportunity for socialization of action; (2) it enables the child to internalize words in the form of thoughts and a system of signs; and most important, (3) it internalizes action so the child does not have to depend on manipulating things physically to solve problems. Instead, the child can represent them by mental images with which she conducts experiments. The child becomes less bound by time and space. He or she can increasingly imagine things that are out of sight, far distant, and in the past. The child can experiment with these things in different mental combinations far more quickly than he or she could manipulate them physically.

Egocentric speech   From age two to four, children learn an increasing variety of words. They begin to talk a lot, and the talk is of two varieties. Some of their talk is *social communication*—a child may ask parents to reach a toy he cannot get, tell his sister he wants the doll back, or tell mother he wants to go to the toilet.

But a far larger proportion of the child's talking and listening is *ecocentric,* a running oral commentary that accompanies what the child is doing at the moment and is not intended to communicate anything to anyone else. Since this kind of talk often appears in social situations, such as in a group of children at play, it can at first glance be mistaken for social communication. However, on closer inspection it becomes apparent that everyone is talking to herself or himself without listening to the others. For this reason, Piaget labeled such speech *collective monologues.* An important causal factor behind this discourse, in Piaget's opinion, is the child's lingering self-centeredness. The child still views life from his or her own perspective and has difficulty seeing things from the perspectives of others. Hence the child does not try to comprehend what others say in order to respond from the viewpoint they express.

To check this hypothesis, Piaget observed preoperational children in situations requiring them to explain something to another child, and then noted, from the other child's behavior, how well the explanation or directions had been understood. The observations revealed a systematic egocentricity in the sense that the child giving directions had great difficulty adopting the other's viewpoint, so as to cast the explanation in a form readily comprehended from the second child's perspective (Piaget & Inhelder, 1969, pp. 120–122).

While children's growing language skills aid their mental development, they do not free reasoning abilities from the influence of immediate perception. Children of age two through four or five base their problem solving heavily on what they see or hear directly rather than on what they recall about objects and events. What they perceive about an object is what dominates their conclusions, not what they conceive about the object based on memories of the object's permanent characteristics. Children at this age suffer from the limitations of what Piaget called *centration.* Presented with a visual stimulus, a child centers on one aspect and believes that this aspect completely characterizes the stimulus. The child cannot consider two dimensions, such as height and width, at the same time. For instance, if there is the same amount of water in two glasses of identical size and shape, the four-year-old will agree that both contain the same amount of water. But on seeing the water from one glass poured into a taller and thinner glass, the child will center on the height dimension only and conclude that the taller glass contains more water. It may be apparent that centration is not the only factor involved in the child's error of judgment. Other characteristics of immature logic also contribute to the error. For example, the preoperational child fails as well to comprehend the principle of *compensation*—that is, that the dimensions of an object can operate in coordination so that one dimension compensates for another. The greater width of the original glass compensates for its lack of height.

Intuitive thought   By the time children reach age five or six or so, they enter the stage Piaget labeled *intuitive thought.* It is a transition period between depending solely on perception and depending on truly logical thinking. An experiment with beads illustrates the characteristics of such transitional thinking. Six red beads are lined up on a table, and the child is told to put as many blue beads on the table as there are red ones. At age four or five the typical child makes a row of blue beads about the same length as the red row, without bothering to make sure there are six

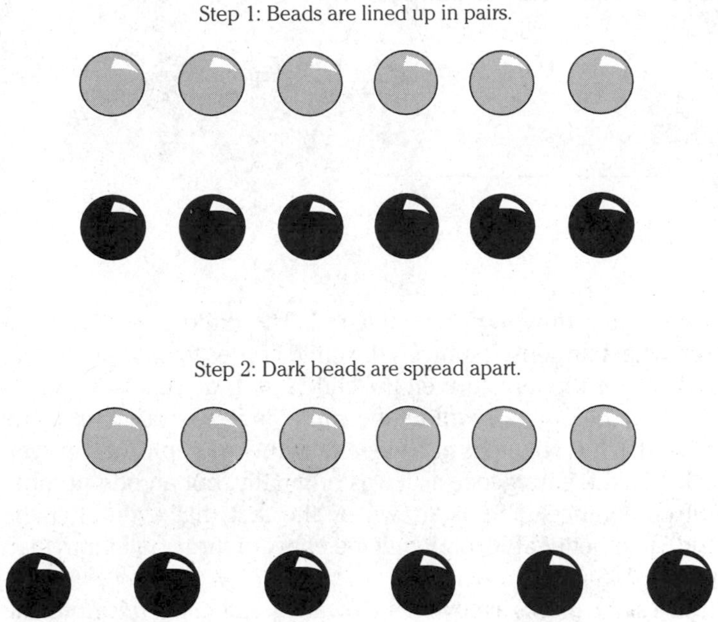

Step 1: Beads are lined up in pairs.

Step 2: Dark beads are spread apart.

FIGURE 9.1
A Piagetian experiment in conservation

blue ones. But a child a year or two older lines up six blue beads opposite the red ones, thus displaying progress toward recognizing equivalent quantities. There are still shortcomings in the child's logic, however, for if the experimenter then spreads out the red beads to form a longer line, the six-year-old thinks the number of red and blue beads is no longer equivalent (Figure 9.1). The child is still unduly influenced by perception of line length rather than the logic of quantity. In the terminology used by Piaget, the child has not recognized that the number of beads has been *conserved* or is *invariant* even though the length of the two lines has been altered (Piaget, 1950, p. 132).

Another Piagetian experiment also illustrates the transition—between dependence on perception (on how things look) and on logic (on what principles govern their operation)—occurring in the child's thinking during this stage of intuitive understanding. Three beads—one red, one blue, one yellow—are on a string that passes through a cardboard tube (Figure 9.2). A child is asked to observe the order of the beads before they are slipped into the cardboard tube where they cannot be seen. Then the child is asked to predict the order in which the beads will emerge from the other end of the tube. All children can predict correctly. But if asked to tell in what order they will emerge if poured back out through the same end they entered, the child under age four or five will be confused. The child fails to see that they will emerge in the opposite sequence if they are backed out of the tube. Furthermore, while the beads are in the tube, if the apparatus is turned 180 degrees and the child is asked the order in which the beads will emerge, the child from about age four to about age seven will fail to see that half a turn will change the order

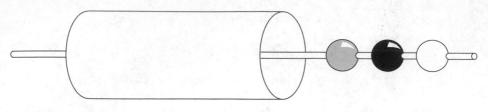

FIGURE 9.2
Piaget's beads and tube task

of emergence from red-blue-yellow to yellow-blue-red. The child then is given a chance to try it and see what happens. Intuitively the child comes to recognize what the half turn will do. By experimenting further, the child finally admits that if given two half turns, the order of emergence will be the same as it was originally. The child intuitively gets the idea, yet still does not understand the principle that an even number of half turns keeps the emergence as it was originally, but an odd number reverses the order of emergence. This is shown by the fact that even after the experiments, the child is no better able to predict the effect of three half turns than before (Piaget, 1950, pp. 135–136).

In short, the intuitive stage marks a movement toward greater *decentration.* The child is better able to see more than one factor at a time that influences an event. The child is on the verge of a major advance in logical thought.

To summarize, children make several important growth gains during the pre-operational thought level between ages two and seven. They acquire facility in spoken language as a tool for communicating with others and for helping themselves think aloud. By age seven their communicative language greatly increases as collective monologues decrease. They also gain skill in solving problems intuitively when the objects involved in the problems are in front of them. They become less self-centered in that they recognize that objects have an existence and permanence of their own that does not depend on the child's wishes or actions. Specifically, children recognize the permanence of an object's substance when its location or shape is changed. Water poured from a bowl into a tall glass is still water. A ball of clay rolled into a sausage shape remains the same clay. But preoperational children are still in the process of transition toward decentering, for they do not yet recognize that volume, weight, and mass are also conserved in the acts of pouring and rolling. Even though they have made great advances by age seven in comprehending how the universe of things operates, they are still strongly dependent on perception (how events seem to the eye) rather than on logic (what principles govern events).

Level 3: The Concrete-Operations Period
(about Age Seven to Age Eleven)

At the concrete operations stage, children become capable of performing operations that are directly related to objects. In the formal operations period, which comes later, they learn to perform operations on verbally stated hypotheses and propositions that are not limited to particular objects (Piaget & Inhelder, 1969, p. 100). The term *concrete* does not mean children must see or touch actual objects as they work through a problem. Rather, *concrete* means that the problems involve identifiable objects that are either directly perceived or imagined. In the later formal operations period, children are able to move ahead to deal with problems that do not concern particular objects. To illustrate this difference, we can consider the following two items, the first suitable for the concrete operations child, the second for the more advanced formal operations child or adolescent:

> **Concrete:** If Alice has two apples and Caroline gives her three more, how many apples will Alice have altogether?
> **Formal:** Imagine that there are two quantities which together make up a whole. If we increase the first quantity but the whole remains the same, what has happened to the second quantity?

It may be apparent that even though children do not need to see the objects in order to carry out the operations, in the early transitional phase toward learning and mastering such operations, they will be aided by viewing the actual objects or pictures of them.

In the earlier brief introduction to the term *operations,* I defined it but did not illustrate its several characteristics. I will do so now. Piaget said that for an action of the child to qualify as an operation, it had to be internalizable, reversible, and coordinated into overall systems. Furthermore, operations are not unique to an individual child but are common to all people of the same intelligence level. Finally, an operation assists the child not only in private reasoning but also in "cognitive exchanges," which bring together information and combine it in various ways (Piaget, 1953, p. 8; Piaget & Inhelder, 1969, pp. 96–97).

By *internalizable* Piaget meant the actions can be carried out in thought "without losing their original character of actions" (1953, p. 8).

By *reversible* he meant they can be readily inverted into their opposite. For example, two groups of apples that have been combined (added together) to form a whole group can easily be reduced (subtracted from the whole) to their original status. Hence adding is an operation. In contrast, Piaget said, writing from left to right is only a simple action and not an operation, for it cannot be inverted into writing from right to left without the child's having to develop an entirely new set of actions (1953, p. 8).

Reversible transformations may be of two varieties: *inversions,* where $+A$ is reversed by $-A$ (addition reversed by subtraction, multiplication reversed by division) and *reciprocity,* where $A < B$ is reciprocated by $B > A$ (the width of the bowl of water compensates for its lack of height, and the height of the glass of water compensates for its lack of width). When an object is moved or transformed in some way, in a transformation that qualifies as operatory, not everything about the system changes. Some features remain constant. As we have seen, Piaget gave the label *conservation* to this feature of constancy or invariance of objects. So we can say that a child's scheme or idea of a permanent object consists of that combination of features of the object that do not change when the object is moved or acted on. How adequately the child's scheme matches that of adult logic or "reality" can be judged if we assess which aspects of objects the child believes have been conserved during the transformation. Many of the problem situations Piaget contrived for children to solve are designed to test children's notions of conservation. And his investigations have shown that the particular aspects a child sees as being conserved depend on the child's age, or more accurately, on the child's developmental level.

For example, when two lumps of clay the same size and shape are shown to a child and then one lump is rolled into a sausage form, the child of age seven or eight discovers that the substance has been conserved. But not until age nine or ten does the child discover that the weight has been conserved as well. And not until age eleven or twelve does the child discover the conservation of volume that occurs when an object is immersed in water and the displacement measured (Piaget & Inhelder, 1969, p. 99).

Thus during the concrete operations period, from age seven to around eleven or so, children gradually discover more of the properties of objects and transformations and master mental operations that can be applied to their concrete world.

During the concrete-operations period, children not only gain greater command of the notions of conservation and reversibility but also become capable of decentering their attention, of recognizing the way two or more dimensions of an event interact to produce a given result. Children no longer center their attention solely on the height of the water glass or only on its width but consider both dimensions simultaneously and recognize their interaction. When presented with twelve wooden beads (nine red, three white), children no longer say there are more red beads than wooden beads when asked to compare red ones with wooden ones. At the concrete operations level children now recognize that color and construction material are two different classifications, and they are not stuck by centering on only color or material. They also can now order things in a series according to a stated criterion, such as size or number.

Whereas the preoperational child focused on the static beginning state and final state of an object in a transformation, the concrete-operations child can comprehend the transformation as a process. For example, typical preoperational children at age three or four think there is more clay in five small balls than in the original large ball from which the five were made. Even when the transformation, and its reverse of recombining the five into one, is performed before their eyes, three- and four-year-olds still say that the five contain more clay than the one. But by age six or eight, children agree that the quantity remains the same in the change from one to five balls and back again.

The egocentrism that caused younger children to see things only from their own viewpoint changes as older children achieve the aspects of cognitive growth just mentioned and as their increased facility with language leads to greater socialization. The child in the concrete operations period now has a more objective view of the universe and better understands how others see things.

Children's concepts of causation also mature during this period. For instance, a comparison of a child aged six years and eight months and a child aged ten years and three months illustrates the development of the concept of displacement of volume. The experiment involves dropping a small stone into a container of water (Piaget, 1930, pp. 169–172).

When the experimenter asks the six-year-old what will happen if the stone is dropped into the water, the child says the water will rise *"because it is heavy in the water."* The experimenter says, "You see the pebble hanging on this thread: if I put it in the water as far as this (half-way), will it make the water rise?" *"No, because it is not heavy enough."*

In contrast, the ten-year-old says the water will rise *"because the pebble takes up space."* The experimenter asks, "If I put this wood in, what will happen?" *"It will lie on the water."* "And what will the water do?" *"It will rise because the wood also takes up space."* "Which is the heavier, this pebble (small) or this wood (large)?" *"The pebble."* "Which will make the water rise the most?" *"The pebble takes up less space, it will make the water rise less."*

So the child arrives at the early teen years with increased skill in accounting for the cause of physical events and is ready to solve not only problems that involve objects, but also problems concerning hypotheses and propositions about relationships.

Level 4: The Formal-Operations Period (about Age Eleven to Age Fifteen)

In adolescence children are no longer limited by what they directly see or hear, nor are they restricted to the problem at hand. They can now imagine the conditions of a problem—past, present, or future—and develop hypotheses about what might logically occur under different combinations of factors. For example, if we begin a problem, "Imagine that water in the river ran up hill . . . ," children younger than twelve will claim that the subsequent problem cannot be solved because water does not run uphill. But by the close of the formal-operations period teenagers can accept the hypothetical condition of upward flow and can apply it in solving the posed problem.

Another of Piaget's favorite examples further illustrates the difference between the concrete-operations child and the one who has attained formal-operations ability. This is a problem involving *transitivity,* meaning that a relationship between two elements or objects is carried over to other elements logically related to the first two. For example, a child has solved the problem of transitivity if he recognizes that when $A = B$ and $B = C$, then $A = C$. Or if $A < B$ and $B < C$, then $A < C$. So the question posed to the child is this: "Edith is fairer than Susan; Edith is darker than Lily; who is the darkest of the three?" Piaget (1950, p. 149) found that before age twelve, children rarely could solve this. Instead, they engaged in such reasoning as "Edith and Susan are fair, Edith and Lily are dark, therefore Lily is darkest, Susan is the fairest, and Edith is in between." However, the adolescent in her midteens can solve the problem accurately, for she comprehends the transitivity it involves.

Prior to early and middle adolescence, therefore, children are still bound by their perceptions. But during the formal operations period they are able to engage in "*pure* thought which is independent of action" that they see or carry out themselves (Piaget, 1950, 149). Adolescents can hypothesize and draw deductions from the hypotheses. They can understand general theories and can combine them to solve assumed problems. In effect, by age fifteen, the framework of the average youth's thinking has evolved into its mature state. The types of thought of which the adult is capable are now all within the youth's repertoire of mental functions.

Does this mean, then, that there is no intellectual growth beyond mid-adolescence in Piaget's model of the mind? No, it does not. It means that the framework of thought is complete, but the framework is not all filled in. Further experiences during the years of youth and adulthood fill in the outline with addition-al, more complex schemes or greater knowledge, so the adult *does* know more than the adolescent. However, the adolescent is capable of all the forms of logic that the adult commands.

According to Piaget, the most obvious distinction between adolescent and adult thought is the greater lingering egocentrism displayed by adolescents. Teenagers, with their newly acquired skills of logical thought, are idealists who expect the world to be logical. They fail to recognize or accept the reality that people do not operate solely on the basis of logic, and they become reformers and critics of the older generation, foreseeing a glorious future in which they and their peers will right today's wrongs. In Piaget's opinion, this egocentrism and idealism is rendered more realistic and social by the youth's entering the occupational world or by her taking on serious professional training.

> The adolescent becomes an adult when he undertakes a real job. It is then that he is transformed from an idealistic reformer into an achiever. In other words, the job leads thinking away from the dangers of formalism back into reality. (Inhelder & Piaget, 1958, p. 346)

This move from adolescence into adulthood, then, completes the sequence of stages through which the intellect develops during the first two decades of life.

Piaget's notion of periods of development was not limited to the set of general intelligence stages described above. He also identified minor sets of stages for special aspects of cognitive growth. For example, his pioneering studies of moral development led him to distinguish three phases in children's conception of lying. Below age five or six, children equated lying with saying something naughty—that is, with saying something forbidden by adults. Around ages five to seven, children could distinguish between an intentional falsehood and an unintentional error, but they still applied the word *lie* to each of these sorts of acts. Not until age ten or eleven did most children accurately define lying as intentionally giving a false statement (Piaget, 1948, pp. 139–144).

Four Concepts: A Closer Look

The foregoing introduction to Piaget's system serves as a backdrop to a more detailed examination of four concepts mentioned earlier: genetic epistemology, stages or periods of development, functional invariants, and equilibrium.

Genetic Epistemology

At the beginning of this chapter *genetic epistemology* was defined as the study of changes in the relationship between the knower and the known with the passing of time. I noted as well that Piaget's investigations of children's cognitive development were stimulated by his interest in clarifying issues of genetic epistemology rather than by his desire to catalogue ways children at different age levels think about the world around them. And because this epistemological intention led to Piaget's publishing findings about how children's minds operate, some people have inferred that genetic epistemology and Piaget's proposals are one and the same. To correct this impression, Jacques Vonéche, who occupies the Piaget professorial chair at the University of Geneva, suggested that the general discipline of genetic epistemology should be

> disembarrassed from the unhappy fusion it has undergone, in recent times, with Piaget's specific attempt to orient that discipline along certain lines. . . . [Furthermore] besides limiting genetic epistemology to the sole attempts of Jean Piaget, there is another confusion generally made by philosophers and scientists alike, that of fusing Piaget's epistemology with his psychology. Numerous examples can be given of people who sincerely think that genetic epistemology is the title Piaget bestowed upon his theory of intellectual development in human ontogeny, although it should have seemed unlikely that a person of Piaget's considerable historical erudition and critical acumen would conflate individual developmental psychology with genetic epistemology. (1985, pp. 1997–1998)

Piaget's approach represents only one of a variety of solutions scholars have attempted for studying "the mechanisms of the growth of knowledge" ever since James Mark Baldwin coined the term *genetic epistemology* in 1906 (Baldwin, 1906, 1908, 1911). And as Vonéche implied, *genetic epistemology* and *genetic psychology* are not the same thing, even though there is a connection between them. Genetic psychology can be defined as the study of how the intelligence or the behavior of a typical member of a species changes over a lifetime. However, genetic epistemology involves not only this question of how intelligence develops but also such philosophical issues as the nature of being (ontology), the way knowledge should be defined, and the kind of evidence admissible for establishing the validity of knowledge.

The theory we have reviewed in the foregoing pages has been Piaget's psychology of cognitive development, not his complete version of genetic epistemology. However, it is useful to note ways in which certain of his assumptions about epistemology influenced his research methods and theoretical conclusions. For example, Piaget did not assume, as philosophical solipsists do, that the "real world" is simply what individuals' experience tells them is real. Rather, Piaget assumed that there is a "real world" outside of the individual "knower"; as children develop they achieve an increasingly accurate match between most adults' conception of a real world and the child's own conception. And, as noted earlier, Piaget also defined knowledge in a particular way—as physically or mentally acting on things, rather than as a fund of beliefs shared by members of a given society or as an individual's own storehouse of information. Furthermore, Piaget held that evidence obtained by the methods of modern science constitutes genetic epistemology's proper way of knowing. Finally, he viewed genetic epistemology as an interdisciplinary undertaking in which developmental psychologists participated with other scientists.

> The first rule of genetic epistemology is therefore one of collaboration. Since its problem is to study how knowledge grows, it is a matter then, in each particular question, of having the cooperation of psychologists who study the development as such, of logicians who formalize the stages or states of momentary equilibrium of this development, and of scientific specialists who show interest in the domain in question [such as physics, biology, sociology]. Naturally we must add mathematicians, who assure the connection between logic and the field in question, and cyberneticians, who assure the connection between psychology and logic. (Piaget, 1972, p. 8)

Stages of Development

Among scholars of Piagetian theory, the terms *stages, steps, levels, periods,* and *phases* of development are sometimes employed interchangeably. Or, as found earlier in this chapter, a major plateau in development may be called a *level* or *phase* and a subplateau called a *step* or *stage* or *substage*. But whatever the term used, the idea behind all such designations is that children's development is marked by times of noticeable change that are interspersed with times of stability.

Although all stage theorists agree that stages involve alternating times of change and of stability, few believe that change and stability is the *only* quality that defines a stage theory. Instead, most theorists propose additional factors they believe a growth pattern should exhibit in order to qualify its stable times as *stages*. As for Piaget, he contended that stages should have five further qualities: they must be universal, invariant in sequence, transforming and irreversible, gradually evolved, and ultimately in equilibrium.

1. *Universality*: The quality of universality means that stages are the same for all members of the species. A pattern of behavior that is found only in some children does not qualify as a stage. The pattern must be found in all children.

2. *Invariant sequence*: In Piaget's view, as well as in the opinion of most developmentalists, sets of behaviors do not compose a hierarchy of stages unless everyone goes through the sets in exactly the same sequence. For example, if some children exhibited formal operational thinking directly after the sensorimotor phase, whereas other children moved from sensorimotor to preoperational thought, then Piaget's sets of sensorimotor, preoperational, and formal operational thinking would not be stages. All children must pass through all the stage gates in the same order.

3. *Transformation and irreversibility*: When children enter a new stage, they not only interpret all future experiences through the lens of the new stage, but problems solved in the past by the methods of the previous stage are all now tranformed, seen through the conceptual lens of the new stage. In effect, the child who has thoroughly progressed into formal operational thinking will seldom if ever

go back to thinking in concrete or preoperational terms. This means that the naivete of early childhood is "spoiled" by progress into the more sophisticated thought of middle childhood. In short, stage progression is irreversible. For instance, after children in the concrete operations stage discover the principle of compensation (that the width of a glass bowl compensates for its lack of height, enabling the bowl to hold as much water as does a tall glass), they no longer limit their attention to only one dimension of containers whenever they are asked about the quantities and weights of a substance that might fit into various containers. With this discovery, children are never again amazed by the kinds of results that surprised them at an earlier age when they saw liquid poured from one vessel into another of a different shape.

4. *Gradual evolution*: Elevation to a new level or stage does not occur all of a sudden, or even within a period of a month, a few months, or a year. Instead, in Piaget's system movement to a new stage occurs gradually, a bit here and a bit there, until finally enough of a child's behavior exhibits the traits of the new stage to say that the transformation to the next level is complete. For example, children do not grasp the conservation of substance, quantity, mass, or volume of objects all at the same time, but instead only over a period of years.

5. *Equilibrium*: Once a child consolidates his thinking patterns into a coherent way of acting in the world, this new stage of cognitive development is said to have reached a state of stability and balance. The stage is now in equilibrium.

Piagetian stage theory does not require that children pass through the stages at the same speed nor that all children eventually reach the highest level. Piaget expected individual differences in the rate of progress, and he noted that some children would fall short of the formal operations level or, in the case of severe mental retardation, might not even get past the sensorimotor or preoperational levels.

However, while the five attributes of stages may seem clear at a conceptual level, some of them have posed awkward problems about child nature as observed in daily life. For example, when children's thought processes about a variety of aspects of their life are compared, it is clear that there is considerable unevenness in the kinds of thinking they exhibit in solving different types of problems. For example, in mathematics it is typical for children to conceive of the conservation of number and length before that of area and volume. And the differences in the stages of children's thought processes in one domain, such as mathematics, and another, such as that of moral reasoning, are even greater. This brings up the question of whether the general stages of mental growth Piaget postulated really do form a valid description of how children's thinking develops. Perhaps there are only special stages for different aspects of life that cannot legitimately be compounded into a single general system.

One way that Piaget accounted for this lack of coordination of children's thinking processes was the notion of gradual evolution, described under item 4. He gave the term *horizontal décalage* to the apparent lag in a child's applying in all aspects of life a mode of thinking that Piaget proposed was characteristic of a single stage. For example, during the concrete-operations phase of development, when children see a ball of plasticine clay divided to become five smaller balls, they do not simultaneously discover that both the substance and the weight have been conserved as the number of balls has changed from one to five. Instead, children comprehend the conservation of substance (clay remains clay) at an earlier age than they comprehend that the weight also remains unchanged. In effect, there is some horizontal *décalage* (meaning *displacement*) between the time a child applies a new stage of thinking to one facet of life and the time he or she applies that same stage to other facets. However, we may ask, Does labeling this phenomenon *horizontal décalage* really explain the apparent unevenness in the way children apply a particular level of thought to different aspects of life, including different subject-matter areas in school? We will examine this further in the assessment of the theory at the end of the chapter.

Piaget called *vertical décalage* a child's applying increasingly complex modes of thought to the same phenomenon or problem in life. For example, in the beads-and-tube task pictured earlier, a kindergarten child may physically reverse the tube and thereby be able to tell the order in which the colored beads will emerge from the tube, although she cannot explain why she knows. In contrast, in the primary grades, the child not only can predict the order of the beads without physically turning the tube but also can explain how her mental image of the tube has enabled her to solve the problem. Subsequently, the youth who has achieved formal-operations thought patterns can even explain the abstract principle that enables her to accurately predict the order of the beads, no matter how many times the tube is turned. Thus *vertical décalage* refers to the displacement of one mode of thought by a sequence of more sophisticated modes as the child matures. Although the notion of horizontal décalage seems somewhat at odds with Piaget's theory of broadly encompassing stages of mental development, the idea of vertical décalage fits quite logically into his stage model.

Functional Invariants

It is apparent that Piaget's model accounts for the ways in which children's thought structures vary from one stage of development to the next. He also points out that, as children grow up, their schemes change by increasing in number, in precision, and in interconnections. But not everything about development changes as the years pass. Certain aspects continue unaltered over the entire life span. Piaget called these aspects *functional invariants* to signify not only that they are stable but also that they are *processes* or *functions* rather than structures.

Two such functions are *adaptation* and *organization.* Throughout life, people adapt to their environment and reorganize their schemes in ways that promote survival. Three other invariant functions—*assimilation, accommodation,* and *equilibrium*—serve as the chief instruments for promoting adaptation and organization. The lifetime process of adapting and organizing consists of a never-ending cycle of assimilation, of accommodation, and of the achievement of a temporary state of equilibrium that is soon disturbed by events that stimulate further assimilation, which starts the cycle over again.

Among these invariants, the one whose meaning seems most elusive is equilibrium, so let's inspect it in more detail.

Equilibrium

At least part of the reason people have difficulty comprehending *equilibrium,* or the companion term *equilibration,* is that Piaget seems to have used it to mean different things at different times. In general, *equilibration* seems to mean a process of movement toward a state of *equilibrium* or of balance, a state in which an organism remains until conditions upset the balance. In this sense, "a state of equilibrium is not a state of final rest, but constitutes a new point of departure" (Piaget in Battro, 1973, p. 57). However, these rather gross meanings seem insufficient to clarify Piaget's diverse applications of the term, as the following excerpts from English translations of his publications suggest.

> [We may] (a) conceive of equilibrium as characterized by *maximum* entropy, (b) or as due to the intervention of coordinations which introduce from outside an order diminishing the entropy, (c) or else as due to a sequence of "strategies" of which each one will be oriented by the results of the preceding one up to the moment when the actions become reversible through the very coordination of these preceding strategies that would have been freed from the earlier historic process in order to reach equilibrium.
> Equilibrium [is the] place of specific junction between the possible and the real.
> The structures can be interpreted as . . . the result of an autonomous process of equilibration.
> The best equilibrated states . . . correspond to a maximum of activities and a maximum of opening up of exchanges.
> The system is in equilibrium when the operations of which the subject is capable constitute a structure such that the operations can unfold in two directions (either by strict inversion or negation, or by reciprocity). It is therefore because the totality of possible operations constitutes a system of potential transformations which compensate each other—and which compensate each other as far as obeying the laws of reversibility—that the system is in equilibrium.
> We shall say that a structure has . . . a permanent equilibrium if, when the initial field C is modified to C' the substructure of the elements corresponding to C conserves the same equilibrium as before. (Piaget in Battro, 1973, pp. 49, 56–58)

In addition, Piaget modified his basic conception of equilibrium by attaching to it such adjectives as *momentary, semipermanent, permanent,* and *operational.* However, these adjectives seem to have been of limited help to his reading audience.

P. H. Miller (1983, pp. 75–76) attempted to clarify Piaget's usage by proposing that Piaget differentiated the use of equilibrium according to at least three spans of time: (1) the moment-to-moment encounters a child has with the environment as the child attempts to master the encounters by assimilating, accommodating, and finally achieving the state of satisfactory resolution called equilibrium; (2) the final step in a child's moving gradually out of one stage and establishing himself or herself securely in the next higher stage; and (3) the process of achieving ever better adaptation and organization over the entire series of growth periods, birth through adolescence.

Finally, there are frequent passages in which equilibration seems to mean the unexplainable coordinating power that makes all parts of the developmental system work together in harmony.

EDUCATIONAL APPLICATIONS OF THE THEORY

During the past four decades Piaget's writings have exerted a growing influence on the conduct of education in many parts of the world. Piaget himself pointed out the educational implications of his model. To illustrate some of these implications, we will inspect the Piagetian model's application to questions of (1) the choice of learning objectives, (2) curriculum sequencing, (3) grade placement of topics, (4) the assessment of children's intellectual functioning, and (5) teaching methodology.

The Choice of Learning Objectives

As educators have selected learning goals for pupils to pursue, they usually have based their choices on tradition or on analyses of what children need to learn in order to succeed in the culture in which they are growing up.

The word *tradition* in this context refers to the curriculum of the past. Members of the adult generation recall what they were taught in school and assume that this same pattern of facts, concepts, skills, and values will be equally proper for the coming generation of children. This might be called the conservative approach to selecting objectives, since it emphasizes the conservation or retention of traditional goals.

The phrase *analyses of what children need to learn in order to succeed* identifies the practice of educators who inspect present-day society and predict changes that will likely occur in that society over the coming decades. On the basis of such analyses, they estimate the knowledge, skills, and values that will best equip the growing child or youth to become a happy, constructive member of that society. This could be called the *personal-social adjustment* approach to establishing objectives, for it emphasizes the achievement of objectives that enable the individual to fulfill personal needs within a culture that is continually evolving. A curriculum produced by such a process of analysis can be expected to retain some of the goals of the past, but it also will offer new objectives that result from changes in the society.

There is also a third tack, which derives from Piagetian theory and might be called the *cognitive development* approach. To understand the main focus of this approach, we need to consider once again (1) the distinction Piaget made between *spontaneous* or *psychological* development and *psychosocial* development and (2) his ideas about the interaction of nature and nurture.

As explained earlier, several factors determine when a child will develop through the levels of sensorimotor reactions, of concrete operations, and of formal operations. The first factor is the internal maturation of the neural system. The time at which the maturational steps needed for a given level of cognitive functioning to occur is established by nature, by the child's genetic time schedule. But the developmental potential that this maturation provides cannot be realized unless the child obtains suitable direct experiences in life, experiences that bring the potential to fruition. Piaget called these unguided experiences (the second factor) *psychological* or *spontaneous* development. The third factor is that of more formal instruction, the sort that goes on in school. It needs to be preceded by the first two, maturation and psychological development, if it is to be successful. Piaget called this third factor *psychosocial* development.

This Piagetian view of intellectual growth is the foundation for the cognitive development approach to selecting instructional goals. From such a perspective, the central goal of the school is not to teach particular facts and concepts, nor is it to teach solutions to personal and social adjustment problems. Instead, the purpose of schooling is to promote the optimal development of thinking skills appropriate to each level of growth. As a result of such schooling, by the time children reach adolescence they should be able to efficiently apply formal operational thinking in understanding life and in solving whatever problems they face. In such a curriculum the child does indeed learn facts and concepts. However, these are not selected for any inherent value they might have but rather for their worth in fostering the development of the particular level of cognitive growth that the child is currently working toward.

Curriculum Sequencing

Piagetian theory not only furnishes a vantage point from which to select objectives, but also suggests the sequence in which these objectives and their associated learning tasks should appear in the curriculum. For example, in reasoning about scientific and mathematical phenomena, children at the preoperational level can consider only one dimension at a time, such as only the height or only the width of an object. At the concrete operations level they can comprehend the interaction of two dimensions, such as height and width, simultaneously. Not until they reach the formal operations level can they consider the interaction of more than two variables. A similar sequence has been identified in the realm of moral or ethical judgments.

> At the egocentric stage in the logic of feeling, the self becomes the single dimension around which feelings and social interaction revolve. The second, sociocentric stage corresponds to concrete operations, in interacting with peer-group norms as the other dimension. The allocentric stage is multidimensional like formal operations: the individual can construe himself as a dimension in a matrix, including abstract principles and social norms as other dimensions. (Biggs, 1976, p. 157)

A further example of a sequence is that of understanding the conservation aspects of physical objects. The child's comprehension moves from that of understanding the conservation of the quantity of substance (the space an object appears to take up) to that of the weight of the substance and then to that of the density of the substance.

These sequences, along with a variety of other more specific ones, can suggest to curriculum developers a psychologically sound order in which to confront children with different learning tasks. In the traditional school curriculum, children are often expected to acquire concepts of mass, weight, volume, space, time, causality, geometry, speed, and movement in a sequence that is at odds with the child's natural pattern of comprehending such concepts (Elkind, 1976, p. 196). A curriculum plan founded on Piagetian theory and empirical studies would seek to correct such incoordination between development and school learning activities.

Grade Placement of Topics

Piaget's results also suggest at what general age level each step in a given sequence is likely to occur. For instance, understanding of conservation of substance seems to come around age seven for most children, of weight around age nine, and of volume around age eleven or twelve (J. L. Phillips, 1975, p. 100).

These age points are similar, but not identical, from one child to another and from one ethnic or socioeconomic group to another. Differences among children in the age at which they achieve a particular new level are apparently due to differences in those primary causal factors that Piaget said underlie development: the genetic time schedule for internal maturation, self-directed experience with the world, and instruction or training. Some children are genetically equipped to advance earlier than others. Some have better opportunities to engage in profitable direct experiences and to receive more useful instruction. What these differences in influence mean for curriculum developers is that some flexibility is needed in the grade placement of learning goals founded on Piagetian theory. Not every child will be ready at the same time to accomplish the next step in a cognitive development sequence. However, the general placement of a given objective in the school's grade hierarchy can be estimated. Curriculum developers know whether a particular cognitive skill is more suitable for the preschool years than the primary grades (first through third) or for the upper elementary grades (fourth through sixth). They also know whether a particular understanding is more likely achieved in the junior high (grades seven through nine) than the senior high years (grades ten through twelve).

As already noted, Piaget, besides outlining the stages of development described earlier for general cognitive development, also identified within the general structure a variety of separate sequences, such as one for the understanding of number, another for causality, a third for conservation of physical aspects, a fourth for moral reasoning, and so on. Although the pattern of one such sequence is much like the pattern of another, the timing of steps within different sequences does not always coincide. In other words, there is some unevenness in progress between sequences.

This lack of coordination between sequences can be illustrated by noting that the logic children use to explain their moral or ethical judgments usually lags a couple of years behind the level of logic they use to explain physical phenomena. It is not yet known whether this lag is due entirely to the greater amount of experience and instruction children have with physical events as compared to moral issues or whether some maturational factor also contributes its influence. Piaget's most frequent collaborator, Barbel Inhelder, believed:

> The general succession of stages seems to be confirmed by all authors, but the relationship between different tasks and substructures, apparently requiring the same mental structure, is still far from adequately explored; what is more, the experimental findings on this point are difficult to interpret. (1968, p. vii)

However, the implications of such a finding for curriculum developers seem clear. It is not sufficient to use only Piaget's *general* developmental stages as guides to the placement of learning activities in the school's grade structure. Rather, it is important to assign activities according to the various types of sequences that are involved. For example, activities to promote a given level of moral judgment should be assigned a grade or two later in the school program than activities to promote a similar level of mathematics and science knowledge.

It is possible, though, to use the same general topic or problem situation at both a lower and an upper grade level. For instance, E. A. Peel, a British educational psychologist (1976, p. 181), recommended that a spiral plan for teaching both physical science and social science can be adopted for adolescents. In such a program, students in an upper secondary grade can return to topics they studied three or four years earlier. The virture of this approach from a Piagetian viewpoint is that the pupils are thereby not simply reviewing or repeating their earlier experience, since during the intervening years the *quality* of the students' intelligence has changed. Whereas a child at the beginning of the secondary school could offer only partial and single explanations of a phenomenon, the youth in high school is able to apply "a greater conceptual repertoire and more mature form of intellectual enquiry" (Peel, 1976, p. 181) to the same phenomenon. In effect, the second time the youth studies the topic she or he does so by means of a new, more complex cognitive lens—in other words, a more complex schema.

The Assessment of Intellectual Functioning

Piagetians are critical of the use of traditional intelligence tests for estimating children's cognitive development and readiness for another step in a learning sequence. Their chief complaint is that the typical intelligence test determines whether the child can give a correct answer to questions; it does not reveal the child's thinking processes. Thus the test fails to indicate a pupil's current level of cognitive development. As a result, Piagetians prefer to base their judgments of children's cognitive styles on (1) how children solve the problems posed in the tasks Piaget used in his research studies and (2) teachers' observations of the level of children's reasoning during the regular activities of the classroom (Elkind, 1976, pp. 171–194).

Dissatisfaction with standard intelligence tests has stimulated a pair of researchers at the University of Montreal, Monique Laurendeau and Adrien Pinard, to devise a new scale of mental development, a test that represents "an attempt to combine the advantages of Piaget's method (thoroughness and flexibility of questioning) with those of traditional psychometric methods (standardization of questioning)" (J. L. Phillips, 1975, p. 162). Unlike such tests as the Stanford-Binet or Wechsler Intelligence Scale for Children, the Montreal scale does not involve each child's being asked to answer exactly the same questions. Instead, the way a child responds to one question influences the nature of the succeeding questions the child is asked. Furthermore, the tester is not only interested in the number of right answers the child gives, but is equally interested in "wrong" answers, since they too are valuable in revealing the child's mode of thinking. In sum, the Montreal project represents an extension of Piagetian theory into the realm of formal intelligence testing.

Teaching Methodology

A common way to conceive of teaching methodology within a Piagetian-based curriculum is to define the two most basic responsibilities of the teacher as those of

1. diagnosing the current stage of a child's development in the various growth sequences the curriculum is designed to promote, and
2. offering learning activities that challenge the child to advance to the next higher step of the particular type of sensorimotor cognitive development that the sequence involves.

In other words, the teacher is not viewed as being a fount of knowledge from which the pupils are expected to fill their minds. Nor is the teacher's job simply that of a pleasant clerk who displays equipment and materials in the classroom and then stands back while children explore the objects on their own. Instead, the teacher is expected to achieve a proper balance between actively guiding or directing children's thinking patterns and providing opportunities for children to explore by themselves.

Not all educators have come up with exactly the same picture of teacher behavior for achieving this balance between active guidance and passive permission. H. G. Furth and W. Wachs, who described their experimental Piagetian-type school in their book *Thinking Goes to School* (1975), recommended that the teacher offer a sequence of activities that will enable pupils to achieve their next developmental steps efficiently. The activities give a structure or direction to pupils' work, but each child is free to pursue each activity in his or her own manner or is free not to participate in the activity at all if she or he so chooses.

> The teacher in our school knows that he can do no more than provide the occasion and leave the child free to use it well. He can coach and facilitate and encourage; but in the final analysis it is the child himself who initiates intellectual growth. (Furth & Wachs, 1975, p. 46)

A somewhat different version of the teacher's role within a Piagetian-based curriculum was given by D. Elkind (1976), who identified three modes of learning, each featuring a different combination of the assimilation and accommodation processes.

The first mode Elkind called *operative learning.* It is most prominent when the child's intelligence "is actively engaged by the materials she is interacting with" (Elkind, 1976, p. 113). Working with the materials, the child may face contradictions in the way she supposes they will respond, and the contradictions will force her to abstract new understandings from her actions on the materials.

> Operative learning, in addition to facilitating the development of mental operations, also gives rise to *practical intelligence.* Practical intelligence consists of the operations and knowledge the child requires to get about in the everyday world. Much of it . . . is unconscious. (Elkind, 1976, p. 114)

The second mode Elkind called *figurative learning.* It involves the child's acquiring "aspects of reality" that cannot be reconstructed or rediscovered by the child on his own but "must be largely copied" (Elkind, 1976, p. 114). Perhaps the prime example of this mode is the learning of language—the vocabulary, syntax, pronunciation, and gesture that make the speech of one culture different from that of another. For such aspects of reality, the teacher adopts a more active instructional role, carrying out more "teaching" in its traditional sense.

The third mode is *connotative learning.* It is the "conscious conceptualization of one's own mental processes, what has been called *reflective intelligence.*" It is most prominent during the years of adolescence (Elkind, 1976, pp. 115–116). "Connotative learning is expressly concerned with the construction of meanings, with establishing connections between concepts and figurative symbols. It is no less than the child's efforts to make sense out of her world" (Elkind, 1976, p. 116).

In promoting operative learning, the teacher may bring objects—a bird, a telescope, a toy boat—to the classroom and may pose questions that stimulate pupils to discover aspects of the item. However, to a great extent the pupils are left on their own to explore the objects. For the figurative mode, the teacher furnishes models and gives demonstrations and explanations, such as showing how to carry out arithmetic computation efficiently or how to use phonics to discover the pronunciation of new words met in a reading passage. With connotative learning, the teacher still encourages pupils to make discoveries and use the communication skills they have acquired, but the "teacher's most important role in connotative learning is to help children do work of the quality that they are really capable of doing" (Elkind, 1976, p. 231). In other words, the teacher stimulates them to produce to the best of their ability.

Whether teachers adopt a Furth and Wachs version or an Elkind version of a Piagetian-based instructional style, they need to carry out their teaching in a setting that is conducive to a substantial amount of small-group and individual activities. Tables, desks, and chairs need to be movable. Different interest centers around the classroom need to be available for use by pupils who are at a given developmental level and can most profitably pursue activities and use materials suited to promoting progress to the next level.

In summary, Piaget's theory and his empirical research findings suggest guidelines about how children's sensorimotor-cognitive development can best be nurtured.

PIAGET'S THEORY: AN ASSESSMENT

By the 1990s, the status of Piaget's model had reached a phase that occurs in the life of nearly every influential model in developmental psychology. A typical theory's life span begins when the scheme is newly formulated, then announced publicly in a journal or book. Initially this innovative proposal has a difficult time gaining widespread acceptance, since most developmentalists already subscribe to some existing model. However, as the new theory's proponents extol its virtues to a growing audience, and as empirical investigations and applications of the proposal multiply, the throng of believers increases. Subsequently, when the theory reaches the apex of its prominence, it is placed under critical surveillance by professionals in the field who test its hypotheses and scrutinize its logic. Any weaknesses found in the clarity of the theory's definitions or in its ability to explain and predict can undermine people's faith in its worth. A subsequent decline in the theory's status is accompanied by the appearance of other scholars' ways of explaining growth and behavior. Such has been the fate of Piagetian theory as its popularity among developmentalists has waned in recent years. C. J. Brainerd (1983, p. vi) stated that the early 1980s witnessed

> a rapid decline in the influence of orthodox Piagetian theory, a fact that is now acknowledged by Piagetians and non-Piagetians alike. Until the mid-1970s, Piaget's ideas dominated the landscape the way Freudian thinking once ruled abnormal psychology. Since then, however, the picture has changed dramatically. Empirical and conceptual objections to the theory have become so numerous that it can no longer be regarded as a positive force in mainstream cognitive developmental research, though its influence remains profound in cognate fields such as education and sociology.

Other observers, while admitting to shortcomings of Piaget's formulations, have been more positive than Brainerd in recognizing the Swiss theorist's contributions. R. Case (1985, p. 24) concluded that

> Piaget played the same role for intellectual development as Darwin had played for the development of the species. He gathered a vast fund of empirical data on the intellectual behavior of the human organism over time. He developed and integrated a number of previously existing notions within a framework that not only explained the existing data, but led to the discovery of a wide variety of new data. Finally, he provided a view of mankind the significance of which transcended the particular discipline and data from which it was derived, and which was of great social significance.

PIAGET'S THEORY

How well do I think the theory meets the standards?

Standards	Very well	Moderately well	Very poorly
1. Reflects the real world of children		X	
2. Is clearly understandable			X
3. Explains the past and predicts the future			X
4. Guides child rearing		X	
5. Is internally consistent	X		
6. Is economical	X		
7. Is falsifiable		X	
8. Is supported by convincing evidence	X		
9. Adapts to new data		Xo	Xp
10. Is novel	X		
11. Is comprehensive		X	
12. Stimulates new discoveries	X		
13. Is durable		X	
14. Is self-satisfying		X	

Some of the reasons for the recent decline in the popularity of Piagetian theory are described in the following paragraphs in which the fourteen standards of judgment from Chapter One provide the framework for evaluating Piaget's contributions.

In regard of the theory's fertility (item 12, stimulates new discoveries), Piaget's work deserves a top rating. As E. R. Hilgard and G. H. Bower (1975, p. 327) remarked: "One of the great problems that have beset psychology as a science is that there are so few discoveries of genuinely new phenomena. . . . Consequently, it is worth noting that the facts of conservation, as pointed out by Piaget and his associates, represent one of the genuine 'discoveries' within his experimental observations."

Not only did Piaget conduct pioneering studies on multiple facets of cognitive development, but his work has stimulated thousands of other investigators to expand and refine his notions. By 1995, the *psychINFO* bibliographic data base listed nearly 3,600 journal articles, books, and book chapters bearing on Piaget's work, with at least 15 percent of them focusing particularly on the structure and use of the theory itself. Rather frequently, follow-up studies have cast doubt on certain of Piaget's conclusions, thereby inspiring critics to offer alternatives to the traditional Piagetian model. Thus, in recent decades, a substantial body of neo-Piagetian or post-Piagetian literature has evolved (Bruner, 1964; Case, 1985; Dason, 1977; Pascual-Leone, 1976; Scholnick, 1983; Valsiner, 1987; Zimmerman, 1983). As an example, Klaus Riegel (1973, pp. 346–370), who styled his own theory of development as *dialectical,* criticized Piaget for ending the stages of intellectual growth with the formal operations period of adolescence. Riegel accepted the Piagetian stages as being reasonable as far as they went, but proposed a dialectical scheme of his own whereby one set of psychological forces struggled against other sets to produce development beyond the middle teen years. In short, no other developmental psychologist has ever inspired as much discussion and empirical research as Piaget has.

Piaget's model has also been judged internally consistent and parsimonious (standards 5 and 6). Case (1985, pp. 23–24) maintains that the model's basic elements represent "a sophisticated, coherent, and tightly interrelated system. . . . Given the great diversity of phenomena for which it accounted, it utilized remarkably few constructs and postulates."

As for reflecting the real world of children (item 1), the theory gains strength from the host of empirical studies on which the author based his speculation. Nevertheless, in several respects it falls short of accurately reflecting reality. The first shortcoming concerns individual differences among children. Piaget's great emphasis was on what the average child does. It is true that Piaget did recognize some diversity in rate of development, and he suggested that the social milieu within which a child is reared will affect this rate. But he did not offer any careful analysis of how different factors or agents in the social setting influence the attainment of the wide variety of differences in cognitive functions that children exhibit. As B. J. Zimmerman (1983, p. 4) noted, "Piaget gave little attention to the effect of the social dimensions of the environment—the individual and collective behavior of other people—on children's reasoning. The concepts that he studied were generally nonsocial in nature (e.g., space, number, time, conservation, and mathematics) and thus were less likely to be contextually dynamic."

In judging how readily Piaget's work can be understood (item 2), I have marked the theory just slightly above the middle. A variety of notions proposed by Piaget seem rather easy to comprehend, at least on the surface. That seems to be the case for the concepts of assimilation, accommodation, and conservation; for the general nature of levels through which children develop; and for the proposal that the sequence of levels is the same for all children. However, this clarity can dissipate when readers seek precise meanings for *cognitive structure,* for how equilibration functions, and for the apparent inconsistency between the concepts of *stage* and *horizontal décalage.* Brainerd (1983, p. ix) complained that conflicting interpretations abound and, more important, we do not know how to set about measuring the relevant variables. For some years, it was fashionable to suppose that Piagetian constructs, like the ideas of quantum physicists, were merely difficult for the average mind to comprehend and that careful study of the theory would dispel the conceptual fog. As this has not happened, a more plausible hypothesis is that the theory is intrinsically opaque.

Although I find much of Piaget easy enough to understand, I must agree with Brainerd's concern, since I have difficulty comprehending certain key aspects of Piagetian thought. For instance, I find an unsatisfying circularity in some of Piaget's explanations, as when he suggested in publication *A* that equilibrium explains reversibility ("The equilibrium finally reached between assimilation and accommodation explains then the reversibility of the operational grouping") and in publication *B* that reversibility explains equilibrium ("Equilibrium will thus be defined by reversibility") (Piaget in Battro, 1973, pp. 56–57).

As for the scheme's value in explaining the past and predicting the future (item 3), it does rather well both (1) for the sorts of cognitive behavior on which the model focuses and (2) for the average child. Piaget claimed that the sequence of the changes plotted in his stages of mental growth is invariant from one child or one society to another. Empirical investigations conducted in many nations support this claim (Dason, 1977; Piaget, 1973, p. 7; Sigel & Hooper, 1968). He further noted that the rate of passage through stages may vary by as much as two years between the average children of one culture and those of another (Piaget, 1973, pp. 25–27). So he predicted accurately the types and sequence of cognitive behaviors children can be expected to exhibit, but he did not furnish adequate explanations of deviations from the average.

In terms of guidance for child rearing (item 4), the theory has proven of great interest to educators, who have been making increasing use of Piaget's description of developmental stages to determine the sequence and grade placement of cognitive skills to be learned, particularly skills in mathematics and the physical sciences. Educators are also using Piagetian tests—the problems from his clinical method—both for assessing children's developmental status and for providing them with opportunities to try the thought processes represented in the developmental stages of the theory (Furth & Wachs, 1975; Tronick & Greenfield, 1973; Piaget, 1970b). In addition, a sequence of annual conferences for members of the helping professions resulted in a series of publications describing applications of Piagetian theory to pediatrics and social work (Magary, Poulsen, Levinson, & Taylor, 1977; Poulsen & Luben, 1979). Thus the Piagetian model offers a good deal of guidance for child rearing in cognitive areas.

The model does not, however, furnish guidance for treating a variety of other problems that confront parents, teachers, pediatricians, and social workers. The problems I refer to are ones reflected in such phrases as "poor self-concept," "lack of friends," "easily frustrated," "too heavily influenced by undesirable peers," and "lacks significant goals or purpose in life." For coping with such matters, Piaget is of little help. But, as he frequently pointed out, his area of concern was genetic epistemology; and the above problems are not central to that concern. In assessing the theory on item 4, I balanced the foregoing positive points against the negative and rated the scheme between "very" and "moderately well."

Next, how falsifiable is the theory (item 7)? Many aspects of Piaget's model are in forms that make determining their validity very testable. Such is true of the developmental stages, both their sequence and their age placement. However, several of the concepts at the core of the theory are not, I believe, susceptible to confirmation or disconfirmation. Included are the concepts of schemes, assimilation, and accommodation. I see no way of testing their validity. Hence I balanced the many falsifiable aspects of the Piagetian model against the apparently few that must be accepted on faith, and marked item 7 somewhat above the center.

The Piagetian model is grounded in a great quantity of empirical data (item 8). Not only was Piaget himself a prolific researcher, but hundreds of additional studies of children focusing on Piagetian concepts have been conducted by other investigators in a wide array of cultures.

Because much of the popularity of Piaget's proposals in recent decades has derived from the innovative character of his ideas, I have given his theorizing a high rating for its novelty (item 10).

The adaptability (item 9) of the theory can be viewed in two ways: (1) how well Piaget himself accommodated new data and reacted to criticisms and (2) how well adherents of Piagetian theory adjusted to new discoveries. Whereas Piaget held fast to many of his basic convictions that others found incongruent with evidence about children's development, he still was willing to alter other of his beliefs in the face of additional data. For instance, in his early work he tended to draw broad generalizations about all children from inspecting just a few, without even reporting how few he had studied. Furthermore, the few he had studied came from a very restricted cultural background, primarily from middle-class Swiss families. In later years he paid far more heed to sampling procedures—that is, to the quantities of children studied and to the different cultural milieus in which they lived. Thus the Xp on item 9 is my estimate of Piaget's adaptability. The Xo rating reflects my estimate of the greater adaptability of those proponents of Piagetian theory who have altered the master's basic model in a variety of ways to meet the demands of evidence derived from additional research.

On comprehensiveness (item 11), I have located Piagetian theory in the upper portion of the "moderately well" category. Whereas Piaget studied many aspects of children's cognitive activity, he paid very little attention to their emotional life or their physical development.

Although the long-term durability (item 13) of the theory cannot be judged adequately at this early date, I imagine that many of his ideas will leave a lasting mark on child-development theory and that Jean Piaget will always be remembered as an important figure in the history of child psychology.

Finally, I find the theory to be overall quite satisfying (item 14). Despite the reservations mentioned above, I am convinced that the greater part of Piaget's writings is valuable and accurate. After studying his works, I feel that I understand the development of children's thinking processes far better than before. And as a consequence, I believe I can work more effectively with children and youths. I feel the theory rates a high mark.

FOR FURTHER READING

Piaget, J., and B. Inhelder. (1969) *The Psychology of the Child.* New York: Basic Books. Although any of the books listed under Piaget's name in the bibliography at the end of this volume offers useful insights into his many-sided theorizing, this volume by Piaget and his long-time colleague, Inhelder, is particularly helpful in reviewing not only the principal aspects of basic cognitive development but also the associated social and affective interactions, including moral feelings and judgments.

Battro, A. M. (1973) *Piaget: Dictionary of Terms.* New York: Pergamon Press. People who have had difficulty with the meaning Piaget intended for the specialized terms he used will find this book useful. Battro lists Piagetian terms alphabetically and then under each he gives one or more definitions in the form of quotes from Piaget's writings.

Campbell, S. F. (1976) *Piaget Sampler.* New York: Wiley. An autobiography by Piaget (covering the years 1896–1966) appears as Chapter Ten in this potpourri of articles by the theorist.

Many books published in recent years have been designed to offer a condensed version of Piagetian theory, ones more readily understandable than Piaget's original writings. The following two small volumes, one by Phillips and the other by Sigel and Cocking, are among the more readable and up-to-date books of this type.

Phillips, J. L., Jr. (1975) *The Origins of Intellect: Piaget's Theory,* 2d ed. San Francisco: Freeman.

Sigel, I. E., and R. R. Cocking. (1977) *Cognitive Development from Childhood to Adolescence: A Constructivist Perspective.* New York: Holt, Rinehart & Winston.

CHAPTER TEN

VYGOTSKY AND THE SOVIET TRADITION

Because the nation known as the Soviet Union no longer exists, it may appear anachronistic to speak in the present tense about a *Soviet theory of child development*. However, I would defend this usage on the belief that a theoretical position held for seven decades as a society's single official interpretation of human development will not be immediately abandoned just because the political establishment that sponsored the position is dissolved. It seems unlikely that developmental psychologists who have been steeped in a theoretical tradition for so long a time will suddenly shed their convictions in order to embrace or create something quite different. Thus, I assume that the conception of development espoused by Vygotsky and his compatriots is still very much alive in societies formerly within the Soviet Union's sphere of political influence. The purpose of this chapter is to describe key features of that conception.

During the years following the Russian Revolution near the close of World War I, psychologists under the new Soviet Union government struggled with the problem of devising a theory of human development compatible with the Marxist political tenets on which the new state was founded. By the mid-1920s the most successful solution to this problem was that created by Lev Semenovich Vygotsky (1896–1934), a teacher of literature whose first research as a young scholar between 1915 and 1922 focused on artistic creation (Vygotsky, 1971). In 1924 Vygotsky began serious work in the areas of developmental psychology, education, and psychopathology, pursuing these interests at a highly productive pace until he died of tuberculosis in 1934 at the age of thirty-eight.

Although his career as a psychologist was brief, Vygotsky earned high regard in the Soviet Union for establishing an acceptable sociopolitical foundation for much psychological investigation. He did this by casting in suitable research form "the Marxist-Leninist thesis that all fundamental human cognitive activities take shape in a matrix of social history and form the products of sociohistorical development" (Luria, 1976, p. v).

In other words, according to this doctrine, the intellectual skills or patterns of thinking that a person displays are not primarily determined by innate factors— inherited intelligence or mental abilities. Instead, patterns and levels of thinking are products of the activities practiced in the social institutions of the culture in which the individual grows up.

270

It follows that practical thinking will predominate in societies that are characterized by practical manipulations of objects and more "abstract" forms of "theoretical" activity in technological societies will induce more abstract, theoretical thinking. The parallel between individual and social development produces a strong proclivity to interpret all behavioral differences in developmental terms. (Luria, 1976, p. xiv)

From this viewpoint, the history of the society in which a child is reared, and the child's own developmental history in terms of his or her experiences in that society, are both extremely important in fashioning the ways the child will be able to think. Furthermore, advanced modes of thought—conceptual thinking—must be transmitted to the child by means of words, so language becomes a crucial tool for deciding how children learn to think.

It was in an atmosphere of these assumptions that Vygotsky wrote *Thought and Language* shortly before his death. In 1936, two years after its publication, the volume was suppressed in the Soviet Union because of disputes within the nation's psychological community. But when the disputes ended, the book was distributed once again. However, it wasn't translated into English until 1962, so it is only since then that Vygotsky's theory has become widely understood and discussed in English-speaking countries. During the 1970s further works by Vygotsky and his followers were translated into English, providing ample evidence of his talent as a theoretician and practitioner who was skilled in applying research findings to the improvement of child rearing and schooling (Cole, 1977; Luria, 1976; Valsiner, 1988b; Vygotsky, 1978).

This chapter is divided into six sections: (1) a description of key influences on Vygotsky's theory, including the linkage between Marxist social philosophy and Vygotsky's view of child development, (2) an example of Vygotsky's applying his theory to explain the growth of thought and language, (3) a series of generalizations he proposed about child development, (4) a brief review of principal trends in Soviet developmental psychology from the 1920s into the 1980s, (5) practical applications of Vygotsky's model, and (6) an assessment of the theory.

The chapter focuses on Vygotsky's theorizing, not simply because he was the chief architect of Soviet developmental psychology in the early years of the Communist regime, but because his proposals contribute to discussions in contemporary psychology. The late Alexander R. Luria (1902–1977), a world-renowned Soviet developmentalist, before his death wrote:

Vygotsky was a genius. After more than half a century in science I am unable to name another person who even approaches his incredible analytic ability and foresight. All of my work has been no more than the working out of the psychological theory which he constructed. (Vygotsky, 1978, dust jacket)

KEY INFLUENCES ON VYGOTSKY'S THEORY

Three characteristics that marked Vygotsky's work were (1) a sincere dedication to Marxist social philosophy and a conviction that psychological development was intimately linked to the tenets of that philosophy, (2) a thorough acquaintance with the work of leading European and American psychologists of his day and of earlier decades, and (3) great ingenuity in devising methods for studying children and for interpreting the data his methods produced.

Marxism and Vygotsky's Theory

When two German political philosophers, Karl Marx (1818–1882) and Friedrich Engels (1820–1895), in 1847 published their vision of societies evolving toward utopian communism, they founded their proposal on the following three core assumptions.

1. Activity generates thinking.   Marx postulated that people's acting within particular social environments accounts for both (1) the differences in privilege and role among subgroups in society and (2) the particular contents of individuals' minds and modes of thinking. He proposed that people's consciousness (attitudes, conception of reality, psychophysical skills) is constructed from the production and distribution activities in which they engage. Marx stated:

> In the social production of their life, men enter into definite relations that are indispensable and independent of their will, relations of production which corre-spond to a definite stage of development of their material productive forces. . . . The mode of production of material life conditions the social, political, and intellectual life process in general. It is not the consciousness of men that determines their existence, but, on the contrary, their social existence that determines their con-sciousness. (Marx, 1859, p. 389)

Vygotsky concurred with this conviction, so his theory of development pictures children engaging in activities and, from this engagement, constructing the contents of their minds. Thus thinking does not initially create action; instead, action creates thought. Mental development is the process of children's internalizing the results of their transactions with their environment.

2. Development advances by dialectical exchanges.   Marx contended that societies develop through a process of resolving dialectic confrontations. As noted in Chapter Eight, Hegel's dialectical formula for logical thought consisted of an assertion (thesis), its opposite (antithesis), and the resolution of the thesis-antithesis conflict by means of a revised conclusion (synthesis). Marx adopted the dialectical concept to account for the development of societies. As a social system for producing and distributing materials (such as a feudalistic agricultural society with its landlords and serfs) became well established (thesis), advances in technol-ogy (industrial revolution) precipitated conflicts within that system (antithesis). The conflicts could be resolved only by that social structure's transformation into a new one (capitalism). Once capitalism became established, further conflicts arose to render it unsuitable, with the proper resolution in Marx's view being a transforma-tion of the sociopolitical-economic system into one of communal ownership of the production and distribution of goods. Among the several dialectical confrontations that would be involved in such societal development, the one that Marx featured in his theory of dialectical materialism was the struggle between social classes.

Vygotsky applied the dialectical formula to child development by proposing that as children go about the activities of their lives, their established ways of doing things (thesis) don't always work because these ways fail to accommodate to the conditions of the current situation (antithesis). Hence children must devise new problem-solving methods that satisfy those conditions (synthesis). Child development, therefore, consists of an endless stream of dialectical conflicts and resolutions, with the resolutions then internalized to form the child's increasingly sophisticated physical and psychological knowledge. This knowledge then becomes the set of theses (understandings, skills, expectations) with which the child approaches the next of life's activities.

3. Development is a historical process within cultural contexts. Marx conceived of societal development as a process of evolution. Because of technological advances, societies developed from a feudal to a capitalistic and ultimately to a socialistic form of material production and consumption. As he contended in *The Communist Manifesto*, "All property relations in the past have continually been subject to historical change consequent upon the change in historical conditions" (Marx, 1847, p. 231). Thus a society's history is a chronology of purposeful change (development). The phrase "history in the making" refers to the dialectical exchanges occurring at any particular time. By analyzing such change processes, we come to understand how the society develops. The culture (way of life) of a given society at any point in time is not only a product of the society's past history but also the contextual foundation for future development.

Vygotsky adopted such a cultural-historical viewpoint when he formulated his child development model. Understanding how and why children develop as they do requires that we understand the nature of the culture's historical background because the environments that children inhabit confront children with opportunities and demands unique to that culture. Furthermore, the history of the child's own ontogenetic development (the succession of the child's past dialectic confrontations) determines how the child is prepared to resolve upcoming problem situations.

In summary, Vygotsky's theory of human development represented a synthesis of assumptions that fit nicely into the Marxist theory on which Soviet society was constructed.

Vygotsky and the International Psychological Community

A factor of particular importance to the progress of Vygotsky's work was his intimate knowledge of current and past psychological events in Western Europe and North America.

> In contrast to Vygotsky's outright rejection of American and Russian behaviouristic thinking, his positive contribution to psychology was clearly rooted in the continental-European psychology of his time. German Gestalt psychology . . . had a

> strong influence. . . . Kurt Lewin's field theory surfaces in appropriate places in
> Vygotsky's writings. . . . He develops further on Binet's work on memory [and]
> criticizes and follows Piaget. . . . [He] was likewise open to the important ideas that
> Freud and other psychoanalytic thinkers had explicated. (Valsiner, 1988b, p. 121)

To understand something of the climate for psychology in Vygotsky's time, we
need to recall two antithetical views of human thought that were prominent in the
early twentieth century.

The first was a traditional view of the mind that grew out of the faculty
psychology of past centuries. Psychologists in the late nineteenth and early twentieth centuries studied mind and its functions by means of introspection. A person
carefully looked into his or her own mind to analyze the working of perception,
thought, memory, feelings, and the like.

The second movement was in direct opposition to the first. It represented an
effort to be scientific and objective about the study of humans, just as physics,
chemistry, and biology were objective sciences. As described in Chapter Seven, the
movement in North America was known as behaviorism, for its leaders proposed
that the proper study of humans involved observable behavior as measured and
recorded by scientists rather than by the people being observed. In effect, the
staunchest behaviorists of Vygotsky's day had eliminated mind and its functions in
favor of analyzing only observable acts.

Vygotsky saw shortcomings in both of these schools of theory. He did not trust
introspection as a secure methodological base on which to found scientific psychological theory. And as for behaviorists' rejecting mind, he wrote:

> In that psychology ignores the problem of consciousness, it blocks itself off from
> access to the investigation of complicated problems of human behavior, and the
> elimination of consciousness from the sphere of scientific psychology has as its
> major consequence the retention of all the dualism (mind versus body) and
> spiritualism of earlier subjective psychology. (1962, p. vi)

Vygotsky's Research Techniques

Given Vygotsky's basic assumptions (activity generates thought, and development
results from dialectical exchanges in historical-cultural contexts), he now needed
suitable methods for conducting empirical research. But he recognized that the
standard investigative methods of stimulus-response psychologists were poorly
suited to studying children's in-process mental development. He could not expect
to discover children's ongoing thought processes simply by presenting the children
with a stimulus (a test question) and then noting how closely their responses
matched the correct answer. Such a method would show only whether the child
gave the desired response. Instead, what Vygotsky wanted to know was the pattern
of events operating in children's actions and thoughts as they grappled with a task
and, in the midst of grappling, effected a change in their own mental development.
So the child's procedure in constructing an answer was what interested Vygotsky,
not whether the answer was right. During his search for suitable investigative
techniques, he spoke admiringly of Piaget's *clinical method,* which he felt was far

closer to the mark than traditional S-R methods. But for his own empirical studies he placed children in problem-solving situations of his own creation (Valsiner, 1988b, pp. 128–140).

The *double-stimulation method* that Vygotsky devised drew on ideas from P. Janet's psychiatric practice in France and W. Köhler's Gestalt experiments with apes in Germany. The method involves placing a child in a problem-solving setting that contains a collection of objects that form a complex pattern of stimuli. Some of the objects have been purposely selected by the experimenter, while others are incidental parts of the experimental situation. The child has a goal to achieve. The goal is either overtly defined by the researcher or simply inferred by the child from the nature of the context. The child's task is to figure out how to attain the goal by means of the objects in the setting. The term *double stimulation* refers to two sorts of stimuli to which the child can attend in performing the task—stimulus objects and stimulus means. The child is expected to inspect (be stimulated by) the objects at hand and thereby conceive of ways (stimulus means) the objects might be used to achieve the goal. The experimenter's aim is to discover how the child acts and thinks during this event. To achieve such understanding, the researcher tracks the course of the child's actions and listens to the child's remarks that accompany the actions. From the sequence of actions and the child's commentary, the experimenter draws inferences about what sort of intellectual development has occurred during the problem-solving incident. The following segment of a double-stimulation experiment is one I devised to illustrate a research setting and a set of child behaviors that could typify such an investigative approach (Valsiner, 1988b, pp. 134–140).

The same situation was posed on separate occasions to six-year-old Justin and to his eight-year-old cousin, Courtney. The task was a simulated problem introduced to Justin in the following manner:

> *Investigator:* The mother of a six-year-old boy told him, "We're going on a trip this weekend, and we can't leave the cat home alone. So we have to take him over to Aunt Martha's in the cat carrier. The cat's now in the kitchen. Would you please go there and put him in the carrier. But be careful. If he thinks we're going to take him to Aunt Martha's, he'll try to get away." Now, Justin, here's a picture of the kitchen. Look at the things in the room and tell me what you think the boy should do to get the cat into the box. (See Figure 10.1.)
>
> *Justin:* (Studies the picture for a moment, then points to the dish on the rug.) I'd put this milk in the box, and the cat would go in the box to drink the milk.
>
> *Investigator:* All right. But what if the cat tried to run away while you were doing that? Is there anything you could do when you first come into the room?
>
> *Justin:* I'd close the window and door. And then I'd put the milk in the box.
>
> *Investigator:* That sounds good. But suppose there wasn't any milk in the dish. What could you do then?
>
> *Justin:* I'd put cat food in the dish, and the cat would smell it and go in to eat.
>
> *Investigator:* Where would you get the cat food?

FIGURE 10.1
A drawing used in a double-stimulation approach

> *Justin:* (Points to the right-hand cupboard.) I'd get it out of there.
> *Investigator:* Look around the kitchen and see if there's anyplace else to get cat
> food.
> *Justin:* (Studies the picture, points to the box labeled "cat food" and slowly
> reads aloud.) Cat food. (He smiles and nods.) In there. That's cat food.

Justin's cousin, Courtney, is later faced with the same task, but the main
character in her anecdote is an eight-year-old girl. Courtney responds to the
assignment in this fashion:

> *Courtney:* I'd grab the cat and put him in the box and close the door.
> *Investigator:* OK. But when you first enter the kitchen, is there anything you
> might do to make sure the cat doesn't get away before you grab him?
> *Courtney:* I'd close the window and door.
> *Investigator:* Could you think of any way to get the cat into the carrier without
> grabbing him?
> *Courtney:* There's a box of cat food. I'd put some cat food in the cat carrier, and
> when the cat goes in to eat, I'd close the door.

We can now speculate about the nature of the two children's thought patterns
as they dealt with the problem of getting the cat into the carrier. At the outset, neither
child was at a loss for a solution. That is, both were prompt in suggesting a reasoned
means of capturing the cat. And while neither child spontaneously considered the
likelihood that the animal might escape from the room before their solution was put
into operation, once that possibility was proposed by the investigator, both children

immediately suggested closing the window and door. Since both children had cats in their own homes, their own experiences undoubtedly influenced their proposed solutions. For example, when Justin was asked where he would find cat food, he pointed to a kitchen cupboard, which was where the cat food was stored in his own home. The two children's physical size may also have affected their initial solution. Courtney was considerably larger than Justin and thus may have had more success in grabbing cats than Justin had.

We can also speculate about what the two children may have learned during the problem-solving incident. It is worth noting that when Justin was asked where he would find cat food, he pointed to the cupboard rather than to the box of cat food. Only when he was prompted to inspect the picture more closely did he read the "cat food" label. This behavior can be viewed against Justin's acquaintance with reading. He was currently in first grade, where he read simple primers quite adequately, though with studied effort. In his experience, reading was apparently something done in story books rather than a tool used for solving everyday problems. Hence he depended on his own past knowledge of cupboards rather than on the labels in the picture to guide his search for cat food. In contrast, third-grader Courtney immediately pointed to the "cat food" label when asked how she might entice the animal into the carrying case. She appeared to use reading as an instrument of daily problem solving.

When the children later told their parents about the event, both said they would first close the door and window and then they would put the cat in the carrying case. Justin added that he could get cat food out of a box on the floor. Thus it seems likely that each may have learned something new during the activity.

It is instructive to recognize how Vygotsky's approach to research differs from two other experimental models commonly used in child study. One of these models is the S-R variety. The child is furnished a stimulus, and the child's response is then recorded. All sorts of test situations assume this form, including tests to measure intelligence, academic achievement, physical agility, values, attitudes, and more. Surveys that employ questionnaires or interviews are also of the S-R variety. Although these techniques can reveal what the respondent apparently knows or believes at that moment, they tell nothing about how such knowledge and beliefs develop.

A second common experimental design, in its simplest form, consists of a pretest, a treatment, and a posttest. For example, in the area of arithmetic instruction, if we want to discover whether children become more accurate if they learn to subtract whole numbers by an equal-additions method rather than a decomposition method, we can do the following:

1. *Pretest* a large group of children on their subtraction ability, particularly their skill in subtracting quantities that involve carrying.
2. *Divide the large group into two subgroups,* so that the pattern of pretest scores of one subgroup match the pattern of the other subgroup, thereby making the groups equal in skill at the outset.
3. *Provide different treatments* by teaching one subgroup by the equal-additions method and the other by the decomposition method.

4. *Posttest* both groups to discover what difference each treatment has made in the children's subtraction skills.

Although such an approach may help us decide which method of instruction is—on the average—more effective, it tells us nothing about how different children think while they do subtraction, or how their thinking developed during the treatment sessions, or why they got some problems right and others wrong. In the pretest–treatment–posttest design, the *dependent variable* is the posttest score, for it ostensibly has been determined by what occurred during the treatment. The dependent variable is thus the *consequence* of the child's experience. The magnitude of the posttest score in relation to the pretest score is thus of primary interest to the experimenter. However, such is not the case with either Vygotsky's double-stimulus approach or Piaget's clinical method. For them, the dependent variable or consequence of the experiment is found in the record of the child's series of actions and running commentary. The results of their investigations are qualitative, not quantitative. In the opinion of such developmentalists as Vygotsky and Piaget, inferences about the ongoing development of a child's acts and thoughts during a problem-solving session cannot be cast meaningfully into numbers, then summarized as averages, interpreted by means of analyses of variance, and the like.

It is important to note that Vygotsky's methods were not limited to experiments in which the researcher traced the child's pattern of thinking while that thinking was developing. Like Piaget, Vygotsky and other Soviet psychologists also frequently studied children's current mental skills and beliefs, then estimated what kinds of developmental experiences must have contributed to such beliefs.

In assessing the worth of Vygotsky's efforts, J. Valsiner (1988b, p. 140) proposed:

> Vygotsky's major contribution to developmental psychology lies in his efforts to provide the discipline with a methodological strategy that would afford the empirical study of developmental phenomena.... It involves the empirical analysis of the process of development, either "on-line" (i.e., through analyzing the dynamics of subjects' solving of the experimental problem within the setting and resources given), or "off-line" (as in the case of [after-the-fact] efforts to analyze the developmental process of already existing phenomena using the available information).

THE DEVELOPMENT OF THOUGHT AND LANGUAGE

A more detailed review of one of Vygotsky's principal interests illustrates how he used newly created objective methods for studying cognition and speech, methods that did not depend on the introspection or "spiritualism" that he ridiculed.

His investigations were designed to determine which of three possibilities best represented the developmental relationship between thought and language. Was thought identical with language, as Watsonian behaviorists claimed when they said thinking is just silent speaking? Or was thought independent of language, complete in itself, as many introspectionists seemed to believe, with language simply serving as the tool for communicating thought to others—just as a camera is an instrument for communicating visual images? Or, as a third possibility, were thought and language separate functions that could commingle and in so doing modify each other?

To arrive at an answer, Vygotsky (1) analyzed a host of studies of thought and language conducted by psychologists and anthropologists from numerous countries and (2) devised his own investigations of thought and speech as found among children, adolescents, and adults in the Soviet Union. He cast his interpretations of these findings as three sets of conclusions about child development. The first set concerned the development of conceptual thought, the second the development of speech, and the third the connection between the first two. The nature of these conclusions is the subject of the rest of this section. However, we will consider the three sets in reverse order, beginning with Vygotsky's general views on the relationship between the development of thought and the development of language (*language* in this case meaning speech).

In general, Vygotsky concluded that the child's thought and speech begin as separate functions with no necessary connection between them. They are like two circles that do not touch. One circle represents nonverbal thought, the other nonconceptual speech. As the child begins to grow up, the circles meet and overlap (Figure 10.2). The juncture of the two represents *verbal thought,* meaning that the child has now begun to acquire concepts that bear word labels. A *concept* here means an abstraction, an idea that does not represent a particular object but rather some common characteristic shared by—or some relationship among—diverse objects.

The two circles never completely overlap. Even though the common portion becomes more prominent as the child develops (particularly in a highly literate cultural setting), there always remains some nonverbal thought and some nonconceptual speech. An example of nonverbal thought in the adult is skillful use of tools. An example of nonconceptual speech in an adult is singing an old song or reciting a poem or repeating a memorized telephone number. These repetitions by rote are "mental activity" but are not of the conceptual variety that Vygotsky identifies as verbal thought.

Figure 10.2 shows Vygotsky's general idea of the thought–language relationship during a child's development, but the actual coordination between the two circles is probably far more complex. Vygotsky admitted that the pattern of their interaction was not yet clear. But he did contend that

> progress in thought and progress in speech are not parallel. Their two growth curves cross and recross. They may straighten out and run side by side, even merge for a time, but they always diverge again. This applies to both phylogeny and ontogeny. (1962, p. 33)

Vygotsky disagreed with theorists who said that children, as a result of internal maturation, can achieve skill in advanced conceptual thought on their own, distinct from what they are taught. While admitting the necessary role of internal maturation in development. Vygotsky believed that children's informal and formal education through the medium of language strongly influences the level of conceptual thinking they reach. If the language climate within which children grow up (direct

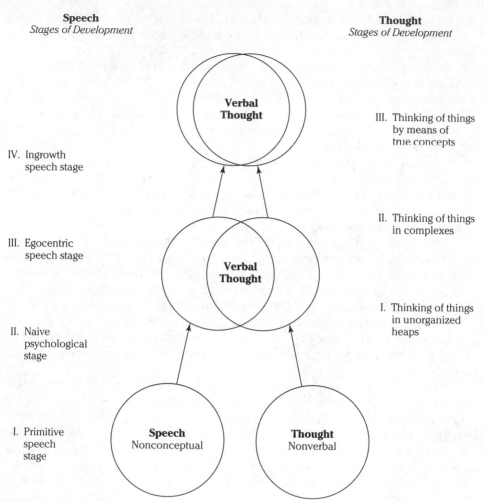

Speech
Stages of Development

Thought
Stages of Development

IV. Ingrowth
speech stage

III. Egocentric
speech stage

II. Naive
psychological
stage

I. Primitive
speech
stage

III. Thinking of things
by means of
true concepts

II. Thinking of things
in complexes

I. Thinking of things
in unorganized
heaps

FIGURE 10.2
Vygotsky's view of speech and thought development

speech, mass communication media) is dominated by simplistic or "primitive" language, then the children will think only simplistically or primitively. But if the language environment contains varied and complex concepts, then children will learn to think in varied and complex ways, given that their initial biological equipment (sense organs, central nervous system) is not impaired.

In extending the scope of his theorizing beyond children's development, Vygotsky suggested that the stages through which a child's thought and language evolve are likely the same as those through which humanity's thought and language have evolved over eons of time. Thus studying children's ontogenetic development not only helps us understand the child's thought and speech but also serves as the most practical method for estimating the phylogenetic development of our species.

These are the general features of Vygotsky's theory. The model is not a completed theory, with all details filled in and each proposal buttressed with a mass of empirical evidence. Rather, as Jerome S. Bruner (Vygotsky, 1962, p. viii) wrote, the book *Thought and Language* "is more programmatic than systematic." It's as if Vygotsky had found only parts of the thought–speech puzzle by the time he wrote the volume, and his theory or "program" represented his assumption that when the rest of the parts were eventually discovered, the final assemblage would take on the general configuration he outlined in his proposal.

Stages in Speech Development

Vygotsky's studies led him to conclude that speech development proceeds through the same four stages and is governed by the same laws as those relating to other mental operations that employ signs—that is, such other operations as counting and memorizing with the aid of mnemonic devices (Vygotsky, 1962, pp. 46–47).

He called the first of these four stages the *primitive* or *natural stage*. This first period, which represents the time before the circle of language overlaps the circle of conscious thought, lasts from birth until about age two in Vygotsky's opinion. The stage is characterized by three nonintellectual speech functions. First are sounds representing *emotional release*: crying with pain or frustration, cooing or babbling with contentment. Next, as early as the second month after birth, these emotional noises are joined by sounds that can be interpreted as *social reactions* to other people's voices or appearance. The noises of social contact include laughter and a variety of inarticulate sounds. The third type of thoughtless speech consists of the child's first words, which are *substitutes for objects and desires*. These are words learned by conditioning, by parents and siblings matching the words frequently to objects, just as some animals can be conditioned to recognize words as labels for things.

Around age two the primitive stage ends and the second period begins, that of *naive psychology*. Children discover that words can have a symbolic function, and they display this discovery by frequently asking what things are called. They no longer are simply conditioned by others to label objects and actions, but actively seek this information themselves. As a result, their vocabulary increases at a great rate. With the advent of the naive stage, the circles of language and thought begin to merge.

During this second period, children exhibit the beginnings of practical intelligence by recognizing characteristics of their surroundings and by starting to use tools—that is, starting to use objects as means to accomplish desired ends. However, their language is considered naive because they use grammatical structures properly without recognizing the underlying functions they serve.

The experience children gain using language in relation to the objects of the world subsequently enables them to move to a third level, the stage of *egocentric speech*. This kind of talk makes up a large proportion of the preschool and kindergarten child's speech, particularly that occurring in play situations. It takes the form of a running monologue that accompanies the child's activities, whether the child works alone or beside others. It requires no response from anyone because it is not directed at anyone but the speaker. This commonly observed phenomenon has been interpreted in various ways by different investigators. Some have viewed egocentric speech as a "running accompaniment" or tune that merely parallels children's thought and activity as they play. But Vygotsky arrived at a different conclusion. He saw egocentric speech as an important new tool of thought. Not only do children think to speak, but what they say to themselves influences what they then will think, so the two interact to produce together conceptual or verbal thought.

To test this hypothesis, Vygotsky arranged for problems to arise during the play-work activities of young children. For example, a pencil for the drawing task would be missing or the paper would be too small or too large. The investigators then observed that the amount of egocentric talk on these occasions was double that observed when children did not face such problems (Vygotsky, 1962, pp. 16–17). This Vygotsky interpreted as evidence that egocentric speech is not just a release of tension or an expressive accompaniment to activity but is also a significant tool "of thought in the proper sense—in seeking and planning the solution of a problem" (1962, p. 16).

Nor did Vygotsky agree that egocentric speech simply died out after age seven or so. Rather, he saw the decline of egocentric speech as a signal of the onset of the fourth stage in his developmental hierarchy, the *ingrowth stage*. Children learn to manipulate language in their heads in the form of soundless speech, thinking by means of logical memory that employs inner signs for solving problems. Throughout the rest of their lives, individuals will use both inner speech and outer speech as tools in conceptual or verbal thought.

In summary, children's speech grows through four stages between the time of birth and the years of primary school, age seven or eight. The process begins with nonintellectual or "thoughtless" speech and develops via naive and egocentric language into inner speech that is inextricably interwoven with conceptual thinking. Now that we have traced development from the vantage point of speech, we will trace the development of verbal thinking from the vantage point of thought.

Stages in Conceptual Thought Development

Vygotsky's method of studying the development of conceptual thought involved two steps: (1) devising a test that would reveal the process a person follows when faced with the necessity to create a concept and administering the test to children, adolescents, and adults; and then (2) comparing the developmental hierarchy revealed in this testing with reports from other psychologists who had longitudinally followed the conceptual growth of individual children from one year to another. The purpose of this comparison was to determine whether the differences observed in testing cross sections of people of different ages accurately reflected the changes in thought processes that occur in the individual as he or she matures.

To begin we will briefly look at the testing instrument Vygotsky created (now known as the Vygotsky blocks), for it reveals something of his research ingenuity. One of the sticky problems faced in testing children's concept-formation process is that of finding concepts for them to generate in the testing situation that we are sure they did not already know. In particular, we want to ensure they have mastered the concept and have not simply memorized a word that suggests they know the concept when they actually do not.

Vygotsky solved this problem by constructing a set of twenty-two wooden blocks of different colors, shapes, heights, and sizes (*size* meaning overall horizontal area). These characteristics vary in such a manner that no two blocks are alike in all ways. On the bottom surface of each block is written one of four nonsense words: *lag, bik, mur, cev.* Irrespective of the blocks' color or shape, *lag* appears on all tall, large blocks; *bik* on all flat, large ones; *mur* on tall, small ones; and *cev* on short, small ones. Each testing session begins with the examiner spreading the blocks before the child in a random mixture, then turning up a sample block and showing the child the name on the bottom. The child is asked to pick out all the blocks the child thinks are the same kind—that is, ones that bear the same name. When the child has done so, the examiner turns up one of the selected blocks the examiner knows is wrong and shows the child that it does not bear the correct word. The child is asked to try again. This process is repeated over and over until the child solves the problem. The solution, of course, requires that the child recognize that the word represents a concept composed of two of the dimensions of the blocks—both height and horizontal size. Since there is no single word in normal language representing this combined concept, the child cannot have known or rote memorized it prior to the testing session (Vygotsky, 1962, pp. 56–57).

Throughout the testing session the examiner carefully watches the combinations the child chooses each time, for the nature of each combination reflects the strategy of thought in which the child has engaged. Using the block problem with several hundred subjects of different ages enabled Vygotsky to identify a hierarchy of three major stages children pass through in achieving true conceptual thought between the preschool years and middle adolescence. Within each stage, children also traverse a series of subphases.

Conceptual thinking is really a mode of organizing one's environment by abstracting and labeling a quality shared by two or more phenomena. The major steps in children's intellectually organizing perceived phenomena are (1) clustering things into unorganized heaps, then (2) putting things together in complexes, and, as puberty arrives, (3) beginning to think in genuine concepts. But even when adolescents achieve the ability to think conceptually, they do not entirely abandon the two earlier forms of thought; these earlier forms merely subside in frequency and reappear on certain occasions.

The three major stages and the subphases, based upon children's and adolescents' solutions to the Vygotsky-blocks problem, are as follows (Vygotsky, 1962, pp. 58–81):

Stage I: Thinking in unorganized congeries or heaps   During this period the child puts things in groups (and may assign the group a label) on the basis of what are only chance links in the child's perception.

Subphase I-A: Trial-and-error grouping   The groups are created at random, on a blind guess.

Subphase I-B: Visual-field organization The child applies a grouping label to a collection of things that happen to appear together in space and time.

Subphase I-C: Reformed heaps The child first produces groupings on the basis of either guess or visual-field organization, then in dissatisfaction tries to reform the heaps by shifting elements in them around, but the items are still not alike in any inherent way.

Stage II: Thinking in complexes Individual objects are united in the child's mind not only by subjective impressions but also by bonds that actually exist among the objects. This is a step away from egocentric thinking and in the direction of objectivity. In a complex, the bonds between components are *concrete* and *factual* to some degree rather than abstract and logical. Five types of complexes succeed one another during this stage of thought.

Subphase II-A: Associative complexes These are based on any bond the child notices, such as color, shape, or nearness of objects to one another.

Subphase II-B: Collection complexes Items are grouped by contrast rather than by similarity. For example, one block of each color may be put in a group and given a label. (At a dinner table, a knife, fork, spoon, plate, cup, and saucer would make up a set of a collection variety.)

Subphase II-C: Chain complexes These involve a consecutive joining of individual items with a meaningful bond necessary only between one link and the next (as in the game of dominoes). A *large* green block may be linked to a *large red* block, then a *red* small *round* one followed by a *round* yellow middle-sized one.

Subphase II-D: Diffuse complexes These are groupings in which there is a fluidity in the attribute that unites the individual elements. The child may put triangles together, then add a trapezoid to the group because the trapezoid's points remind her of a triangle's points.

Subphase II-E: Pseudoconcept complexes These at first view appear to be groupings based on true conceptual thinking. But when the label the child has applied is challenged, he shows he is unable to rationalize the grouping condition adequately. If he has put all red blocks together and the experimenter turns two blocks over to show they do not bear the same name (one is *mur* and the other *bik*), the child is unable to give up his first basis for grouping and to seek a different one, a different characteristic that unites the objects. Pseudoconceptual thinking represents a transition from thinking in complexes to thinking in true concepts.

Vygotsky made an important distinction between pseudoconcepts and true concepts: true conceptual thinking requires that the child spontaneously group objects on the basis of abstract characteristics that she perceives and not simply apply ready-made labels that she has been taught to use with other, common groupings. Vygotsky explained this phenomenon, which causes many adults to mistakenly assume that young children think conceptually, in this way:

Pseudoconcepts predominate over all other complexes in the preschool child's thinking for the simple reason that in real life, complexes corresponding to word meanings are not spontaneously developed by the child: The lines along which a complex develops are predetermined by the meaning a given word already has in the language of adults. (1962, p. 67)

Stage III: Thinking in concepts   On the threshold of this final major stage, we will pause and inspect two paths of thought development—*synthesizing* and *analyzing*—that have now converged to make conceptual thinking possible.

The first path was through the sequence of complexes. The main function involved in such complex thinking was the *drawing together* or synthesizing of phenomena that share common aspects. The second path leading to conceptual thinking followed the process of *separating* or analyzing phenomena by singling out or abstracting elements from them. In Vygotsky's opinion these two processes, uniting and separating, arise from different sources in the child's development. We have already traced the path of drawing together or synthesizing. We will now move back to find the beginnings of the other path, that of abstracting or analyzing.

In his experiments, Vygotsky located the beginnings of abstracting at the point where children identified ways in which objects were *maximally similar*—that is, alike in as many ways as possible. For example, they pick two blocks that are both tall *and* yellow or both short *and* green. But since such pairs of blocks also differ in shape or horizontal size, the child's abstracting process is somewhat in error. However, at this age the child overlooks the discrepancies and overemphasizes the similarities he first identified.

At the next stage of abstraction, the child identifies a *single characteristic* by which to group objects, selecting only green blocks or only tall ones. Vygotsky called these single-characteristic selections *potential concepts.*

The child then takes the final step into conceptual thinking when she makes a new synthesis of accurately abstracted traits, a synthesis that is stable and convincing in her mind, and this synthesis "becomes the main instrument of thought" (Vygotsky, 1962, p. 78). The child—by now an early adolescent—views things in terms of her synthesized and analyzed concepts. But even among adolescents conceptual thinking is somewhat unstable, being more consistent in concrete situations that have objects present than in solely verbal situations. Furthermore, there is no sharp break between one sort of thought and another. As the child begins to achieve conceptual thought, her thinking in complexes continues, although it diminishes in frequency. A person, even as an adult, is never "purely" a conceptual thinker.

Throughout this process of mental development, language has served as a significant tool or mediator for thinking activity. The intellectual operation of forming concepts, according to Vygotsky (1962, p. 81), "is guided by the use of words as the means of actively centering attention, of abstracting certain traits, synthesizing them, and symbolizing them by a sign."

As mentioned earlier, after Vygotsky conducted his experiments with the blocks and identified his hierarchy of mental acts leading to true concept formation, he studied the literature on children's linguistic development, on the thought processes of primitive peoples, and on the nature of languages as such. The comparison of his own experimental results with those from the professional literature convinced him that the stages he had identified were essentially an accurate description of the development of conceptual thought. He apparently felt that a significant portion of the thought–language puzzle had been solved.

KEY GENERALIZATIONS ABOUT DEVELOPMENT

Vygotsky also produced a variety of other insights that illustrate other facets of development. The following selections reflect some of these beliefs. Each selection in a sense describes a direction that development takes, since each is cast in a form that pictures the way the condition of the young child changes as the child grows toward adolescence.

Structures and Functions

At each level of development, the child's manner of interacting with the world is determined by the particular *structures* of the personality at that time. A given structure equips the child to function in a particular way. By *function*, Vygotsky appeared to mean the way the child interpreted the world and responded. The first structures displayed by the newborn and young child Vygotsky termed *elementary*. They are seated in the conditioned and unconditioned reflexes, in the basic biological nature of the individual, and their functions "are totally and directly determined by stimulation from the environment" (Vygotsky, 1978, p. 39).

As the child grows up, he periodically arrives at new stages at which new structures are built, thereby creating potentials for new functions. Vygotsky termed these *higher structures,* ones that emerge in the process of cultural development and utilize signs (language) and tools. Whereas the elementary functions consist of the child's reacting directly to stimuli from the environment, for "higher functions, the central feature is self-generated stimulation, that is, the creation and use of artificial stimuli which become the immediate causes of behavior" (Vygotsky, 1978, p. 39). The older child, then, "thinks up" things to do and employs language and tools in pursuit of need fulfillment.

Vygotsky proposed that as a child moves from a more elementary to a higher structure, the process at each step of development involves the same sequence of events. "The initial stage is followed by that first structure's destruction, reconstruction, and transition to structures of the higher type. . . . Higher psychological functions are not superimposed as a second story over the elementary processes; they represent new psychological systems" (Vygotsky, 1978, p. 124). Note that Piaget (Chapter Nine) held similar views.

Memory

In keeping with his lower and higher levels of structure and function, Vygotsky defined two separate types of memory. The lower type, corresponding to elementary structures, he called *natural memory.* This sort dominates the intellectual behavior of both young children and nonliterate peoples. Natural memory consists of a person's retaining mental images of actual experiences and objects. Such memory traces resemble pictures and sounds in the mind, revealed in studies of young children's eidetic or photographic records of events. Natural memory is the most basic form of cognition, "the definitive characteristic of the early stages" of mental development (Vygotsky, 1978, p. 51).

In contrast to natural memory is the abstract variety that evolves as the child gains command over signs that form language. Objects and events can be symbolized as words and figures, and these symbols can themselves be manipulated to form new meanings. The older child develops concepts by abstracting a common quality from various events and by comprehending principles that represent relations among the concepts. For the adolescent, remembering is not simply the recall of images. As Luria (1976, p. 11) explained, "although the young child thinks by remembering, an adolescent remembers by thinking." An adolescent girl's "memory is so 'logicalized' that remembering is reduced to establishing and finding logical relations; recognizing consists in discovering that element which the task indicates has to be found" (Vygotsky, 1978, p. 51).

Perception

As children develop, their perception progresses from a natural form to higher forms that are mediated by language. Preverbal infants seem to perceive only immediately present visual and aural fields. Then, as language is gradually acquired, children gain more control over what they attend to and how they perceive it. Vygotsky concluded that the chief function of speech for young children is that of applying labels to things, thereby singling out the object from its background for attention and imposing some of their own structure on the natural sensory field. At the same time, children accompany their first words with expressive gestures, ostensibly compensating with gesture for their shortcomings in communicating with language.

At a more advanced stage of development, speech functions as an instrument for synthesizing and thereby producing more complex forms of perception. Speech frees the child from the immediate visual field.

> The independent elements in a visual field are simultaneously perceived; in this sense, *visual perception is integral.* Speech, on the other hand, requires sequential processing. Each element is separately labeled and then connected in a sentence structure, *making speech essentially analytical.* (Vygotsky, 1978, p. 33)

In summary, then, these examples of Vygotsky's beliefs about elementary and higher functions, about memory, and about perception illustrate his deep conviction that acquisition of tool use and language is essential for the development of higher cognitive processes. And in keeping with his Marxist views about the significance of the social environment for development, Vygotsky saw the language environment—the *culture*—in which a child is raised as being crucial in determining the direction and extent of the individual's intellectual growth. The history of that particular culture and the history of the individual child's experience in that culture mold the child's cognitive abilities.

CENTRAL CONCERNS IN SOVIET DEVELOPMENTAL THEORY: 1920S—1980S

In pointing out the chief interests of Soviet developmentalists during the past seven decades, V. V. Davidov (1985) emphasized the crucial role played by activity at each stage of child development. An *activity* is a person's goal-oriented, genuinely industrious interaction with the world, with the product of this activity becoming transformed in the structure of the individual's intellect. More specifically, as a child engages in a type of social interaction with others in his or her culture, this activity is accompanied by signs or language that represent the activity. The signs or language are then internalized by the child so that the internalization alters the psychic structures that, in turn, produce new psychic functions by which the child interacts with the world.

At the base of such a theory is the concept of a hierarchy of types of activities, with a dominant or *leading activity* at the top of the hierarchy at each stage of development. Thus each period of human development is motivated by a particular leading activity. The change from one leading activity brings about a change in the person's perception of life and signifies the transition from one stage to the next. A leading activity is marked by three features: (1) it is the chief factor establishing a given period in the child's psychological development; (2) it is within the field of this activity that particular psychic functions emerge; and (3) the climax of the activity forms the foundation for the next leading activity.

Thus successive leading activities signify the focus of development over the passing years and become a series of developmental stages. The best-known version of this series was described by Vygotsky and D. B. Elkonin (Davidov, 1985; Elkonin in Cole, 1977, pp. 538–563). It consists of six levels:

1. *Intuitive and emotional contact between child and adults (birth to age 1)*: The basic types of development produced by this contact include feeling a need for interacting with other people, expressing emotional attitudes toward them, learning to grasp things, and displaying a variety of perceptual actions.
2. *Object-manipulation activity (early preschool years, ages one to three)*: Children adopt socially accepted ways of handling things, and through interaction with adults they develop speech and visual-perception thinking (memory images).
3. *Game-playing activity (later preschool years, ages three to seven)**: Children engage in symbolic activities and creative play. They now have some comprehension of how to cooperate together in group endeavors.

---

*Traditionally Soviet children started elementary school at age seven, some of them having been in preschool programs for two or three years.

4. *Learning activity (elementary school years, ages seven to eleven)*: Children develop theoretical approaches to the world of things, a function that involves their considering objective laws of reality and beginning to comprehend psychological preconditions for abstract theoretical thought (intentional mental operations, mental schemes for problem solving, reflective thinking).

5. *Social-communications activity (early adolescence, ages eleven to fifteen)*: Adolescents gain skills in initiating types of communication needed for solving life's problems, in understanding other people's motives, and in consciously submitting to group norms.

6. *Vocational-learning activity (later adolescence, ages fifteen to seventeen)*: Older adolescents develop new cognitive and vocational interests, grasp elements of research work, and attempt life projects.

The transition from one stage of development to another disrupts the stability of the child's ways of thinking and interacting with the world and produces *crises* as the child struggles with the prerequisites for the next activity that is to occupy the leading role. Thus development is composed of cycles of stability interspersed with transitional crises.

Davidov (1985) identified five major concerns that increasingly engaged the attention of Soviet developmental psychologists: (1) elucidating the basic concepts of development concerning humans in general and specific ways individuals' intellects evolve, (2) creating a complete theory of intellectual development incorporating the leading activities of the successive stages of child growth, (3) discovering how the historical development of a society relates to its members' intellectual development, (4) determining methods for studying critical periods over the entire life span of development, and (5) studying intellectual development in middle-aged and elderly people.

Practical Applications

In a society whose entire apparatus—scientific, organizational, artistic, educational, social, athletic—was designed to promote such sociopolitical goals as those of Marxist-Leninism, developmental psychologists were necessarily practical people who focused their theories on the solution of problems in the society. Vygotsky and his fellow developmentalists accepted this responsibility with apparent enthusiasm as they applied their studies to aiding the physically and mentally handicapped, spreading literacy throughout the third largest population in the world, improving instructional methods in the schools, raising the level of intellectual functioning of disadvantaged groups in the society (Luria, 1976), and promoting better child-rearing practices in general (Moll, 1990).

In formulating the theoretical foundations for these practical undertakings, Vygotsky and his colleagues often departed from the dominant views of European and American psychologists. An example from Vygotsky's writings illustrates one of these departures. The issue is that of learning readiness—that is, how does a teacher or parent know when a child is capable of learning to perform a given intellectual function or task? This determination traditionally has been based on aptitude and intelligence test scores. The child's developmental level is determined on the basis of how adequately she or he answers the questions or solves the problems posed by the test. Or Piagetian tasks have been used to reveal the present mode of the child's mental functioning. Ostensibly this assessment informs the educator of the base on which instruction might build. If the child's test performance shows that he or she has mastered the level of thought necessary for a given type of learning, then those learning activities are appropriate for that child at that point. However, if the child's intellectual development appears insufficient for pursuing the proposed learning task, then the task should be postponed until a later date.

However, Vygotsky disagreed with this line of logic and proposed instead that two developmental levels were important for determining whether a given sort of learning could profitably be attempted. The first and lower level, which he called the *actual developmental level,* was the one established by the tests or Piagetian tasks. It showed the stage of development that had already been completed. But Vygotsky contended that this level was not a good indicator of how well a child can learn new material with some hints or help from an instructor. Besides the development that has been completed, there is development that is currently evolving, and this sort of learning potential is not adequately revealed by traditional tests. Rather, it is revealed during the process of teaching a child, by observations of how the child's intellect functions in relation to hints or leading questions or suggestions from a sensitive instructor. Studies conducted by Vygotsky and his associates supported this contention and motivated him to identify a second developmental level that extends above the actual level. He called this the *zone of proximal development.*

> [The zone] is the distance between the actual developmental level as determined by independent problem solving and the level of potential development as determined through problem solving under adult guidance or in collaboration with more capable peers.
>
> The zone of proximal development defines those functions that have not yet matured but are in the process of maturation, functions that will mature tomorrow but are currently in an embryonic state. These functions could be termed the "buds" or "flowers" of development rather than the "fruits" of development. The actual developmental level characterizes mental development retrospectively, while the zone of proximal development characterizes mental development prospectively. (Vygotsky, 1978, pp. 86–87).

Such a notion of learning readiness, when applied to practical teaching situations, significantly influences the teacher's decision about what kinds of learning activities to provide and how to decide whether children are capable of profiting from them. For example, a teacher who knows the sequence in which the zones of proximal development evolve in the field of mathematics can predict the next mathematical skill that a child should be capable of mastering. Equipped with this knowledge, the teacher can design learning activities for the child that will stimulate the early fruition of that skill.

SOVIET THEORY

How well do I think the theory meets the standards?

Standards	Very well	Moderately well	Very poorly
1. Reflects the real world of children	X		
2. Is clearly understandable	X		
3. Explains the past and predicts the future		X	
4. Guides child rearing		X	
5. Is internally consistent	X		
6. Is economical		X	
7. Is falsifiable	X		
8. Is supported by convincing evidence		X	
9. Adapts to new data			X
10. Is novel	X		
11. Is comprehensive	X		
12. Stimulates new discoveries	X		
13. Is durable		X	
14. Is self-satisfying	X		

VYGOTSKY'S THEORY: AN ASSESSMENT

As in previous chapters, the fourteen standards of appraisal from Chapter One provide the framework for evaluating Vygotsky's theory.

Vygotsky's theorizing warrants a rather high mark for how well it reflects the real world of children (item 1). His speculations were founded on the results of experiments with children of various ages, and he sought to check his conclusions with other studies from various nations. I would have rated item 1 even higher if his theory had been further supported with data from studies specifically designed to test his hypotheses (1) by experimental methods in addition to those using such devices as the Vygotsky blocks and (2) with children from more varied cultural environments.

The theory is clearly described (item 2), particularly in its English-language form, which profits from the translators' organizational improvements.

The theory explains the past and predicts the future (item 3) of verbal-thought development for children in general. However, it does not (at least in the form described in *Thought and Language*) provide a means for analyzing the influence of causal factors in a child's life so that the individual child's progress toward conceptual thought can be explained or predicted. Thus I have given it only a moderate rating on item 3.

Implications for child-rearing practices (item 4) in the form of suggestions for teaching scientific concepts have been included in Vygotsky's writings. But as in the case of item 3, I feel the theory's usefulness as a guide to child rearing is limited by the failure to specify how causal factors combine in an individual child's life to determine his or her particular intellectual development. Thus I have rated the theory as moderate on item 4.

I have not located any internal inconsistencies in Vygotsky's model (item 5), and it appears economical (item 6) in that complex theoretical mechanisms are not used to account for phenomena that might be equally well explained by less complex ones. I feel, however, that more elements and a better explanation of their interactions are needed to account for the results he obtained with his block experiments. The theory as it appears in *Thought and Language* is more programmatic than complete and systematic. At the time of Vygotsky's death it was necessarily still in skeletal form. My mark near the center for item 6, therefore, represents my opinion that the theory was somewhat overly economical, barren in detail.

In terms of falsifiability (item 7), I believe all of Vygotsky's hypotheses and proposals, as well as his actual stages of growth, can be tested experimentally to determine whether they are supportable in fact.

Just as Karl Marx's conception of society was highly innovative, so also was the Soviet child development model that Vygotsky erected on Marxist principles (item 10).

As stimulators of new discoveries (item 12), Vygotsky's theoretical proposals were highly regarded in the Soviet Union (Luria, 1976, pp. v, 11–12; Vygotsky, 1962, pp. ix–x). And ever since his work was first published in the West, it set off new speculations and investigations that are appearing at an increasing rate outside of Eastern Europe. Over the sixteen-year period from 1964 to 1980, *Psychological Abstracts* listed only 34 journal articles that drew on Vygotsky's work. In contrast, over the ten-year span from 1980 to 1990, more than 120 such studies were cited from publications both inside and outside the Soviet Union. Thus I have given Vygotsky's contribution a high mark for its fertility.

In terms of durability (item 13), we could expect that the demise of the Soviet government and the decline in people's confidence in Maxist social theory might be accompanied by a declining faith in certain aspects of the Soviet view of child development. I would speculate that, within the populace at large, the earliest challenge to the Soviet tradition will come—or has already come—from Jewish (Hartman, 1990), Christian (Thomas, 1990), and Muslim (Obeid, 1990) conceptions of human development that were suppressed under the Marxist regime. In particular, the large populations of Muslims in former southern Soviet republics (Azerbaijan, Kazakhstan, Kyrgyzstan, Tajikistan, Turkmenistan, Uzbekistan) will likely turn away from the Marxist-based position on child development. Within the Eastern European scientific community itself, I imagine that greater importance will be accorded genetic factors, as compared to social influences, in accounting for children's development. I also expect that a greater variety of theories of development will be openly admitted into those scientific circles that formerly were obliged to follow the imposed party line. In Western democracies, the respect that the Soviet model has been accorded in recent years suggests that at least portions of the Soviet perspective will continue to influence child development theory in those nations (Kozulin, 1990; Newman & Holzman, 1993; Moll, 1990; Rieber & Carton, 1987, 1993; van der Veer & Valsiner, 1994; Wertsch, 1985). Of particular interest are Soviet research methods, such notions as Vygotsky's zone of proximal development, the influence of actions on thought, and attention to how both the society's and individual children's social histories affect development.

I rated the Soviet tradition in the upper "moderately well" region on comprehensiveness (item 11). The theory addresses the development of both cognitive and physical abilities. However, the versions I have read appear to slight emotional factors and the growth of individual children's perceptions of self.

A substantial amount of empirical evidence was produced in the Soviet Union and in other communist societies from the mid-1920s through the 1980s to support the Soviet scheme (item 8). But the need for the Soviet model to adhere to Marxist sociopolitical convictions limited the ways in which data contrary to the model's basic precepts could be interpreted (item 9). The two ways most adherents of Soviet theory appeared to respond to additional data were (1) to interpret the evidence in terms of the theory without altering the theory significantly or (2) to avoid or dismiss data that appeared to cast doubt on the model's validity. For example, empirical results suggesting the significant influence of heredity on people's abilities and on their positions in the social structure were not compatible with a Marxist position and thus were not welcomed by proponents of the Soviet tradition. As a result, I have marked the Soviet theory rather low on adaptability (item 9).

Finally, I find the Soviet theory overall to be highly thought provoking and in many respects sufficiently convincing to rate it between very and moderately satisfying (item 14).

FOR FURTHER READING

Reiber, R. W., and A. S. Carton. (eds.) (1987, 1993) *The Collected Works of L. S. Vygotsky.* New York: Plenum.

Moll, L. C. (ed.) (1990) *Vygotsky and Education: Instructional Implications and Applications of Sociohistorical Psychology.* New York: Cambridge University Press.

van der Veer, R., and J. Valsiner (eds.) (1994) *The Vygotsky Reader.* Cambridge, Mass.: Blackwell.

Vygotsky, L. S. (1962) *Thought and Language.* Cambridge, Mass.: M.I.T. Press.

For Soviet psychological investigations utilizing Vygotsky's proposal that cognitive development as reflected in speech is heavily influenced by the child's sociohistorical background, see:

Cole, M. (ed.) (1977) *Soviet Developmental Psychology*. White Plains, N.Y.: Sharpe.

Luria, A. R. (1976) *Cognitive Development: Its Cultural and Social Foundations*. Cambridge, Mass.: Harvard University Press.

Luria, A. R., and F. Yudovich. (1971) *Speech and the Development of Mental Processes in the Child*. Harmondsworth, England: Penguin.

For Piaget's reaction to Vygotsky's criticism of an early version of Piagetian theory, see:

Piaget, J. (1962) *Comments on Vygotsky's Critical Remarks Concerning the Language and Thought of the Child and Judgment and Reasoning in the Child*. Cambridge, Mass.: M.I.T. Press, 16 pages.

For a detailed, highly readable chronicle of the evolution of Soviet developmental psychology, including Vygotsky's role in that pageant, see:

Valsiner, J. (1988b) *Developmental Psychology in the Soviet Union*. Bloomington: Indiana University Press.

Estimating the Future of Stage Theories

What are characteristics of recent stage theories, and what might be expected of stage theories in the years ahead?

Three of the ways in which theorists have traditionally charted the course of development are (1) in terms of a direction—that is, tracing how development progresses from an initial condition to a final condition; (2) as processes of growth; and (3) as a hierarchy of stages. Some writers have adopted only one of these perspectives. Others have combined two or all three.

Kurt Lewin (1889–1947) and Heinz Werner (1890–1964) are examples of authors who depicted development in the first of these ways. Each proposed a set of dimensions along which, according to their analyses, development naturally advances. Their dimensions, stated as growth principles, were in most cases remarkably alike, even when the labels they applied to the principles were dissimilar (Barker, Dembo, & Lewin, 1943, pp. 441–442; Werner, 1961).

To illustrate, let's consider three of the dimensions on which Lewin and Werner agreed. Their first principle held that the child develops from a simple to an increasingly complex organism in terms of perceptual ability, thought processes, language, social interaction, physical skills, and the like. For Lewin, this was the principle of *differentiation*. For Werner, it was progression from the *syncretic* (global, general, indistinct) to the *discrete* (diverse, numerous, varied). A second principle centered on the gradually improving coordination among the various aspects of the child's differentiating self. Lewin's term for this principle was *organized independence*, whereas Werner's was *articulation*. The two authors also agreed that the growing child becomes ever more *realistic*, in the sense of being able to distinguish between (1) what might be or what we wish to be or what we imagine could be and (2) how things really are.

In contrast, other theorists have portrayed development in terms of growth processes. Such is true of behaviorists and social learning proponents, as well as the information-processing advocates, ecological psychologists, and ethologists whom we meet in later chapters. For supporters of a growth-process perspective, the emphasis is not so much on the direction of development as it is on the operations that produce developmental change. Among radical behaviorists, these operations are reflected in such terms as *operant conditioning, reinforcement, shaping,* and *chaining*. Social learning theorists add such processes as *modeling, attending,* and *coding for memory*. Process-oriented theorists are often referred to as *functionalists* since they focus on the functions of the environment in promoting development.

Our third option for describing development is to characterize growth as a series of stages. Examples are the phases of development proposed by Gesell, Havighurst, Freud, Erikson, Piaget, and the Soviets. The purpose of this perspective is to carry the analysis of stage theories a step further by (1) describing key features of some recently proposed models and (2) estimating what might be expected of stage theories in the future.

THREE RECENTLY PROPOSED STAGE THEORIES

Within the realm of stage theories, several varieties have emerged in recent times. To account for their principal forms, Robbie Case explained:

> An issue that has played a central and controversial role in the field of intellectual development, virtually since its inception, is the question of whether the human mind should be seen as developing in a general or a specific fashion. Those favoring the former position have tended to characterize children's development as proceeding through a sequence of general stages, often ones that are presumed to be universal in their character, whereas those favoring the latter position have preferred to characterize children's development as proceeding along many fronts at once, at different rates, in a continuous and contextually sensitive manner. (1992, p. 343)

Piaget's scheme qualifies as a general system in which stages are universal for all children and are determined primarily by internal maturational functions. In contrast, the proposals of Gelman (1969) and Klahr and Wallace (1976) represent specific-stage perspectives in which development is seen as strongly influenced by children's particular environmental situations. From a specific-stage viewpoint, development in one cognitive domain (such as numerical skill) advances in a different fashion than development in other domains (such as verbal, musical, mechanical, or social skills). Recent attempts to achieve a balance between these two contrasting positions have produced a further class of theories. Several within this class are called *neo-Piagetian*, "because they retain many of Piaget's core epistemological assumptions" (Case, 1992, p. 344). The three perspectives described in the following pages are of this neo-Piagetian ilk.

As a preparation for inspecting these models, we can profitably consider the matter of what constitutes a *structure* and a *stage*. Although not everyone in the field of child development agrees on how *structure* should be defined, I imagine that most would find the following statement fairly acceptable: a cognitive structure is an interpretive framework that an individual applies in giving meaning to stimuli from the environment. Case (1986, p. 58) defined such structures as "order-imposing devices with which children come equipped at birth" and then change in a predictable pattern with increasing age. Children's intellectual development can then be seen as progressive alterations in their cognitive structures—in the mental templates they use for comprehending their world. K. W. Fischer and R. L. Canfield (1986) pointed out that changes in structures can be brought about in more than one way—for example, by intense emotional encounters (religious conversion, child abuse), by vivid learning experiences (producing insight), and by maturational advances in the child's nervous system. The last of these—maturation governed chiefly by the child's inherited genetic timing system—is the type of structural change usually referred to as *developmental*. It is the kind of structural change common to all children, and it forms the basis for many of the stage theories of child development. Such stage theorists typically are labeled *structuralists* because of their stress on how development depends so heavily on the genetically governed physical and mental structures through which the organism interprets events in the environment.

As in the case of structure, there has been—and continues to be—considerable disagreement about the meaning of *stage* (Levin, 1986). But, for present purposes, the following meaning will suffice as a starting point: a new stage of cognitive development has been reached when there has been a marked change in cognitive structures that bear on varied domains of thought, when the nature of the change is similar for children of relatively the same age, and when the new structures will continue in use for some time. In other words, a fairly abrupt change in structures is followed by a *plateau*—an extended period of time when no dramatic alterations occur. The term *domains* in this context refers to such areas as language use, mathematical functions, the explanation of physical events, self-concept, and the like. Ways that such a general notion of stage can be rendered less simplistic and more precise are illustrated in the theories described below.

In the following presentation, the topics addressed under each theory include events that occasioned the theory's creation and its distinctive features.

Case's Four-Stage Scheme

In the mid-1980s, Robbie Case, who is now the director of the University of Toronto Institute of Child Study, published a new version of cognitive development theory grounded in extensive empirical research (1985, 1992). In constructing his model, he drew a portion of his concepts and investigative methods from several pro-genitors, principally J. M. Baldwin (1895), J. Piaget (1963), J. S. Bruner (1964), J. Pascual-Leone (1976), and D. Klahr and J. G. Wallace (1976). Case's stated purpose in devising this new departure was to resolve some of the difficulties encountered in the models proposed by these predecessors.

His stage structure in its gross features is similar to, and generally supportive of, Piaget's scheme of sensorimotor, preoperational, concrete operational, and formal operational periods. However, Case designated the upper three stages with labels he felt more accurately described the sorts of mental processes exemplified in children's thinking from early childhood through adolescence. As shown in Figure D.1, he substituted the term *relational* for Piaget's *preoperational*, the term *dimensional* for *concrete operational*, and *vectorial* for *formal operational*.

Case found much to commend in Piaget's detailed analysis of the phase of mental growth from birth to about eighteen months, and he agreed that the term *sensorimotor* accurately reflected the infant's intellectual functions. But he disagreed that the succeeding phase of early childhood (around two months to about five years) should be called *preoperational*, as if it were simply a preparation for the

Vectorial Stage

+3 Elaborated coordination
15–18 years

+2 Bifocal coordination
13–15 years

+1 Unifocal coordination
11–13 years

0. Operational consolidation
9–11 years

Dimensional Stage

+3 Elaborated coordination
9–11 years

+2 Bifocal coordination
7–9 years

+1 Unifocal coordination
5–7 years

0. Operational consolidation
3.5–5 years

Relational Stage

+3 Elaborated coordination
3.5–5 years

+2 Bifocal coordination
2–3.5 years

+1 Unifocal coordination
1.5–2 years

0. Operational consolidation
12–18 months

Sensorimotor Stage

+3 Elaborated coordination
12–18 months

+2 Bifocal coordination
8–12 months

+1 Unifocal coordination
4–8 months

0. Operational consolidation
0–4 months

F I G U R E D.1
Case's stages of mental development (adapted from Case, 1985, p. 413)

following stage (ages five to eleven). "The period from 2 to 5 years of age is not just a precursor of concrete operational development. It is a distinct stage of its own, with its own sequence of operative structures and its own final operational system" (1985, p. 116). In applying the label *relational* to this period, Case suggested that from around age two until children enter kindergarten, they develop mental skills of comprehending relations between observed phenomena in their lives, such as in recognizing ways that different animals are similar to each other.

According to his analysis, the next period (ages five to eleven) is distinguished by children's ability to mentally manipulate phenomena that can be aligned along dimensions—including such polar dimensions as hot–cold, far–near, more–less, long–short, high–low, frequent–seldom, old–young, and others. Hence the term *dimensional* replaced Piaget's *concrete operational.*

Next, Case concluded that a more accurate descriptive word, *vectorial,* should replace *formal operational* in order to signify the ability of children beyond age eleven to explain or predict what will result from the interactions of two or more dimensions. For example, vectorial thought processes are required to predict how a balance beam will respond to the interaction of *varied weights* at *varied distances* along the beam arms. In its playground form, this problem is encountered with a teeter-totter or seesaw. The matter of judging the interaction of weight and distance can be rendered quite complex when precise estimates of weights and distances, along with certain unknown quantities, are required. Case proposed that within this fourth stage "children are no longer focusing on either of . . . two dimensions separately. Rather, they are focusing on a more abstract dimension: the vector that results from [the dimensions'] opposition" (1985, p. 108).

A key feature of Case's theory is the proposal that within each stage there is a sequence of subphases (*substages*) that advance the child's thought processes from less sophisticated to more sophisticated modes of operation. These sub-stages, common to all four major stages, are entitled (0) *operational consolidation*, (1) *unifocal coordination,* (2) *bifocal coordination,* and (3) *elaborated coordination.* As suggested in Figure D.1, at the operational consolidation phase the child is essentially integrating in a secure form the accomplishments of the previous stage rather than acquiring a significantly new style of thinking. For this reason, Case numbered the first phase 0. In contrast, the subsequent three substages represent added mental skills and thus are assigned numbers 1, 2, and 3. At the unifocal coordination substage, the child is able to center attention on a variety of individual factors, but can only focus on one such factor at a time to solve a problem—one sensorimotor movement at ages 4 to 8 months, one relationship at ages 1.5 to 2 years, one dimension at ages 5 to 7 years, and one interaction of contrasting dimensions (vectorial) at ages 11 to 13 years. However, with additional maturation and experience, children advance to a bifocal coordination substage where they can direct attention at two different factors to solve a problem—two sensorimotor movements at ages 8 to 12 months, two relationships at ages 2 to 3.5 years, two dimensions at ages 7 to 9 years, and two interactions of contrasting dimensions (vectorial) at ages 13 to 15 years. In like manner, at the final elaborated coordination level of a major stage, children can coordinate two or more factors in a sophisticated way to solve a problem.

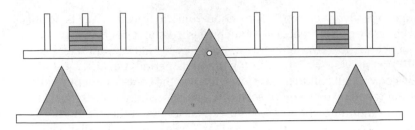

F I G U R E D.2
Balance beam for testing school-age children's reasoning patterns (adapted from Case, 1985, p. 104. Originally appeared in Siegler, 1976)

Although space limitations prohibit my demonstrating each of the stage progressions in detail, an example from the dimensional stage may suffice to illustrate how children's thinking typically advances (Siegler, 1976). Children ages 3.5 through 10 years were shown a balance beam with four pegs at equal intervals on either side of the fulcrum, along with a stack of doughnut-shaped weights that could be slipped onto the pegs (Figure D.2). The task was to predict how the beam would behave if the weights were arranged in various quantities and at various distances along the beam. Children operating at the unifocal coordination substage (ages five to seven) approached this problem by concentrating their attention on the dimension of weight, with their focus on the number of separate weights. Their strategy involved counting the number of weights on each side, noting which side had the larger number, and choosing that side as the one that would go down when the beam was free to move.

At the next substage (bifocal coordination, ages seven to nine) children could solve the problem by coordinating two dimensions: (1) noting which side had the greater number of weights, (2) noting the side that had weight at a greater distance, and (3) concluding that if the weights were about equal, the side with the greater distance would go down; otherwise, the side with the greater weight would go down. At the third substage (elaborated coordination, ages nine to eleven), children appeared to use addition and subtraction to solve problems involving more complex combinations of weights and distances than could be managed by children still operating at substages 1 and 2.

> The addition strategy is quite simple. Children merely add the number of weight and distance units on each side, and pick the one with the greater total value as the one which will go down. The subtraction strategy is more complicated, but follows the same basic logic. Children first compute the difference between the two weights, and the difference between the two distances. They then base their decision on the dimension with the greater difference. For example, if the weights are 2 and 8, and the distances are 4 and 3, they pick the side with the greater weight to go down, because the difference along this dimension is greater than that along the distance dimension. (Case, 1985, p. 106)

Case has used his model not only for charting children's reasoning about inanimate objects but also for interpreting children's language development and the way they think about people's social interactions. The model is thus conceived to be a general theory of intelligence, applicable to a variety of aspects of mental development.

In a number of ways Case's scheme has advanced development theory by accounting for phenomena that were not adequately explained by earlier models. For instance, as noted in Chapter Nine, the fact that children conceive of the conservation of substance, quantity, weight, and mass at different ages rather than simultaneously casts in question the existence of a single qualitatively distinct mode of thinking (concrete operational) covering the entire range of elementary-school years. The term *horizontal décalage* serves as a label for such inconsistency but not as an explanation. However, Case's notion of substages within each major stage permits him to rationalize the inconsistency. That is, in the early unifocal coordination phase of a stage (ages five to seven), the child focuses on separate factors (such as dimensions of height, width, weight, mass), each of which may develop at a different time. Only by the third substage (elaborated coordination) do all of these separate insights become integrated into a general, qualitatively distinct mode of thought governing a broad spectrum of mental activities.

In searching for a way to resolve the conflict between general-stage and specific-stage theories, Case and his colleagues conducted a series of studies focusing on how children between ages four and ten (Case's *dimensional stage*) solve problems involving diverse cognitive domains (quantitative, musical, motor, spatial-relations, social-perception) as well as diverse tasks within each domain. The findings support the notion that the foundation of each stage consists of a core set of elements that make up the child's *central conceptual structure*. But the findings also recognize that mental activity can be divided into various *domains of functioning*, such as the logico-mathematical, verbal, visual-perception, social-perception, musical, motor, and more. To a great extent, children perform in one domain at nearly the same level as they do in another. This suggests that the central conceptual structure permeates all of the domains. In other words, all domains share a basic way of conceiving the world within each of Case's four principal stages. However, every domain also displays a particular level of functioning that may not be precisely the same as the level of other domains. Perhaps the human nervous system is constructed in the form of *modules*, each designed to process the stimuli specific to a given domain; and the pattern and rate of development of different modules may not be the same. Furthermore, the particular experiences children have with a domain can be expected to influence their development in that domain's mode of thought.

Case proposes that in very young children, the central conceptual structure is heavily dependent on genetic factors—on an inherited biological clock. However, with advancing age, "the experience that is relevant to the formation of central conceptual structures becomes less universal, and more highly dependent on technologies and bodies of knowledge that are unique to the culture in which they were developed. . . . [As age progresses] social institutions, such as schooling, play an increasingly important role . . . in providing this experience . . . [by familiarizing] children with the culture's symbol systems and the concepts and conventions underlying their use" (Case, 1992, pp. 367–368). Hence, one culture can be expected to promote somewhat different levels of development in certain domains than does another culture.

Thus the idea that cognitive development involves domains (specific) that are built within a central conceptual structure (general) enabled Case to rationalize the ostensible contradiction between specific-stage and general-stage theories. Mental activity is seen as a combination of general and specific levels of intellectual functioning.

In conclusion, although the summary just given identifies a few central elements in Case's scheme, it is far too brief to reveal the tightly knit logic that renders the theory internally consistent, understandable, and generally falsifiable. And the quantity of empirical evidence on which it is founded suggests that the scheme accurately reflects the real world of childhood. Finally, Case appears judicious in recognizing limitations in what he has accomplished. He wonders whether his postulated set of horizontal structures (his subphase and stage characteristics) is the best model of children's mentation. Other puzzles that he considers not yet solved are ones of short-term-memory storage space, the number of cognitive transitions that take place during the preschool years, and the relationships between children's emotional and cognitive development as well as between their procedural and declarative knowledge (Case, 1985, pp. 420–424).

Fischer's Skill Development Theory

Kurt W. Fischer, a professor of psychology at Harvard University, has proposed a *skill theory* that "treats cognitive development as the construction of hierarchically ordered collections of specific skills" (1980, p. 477). Because explaining Fischer's model in its complete form would require a great many pages, the brief version I offer here is admittedly bare-bones. I shall describe only a few of the main features of his proposal, only enough to suggest his general approach to the problems he seeks to solve.

At the outset, Fischer acknowledged virtues in both Piaget's and Skinner's work, as well as in proposals of information-processing psychologists and skill learning theorists. However, he felt that Piaget placed too much emphasis on children's internal maturation and neglected environmental contexts while Skinner did just the opposite. Therefore Fischer developed a model intended to represent an evenly balanced interaction between nature and nurture:

> The skills in the theory are always defined jointly by organism and environment. Consequently, the skills are characterized by structures that have properties like those described by organism-oriented psychologists and that simultaneously are subject to the functional laws outlined by environmentally oriented psychologists. (Fischer, 1980, pp. 478–479)

The skills on which the theory focuses are those techniques children acquire for acting on their world. Such acting can be motor (observable physical movements), perceptual (constructing meanings for what is observed), or mental (manipulating percepts and concepts). Thus Fischer's skills are analogous to Piaget's

TABLE D.1
Fischer's levels of cognitive skills development

Cognitive tiers and levels	Age of first development
Tier 1: Sensorimotor	
Level 1: single sensorimotor sets	several months after birth
Level 2: sensorimotor mappings	middle of first year
Level 3: sensorimotor systems	end of first year, start of second year
Level 4: systems of sensorimotor systems	early preschool years
Tier 2: Representational	
Level 4: single representational sets	early preschool years
Level 5: representational mappings	late preschool years
Level 6: representational systems	grade school years
Level 7: systems of representational systems	early high school years
Tier 3: Abstract	
Level 7: single abstract sets	early high school years
Level 8: abstract mappings	late high school years
Level 9: abstract systems	early adulthood
Level 10: systems of abstract systems	

Adapted from Fischer, 1980, pp. 479, 522.

schemes and Skinner's operants. Like Piaget and Case, Fischer has pictured development as proceeding from the simplest sensorimotor acts in infancy to the manipulation of abstract systems in early adulthood. But rather than describing such development as a progression through a series of stages, Fischer has chosen to depict it as movement through ten levels that are subsumed under three tiers (Table D.1).

As shown in Table D.1, within each tier, cognitive development advances through four types of levels—single sets, mappings, systems, and systems of systems. A *set* in Fischer's usage means "a source of variations that the person can control" by physically or mentally acting on things (Fischer, 1980, p. 486). A set on the sensorimotor tier is very simple, such as the infant's reaching actions (*variations*). Sets on the higher tiers are more complex, such as a child's conception (mental representation) of the kinds of actions (variations) suitable for playing the role of doctor or of mother (*thing*).

The first level on a tier involves single sets. This means that the child can act on (perceive, conceive, think about) a set by itself but not one set in relation to another. The very young infant may follow with her eyes the motion of a toy passed across her crib, and she may also be able to reach and grasp, but she does not connect the seeing and the reaching so as to catch the toy. The means–end combination of seeing and reaching to grasp the toy occurs at the second level, that of *mapping* (connecting) one set onto another. For the older child, mapping may occur when the child, in imaginative play, integrates the doctor role with the role of mother—the doctor converses with the mother about the treatment of the patient (a doll).

At level 3, the child can relate not just one, but two aspects of each action that forms a system. On the sensorimotor tier, the toddler can recognize the distance and speed of a moving toy and adjust his reaching motion to catch it. The older child, playing doctor, may coordinate different aspects of the medical role with different aspects of the mother's role to produce a more complex form of play. Finally, at level 4, the child relates one system to another. For instance, at the sensorimotor level, the child understands that any "object is in fact the focus of a number of different sensory-motor systems; that is, every object can be made to . . . produce many types of actions. The ability to understand objects in this way (as independent agents of action) first develops at level 4" (Fischer, 1980, p. 493).

As shown in Table D.1, the fourth level in each tier serves as the foundation of the next higher tier. Children's being able to perceive relations between two systems of sensorimotor actions—sights, sounds, touch sensations, movements—is their first step in developing the ability to represent mentally such single attributes as weight, length, and width. Then in the latter preschool years, children are able to correlate (map) two such attributes of things. During their time in the elementary grades, their ability to conceive of these attributes as operating in systems progresses, so that "with only level 6 skills, the person can understand most of the individual kinds of conservation that Piaget and his colleagues have documented . . . but cannot integrate those separate conservations into an abstract concept of conservation" (Fischer, 1980, p. 495). Such integration begins to occur at level 7, where "in an abstract set, the person abstracts an intangible attribute that characterizes broad categories of objects, events, or people" (Fischer, 1980, pp. 494–495). Then, as a high school youth and young adult, the individual develops growing sophistication in mapping one abstract set onto another, conceiving of abstract sets as systems and as interrelating systems. Youths who have advanced to level 10 can now meaningfully discuss such matters as (1) the effect of gravity on the ocean tides, the movement of the planets, and space travel; (2) the relation of supply to demand in capitalist and communist economic systems; (3) the relation of the surface grammatical structure of languages to their deep structure; and (4) theories of child development.

Fischer's substituting the word *tier* for *stage* was apparently motivated by a desire to preclude readers' bringing existing notions of *stage* to his model. In contrast to a traditional Piagetian idea of stages, Fischer's levels and tiers involve a good deal of flexibility. Whereas the genetic human nature common to all children furnishes a basic maturational time schedule that conveys all children through the same general tiers and levels, each child's unique environmental experiences and particular genetic structure leads to differences among children in skills they acquire, in when they gain the skills, and, to some extent, in what order. For example, the pattern of two children's development can vary because of their different learning opportunities, the instructional methods they experienced, and the emotional environment in which their learning took place. Thus it should not be surprising that a child may display different levels of skill in reading, calculating, drawing pictures, operating a computer, and speaking a foreign language.

Not only do children's learning histories result in different levels of development of different sets of skills, but the context in which a given skill is displayed can influence the level a child exhibits on a particular occasion. Fischer has applied the term *environmental support* in reference to how much the context may guide the child toward utilizing a skill at one level rather than at another. Take the example of a teacher who is providing primary grade children the opportunity to engage in creative dramatics by playing a medical doctor. The teacher would provide a high level of environmental support by demonstrating (with such objects as a stethoscope, thermometer, or doll) a doctor treating a patient and then allowing the children to play as they wish. In contrast, a low level of environmental support would involve simply furnishing the objects and suggesting that "you might want to play a doctor" without providing any demonstration. In experiments of this type, Fischer found that children aged seven and a half typically showed in their free play a functional level 4 under the low-support condition but level 5 in the high-support context (Fischer & Canfield, 1986, pp. 252–255).

In summary, then, Fischer built into his theory several ways to account for the unevenness of children's development across skills (Piaget's *horizontal décalage* problem) and for the varied paths of cognitive skill development that are sometimes found in empirical investigations.

A further way Fischer adjusted his theory to empirical findings is by proposing five transformation rules that specify how a skill is converted into a new, more advanced skill. The five rules are "the heart of the mechanism for predicting specific sequences of development" (Fischer, 1980, p. 497). He labeled them *intercoordination, compounding, focusing, substitution,* and *differentiation.* The first two rules designate how existing skills are combined to produce new ones. Intercoordination identifies combinations that produce development from one level to the next (macrodevelopment), while compounding identifies combinations that result in small increments of development within a level (microdevelopment). Focusing and substitution identify smaller microdevelopmental steps than does compounding. Specifically, focusing accounts for "moment-to-moment shifts from one skill to another, and substitution designates certain cases of generalization of a skill" (Fischer, 1980, p. 497). The last rule, differentiation, identifies how sets of skills may become divided into subsets while the other four transformations are taking place. Although Fischer does not believe that his five rules cover all the factors governing skill development, he contends that applying the five can furnish better predictions of cognitive growth than have previous theories.

In assessing this skill development model, I would give nearly the same sort of ratings as I proposed for Case's theory. Fischer's carefully reasoned presentation of his theory makes it appear internally consistent and disconfirmable. His explanation is well illustrated with empirical studies of children's reasoning skills. His incorporating children's learning histories, emotional conditions, and the notion of environmental support appear to furnish reasonable interpretations of empirical findings not adequately explained by classical Piagetian theory. I found the major features of the theory understandable. However, a number of details seemed unclear. For example, I did not know precisely how to distinguish one set or system from another in aspects of life that were not specifically illustrated in Fischer's explanation. The exact criteria to use in making such distinctions in a divesity of life situations appears to need clarification. But overall, this recent stage theory (or *tier theory*) appears to be an advance over Piaget's scheme—a move in the right direction.

Mounoud's System of Coding Capacities

Pierre Mounoud is a professor in the Faculty of Psychology and Educational Sciences at the University of Geneva in Switzerland. While still following Piaget's general lead in formulating stages of development, Mounoud has revised Piaget's conception in several respects—in how to name the stages, how much time is spent in a stage, what subphases occur within a stage, and what the child *constructs* while advancing through a stage. The names of the stages and the age levels at which they occur in Mounoud's model are shown in Table D.2.

Mounoud has retained the notion of four major stages but has renamed the last three to represent more accurately his notion of their essence. To grasp this point, we need first to understand what Mounoud believes children construct at each stage of development.

> Piaget's psychogenetic theory regarding the construction of structures appears to me to be extremely vulnerable to criticism. From my point of view, what the child constructs are not structures but *representations or internal organizations of contents*. The child arrives at them by means of structures, which I feel are more economically considered as preformed. Now it is possible to reinterpret the process of reflective abstraction as a *process of construction of representations* and no longer as a process of construction of logical structures (internalization of general coordinations of action). (Mounoud, 1986, p. 51)

In other words, Mounoud chooses to regard the general sensorimotor and mental lenses through which children interpret their world as already existing in the child's nature and evolving by means of a genetically set timing system. He does not accept the notion that the child constructs these general capacities or viewpoints during the process of growing up. Instead, these preformed, evolving structures periodically equip children with new capacities for coding their experiences with the environment. Infants gradually develop coding abilities limited to what is directly perceived: "How it looks and how it sounds and how it feels is what it means." So in Mounoud's system, what the child constructs during these early years are not basic sensorimotor structures (the basic lenses) but, rather, psychomotor records (representations) of the child's encounters with the environment (internal organizations of contents).

During the preschool years (ages two to eight), the child's perceptual capacities are well developed so that environmental encounters are interpreted (internal representations are constructed) in terms of their appearance, sound, and touch. In other words, children internalize perceptuomotor organizations of the world. At the same time, children are beginning to develop new coding capacities, ones based not just on how things look, but on logical properties of things—on concepts rather than merely on percepts. The process of development during these years carries

T A B L E   D. 2
Mounoud's stages of cognitive and motor development

Stages	Child's internal representations	Type of organization
birth	sensorial representations (preformed) linked with preformed structures + new coding capacities (the perceptual code)	sensorimotor organization (preformed)
18–24 months	perceptual representations (constructed) + new coding capacities (the conceptual code)	perceptuomotor organization (constructed)
9–11 years	conceptual representations (constructed) + new coding capacities (the semiotic code)	conceptuomotor organization (constructed)
16–18 years	semiotic representations (constructed)	semioticomotor organization (constructed)

Adapted from Mounoud, 1986, p. 52.

children fully to the next major stage of how they code their experiences, that of conceptual thought (ages nine to fifteen). Their mental organizations of the world are now chiefly in terms of concepts. And it is during this third stage that they gradually develop a new way to represent the content of their world, that of abstract symbols and signs (semioticomotor organization), a capacity that can be fully achieved by age sixteen or eighteen.

It should now be apparent that in Piaget's system of four stages (sensorimotor, preoperational, concrete operational, formal operational), the beginning of the upper three stages occurs considerably earlier than in Mounoud's system. This difference can be explained by Mounoud's assumption regarding the process of development within a stage. He proposes that within each stage there occur two levels of behavioral organization or of object elaboration that represent "two qualitatively distinct levels of organization of exchange between subject and environment. These two levels would characterize an *invariant developmental sequence* which defines the internal dynamics of each stage" (Mounoud, 1986, p. 51).

On the first level within a stage, the child's newly evolved coding capacities equip the child to produce what Mounoud calls "the first revolution" in organizing the child's interactions with the environment. This revolution consists of the child's analyzing actions and objects into constituent parts in order to form new elementary representations that are "partial, local, and juxtaposed" rather than integrated and interrelated. This segmenting of experiences "comes to an end with the integration of these elementary representations into *new or global representations* which are momentarily rigid and nondecomposable, nonsegmentable. The second revolution consists precisely in the decomposition of these total representations into parts or units in such a way as to establish relationships between their components" (Mounoud, 1986, p. 53).

In summary, within each stage, the child's encounters with the environment elicit an innate, evolving general capacity for segmenting a whole into abstract units and then reforming the units into new, more sophisticated patterns of how to represent the world (Mounoud, 1986, p. 45). This second, reformulating revolution occurs near the middle of a stage and is consolidated over the months or years prior to the next stage. Thus, within the perceptuomotor stage, this second revolution appears around age six, when the child enters school and now has the coding capacity to learn reading, writing, calculating, and the conservation of weight, mass, and number. Consequently, Mounoud's second revolution during the per-ceptuomotor stage coincides with the beginning of Piaget's concrete operations stage.

In the nature–nurture debate, Mounoud admits that his model credits genetic forces with greater influence on development than environmental factors:

> This conception ascribes a more important role to the process of neural maturation and the biological substrates of behavior which determine the origin of the steps in this developmental sequence. The maturation of the neural system itself depends on the nature of the interactions of the organism with the environment but in a nonspecific way, these interactions at the most being able to accelerate or slow down the process. (Mounoud, 1986, p. 55)

My assessment of Mounoud's scheme is much the same as for Case's and Fischer's theories. I find his line of logic reasonable, his explanation understandable, his hypotheses testable, and his contentions convincingly illustrated with empirical studies. His model offers abundant research possibilities, as there are numerous details yet to be clarified and hypotheses to be tested in situations other than those from which Mounoud generated his scheme.

A Likely Future for Stage Theories

A number of writers in recent decades have forecast, or at least implied, the demise of stage theories on the grounds that the theories' predictions too often fail to match the picture of child development revealed in empirical studies (Case, 1986, pp. 59–61; Klahr & Wallace, 1976). However, as illustrated by Case, Fischer, Mounoud, and a number of other authors (Bruner, 1964; Halford, 1982; Pascual-Leone, 1976), revised versions of stage theory are alive and thriving in the realm of developmental psychology. To characterize this collection of new schemes, I. Levin (1986, p. viii) noted that they "all agree with major features of the Piagetian structure-based stage model but liberate it from certain constraints so as to make it fit the current state of the art."

Case (1986) suggested that a key feature of recent progress in stage theorizing has been increased dialogue among proponents of the three traditional views of development—one emphasizing process (the empiricists), another emphasizing structures (the rationalists), and a third emphasizing historical and cultural factors (the social contextualists). In other words, theorists operating from each of these three basic worldviews have increasingly sought to incorporate features of the other two perspectives into their own models. Consequently, stage proponents have attempted to account for the day-by-day processes that contribute to development and for the contexts in which development occurs. As a result, they draw such conclusions as that offered by K. W. Fischer and R. L. Canfield:

> Stage and structure do not appear to be monolithic, unitary, fixed characteristics of a child. Instead, they seem to be dynamic, variable properties of the child-in-a-context. Different children show different stages in a given context, and different contexts produce different stages in the same child. To deal with the ambiguity of stage and structure, investigators need to use methods that allow them to detect variations in stage and to expand their range of observations to include likely sources of such variation. These sources include not only the age and learning history of the child, but also factors that specifically relate to short-term variations in stage such as degree of environmental support and task complexity, and factors that are likely to produce long-term individual differences in developmental sequences such as emotional experiences and strategies of approaching tasks. (1986, p. 259)

The future is likely to witness more of this cross-fertilization, so that some investigations of unsettled issues

> will lead to interesting discoveries about children's cognitive development. [In contrast, other issues that arise] will probably have the fate of many thought-provoking problems in the past, and either lead to a blind alley or simply become too boring to the community at large. However, the basic questions of how and what develops, [as] concealed behind the concepts of stage and structure, are still the crux of our domain. (Levin, 1986, p. xix)

In effect, stage theories, in some form, seem destined to be with us forever.

Computer Analogues and the Self

A search for the way children gain skill in processing information and for how a child's innermost self develops

The two types of theories analyzed in Part Six are distinctly different from each other, but not necessarily incompatible. While both are primarily products of the past three decades, they differ dramatically in their philosophical underpinnings, their investigative methods, the aspects of child nature that their proponents consider most important, and the precision of their conceptual structures.

The first type is concerned with information processing (Chapter Eleven). The principal exemplar on which information-processing theories are built is the electronic computer, an analogue chosen on the assumption that advanced forms of computers carry out many of the same functions as the human brain. Thus we might presume that attempts to simulate all sorts of human thought processes with computers could be a fruitful way of discovering the nature of human mental operations and of how such operations develop during childhood and adolescence. Investigative techniques typically employed by information-processing advocates have included (1) the creation of computer programs intended to replicate human mental functions, and (2) the analysis of how people apparently carry out steps of human thought that form an information-processing chain: (a) receiving sensations from the environment, (b) interpreting these sensations, (c) storing the results of the interpretation in long-term memory, and (d) retrieving the contents of memory when they are needed for acting on the environment.

The second type (Chapter Twelve) involves theories of the self. The presentation features humanistic psychology. However, it also includes an additional pair of theories created outside the humanistic tradition.

The prototype humanistic paradigm has been characterized by K. P. Hillner as a conception of development that

> focuses on the person, personality, ego, self, the essence of one's being and existence. Humanism is concerned with such psychological phenomena as creativity, love, self-regard, growth, autonomy, identity, responsibility, and adjustment. As a remedial or interventionist endeavor, humanism amounts to a psychotherapeutic process that strives to make the individual understand himself/herself better and be more aware, independent, open, integrated, and stable. (1984, p. 238)

Because the essence of humanistic psychology is found in individuals' unique views of themselves in relation to their world, research methods that involve measurements and observations of a person by outsiders are of far less interest than individuals' feelings about themselves. Likewise, drawing generalizations about groups (normative-descriptive studies) and making comparisons of one person with another are of little or no use to humanists.

As for theoretical precision, information-processing models are more detailed and specific than humanistic views, whose misty dimensions are often rather difficult to make out. Information-processing theory is readily communicated through verbal descriptions, diagrams, equations, and computer programs. In contrast, humanistic views involve a large measure of emotions and self-perceptions that are not easily conveyed through words, graphs, statistics, or formulas.

By saying that these two very different perspectives on development are not necessarily incompatible, I am suggesting that it is possible to include a concept of *self* as one component of long-term memory in an information-processing model.

Perspective E, at the close of Part Six, addresses matters of causation as they relate to theories presented in this book. The issue, when stated as a question, becomes: In different theories of child development, what is meant by *cause?*

CHAPTER ELEVEN

INFORMATION-PROCESSING THEORIES

As a way of explaining children's behavior, information-processing theories attempt to picture what happens between (1) the moment a child receives impressions from the environment through the senses (mainly through the eyes and ears) and (2) the moment the child visibly responds with such behaviors as speaking, writing, manipulating a toy, catching a ball, or the like. This process has often been compared to the operation of an electronic computer. Data are entered into the computer *(input),* manipulated within the machine *(throughput),* and then the results are printed on paper or displayed on a television screen *(output).* Whereas we can directly witness the first and third steps (input and output), the middle step—the internal operation of the computer—is unseen. Unless we open the computer and have the skill to analyze the inner works while they function, the computer remains a mystery, and we must be satisfied with theorizing about what may be going on inside.

The problem of analysis is essentially the same when we view children from an information-processing perspective. Only the input stimuli (observed environment) and the output behavior (observed actions) can be directly witnessed by people outside the child. We are left to speculate about the throughput segment of the process. And although children can, by introspection, witness this segment and report the way they believe they "think," there is a host of evidence to suggest that such introspection leads to incomplete and faulty descriptions. Not only is the immature child's interpretation of his or her thinking process inadequate, adults' analyses of their mental operations appear incomplete and flawed as well because thinking is a highly complex activity whose elements are not readily apparent in our consciousness.

Information-processing theorists speculate about the nature of the throughput portion of the sequence. (This is the portion that, over the decades, has been identified by diverse terms: *mind, self, personality, the inner child, the organism,* and *the mysterious black box.*) Information-processing theorists attempt to specify the components of the child's internal mechanisms for manipulating information and to delineate how these components interact to produce the child's behavior.

So far, I have spoken of information-processing theory in the singular, as if it were one unified model consisting of a single set of agreed-upon characteristics. However, this is hardly the case. Within the well-populated camp of information-processing theorists, debates abound about the types of components that compose a person's processing system and about how the components interact. Developmental psychologists Robert Kail and Jeffrey Bisanz (1982, p. 47) propose that information processing, at least in its present state, should properly be dubbed a framework, not a theory, since within this framework are a multitude of different theories that have been created over the past two decades or so. Although it is beyond the scope of this chapter to review all these versions, we can look at some of the widely agreed-upon components and can identify key issues that are debated.

As noted in earlier chapters, among people who write about human development theories it is customary to speak of the earliest forms of a theoretical proposal as *standard* or *classical* models and then append some other adjective (*neo* or *post* or *revised*) to subsequent varieties as a means of differentiating among the successive versions. Such has been the case with information-processing theory. The pioneering schemes created in the 1960s and early 1970s are now labeled *standard, early,* or *classical* to distinguish them from types introduced more recently (Pylyshyn, 1989). In this chapter, we first look at a typical classical model that illustrates an early version of information-processing theory. Subsequently we inspect recent reformations of the information-processing paradigm.

Information-processing theories frequently imply that people of all age levels treat information the same way. In other words, the developmental dimension is often overlooked. But because our concern throughout this book is with children, our discussion includes material about how information may be processed differently at various stages of children's growth. The topics are presented in the following sequence: (1) the interacting components of classical information processing, (2) modes of investigation, (3) reformations of classical models, (4) information processing and development, (5) practical applications, and (6) a summary assessment.

CLASSICAL COMPONENTS OF THE INFORMATION-PROCESSING SYSTEM

The general notion that people function as processors of information is nothing new. Historical accounts show that from ancient times people have speculated about how they receive information from the environment, how they think about and remember this information, and how they reach a decision and act on it. What is new is that recent investigations have added greater precision to describing the likely parts of the processing system and their ways of operating.

As typically conceived today, the human processing system consists of four principal elements: (1) *sense organs,* such as eyes, ears, taste buds, pressure and pain nerves in the skin, and others, which receive impressions from the environment; (2) *short-term memory* or working memory, which holds a very limited amount of information for a short period of time; (3) *long-term memory,* which stores large amounts of information perhaps indefinitely; and (4) *muscle systems* energized by nerve impulses to perform all of the motor acts people carry out, such as reading, speaking, running, assembling machines, and the rest. The system also involves functions or processes within each element and the interactions among these elements.

At first glance it might appear that the system operates in the sequence just listed: sensations from the environment are entered into short-term memory where they are interpreted (perceived), then moved into long-term memory where they are stored until needed for action, at which time they are retrieved to determine what motor acts, if any, to perform. However, because such a sequence is much too simple to account for the way people actually think and behave, theorists have proposed more complex models comprising networks of interaction, with various kinds of information passing instantaneously back and forth among the elements rather than simply traveling in one direction along a single track from the sense organs' input to the muscles' output. The following description is one version of such a processing network.

This version is a model I have assembled from the work of various theorists in order to offer a relatively simple illustration of what can be involved in information-processing explanations of human thinking.* I will illustrate the system with an imagined problem-solving situation faced by an eighteen-year-old who is trying to decide which route to take to a city 300 kilometers away. But before tracing the way the eighteen-year-old would process information according to the theory, I need to describe the system in terms of each component's (1) function, (2) type of contents, (3) capacity or quantity of contents, (4) processing time, and (5) interactions with other components. The hypothetical system is displayed schematically in Figure 11.1.

The Senses

The open region at the far left in Figure 11.1 represents the world outside the person. The large box enclosed by the black line is the person. The individual's intercourse with the environment is mediated by (1) the sense organs as input channels or "windows to the world" and (2) the muscle systems as output channels or actors on the world.

To simplify the explanation, Figure 11.1 shows only three sense modalities— eyes, ears, and the pressure receptors under the skin that people commonly call touch or the tactile sense. Although the organs for detecting smell, taste, temperature, pain, and body position are not pictured, remember that they also feed environmental information into the system.

Each sense organ is obviously a very specialized instrument, attuned to just one kind of stimulation from the environment—the eyes receive only a narrow segment of the wide spectrum of light waves, the ears a narrow range of sound waves, and the tactile receptors only a portion of the impulses that impinge on the skin. Thus, while the sense organs gather information from the environment, they do so in a highly selective way, filtering out far more of the world's potential information than they allow to enter the human processing system.

*See Anderson, 1983; Broadbent, 1958; Kail & Bisanz, 1982; Klahr & Wallace, 1976; Newell & Simon, 1972; Uttal, 1981.

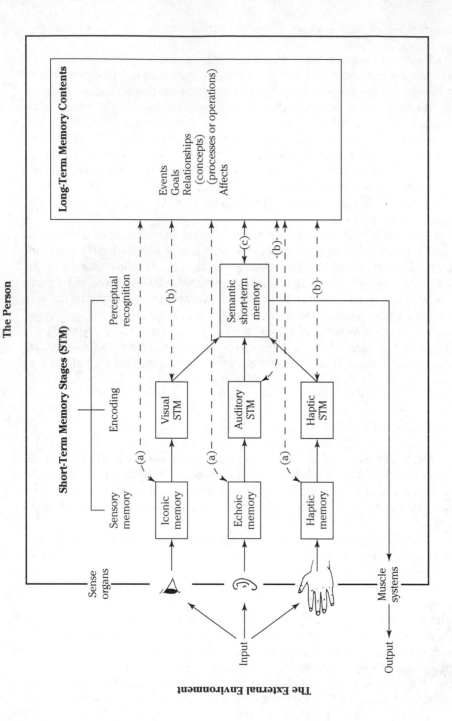

FIGURE 11.1

One classical version of the human information-processing system

Short-Term Memory

Stimuli collected by the sense organs are initially processed in what different theorists have variously called *short-term memory, primary memory, active memory,* or *working memory.* Some writers use these terms as synonyms; some make distinctions among them. For example, R. L. Klatzky (1980, p. 87) divides short-term memory into two functions: (1) that of storage, meaning the retention of recognized impressions for a brief time, and (2) that of working memory, meaning "ongoing cognitive activities—for instance, meaningful elaboration of words, symbol manipulation such as that involved in mental arithmetic, and reasoning."

Sensory memory   In the version of the traditional information-processing approach offered in these pages, short-term memory consists of three stages. The first, *sensory memory,* is apparently located in the sense organ itself and is a stage of momentary image retention. Sensory memory is an unselective form of memory for everything that strikes the particular organ within the range of its receptiveness. The eye's sensory memory holds all receivable light impulses striking the eye, the ear holds all receivable sound waves striking the ear, and the pressure receptor holds all tactile sensations on the skin.

Labels applied to memory at this early stage reflect the notion that information is still in a relatively "original" form—*iconic memory* for visual images, *echoic memory* for auditory impressions, and *tactile* or *haptic memory* for touch sensations. The storage of this information is only momentary, perhaps no longer than half a second for visual stimuli before the impression dissipates. Auditory information apparently can last as long as one to two seconds before decaying (Klahr & Wallace, 1976, p. 174). During this momentary retention of stimuli impressions, an interchange occurs between sensory memory and long-term memory (indicated by the lines labeled *a* in Figure 11.1). To clarify the nature of this interchange, we need to take a brief look at the contents of long-term memory.

In this version of information processing, long-term memory is the storage location of ideas or *mental constructions* derived from the person's past experiences. This collection of ideas is the person's *knowledge base.* At each of the three stages of short-term memory, an interchange or transaction (*a, b,* and *c* in Figure 11.1) takes place between the particular short-term stage and long-term memory. The transaction both (1) informs pertinent portions of long-term memory of the nature of the information received at that juncture and (2) permits long-term memory to tell that particular short-term stage which aspects of the stimuli to filter out and which to send along to the next stage. We assume that interchange *a* results in sensory memory identifying certain gross characteristics of the stimuli—such as distinguishing figure from ground—and sending the resulting crudely defined information to the next step along the pathway. An example of distinguishing figure from ground could be separating the outline of a nearby person from the pattern of colors produced by the foliage and buildings behind the person. In the auditory mode it could be separating the sound of a voice from the background sounds of birds chirping, leaves rustling, and a truck rumbling by.

Encoding The second stage is that of *encoding* or recasting the sensory-memory information into a form that can be used at the third stage. This notion of *encoding* reflects a key assumption made in information-processing theory—that sense impressions are not manipulated or stored in memory in their original form. Instead, impressions are translated into codes, into symbols or *representations* suitable for manipulation by the nervous system. At this second stage of our model, such encoding is accomplished through transaction *b* with long-term memory, in which instructions are issued by long-term memory for how the stimulus information from stage 1 should be symbolized for use at stage 3. As shown in Figure 11.1, stage 2 short-term memory is still divided according to the sense modalities in which the stimuli were originally received. Visual, auditory, and haptic memories are still separated from each other. Stage 2 memory is assumed to last only a brief time and to be of very limited capacity, unable to hold much information, with auditory capacity perhaps greater than visual capacity (Broadbent, 1970).

Semantic memory The third stage is called *semantic* short-term memory because at this point the coded materials from the three channels of stage 2 are combined and compared to selected contents of long-term memory to yield meaning (transaction *c*). Stage 3, in effect, is that of *perceptual recognition*, where the person identifies the information for what it represents in terms of his or her memory (long-term) of past experiences. In conscious thought, this is the "Aha!" juncture at which a person discovers "So that's what it is!"

Studies of how much information people are able to keep immediately in mind—that is, to maintain in semantic short-term memory—firmly suggest that the average adult can hold seven "chunks" of information at one time, although some people can manage as many as nine chunks while others can manage no more than five or six (G. A. Miller, 1956). A *chunk* can be defined as "a portion of a person's knowledge base that is always activated and deactivated as a unit" (Kail & Bisanz, 1982, p. 59). A chunk may be either simple, such as a specific person's name, or complex, such as the concept of a television receiver's tuning system, which may, in a single phrase, represent an electronic engineer's entire knowledge of the network of elements that comprise the tuning mechanism of a television receiver.

In speaking of seven chunks, it's important to recognize a distinction between immediate *memory* and immediate *consciousness*. Experiments conducted by S. Sternberg (1969) have suggested that while an individual can immediately recall seven chunks of information, the amount he or she is consciously using in a given instant is more likely to be a single unit or chunk.

Long-Term Memory

I am assuming that long-term memory has two principal functions: (1) directing the operation of the entire information-processing system and (2) storing coded material derived from the person's past experiences. While short-term memory has very limited capacity, long-term memory can apparently accommodate infinite amounts of material. And, as implied in their names, short-term memory retains material very briefly, while long-term memory may retain material indefinitely.

In this version of information processing, I am proposing that coded material stored in memory is of several sorts: single events or episodes, goals, relationships (including concepts and processes), and affects. A *single event* is the memory trace about a specific person or object from a particular incident in the past. E. Tulving (1972) labeled this sort of memory *episodic* to indicate that it is a kind of knowledge specific to a given context—that is, knowledge of how things appeared and when they happened. He contrasted episodic knowledge with what he called *semantic* memories, which consist of more generalized instruments of thought, such as concepts and processes that are not limited to one place or time.

A *goal* is something the individual seeks to accomplish. Goals are the motivational components of information processing. They energize the individual to focus attention on particular facets of the environment and to draw from long-term memory particular contents for interpreting sense impressions.

A *relationship* is a connection between one item in memory and another. Relationships may be of various types. One of the most important is that of concepts, with *concept* being defined as an abstraction of specified characteristics that are shared by individual people, objects, or incidents from the past. Typically a label is attached to the abstraction. For example, *square, red, weather, weaponry, religious,* and *theory* are concept labels. Another relationship is the comparison of one concept with another. For example, the relationship between the concepts *square* and *circle* is defined by the ways in which square and circle are both alike and unalike. (While I define concepts as relationships, some writers prefer to categorize concepts as *associations* rather than relationships and to reserve the term *relationship* for the usages below.)

Some relationships can be called causal because the individual assumes that one concept is the producer of another—as when the idea of heat under a pan of water produces the idea of boiled water. Many causal relationships are complex, with more than one prior condition (the assumed cause) combining to produce a resulting condition (the assumed effect). The idea of how long it will take water to boil can be conditioned by ideas of the amount of water, the water's original temperature, the degree of heat, the heat source, the shape of the pan, atmospheric pressure, and more.

A *process* is a kind of procedural knowledge: a series of steps performed to accomplish some end. Examples of processes are the series of operations required for multiplying 27 by 64, for defining *hypothesis,* for diagraming a sentence, for reading a map, and for driving a car.

Affects are emotions, as suggested by such words as *anger, pity, affection, frustration, attraction,* and *disappointment.* In long-term memory some type of affect or emotional tone is often associated with events, goals, and relationships.

The structure of long-term memory   Of particular interest to information-processing theorists is the anatomy of long-term memory. What are the structural components of memory and how are they interlinked? One popular suggestion is that long-term memory is organized something like a fishnet, with each node or intersection where the strands are knotted together representing an individual memory trace, such as an event or concept. The multiple strands extending out from the node are the links to other nodes; that is, the strands lead to other events or concepts that the person associates with the memory trace at the original node. The links between some nodes are stronger than between others, meaning that communication across the strong linkages is more frequent and more rapid than between weak linkages. In other words, strong links represent close associations between memories, whereas weak links represent distant associations, ones more difficult to conceive. Obviously such a memory network is infinitely more complex than a simple fishnet in order to account for the intricacies of human thought (Anderson, 1983).

Let us look again at the interactions between long-term memory and the three stages of short-term memory. One of the most important interactions is that of matching the stimuli received from the environment with the contents of long-term memory. In particular, perceptual recognition results when the newly coded material from short-term stage 3 matches identical or similar coded material in the long-term memory network. In this theory, the person "understands" the sensory input or "sees what it means" by accomplishing a satisfactory match. In other words, the person assigns a "meaning" from long-term memory to each new recognizable sensory encounter with the environment.

I am suggesting as well that active decision making and problem solving are carried out through transactions between semantic short-term memory and long-term memory. Not only is information from the environment entered into semantic short-term memory, but material from long-term memory (incidents, goals, relationships, affects) is also inserted into semantic short-term memory and used there. Since short-term memory has such a limited capacity, it is necessary during problem solving for the contents of short-term memory to be constantly changing. Thus there is a great flow of extremely rapid transactions going on all the time, producing the "stream of consciousness" of the person's awareness.

Influences on long-term memory   The source of most, if not all, of the contents of long-term memory is the person's earlier experiences. This is hardly a surprise, for it accords with the commonsense notion that what people remember is what they have learned in the past. But not so apparent is the discovery from experimental studies that the material entered into memory may be distorted during the encoding and storing activities—that is, during the *memory-construction* process. People who hear or read a series of sentences relating to an incident do not simply memorize the sentences. Instead, they tend to abstract the main ideas conveyed in the sentences, and they store this abstracted or more economical version in long-term memory, often omitting some of the original details or the exact phrasing of the incident. Furthermore, ideas already in memory about a given topic will influence how coded traces of a new experience are constructed and stored. For example, hearing about possible dishonesty in public office may well be interpreted and stored differently if the incident is said to involve George Washington or Abraham Lincoln than if it is said to involve some other president whose reputation is less admirable. In effect, new information tends to be coded and stored in ways that make it accord with logic, with one's emotions, and with the contents of one's current knowledge system.

In addition, the coded traces of experiences—called *representations*—may not reside in the long-term state in their original condition but, rather, may be revised in various ways. With the passing of time, or at the moment the memory is retrieved, the memory may be altered by new experiences that have entered the knowledge system since the original memory was recorded, thereby causing one's recollection to differ from the originally stored representation. The new experiences may have distorted the original memory by casting doubt on its logic, by making it more elaborate, by simplifying it so as to fit a stereotyped pattern, or by coloring it with emotions of pleasure or distaste (Dooling & Christiaansen, 1977; Klatzky, 1980, pp. 301–305; Loftus, 1975).

The combined short-term and long-term memory components make up the human knowledge system. Kail and Bisanz concluded:

> Despite discrepancies among various theories, most theorists generally agree on the general properties of the human knowledge system. (A) There are, theoretically, no limits on the quantity of knowledge that can be stored. (B) Knowledge is not lost; "forgetting" reflects an inability to access knowledge. (C) Most knowledge can be accessed by multiple routes and multiple cues, reflecting the fact that knowledge is rich in interconnecting links. (D) Knowledge is characterized by a weak form of *cognitive economy:* not all of one's knowledge about concept X need be associated directly with X. . . . Instead, some of this knowledge is available only indirectly, via inference. (E) A process can operate on itself as well on other representations and processes. (1982, p. 50)

The System's Behavioral Output

After having described short-term and long-term memory, let's look at the final link in the information-processing chain, that of behavioral output, such as speaking to a classmate, climbing stairs, stepping on the car's brake pedal, writing a homework assignment, and the like. Each decision made in semantic short-term memory elicits from long-term memory coded directions for activating the appropriate muscles. These coded directions are transmitted through the efferent nerve system to the proper muscle locations to perform the behavior. The action completes the information-processing cycle.

Although overt action has thus been described as the final link in the processing chain, it should be apparent that overt action does not have to occur in order for cognitive development to take place. As our own introspection informs us, we can record events in memory, acquire new concepts, and attach different emotions to memories simply by "thinking things over" or "coming to a conclusion" or "changing our mind" without displaying this in an observable act. However, eventually such development will be reflected in the ways we act on the world.

The Central Phenomena:
Attention, Perception, and Memory

As perhaps can be inferred from the foregoing discussion, information-processing theories are designed particularly to explain relationships among a trio of phenomena of traditional interest in psychology, those of attention, perception, and memory.

In regard to *attention,* theorists have attempted to account for several factors studied by psychologists for more than a century, from the time of William James and even earlier (James, 1890, pp. 402–404). James and others observed that attention is a purposeful operation, so that people actively seek stimuli rather than only passively record impressions imposed on them by the environment. Furthermore, people seek selectively. They focus on certain items for conscious analysis while ignoring others. Such selectivity is necessary because the human attention-directing mechanism has limited capacity and apparently can operate on only one item at a time rather than on several simultaneously. To account for such observations as these, theorists have proposed that the information-processing mechanism includes (1) filters to keep the system from being overloaded and (2) special storage provisions, as suggested at the initial stages of short-term memory, to extend the time available for extracting information from relatively short-lived inputs (Horton & Turnage, 1976, p. 205). Theorists have also proposed cycles of interaction between short-term and long-term memory in order to explain how a person's goals help filter stimuli and how an individual assigns meaning to impressions received from the sense organs.

The phenomenon of *perception,* in which the act of attention is embedded, typically involves all the steps of the information-processing chain from the environmental stimuli through the stage of semantic short-term memory of Figure 11.1. Different theorists have proposed different stages in the process of perception, with some offering more stages and some fewer than the ones in the version we are using here. Some theorists have hypothesized that the most significant stage in perception occurs at the sense organ itself—at the eye, ear, or skin. Others have proposed that the most significant stage is in the brain at the semantic-memory level. In short, a variety of theories of perception exist, with no one of them yet earning general acceptance within the information-processing community (Uttal, 1981, pp. 986–987).

As for *memory,* some writers have sought to explain its complex operations by hypothesizing the existence of such subdivisions as short-term and long-term memory and by identifying a variety of factors affecting the storage and retrieval of information. Others have rejected the notion of such components as short- and long-term memory and speak instead of different depths or levels of processing (Craik & Lockhart, 1972). In effect, there continues to be a diversity of notions about how memory operates.

An Example of the System in Operation

To illustrate how our sample theory can be used to interpret everyday behavior, let's apply the theory's elements to analyze our fictitious eighteen-year-old's trip to a city 300 kilometers away.

As the young woman walks through the business district of her home town, her long-term memory alerts the three stages of her short-term memory to her general goal—to take the trip—as well as to the steps of a process or *strategy* for achieving the goal. This strategy, constructed from her experiences in past years and stored in long-term memory, consists of (1) locating a map of the area, (2) identifying on the map alternative routes to the city, and (3) comparing the desirability of the various routes by testing the alternatives against a series of criteria, including those of distance to travel, road conditions, amount of traffic, safety, attractiveness of the scenery, and others. As she strolls along the street under the influence of this "mental set," she scans the environment for sources of road maps. Her visual attention is caught by a travel agency sign on a store window. For this girl at this moment, that particular sign is a "salient stimulus" in the environment because it matches one of the relationships she has stored in long-term memory (travel agency = maps and road information). Her decision to enter the agency (a decision reached in semantic short-term memory) evokes from long-term memory sequences of operations that cause her efferent nerve system to order the muscular movements that allow her to walk into the shop.

Another process now drawn from long-term into short-term memory starts her scanning the walls to locate sensory stimuli to match the concept of *road map* whose defining features, stored in long-term memory, have now been entered into her short-term memory. By the time she scans halfway across the back wall, she finds the desired match. This accomplishment evokes from long-term memory a process that directs her muscles to transport her to the wall to pick up the map. Next, her inspection of the map is guided by a map-analysis process that has just been transferred into short-term memory from long-term memory. The map-analysis process or strategy, constructed in the past from her experiences in reading maps, is composed of a series of steps that include locating the map legend that defines symbols for types of roads, distances, directions of the compass, and cities and towns. As an aid in visually following the alternative routes on the map, the girl adds another modality by tracing each route with her right index finger. At the same time she listens to an employee of the travel agency answer the question she has asked about traffic conditions on the different routes. She is, in effect, simultaneously receiving visual, haptic, and auditory input that is being encoded into semantic short-term memory where it will contribute to her decision about which route to follow.

At this point we leave the young woman, on the assumption that this brief and admittedly simplified analysis has illustrated how incidents from everyday life can be interpreted with one version of the information-processing perspective. We are now prepared to consider the principal methods of inquiry that have led to such theorizing.

MODES OF INVESTIGATION

Classical information-processing theorists have employed two modes of investigation for generating and refining their proposals.

The first mode involves using human subjects in experiments designed to answer questions about such matters as how patterns of reflected light stimulate receptor nerves in the eyes, what number of chunks of information can be accommodated in short-term memory, and how material from short-term memory is encoded for storage in long-term memory.

The second mode, which utilizes information from the first mode's experiments, involves employing electronic computers to simulate human mental operations. Theorists working in this rapidly growing field of *artificial intelligence* propose that if they can program a computer to produce the same sorts of solutions to problems that a human would produce, they will have taken a significant step toward understanding human thought processes. In making such a proposal, they are assuming that if a computer program is given the same problem-solving input as a human and the computer produces the same output as the human, then the program may well contain the same sorts of components and processing steps as those operating in the human nervous system.

In applying this same line of logic to explaining children's intellectual development, psychologists face two tasks: (1) devising a series of computer programs so that each program accurately simulates children's thinking processes at a particular stage of mental growth and (2) explaining the means by which the program at one stage can be transformed into the next program in the series. So far, theorists designing computer programs to represent children's thinking processes have been more successful with the first of these tasks than with the second. For example, D. Klahr and J. G. Wallace (1976) managed to prepare what they judged to be rather satisfactory computer simulations of Piagetian preoperational and concrete operations substages for the task areas of class inclusion, conservation, and transitivity. However, the two investigators admitted to being far less successful in fashioning an adequate explanation of how a child makes the transition from preoperational to concrete operations thinking. They decided that more experimentation was needed.

With this overview of classical information-processing models as a foundation, we next consider revisions of such theory that are intended to solve problems encountered with the classical versions.

MODIFICATIONS OF CLASSICAL THEORY

Most critics of information-processing models have not faulted the standard theory for being entirely wrongheaded but, rather, for being incomplete and thereby distorting the picture of human development. My purpose in this section is to describe (1) refinements of classical information-processing theory proposed since the mid-1970s and (2) further conditions of human experience that need to be recognized in future models if they are adequately to account for cognitive development. The discussion is organized around two questions: (1) What revisions of the original information-processing model have appeared in recent times? (2) What suggestions for the improvement of information-processing theory can be derived from comparing computers and humans?

Recent Refinements of Classical Theory

B. J. Zimmerman (1983, p. 3) illustrated one form of disenchantment with early cybernetic (electronic computer) models by noting that "Neisser's 1967 book, *Cognitive Psychology,* was a widely read, generally sympathetic description of the cybernetic version of information processing. However, in his 1976 text, significantly entitled *Cognition and Reality,* Neisser renounced the utility of cybernetic models of human thought because of their limited capacity to describe the complex reciprocal relationship between people and their proximal environment." Thus, to render information-processing theory sensitive to different environmental conditions, revised models need to portray contexts far more precisely than the general provision of "the external environment" in Figure 11.1.

M. H. Ashcraft (1989, p. 64) cited further shortcomings of classical theory in relation to the following seven current themes of cognitive psychology. Each theme in some way will either alter the patterning of the cognitive functions pictured in Figure 11.1 or will require an elaboration of how those functions operate.

1. *Attention*: Whereas the phenomenon of attention was not entirely ignored in standard models, critics charged that its importance was not adequately recognized in most early versions of the theory—that is, the key role of attention in the transfer of information from sensory memory to short-term working memory and attention's essential function in any conscious or partly conscious mental operation need to be featured more prominently.

2. *The conscious to automatic dimension*: An analysis of the amount of conscious effort needed to perform a given mental act suggests that mental processes can be aligned along a scale ranging from *highly conscious* at one end to *entirely automatic* or nonconscious at the other. Actions that are simple and have been practiced frequently become automatic, in the sense that no intentional effort is required to carry them out. For example, when people are first learning to drive a car, they need to concentrate on each movement in the sequence of sensorimotor acts that lead from turning on the ignition to finally guiding the auto through traffic. For the experienced driver, this series of decisions becomes essentially nonconscious. If an information-processing theory is to be complete, it needs to include such a conscious-to-automatic dimension among its features.

3. *Serial and parallel processing*: When a person is learning something new or working on a complex problem, information is apparently processed serially—that is, step after step. But in the case of well-practiced, simpler tasks, two or more acts may be carried out in parallel, as in the case of a motorist listening to the radio or talking with a companion while driving down the highway. Classical models of information processing tended to picture all cognitive and motor activity as serial.

4. *Data-driven versus conceptually driven processes*: In earlier chapters we met both empiricists and structuralists. Empiricists (Skinner, contextualists) propose that what we come to understand is determined primarily by the environment—that is, by the nature of the events people witness. Such a process of

understanding can be labeled *data driven*. In contrast, structuralists (Piaget, Case, Mounoud) emphasize the importance of people's mental templates in fashioning the understandings derived from environmental encounters; people impose meanings on events they witness, so their understandings are *conceptually driven*. Ashcraft proposed that both of these processes operate in the cognitive system, with the particular relationship between a stimulus and the person's memory structures determining which of the processes dominates at a given moment.

> Whereas data-driven processes are assisted very little, if at all, by already-known information, conceptually driven processes are those that rely heavily on such information. Thus, a conceptually driven process uses the information already in memory, and whatever expectations are present in the situation, to perform the task; data-driven processes use only the stimulus information. (1989, p. 64)

Information-processing theories can profitably incorporate this data-driven versus conceptually driven dimension among their components.

5. *Knowledge representation*: As noted earlier, an issue still far from being resolved is the question of how knowledge is stored in long-term memory. Various answers to this question continue to be offered by different theorists without a consensus being achieved. One conception is Tulving's (1972) division of memories into episodic and semantic knowledge. Another is J. R. Anderson's (1983) division of mental storage into *declarative memory* (events, facts, concepts—the nature of things) and *production memory* (procedural knowledge, operations—how to do things). It seems clear that any adequate version of information processing needs to include some such conception of knowledge representation.

6. *Tacit knowledge and inference*: Another matter given too little attention in early models is the issue of how a person's tacit knowledge (the backlog of information already available in long-term memory) leads to inferences that embellish the meaning derived from environmental stimuli. An explanation of how people's systems of tacit knowledge and inference operate to determine their understandings can usefully be inserted into versions of information processing.

7. *Metacognition*: The final item in Ashcraft's list is metacognition—our self-awareness and monitoring of how our cognitive system operates. This factor was essentially overlooked in much of the early theorizing about information processing.

With Ashcraft's seven updated features in mind, we can now consider two ways they can be used to elucidate the nature of children's cognitive development. First, they can alter the method of diagramming an information-processing model. Second, they can be applied in our estimating the manner in which children's cognitive processes develop over the years.

Diagramming Additional Components

The task of recasting information-processing models into a refurbished graphic form requires a somewhat different approach than that used in Figure 11.1. One way this might be attempted is shown in Figure 11.2. The first obvious feature of this

INCIDENT A

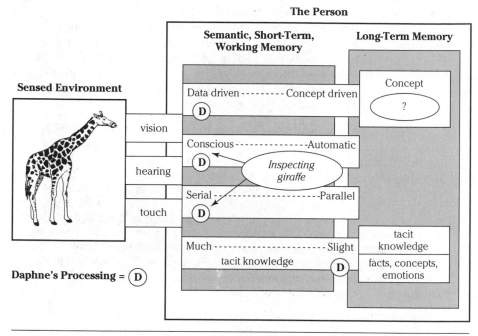

INCIDENT B

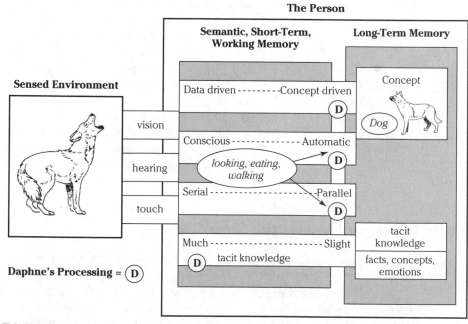

FIGURE 11.2

A version of a child's information-processing system during a visit to the zoo

approach is that a single static diagram is insufficient to illustrate a system that varies in relation to different environmental contexts, different points along a conscious–automatic dimension, and different patterns of tacit knowledge. At least two diagrams are needed to suggest how such variables can affect cognitive processes. Even more diagrams that picture additional combinations of the variables would be even better. The two diagrams in Figure 11.2 can properly be accompanied by the following kind of explanation in order to clarify the conditions that distinguish incident A from incident B:

> Four-year-old Daphne is taken by her father for her first visit to the zoo, where they buy popcorn that Daphne munches as they walk from one exhibit to another. *(Incident A)* At the giraffes' enclosure, Daphne stops eating popcorn to stand and stare at a mother giraffe and her offspring. Daphne asks, "What's that thing?" Her father explains, "It's a giraffe—from Africa." The girl inspects the tall animal from head to foot. Her father asks, "Didn't you ever see one in a picture book?" Daphne shakes her head and continues staring. *(Incident B)* Later, as she and her father come to an enclosure labeled *Coyote,* Daphne glances at the two animals standing beside a tree and comments between bites of popcorn, "Like Ranger." Ranger is the name of the German shepherd dog that lives across the street from Daphne's home. This time, rather than stopping to stare at the animals, Daphne continues walking and consuming popcorn.

To interpret the child's behavior in terms of Figure 11.2, we can speculate that the processing of the giraffe encounter (incident A) was strongly data driven, required much conscious attention, was serial (Daphne stopped eating and walking as she inspected the giraffes), and was unembellished by tacit knowledge because Daphne had no readily applicable concept in memory to apply to such a towering, long-necked, mottled creature. In contrast, the coyote encounter (incident B) was more conceptually driven (Daphne had a readily available concept into which the stimulus fit), was more automatic (required little conscious attention because the animal seemed so familiar), was bolstered by tacit knowledge (her experience with Ranger's characteristics), and thus enabled Daphne to engage in parallel processing (she could simultaneously perceive the animal and continue walking and eating popcorn). Therefore, compared to the graphic model in Figure 11.1, the revised form of diagramming of Figure 11.2 more adequately reflects the way differences in environmental stimuli can influence how information is processed.

Child Development and the Seven Themes

Ashcraft's themes can also be used for answering the question, As children grow up, what is it that develops? In response, we can suggest that development from infancy through adolescence is marked by an increase in the proportion of mental and psychomotor operations that are (1) automatic rather than conscious, (2) processed in parallel rather than serially, and (3) conceptually driven rather than data driven. Furthermore, as the years advance, (4) children's tacit knowledge expands so they can draw increasingly complex and accurate inferences, (5) their metacognition skills become more elaborate, and (6) knowledge in long-term memory is represented in more refined, complicated patterns. Children also (7) gain greater conscious control over directing their attention.

Computers and People Compared

In addition to Ashcraft's themes, other pertinent features of information-processing models can be identified by comparing characteristics of computers and of humans. Such an exercise can help suggest (1) what cautions should be observed in interpreting human cognition in terms of computer operations and (2) what changes in computer hardware and software might more adequately simulate the ways children think.

One simple way such comparisons can be pursued is shown in Table 11.1, which contrasts present-day computers and humans on a series of characteristics. While it is apparent that computers and people can be compared along far more dimensions than those listed in Table 11.1, for our present purpose these twelve characteristics should suffice. The twelve are ones that seem to me particularly significant from the viewpoint of basing a theory of children's cognition on a cybernetic model.

Researchers in the field of artificial intelligence use such comparisons in their efforts to produce computer simulations that more adequately mirror human thinking. Hence, as advances in these efforts are achieved, information-processing theories that rely on a cybernetic design can be expected to represent human thought more adequately. But even before more sophisticated computers are created, child development theorists who are guided by computer designs when creating models of children's cognitive functions can properly extend their theories beyond the confines of existing computer designs in order to accommodate for such differences between machines and people as shown in Table 11.1.

Perhaps the most dramatic shortcoming of existing cybernetic models as analogues of child thought is found in the final item in the table, "operating condition over the unit's lifetime." Cybernetic models fail to show how sensorimotor and cognitive abilities systematically change with the passing of time. In effect, computer simulations—at least at present—are not developmental. Thus more than just the elements contained in cybernetic models is required to account for the advances from infancy through adolescence in the characteristics depicted in Table 11.1. Extensions beyond computer designs are needed to explain changes in children's sources of stimulation, mobility, standardization (extent of individual differences), memory, sources of processing "programs," and the rest.

In summary, then, comparing computers and humans can be useful for identifying (1) human characteristics that designers of computers can seek to simulate in their cybernetic models and (2) ways that human development theories based on cybernetic analogues need to be extended to reconcile the differences between computers and people.

Comparing people and computers led Niels Bernsen (1989, pp. xi–xii) to observe that the classical artificial intelligence paradigm portrayed the *throughput* aspect of information processing as consisting largely of automatic compu-

TABLE 11.1
Comparison of computers and people

The computer	The person
Source of stimulation	
Waits for environmental input.	Searches the environment for input and also has input imposed by the environment.
Mobility	
Is stationary, cannot move itself except when built in a movable robot form, and even then the flexibility and adaptability of its movements are quite limited.	Is self-moving (auto-mobile), can view environments from various perspectives; movements are highly flexible and adaptable.
Level of standardization	
Highly standardized. Within a given type of computer, the structure and function of all members of that type are essentially identical. The influence of typical environmental conditions (temperature, length of use, skills of the operator) on the function of the computer is quite limited. Thus knowing the traits of one member of that type permits highly reliable predictions about the operation of any other member. A computer's operation is highly similar in different contexts.	Standardization is limited to those characteristics that make up "human nature" at any stage of development. Such human nature permits marked variability in how one member of the species functions compared to another member. Even monozygotic twins, who start off with identical genetic potential, soon differ from each other as a consequence of varying environmental forces in their lives. Thus knowing the characteristics of one member of the species permits no more than gross, somewhat unreliable predictions of specific characteristics of another member, even when the two members are the same chronological age. And a given individual's functions often vary from one context to another.
Condition of memory	
Static, stationary, retains input in precisely the state it was received.	Active, alters stored material as the result of new input, of alterations in the biological structure, and of the passage of time.
Nature of programs for processing data	
Stable—programs remain in the same form in which they were originally prepared. Except in rare cases, programs must be changed by an outside operator.	Active—processing continually reconstructs "programs" in relation to input and to biological alterations in the organism. Person can be instructed by others in ways to alter programs. Person can also discover how to alter own programs.
Damageability	
Can be damaged by accidents or wearing out of building materials so that memory is lost or processing goes awry.	Can be damaged by accidents or wearing out of "building materials" so that memory is lost or processing goes awry.
Maintenance of structure	
Can monitor the condition of many of its own functions and can report when certain components or functions go wrong. Usually cannot repair itself.	Can monitor the condition of many of its own functions and can report when certain components or functions go wrong. Often can repair self, though the repair process may require that certain usual functions cannot be performed for some period of time.

The Computer	The Person
Maintenance of operating efficiency	
Stops operating when capacity is overtaxed, but is not subject to boredom, lack of motivation, fatigue, and emotional disturbance.	Stops operating when capacity is overtaxed, and is highly subject to boredom, lack of motivation, fatigue, and emotional disturbance.
Scope or range of functions	
Confined to a limited set of programs. Compared to humans, deficient in potential for creating novel solutions.	Extends to a far greater variety of "programs" than are available in present-day computers, particularly ones involving creativity in literature, science, social science, and the arts.
Processing speed	
Faster than people in performing routine computations and in storing large quantities of data in long-term memory.	Slower than computers in performing such functions as computing and storing large quantities of data in long-term memory.
Processing complexity	
Far more accurate than people in combining, comparing, calculating, summarizing, and reporting results for large quantities of data of a kind readily manipulated by rules of logic.	Far more competent than computers in manipulating variables that have not been clearly defined or predicted ahead of time and whose weightings (degrees of importance for arriving at a solution) have not been specified. (These cognitive functions are sometimes referred to as intuiting, estimating, guessing, imagining, and envisioning.)
Operating condition over the unit's lifetime	
Essentially constant, barring relatively rare breakdowns of the machine's hardware components or faults that humans have built into software, either unintentionally (programming errors) or intentionally (viruses).	Very inefficient at the beginning. Efficiency typically improves markedly over the first two or three decades, then is likely to decrease for some functions and remain constant or gradually increase for others over the next three decades or so, and finally during the sixth and seventh decades will deteriorate in varied degrees for different individuals.

tation over language-like, discrete, and combinatorial symbolic codes, as in conventional serial or more recent parallel computers. [But] computation over discrete combinatorial symbols exists to a lesser extent, or does not exist at all, in intelligent biological systems. Instead, the complex cognitive abilities of higher organisms are based on the information processing abilities arising from the collective behaviour of large populations of highly interconnected and very simple processing elements such as nerve cells. . . . Consequently, it is maintained, cognitive scientists should develop and implement their theories of intelligent information processing in ways that resemble much more closely the way in which the brain actually operates.

INFORMATION PROCESSING AND DEVELOPMENT

By conducting experiments with children at different age levels and by devising additional computer simulations, investigators in recent years have been furnishing a rapidly growing quantity of data about changes that occur in human information processing as people advance in age. Let's now look at examples of the kinds of data resulting from such studies. We begin by focusing on (1) sensory intake and short-term memory, (2) long-term memory, and (3) interactions between components of short-term and long-term memory.

Sensory Intake and Short-Term Memory

One notable difference between the infant and the older child concerns elements in the environment to which children attend.

A strong environmental characteristic for attracting attention is that of *novelty,* of things out of the ordinary. The infant, with such a limited store of experience with the world, can be expected to find novelty in events that are quite usual to the more experienced older child. Thus the younger child pays attention to events the older child ignores because such events are so ordinary for the older one.

> We see in the behavior of the developing infant that many aspects of attention . . . involve largely automatic reactions to rather simple characteristics. That is, the early responses of infants can be accounted for by assuming the infant is automatically "captured" by sensory input to a greater degree than is an older child or an adult. As the infant develops through childhood to adulthood, he seems to be less and less a "captive" of sensory stimulation and more and more a "capturer" of sensory input. (Horton & Turnage, 1976, p. 203)

In brief, the growing child increasingly sets his or her own goals and then purposely seeks out situations in which to invest attention in order to achieve the goals. J. F. Mackworth divided this process of the development of attention into three main stages. At the first stage the very young infant focuses on patterns or objects in his visual and auditory environment, attending to them frequently and at great length, since

> his task at this time is to construct internal models of the environment, and everything that he sees is new. Throughout life he will continue to construct such models, but as he grows older his attention is devoted more to comparing new experiences with already stored models. Since the neonate has no such stored models, he must spend a great deal of time on assimilating the stimulus, and therefore he shows little or no habituation. (1976, p. 145)

The second of Mackworth's major stages extends from around age one until four or five. It consists of the child's beginning to show acquaintance with, or *habituation* to, patterns she has seen or heard before and to select for study those patterns that exhibit novelty. However, at this stage the child may center attention chiefly on a few features on which to base a decision and may overlook other features that would contribute to a more accurate judgment about the significance of the observation. E. Vurpillot (1976, p. 231) noted that the young child's responses to what he observes are often fluctuating and contradictory from one moment to the next "because he focuses his attention first on one detail, then on another. . . . Thus, his greatest weakness lies in an absence of coordination between all the cues he is capable of perceiving and the rules he is capable of using."

At the third stage, the older child or adolescent achieves better cognitive control over attention. She is not so hasty as the young one and can search a display until she acquires all the needed information. She is also better at selecting important details, at altering judgment on the basis of feedback, at abstracting a rule from a sequence of events, and at changing the rule if necessary.

In addition to the matter of how children's ways of attending change with time, another developmental factor in the early phase of processing appears to be the capacity of short-term memory. In discussing the model pictured in Figure 11.1, I proposed that semantic short-term memory in the average adult can accommodate seven chunks of information. Or, stated another way, the average adult has an *apprehension span* of seven chunks, a capacity that apparently was not present at birth but, instead, evolved during the years of childhood. According to some studies, at eighteen months the average child's span is one chunk, a capacity that by age five appears to have increased to four chunks, then to five chunks a year or so later, and finally to seven by adolescence. Such changes in short-term memory capacity could help account for the differences in children's thinking and acting at different age levels. For example, observations of children between ages one and two show that they commonly employ a single word to represent a set of ideas (the phenomenon of *holophrasis*) an older child would describe in several words. Whereas the six-year-old might say, "Mother's bringing the cake out now," the eighteen-month-old is likely to say only "mom" or "cay" in the same situation. S. Farnham-Diggory (1972, p. 62) speculated that "the one chunk span of the eighteen-month-old may be the basic factor in his production of holophrases."

However, not only the number of chunks a child can accommodate but other factors as well contribute to the improved operation of short-term memory with increasing age. One such factor is the structure of the chunks. A chunk that is a concept—such as *transportation*—carries a broader range of meaning by encompassing more of the world's phenomena than does a chunk that represents only a single event or fact—such as *mother's blue dress*. A chunk that represents an entire operation or process, such as the sequence of steps involved in mounting a bicycle and riding it along a winding path, is more encompassing than a chunk that represents only the licking of a postage stamp. Thus, according to one explanation of the contents of short-term memory, a chain consisting of actions that have been practiced so thoroughly that they come to compose an automatic process can be considered a single chunk since when the first action or idea in the chain appears in short-term memory it can trigger the rest of the sequence without the individual having to apprehend—that is, intentionally have to "think about"—the subsequent links in the process. And when an entire chain can be represented as a single chunk, the remaining spaces in short-term memory are available for other chunks of information. According to the theory, this greater complexity of the chunks in the older child's repertoire of memories helps her short-term memory function more efficiently than the younger child's.

The capacity of a child's processing system may also influence what the child attends to in the environment. Infants are attracted by simpler stimuli, such as simpler geometric forms, than are older children because, perhaps, infants lack the capacity to manage complex forms in immediate memory. However, the issue of whether, and how much, the capacity of short-term memory increases with age is neither simple nor settled. Certain investigators have proposed that older children's superiority to younger ones in performance that depends on memory does not result from any larger short-term capacity but rather from the older child's greater fund of knowledge in long-term memory and from his greater facility in using such mnemonic strategies as rehearsal and the clustering of items to be remembered (Chi, 1976, p. 559).

Development of Long-Term Memory

While changes in the sense organs and in short-term memory account for a portion of the age differences in information processing, by far the largest part of the differences is caused by changes in long-term memory. The changes are apparently of two general types: (1) alterations in the nerve structures as determined by genetically timed growth processes and (2) changes in the knowledge base or contents of memory as the result of experience. It is likely that these two types are not independent but that they interact. In other words, the gradual maturation of nerve tissues and changes in their patterning provide increasing potential for the individual to profit from interactions with the environment. And, in turn, as time passes, the kinds of memories or knowledge the person accumulates as a result of experiences may hasten or retard the maturation of the electrochemical structures of the nervous system.

Perhaps the most obvious developmental difference between the older and younger child's knowledge base is the quantity of contents stored there, available for interpreting environmental stimuli and for problem solving. The typical older child has compiled a greater number of memory traces (nodes) of events and relationships as the result of more years of experience and a more mature nervous system.

Besides having a greater fund of items in their knowledge base, older children have a greater number of associations between the items or nodes than do younger ones. For example, the typical older child recognizes more ways that the concepts *bucket, string, food, sea,* and *tuna* can be connected than does the younger child. In a sense, the young child's knowledge base is like a small, very loosely woven fabric, knit with only a few strands of memory traces and with the simplest of stitches. In contrast, the adolescent's long-term memory is more like a widespread fabric of intricately interwoven strands forming complex patterns. And it is both the number of items and their patterning of connections that determine how complex a chunk of knowledge will be when it is summoned for action into semantic short-term memory. For instance, a chunk identified by the label *arithmetic* encompasses a

great number of items linked in complex patterns in the knowledge base of the typical adolescent, but the chunk *arithmetic* has far fewer items with simple links in the long-term memory of a typical six-year-old.

Furthermore, the processes (sequences of steps for accomplishing a goal) that a child has available in his knowledge base increase in both number and sophistication with advancing age. For instance, if children are asked to memorize a telephone number or a list of street names, the younger ones are likely to depend on only one strategy, such as *rehearsal* (saying the number or list over and over). However, as J. H. Flavell (1977, p. 195) noted, "rehearsal is by no means the most effective mnemonic strategy available to a sophisticated and resourceful informa-tion processor." Adolescents not only rehearse the items but *cluster* or *group* them according to some common factor, such as their ordinal or alphabetical sequence. Adolescents may also intentionally *associate* the items with others already in memory, such as comparing the phone number to their own phone number or to a similar number from history, for example, 1492 or 1776 or 1945.

Besides the increase in the variety of mnemonic techniques used, the way a given technique is used also changes as children grow older. For instance, in rehearsing a sequence of items to recall later, children in the lower primary school grades repeat each new item several times, but they usually do not connect that item with others during the rehearsal process. In contrast, adolescents cluster the items to be memorized into groups, attaching each new item of the sequence to a group, and then practice the group as a whole. In effect, older children are more conscious of their rehearsal technique and more actively fashion their approach in ways that improve the storage and later recall of the information (Ornstein & Naus, 1978). Their superior ability to recall material may thus be caused to a great extent by their imposing some kind of organization on the material when it is first met, whereas younger children do not tend to impose organization.

> Until the age of 7 or 8, children do not ordinarily elaborate and transform stimuli that are to be recalled later. Older children, 11 or 12 years of age, begin to rearrange items and construct additional relationships spontaneously, as adults commonly do. (Paris, 1978, p. 153)

In addition, older children more readily recognize when a process learned in one setting will be suitable to apply in a different setting.

> There . . . appears to be an identifiable transitional stage during which the child can use a strategy under certain conditions or can learn to use it during a relatively brief training session. However, the strategy is not used spontaneously nor does it show the characteristics of durability or generality. . . . It appears that learning, whether it be through spontaneous experience, informal education, or formal training, is critical in the development of the use of strategies. (Hagen, Jongeward, & Kail, 1975, p. 73)

A growing quantity of empirical evidence suggests a further developmental change in memory processes—a shift from verbatim-recall to gist-recall that has been labeled the *fuzzy-trace theory* (Reyna, 1992). Whereas young children tend to recall information word-for-word, adolescents tend to retrieve only the essence or

fuzzy trace of the message. For example, young children learn thousands of words of their home language (their first language) at the rate of

> roughly 14 new words per day by some estimates, [thereby attesting to the children's] powerful verbatim memory capabilities. . . . [In contrast] the ability to acquire the vocabulary of a second language decreases steadily after about age 8, and is very limited after early adolescence. . . . Hence, fuzzy-trace theory's basic claims are simply (a) that the memory systems that support retention of verbatim information exhibit rapid maturation and complete their ontogenesis rather early, (b) that the corresponding systems that support retention of senses and patterns [that is, gists or fuzzy traces] exhibit slow maturation and complete their ontogenesis rather late, and (c) that there is a point (probably in early adolescence for most individuals) when verbatim systems begin to deteriorate while gist systems continue to improve. (Reyna, 1992, p. 112)

In summary, children's mnemonic strategies are not present in long-term memory at birth nor do they automatically appear full-blown at particular times of life; rather, they are acquired through experience. The question of whether—and when—they are acquired appears to depend on both the maturity of the child's nervous system and the child's particular foundation of experiences from which to construct the strategies.

Interactions of System Components

As diagrammed in Figures 11.1 and 11.2, the human information-processing system includes a constant series of transactions between the contents of long-term memory and the stages of short-term memory. Likewise, the stages of short-term memory constantly interact with each other. The complexity of these interactions is one of the most important factors that render theorizing about information processing so difficult. This assumed complexity can be illustrated by the *verbal-loop hypothesis*, which is an explanation of the changes in children's memory skills with the passing years. In the earlier explanation of Figure 11.1, I proposed that incoming sensations are not perceived or stored in their original form but instead are translated into some sort of code for perception and storage. This encoding likely involves different stages of translation and appears to vary according to the developmental level of a person's cognitive system. In particular, encoding appears related to a person's level of verbal ability—that is, the person's facility in using words. For instance, experiments in which people were asked to reproduce visual forms or to write digits they heard suggest that people perform this task by first translating the visual forms and digit sounds into words and then drawing the forms and digits under the guidance of the verbal descriptions they had stored in memory (Kaufman, 1974, p. 533). The path from input to output was mediated by a *verbal loop* in the middle. If this hypothesis is true, then it may help explain the superiority of older children over younger ones in reproducing visual and auditory stimuli—the older children have greater verbal facility for coding stimuli into words. But while the verbal-loop notion offers some insight into information processing, it is admit-

tedly a crude and very incomplete explanation of the complex relationships that account for people's perceiving and storing and recalling information.

Another facet of the interaction of long-term and short-term memory is speed. Studies of information processing suggest that even when younger and older children both use the same mental procedures in problem solving, the older ones do so more rapidly. The reason is perhaps that the older children's longer experience with the steps of a strategy equips them to manipulate messages through the components of the system with greater facility than can younger children.

Finally, we may summarize the main developmental characteristics of the human information-processing system by concluding that as age increases, processing increases in speed, in complexity, and in the integration of the system's parts. Furthermore, the data stored in long-term memory grow in quantity, variety, and complexity.

PRACTICAL APPLICATIONS

The most obvious applications of information-processing theory occur in teaching, where the information-processing perspective is helpful in two major ways.

First, information-processing models alert instructors to the stages by which children ingest information from the environment, commit it to memory, and retrieve it to solve problems. By understanding this sequence, a teacher can provide experiences that give learners practice with each stage. Teachers can also help children analyze their own acts of perceiving, storing, and recalling so that they gain greater conscious control over each stage of the process. For instance, children can be taught such memory-enhancing strategies as rehearsal, grouping items, keyword associations, acronyms and rhymes as mnemonic devices, and multiple associations. In other words, teachers can help children's metaperception and metamemory, helping them "learn how to learn."

The second application is one I have found particularly valuable, that of using the model as a guide to the diagnosis and treatment of children's learning difficulties. Diagnosis involves first identifying how each component of the model can be assessed through tests, observing the child in learning situations, and interviewing the child. These assessment techniques are used to determine how efficiently each component of the child's information-processing system is operating so that the location of the cause of the child's learning problem may be discovered. Are the child's sense organs faulty, causing either poor eyesight or distorted hearing? Is the child motivated to attend to learning stimuli; that is, does he or she have the goal of attending to learning stimuli? Was the stimulus encoded inaccurately or not recorded at all during the exchange between short-term and long-term memory (perhaps accounting for the reading disorder of dyslexia or the quantitative-comprehension disorder of dyscalculia)? Or was the stimulus perceived accurately but not stored in a manner that permits ready retrieval, so that when the child needs to recall the memory he or she cannot? Or have all of the foregoing steps been performed adequately, but a faulty system of sending messages to the muscles has prevented the child from accurately expressing in behavior the results of his or her learning, as is apparently the case with at least some children who suffer from cerebral palsy?

Once a decision is reached about which components in the system, or which relationships between components, are at fault, then methods designed for treating those specific faults are applied. The methods may consist of special training procedures, medical interventions, or both (Thomas, 1989c).

In addition, research studies describing the pace at which various components of the information-processing system develop let parents and teachers know what sorts of learning children can reasonably be expected to exhibit at different stages of growth. For example, studies of this sort already suggest at what age children typically can learn a particular mnemonic technique, such as that of creating key words to associate with items to be learned. A growing number of research reports also illustrate ways of teaching such mnemonic techniques and of assessing how well children master them (Ashcraft, 1989, pp. 684–685; Brown & DeLoache, 1978; Chi, 1976; Hagen, Jongeward, & Kail, 1975; Schneider & Pressley, 1989).

INFORMATION-PROCESSING THEORIES: AN ASSESSMENT

Once again, my assessment is guided by the fourteen criteria introduced in Chapter One.

To begin, I rated the information-processing approach high on item 1 (the real world of children), because the model is founded on a growing body of empirical research with children, and computer simulations of child thought and behavior use such research to devise the relationships that make up the computer programs.

I also placed information-processing models high on the clarity scale (item 2) because theorists who write about information processing usually are careful to define their terms and illustrate their definitions with examples from research studies or observations of children. Nevertheless, a number of matters are still unclear. Yet the fault, I believe, lies in the complexity of the problems the theorists are attempting to solve rather than in their lack of skill in explicating what they believe. They typically admit that they have yet to find satisfactory solutions for numbers of the issues they face. Examples of difficult areas are those of the structure and function of short-term and long-term memory, of the process for encoding stimuli sensations, and of the way a person's goals arise to direct attention to selected aspects of the environments.

These theories appear to explain the past and predict the future (item 3) for the elements of child development on which their components focus: the sense organs, attention and perception, and operations of memory. When the present status of these components is assessed, the information-processing theorist is able to propose what has happened in children's past to account for the components' present status. Research performed under the guidance of such models furnishes an expanding pool of information about the development of the sense organs, perception, and memory. As a consequence, predictions about children's future status in relation to these elements can be made with increasing confidence. It is

THE INFORMATION-PROCESSING PARADIGM

How well do I think the theory meets the standards?

Standards	Very well	Moderately well	Very poorly
1. Reflects the real world of children	X		
2. Is clearly understandable		X	
3. Explains the past and predicts the future		X	
4. Guides child rearing		X	
5. Is internally consistent	X		
6. Is economical	X		
7. Is falsifiable		X	
8. Is supported by convincing evidence	X		
9. Adapts to new data	X		
10. Is novel		X	
11. Is comprehensive		X	
12. Stimulates new discoveries	X		
13. Is durable	G	Sp	
14. Is self-satisfying		X	

true, however, that predictions about the "average" child of a given age continue to be more reliable than predictions about any particular child. Before more precise judgments can be made about the future of individual children's information-processing systems, more evidence is needed about the causes of children's individual differences in their processing styles.

I have rated the approach high as a guide to child rearing because the results of empirical research offer specific suggestions about what to expect of children at different age levels and about how to promote the development of the information-processing constituents. Parents and teachers can draw on an extensive body of information about care of the eyes and ears, about directing children's attention toward constructive activities, and about strategies for improving memory and for retrieving stored information.

I did not find internal inconsistencies in the versions of the theory I inspected, so I have given the model a high rating on item 5. Likewise, the components and their interactions as proposed by various theorists have not appeared unduly

elaborate to account for the data they intend to explain, so a high rating for economy (item 6) seems warranted as well.

To a great degree both the proposed elements of the information-processing system and the interactions among them seem testable, at least potentially (item 7). Some concepts—such as those of working memory and long-term memory—have not been specified precisely enough to determine very well how they can be isolated and their interactions measured, but progress toward this end is being made in empirical studies, particularly with the aid of computer technology. As a consequence, the future of achieving the operational specificity needed for testing the truth of the theories seems to me very promising.

A high rating for the theories' ability to stimulate new discoveries (item 12) appears justified on the basis of the growing quantity of research (item 8) related to the senses, to the encoding of stimuli from the environment, to the process of memorizing, to problems in the retrieval of stored information, to the mechanisms that guide the muscles to act, and to computer simulations of human information-processing functions.

As the decades have advanced, information-processing theorists have displayed a noteworthy ability to accommodate new data (item 9) by altering the theories themselves rather than by simply dismissing confounding evidence as irrelevant. Models of information processing that were seen as somewhat removed from the mainstream of cognitive psychology in the 1960s have since entered that mainstream by incorporating an increasing array of cognitive psychology's concepts and empirical findings.

The general idea of people receiving sensory impressions, thinking them over, and then acting on the results of their thought is not new (item 10). However, the analysis of this input-throughput-output process in recent times has provided many novel insights. Therefore, I have marked the model between the "very well" and "moderately well" positions.

Information-processing theories focus primarily on how people think rather than on how they develop physically, emotionally, and in their sense of self. Hence, I have judged that the theories fulfill the comprehensiveness criterion only moderately well (item 11).

On the durability scale (item 13), the G is to suggest that the information-processing model as a general approach to understanding children's mental development will likely be with us for a very long time. The Sp reflects my impression that specific forms of the theory are bound to be short-lived as they are replaced by improved versions.

All things considered, I find the information-processing approach very satisfactory (item 14). For me, it provides a convincing, integrated structure within which to explain such disparate phenomena as environmental stimuli, the operation of the sense organs, attention and perception, memory, and observable behavior. I rated it somewhat below the maximum "very well" level because only recently have variations of the paradigm addressed the relationship between conscious and unconscious mental operations and ways that different environments influence mental processes. Furthermore, theorists have not focused sufficient attention on such issues as the role of the emotions and of how people generate

their goals. These matters I believe need to be formally incorporated into the approach if it is to furnish a balanced conception of thought and action.

FOR FURTHER READING

Ashcraft, M. H. (1994) *Human Memory and Cognition,* 2d ed. New York: Harper Collins. Ashcraft's detailed description of information-processing theory, of diverse viewpoints, and of empirical studies is thorough and written in a most engaging style.

Posner, M. I. (ed.). (1989) *Foundations of Cognitive Science.* Cambridge, Mass.: M.I.T. Press. An in-depth description of "the mind as a symbol processor" and "intelligence from the perspective of computation."

Classical versions of information-processing theory from a child development perspective are described in the following sources.

Flavell, J. H. (1977) *Cognitive Development.* Englewood Cliffs, N.J.: Prentice-Hall.

Kail, R., and J. Bisanz. (1982) "Information Processing and Cognitive Development," in H. W. Reese and L. P. Lipsett (eds.), *Advances in Child Development and Behavior,* Vol. 17. New York: Academic Press.

Klahr, D., and J. G. Wallace. (1976) *Cognitive Development: An Information-Processing View.* Hillsdale, N.J.: Erlbaum.

CHAPTER TWELVE

CONCEPTIONS OF THE SELF: HUMANISTIC AND OTHERWISE

I presume that everyone has a conception of *self*, a notion of "who I am" that continues relatively intact day after day and month after month, providing a central theme of internal perceptions that runs from early childhood throughout the life span. This is not to suggest that one's *self* goes forever unchanged. Rather, it is to say that changes in one's sense of identity are gradual—barring cataclysmic events—so we maintain our sense of continuity or sameness of *self* with the passing of time.

The self is assigned a key position in various theories of personality development, both humanistic and otherwise. The purpose of this chapter is to inspect views of the self and of how it develops during the first two decades of life. The chapter is presented in three segments. The first addresses the question of how the self has been defined by different writers. The second focuses on the humanistic tradition in psychology that places self at the center of its concerns. The third considers two other conceptions of the self and its development that lie outside humanistic models.

DEFINING THE SELF

Although there is a kernel of agreement among theorists about the meaning of *self*, the concept is not described in exactly the same way by different writers or even in the same way at all times by a single writer.

Arthur Combs and Donald Snygg (1959, p. 124) proposed that the *phenomenal self* "is not a mere conglomeration or addition of isolated concepts of self, but a patterned interrelationship or Gestalt of all these. It is the individual as he seems from his own vantage point."

Rollo May called the self "the organizing function within the individual . . . by means of which one human being can relate to another; consciousness of one's identity . . . as a thinking-intuiting-feeling and acting unity; . . . not merely the sum of 'roles,' but the capacity by which one *knows* he plays these roles; it is the center from which one sees and is aware of these 'sides' of himself" (quoted in Reeves, 1977, pp. 286–287).

Gordon Allport (1961, p. 110) described the self as a "kind of core in our being. And yet it is not a constant core. Sometimes the core expands and seems to take command of all our behavior and consciousness, sometimes it seems to go completely offstage, leaving us with no awareness whatsoever of self."

Frederick Perls called the self the integrator, the synthetic unity, and "the artist of life." And while it is "only a small factor in the total organism/environment interaction, . . . it plays the crucial role of finding and making the meanings that we grow by." It is the "system of contacts [with the environment] at any moment" and is "flexibly various, for it varies with the dominant organic needs and the pressing environmental stimuli; it is the system of responses; it diminishes in sleep when there is less need to respond" (Perls, Hefferline, & Goodman, 1951, p. 235).

Michael Lewis (1990, p. 279) equated *self* with *identity*, which "is mostly cognitive—a set of beliefs about oneself that we refer to as a 'self-schema.' Identity, for the mature human, refers to our beliefs about ourselves, including consciousness and our similarity to and difference from other humans and nonhumans around us." Achieving identity "allows the organism to determine 'who it is and where it belongs.' "

Although these descriptions view the self as being entirely conscious, such theorists as Earl Kelley include unconscious functions as well:

> The self consists of an organization of accumulated experience over a whole lifetime. It is easy to see, therefore, that a great deal of the self has been relegated to the unconscious, or has been "forgotten." This does not mean that these early experiences have been lost. It merely means that they cannot readily be brought into consciousness. (1962, p. 9)

With these slightly disparate notions of the self as a background, we turn now to a cluster of beliefs that exemplify humanistic conceptions of development.

THE HUMANISTIC PERSUASION

The realm of humanistic psychology over the past few decades can be pictured as two circles, with the smaller inside a larger. The smaller one represents a publicly declared movement launched in the United States in 1962 with the formation of the Association of Humanistic Psychology (AHP), and the initial publication of the *Journal of Humanistic Psychology.* The larger, surrounding domain includes not only the inner circle of people who subscribe to the association's tenets, but also other theorists who differ in certain respects from members of the inner coterie. While there actually is no precise borderline separating inhabitants of the inner domain from those in the surrounding territory, for purposes of discussion it is convenient to distinguish between the two. The humanistic version of development offered in this chapter reflects convictions of theorists from both the inner circle and the outer realm. Other versions of a humanistic approach, from both the inner and outer domains, can be found in the writings of Gordon W. Allport (1968), Arthur W. Combs and Donald Snygg (1959), Earl C. Kelley (1962), Rollo May (Reeves, 1977), Frederick S. Perls (Perls, Hefferline, & Goodman, 1951), Carl Rogers (1961, 1973), and other authors who write for such publications as the *Journal of Humanistic Psychology, The Humanistic Psychologist, Journal of Phenomenological Psychology, Review of Existential Psychology and Psychiatry,* and *Self and Society.*

Humanists, in contrast to behaviorists' practice of analyzing people from the outside, analyze them from the inside. Introspection becomes the chief investigative technique, for humanistic psychologists believe that the quintessence of an individual is found not in overt acts but in one's thoughts and feelings about one's personal experience. This inward view of personality has appeared over the centuries in numerous versions, each bearing its own name: humanism, existentialism, phenomenology, mysticism, and others. Philosophers of a humanist persuasion have stressed a belief in each person's possessing a free will that permits one to make choices and display creative powers as an individual. One variety of this viewpoint, developed in nineteenth-century Europe under the name *existentialism,* proposed that the reality of life resides in each individual's interpretation of his or her personal existence. Existentialists have emphasized the importance of a person's fully experiencing each moment of life. In a similar manner, *phenomenologists* have proposed that the "truth" about life is found in experiencing rather than in objective descriptions of people's behavior as measured and tested by the techniques of natural science. A mid-twentieth-century variant of phenomenology appeared in a book entitled *Individual Psychology* by two U.S. psychologists, Combs and Snygg, who accorded prime attention to the *phenomenal self,* meaning the personally recognized "I" or "me."

Humanistic psychologists in their research methodology "do not claim to be 'objective.' They are intent on the discovery of methods within the highly subjective interchange of a relationship which will garner 'personal knowledge' of another human being" (Buhler & Allen, 1972, p. 24). As a result of this viewpoint, other psychologists who regard experimental methods as the best source of information about child growth often believe that humanistic approaches do not qualify as proper theories of development. However, under the broad definition of *theory* adopted in this book, humanistic views can form theories of development, for they furnish answers to most of the questions posed about development in Chapter Two. The humanistic theory described in this chapter is a composite version built mainly around beliefs extracted from the writings of Abraham Maslow, Charlotte Buhler, and Alvin R. Mahrer, with the first two authors representing the inner circle of humanistic psychologists and the third representing a position that differs in several ways from the beliefs of the inner group.

The following discussion opens with (1) a brief introduction to the humanistic movement that arose in the 1960s. The presentation then continues with humanistic perspectives on (2) the original nature of the child, (3) the importance of needs and goals, (4) the nature of the self, (5) directions and stages of development, (6) healthy growth, disease, and deviance, and (7) nature and nurture. The section closes with (8) practical applications of such a theory and (9) an assessment of the humanistic approach.

The Roots of Modern-Day Humanistic Psychology

The movement represented by the creators of the Association of Humanistic Psychology (AHP) in the early 1960s was primarily an attempt to focus attention on the growth of *self.* At the same time, it was a reaction against two current streams of psychological thought and thus was dubbed "a third force" in psychology by a Brandeis University professor, Abraham Maslow (1903–1970).

The two theoretical positions that humanistic psychology rejected were behaviorism and psychoanalysis. Behaviorism was accused of reducing individuals to a system of observable acts and thereby missing such human aspects as people's values, feelings, hopes for the future, choices, and creativity. Behaviorists were charged with neglecting to picture the human being as a unitary person in pursuit of goals and ideals (Maslow, 1968, 1970). Freudian psychoanalysis was accused of adopting a negative model of humanity, of espousing a morbid emphasis on neurotic behavior, and of failing to define the nature and the path of positive, healthy personality development.

Humanistic psychology, as reflected in the association's tenets, is marked by the following:

1. A centering of attention on the experiencing *person,* and thus a focus on *experience* as the primary phenomenon in the study of man. Both theoretical explanations and overt behavior are considered secondary to experience itself and to its meaning to the person.
2. An emphasis on such distinctively *human qualities* as choice, creativity, valuation, and self-realization, as opposed to thinking about human beings in mechanistic and reductionist terms.
3. An allegiance to *meaningfulness* in the selection of problems for study and of research procedures and an opposition to a primary emphasis on objectivity at the expense of significance.
4. An ultimate *concern with and valuing of the dignity and worth of man* and an interest in the *development of the potential inherent in every person.* Central in this view is the person as he or she discovers his own being and relates to other persons and to social groups (the AHP brochure).

In effect, humanistic theorists propose a positive, optimistic picture of humans and believe that life "is to be lived subjectively, as it takes place."

Ideas arising within the humanistic movement have not been molded into one system, nor do the beliefs of one theorist always agree with those of others, as this chapter demonstrates. Furthermore, humanistic theory is not specifically a child development theory, for most of its materials focus on adults or speak about the life span in general without distinguishing very clearly between one age period and another. However, from the writings of certain humanistic psychologists it is possible to derive answers to many questions about child development.

Three theorists whose works are particularly useful as sources of such answers are Abraham Maslow, Charlotte Buhler (1893–1974), and Alvin R. Mahrer (born 1927). Maslow was first trained in experimental psychology and psychoanalysis, but he concluded that both of these traditions failed to give proper attention to what he considered the essence of human personality—that is, to a person's sense of *self* and to the immediate experiencing of life. Buhler was a well-known European psychologist who made her first contributions to the child development literature in Austria before establishing her home in the United States. Mahrer, now a professor of psychology at the University of Ottawa in Canada, was raised in the United States by Czech-immigrant parents. He earned a doctorate at Ohio State University before entering private practice as a psychoanalytic therapist, and then gradually moved away from psychoanalysis to an existential-humanistic position, which he refers to as *experiential psychotherapy*. His book *Experiencing: A Humanistic Theory of Psychology and Psychiatry* (1989) offers extensive proposals about the process of development. As will be illustrated, Mahrer's views in several respects differ from those of Maslow and Buhler. Mahrer admits that he "cannot feel very much at home with the typical humanistic psychologists."

The Original Nature of the Child

In most versions of humanistic theory, the biologically determined inner nature of the human consists of basic needs, emotions, and capacities that are either neutral or positively good. Such "bad" characteristics as destructiveness, cruelty, and malice are not innate, according to Maslow (1968, pp. 3–4), but are "violent reactions *against* frustration of our intrinsic needs, emotions, and capacities. . . . Since this inner nature is good or neutral rather than bad, it is best to bring it out and to encourage it rather than to suppress it. If it is permitted to guide our life, we grow healthy, fruitful and happy."

Therefore the goal of guiding child development is to foster the expression of the child's inner nature. This task is difficult because the inner essence of the child's personality is not very hardy but, rather, is delicate and easily damaged by unfavorable experiences. Suppressing or distorting the expression of the inner nature causes some degree of sickness, bodily ailment, or behavior deviation that sometimes shows up immediately but other times may surface months or years after the maltreatment. Nevertheless, even when the inner essence is suppressed, it continues to live in the depths of the unconscious, always striving for expression or, in Maslow's language, for *actualization.*

Although Buhler and many other humanistic theorists would agree with Maslow's conception of the child's original nature, Mahrer offered a different proposal. He claimed that it is a *humanist* rather than a *humanistic* belief that "the infant has a basic nature which is inherently free, spontaneous, creative, loving, active, striving, actualizing" (Mahrer, 1978, p. 634). As an alternative to such a notion of inherent human nature, Mahrer proposed what he regards as a true humanistic concept of the initial state of infancy, a state he labels *primitive personality.* The primitive personality is not simply something inside the newborn but rather is composed of (1) the physical characteristics and inner potentials of the infant, (2) the parents' convictions of what an infant should be like, and (3) the relationships that exist between the infant and parents as a result of the parents' ideas of how to treat such an infant (Mahrer, 1978, p. 619). The interaction of these internal and external forces, Mahrer contended, determines what the infant experiences, so the interaction is properly identified as the *primitive personality* or original state of the child.

In summary, the dominant conception among humanistic theorists—and humanists—is that the child's original nature is one of positive striving to actualize an inner essence that is good and constructive. But there are other theorists, such as Mahrer, who also identify themselves as humanistic but who subscribe to a somewhat different view of the initial condition of the child.

Human Needs and Goals

A key concept to which humanistic psychologists subscribe is that human behavior is motivated primarily by the individual's seeking to fulfill a series of needs. However, not all theorists use the word *needs* to label the internal force they believe drives people to thought and action. Some theorists prefer such terms as *wishes, drives, goals, impulses,* or *potentials* (Mahrer, 1978, pp. 20–23).

To differentiate a humanistic view from the concept of needs in other theories, Maslow distinguished two types. The first he called *deficiency needs.* Examples of this variety are the needs for food, for drink, for a comfortable temperature, for safety from bodily harm, for close love relationships, for respect, and for prestige. He proposed that deficiency needs can be recognized by five objectively observed characteristics of the person and by two subjectively experienced feelings. Objectively, a need for something exists if (1) its absence breeds illness, (2) its presence prevents illness, (3) its restoration cures illness, (4) under certain free choice situations, it is preferred by the deprived person over other satisfactions, and (5) it is found to be inactive, low, or functionally absent in the healthy person. Subjectively, a deficiency need is felt as (6) a conscious or unconscious yearning and desire and (7) a lack or deficiency (Maslow, 1968, p. 22).

Beyond these deficiency needs, which are included in other theories of child development, humanistic psychologists postulate a second cluster called *growth* or *self-actualization* needs. Theorists have had far more trouble in specifying this second group than in identifying deficiencies. Maslow admitted that

> growth, individuation, autonomy, self-actualization, self-development, productive-
> ness, self-realization, are all crudely synonymous, designating a vaguely perceived
> area rather than a sharply defined concept. . . . We just don't know enough about
> growth yet to be able to define it well. (1968, p. 24)

But in an initial attempt at a general definition, Maslow proposed that the self-actualizing need is a striving to realize one's potential, capacities, and talents; it is a seeking to fulfill a mission or destiny or vocation; it can be a fuller knowledge and acceptance of one's own personality and "an unceasing trend toward unity, integration, or synergy within the person" (Maslow, 1968, p. 26).

The highest stage of growth in humans, then, is the achievement of such self-actualization. Commenting on this highest stage, Buhler and M. Allen (1972, p. 45) have said, "All humanistic psychologists see the goal of life as that of using it to accomplish something in which one believes."

The human needs in Maslow's system, then, form a hierarchy ranging from the most basic physiological deficiency needs at the foundation to the self-actualization needs at the apex. Maslow proposed that the lower needs must be filled before the upper-level needs receive attention. In descending order from the apex, they can be placed in five clusters (Maslow, 1970, pp. 80–89):

1. *Self-actualization need:* doing what one, *individually,* is fitted for—"What a man *can* be, he *must* be. He must be true to his own nature."
2. *Esteem needs:* for self-respect and self-esteem and for the esteem of others.
3. *Belongingness and love needs:* for family, friends, lover; affection, rooted-ness, intimacy.

4. *Safety needs:* for security and stability, for freedom from fear, anxiety, and chaos. This includes a need for structure, law, and limits.
5. *Physiological needs:* for air, food, drink, rest, fulfilling the appetites, and for achieving balance or homeostasis within the body.

The Mind and the Self

Both Maslow and Buhler, like many other humanistic theorists, accept the principal agents that Freud defined as composing the personality or mind: id, ego, and superego. They also accept the various Freudian instincts, impulses, and defenses, as well as the primary process (seeking immediate pleasure) and the secondary process (the ego's recognizing the real world and fulfilling the id's demands in the light of reality). But for the humanistic psychologist these separate and often conflicting agents and tendencies become increasingly integrated into a compatible unity—into the *essential self*—as the person matures. Thus the individual who is fulfilling all of her or his needs, basic as well as self-actualizing ones, is marked by a smooth working together or *synergy* of the composite elements of personality (Buhler & Massarik, 1968, p. 19).

Likewise, humanistic psychologists often subscribe to the levels of consciousness postulated by Freud, even if they do not always include the unconscious level in their concept of the essential self. They feel that much of human behavior arises from unconscious motives and that "those portions of ourselves that we reject and repress out of fear and shame do not go out of existence" (Maslow, 1971, p. 158) but go underground into the unconscious. However, humanistic writers strongly disagree with Freud's idea that the contents of the unconscious are principally (if not entirely) antisocial—that is, selfish and resistant to moral values. They believe that the contents also include the roots of creativeness, joy, and goodness.

In humanistic belief, conscience differs somewhat from the punitive Freudian superego whose contents derive exclusively from the rules and expectations imposed by the environment, particularly expectations imposed by parents. Maslow proposed that in addition to values that the child ingests from people around her, her conscience also has a genetic source, a kind of intrinsic feeling or knowledge of the right thing to do. This faint voice has its beginnings in the ancient nature of humans and is linked to the instincts of lower forms of life. It is an inner knowledge of one's true self. Maslow said that intrinsic guilt arises when an individual senses he has betrayed his own inner nature and has deviated from the path of self-actualization.

In Maslow's view, intrinsic guilt is a most desirable thing for it warns the child that she is straying from her true destiny. On the other hand, guilt based on unreasonable expectations from the environment is frequently nonconstructive and detracts from the pursuit of one's identity and self-fulfillment.

A question of continuing debate among humanists is whether the self is an entity or a collection of separate selves, each of which comes into play under particular conditions. P. D. Ouspensky suggested:

> The principal mistake we make about ourselves is that we consider ourselves one; we always speak about ourselves as "I" and we suppose that we refer to the same thing all the time. . . . We do not know that we have not one "I," but many different "I's," connected with our feelings and desires, and have no controlling "I." These "I's" change all the time; one suppresses another, one replaces another, and all this struggle makes up our inner life. (1957, p. 3)

This notion of multiple selves was expressed in its most popular form by the psychiatrist Eric Berne in such books as *Games People Play* (1967) and *What Do You Say after You Say Hello?* (1972). In Berne's theory, the three selves that contend for attention on different occasions are those expressing (1) vestiges of the person as a young "child," (2) an internal representation of the person's "parent," (3) and the person as a rational "adult."

In summary, then, despite some lack of consensus about the exact features of the self, all humanistic theorists consider the self the focal object of human development.

Directions and Stages of Development

As noted earlier, humanistic psychology was not created as a child psychology. It was devised by theorists concerned mainly with helping adults achieve better personal and social adjustment or, in more positive terms, achieve greater self-actualization. Hence the attention of most humanistic psychologists has focused on childhood only in incidental ways. Our picture of the direction of development and stages of growth in childhood must therefore be gleaned from passing comments. In effect, humanistic psychology, as outlined by its best-known proponents, has not been organized as a system of phases of childhood and adolescence as correlated with chronological ages. To some degree Mahrer is an exception, for he has identified what he calls a sequence of *plateaus* in the development of self. This hierarchy of plateaus represents the closest approximation in humanistic theory to the stages of growth identified in such development models as those of Piaget, Freud, Gesell, and Havighurst.

Despite this lack of precisely defined growth steps for the first two decades of life in most humanistic theories, Maslow and Buhler have identified at least two general levels of change, those of *childhood* and *adolescence.* In discussing these levels, Buhler distinguished biological from psychological development. From a biological standpoint, she divided the first twenty-five years of life at age fifteen. During childhood, from birth to fifteen, there is progressive physical growth without reproductive ability. During adolescence or youth, ages fifteen to twenty-five, there is continued growth following the onset of reproductive ability (Buhler & Massarik, 1968, p. 14).

Psychological development can also be viewed as two general segments, childhood and adolescence, but the distinctions are not nearly as clear as in the biological realm. Psychologically, the child grows toward self-actualization, toward achieving clearer goals in life and better integration of needs and values. This development of *self* is somewhat correlated with biological growth, in that the very young child is not very self-actualized. Time and experience are required for the child to achieve greater self-realization and synergy. But time alone is not enough. Just becoming older does not assure self-actualization. There are many adolescents and adults who still have not achieved psychological maturity. So the passing of childhood and the arrival of adolescence provides *opportunities for becoming mature*, but such maturing is not automatic.

Buhler concluded that the first appearance of a self-conscious ego occurs when the young child is between ages two and four. During this time "I want" behavior is prominent as "the child begins to discover his own self and the possibility of giving himself a direction of his own" (Buhler & Massarik, 1968, pp. 30–31). The way a child expresses this self-consciousness varies greatly from one child to another, with such individuality being both genetic and environmental in origin. "The child with creative potential begins his first attempts toward self-realization when he is between two and four years" (Buhler & Massarik, 1968, p. 32).

Motivational Trends

Throughout the next eight or ten years the child's personality gradually evolves until the arrival of marked psychological change around age ten to twelve or so. At this time, according to Buhler, several *motivational trends* appear, trends that extend into the future and mark the child's individuality in rather permanent ways.

One trend concerns a constructive–destructive dimension that involves the person's basic attitude toward life, an attitude that is becoming well set during this period of development. The attitude either can be one of building up positive human relationships and optimistic plans for the future, or it can be one of tearing down relationships by attacking others and despairing of the future. Which of these tendencies is dominant is most clearly evidenced in the way children interact with their parents, particularly in the way conflicts between child and parent are either resolved or expanded.

A second trend relates to *achievement motivation.* The extent to which a child will strive to achieve in her adult life and the form of this achievement will show up most clearly after puberty.

Beliefs and values that are based on more than blind acceptance develop in the early adolescent years, along with *love* and other *commitments* to a cause or to other people. Buhler said that the voluntarily chosen bonds of intimacy and commitment in a mutually shared sex and love relationship may result in "the ecstatic experience of unity . . . one of the most, if not *the* most, essential aims of the maturing person." Maslow called this feeling of unity one of the individual's *peak experiences* (Buhler & Massarik, 1968, p. 37). (The term *peak experiences*, frequently found in humanistic literature, identifies the most wonderful experience or experiences of your life, happiest moments, ecstatic moments, moments of rapture [Maslow in R. Wuthnow, 1978, p. 57]. The attainment of increasing numbers of peak experiences is, from a humanistic perspective, an important goal of human development.)

But even with adolescents' new concern for personally adopted values and immediate ambitions, they usually have only vague and tentative life goals. Rarely do they view life as an entirety, as a complete span of years with possibilities of an integration of all its aspects. "It is the exceptional youth who asks what life is all about" (Buhler & Massarik, 1968, p. 42).

Like Buhler, other writers in the humanistic vein consider adolescence to be a time of increased awareness and searching in the realm of values, goals, and commitment for something considered worthwhile. It is also a time of significant confusion. In this sense, the typical humanistic psychologist would agree with Erikson's notion that adolescence is experienced as an identity crisis. Maslow commented that the uncertainty of many adults in the United States about their own values has led many young people to live not by clear adult values but by "adolescent values, which of course are immature, ignorant, and heavily determined by confused adolescent needs" (Maslow, 1968, p. 206).

In summary, while most humanistic psychologists recognize at least prepubertal childhood and postpubertal adolescence as separate stages in personality development, they do not define substages within these periods, nor do they discuss even these two broad periods in any systematic way. Instead, they give only incidental attention to any idea of growth stages being correlated with age.

A Hierarchy of Plateaus

As mentioned earlier, Mahrer has proposed a sequence of five *plateaus* of personality growth and has linked the sequence to age levels, albeit in a rather vague manner. To contrast his system with the typical sets of growth periods postulated in other theories, Mahrer "sets aside the whole framework of biosocial, biopsychological stages of development" since he contends that "there are no intrinsic forces moving the child from one plateau to another, no biological factors, no built-in developmental sequences, no neurophysiological or hereditary or cultural lines of development" (1978, pp. 788, 790). Instead, he proposed that "people are responsible for an individual's staying on one plateau or moving to another. Those people may include the individual himself, his family, the groups in which he lives, significant strangers" (1978, p. 788).

The hierarchy of plateaus begins after birth with the *primitive personality*, which is the condition of the child encompassed within a *primitive field*. This primitive psychological field is created by parents and others in the child's environment who have a concept of what the infant should be like and who base their treatment of the infant on that concept. During this period children have no sense of self but are dependent for their identity on the way others act toward them. "What I am is a function of how others see me" (Mahrer, 1978, p. 791). Whether children advance out of this early condition and onto the next plateau depends on how they are treated by the people in charge of their welfare. If not treated constructively, the child could remain a primitive personality all his or her life, forever relying on the external world as a mirror of his or her identity.

With proper nurturing, the individual advances to the second plateau, where a sense of self is born. Mahrer estimates that for some people this occurs in early childhood, but for most it happens during middle childhood between ages six and twelve. For still others it does not appear until adolescence or adulthood, or perhaps never. He further proposes that this second state is not achieved suddenly but occurs "in bits and pieces, little juttings and bursts" (1978, p. 799).

On the third plateau children become active seekers, constructors of experience, employing their growing potentials to select activities and to organize their world so that particular kinds of experiences occur. Instead of being manipulated by their environment, they actively fashion and utilize their surroundings for their own purposes.

Whereas the third period witnesses the individual initially developing skills or "operating potentials," on the fourth plateau new and more sophisticated skills are devised, ones that enable the person to experience life in greater depth and complexity.

The fifth, optimal state of being is that of self-integration and self-actualization, a plateau "beyond normal, mature, adjusted, healthy . . . achieved by a very small proportion of individuals. . . . Our concept is like that of a yogi, an individual who has attained the goal of yoga . . . the union of self with the supreme reality or universal self" (Mahrer, 1978, p. 833).

Mahrer pictures the plateaus as representing a sequence of three struggles, first to acquire selfhood or personal identity during infancy and early childhood, next to preserve one's identity against the pressures of a changing environment, and finally to "lose selfhood" in ultimate self-actualization.

In conclusion, some developmental periods can be extracted from the works of a few humanistic authors. However, humanistic writers generally do not offer a *growth-stage* theory, but rather a *growth-directions* theory, meaning that a person grows gradually out of being one kind of individual toward being a different kind. But, to recognize whether a child is indeed developing in a proper direction, we need a definition of the desired end product or the desired goal that development is to pursue. Maslow defined this *direction of healthy growth* in two ways, one general and the other more specific.

As a general definition, he said that people are motivated in their development toward "ongoing actualization of potentials, capacities and talents, as fulfillment of mission—or call it fate, destiny, or vocation—as a fuller knowledge of, and acceptance of, the person's own intrinsic nature, as an unceasing trend toward unity, integration or synergy within the person" (Maslow, 1968, p. 25).

But many people found this definition unduly vague, so he provided a more specific description of the end condition of healthy development by specifying a series of traits displayed by a self-actualized person. Such a paragon of excellence exhibits (Maslow, 1968, p. 26) the following:

1. superior perception of reality
2. increased acceptance of self, of others, and of nature
3. increased spontaneity
4. increased problem solving
5. increased autonomy, and resistance to enculturation
6. increased detachment and desire for privacy

7. greater freshness of appreciation, and richness of emotional reaction
8. higher frequency of peak experiences
9. increased identification with the human species
10. changed (the clinician would say improved) interpersonal relations
11. more democratic character structure
12. greatly increased creativeness
13. certain changes in the value system

Other humanistic theorists besides Maslow have proposed their own set of directions in which development should proceed. For example, Combs (1962, pp. 53–62) has contended that the truly adequate personality (1) both gives love to others and feels loved by them; (2) is open to new experiences; (3) closely identifies with others so that he or she treats them in a highly responsible, trustworthy fashion; and (4) has a "rich and available perceptual field," meaning that she or he is well enough informed about the world to clearly understand events in which she or he is enmeshed.

Carl Rogers (1973, p. 12) pictured proper development as proceeding from rigidity toward flexibility, from static living toward "process living," from dependence toward autonomy, from being predictable toward an "unpredictable creativity," and from defensiveness toward self-acceptance.

Healthy Growth and Deviance

In place of the terms *normal* and *abnormal,* Maslow spoke of *health* and *illness* or of *mature* and *immature* development. For example, he distinguished between two sorts of immaturity, *chronological* and *unhealthy.* Chronological immaturity is found in the child as he grows up; it is expected, even necessary, for it consists of the healthy process of developing from a state of weakness, ignorance, and lack of direction to an adult state of self-fulfillment. But when the same sorts of symptoms are found in the adult, they are considered unhealthy, for by adulthood the individual should have become strong, wise, well integrated, and clear in his values and goals.

Deviance—that is, being different from others or failing to fit the norms—is not regarded as necessarily unhealthy. Indeed, being deviant in terms of expressing one's own talents and of following the guidance of one's unique inner gyroscope was viewed by Maslow as essential to achieving self-actualization. If a person adopts the typical behavior or norms of a culture that blocks the expression of her inner nature or personality core, then she is not considered to be normal in the sense of developing properly or in a healthy pattern. Instead, she is regarded in Maslow's system as being immature and unhealthy, for "the main source of illness (although not the only one) is seen as frustrations (of the basic needs, . . . of idiosyncratic potentials, of expression of the self, and of the tendency of the person to grow in his own style and at his own pace) especially in the early years of life" (Maslow, 1968, pp. 193–194).

So it is not deviance from the common or typical behavior of a society that is viewed with disapproval in the humanistic model; it is deviance from one's potential. A child who does not "fit in" to his culture or who "stands against the crowd" is a psychologically healthy child by humanistic standards if that culture is a bad one. And by *bad* Maslow meant a culture that is growth-inhibiting rather than growth-fostering. "The 'better' culture gratifies all basic human needs and permits self-actualization. The 'poorer' cultures do not" (Maslow, 1968, p. 211).

Nature and Nurture

The general humanistic position on heredity–environment issues is that the infant is born with inherited potentials—for growth and for self-fulfillment by pursuing constructive missions—but that these potentials will not flower at all unless they are properly nurtured by the people with whom the child interacts during the growing years. As the discussion of Maslow's views has already suggested, he assigned heredity a strong role in personality development. The essence of the sort of person a child should become is established in the genetic structure as a unique *self* composed of latent talents and interests. The environment then determines how adequately this idiosyncratic self or identity unfolds or becomes actualized. So while humanistic theorists recognize the significance of innate potentials as the seeds of personality, they still place great emphasis on the function of the social environment in producing the actual personality the growing child displays. The self "is built almost entirely, if not entirely, in relationship to others. While the newborn babe has the equipment for the development of the self, there is ample evidence to show that nothing resembling a self can be built in the absence of others" (E. C. Kelley, 1962, p. 9). "People discover their self concepts from the kinds of experiences they have had with life—not from telling, but from experience" (Combs, 1962, p. 84).

Practical Applications

Although the most extensive applications of humanistic psychology have been therapeutic and consciousness-raising activities for adults, a substantial body of literature has been produced as well on child-rearing practices and on schooling and therapy during the first two decades of life. Such child-focused literature can be divided into two types. The first consists of general guidelines and warnings about raising children. The second consists of specific activities for promoting humanistic goals of development.

Examples of general guidelines are such observations as the following:

> A high quality of maternal love and care . . . seem to prepare the child for emotional contacts with other people and to supply enough confidence to encourage the exploration of new situations. . . . Among the greatest benefits of psychoanalysis is the fact that it has disclosed the damaging consequences of extreme parental demands and discipline. . . . On the whole, it may be assumed that warmth and permissiveness facilitate the growth of sociable, yet independent children, and that parental hostility has debilitating effects. (Buhler & Massarik, 1968, pp. 174–178)

Once the infant puts forth a rudimentary nubbin [of individuality], parental figures can develop that behavior by [an] . . . integrative relationship that is expressed in warmth, love, closeness, acceptance. . . . To relate disintegratively is to relate with fear and hate, depression and anger, meaninglessness and menace to the behavior bit put forth by the infant. (Mahrer, 1978, pp. 698–699)

Anytime a pupil's actions suggest that he can profit from expressing and comprehending (emotionally as well as intellectually) his feelings, the teacher should use methods suitable for promoting such expression and comprehension. (Thomas & Brubaker, 1971, p. 260)

We know only too well that a parent cannot make his children into anything. Children make themselves into something. The best we can do and frequently the most effect we can have is by serving as something to react against if the child presses too hard. . . . Schools should be helping children to look within themselves, and from this self-knowledge derive a set of values, . . . spontaneity and . . . naturalness. (Maslow, 1971, pp. 169, 185–186)

Maslow's faith in the correctness of the child's natural inclinations caused him to recommend a *permissive regime,* meaning that parents should begin meeting the child's needs directly and with as little frustration as possible in early infancy. But as the child acquires greater strength and experience, adults should gradually cease gratifying his needs directly. They should now arrange the child's environment so he can gratify his own needs and make his own choices, for "he 'knows' better than anyone else what is good for him" (Maslow, 1968, p. 198).

The intention of Maslow's educational scheme is not to prevent developing children from ever experiencing frustration, pain, or danger. But, with a good foundation in the early years of safety, love, and respect, children should increasingly be allowed to face difficulties that enable them to acquire frustration tolerance. Part of self-realization comes as the older child and the youth learn about their strengths and limitations and learn ways to extend their abilities by overcoming difficulties, "by straining . . . to the utmost, by meeting challenge and hardship, even by failing" (Maslow, 1968, p. 200). Curiously, this general pattern of child raising—except for the desirability of failing—sounds much like the pattern found in Skinner's *Walden Two,* illustrating the observation that children may be treated in similar ways from quite different theoretical viewpoints.

Some humanistic writers have gone beyond offering general suggestions and have described specific activities for implementing their suggestions. For example, Mahrer (1978, pp. 766–771) proposed a regimen for promoting an infant's development out of the condition of primitive personality into an initial sense of self. The routine to be carried out with the six- to nine-month-old child consists of the adult playing with the baby for thirty minutes to an hour each day. However, it is the infant, not the adult, who determines the direction of the play. The adult's role is first to furnish *effectance-promoting objects* that the child can touch, grasp, squeeze, shape, mouth, crumple, push, throw, hit, release, roll, take apart, open, and close. The objects should also make noise, have odors, and be different colors. And all the objects should be started, stopped, and manipulated by the baby himself, not by the adult. With such equipment at hand, the adult's task is to remain within *interactive distance* of the infant, meaning that the adult's face is within two feet of the child.

The baby is then allowed to initiate his own behavior, with the adult focusing attention on and commenting about what the baby is doing, being careful all the while not to interfere with or redirect the infant's activity.

For school-age children and youths, a variety of other writers have proposed specific learning activities. These can be illustrated by examples from *confluent education,* which is a variant of the humanistic movement that emphasizes a confluence or compatible flowing together of the cognitive and emotional aspects of experience. For instance, to help children investigate their feelings about communicating with others under unusual circumstances, one set of activities consists of pupils dividing into pairs. Each pair first sit back to back to converse with each other orally, then sit facing each other to communicate only with their eyes, and finally—with eyes closed—to communicate only with their hands. To foster greater "self-awareness and other-awareness," each child is next asked to "close his eyes and with his hands explore his own face very slowly and get in touch with the various textures and parts of his face" and then to explore the face of his partner (G. I. Brown, 1971, pp. 29–32). An opportunity to investigate feelings of trust and distrust is provided by the *blind walk,* which involves one of the pair of children being blindfolded and then led by her partner around the classroom and other areas of the school. An additional activity to promote self-awareness has been labeled a *fantasy body trip.* Students close their eyes, assume comfortable positions, and "move into themselves" by concentrating on different parts of the body, with each student "beginning with his toes, moving gradually up to his head, experiencing any sensations he might feel emanating from that part of the body" (G. I. Brown, 1971, p. 35).

Numerous additional activities devised by proponents of humanistic development demonstrate ways to plumb the experiences of loneliness, affection, responsibility, anxiety, faithfulness, prejudice, social acceptance and rejection, confidence, insecurity, emotional dependence and independence, and more. Over the past three decades an increasing number of such activities have been included in elementary and secondary school curricula and in nonformal educational programs.

HUMANISTIC THEORY: AN ASSESSMENT

Three of the greatest strengths of the humanistic approach are its attention to children's feelings and values as part of their real world (item 1), its concern for the individual's hopes and plans for the future (item 3), and its application of a humanistic view to child raising (item 4).

I agree with humanistic psychologists that the world that is most significant to children or adolescents is the one they feel that they are experiencing at the moment. This attention to the phenomenal self seems to be a proper counterbalance to the heavy dependence on objectively observed actions of behaviorist views. The typical humanistic theory seeks to devise general principles that underlie different facets of growth, not just one aspect such as cognitive development. However, by concerning itself only with general principles, it has failed to trace the specific ways one aspect, such as language usage, develops in comparison to the

HUMANISTIC THEORY

How well do I think the theory meets the standards?

Standards	Very well	Moderately well	Very poorly
1. Reflects the real world of children	X		
2. Is clearly understandable		X	
3. Explains the past and predicts the future	X		
4. Guides child rearing	X		
5. Is internally consistent		?	
6. Is economical		?	
7. Is falsifiable			X
8. Is supported by convincing evidence		X	
9. Adapts to new data		X	
10. Is novel	X		
11. Is comprehensive		X	
12. Stimulates new discoveries	X		
13. Is durable	G	Sp	
14. Is self-satisfying	X		

ways other aspects, such as physical agility, grow. Hence I have rated humanistic psychology high on item 1 but not at the top.

Some critics have faulted present-day humanistic theory for ostensibly limiting its focus to a limited segment of society, so they would rank the theory low on item 1 for being only relevant to the "haves" (i.e., those who have achieved sufficient economic wealth) and completely irrelevant to the "have-nots" (i.e., in Maslow's terms [1968], those too busy concerning themselves with lower-level needs rather than higher-level needs such as self-actualization). Herein lies the contradiction in the practice of contemporary "humanistic" psychology—a contradiction that must be resolved in order for "humanistic" psychology to evolve into a truly *humanistic* psychology (Buss, 1976, p. 258).

The humanistic approach is notable for recognizing the influence on development of the child's hopes, expectations, and plans for the future, which are facets of experience neglected in many other theories. I have sought to recognize this contribution by a relatively strong rating on item 3. That rating would have been higher if the manner in which humanistic theory explains the past were more precise.

Two general principles of child rearing that humanistic theorists appear to support are that (1) the adult should seek to perceive life from the emotional and cognitive perspectives of the child and, through such empathy, should treat the child in ways that show respect for and understanding of the child's phenomenal self; and (2) the adult should respect the child's right to be an individual with interests, talents, and emotions of her own. I am convinced that these principles are desirable guides in child raising, so I have rated the humanistic approach high on item 4. But again, the rating is not at the top of the scale, for I believe humanistic theory lacks the specificity that parents and teachers look for in their search for ways to treat the growing child. However, a lack of precise directives to parents is perhaps a necessary part of any theory that emphasizes the unique character of each child.

On other dimensions, I have judged that humanistic theory doesn't fare so well. One problem is its lack of clarity (item 2). Humanistic writers describe their ideas in terms that can carry quite different meanings for different readers. When you speak of your *peak experiences,* of your *self-realization,* of *authenticity* and *synergism,* and of your *identity,* how am I to know whether I have experienced the same things that cause you to use these words? Likewise, when I seek inner guidance in making a decision, how do I know which of my impulses represents my *true* inner self, the one that directs me toward self-actualization, and which impulses represent values I have learned from my environment, values that may conflict with my innate essence or calling?

Further puzzles have arisen from seemingly self-contradictory principles offered by humanistic writers. For example, Maslow wrote that "for self-actualizing people, there is a strong tendency for selfishness and unselfishness to fuse into a higher, superordinate unity" (1968, p. 207).

In addition, Maslow's system proposes that children are immature because they are at lower levels in the needs-fulfillment hierarchy and at lower levels on the scales of maturity. Yet he stated that "the highest maturity is discovered to include a childlike quality" (1968, p. 207). If this is true, then the development of maturity requires a clearer explanation than the existing humanistic literature seems to provide.

In effect, one of the very strengths of humanistic theory, its insistence on the importance of unique personal experiences, leads also to one of its serious weaknesses—its imprecision in communicating the essence of one person's experience to another.

The same personal or existential quality of humanistic thought also contributes to the theory's lack of falsifiability (item 7). The difficulty here rests to a great degree in humanistic theorists' preference for using introspection as their principal investigative technique. Although Maslow accepted the objective, scientific modes of studying people that have evolved over the past century or so, he criticized the adoption of behaviorism and of logical positivism as the exclusive, or even as the preferred, mode of understanding human development. He claimed that such approaches to studying the growing child result only in verbal, analytic, conceptual rationality and ignore the more significant aspects of personality: the hopes, feelings, fears, and ambitions of the experiencing self. For example, in discussing motivation, Maslow stated:

> The original criterion of motivation and the one that is still used by all human beings except behavioral psychologists is the subjective one. I am motivated when I feel a desire or want or yearning or wish or lack. No objectively observable state has yet been found that correlates decently with these subjective reports, i.e., no behavioral definition of motivation has yet been found.
>
> Now of course we ought to keep on seeking for objective correlates or indicators of subjective states. . . . But until we find [them] we ought not make believe that we have. Nor ought we neglect the subjective data that we do have. (1968, p. 22)

Not only does humanistic theory draw upon self-reports, but it accords a key position to nonlogical, or even illogical, intuitive impressions or feelings, which it claims are so often expressions of the true inner self.

> If our hope is to describe the world fully, a place is necessary for preverbal ineffable, metaphorical, primary process, concrete experience, intuitive, and esthetic types of cognition, for there are certain aspects of reality which can be cognized in no other way. (Maslow, 1968, p. 208)

This attitude about the proper sources of evidence about personality development influences the humanistic view of the way the theory is validated. In earlier chapters I noted that behavioristic theories depend upon the experimental or field-study testing of hypotheses as the appropriate way to determine whether the theory or some part of it is true. But humanistic psychologists trust their own feelings and logic more than many sorts of objective data to validate their theory. To most if not all humanistic psychologists, it appears to be enough to contend that "I know that's the way things are because it makes sense and feels right to me." But such a testimonial would less likely satisfy a behaviorist, a Piagetian, or a psychoanalyst.

In terms of the theory's internal consistency (item 5) and economy of explanation (item 6), I have placed question marks in the lower reaches of the appraisal scales. My puzzlement regarding these matters is occasioned by a lack of precision in the definition of terms and of the relationships among variables. I find myself unable to make a careful estimate of internal consistency and economy of explanation when I fail to understand the elements of the system adequately. To a considerable extent, humanistic writing appears cast in unscientific, literary language. Rhetoric and obvious enthusiasm do not, I feel, sufficiently make up for what seems to be a structural imprecision in the theory.

During the past four decades or so, humanistic views have gained wide public attention and have influenced the way teachers, parents, social workers, and others perceive children (G. I. Brown, 1971; Fantini & Weinstein, 1968; Leff, 1978). However, this success in attracting people's interest in perceiving children in ostensibly more "humane" ways has not led to a significant number of new discoveries about children. It is true that such proposals as Maslow's hierarchy of needs have been innovative. But in many instances, the matters of which humanistic writers speak have been matters that people of earlier times sensed intuitively, and the humanistic theorists' contribution has been to stimulate the rediscovery of these insights about self, about feelings, and about hopes for the future. As a case in point, humanistic literature includes frequent allusions to concepts from Eastern religions, especially to Hindu and Buddhist notions (Muzika, 1990; Tart, 1990). In more than three hundred articles bearing on humanistic psychology in the standard psychological journal literature for the period 1974–1990, the objects of discussion were adults or people in general. Attention was rarely directed at development during childhood, and even then the mention was chiefly incidental. If you search through current child development textbooks, you will find very few new items of knowledge about child growth contributed by theorists and researchers using humanistic approaches. Hence I have marked the theory in the lower ranges of item 12. My purpose in giving such a rating is not to downgrade the importance of the humanistic persuasion but only to note that humanistic psychology has not stimulated significant amounts of new information or innovative perspectives on child development.

By concentrating on the self, humanistic explanations address only a limited aspect of development. Such features as children's bio-electrochemical nature, their modes of processing information, their analytical abilities, and their memory systems are generally left untouched. Therefore, I have rated humanistic approaches between "moderately well" and "very poorly" on comprehensiveness.

The low mark on item 8 (supporting evidence) derives from humanistic theory's great dependence on people's feelings about what is true rather than on experimental studies and objective observations of behavior. Humanistic approaches appeal most to people who place great trust in introspection and intuitively affirmed testimonials about how the self develops. Such heavy reliance on intuition rather than on traditional canons of scientific investigation often leads to humanistic theorists' rejecting results of a wide range of studies as being irrelevant to their concerns (item 9).

In rating the novelty (item 10) of humanistic theory, I judged that placing the experiencing self as the centerpiece of a theory is not a new idea, since the self in various guises has been an item of philosophical inquiry over the centuries. However, certain features of the humanistic proposals of Buhler, Maslow, and Mahrer appear to be original. Hence, on balance I rated humanistic theory in the "moderately well" range.

The durability scale (item 13) contains two marks. The G represents my estimate of the general lasting interest to be expected for theories of the developing self. They will always be with us. On the other hand, I believe that the specific versions (Sp) offered in this chapter will likely disappear with passing time, replaced by new or revised conceptions. Such an estimate accords with the opinion of humanistic theorists themselves, since they make no claim for having produced a finished, close-knit theory of child development. Instead, they see their proposals as constituting only a beginning toward a model of human nature "as a total, single, comprehensive system of psychology" (Maslow, 1968, p. 189). At the same time, humanistic theorists claim that their approach, with its emphasis on the experiencing self, holds more promise for revealing the essence of human personality than do such systems as psychoanalysis and behaviorism. Overall, I find humanistic theory moderately self-satisfying (item 14).

OTHER CONCEPTIONS OF THE SELF

Interest in the self is not the exclusive province of humanistic psychology. Theorists operating from a variety of other perspectives—psychoanalytic, social-learning, information-processing, general-cognitive, and more—often include a version of self in their models of development. As a result, Banaji and Prentice (1994, p. 297) were able to report that "the self continues to occupy a center-stage position in psychology. Over 5000 articles about the self" were published over the period 1987–1994.

The purpose of this section is to sketch two current theories relating to the self, with particular attention to child development. For convenience of analysis, I have organized the discussion around one version of the self that seems to be popular among a goodly number of writers in the field (Hattie, 1992; Jersild, 1952; Montemayor & Eisen, 1977; Shavelson, Bolus, & Keesling, 1983). This version holds that whereas a person's self is a unified conviction about "who I am," that conviction is many-sided. Consequently, to identify the constituents that make up the self, we must view the self from diverse perspectives. Two examples of such theories have been selected for attention in the following paragraphs. In each example, the components are first identified by a typical label and defined. The definition is then followed by the theorists' proposals regarding how components develop during childhood and adolescence.

Self-Understanding

An aspect of self called *self-understanding* has been defined by William Damon and Daniel Hart as "one's cognitive representation of self, self-interest, and personal identity" (1988, p. 14). Damon and Hart's theory of self-understanding is founded on a distinction William James drew a century ago between what he called the "I" and the "me" facets of self (James, 1892/1961).

The "me" component, defined as "the sum total of all a person can call his," includes three constituents of the person's self-as-known: (1) all material characteristics (body, possessions), (2) all social characteristics (relations with others, roles played), and (3) all "spiritual" characteristics (consciousness, thoughts, psychological mechanisms) "that identify the self as a unique configuration of personal attributes" (Damon & Hart, 1988, p. 5). A researcher can learn the configuration of a person's "me" by extensively questioning the person, since "me" constituents are characteristics an individual is able to describe: "I'm tall and thin, my family's pretty well off financially, I get along better with boys than with girls, I'm good at math, and I plan someday to be an architect."

However, discovering a person's "self-as-I" is quite a different matter, since the "I" is highly subjective, not readily communicated to others. Whereas the "me" is the self-as-known, the "I" is the self-as-the-knower. Its elusive nature comes from the fact that it consists of four kinds of awareness not easily cast into words— awareness of one's influence over life events, of the unique quality of one's life experience, of one's personal continuity over time, and of one's own awareness.

With James's proposal as a starting point, Damon and Hart devised a model of how self-understanding develops from early childhood through late adolescence. Although their theory is too complex to describe fully in a few pages, something of its character can be conveyed by an example from the self-as-me (self-as-known) component. The authors began constructing their model by adding a fourth constituent subself—the active self—to James's original physical, social, and psychological (spiritual) selves. They then identified four developmental levels through which the normal child would be expected to progress within each these subselves during the first two decades of life. Each level is identified by a label that reflects the general principle children appear to use in organizing their self-understanding at that stage of life. The relationship between organizing principles and subselves can be illustrated with the following examples of children's understanding of their social self.

Early childhood The organizing principle is *categorical identification.* The social self is described in terms of the child's association with others—family, friends, acquaintances—or by memberships in designated social groups.

Example: *What can you tell me about the kind of person you are?* Well, I have a little sister named Samantha. . . . And I have a mother and father. *Why is it important to tell me about all those people?* I don't know, they're just my family (Damon & Hart, 1988, p. 60).

Middle and late childhood The organizing principle is *comparative assessments.* The child's abilities are revealed by the reactions of other people, including others' affective responses that reflect approval or disapproval.

Example: *What makes you feel proud?* When my Mom and Dad come and watch a game, and I play really well, like I hit a lot of homers, and I can hear them cheering real loud. *Why does that make you proud?* 'Cause they're letting me know how I did good (p. 63).

Early adolescence The organizing principle is *interpersonal implications.* Young teenagers understand their social self in terms of social-personality features that affect their social interactions, social appeal, or group memberships.

Example: *What are you like?* I'm an honest person, and I was raised that way, and people trust me because of it (p. 66).

Late adolescence The organizing principle is *systematic beliefs and plans.* The social self is understood in relation to the youth's personal philosophy, ideology, moral beliefs, or life plans.

Example: *What else is important about you?* I'm a Girl Scout. *Why is that important?* Because we do good things. We help people and stuff. If more people did what we did, the world would be a better place (p. 68).

In a similar manner, Damon and Hart also depict the four developmental levels for each of their other "me" constituents (physical, active, and psychological selves) as well as for three self-as-I components—self-continuity, self-distinctiveness, and self-agency (influence).

Self-Concept

John Hattie (1992) suggested that the term *self-concept* is shorthand for "conceptions of our self." In what he called "a facet analysis of self-concept," Hattie defined conceptions of self as our cognitive appraisals—expressed in terms of descriptions, expectations, and prescriptions—that are integrated across various dimensions that we attribute to ourselves. The integration or unification of the diverse dimensions is achieved via self-verification, self-consistency, self-complexity, and self-enhancement. The attributes of our self-concept can vary in their consistency as a result of how well other people and we ourselves confirm or disconfirm them (p. 37).

By inspecting the elements of this definition, we may grasp more precisely the nature of Hattie's theory. The "various dimensions" relate to three major facets or *content domains* within a school-age child's general self-concept—academic self-concept, social self-concept, and self-regard/presentation self-concept. Each of these domains subsumes more specific facets. For instance, the academic self-concept comprises achievement, ability, and classroom self-concepts.

> Ability self-concept denotes the extent to which the individual believes he or she is *capable* of achieving, whereas achievement self-concept relates to feelings or *perceptions* of actual achievement. [On self-concept questionnaires, the achievement self-concept] can be measured by items such as "I am proud of my report card" and "I am satisfied with my school work." Ability self-concept can be measured by items such as "I think that I have the ability to get good grades in schoolwork. [Classroom self-concept] relates to confidence in classroom activities and is measured by items such as "I feel left out of the things in class. . . ." (Hattie, 1992, p. 83)

Beneath the achievement and ability self-concepts, Hattie subsumed specific subject-matter self-concepts, which "are most likely to be situation specific, sensitive to change, and probably can be grouped into arts/verbal and science/mathematics factors" (1992, p. 83). (See Figure 12.1.) A child's overall self-concept consists of an amalgamation of this entire array of specific components.

Hattie proposed that in each content domain, individuals appraise themselves in terms of descriptions, prescriptions, and expectations, with descriptions of themselves being the dominant constituent of the self-concept. "I'm a redheaded girl, about medium height, kind of skinny, a pretty good swimmer, in school I'm better in art than in music, and I like books about horses and dogs." In Hattie's opinion (1992, p. 43), some people rarely think about who they are, since they consider conceptions of self unimportant. Others, however, assign much significance to their self and thus often puzzle over the question, "Who and what am I?"

In addition to self-descriptions, children have *expectations* for their physical

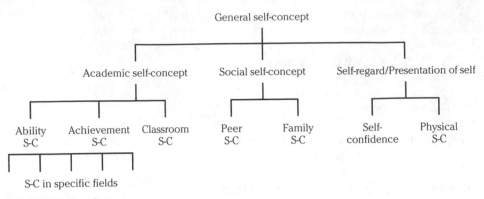

FIGURE 12.1
Song and Hattie's self-concept model (adapted from Hattie, 1992, p. 84)

appearance, their academic performance, their social success, their athletic pro-wess, and more. Daily experiences, particularly the way a child is treated by others, can either corroborate or disconfirm these expectations, thereby influencing the child's self-concept and subsequent self-description. *Prescriptions* are an individual's standards of correctness or desirability. How well children's performances match the standards they have acquired affects how they feel about themselves.

Hattie postulated seven processes that interact during the first two decades of life to fashion an individual's self-concept. The seven, along with the theorist's estimate of the importance of each during different age periods, are summarized in Table 12.1.

The theory assumes that neonates have no sense of self, in that they fail to recognize any difference between their own body and the people and objects in their surroundings. But infants' daily experiences equip them to begin making this distinction in the early months of life, so that the division between self and environmental objects is securely established by the early preschool years. However, separating one's concept of self from one's concept of other people develops far more gradually, extending into early adulthood. This continuing attachment of self to others is reflected in a child's so closely identifying with selected others that their successes and failures affect the child emotionally nearly as much as the child's own successes and failures.

The term *recognitive development* refers to children's growing ability to recognize aspects of themselves and distinguish those from aspects of other people. Acquiring language that equips the child to label things *(mine, yours, ours, theirs)* contributes to the recognitive process. As indicated in Table 12.1, Hattie suggested that this process is very important in infancy, declines somewhat in childhood, and assumes a major role in defining self during early and middle adolescence. In accounting for this pattern of change, Hattie drew on David Elkind's (1971, p. 111) observation that

> [even though younger children] are aware of themselves, they are not able to put themselves in other pupils' shoes and to look at themselves from that perspective.

TABLE 12.1
Seven processes in the development of one's self-concept

Processes	Ages:	0–2	3–9	9–17	17–25
1. We learn to distinguish self from others.		xx	xx	xx	x
2. We learn to distinguish self from the environment.		xx	x		
3. Our major reference groups change.			xx	x	x
4. We change our source of personal causation.		xx	x	xx	
5. We change recognitive development.		xx	x	xxx	
6. We change and/or realize cultural values.			xx	x	x
7. We change our reception of confirmation and disconfirmation.			xx		x

Codes: x = fairly influential   xx = very influential   xxx = extremely influential
Adapted from Hattie, 1992, p. 119.

Adolescents can do this and do engage in such self-watching to a considerable extent. Indeed, the characteristic "self-consciousness" of the adolescent results from the very fact that the young person is now very much concerned with how others react to him.

The matter of personal causation is reflected in the question: Which events do I cause, and which ones are caused by other people or by forces of nature? Or, to what extent am I responsible for what happens? Hattie assumed that the infant's experiences are very important for identifying distinctions of cause in simple matters, and that in more complex philosophical and scientific ways the process is again very important for the adolescent.

The three remaining processes in Table 12.1 are seen as playing their most significant roles during early and middle childhood. The principal *reference group* for the infant and toddler is the family. But this changes dramatically when the child enters preschool and the elementary grades, where an entirely new, expanded array of people react to the child's appearance and behavior and thereby strongly influence the child's view of self. Shifts in the older child's and adolescent's reference groups are viewed as important, but less so than the young child's experience in shifting from the immediate family to the school and encountering greater diversity of people and *cultural values.* In the confrontation among different values, children are obliged to decide which ones they embrace as part of their own selves and which they reject or simply recognize as being part of other people's selves.

"Some kids cheat in games, but I never cheat even if it's important to win."
"If somebody tries to give me drugs or alcohol, I'll just say no."

"I don't believe in telling lies, but sometimes I'll tell a lie to keep from hurting somebody's feelings."

The final development process in Hattie's scheme concerns changes in how children verify or disconfirm their views of themselves. Whereas the infant depends primarily on reinforcement schedules (rewards and punishments for their acts), preschool and primary grade children use other sources of feedback regarding their appearance and behavior—how well they perform compared to others, vicarious experiences (seeing others perform), verbal persuasion (being convinced by others' lines of reasoning), and emotional arousal (how they feel about their appearance and actions).

Finally, Hattie implied that devising generalizations about self-concept formation that can validly be applied within or across age groups is a difficult task, since "there is no doubt that every person has a unique self-concept because every person has a different upbringing, has a different location in time and space, and has developed a different belief system from which to view the world" (Hattie, 1992, p. 98).

FOR FURTHER READING

Buhler, C., and M. Allen. (1972) *Introduction to Humanistic Psychology.* Pacific Grove, Calif.: Brooks/Cole.

Damon, W., and D. Hart. (1988) *Self-Understanding in Childhood and Adolescence.* New York: Cambridge University Press.

Hattie, J. (1992) *Self-Concept.* Hillsdale, N.J.: Erlbaum.

Mahrer, A. R. (1989) *Experiencing: A Humanistic Theory of Psychology and Psychiatry.* Ottawa: University of Ottawa Press.

Maslow, A. H. (1968) *Toward a Psychology of Being.* New York: Van Nostrand Reinhold.

Maslow, A. H. (1970) *Motivation and Personality,* 2d ed. New York: Harper & Row.

Speaking of Cause

*In theories of child development,
what is meant by cause?*

A prime purpose of all theories of human development is to account for why people grow up the way they do. In other words, theories represent speculation about what causes people to evolve from a single cell in the mother's womb into a newborn infant and subsequently into a child, an adolescent, and an adult who displays a configuration of features unique to that individual.

The purpose of the following perspective is to identify a variety of meanings that philosophers and scientists have assigned to the term *cause* and to suggest which of these meanings have been implied in the theories described in Chapters Three through Seventeen. The first part considers the usefulness of identifying causes and the second describes diverse meanings of cause.

THE USEFULNESS OF IDENTIFYING CAUSES

At the outset, it may be helpful to compare a commonsense view of cause with a contrasting view espoused in recent times in the physical sciences.

Common sense would agree with the proposal of the early American theologian Jonathan Edwards (1703–1758) that "nothing ever comes to pass without a cause" and with the contention of Dutch philosopher Baruch Spinoza (1632–1677) that "nothing exists from whose nature some effect does not follow" (D. Lerner, 1965, p. 2). In other words, events don't "just happen"—rather, one thing produces another. Parents' engaging in a sexual act causes a child to be born nine months later. A three-year-old's knocking a tea cup off the kitchen table onto the floor causes the cup to shatter. That is, common sense holds that life's reality is reflected in the phrase "all events have causes."

In contrast to this belief is the view expressed by such thinkers as Bertrand Russell (1872–1970), the English philosopher of science who observed early in this century that "the Law of Causality . . . is a relic of a bygone age, surviving like the [British] monarchy, only because it is erroneously supposed to do no harm" (D. Lerner, 1965, p. 5). In keeping with Russell's conviction,

> many influential scientists and philosophers have argued that the notion of cause plays a diminishing role in modern science, especially in the more advanced branches of it, such as mathematical physics, and that the notion is . . . a primitive, anthropomorphic interpretation of the various changes occurring in the world. It is

beyond serious doubt that the term "cause" rarely if ever appears in the research papers or treatises currently published in the natural sciences, and the odds are heavily against any mention in any book on theoretical physics. (Nagel, 1965, pp. 11–12)

What such scientists substitute for traditional cause-and-effect relationships is simply a statement of the probability that two or more conditions or events occur together. They speak of *functional relationships* between the two conditions, such as "whenever water is present and the air temperature at sea level is changed from 90 degrees above 0 Celsius to 105 degrees above 0, the water vaporizes 100 percent of the time." Or "in 50 percent of fatal auto accidents, alcohol was found in the blood of at least one of the drivers, so it is probable that in half of future accidents one or both drivers will have alcohol in their blood." In other words, these scientists claim that such probability statements suffice for predicting events without the need to speculate that one of the variables caused the change in the other variable, or that a third factor caused the changes in the original two. Although the reason the variables are correlated is unexplained, the fact that they interact in a consistent manner enables us to predict changes in one by knowing what changes are occurring in the other.

However, critics suggest that people who subscribe to this *noncausality* position are not settling the sticky question of cause; they are merely avoiding it (D. Lerner, 1965, p. 7). And observing physicists outside of the laboratory would imply that they conduct their daily lives on the conviction that there are such things as identifiable causes, so that events are not simply baffling correlations. Consequently, the physicist will turn the television set to a different channel when he fears that the sex and violence on the present channel may have a "bad influence" on his five-year-old daughter.

It appears to me that the noncausality trend in certain sectors of modern science might well be the result of theorists' puzzlement over (1) the multiplicity of ways causation can be interpreted, (2) the great complexity of the factors involved in cause, and (3) the difficulty—or perhaps impossibility—of identifying an *ultimate* or *final* cause. In any event, for purposes of the present perspective, I am assuming that there are such things as causes behind the way children develop and that the kinds of cause posited in one theory can differ from the kinds posited in another. In the practical world of child rearing, it is obviously useful to identify causes underlying development because then attempts can be made to manipulate causal factors to optimize favorable types of development and remedy those types deemed undesirable.

DEVELOPMENT THEORIES AND THEIR PERSPECTIVES ON CAUSATION

The following review of viewpoints of cause is organized under three topics: varieties of causal factors, the chronological location of cause, and nature's plan. Each topic is illustrated with examples from theories reviewed in this book.

Varieties of Causal Factors

Perhaps the most obvious differences in theorists' views of causality is in (1) the types of causal factors they posit, (2) the relative strengths of the different types, (3) the manner in which the types interact, and (4) the importance of various types at different times in a child's life.

Types of factors   A convenient way to think of types is in terms of principal causal factors and of the subfactors subsumed under them. For instance, the most commonly cited broad types of cause are *heredity* and *environment*. Under each of these, constituent subtypes can be listed. Under *heredity*, particular gene combinations might be postulated as responsible for different kinds of development: physical, cognitive, emotional, or the like. Then within each kind, more specific gene patterns might be proposed. Hence, within the cognitive domain, different sets of genes could be presumed to account for the development of such abilities as verbal reasoning, quantitative reasoning, spatial relations, musical talent, and others. In a similar fashion, *environment* might be dissected into causal components: home and family, school, peers, mass communication media, and more. These components might be decomposed into even more detailed subtypes, such as, within the home-and-family category, the influence of each parent and each sibling might be analyzed separately.

In summary, a significant way theories differ is in the patterning of general and specific causal factors proposed to account for children's development. For example, the version of commonsense attribution theory described in Chapter Four was divided into three general types of cause: characteristics of the self, characteristics of the environment, and such indeterminate influences as supernatural intervention and luck. And under each of these general categories, constituent subfactors were listed. In Havighurst's model, developmental tasks arise from three sources: the child's biological structure, the society's demands, and the personal values of the individual. Piaget proposed four general causal variables that contribute to the individual's survival: heredity, the child's physical experience, social transmission (people instructing the child), and equilibration. In Skinner's operant conditioning, a single type of causal factor—the nature of the consequences that follow the child's actions—is considered sufficient to explain development. In a similar way, each of the other theories offers its own propositions about general and specific sources of cause.

Strength of factors   A second way theorists differ is in the amount of influence they assume that each factor exerts on development. Gesell attributed far more power to genetic factors than to environmental influences. Piaget credited heredity with more influence than did Vygotsky. Skinner, social learning theorists, and ecologists assume that environmental factors are dominantly responsible for shaping children's growth.

Patterns of interaction   The manner in which causal factors relate to each other also varies from one theory to another. Piaget described a sequence of three steps by which causal elements play their roles. He contended that a genetic timing plan first establishes the sequence of neural development that equipped children to learn different cognitive skills. Next, children develop cognitive structures through their unguided encounters with the environment. Only after unguided experiences prepare the cognitive structures can instruction profitably take place.

The essence of information-processing theory lies in its system of interactions among the individual's sensori-cognitive-motor elements and selected aspects of the environment.

From a humanistic perspective, Maslow stated that *needs,* as causal forces, operate in a hierarchical fashion, with basic physical needs demanding fulfillment before self-realization needs could be pursued.

In Riegel's dialectical theory, the pattern of interaction that plays itself over and over during the process of development consists of this sequence: a presently existing condition of the child (thesis) encounters a contradictory life situation (antithesis) that stimulates the child to revise the existing condition in a way that resolves the contradiction (synthesis).

Factors related to phases of growth   Theorists often assume that the significance of a given factor differs from one period of development to another. In psychoanalytic theory, the influence of parents on the child's psychosexual development is more important during the early years of childhood (oral, anal, early genital periods) than during adolescence (mature genital period), when peer influence increases. In Erikson's system of psychosocial stages, parents play a more crucial role during the child's trust-mistrust and autonomy-doubt crises (from birth to age 3) than during the industry-inferiority crisis (ages seven to twelve) when school becomes an increasingly potent influence. Likewise, in the scheme of stages proposed by Vygotsky and Elkonin, the *leading activity* that becomes a key causal factor within a growth stage will differ from one stage to another. For instance, the leading activity for ages three to seven is game playing, whereas at ages fifteen to seventeen the activity is vocational learning.

To conclude, the foregoing examples suggest that one useful way to compare how different theories account for development is to analyze the theories in terms of (1) the general and specific types of causal factors proposed, (2) the presumed strength of each factor in affecting development, (3) the manner in which the factors are believed to interact, and (4) the relative importance of different factors at successive age levels.

The Chronological Location of Cause

An entirely different way to perceive causes is in terms of their chronological location—in the past, the present, or the future.

Looking to the past   Psychoanalytic theory, in its psychotherapeutic form, focuses on causes in the past, particularly on those distressing experiences in an individual's childhood that were repressed and, since that time, have seethed unresolved in the unconscious, precipitating physical or psychological disorders that now require the attention of a psychoanalyst. Therapy involves identifying events from the past responsible for present disorders so they can be relived vicariously in a way that places them in an acceptable, realistic perspective. A cause residing in the past is also the concern of developmental-task adherents when they contend that the reason children may be having difficulty with a task at their present stage of growth is that they failed to complete an earlier task.

When theorists conduct a retrospective search for cause, they are often assuming that causes are linked together in a cumulative chain of cause and effect relationships that recede endlessly into the past. This historical mode of reasoning has been called a *genetic* explanation, since it involves "the use of statements of initial conditions that require mention of sequentially ordered events occurring at different times" (Nagel, 1965, p. 17). How such a chain may be formed can be illustrated by the following line of reasoning:

> A six-year-old girl is judged to be shy because her father has so often criticized the child for not achieving up to the father's expectations. The father's high expectations, in turn, are the result of his growing up with eleven siblings in a family that was constantly in financial distress; and in order to work his way out of his family's poverty condition, he developed the habit of setting high standards of productivity for himself and of working hard to achieve them. Now that he is financially well to do and has children of his own, his lasting fear of poverty causes him to set high standards of performance for his offspring as well. The reason for the father's poverty-ridden childhood was that his own parents had been poorly educated peasants from Europe who had immigrated to the United States when their ancestral farmland had been inherited by their older siblings, so they had no source of income.

And in like manner we could continue to trace back over the centuries the linkages of cause and effect that we assume have contributed to the shyness of our present-day six-year-old. Each cause produces an effect, and that effect itself becomes a cause of a subsequent effect. However, to do a proper job of it, we would need to identify not just one cause behind each effect but, rather, to cite a network of causal factors that converged to produce each effect. By engaging in such a mode of reasoning, we have adopted a historical approach to explain development. This attempt to move progressively back into the past is what philosophers have labeled the *infinite regression*—there seems to be no beginning to the chain of cause and effect relationships. One solution to this problem has been to adopt a theological position and identify the *first cause* or *final cause* as God, Allah, the Cosmic Soul, the Great All-Knowing, or the like. Such a solution is offered by the familiar proposal of a final cause in the opening phrases of the Judeo/Christian/Islamic scriptures: "In the beginning, God created the heaven and the earth. . . . And God said, Let us make man in our image, after our likeness" (Genesis, verses 1, 26). Or, we could eschew a theological explanation and, instead, cite the secular scientists' first cause, the *big bang.* But this hardly settles the question of the *ultimate* cause, since we still need to account for what caused God or the big bang. Commonsense explanations often involve some version of genetic explanation, with people arriving at the ultimate cause rather quickly. After proposing one or two links to the past, they conclude that the cause was "God's will" or "nature's way."

A historical approach to causality is often used in accounting for the ostensible *national character* displayed by a particular social group, such as the Slovaks, Scots, Arabs, or Malays. Ways that members of the group are alike are seen as resulting from a common developmental history that can be estimated by tracing cause and effect forces in the group's past. And Darwinian theory represents a historical endeavor to explain the origin and characteristics of all species.

Looking at the present   Contextualists and ecological theorists, rather than looking at the past, stress present conditions as the causes of present behavior. Kurt Lewin, as a founding father of contextualist perspectives, proposed that an individual's thoughts and actions at any one time are the result of the entire configuration of forces within that person's current life space. The term *life space* refers to all internal (physiological, mental) and external (environmental) factors that affect the person consciously or unconsciously at the moment. These forces can include events of the past. However, it is not the past events themselves but, rather, the current residue in memory that influences present behavior (Lewin, 1942, p. 217). Hence it is not important to resurrect the past. Instead, we need to identify present environmental and internal conditions (including memories) that currently affect the person.

Looking to the future   Humanistic psychology illustrates a theoretical position that locates cause in the future. Humanists pay particular heed to how a person's ambitions, hopes, dreams, and expectations for the months and years ahead influence development. The notion that children are goal directed and actively pursue self-realization is used by humanistic theorists to help account for why the young develop as they do.

Although this discussion has separated the retrospective, the immediate present, and the prospective views of cause, it should be apparent that a given theory may reflect two or three of these perspectives. Psychoanalysts do not completely ignore the present, nor do humanists concentrate entirely on the future. Piaget and Vygotsky concerned themselves with both the past and the present. Nevertheless, even when theorists include more than one chronological location, they still differ in regard to which location they emphasize in explaining cause.

Nature's Plan

The phrase *nature's plan* identifies a belief that the pattern of children's development follows a predetermined program built into the species' gene structure. Growing up is simply the gradual unfolding of that plan. This belief is a form of teleological explanation—that development is a revelation of nature's purpose and design. As noted in Chapter Six, Erikson labeled this plan *the epigenetic principle.* Gesell and his colleagues have been strong advocates of a teleological position. And neo-Darwinism is the form of nature's plan in which sociobiologists and other varieties of ethologists (Chapter Fourteen) anchor their theories of development.

CONCLUSION

Statements about child development are of three major varieties: descriptive, prescriptive, and explanatory. Descriptive statements tell what children are like at any given time and how they change from one time to another. Description is based on observations, measurements, and children's introspective testimonials about what they think and how they feel. Prescriptive statements tell what children should be like and are based on the ideals or set of values held by the person offering the prescription. Explanatory statements are estimates about what causal factors account for the way children develop. The present perspective has focused on explanatory statements. I have suggested that the task of understanding the conception of cause represented in a particular theory can be profitably pursued by identifying (1) the types of general and detailed causal factors that the theorist delineates or implies, as well as the strength and interaction of these factors at different periods of children's development, and (2) the chronological emphasis implied in causal attributions—emphasis on the past, present, or future. Furthermore, identifying the assumptions that a theorist may make about "nature's plan" can also prove enlightening.

PART SEVEN

ENVIRONMENTS, GENETIC PLANS, AND THE BIOLOGICAL CHILD

A search for patterns of environmental influence and for biological sources of development

The first two varieties of theory described in Part Seven have been devised in recent times as correctives to what their creators have claimed are simplistic or distorted features of existing models. The third variety views the growing child as a biological organism whose composition can be analyzed through six descending levels of specificity, progressing from the top (the organism as a unified person) to the bottom (the organism as no more than an aggregation of quadrillions of subatomic particles).

The first of this trio of theories, ecological psychology (Chapter Thirteen), is intended to remedy *intra-individual stage theorists'* neglect of the complex ways environments influence children's development. People espousing ecological models accuse such theorists as Sigmund Freud and Jean Piaget (or at least Piaget's interpreters) of explaining "development either by reference to elementaristic traits or systemic mechanisms which are supposed to locate strictly inside the organism. . . . Very often psychologists who use this [framework] model their thinking along the lines of traditional genetics, positing the existence of psychological analogues of genes that are supposed to cause temporal unfolding of predetermined developmental sequences of phenomena" (Valsiner, 1987, p. 46). Thus ecological theorists, rather than looking chiefly inside the individual to answer the "why" of development, focus primary attention on the environments the child inhabits—or, perhaps more to the point, the individual's interactions with those environments (the individual-ecological frame of reference). Chapter Thirteen briefly reviews the evolution of ecological theory in the line following Kurt Lewin and Roger Barker, then provides a more detailed description of Urie Bronfenbrenner's (1979) ecological model.

The second general kind of theory in Part Seven is offered in Chapter Fourteen, "Ethology and Sociobiology." Ethologists, in contrast to ecologists, seek to remedy what they consider to be the neglect of human biological inheritance in explanations of why children develop as they do. In the opening paragraphs of his book *Human Ethology* (1989), Irenäus Eibl-Eibesfeldt reproached sociologists, psychology's behaviorists, and anthropology's cultural relativists for assigning no role to inherited biological tendencies in the development of human communication skills, social behavior, ethics, and aesthetics. In depicting the state of these three social science disciplines prior to the mid-twentieth century, Eibl-Eibesfeldt argued:

> The possibility that some aspects of behavior might, through phylogenetic adaptation, be genetically programmed was not even considered. . . . As late as the 1970s, the majority of behaviorists and sociologists viewed humans as primarily passive beings subject to the formative influences of their surroundings. . . . Parallel to the development of behaviorism in psychology there developed in anthropology a pronounced cultural relativism according to which culture is a construct on which the laws of biology have no influence. . . . The decisive impetus for revising this extreme environmental approach came from behavioral biology (ethology). . . . [In the 1930s and 1940s, the pioneers of ethology] Lorenz and Tinbergen demonstrated that phylogenetic adaptations determine behavior in well-defined ways. . . . By introducing the dimension of phylogeny into the science of behavior, their work incorporated Charles Darwin's findings. (1989, pp. ix–x)

Eibl-Eibesfeldt's reference to Darwin raises the issue of the relationship between phylogeny and ontogeny in child development. Phylogenetic theories are designed to answer the question, By what process has the human race—species *Homo sapiens*—developed in comparison to the process by which other species have developed? Ontogenetic theories, on the other hand, are intended to answer the question, By what process does an individual human being change from the moment of biological conception until the time of death?

The two most popular present-day phylogenetic theories are Darwin's and the biblical account to which fundamentalist Jews, Christians, and Muslims typically subscribe. The biblical version holds that God created the first humans, Adam and Eve, on a particular day several thousand years ago, completing these initial ancestors of the human race in a form that has remained essentially the same in all their descendants down to the present day. Darwin, in contrast, proposed that all living things trace their origins back to a common simple organism. Since that time millions of years in the past, certain descendants of the earliest organisms have become more complex and differentiated as a result of both genetic mutations and the extent to which the mutants' characteristics have equipped them to survive changes in environmental conditions. Ethologists are much concerned about the way such phylogenetic development has produced different species, and are particularly concerned about the ways genetic composition makes members of a given species alike. In other words, ethologists are especially interested in understanding children's *human nature*—what one child has in common with all other children. On the basis of this understanding, the ethologist is subsequently interested in knowing the way such a phylogenetically developed nature contributes to ontogeny—that is, contributes to the individual child's development through transactions with his or her daily surroundings.

In summary, both ecologists and ethologists are much interested in environments. However, the focus of their interest differs. Ecologists are most concerned with how the patterning of a child's daily environments influences that child's development. Ethologists, on the other hand, are more concerned with the way environments of the species' past (phylogenetic environments) have fashioned those inherited genetic structures that serve as templates for the propensities, potentials, and limitations that govern how children can behave and what they can learn from their present environments.

The third conception of development in Part Seven views the child as kind of living machine whose growth and behavior can be interpreted as interactions among electrochemical substances. Such an approach to development derives chiefly from the efforts of biochemists, geneticists, molecular biologists, physiological psychologists, and atomic physicists. They endeavor to explain all development phenomena, including children's emotions and patterns of thought, in terms of bio-electrochemical changes within the child and transactions the child carries out with the surrounding environment.

The perspective that closes Part Seven is entitled "Charting Trends of the Times." It is designed to answer the question of what major shifts have occurred over time in the popularity of the principal theories described in Chapters Three through Fifteen.

CHAPTER THIRTEEN

ECOLOGICAL PSYCHOLOGY

Urie Bronfenbrenner (born 1917) credits his own childhood environment with directing his attention to the crucial role children's social and physical settings play in fashioning their development.

> It was my good fortune to have been brought up on the premises of a state institution for those who were then called "the feebleminded," where my father was a neuropathologist. Along with his medical degree, he had a Ph.D. in zoology, and he was a field naturalist at heart. The institution's grounds offered a rich biological and social terrain for his observant eye. (Bronfenbrenner, 1979, p. xi)

From such a vantage point, young Bronfenbrenner learned how plants' and animals' surroundings affect their growth as well as how the social and physical environment of an institution can influence the development of its residents. Specifically, he noted that the social behavior, personalities, and tested intelligence of people held at the institution changed in relation to the social situations in which they were placed. This early introduction to the influence of environments on the developmental fate of living things had a strong effect on Bronfenbrenner's later career as a developmental psychologist at Cornell University. Much of his academic life there was dedicated to cross-cultural research in such diverse locations as Nova Scotia, the Soviet Union, China, Eastern and Western Europe, Israel, and the United States. As a result of his observations, he concluded:

> Seen in different contexts, human nature, which I had previously thought of as a singular noun, became plural and pluralistic; for the different environments were producing discernible differences, not only across but also within societies, in talent, temperament, human relations, and particularly in the ways in which the culture, or subculture, brought up its next generation. (1979, p. xiii)

He also recognized that the environments in which children live are so multifarious and intertwined that the task of understanding their effect on children is extremely demanding. To simplify and systematize this task, he devised the ecological theory of development whose principal features are described in this chapter. But before we concentrate on Bronfenbrenner's scheme, we may profit from recognizing some of the events in the realm of ecological psychology that preceded and paralleled his work.

BACKGROUNDS OF ECOLOGICAL PSYCHOLOGY

An important ancestor of ecological theory is Gestalt psychology, which evolved as a significant movement in Germany during the early decades of the twentieth century. Gestalt views became disseminated in America during the 1920s and the 1930s when such prominent figures as Kurt Koffka (1886–1941), Kurt Lewin (1890–1947), Heinz Werner (1890–1964), and Fritz Heider (1897–1988) immigrated to the United States to accept university posts. Gestalt theory, when applied to child development, conceives of the child as a whole, integrated organism. The word *Gestalt* in the German language means "configuration," thus reflecting the holistic viewpoint typical of European theorists in many scientific fields, in contrast to the British associationism from which behaviorism partially derived. *Associationism* represents a tradition that conceives of development as proceeding by small, additive increments that gradually accumulate to form the personality or to make up the child's repertoire of acts. But to the holistic or field theorist, a new stimulus or experience does not simply add a new element to a child's store of actions or knowledge, leaving the previous elements undisturbed. Instead, every significant new experience can alter the relationship of many or all of the existing elements that have made up the personality to this point, so the patterning of the child's entire individuality is influenced.

The holistic or field-theory concept of development is sometimes explained by the use of an example from astronomy. Assume that a new planet the size of Saturn is added to the solar system between Earth and Mars. This addition does not simply place a new speck of light in the sky of Earthlings and Martians. Rather, its gravitational pull influences the paths of all the planets in the solar system, having more effect on the closer bodies than on the distant ones. So with the entire pattern of the solar framework altered, the system itself becomes something new. In psychology, holistic or Gestalt theorists propose that a similar effect occurs in the development of a child's personality each time the child encounters impressive new experiences or each time an internal physiological change is triggered by the individual's genetic structure.

What is now known as *ecological* or *environmental* psychology owes part of its evolutionary background to the work of Lewin and his colleagues during the 1930s and 1940s, principally at the University of Iowa. Lewin labeled his Gestalt perspective *topological psychology,* a term adopted from the field of mathematics, where *topology* is a type of geometry that gives attention to the relationships among spaces, especially to the distance between one space and another and to the barriers between the two. He coined the term *life space* to encompass all of the facts that influence a child's behavior at a given time. As mentioned earlier, in this system a *fact* is not an objectively verifiable observation from the "real world." Instead, a fact is any element within the child's psychological environment that affects that individual's behavior or thought; this includes forces of which the child is unaware as well as elements the child accepts as real or true.

In 1947, the year Lewin died, two of his coworkers, Roger W. Barker and H. F. Wright, accepted academic appointments at the University of Kansas, where they gave topological psychology a particularly strong environmental bent by concentrating on the role of environmental forces in a child's life space (Barker, 1978). They noted that in biology the term *ecology* refers to the interrelationship between a plant or animal and its environment, so they borrowed the term to describe their way of studying how children's surroundings affect behavior and development.

Barker (1968) noted that traditional psychology showed ways in which people differed from one another but failed to trace the great variations in thought, feeling, and action that an individual child experiences during a typical day. Furthermore, according to Barker, a large proportion of the variation within a single child's life can be accounted for by the environments or *behavior settings* through which that child commonly moves. In effect, ecological theorists contend that we can account for a great deal of a child's behavior if we know the child's current environment. For example, we can predict that if a typical teenager is in church, she will not be shouting, but if she is at a basketball game she will shout loud and long. If she is walking to the drugstore, we can predict that she will not be walking in line, but if she is marching in the school band during the Fourth of July parade, she will be carefully keeping in line and in step with her companions.

To move ecological theory beyond these commonsense observations, Barker and his colleagues identified a variety of components of behavior settings so that the nature of a child's significant surroundings could be analyzed more systematically. For instance, they proposed that a behavior setting (such as a history class or a dinner party) comprises two main elements: (1) the typical ways people act (called *standing patterns of behavior*) and (2) the *milieu,* which is made up of two components. The first component is *physical things:* desks and wall maps in history class, the dining table and silverware at the dinner party. The second is *time boundaries:* a forty-five-minute class period, a two-hour dinner party. The milieu is said to be circumjacent to (that is, it encompasses) the behavior of the people in the setting. Such terms were created to help ecological analysts organize their observations of the environments in which children grow up. One of the Kansas group's most detailed investigations focused on the effect school size exerts on students' development (Barker & Gump, 1964; Barker et al., 1970). The group accurately predicted that students of smaller high schools engage in a wider variety of activities, assume more responsibility, hold more extracurricular positions of importance, and are more highly motivated to take active part in voluntary activities than is the case with students in larger schools (Ross, 1985).

One important branch of environmental psychology focuses on issues of particular concern to community planners, architects, and social service agencies. The issues relate to questions of how human behavior is affected by urban crowding, inner-city decay, suburban growth, sparsely settled rural regions, resource availability, institutional size, and the like. Attempts to understand the influence of physical settings on people's lives have spawned a variety of theories. For instance, an *information-overload* model holds that people have a limited capacity to process information, so when excessive stimulation from the environment occurs, they ignore peripheral inputs in order to give adequate attention to primary tasks. "The result is that responses to these peripheral nonsocial or social stimuli are minimal or nonexistent" (J. D. Fisher, Bell, & Baum, 1984, p. 83). An *understimulation* theory proposes that monotonous environmental stimulation causes boredom and less reason for people to take action. A *behavior-constraint* model suggests that when children feel they have lost control over their environment, they behave in ways they think will recover their control and freedom of action.

Among investigators toiling in this domain are developmentalists seeking to discover valid generalizations about the interactions of specific types of physical settings on child growth and adjustment. J. F. Wohlwill and W. van Vliet's book, *Habitats for Children* (1985), illustrates this type of inquiry. For instance, van Vliet derived the following generalizations from reviewing studies of the role of housing type, household density, and neighborhood density on children's peer interactions and social adjustment:

> Neighborhood density may be conceptualized as a factor contributing to the field of opportunities for interactions with peers. Such interactions may be either socially desirable or deviant. Except possibly for situations of extreme crowding or isolation, the acceptability of children's social relations does not appear to be related to the conditions of neighborhood density under which they come about. . . . Research findings do not demonstrate convincingly that high neighborhood densities contribute to maladjusted behavior. . . . Some studies suggest that, in suburbs, children's interactions with peers are less frequent and less spontaneous and fewer times revolve around common interests than is the case in city environments. In these investigations neighborhood density has not been singled out for study as a variable which may, in part, be responsible for these differences. (van Vliet, 1985, p. 194)

Developmentalists have proposed a variety of approaches to understanding environmental influences in children's lives. One of the most systematic of these schemes is the one created by Bronfenbrenner, which we will now inspect in some detail.

BRONFENBRENNER'S ECOLOGICAL THEORY

In a heavily laden definition, Bronfenbrenner portrayed the ecology of human development as

> the scientific study of the progressive, mutual accommodation, throughout the life course, between an active, growing, highly complex biopsychological organism— characterized by a distinctive complex of evolving interrelated, dynamic capacities for thought, feeling and action—and the changing properties of the immediate settings in which the developing person lives, as this process is affected by the relations between these settings, and by the larger contexts in which the settings are embedded. (1993, p. 7)

In Figures 13.1 and 13.2, I have sought to diagram the relationship that Bronfenbrenner posited among the principal components of his definition.

The model's most basic unit of analysis is the *microsystem*—"a pattern of activities, roles, and interpersonal relations experienced by the developing person in a given setting with particular physical and material characteristics" (Bronfenbrenner, 1979, p. 22). Figure 13.1 pictures three typical settings for such microsys-

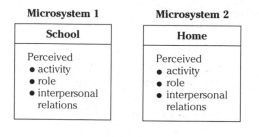

FIGURE 13.1
Children's microsystems of experience

tems: school, home, and peer group locations. (Barker would label these locations *behavior settings* [1968; Schoggen, 1989].) A crucial conviction in Bronfenbrenner's scheme is that the influence of a behavior setting on a child's development is not exerted by the "objective" or "real-life" nature of the activities, roles, and interpersonal relations seen there. Rather, the influence derives from the child's perception or interpretation of these factors. Bronfenbrenner agrees with Lewin's early proposal that (1) the phenomenological (internally interpreted or experienced) environment dominates the real environment in guiding behavior; (2) it is folly to try to understand a child's action solely from the objective qualities of an environment without learning what those qualities mean for the child in that setting; (3) it is important to discover how the objects, people, and events in the situation affect the child's motivations; and (4) it is essential to recognize the influence on behavior of "unreal" elements that arise from the child's imagination, fantasy, and idiosyncratic interpretations (Bronfenbrenner, 1979, pp. 24–25).

An analyst is best equipped to comprehend a child's behavior by learning how the child perceives the activities, roles, and interpersonal relations displayed in that setting. The term *activities* refers to what people are doing. *Roles* are the actions expected of people holding a position in society, such as the position of parent, infant, sibling, teacher, friend, coach, or the like. *Interpersonal relations* are the ways people treat one another, as shown by what they say and do as a result of their being together. Bronfenbrenner adopted the term *microsystems* to reflect his conviction that behavior settings provide the smallest unit of analysis (micro) and that the three most significant components of a setting (activities, roles, and interpersonal relations) form a Gestalt or interacting behavior field (system) in which a change in one component could affect the entire configuration and produce a new

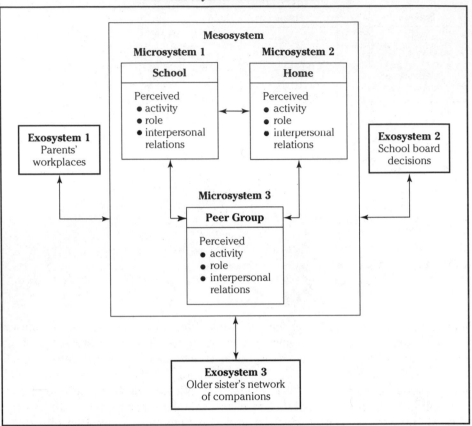

FIGURE 13.2
Embedded systems of children's environmental experiences

meaning for the child. An obvious methodological problem faced in the analysis of a microsystem arises from the fact that the components are often in flux, as determined by shifts in the ongoing activities and by readjustments occurring in the participants' roles and relations. An analyst of the microsystem is thus obliged to aim at a moving target.

In a recent explication of the microsystem level of analysis, Bronfenbrenner (1993) proposed two broad kinds of processes that promote development: (1) children's interactions with people, and (2) activities in which children engage. The nature of these relationships is influenced by four attributes children bring to their encounters with people and activities. First is the set of a child's personal characteristics that either invite or discourage the sorts of responses from the environment that will disrupt or, in contrast, promote that child's psychological growth. For example, a very pretty girl often elicits a different reaction from other people than does a very plain girl. A diffident boy may draw a different response from classmates than an outspoken one does.

The second attribute is a child's interest in, and exploration of, certain aspects of the physical and social environment, in preference to other aspects. Bronfenbrenner labeled this trait *selective responsivity*. One child is inclined to engage in active sports, while another favors video games. Other children favor reading, acting out make-believe dramas, or collecting pictures of movie personalities or baseball stars.

A third influence on development is the degree to which children are disposed to pursue increasingly complex activities—that is, to restructure their environment in more elaborate ways. A four-year-old girl, not content with merely holding a new doll, creates a spontaneous drama in which she is a mother introducing her child to the group of stuffed animals that inhabit the playroom. A twelve-year-old boy suggests to several friends that they form a club and build a tree house where club members can meet. Bronfenbrenner called this tendency of children to reorganize their environment a *structuring proclivity*.

Fourth is children's propensity as they grow older to conceptually organize their experiences, to devise increasingly elaborate plans and ways to carry their plans to fruition. Bronfenbrenner identified these conceptualizations as *"directive belief systems about the relation of the self to the environment,* or, for short, *directive beliefs"* (1993, p. 13).

Bronfenbrenner called these four attributes *personal stimulus characteristics*, since the way a particular child displays the four can affect what activities the child pursues and how people will treat the child.

> I propose that the attributes of the person most likely to shape the course of development, for better or for worse, are those that induce or inhibit dynamic dispositions toward the immediate environment. For great want of a better term, I refer to such qualities as *developmentally instigative characteristics*. (Bronfenbrenner, 1993, p. 11)

But it's not only the child's personal characteristics that instigate development. The environment also initiates transactions with the child that either promote or thwart development. In effect, how the child grows up is also strongly affected by what is said or done to the child—or in the child's presence—by parents, siblings, other relatives, peers, teachers, coaches, club leaders, and the like. Influences on development can also be instigated by such physical conditions of the environment as the size and furnishings of the child's dwelling, the child's diet, the quality of the air, the surrounding noise, threats of danger, and far more.

As Bronfenbrenner over the years has continued to elaborate his theory, he has rendered the definitions of key terms more complex in order to accommodate his recent embellishments to the scheme. Consider, for instance, his definition of *microsystem*. The portion in roman type is his earlier version (1979); the portion in *italics* is an addendum (1993) that reflects the developmentally instigative characteristics described above.

> A *microsystem* is a pattern of activities, roles, and interpersonal relations experienced by the developing person in a given face-to-face setting with particular physical, *social, and symbolic features that invite, permit, or inhibit, engagement in sustained, progressively more complex interaction with, and activity in, the immediate environment.* (1993, p. 15)

As the theory has grown more complex, so also have the demands it places on the ingenuity of researchers who choose to found their investigations on the author's *process-person-context* model. Studying a child at the microsystem level calls for gathering information about the multiple *instigative characteristics* of both the child and the environment. But it's not enough just to study these characteristics at a given point in time. Instead, they must be studied over a sufficient period to reveal the ongoing process of the child's development and not simply the child's status at a single juncture of growth. Bronfenbrenner recognizes that having to provide such investigative techniques is a very tall order, since few if any of the research methods of the past would seem to suffice unless combined in novel ways that are as yet only vaguely recognized. What's more, the researcher's challenge does not end with the microsystem. The endeavor becomes even more daunting when three other dimensions of the model are added: mesosystem, exosystem, and macrosystem.

The *mesosystem,* the first phase beyond the child's single immediate behavior setting, is symbolized within the second largest box in Figure 13.2. In the following definition, the segment in roman type is an earlier version (1979); the portion in *italics* is a later elaboration (1993).

> A *mesosystem* comprises the linkages and processes taking place between two or more settings containing the developing person. *Special attention is focused on the synergistic effects created by the interaction of developmentally instigative or inhibitory features and processes present in each setting.* (1993, p. 22)

As the double-pointed arrows suggest, the pattern of interrelationships among microsystems can influence the child's perceptions and behavior within any of the settings in which the child is presently located. For instance, children's experience in the classroom on any given day is typically affected by their impressions of the attitudes of their parents and their peers.

Bronfenbrenner applied the label *exosystem* to the next phase outside the mesosystem.

> The *exosystem* comprises the linkages and processes taking place between two or more settings, at least one of which does not contain the developing person, but in which events occur that indirectly influence processes within the immediate setting in which the developing person lives. (1993, p. 22)

The three illustrative exosystems in Figure 13.2 are the workplaces of the child's parents, school board decisions that affect the child, and an older sister's network of companions. If the parents' workplaces are nearby rather than hundreds of miles distant, then parents will have more time to spend with the child. If the child is a slow learner and the school board decides to "mainstream" slow learners into regular classes rather than providing such pupils with special instructional help, then the child's progress in school can be affected. In addition, the child's development can be somewhat different if an older sister's companions engage in activities that draw her away from home much of the time so she rarely is available to baby-sit her younger sibling.

Finally, the source of influence most remote from the children's immediate experience is the array of attitudes, practices, and convictions shared throughout society at large. This *macrosystem* is composed of the *cultural milieu,* which is represented in Figure 13.2 by the large box encompassing the microsystems, mesosystem, and exosystems of the child's environment.

A question may now be asked about what implications this model holds for researchers and others (parents, teachers, social workers, club leaders) who try to understand children's development. First, the model suggests which aspects of the child's environment should be the principal foci of data gathering. These aspects include

1. *the behavior setting* of the child's immediate microsystem (e.g., the school playground during recess)
2. *the activities, roles, and interpersonal relations* of the primary participants in that setting (e.g., the playground supervisor and the boys and girls on two competing soccer teams)
3. *the mesosystem*—the influences of other microsystems on the child's perceptions in this setting (e.g., the child's recollection of recent soccer games and what parents might say if the child performs well or poorly in this game)
4. *the exosystems* (e.g., the school's "sports committee" that established the rules for such games, and the length of the recess period as determined by the school's time schedule)
5. *the cultural milieu* (e.g., the expectations widely held in the society about such matters as abiding by the rules, being "a good winner and a good loser," placing the team's welfare above one's own welfare, and obeying people in authority)

Second, the model's use of the term *systems* implies that an analyst not only should gather evidence about the foregoing five components, but also about the transactions among them. The analysis of transactions can profitably involve decisions about (1) which elements apparently have influenced which others, (2) the nature of this influence (what did A cause B to do), (3) to what extent was the influence reciprocal (did B also alter A's performance or characteristics), and (4) which of the elements appeared to exert the most powerful effects (was element C's influence great but D's negligible).

It is obviously impossible to chart moment-to-moment alterations in the model's complex of components and their interactions. Thus, to render the task of analysis feasible, it is necessary for an investigator to select occasions for taking ecological "snapshots" or for making summaries of ecological events. These occasions should be chosen for their likely significant effect on the child's long-term abilities and attitudes. To aid with this decision about when a new snapshot is warranted, Bronfenbrenner has suggested the notion of *ecological transition,* meaning a shift that occurs whenever the child's position in the ecological environment is significantly altered due to a change in role, setting, or both. We might infer that there can be major and minor transitions. Major ones include the newborn's coming home from the hospital, the child's learning to walk and talk around age eighteen months, entering nursery school at age three, starting the primary grades at age six, going to summer camp, moving with the family to a new city, and witnessing the parents' divorce (Bronfenbrenner, 1979, pp. 26–27). Minor transitions can involve less dramatic changes that, nevertheless, leave some residue of attitudes or skills that contribute to long-term development. A minor transition might occur with a girl's membership in a high school choir, with a nine-year-old's having a grandmother live in the home for six months, and with a teenager's developing acne. The task of the researcher becomes one of charting the child's ecology before and after the transition point and noting both (1) the factors that apparently have precipitated the transition and (2) the effects the transition produced on the child.

> I shall argue that every ecological transition is both a consequence and an instigator of developmental processes. . . . [Thus] from the viewpoint of research, every ecological transition constitutes, in effect, a ready-made experiment of nature with a built-in, before-after design in which each subject can serve as his own control. In sum, an ecological transition sets the stage both for the occurrence and the systematic study of developmental phenomena. (Bronfenbrenner, 1979, p. 17)

A critical feature of research methodology in Bronfenbrenner's scheme is what he calls *ecological validity,* meaning "the extent to which the environment experienced by the subjects in a scientific investigation has the properties it is supposed or assumed to have by the investigator" (Bronfenbrenner, 1979, p. 29). His emphasis on ecological validity derives from a concern that too often research on children is conducted in laboratories or other unique settings, and then broadly inclusive generalizations are drawn about development without regard for how children's interpretations—their phenomenological perceptions—are affected by the different configurations of different environments. Several lessons about research methods are suggested by this notion of ecological validity. First, reports of research should describe the study's influential environmental variables, and investigators should limit their conclusions to ones applicable to children who experience life within similar ecological domains. Second, the focus of analysis should be the children's perceptions of the environment rather than the environment's "objective" characteristics. Thus the research methods need to be ones that reveal children's phenomenological interpretations, instead of ones that merely identify observable characteristics of the setting. But the task of accurately eliciting children's perceptions is far more difficult than that of simply describing the setting. Such a job can most adequately be performed by investigators who themselves are intimately acquainted with the culture and thus able to discern the nuances of language and the undercurrent of attitudes embedded in children's responses. Derek Freeman (1983), in his caustic criticism of Margaret Mead's *Coming of Age in Samoa* (1968), faulted her for drawing erroneous conclusions about Samoan adolescent girls' development because of Mead's failure to comprehend the Samoan cultural milieu and her approaching the research task with the aim of "proving" a hypothesis rather than of understanding the significance of Samoan adolescents' remarks from the perspective of the Samoan macrosystem. Bronfenbrenner and his coworkers have admitted that existing research techniques are still inadequate for achieving the desired ecological validity. He sees the task of creating such techniques as an item developmentalists need to include on their future agenda.

An additional consideration in Bronfenbrenner's scheme is the concept of *developmental validity*. In order for an observed change in a child's perceptions or activities in one setting to qualify as developmentally valid, that change must be shown to carry over to other behavior settings and other times. In effect, changes that are unique to a given time and place and fail to appear in other ecological settings are not credited as developmental, since they fail to exert a lasting effect on the child's attitudes or skills.

In addition to identifying the components of his theory, Bronfenbrenner spelled out in considerable detail the way research can be conducted from the perspective of the model. In his analysis, he described studies that can be conducted in either laboratory situations or such natural settings as children's institutions (foundling homes, children's hospitals), child-care centers, and nursery schools. However, "well-designed ecological experiments are, as yet, not easy to find. I have therefore had to invent some examples where they did not exist. Moreover, in many instances there was a dearth not only of relevant research but also of relevant research ideas. Accordingly, [this discussion offers] . . . even more proposed hypotheses than proposed investigations" (Bronfenbrenner, 1979, p. 42). In short, the theory's potential for generating widespread, fruitful research still remains to be demonstrated.

PRACTICAL APPLICATIONS

Ecological theory appears to hold considerable promise for guiding child rearing, educational practices, social work, and child therapy as soon as more adequate appraisal techniques are created and an expanding range of empirical investigations produce a growing fund of convincing generalizations about relationships within the theory's four levels of systems (micro, meso, exo, and macro).

The focus of Bronfenbrenner's theory is on children's interpretations of their surroundings rather than on the objective characteristics of those surroundings. Thus practical applications must involve methods of effecting contructive changes in children's perceptions of their environments. Such perceptions could be improved by one or more of the following methods: (1) changing the damaging components of an environment (a microsystem), (2) transporting children out of unsuitable environments and into favorable ones, (3) assigning to other microsystems the child-raising responsibilities that are not being performed adequately in a current microsystem (changing the mesosystem), or (4) altering children's perceptions of those environments that they must continue to inhabit. To illustrate, consider the situation of a boy whose development is deemed to suffer from his living with neglectful parents. The neglect takes the form of the parents' failing to teach the boy appropriate social behavior, failing to offer him affection and emotional support, and blaming him for being an unsatisfactory son. Such neglect is judged to contribute to the boy's unsuitable behavior in microsystems outside the home (the school, the Scout troop, the neighborhood peer group) where he is rude to peers and adults, resists assuming responsibility, and seeks attention by bragging and criticizing others. Attempts to alter these characteristics could include

(1) changing the parents' child-rearing practices through counseling, (2) placing the boy in a boarding school, (3) having school personnel and the Scout leader teach proper social behavior and furnish emotional support, and (4) counseling with the boy to alter his perception of his home life, thereby equipping him to accept his parents for what they are, to stop blaming himself for the way his parents treat him, and to adopt people outside the family as models to emulate.

In summary, the ability of Bronfenbrenner's type of theory to produce practical applications depends on the success with which ecological investigative techniques reveal where within the four levels of systems (micro, meso, exo, macro) counterproductive components are operating. Then steps can be taken to change those components in ways that constructively alter the child's perception of environments in relation to self.

ECOLOGICAL THEORY: AN ASSESSMENT

In rating Bronfenbrenner's model, I have qualified my judgments on several of the nine standards with the symbol *P,* signifying *potential.* This is because the details required for translating the theory into practice do not appear well worked out as yet. I do find Bronfenbrenner's basic argument convincing (though hardly novel)— that the environmental forces he identifies significantly influence children's development. I believe he is correct in both (1) alerting us not to neglect these forces and (2) proposing a heuristic scheme for categorizing the multitudinous forces into four interlocking systems. What is now needed is a set of more precise guidelines than the author has so far provided to render the model operational (item 2, clarity). As a way of illustrating only three of the numerous aspects of the theory that call for more detail, imagine that we wish to study a thirteen-year-old girl's development from the perspective of the ecological model. Then we face such questions as the following:

1. *Discriminating among microsystems:* How do we decide where one microsystem leaves off and another begins in the following episode: the girl walks to school with companions, is joined by additional companions, accompanies them into a video store for a few minutes, then continues with the group to school where she chats with a teacher before entering class? Perhaps more important, how can we determine if this series of incidents exerts a significant enough effect on the girl's development to warrant our bothering to seek her interpretation of the events?

2. *Identifying roles:* If we define a microsystem by its physical setting during a period of time (Tuesday's seventh-grade forty-five minute math class), which roles should we identify for people in that setting when some of the people may be evincing more than one role or may shift from one role to another? For instance, our thirteen-year-old assumes the role of learner as the teacher explains a new math function, the role of monitor when she passes out rulers and compasses to her classmates, the role of tutor when she helps a boy with a difficult problem, and that of student representative when she requests on behalf of the others that the teacher not assign homework the night of the championship basketball game. Should each

BRONFENBRENNER'S THEORY

How well do I think the theory meet the standards?

Standards	Very well	Moderately well	Very poorly
1. Reflects the real world of children	P*	X‡	
2. Is clearly understandable	P	X	
3. Explains the past and predicts the future	P	X	
4. Guides child rearing	P	X	
5. Is internally consistent	X		
6. Is economical	X		
7. Is falsifiable	P		X
8. Is supported by convincing evidence	P	X	
9. Adapts to new data		?	
10. Is novel		X	
11. Is comprehensive	X		
12. Stimulates new discoveries	P	X	
13. Is durable		?	
14. Is self-satisfying		X	

*P = potential status   ‡ X = present, actual status

of these roles be identified in our study? If not, what criteria should we use for choosing those roles that are to be depicted?

3. *Assessing the strength of system components:* Implicit in the theory is the assumption that some elements of the model will exert greater influence on the child's perceptions and behavior than will others. Although Bronfenbrenner has proposed some general principles for judging the relative power of elements or subsystems, the way one would make this judgment in a specific case is still unclear. In the case of our thirteen-year-old girl, how do we estimate the degree to which such exosystems as the girl's parents, her television viewing habits, or her study of "the democratic process" in history class has caused her to represent the group in requesting that homework not be assigned?

My intention in citing these ambiguous and clouded features of ecological theory is not to suggest that the model lacks potential value. Rather, my purpose is simply to explain why I have employed two symbols, X and P, in rating the theory. I have used X to indicate what I judge to be the theory's present status on the fourteen assessment standards and then have placed a P on several of the scales to suggest the potential the theory might hold if the current imprecision of its key features can be rectified. Bronfenbrenner himself has been frank in recognizing that his model is still in an early formative stage, particularly in regard to the details of devising suitable investigative techniques and applications to child rearing and education. Thus, because his version of ecological psychology is so new in the developmental marketplace, there is as yet a paucity of empirical examples to illustrate its applications or to test its hypotheses. Even the number of hypotheses that might be tested is as of yet quite small. Therefore, compared with such theories as Freud's, Piaget's, Vygotsky's, Skinner's, and Bandura's, his ecological model is still very much a baby, so its contributions to developmental psychology—whatever they may be—lie necessarily in the future.

In terms of the theory's present, actual status, I have given the highest ratings for its internal consistency and economy (items 5 and 6). The model's components do not appear to conflict with one another, nor do they seem unduly elaborate as a means of accounting for the phenomena they are intended to explain.

I have given the lowest rating to item 7 because the theory presently is at such a high level of abstraction. Only when specific hypotheses are spelled out for particular aspects of the model can empirical tests be applied to confirm or disconfirm those aspects. I have also rated the theory low for its value in explaining the past and predicting the future (item 3) because of the problems of imprecision illustrated in my example of the thirteen-year-old girl. If past development is to be convincingly explained and future development predicted, there need to be precise ways of (1) identifying the strengths of significant components in each system (micro, meso, exo, macro), and (2) plotting the interactions among components and systems. Such precision is apparently not yet available for Bronfenbrenner's scheme. And the adequacy of the theory for guiding child rearing (item 4) is governed by its ability to explain and predict.

My rating of item 12 (stimulates new discoveries) between "moderate" and "poor" recognizes (1) on the plus side, the new insights Bronfenbrenner arrived at in the process of creating his scheme, and (2) on the minus side, the fact that the theory is still in its infancy, not widely adopted by other researchers for empirical investigation nor yet subjected to extensive critiques that might lead to additional novel insights by means of comparisons with existing data and models.

I have estimated that the model is moderately good in terms of clarity (item 2). While I find the basic structure of the model easy to understand, I am left puzzled about a variety of the theory's more specific aspects, as suggested in the illustration of the thirteen-year-old. As for reflecting the real world of children (item 1), my own experience suggests that the environmental factors featured in the model all seem to be significant forces in fashioning children's development. But once again, the lack of sufficient detail and precision in explaining how the components interrelate to produce the development that a particular child exhibits causes me to rank the theory as being only moderately realistic.

I rated the theory's comprehensiveness (item 11) between "very well" and "moderately well." The scheme's strength is found in its attention to environmental influences on physical, cognitive, social, and emotional development. However, I believe the theory pays too little heed to the role played by the child's genetic endowment.

In regard to the evidence supporting the theory (item 8), I have rated the scheme high on potential but rather low in terms of its current status. As already noted, the theory is still quite new so it has not yet served as the model on which a substantial amount of empirical research has been based. Most of the support that the proposal enjoys comes from the logic of the argument its author adduces. For instance, the notion of the four *systems* of a child's environment makes sense to me, as do the *instigative characteristics* of the child and the environment. Some researchers, such as C. Wright (1988) in her survey of home-school studies, have used Bronfenbrenner's scheme as a framework within which to review empirical research. However, few studies have been designed precisely to test or explicate hypotheses deriving from the model. Thus, most empirical research founded on the theory is still in the offing.

The rather low rating on novelty (item 10) is not intended to discount the contributions Bronfenbrenner's proposal makes to the field. Rather, the rating simply recognizes that there is nothing really new in the basic notion underlying his model—that children's development is significantly affected by the environments they inhabit. Bronfenbrenner's theory is just one among numerous variations of contextualism. Nevertheless, parts of his conception do qualify as innovations, so I have recognized these creations by rating the theory "moderately well."

I declined to appraise the theory's adaptability (item 9) and durability (item 13) on the grounds that it is of such recent vintage that there is little evidence of how well it responds to criticism and new data, or of how long it is likely to last.

Finally, as the locations of the *P* ratings on the chart suggest, if the issues of precision can be resolved, I think Bronfenbrenner's scheme might serve as a valuable instrument for explaining and predicting the role of environments in children's development. In view of the theory's present state and likely potential, I find it moderately satisfying (item 14).

FOR FURTHER READING

Barker, R. (ed.). (1978) *Habitats, Environments, and Human Behavior.* San Francisco: Jossey-Bass. Descriptions of nineteen studies conducted by Barker and his associates between 1947 and 1972 at the Midwest Psychological Field Station, University of Kansas.

Bronfenbrenner, U. (1979) *The Ecology of Human Development.* Cambridge: Mass.: Harvard University Press. An elucidation of Bronfenbrenner's four-level environmental systems model, with examples of its application, especially in early childhood.

Bronfenbrenner, U. (1993) "The Ecology of Cognitive Development: Research Models and Fugitive Findings," in R. H. Wozniak and K. W. Fischer (eds.), *Development in Context: Acting and Thinking in Specific Environments.* Hillsdale, N.J.: Erlbaum. An updated version of Bronfenbrenner's process-person-context model.

Schoggen, P. (1989) *Behavior Settings.* Stanford, Calif.: Stanford University Press. A revised, extended version of Roger Barker's 1968 volume, *Ecological Psychology.*

CHAPTER FOURTEEN

ETHOLOGY
AND SOCIOBIOLOGY

Ethology, in its most general sense, is the study of the behavior of animals (including humans), especially as that behavior occurs in natural environments. *Sociobiology,* as a subcategory of ethology, is the study of the biological bases of the ways members of a species act toward one another and toward members of other species.

Although ethology traces its historical roots back to Charles Darwin (1809–1882) and other naturalists of the nineteenth century, its modern version is of rather recent origin, beginning with the animal studies of two Europeans shortly before World War II. The two—Austrian Konrad Z. Lorenz (1903–1989) and Dutch Nikolaas Tinbergen (born 1907)—were awarded the Nobel Prize in physiology in 1973, the year that Lorenz assumed the directorship of the Department for Animal Sociology in the Austrian Academy of Science. Tinbergen spent most of his professorial life at Oxford University in England. Lorenz (1977) is perhaps best known for describing the phenomenon of *imprinting,* which is the propensity of a newborn animal to attach itself emotionally to the first being it encounters as a nurturing guardian, such as the mother. This imprinting attachment was demonstrated by Lorenz when goslings followed him as their nurturing guardian. Tinbergen (1973) is recognized for directing his work toward answering four questions he considered essential for a proper understanding of behavior (Hinde, 1983, p. 28): What causes this behavior? How did it develop? What is its biological function? How did it evolve?

From the 1930s well into the 1960s, ethologists were chiefly zoologists whose work centered almost exclusively on nonhuman species. However, by the latter 1960s, increased communication between ethologists and psychologists led to the application of ethological concepts and research methods to humans, particularly to children. A leader in this effort was John Bowlby, a London psychoanalyst who studied the emotional bonding of a newborn child to a nurturing adult (1969, 1980). Throughout the 1970s and 1980s, the adoption of ethological approaches for understanding child development grew at an accelerating pace, and even greater advances are expected in the 1990s.

It is not proper to speak of ethology as a *theory* or to think of ethologists as all subscribing to a unified conceptual system from which particular hypotheses are derived. Rather, ethology is more accurately defined as a set of "orienting attitudes" shared by those who engage in comparative animal studies. Such attitudes derive in large part from Darwin's theory of evolution and from the research techniques on which this theory was founded. R. A. Hinde (1983, p. 29) noted that the early ethologists, in keeping with Darwin's model and investigative techniques, were convinced

> that the description and classification of behaviour is a necessary preliminary to its analysis; that the behaviour of an animal cannot be properly studied without some knowledge of the environment to which its species has become adapted in evolution; and that questions about the evolution and biological function of behaviour are, in principle, as valid and important as those about its immediate causation (and, it may be added, development).

It is thus impossible to understand ethologists' viewpoint unless we first recognize assumptions they hold in common. So in the following discussion I will review in an elementary fashion a number of those beliefs, asking your forebearance if the review is unduly reminiscent of a class in high school biology.

A FOUNDATION OF NEO-DARWINISM

At the outset it is important to establish the definitions of two terms: *species* and *population*. A *species* is a collection of individual organisms capable of interbreeding under natural conditions. The phrase *natural conditions* is an essential part of this definition for it requires that we establish separate species categories for two organisms that can be induced to mate under experimental conditions but that do not interbreed in a natural setting. Hence lions and tigers form two separate species, even though they can be successfully interbred in captivity (Wilson, 1975, pp. 8–9).

A *population* is a set of organisms of the same species occupying a clearly delimited geographical area at the same time. Thus a single hill of ants is not an entire population—a population in this case is all the colonies of ants of the same species in that particular area. Or a population can comprise all the indigenous people living in a cluster of interlinked islands of the South Seas.

With these definitions of species and populations in mind, let's turn to five propositions that our theorists appear to subscribe to as underlying assumptions.

1. *Species reproduction:* For humans, as well as for all other species that require two parents as the source of reproduction, a new member of the species is conceived when a sperm cell from the male combines with an ovum from the female. This combination produces a new cell that immediately divides. The resulting pair of cells also divide, and this process of dividing to produce increasing numbers of cells continues over and over. Each step in the sequence creates cells of slightly different properties, cells capable of specialized functions, until finally they represent a fully constructed new member of the species, including such variegated, coordinated parts as heart and spleen, throat and lungs, skin and hair, eyes and brain.

2. *The genetic plan:* The architectural design for this new fish or fowl or human is provided by thousands of genes carried by chromosomes contained in the sperm cell of the father and in the ovum of the mother. In humans the chromosomes total forty-six, with twenty-three contributed by the female and twenty-three by the male. The inherited genes determine both (1) the border limits within which develop-

ment normally can occur and (2) potentialities for variation within these limits. By *border limits* I mean the identifying features of the species, the common elements that all normal individuals in the species share. As a simple example, humans normally are born with two eyes in front of the head, one on each side of the upper bridge of the nose. In contrast, rabbits and frogs are normally born with eyes farther to the side of the head. By *potentialities for variation* I mean that within these limits particular gene combinations determine some variation of the general characteristic. So eye color and acuity of sight can vary from one normal child to another, depending on the specific mix of genes received.

The connection between a gene and a given characteristic—such as skin color, intelligence, or competitiveness—is not a simple one. A chromosome does not merely contain a skin color gene or competitiveness gene that by itself determines the hue of the person's skin or the degree of competitiveness. Rather, the inherited foundation of such characteristics is determined by a number of genes located at various places among the chromosomes. Within the same family, one child will inherit a different mix of genes than his siblings, except in the case of identical (monozygotic) twins. Hence it is obviously not only the variations in the environment that cause differences among children in the same family, but also variations in the combination of genes received by each child.

3. *The network of species:* Ethologists subscribe to Darwin's proposition that none of the species, human or otherwise, is a separate creation, unrelated to the others. Rather, all species are links in a network of living things. The network extends from the simplest one-celled organisms—or from even more primitive stages of matter—to the most advanced species, that of the human being.

4. *The natural purpose:* If there is a natural purpose to life, a goal toward which all living things are driven by their nature, then that is *survival.* In its most basic sense, this is not the survival of the individual organism, since all individuals die. Nor is it even the survival of the species, for species are eliminated or altered with the passing of time. Rather, the basic aim seems to be the survival of the genes, which are the carriers of life itself (Wilson, 1975, pp. 3–4).

5. *Natural selection:* Living things obviously do not develop in a vacuum. They develop in environments that can vary in temperature, humidity, oxygen content, food supply, type of predator, and the like. Only those species survive and thrive that are well suited to changes that occur in their environments. Those poorly suited to environmental changes die off. This is the process of natural selection, the survival of the fittest. Such a point of view, refined since Darwin published his theory of evolution in 1859, is the new Darwinism that undergirds much of the work conducted today on the biological origins of human behavior, and thus is the foundation for the origins of child development.

ETHOLOGY'S PLACE IN THE STUDY OF CHILDREN

Since most ethological studies have been conducted on nonhuman species, the question is often asked, Why use studies of animals to elucidate the development of humans? Why not simply study humans directly? A typical answer is that provided by Hinde in *Biological Bases of Human Social Behaviour:*

Understanding human behaviour involves problems infinitely more difficult than landing a man on the moon or unravelling the structure of complex molecules. . . . If we are to tackle them, we must use every source of evidence available to us. Studies of animals are one such source. Sometimes such studies are useful to the extent that animals resemble man, and sometimes they help just because animals are different and permit the study of issues in a simplified, isolated, or exaggerated form. They may assist us in understanding the behaviour of man not only through factual comparison between animal and man, but also by helping us to refine the categories and concepts used in the description and explanation of behaviour and social structure. But the use of animals involves dangers: it is so easy to make rash generalizations, to slip from firm fact to flight of fancy, to select examples to fit preconceptions. Studies of animals must therefore be used circumspectly, and the limitations of their usefulness specified. (1974, p. xiii)

The following sketch of ethologists' contributions to the field of child development is presented in two parts: (1) propositions from animal investigations that may profitably guide the study of children and (2) fruitful research methods.

Relevant Propositions from Ethology

Substantive contributions that ethology may offer the field of child development can be illustrated in the form of six propositions related to the concepts of bonding, altruism, social intelligence, dominance and submission, temporary social separation, and sensitive periods. A *proposition*, as the term is used here, is a generalization from the study of animals that may apply as well to humans and, as such, may explain some aspect of child development.

> *Proposition 1: Bonding* In the earliest hours and days of life a strong mutual emotional attachment or bond occurs between the newborn and an immediate nurturing adult. This bond tends to continue over the following years, even in the face of harsh treatment of the child by the adult.

No newborn creature from species in the upper levels of the animal kingdom is able to fend for itself. In order to survive, all neonates require the aid of at least one nurturing adult until they mature enough to find their own food and shelter and to protect themselves from predators, illness, and accident. An early mutual emotional attachment helps ensure that a specific adult assumes the responsibility for each newborn and that the newborn identifies a particular adult as the one to whom she has a right to turn in time of need. This attachment increases the likelihood that the newborn will survive and will later produce offspring of her own. As interpreted from the perspective of Darwinian theory, within each animal species those genetic lineages that have fostered a strong reciprocal emotional bond between an offspring and a parent at the outset of the newborn's life have survived better than genetic lines that have not. As a consequence, over succeeding generations the gene strains that have fostered bonding have become widespread throughout the species, making bonding a "natural" developmental characteristic of the species.

The notion of early parent-offspring bonding, first generated from observations of nonhumans, stimulated Bowlby (1969, 1980) to try to determine whether the generalization about bonding was also true for humans. Following Bowlby's lead, M. H. Klaus and J. H. Kennell (1976) showed that there appears to be a critically sensitive period for bonding during the first few hours following birth. During this period, readiness to establish emotional attachment seems particularly strong. Comparisons between a group of mothers who had close contact with their newborns during the first few hours and a group who did not showed that the close-contact mothers in subsequent months displayed more fondling behavior and eye contact with their infants than did the other group of mothers. Bowlby's research and similar evidence have since affected infant-care routines in hospitals by influencing growing numbers of hospital personnel to have mothers spend more time with their babies in the hours and days immediately after birth.

Stimulated by Bowlby's pioneering efforts, a substantial literature has developed around what is referred to as *attachment theory,* a literature that is not limited to the newborn's bonding behavior but that extends into childhood and well beyond. The focus of attachment models is on the relationship between a dependent individual (called the *attached person*) and one or more nurturing protectors *(attachment figures).*

> Attachment behavior tends to be most obvious when the attached person is frightened, fatigued, or sick and is assuaged when the attachment figure provides protection, help, and soothing. The mere knowledge that an attachment figure is available and responsive provides a strong and pervasive feeling of security and so encourages the person to value and continue the relationship; . . . although attachment behavior is most noticeable in early childhood, it can be observed throughout the life cycle, especially in stressful situations. (Bretherton, 1985, p. 6)

The bonding of the newborn to a nurturing figure received the initial attention of researchers, but since that time further studies have shown that the child's attachment system does not become organized in a lasting form until sometime during the second half of the first year of life, most evident when the child begins to walk and talk. Interpreting this phenomenon in a manner that can apply to more species than just humans, Bretherton suggested:

> The fact that this change is roughly associated with the onset of locomotion makes evolutionary sense. . . . Independent locomotion enables the child [of whatever species] to leave the mother. A system that ensures that a child's explorations do not take it too far from a protective figure can thus plausibly be viewed as having survival value. (1985, p. 8)

The bonding/attachment example illustrates the process through which ethology can influence child-raising practices. First, a generalization about development is drawn from observations of nonhuman species. Next, the generalization is tested out in laboratory experiments and field studies of humans. If the generalization appears supported by the research on humans, then child development specialists recommend child-rearing techniques that incorporate the new knowledge.

Proposition 2: Separation Short-term separation of infants from their mothers can result in long-term effects on the psychological development of the infants.

This principle was initially proposed by such investigators as Bowlby (1951) and R. A. Spitz (1950) on the basis of observations of human mother-infant separation in such settings as foundling homes and hospitals. However, confounding factors in these real-life settings prevented researchers from drawing clear conclusions about the conditions determining the apparent effects. Since it would be inhumane to manipulate mother-infant relationships in controlled experiments in order to control various factors, a number of ethologists took on the task of performing experiments with nonhuman species, such as rhesus and macaque monkeys (Hinde, 1983; Hinde & McGinnis, 1977).

The studies showed that the symptoms displayed by primate infants were similar to those observed in human babies separated from their mothers—initial active protest and distress followed by depression, decreased movement, and reduced play activity. However, the avoidance of the mother upon reunion that is frequently seen in children was seldom observed in primates. The primate experiments have suggested that the effects of separation on infants can be influenced by such variables as the mother-infant relationships before and after separation, alternative sources of mothering during the separation, and the infant's sex, age, peer relationships, and more (Hinde, 1983, p. 73).

The primate experiments are deemed useful for the study of child development in at least three ways: (1) the nonverbal responses to separation that are similar in human and monkey infants may not require explanations at a high level of complexity, (2) variables observed in primate relationships may warrant closer attention as possible sources of influence in human mother-child relationships, and (3) results of the primate studies may serve as material for generating and testing theories about the nature of early attachment in human development.

> *Proposition 3: Sensitive periods* A specified event in an individual's life produces a stronger effect on development if it occurs at a particular time than if it occurred earlier or later than that time. Or, stated differently, a given result can be produced more readily during a particular time period than at either an earlier or later period.

This proposition comes in both rigid and flexible versions. The rigid version is the *critical-period* principle, and the flexible version the *sensitive-period* principle. The critical-period proposal holds that unless an environmental event happens during a strictly delimited time frame in an organism's development, the effect that event could produce will not occur. Lorenz is credited with popularizing the notion of critical periods after he observed that the young of many bird species react to a moving object in the way they would react to a parent, provided the object is displayed within a period extending from a few hours after birth to a few hours or days later (Hinde, 1983, p. 41). Since Lorenz considered this period unchangeable, he labeled it *critical.* "However, it soon became apparent that the limits of the period were not irrevocably fixed by inherent developmental processes . . . and that imprinting was not irreversible. . . . The term sensitive period, thus, became more popular" (Hinde, 1983, p. 41).

The sensitive-period proposal, in effect, is more lenient. It holds that a particular result is more readily produced during a certain time frame than would be true earlier or later. It does not imply that the period is precisely defined by chronological age or that similar results cannot be produced later. Studies of primates, in particular, have suggested relationships between time periods and attachment and the learning of various skills. The term *readiness* has been commonly used to reflect the concept of sensitive periods for learning in humans. A comparison of both the similarities and differences between human and nonhuman subjects in their sensitive periods has proven useful in the understanding and application of the idea of readiness in child rearing and education.

Proposition 4: Altruism The greater the genetic similarity between two individuals, such as two children, the greater the degree of altruism they will display toward each other.

This proposition is an extension to humans of a kinship theory that zoologists have recently built from studies of altruistic (self-sacrificing) behavior among insects—ants, bees, wasps, and termites—that differ in the extent of their sociality (Alexander & Sherman, 1977; Hamilton, 1964; Trivers & Hare, 1976; Wilson, 1975).

In this kinship theory, an act is called "altruistic" if it benefits another organism while harming the organism performing the act. And to make *benefit* and *harm* easy to measure objectively, benefit and harm are assessed in terms of the reproductive success of an organism—that is, the organism's success in producing its own offspring. An act is thus altruistic if it harms the individual's chances of producing its own offspring while aiding another organism in producing and maintaining its own. At this point the line of reasoning will not make sense unless we recall that within neo-Darwinism the goal of nature is not the survival of the individual but the survival of the genetic line. And in some cases in which organisms are struggling against difficult environmental circumstances, a self-sacrificing act will better ensure that the organism's genetic line, as carried by a close relative of the individual, will prosper than if each individual behaved entirely selfishly without regard for the welfare of others. When the males of the tribe array themselves in the front line of defense against dangerous predators, each of them is reducing his chances of personal survival and reproductive success more than if he tried to escape on his own, leaving the females and young at the mercy of the predators. But his cooperative, altruistic act helps maximize the chance that the large proportion of his genes, which are also carried by the close relatives he is defending, will survive through future generations.

This general line of logic suggests why natural selection over the centuries has encouraged the development of altruistic behavior by promoting the survival and reproduction of genes particularly conducive to such acts. However, in such a general form, the logic does not help us specify the conditions under which an altruistic act rather than a selfish act can be expected. And it is here that zoologists' recent work on kinship theory may offer some help. Scientists have now devised formulas for estimating under what conditions natural selection will favor genes conducive to altruistic acts. The formulas include two main factors: (1) the degree of genetic relatedness of the two organisms concerned (that is, the proportion of genes common to the two individuals) and (2) the comparative cost and benefit to the organism carrying out the act and to the recipient of the act. As R. L. Trivers and H. Hare have put it:

> For natural selection to favor an altruistic act directed at a relative, the benefit of the act times the altruist's r (degree of relatedness) to the relative must be greater than the cost of the act. (1976, p. 249)

In other words, the theory proposes that, through the evolutionary process, genes have been selected that encourage an organism to engage in more self-sacrificing behavior for the benefit of close relatives than for distant relatives. But in all instances, altruism has limits. The individual will bear a higher personal cost for the sake of closely related individuals, but when the cost becomes so high that it exceeds the product of (1) the benefit to the relative times (2) the degree of relatedness, then the actor can be expected to behave selfishly rather than altruistically.

Such, then, is the general direction of reasoning and the beginnings of specifying conditions in kinship theory as based on and tested in altruistic-versus-selfish behavior among social insects. But what might all this have to do with child development? It provides some hypotheses about the bases and conditions of altruism in humans. It suggests some lines of inquiry for investigating such hypotheses as proposition 4, the hypothesis that natural selection for the human species has operated in such a way as to genetically predispose children to display more altruism toward others who are closely related to them than toward people more distantly related. The proposition implies such research questions as the following:

1. To what extent do children exhibit self-sacrificing behavior toward members of their family because the children have been taught to do so, and to what extent is such behavior a result of genetic predisposition?
2. A common ideal of social democracy is to have children treat other people on the basis of each person's individual behavior rather than a person's membership in some subgroup of society (a family, tribal, religious, ethnic, or socioeconomic subgroup). Does this mean that in order to achieve the ideal, those people in charge of child rearing must counteract a natural (genetically based) propensity of children to behave more altruistically toward people who are closely related to them than toward people with whom they have fewer genes in common?

Proposition 5: Social intelligence The majority of problems people face in daily living are ones involving interactions with other people. The ability to solve these problems can be labeled "social intelligence." Such ability is not accurately assessed by means of traditional intelligence tests but, rather, requires different appraisal techniques, ones that directly confront the individual with social-interaction problems.

Throughout the twentieth century, the most popular way of formally appraising a person's problem-solving ability has been by means of intelligence tests that consist of oral or printed questions. This line of appraisal began in France with the work of Alfred Binet during the first decade of the century, and the tradition continues strong today. However, a number of critics, including Jean Piaget, have charged that such tests tell only whether a respondent gives an acceptable answer; they do not reveal the thought processes involved in arriving at the answer. Hence Piaget and others have created different techniques for assessing human mental abilities, techniques that involve a tester's posing problem situations for a child and then observing how the child's thought processes operate as she or he seeks a solution.

But studies by ethologists have called into question the suitability of both traditional intelligence measures and Piaget's problem-solving tasks. The question has arisen from ethologists' observations of animals during the animals' daily living routines in their natural habitats. What constitutes intelligent behavior in such real-life social environments may be rather different from the things measured by typical intelligence tests. In particular, the kinds of problems that appear on intelligence tests are seldom ones involving decisions about how to act in social situations, nor does the contrived laboratory setting in which intelligence tests are typically administered include the same sorts of forces that can affect people's decisions in social settings. So ethological studies have helped alert psychologists to the limitations of both Binet-type and Piaget-type measures of intelligence, thus stimulating the search for better ways of formally assessing children's development in solving problems met in the social intercourse of real life.

> *Proposition 6: Dominance/submission* A genetic line best survives if in-
> dividuals from the line's gene pool are organized socially in such a way that the
> most capable members are in positions of leadership and control, while
> members who are less powerful, less inventive, or less talented accept sub-
> servient positions.

This proposition derives from neo-Darwinism via the following line of logic. The *gene pool* of a population consists of all varieties of genes possessed by the members of that population. Each new member of the population is constructed from one particular combination of genes from that pool. This means that not all members born into the population have the same characteristics, nor are all combinations of genes that compose individuals equally suited for promoting survival. Furthermore, the genetic line thrives best when individuals of the species do not live isolated from one another, solving the problems of survival alone. Instead, the lineage thrives when its members are organized as a social system that exhibits a division of labor and power, and the inherited differences among individuals in the group equip members better for some roles than for others. As the generations pass, the greater the effectiveness of the social system in fostering survival, the greater will be the survival rate of those members who carry genes that fit them well for that system. That is, more of the fittest members will survive and pass on their socially suitable genes to future generations. Through this process, newborns of the species are increasingly equipped with genetic tendencies that in the past have supported the social organization that has become the norm for the given species, whether it be ants, sharks, bees, baboons, or dogs.

Among the range of social characteristics that ethologists trace to such genetic foundations is the dominant/submissive behavior noted among animals in the upper reaches of the evolutionary system, particularly among primates. The dominance/submission hierarchy is defined in animal societies by the way power and privilege are apportioned among the members, especially in matters of access to mates, to food, to desirable resting spots, and the like. Some animals rather readily assume submissive roles, displaying their submission by such ritualistic postures as rolling onto their backs and exposing their bellies or lowering their heads and cowering. Others do not so easily submit but, instead, challenge their rivals for positions of dominance. Yet, once the less powerful are intimidated by threats or defeated in combat, they accept a subservient role, permitting the group to get on with daily living under stable social conditions.

Studies of dominance/submission patterns in animals have stimulated similar studies with children. As a consequence, a growing body of knowledge has accrued about the unstated rules children follow for regulating relationships in childhood groups and about the effectiveness of the adjustment strategies they attempt, such as physical attack and defense, teasing, name-calling and casting insults, verbal threats, escape, gifts of appeasement, weeping, joining forces with peers to gain strength in numbers, and so on. Such studies have shown that in the early stages of a group's formation, as at the beginning of the school year, conflicts are frequent until dominant members prove themselves and the losers in the struggle accept positions lower in the social hierarchy. Thereupon, conflicts diminish dramatically and the work of the group moves ahead more peaceably (Savin-Williams, 1976; Sherif, 1966; Strayer & Strayer, 1976).

The list of six propositions just given is intended to be merely illustrative, certainly not definitive. Other propositions derived from ethology that prove of aid in understanding child development are those bearing on (1) communication and sign stimuli that affect social relationships (smiling, eye movements, frowning, posturing, emitted sounds), (2) adaptiveness to new environmental conditions, (3) parent-child relationships, (4) displays of affection, (5) aggression, (6) experiences early in life, (7) self-regulatory mechanisms, (8) aesthetic responses, and (9) moral behavior (Eibl-Eibesfeldt, 1989; Hinde, 1983; Wilson, 1978). Books have also been written comparing humans with other species in terms of play (Mueller-Schwarze, 1978), infanticide (Hausfater & Hrdy, 1984), and maternal influences on early behavior (Bell & Smotherman, 1980).

In summary, explanations of child development from an ethologist's perspective place particular emphasis on biological forces (derived during the evolution of the species) as determiners of tendencies for behavior. For instance, a Harvard University ethologist, Edward O. Wilson, writing on human nature, stated his conviction that genetic factors play a dominant role in determining what an individual can learn:

> The learning potential of each species appears to be fully programmed by the structure of its brain, the sequence of release of its hormones, and, ultimately, its genes. Each animal species is "prepared" to learn certain stimuli, barred from learning others, and neutral with respect to still others. . . . So the human brain is not a tabula rasa, a clean slate on which experience draws intricate pictures with

lines and dots. It is more accurately described as an autonomous decision-making instrument, an alert scanner of the environment that approaches certain kinds of choices and not others in the first place, then innately leans toward one option as opposed to others and urges the body into action according to a flexible schedule that shifts automatically and gradually from infancy into old age. (1978; pp. 67, 69)

FRUITFUL RESEARCH METHODS

Because animals rather than people have been the traditional subjects of ethological investigations, such devices as interviews, questionnaires, diaries, recordings of conversations, and paper-and-pencil tests have necessarily been unsuitable for ethologists' data-gathering purposes. Instead, the basic tool in ethological research has been careful observation of the appearance and actions of individuals and groups within precisely described environments. Because ethologists have concentrated so intently on the use of observation, they have managed to develop observational techniques into a sophisticated array of procedures that might profitably be adopted in the study of children, especially in the study of infants and young children whose verbal abilities are limited.

The following brief examples illustrate (1) basic steps usually followed in observational studies, (2) some alternatives within these steps, and (3) the embellishment of the ethologists' tools with other methods when studies focus on children rather than on nonhuman species.

Basic Steps in Observational Research

Typical phases in conducting ethological studies are as follows (Eibl-Eibesfeldt, 1989, pp. 107–112):

1. *Observing* the subjects' appearance and behavior, preferably in their natural habitats rather than under contrived laboratory conditions, since behavior can vary with the environment in which it is carried out.

2. *Recording* the results of the observation. This can take diverse forms, depending on the sorts of questions the investigator is seeking to answer, on the subjects' characteristics, on the physical and social setting, on the time available, on the equipment used (handwritten notes, videocamera, audio-recording equipment), and on the investigator's skills. The resulting record or behavioral inventory is typically called an *ethogram.*

3. Organizing the observations into *categories*. The selection of categories is governed by the particular problem or question the researcher is seeking to clarify.

> Categorization is often based on function; . . . our knowledge of function is often founded on intuition. Functional categories of this kind include greeting, courting, comforting, or appeasing. If such category names are used, they must be precisely defined and their function also verified. . . . A greeting consists of several behavioral patterns such as head nodding, smiling, rapid raising of the eyebrows, and more. (Eibl-Eibesfeldt, 1989, p. 108)

4. In a subsequent step of synthesis, individual categories of behavior can be connected to represent *behavior patterns*. One common approach to combining subunits is to interpret them as steps in a subject's strategy for reaching a goal, such as a sequence of behavior units involved in finding a lost object, playing a game, or preparing a meal.

5. *Broader-ranging generalizations* can be derived when selected behavior patterns are compared for their likenesses and differences. For instance, in a study of mother-child relations, a series of behavior patterns from observations of a particular mother interacting with her child on various occasions can be analyzed to determine what is common across occasions and what varies by occasion. At a broader level of abstraction, a collection of behavior patterns from observations of a number of mothers and their children in the same community can be compared to provide generalizations about similarities and differences within that group. At still higher levels of generalization, conclusions about mother-child relations for one community can be compared with those from other communities, one ethnic group can be compared with another, and, ultimately, one species can be compared with others.

Options among Observation Techniques

The first step in the sequence just listed will be used to demonstrate that a variety of alternatives are available under each of the steps. Eight modes of observing are identified along with suggestions about the function each serves (Hinde, 1983, pp. 37–38).

1. *Spontaneous sampling (ad libitum sampling):* The observer notes everything possible that comes to her attention or that interests her. This is the most typical initial form of observation carried out in natural history studies. As a form of observational "browsing," it furnishes a record of the most conspicuous events. It then needs to be followed by more precisely directed observations.

2. *Sociometric charting:* This technique involves filling out a matrix or charting social interactions to reveal the relative social positions of individuals within a group of two or more children. In one form of matrix completion, the names of the individuals in the setting can be listed across the top (columns) and down the side (rows) of a chart. Then interactions between pairs of individuals can be tallied in the cell that is the intersection of the two individuals' names. The number of tallies in a cell indicates the frequency of the pair's interactions, while special tally symbols are used to indicate such relationships as dominance and submission or friendliness and antagonism. Sociometric maps can also be constructed to display the amount, direction, and quality of participation of different children in the group (Thomas, 1960).

3. *Focal individual sampling:* All behavior of one individual during a specific period of time is recorded in detail. Responses of others to that individual may also be noted. Such information is valuable in studies of the pace and variety of a child's activities, permitting comparisons among children as well as across situations in which the child participates.

4. *Sampling all instances of selected behavior types:* This method is useful for revealing the frequency, length, quality, nature of participants, and consequences of such forms of child behavior as arguing during games, settling a dispute in the classroom, or planning a small group project. Such a mode of observation is suitable when the events are easily seen and do not move too fast to be recorded adequately.

5. *Sequence sampling:* The purpose with this approach is to trace the series of actions that comprise a given behavior pattern. The recording begins with the initial act of a behavior episode, such as when a baby cries or when a six-year-old starts to prepare her own lunch. Recording of each subsequent step in the sequence continues until the episode is over. Results of sequence sampling enable the investigator to compare different children's modes of addressing the same kind of life situation, or comparisons can be made of the same child's modes over time— that is, from one developmental stage to another.

6. *One–zero sampling:* This is a somewhat crude but easily conducted form of recording observations. It consists of the investigator making a tally mark each time the target behavior occurs, such as each time a child asks a question in class, each time a baby is asleep, or each time a parent disciplines an eight-year-old. Although one–zero sampling is useful for determining how often a given behavior appears, it fails to show either the length of time involved in each occurrence or the quality or consequences of the behavior.

7. *Time sampling* (also known as *instantaneous sampling*): During a pre-determined time interval, an investigator records every act carried out by a child. For example, in a nursery school, a researcher may observe a particular child at three five-minute time periods during the morning. Time sampling is particularly useful for estimating the percentage of time children spend in rather common activities.

8. *Multiple-scan sampling:* This is an extended form of time sampling in which the observer records all the behaviors of one individual in a group for a specified time interval, then does the same for another individual, continuing in this fashion until all members of the group have been observed. The sequence may then be started over with the initial child and continued through a cycle of group members. Such a method is appropriate when time sampling for a single child is inadequate for revealing the behavior shown (since it fails to reflect the group's influence) and when the researcher wants information about a number of children during that same time period.

It should be apparent that variations and combinations of these eight approaches can expand even further the investigator's observational tools to suit diverse research goals and behavior settings.

Amplifying Methods for the Study of Children

As ethologists have increasingly turned their attention from nonhuman species to people, they have added further techniques to their customary observation methods.

First, they distinguish between *distanced observation* and *participatory observation*. In distanced observation, the investigator is an outsider who views, but not does not enter, the effective environment of the subjects being studied. Claims made for distanced observation are that it enhances objectivity and avoids contaminating the naturalness of the subjects' behavior with the observer's influence. Participatory observation, on the other hand, involves the investigator's intentionally interacting with the subjects. Claims made for its value are that the role of participant equips the researcher with opportunities to learn subjects' motives, attitudes, and conceptions that are either difficult or impossible to discover from a distanced vantage point (Eibl-Eibesfeldt, 1989, pp. 107–108).

It is apparent that distanced observation is the dominant, traditional approach in ethology since participation with nonhuman species is relatively rare and of a low level of usefulness. The type of participation with nonhuman species that yields the greatest information is customarily that which involves people interacting with domesticated pets—usually dogs and cats, but also primates, pigs, horses, and the like. The most common forms of participant observation in ethological studies of humans occurs when a researcher, investigating child development in an unfamiliar culture, lives with the people of that culture for an extended period of time in an effort to understand customs and attitudes that typically underlie their behavior.

To supplement their distanced and participatory observations of child development, ethologists have increasingly adopted such devices as interviews, questionnaires, attitude surveys, projective methods (ink-blot tests, picture-story tests), aptitude tests, and achievement tests. As a consequence, the ethologist's repertoire of investigative techniques has become very extensive indeed.

PRACTICAL APPLICATIONS AND RESEARCH CHALLENGES

I have combined applications and research challenges here because the practical applications of ethology to child development take the form of suggestions for research studies. The purpose of such studies is to discover the extent to which generalizations derived from observing nonhuman species can validly be applied to interpreting children's growth and behavior. In addition to the propositions from ethology mentioned above, let's consider several more in the form of questions that demonstrate the broad range of child development research topics that can be generated from ethological theory.

E. D. Wilson (1978, p. 99) wrote: "Are human beings innately aggressive? . . . The answer . . . is yes." But in disagreement with Wilson, there are those who contend that aggressivity, although widespread, is the result of living conditions that precipitate conflict and competition and is not the result of an inborn human tendency. From this difference of opinion a variety of research questions can be evoked. For instance, in what ways can children's environments be arranged to eliminate aggressive behavior at successive stages of growth? And if aggressivity cannot be eliminated, what child-rearing practices can be used to channel it into constructive acts (ones aiding other people in fulfilling their needs) rather than destructive acts (ones frustrating others' need-fulfillment attempts)? To what extent do models of aggression the child observes in the family, in school, and on television influence the amount and type of aggression the child exhibits at different age levels?

Wilson (1978, p. 128) further observed, "Women as a group are less assertive and physically aggressive." Is this true of children of all ages? Or is it simply that boys and girls are equally assertive but use different techniques for expressing assertiveness? And if this is so, to what extent are the differences innate and to what extent the result of cultural influences? More precisely, how can child-rearing practices alter possible sex differences in assertiveness?

As for sexual behavior, to what extent are preferences for heterosexual versus homosexual activities inborn? How do different models of sexual behavior in a child's environment influence the child's sex preferences and activities at different age levels? In terms of vocations, are there certain roles for which females are innately better suited than males, and vice versa?

To what extent are a child's competitive–cooperative and introversive–extroversive actions a result of a genetic tendency to behave in such a manner? How much room is there for environmental forces at different age levels to alter the course of such traits or tendencies?

Is there any truth in beliefs of the past that antisocial acts of children and youths are based, at least partly, on a "bad blood line" or "bad seed"? Or, in more modern parlance, are there actually "psychopathic personalities"—people whose underlying genetic endowment so predisposes them to antisocial acts that efforts to teach them prosocial behavior are destined to fail?

How much are children from a given population (such as an inbred tribal or ethnic group) genetically predestined to display one pattern of social behavior (such as a tendency to settle disputes by reasoning) than another (a tendency to settle disputes by physical violence)?

These questions and far more that derive from ethological investigations provide an extensive source of research opportunities for the field of child development.

Ethological Theory: An Assessment

In explaining my reasons for the ratings on the accompanying chart, I begin with items awarded high marks and then consider ones with lower ratings.

Item 1, concerning how closely the theory reflects the real world, is divided into two subscales, the first focusing on ethologists' main source of data—nonhuman species—and the second focusing on the chief subject of this book, children. I rated ethological theory high on item 1a because each concept in the major ethologists' writings is profusely illustrated with examples from field studies of a broad variety of species. However, many sociologists and social psychologists would probably give a lower rating on item 1a because they believe ethologists credit genes with too great a role in determining individuals' psychological characteristics and groups' social patterns. Although ethologists do not ignore the place of learning in personal

ETHOLOGICAL THEORY

How well do I think the theory meets the standards?

Standards	Very well	Moderately well	Very poorly
1. Reflects the real world of:			
a. nonhuman species	X		
b. children		X	
2. Is clearly understandable	X		
3. Explains the past and predicts the future		X	
4. Guides child rearing			X
5. Is internally consistent	X		
6. Is economical	X		
7. Is falsifiable			X
8. Is supported by convincing evidence	animals A		children C
9. Adapts to new data		X	
10. Is novel		X	
11. Is comprehensive			X
12. Stimulates new discoveries	potential P		actual A
13. Is durable	X		
14. Is self-satisfying		X	

traits and social organization, they do see genetic structure as setting narrower boundary lines within which learning can take place than many social scientists would likely accept. The strong genetic preference exhibited by typical ethologists is reflected in Wilson's contention that what evolves in human development is a set of genetically based capacities to learn certain things rather than others with a certain degree of ease:

> Pavlov was simply wrong when he postulated that "any natural phenomenon chosen at will may be converted into conditioned stimuli." Only small parts of the brain represent a tabula rasa; this is true even for human beings. The remainder is more like an exposed negative, waiting to be dipped into developer fluid. (1975, p. 156)

While ethologists may be criticized for taking a position toward the hereditarian camp in nature–nurture controversies, when more data have been compiled it may turn out that they are correct, or nearly so. In any event, I have given them the benefit of such doubts in marking item 1a on the basis of the wide range of field studies with which they have buttressed their theoretical generalizations and principles of development.

In judging the theory's clarity (item 2), internal consistency (item 5), and economy of explanation (item 6), I have concluded that the main books and articles on ethology available to the public are clearly written and contain ample illustrative descriptions of behavior among many species (see, for example, Eibl-Eibesfeldt, 1975; Hinde, 1974; Lorenz, 1977; Wilson, 1975, 1978). Likewise, neo-Darwinism as expressed in ethological theories does not seem encumbered with more concepts than the minimum needed to explain the phenomena ethologists discuss.

Items 3 and 7 (explains past and predicts future; is falsifiable) can conveniently be considered together for they share a common weakness. The weakness is that ethological theory, at its present stage of development, comprises a set of broad concepts and principles intended to explain the evolution of all psychological and social behavior in all species; but as yet the theory is not sufficiently detailed and precise to produce an unequivocal description of any population's past development or future evolution. The theory does not provide the information needed to judge specifically the genetically set limits or potentialities for various aspects of human development. Nor does the theory elucidate the way different environmental influences complement the genetic pattern to produce the characteristics individual humans display at various stages of growth. Ethology is still at the stage of a natural history, with theorists observing social behavior in one or two species, proposing concepts that could explain such behavior, then extending the application of these concepts by "logical reasoning" to other species without rigorously testing the validity of this extension. As Wilson pointed out in discussing the subrealm of ethology known as sociobiology:

> The greatest snare in sociobiological reasoning is the ease with which it is conducted. Whereas the physical sciences deal with precise results that are usually difficult to explain, sociobiology has imprecise results that can be too easily explained by many different schemes. (1975, p. 28)

The cure for this shortcoming, Wilson says, lies in adopting methods of "strong inference." This means deriving alternative hypotheses from the theory, creating crucial experiments or field observations that will reveal which of the competing hypotheses is the most tenable, and then accepting or revising the theory's concepts in light of these test results (Wilson, 1975, p. 28). Until ethological models reach this stage of methodology, they will continue to be nonfalsifiable and will furnish inconclusive explanations of past and future.

The ratings on items 1b and 4 (children's real world and guidance for child rearing) are somewhat below "moderate," since most ethological studies have not dealt directly with children's lives. Bowlby's work (1969, 1973, 1980) in the 1950s and 1960s provided the most specific early applications of ethological theory to child development. Such applications have become far more extensive in recent times, as attested by the writings of N. G. Blurton Jones (1972), P. K. Smith and K. J. Connolly (1980), Hinde (1974, 1983), and Eibl-Eibesfeldt (1989).

On item 12, I have marked ethological theory for both its actual and its potential value in stimulating new discoveries. As demonstrated in the discussion of research challenges, ethological theory has great potential for stimulating new discoveries in child development. However, so far the direct applications of ethological findings to child development research have been quite limited.

A host of evidence (item 8) buttresses ethological theory as it applies to subhuman species. Yet the applications to child development are still quite meager.

Serious studies of the evolution of nonhuman species have a history extending over more than a century and a half, so ethology as a scientific pursuit is hardly new. But as an approach to studying child growth, ethological theory is of quite recent origin, so I have ranked it rather high on novelty (item 10). A similar rating has been awarded for the model's adaptability (item 9), in recognition of the willingness of ethologists to incorporate new empirical findings into their schemes. However, as Wilson (1975, p. 28) noted, ethological studies often yield "imprecise results that can be too easily explained by many different schemes." Thus, the validity of an ethologist's interpretation of new data may often be subject to question.

Up to the present time, ethological theory has been applied to a rather narrow range of child-development phenomena. Furthermore, the approach has focused primarily on the child as a typical member of a species, rather than on factors that cause individual ontological differences among children. Consequently I have placed it rather low on the comprehensiveness scale (item 11).

As for durability (item 13), I believe that the potential contributions ethology theory can make toward understanding the biological foundations of growth and behavior will ensure ethologists a secure role in the study of child development for many years to come.

For the final assessment standard—how satisfying ethological theory is from a child development perspective—I have marked ethology in the "moderate" range to reflect a counterbalancing between (1) the strengths of the theorists' line of reasoning about species in general and (2) a lack of conclusiveness that surfaces when they apply this reasoning to explain complex human behavior. In particular, I would like the kind of detailed extension of the theory that would account for why children develop psychologically and socially the way they do during the first two decades of life.

FOR FURTHER READING

Eibl-Eibesfeldt, I. (1989) *Human Ethology*. New York: Aldine de Gruyter. This textbook, written by the president of the International Society for Human Ethology, addresses basic concepts and methods of ethology, social behavior, communication, ontogeny (including various development theories), humans in their habitats (ecology), ethology's contribution to aesthetics, and biology's contributions to ethics.

Hinde, R. A. (1987) *Individuals, Relationships, and Culture: Links between Ethology and the Social Sciences*. New York: Cambridge University Press. In analyzing the relationship between biology and human socioculture, Hinde proposed that "sociocultural structure is the product of brains that were shaped by selection acting in the empirical world of actual behavior." Understanding the dialectical interchanges between humans' biological structure and their environment so as to produce individuals' cultural characteristics "requires both a psychological analysis of the ways in which the sociocultural structure is formed by the propensities of the human mind, and a sociological analysis of the ways in which individuals, internalizing the symbols of the culture, come to experience the culture as part of themselves and themselves as part of the culture" (p. 145).

CHAPTER FIFTEEN

A BIO-ELECTROCHEMICAL MODEL

The position argued in this chapter is that one useful way to view development is in terms of the child's bio-electrochemical composition as seen at six levels of specificity. The levels descend from the most unified at the top to the most diversified and detailed at the bottom. The chapter, in effect, is an exercise in reductionism, an exercise that involves decomposing the visible, active child by gradual steps until we reach the subatomic level where the young one is conceived to be simply an aggregation of quadrillions of interacting, electrically charged and electrically neutral particles. The levels can be represented by the titles and principal components in Table 15.1.

In contrast to this book's other chapters, the present one does not describe a particular established theory of development. When I searched for such a theory to fit the intention of this book, I failed to find one that addressed all of the issues I believed were most useful for explaining—in a limited space—child development from a bio-electrochemical perspective. Consequently, I am offering this six-level scheme as a convenient framework within which to display a variety of widely held conceptions of human development that derive from such disciplines

TABLE 15.1
The components of a child

Level	Principal components
Unitary child	The growing child—a singular, integrated person interacting with the surrounding environment—is composed of
Organic	organs (brain, heart, lungs, kidneys, etc.) that are built of
Cellular	cells (nerve cells, blood cells, skin cells, etc.) that are built of
Molecular	molecules (proteins, enzymes, fats, etc.) that are built of
Elemental/atomic	chemical elements (oxygen, hydrogen, iron, etc.) that consist of atoms built of
Subatomic	electrically charged and neutral particles (electrons, protons, neutrons), which are composed of more basic particles (quarks) that themselves may consist of even more fundamental components.

as human ecology, physiology, molecular biology, genetics, biochemistry, and atomic physics.

The levels represent not only descending steps in the process of reductionism, but also successive historical eras of scientific discovery. The first level, that of the unitary child, has been in common use since prehistoric times; but only in the last few years has the sixth level (subatomic particles) been sketched with even a modest degree of clarity.

Another feature of the framework is that some levels may seem to represent "the truth" or "the way things really are" whereas others represent "theory about how things might be." It could thus be argued that a description of the structure and functions of body organs—brain, lungs, stomach, and the like—is not theory but, rather, is a portrayal of factual reality. It might also be argued that picturing the growing child as an aggregation of subatomic particles whose characteristics are not entirely clear is not a description of factual reality but, rather, is a theoretical estimate of how things might be. However, I would suggest that the difference between an organic and a subatomic-particle description is not an issue of reality versus theory, because the proposals at both levels are indeed theory in the way it has been defined in this book—an identification of facts and of how they are interrelated. Instead, the difference between the levels resides in the amount of convincing evidence compiled in support of the postulated relationships. In the distant past, certain theorists estimated that the human heart was the source of such psychological faculties as compassion (kindhearted versus hard-hearted), generosity (good-hearted), and affection (loving-hearted). However, empirical studies over the centuries have failed to endorse such estimates and, instead, have supported the notion that the heart functions solely as a pumper of blood. A multitude of other studies have likewise explicated explanations of other body organs' functions with such consistency that we now tend to regard those explanations as factual reality when they might more properly be regarded as theories that enjoy strong empirical support. Within our six-level framework, the topmost levels tend to be more securely buttressed with convincing evidence than do those at the bottom. And at all levels, the accepted models are always subject to revision or replacement in light of incompatible data.

Our six-level framework embraces a great abundance of macrotheories, minitheories, typologies, hypotheses, and facts; so it is clear that this one short chapter cannot hope to describe such a vast territory with any degree of completeness. The chapter can, however, describe the defining nature of the levels that compose the framework and can illustrate the unique way development is depicted at each level. The design of the chapter has been particularly influenced by the following four convictions.

Understanding development   A different kind of knowledge derives from the study of each level. In other words, each level makes a special contribution toward our comprehending how children develop.

Types of knowledge   Among the kinds of knowledge that can be extracted about each level, the ones of special importance are those that answer questions about (1) the level's types of components, (2) the components' structures, (3) the components' functions or uses, (4) the components' roles in systems, (5) how and why the components change during the process of development, and (6) the symptoms, causes, and cures of disorders in the components. Two key questions that dictate the types of information to be drawn from the disciplines of biology, physiological psychology, chemistry, and physics are these: (1) What can we learn at each level that increases our understanding of how children develop? (2) How can knowledge gained at this level aid us in promoting the kind of development we hope the child will achieve?

The bio-electrochemical nature of development Development consists of biological-electrical-chemical changes that follow a characteristic pattern for the human species. A human being typically begins as a single fertilized bio-electrochemical cell in a female's womb, where the cell multiplies into specialized kinds of cells to produce a system of organs that first form an embryo, then a fetus, and finally an infant that is able—after about nine months—to survive as an independent organism outside the womb. Over the ensuing seven or eight decades, this bio-electrochemical organism evolves in a representative pattern of change that ends when such change assumes a form that no longer enables the individual to exist as an active, sentient entity. With death, the "bio-" (life) portion of the formula has been lost, and only inert chemicals remain.

Defining desirable development Proper or optimal development is first de-fined in psychosocial terms—that is, in terms of how people want (1) to look (physical appearance), (2) to be able to act (cognitive and physical abilities), and (3) to feel (affective states). Then the bio-electrochemical correlates of these desired conditions are identified, and those correlates form the bio-electrochemi-cal definition of the sort of development people hope to achieve. In other words, the kinds of personal and social characteristics that people value in a growing in-dividual become the criteria for determining what kind of bio-electrochemical conditions are worth fostering in the developing child.

As the chapter progresses, every level is discussed in turn, with our attention focusing on those types of knowledge identified above as "of special importance." To illustrate the way different children's development might be described at each level, we will inspect the cases of four young people. In discussing the cases, we will discover what more can be learned about the four hypothetical youngsters' development at each descending step of reductionism analysis. Our four subjects are Larry, age five; Charmaine, age eleven; Ronald, age fourteen; and Stephanie, age seventeen.

LEVEL I: THE UNITARY CHILD

The *components* or *units of analysis* at Level 1 are (1) the child as a biochemical entity that interacts with (2) separate biochemical and inert-chemical entities that populate the child's social and physical environment. The environment's biochemi-cal entities, each functioning as a separate unit, are people (Mom, Dad, a teacher, a television hero), animals (Rover, Kitty, that gray rat), and living plants (the backyard tree, Uncle Bill's flower garden). Inert-chemical entities include such things as diapers and high chairs, dollhouses and toy trains, hamburgers and bicycles, bikini swimsuits and textbooks, ski slopes and automobiles, and much more.

As children grow up, their development is influenced by electrochemical materials that they breathe, swallow, view, hear, smell, and touch. This is the experiential/behavioral level. The experiential consists of children's thoughts and feelings about what is happening to them. Introspection becomes the chief method of identifying such experience. The behavioral consists of the way the developing child is viewed by others. Proper or desirable development (orthogenesis) is first defined in experiential/behavioral terms. Then the bio-electrochemical correlates of this development become the definition of desirable development. Likewise, the definition of undesirable development begins with judgments about how children should not grow and should not act. Then the bio-electrochemical correlates of these undesired characteristics provide the bio-electrochemical definition of improper development. It is thus assumed that discovering ways to change the undesirable bio-electrochemical correlates into desirable ones is the proper method of promoting desirable growth. Dietary, ergonomic (physical therapy, exercise), medicinal (drugs, chemotherapy), surgical (including implants), and radiation treatments represent principal ways of correcting development that has gone awry.

In everyday life, a great many observations about development are in Level 1 terms. These are statements describing in a gross fashion the child's transactions with components of the surrounding environment, statements that omit any speculation about what is happening within the unitary child or within any of the environmental units.

> "When he saw the bully coming, he ran home."
> "If you keep eating junk food, you're going to get sick."

Explanations on Level 1 are, in effect, of the commonsense or folk-culture variety. *Commonsense* in this context means readily observed correlations between apparent inputs and outputs. *Folk culture* means the commonsense beliefs about causes of behavior and development that are shared throughout a community and are passed on as knowledge from one generation to another. The originators of these beliefs are often well-respected adults who appear to have more than ordinary perceptual skills and who explain their beliefs in a convincing manner. Level 1 conceptions of development have apparently existed ever since humans first learned to communicate their observations to each other.

Two examples of commonsense or folk-culture descriptions of development are these:

> "That kid has endless energy—constantly on the move, day and night."
> "She's a real whiz at reading, and at such a young age."

Other commonsense statements go beyond description to include explanation—that is, they include estimates of cause.

"No wonder the child is tall for her age—her parents are both over six feet."

"If the boy keeps smoking cigarettes, he's going to stunt his growth."

"He's exhausted before the game's half over, because he hasn't trained consistently enough to get in shape."

"She's very flighty, jumping from one thing to another. It's not that she isn't bright enough. It's just that she'll never stick at a task."

A fair amount of puzzlement can be expressed on Level 1 when individual cases fail to conform to some general explanatory principle to which an observer sub-scribes, such principles as "The more food people eat, the more weight they gain" and "Practice makes perfect."

"I don't understand why she's so skinny when she eats like a horse."

"No matter how many times he repeats it, he can never recall it when he needs it."

Keeping in mind the general nature of Level 1, we next consider how Level 1 analysis can be applied in describing and explaining the development of our four illustrative young people.

Level 1 Case Analyses

Larry, age five   In the words of Larry's mother: "He loves kindergarten, but unfortunately he often finds it frustrating when he can't keep up with the other children. It's because he tires so easily. His teacher says he tries to do what the others do but just gets worn out—gasps, turns rather pale, and has to rest. Some-times I have to keep him home. He seems worse when there's heavy air pollution over the city. Then he finds it hard to breathe and often has to lie down."

Charmaine, age eleven   The school nurse explains: "Charmaine has been sent to me several times this year. She had to drop out of swimming class because of a persistent cough that casts up sputum (phlegm). It's not a regular cold but more of a smoker's hack. Apparently she smokes a pack or more of cigarettes a day and has been doing so for nearly three years. Since her parents and her nineteen-year-old brother all smoke, they always have cigarettes around the house. Her parents don't seem much concerned about the girl's habit. Apparently they think it's rather cute. And then Charmaine's menstrual periods began two months ago, so she came to see me about that. Her advice about such things seems to come from her friends rather than her family, so she's ended up with a lot of disturbing misinformation. I've tried explaining things to her in a more factual, nonfrightening way."

Ronald, age fourteen   A physical education instructor at the high school reports: "Ron has the makings of a fine athlete. He's just a freshman, but he's big for his age and he's strong and getting better coordinated. At home he does some weight lifting, and in gym class he's very diligent about calisthenics and running laps around the track. He's intent on developing the strength, endurance, and agility he needs to excel at sports. I'm trying to help him do that without harming himself. But one thing about Ron that the other kids find amusing is his color-blindness. In gym class when we divide up to play basketball, he can't tell the red shirts from the green shirts. I should also mention that he's not just a promising athlete, but a good thinker as well. In my health education class his contributions to discussions are well reasoned, and he's always near the top on the tests I give."

Stephanie, age seventeen   The head of the high-school science department says: "This girl is a science teacher's dream. I never saw a kid catch on so quickly to new concepts. And she memorizes so well that she invariably has a great load of facts immediately in hand. I think much of the credit goes to her parents and her teachers in the past. She seems to have been well taught. I imagine she's always had lots of compliments on her performance—a lot of rewards for doing well. Her parents continually encourage her and get her things that support her interests. At home she has a sophisticated computer, a good microscope, a large aquarium, and plenty of books. I suppose the reason she doesn't engage in sports is that she's so nearsighted, but maybe that's helped make her a dedicated scholar."

LEVEL 2: THE ORGANIC CHILD

At Level 2, the child is depicted as a collection of organs, each of which has particular functions in sustaining life and promoting development. The organs are interconnected to form an overall system that is itself composed of constituent subsystems. Each subsystem has an identifying name and an assigned role that is necessary to life and growth.

The scientific disciplines of greatest involvement at this level are *systematic anatomy* (the study of the organs' structures) and *physiology* (the study of the organs' functions). The formal pursuit of these two sciences has a long history, extending back at least to early Egyptian times. The Greek physician Galen produced a variety of medical treatises in the second century A.D., many of which contained anatomical descriptions that for many centuries were considered authoritative in Greek, Roman, and Arabic medical practice. Although some of his descriptions are still in use today, others displayed gross errors that were accepted until the Flemish scientist Andreas Versalius in 1543 issued the first accurate, comprehensive anatomical text, *De Humani Corporis Fabrica* (On the Structure of the Human Body). Since then investigations of the operation of each organ and its interactions within the entire system have become more and more refined. This increasingly accurate understanding of the organic level has equipped medical personnel to repair or replace faulty organs or to enhance the organs' operation through dietary, surgical, ergonomic, and pharmacological interventions, thereby enabling affected children to grow up in a more favorable fashion.

The chief method of studying organs in the past has been that of dissecting corpses. While dissection continues to be practiced, especially in postmortem diagnoses of the cause of death, scientists today have at their service a variety of other methods that enable them to inspect organs in living people. These include X-rays, CAT scanning (computerized axial tomographic scanning using X-rays and a computer to combine images of organs from different angles), and ultrasound scanning (sonography, in which very high frequency sound waves passed through the body produce reflected echoes that are analyzed to build a picture of internal organs).

In modern societies, the organic subsystems are so familiar that they need little or no explanation, since descriptions of the organs now generally qualify as common sense. However, in order to maintain a measure of consistency in presenting the six levels, I include the following simplified description of several of the subsystems to illustrate their roles and interrelations.

The circulatory system consists of the heart and the network of blood vessels that extend throughout the body. The heart operates as a pump sending a constant supply of blood to all parts of the boy. The blood vessels' assignment is to transport nutrients required by the other organs and to pick up waste products that should be discarded so they will not interrupt the child's efficient functioning.

The pulmonary system is designed to intake air from the atmosphere, conduct it from the nose and mouth, through the throat and trachea (windpipe), and into the two lungs. The lungs serve as pumps for ingesting clean air and expelling waste gases.

The nervous system is composed of the brain, the spinal cord, and the network of afferent and efferent nerves that extend throughout the body. This subsystem provides the child with internal communication and interpretation services. The decision headquarters are in the brain and spinal cord. In the extended parts of the body, afferent nerves carry messages to the headquarters about stimuli from the environment—stimuli received by the eyes, ears, and the nerve endings that are sensitive to smell, taste, pressure, pain, and the like. Afferent nerves also detect stimuli from within the body to inform the central decision-making operatives about such things as body posture, hunger, and malfunctioning organs. Efferent nerves are the message lines carrying orders from headquarters to the outer regions, giving the muscles instructions about what actions they should take.

The gastrointestinal system is assigned the task of ingesting food and drink and processing them in ways that provide fuel for the body's operation and that furnish the nutrients required for the construction and maintenance of all the organs. The normal initial entry point to this system is the mouth, where food and drink enter and are then transported down the esophagus into the stomach, thence into the small intestines, and finally into the large intestine or colon. At each juncture of this trip, glandular secretions are introduced to decompose the food and drink into new substances that can be absorbed into the blood stream and sent to nourish organs throughout the body. The gastrointestinal system also extracts waste products received from the tissues and expels them through the anus as feces.

The urinary complex is composed of the kidneys, bladder, and tubes for expelling liquid wastes. The reproductive system, which differs between females and males, contains the components necessary for conceiving and nurturing new members of the species. Furthermore, a variety of glandular systems generate secretions that assist other organs in carrying out their assignments. In like manner, other subsystems contribute their own unique services to promoting growth and behavior. And the bones that compose the child's skeleton furnish the scaffolding on which all the other organs are assembled.

At some point in their operation, each of these subsystems carries out transactions with others. For example, the nervous system provides the control mechanism that determines how rapidly the heart pumps. The gastrointestinal system interacts with the circulatory system to transfer nutrients into the blood and extract waste products that need to be eliminated. The blood vessels not only pass through the lungs to pick up air that is transported to all parts of the body, but also circulate through the kidneys to drop off waste to be discharged as urine.

Such, then, is the general nature of the organ level of human development. Consider, now, how a portion of the development and behavior of our four subjects—Larry, Charmaine, Ronald, and Stephanie—can be depicted at this level.

Level 2 Case Analyses

Larry, age five   The physician who has examined Larry reports: "The main problem here is with the boy's heart. The heart has four main chambers, a pair on each side. In each pair, the smaller upper chamber is called the atrium and the lower the ventricle. The right side receives used blood from the tissues and pumps it into the lungs to be regenerated. The left side receives this regenerated blood and pumps it out to the rest of the body. We've used a chest X-ray, an electrocardiogram, and ultrasound imaging to discover that the boy's troubles seem caused by an obstruction of the opening through which blood is pumped out of the right ventricle on its way to the lungs. The valve at that exit is too narrow, so the heart muscle has to work exceptionally hard to pump blood to the lungs. It's a disorder called pulmonary stenosis. And when the blood supply to the lungs is inadequate, the boy gets breathless. That's why he can't keep up with the others when they play active games. We could also expect his difficulties to increase if has to inhale polluted air rather than clean air."

Charmaine, age eleven.   The school nurse explains: "Lungs were made to take in pure air, not tobacco smoke. Smoke not only irritates the lungs but also chafes the throat (pharynx), trachea, and the bronchi that connect the trachea to the lungs. I would guess Charmaine is on the verge of chronic bronchitis. So much smoking stimulates the production of mucus in the lining of the bronchi, thickening the muscular walls and the smaller airways in the lungs (bronchioles) so the air passages are constricted and susceptible to infection. Chronic bronchitis often is accompanied by emphysema, a disorder in which the air sacs (alveoli) in the lungs become distended. Charmaine could be suffering from a combination of the two, bronchitis and emphysema.

"As for Charmaine's first menstrual period, I explained to her that it's quite a normal event. It's the menarche that all girls experience sometime between about ages ten and fifteen, most frequently around age thirteen. I showed her this diagram of the ovaries, fallopian tubes, and uterus so she could see how the uterus lining was prepared for an egg; then if the egg was not fertilized, the unneeded temporary lining of the uterus flowed gradually out of her body through the vagina. She seemed relieved to learn that she didn't have some awful disease."

Ronald, age fourteen   The physical education instructor reports: "Ron is a curious guy. He not only wants to know the proper way to exercise to build up his body, but he also wants to know exactly how the muscles work. So I explained to him that skeletal muscles are the ones connected to bones, such as those in the arms and legs. They're called voluntary, because you consciously control them to move whatever way you choose. You have about six hundred skeletal muscles that make up about 45 percent of your body weight.

"Muscles have the ability to do two things—contract (tighten) and extend (relax). When you tighten the biceps in your upper arm, the biceps shortens and gets thick, thereby pulling your lower arm upward. When you want to straighten out your arm again, the triceps on the back of your upper arm tightens to pull the lower arm down. In order for your triceps to pull the lower arm down, the biceps on the front of the arm has to relax. So if you are to move a part of your body, one muscle has to contract while one or more opposing muscles have to relax. Regular exercise is what strengthens muscles and improves their coordination.

"Since Ron is intent on developing strength and endurance, this is a good time of his life to be exercising, since studies have shown that weight training brings greater gains in muscle strength during early and middle adolescence than during later adolescence or adulthood [Westcott, 1987, pp. 36–37].

"I recommend periodic changes in the exercises Ron concentrates on. This is because the greatest gains come in the early days and weeks of performing a particular routine, such as doing curls with barbells to build the biceps. So when Ron reaches a plateau in building the biceps, he can profitably emphasize something different, such as pushups to increase the chest and triceps muscles. Later he can return to curls and expect further increase [Westcott, 1987, p. 37]."

Stephanie, age seventeen   The science teacher proposes: "Stephanie has been blessed with a very efficient nervous system—a good brain that processes information extremely well. Her hearing is obviously acute, so her auditory mechanism must be in good shape. That mechanism would include the ear drums that receive sound vibrations and also the bones of the middle ear (hammer, anvil, stirrup) that convey the vibrations to the fluid of the inner ear where microscopic hairs (cilia) stimulate nerve cells that transmit the information to the brain. In addition, the system for translating sounds into meanings in her brain is obviously efficient, since she seldom mistakes what she hears. She has a great sense of touch, too, which shows up when she tries to assemble small objects or identify textures and warmth by feel. This suggests that the several kinds of nerve endings in the skin for sensing pressure, pain, and temperature must be in good order. Granted, her eyes are faulty. She's pretty nearsighted—myopic. The problem with myopia is that the distance inside the eyeball is too great between the lens in the front and the optical nerve endings (retina) in the back. The person can see things up close but things at a distance are fuzzy, because distant images come to sharp focus too far in front of the retina. As a result, myopia doesn't hinder Stephanie's reading or working with a microscope. And since concave lenses in eyeglasses shift the sharp focus farther back in the eyeball, when Stephanie wears her glasses she can see distant objects quite clearly." (See Figure 15.1.)

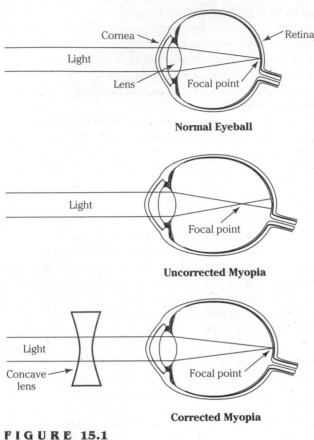

FIGURE 15.1
Correcting nearsightedness

LEVEL 3: THE CELLULAR CHILD

At Level 3, all of the organs are seen as composed of cells, which number in the billions. It was early in the nineteenth century, following the introduction of improved microscopes, that the concept of the cell furnished an important simplifying principle for biology. All organisms could now be viewed as single, free-living cells or, in the case of humans, as collections of cells (Singer & Berg, 1991). F. W. Price (1979, p. 424) proposed: "The cell is the material unit of what we call life."

Although the cells of a particular organ are specialized—designed to perform the tasks assigned to that specific organ—all cells share certain characteristics in common. Every cell is an invisibly small bag containing a fluid called cytoplasm encased in an outer skin known as the cell membrane. Within the fluid are a nucleus (except in red blood cells) and certain specialized structures that are collectively known as organelles. The cell membrane holds the cell together and governs the passage of nutrients into the cell and the expelling of waste products out of the cell. The nucleus is the control center that regulates all of the cell's principal functions. The kinds of organelles found within a given cell are designed to carry out the specialized tasks assigned to the particular organ. Cells can differ markedly in size. Mature red blood cells measure about 0.0003 of an inch, whereas certain nerve cells can be more than three feet long (Clayman, 1989, p. 245).

Each cell's nucleus contains *chromosomes* in the form of DNA (deoxyribonucleic acid) that provide the coded instructions or blueprint for how the child will develop. The chromosomes have been inherited from the child's parents, half from the mother and half from the father. Another nucleic acid, RNA (ribonucleic acid), helps transport, interpret, and implement the DNA instructions. Every child's bio-electrochemical characteristics, and the times at which these characteristics will be manifested during the years of development, are basically determined by the DNA code.

Human development, viewed in terms of cells, begins with conception, when a spermatozoon (male reproductive cell) merges with an ovum (female reproductive cell) in the woman's womb to produce a combined cell that immediately divides to form two cells, which also divide. Those cells divide once more, and this process continues on and on. By means such divisions, the collection of cells multiplies rapidly. Guided by the DNA control mechanism in the nucleus, cells also begin to assume different forms and functions. The resulting aggregation of specializing cells is called an *embryo* during the first eight weeks of pregnancy, and then is known as a *fetus* over the ensuing months until the child is born.

Between the time of birth and the time of death years later, human development consists of a never-ending succession of cells dividing to form new organ components and of cells dying and passing out of the body. The word *cancer* is the pejorative umbrella covering types of cells whose wild increase disrupts the function of a person's benign, constructive cells that operate under the governance of the body's life-preserving, life-enhancing control system.

Level 3 Case Analyses

Larry, age five   The physician estimates: "There could be several reasons that Larry lacks much stamina. One is that his muscles are not receiving enough of the fuel and nutrients carried to the tissues by his blood—by the red blood cells and the plasma fluid. The narrowing of that valve in his heart could account for the inadequate transport of nutrients, since the task of getting enough red cells to the tissues is beyond his heart's ability.

"Of course, there could be other complicating conditions. Red blood cells are manufactured in the bone marrow. If that manufacturing system doesn't work properly, Larry could have a shortage of red cells and therefore an inefficient number of nutrient carriers. We can check out that possibility, but I think the heart-valve problem could be quite sufficient to cause his breathlessness."

Charmaine, age eleven   On the cellular level, the school nurse addresses Charmaine's breathing difficulty by noting: "In the lungs, there are millions of tiny

air sacs (alveoli) with thin cellular walls through which inhaled oxygen is transferred into the blood stream while carbon dioxide is removed from the blood to be
exhaled. Air pollutants, like tobacco smoke, appear to cause emphysema by
encouraging the release of chemicals that damage the air sacs' delicate walls.
Habitual heavy smoking hastens the damage until eventually the alveoli burst and
merge together to form fewer, larger sacs with less area and, therefore, less ability to
exchange oxygen for carbon dioxide. The result is a shortness of breath and, in
severe cases, respiratory and/or heart failure [Clayman, 1989, pp. 399–400]."

The nurse also tells how she discussed menstruation with Charmaine at the
cellular level: "When I showed her the diagram of the female productive system, I
explained that each month an ovum cell was sent from the ovaries down the
fallopian tube to meet one of the many male sperm cells that might appear in the
uterus if there happened to be intercourse with a male. In preparation for this
monthly event, an expanse of cells grew on the inner wall of the uterus to receive
and nourish the ovum if it did indeed merge with a sperm cell. But if this merging
didn't come about, then there was no practical use for either the ovum or for the
nourishing cells, so they all passed out through the vagina as a flow of blood."

Ronald, age fourteen   The physical education instructor explains: "Each of
Ron's skeletal muscles is composed of bundles of long, thin, elastic cells that give
the appearance of fibers. Small muscles may have only a few bundles. Large ones,
like the gluteus maximus that makes up the bulk of the buttocks, have hundreds of
bundles of cells. The cells are not all identical in structure or function. For example,
some act more slowly (slow twitch) than others (fast twitch). Most human muscles
are composed of approximately 50 percent fast cells and 50 percent slow cells.
Slow-twitch cells (Type I fibers) produce low-force contractions for an extended
period of time, thus contributing to greater endurance. Expert distance runners
have up to 75 percent slow-twitch cells in their leg muscles. On the other hand,
fast-twitch cells (Type II fibers) produce high-force contractions for a short time,
providing a high burst of power for relatively brief periods. Olympic sprinters and
jumpers have up to 75 percent fast-twitch cells in their leg muscles. The peak power
output of fast fibers is four times greater than that of slow fibers [Faulkner, Claflin, &
McCully, 1986, p. 83]. Since Ron wants to have both endurance and immediate
power, he'll need exercises that contribute to the development of both fast- and
slow-twitch muscle fibers [Westcott, 1987, p. 18].

"Now, about Ron's inability to distinguish red from green. That's the most
common kind of color blindness. Inside each eyeball, the curved neural surface at
the back (the retina) is comprised of two types of nerve cells, rods and cones, for a
total of more than 125 million cells. Ron's problem results from a defect in the
light-sensitive pigment in one or more of the classes of cone cells. Or such color
blindness could also result from an abnormality of the cells themselves or from a
reduced number of cells."

Stephanie, age seventeen   When Stephanie's science teacher is pressed to
clarify what he meant in crediting the girl with a "good brain," he explains at the
cellular level: "As Stephanie is essentially an adult in stature, her brain would be

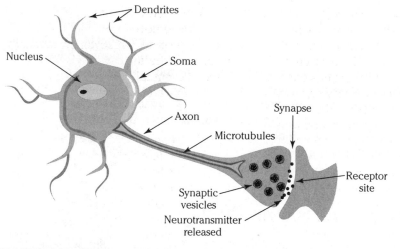

FIGURE 15.2
Typical nerve cell

expected to weigh about three pounds. The largest part of the brain, called the *cerebrum,* constitutes nearly 70 percent of the weight of the entire nervous system. The cerebrum is divided into two hemispheres, the left and the right. The outer surface of each hemisphere (the cerebral cortex) consists of pinkish-gray matter organized in six layers of nerve cells called neurons. The cortex is folded into deep clefts, giving it the appearance of a walnut, with only one third of its total surface visible. Sandra Ackerman [1992, p. 13] likened the cortex to 'a fantastically wrinkled tissue wrapped around an orange,' with the orange representing the much smaller lower brain that includes the cerebellum, which coordinates the brain's instructions for skilled movements and for maintaining posture and balance. The cortex itself is in charge of conscious thought, mental imagery, the production and understanding of language, and the processing of visual information.

"The basic building block of the brain is the *neuron.* While the unborn infant is still in the mother's womb, the brain must grow at an average rate of 250,000 nerve cells per minute to produce the one hundred billion cells that compose the brain of the newborn child. From each neuron's central body or headquarters (the soma) an axon extends like a long arm to conduct signals from the soma out to other neurons. From a different part of the soma, numerous shorter arms (dendrites) receive signals from other neurons and conduct them back to the headquarters (Figure 15.2).

"The nerve cells of the cerebral cortex are interconnected so as to form an extremely intricate network in which the individual neurons send signals to each other across infinitesimally short gaps called synapses. In some cases, signals are passed across a synaptic gap by chemical neurotransmitters. In other cases, signals are sent as electrical charges over a tiny synaptic bridge (three-billionths of a meter long) that connects two adjacent neurons. Nerve impulses fire from one neuron to another at prodigious speeds, sometimes several hundred per second. By the time the child is well into adolescence, there are one hundred trillion or more synaptic connections throughout the neuron network to account for the complexity and speed of brain activity [Ackerman, 1992]. Life's experiences—that is, daily learning experiences—establish, alter, and increase synaptic connections. Consequently, learning something new becomes represented in the nervous system by a new pattern of synaptic associations among neurons. In Stephanie's case, she must have plenty of neurons in excellent working order. Her great array of brain cells are apparently interconnected in more highly sophisticated patterns than is true of many of her age-mates, who don't display Stephanie's remarkable ability to grasp abstract concepts, to recall facts, and to put them all together in such a creative way."

LEVEL 4: THE MOLECULAR CHILD

According to modern-day cell theory, the building blocks of all cells are molecules. A molecule is the smallest complete unit of a substance that can exist independently and still retain the characteristic properties of that substance. Nearly all molecules are composed of two or more linked atoms. Molecules can be dramatically different in size and complexity. They range from such small, simple ones as oxygen, which consists of two linked oxygen atoms, to extremely large and complex varieties, such as DNA (deoxyribonucleic acid), that are constructed from thousands of atoms of carbon, hydrogen, oxygen, nitrogen, and phosphorus. Such complex molecules are composed of simpler molecules (Clayman, 1989, p. 693).

The most important molecules forming the growing child are proteins. Each protein is constructed from hundreds of thousands of amino acids linked in long chains. Twenty different amino acids make up all of the proteins in the human body. What differentiates one protein from another is the arrangement of these amino acids. Enzymes are special proteins that regulate the rate of chemical reaction in the body.

As implied above, the most critical type of protein molecules is DNA. Each cell's nucleus (except for egg and sperm cells) contains twenty-three pairs of chromosomes that are identical in every cell of the child's body (except for red blood cells, which are without a nucleus). One member of every pair was received from the child's father, the other member from the mother. Each chromosome contains a long threadlike strand of DNA molecule. Chemical segments distributed along the DNA strand are called genes. The function of each gene is to direct the manufacture of one variety of protein, with the instructions for this function encoded within the structure of that gene's portion of DNA. Most activity in the child's body derives from the manufacture of proteins that is directed by the genes.

The notion of the gene began with Gregor Mendel in the 1860s, while he was breeding flowers of various colors. The word *gene* itself, as introduced by W. Johannsen in 1910, referred to a hypothetical unit of information that followed Mendelian laws governing the inheritance of an organism's individual characteristics. These early studies necessarily dealt with genes as no more than abstract

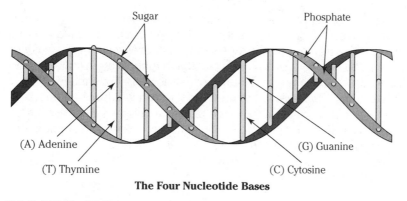

The Four Nucleotide Bases

FIGURE 15.3
DNA's double-helix structure

statistical entities, because there was no information regarding the chemical basis of the traits being studied (Singer & Berg, 1991, p. 17).

Subsequently, continuing improvements in biochemical technologies enabled scientists to effect gradual refinements in understanding genetic inheritance. As a result, in the early 1950s two Britishers, Francis Crick and M. H. F. Wilkins, along with an American, James Watson, could finally put together the double helical model of the DNA molecule that today is widely accepted as essentially correct. For this contribution they were awarded the Nobel Prize in 1962.

The double-helix structure of DNA is often likened to a spiral staircase or a twisted rope ladder. The borders of the staircase, or the vertical side-ropes of the ladder, consist of sugar and phosphate compounds, whereas the steps of the staircase or the ladder are built from four different *nucleotide bases* whose particular permutations determine each gene's unique role in directing the child's development (Figure 15.3).

Recent years have witnessed rapid progress in the ability of scientists to identify which gene segments of DNA carry the directions for which aspects of development. For example, in 1994 researchers identified the defective gene responsible for about one third of the cases of people with shortened ribs—that is, of dwarfism (achrondoplasia). Practical applications of these advances are found in genetic counseling and genetic engineering. Genetic counseling usually consists of someone well versed in genetics providing information to persons who contemplate having a child about how likely that child would be born with inheritable disorders that would derive from the genetic backgrounds of the child's parents.

Genetic engineering involves altering the "inherited, genetic material carried by a living organism to produce some desired change in the characteristics of the organism" (Clayman, 1989, p. 484). For instance, biotechnologists have altered the gene structure in a strain of tomato so as to create a new tomato variety that becomes soft quite slowly, thereby permitting the fruit to remain on the vine a few extra days to ripen and gain flavor without becoming too mushy to ship (Shapiro et al., 1994, pp. 80–82). As yet, no such direct alteration of human genes has been attempted. Up to now the applications of genetic engineering to promote human development have taken an indirect route, that of producing medications for treating anomalies. Among many medically useful substances resulting from genetic engineering are the human growth hormone and insulin, proteins for vaccines against such disorders as hepatitis, and interferon, a substance potentially useful in treating virus infections. The prospect that scientists soon will be able to directly manipulate human genetic material has precipitated a vigorous debate over the potential dangers as well as the potential benefits that could result from tinkering with people's genes (Karp, 1976; Kevles, 1985; Rifkin, 1985).

With this brief sketch of Level 4 in mind, we turn now to a cellular view of certain aspects of our four young subjects.

Level 4 Case Analyses

Larry, age five   The physician judging Larry's condition explains: "If Larry's bone marrow is to manufacture enough healthy red blood cells, the manufacturing process will require an adequate supply of nutrients, which include iron, amino acids, and the vitamins B-12 and folic acid. Each red cell is packed with large amounts of hemoglobin, a protein that is highly efficient at chemically combining with oxygen in the lungs, at carrying oxygen through the bloodstream, and at releasing the oxygen in the tissues. Each red blood cell includes molecules of enzymes, minerals, and sugars that provide the energy to sustain the cell's operation."

Charmaine, age eleven   The school nurse, in speculating about Charmaine's breathing problems, includes the molecular level by noting: "Whereas in nearly all instances emphysema is caused by cigarette smoking, in the rare case the inheritance of an infelicitous pattern of genes on the DNA strands causes a deficiency of a chemical in the lungs called alpha-antitrypsin. This deficiency renders the child susceptible to emphysema, with the vulnerability intensified and hastened by smoking. It's possible that Charmaine has inherited such a predisposition.

"Perhaps Charmaine should be treated with enzymes that loosen phlegm in the airways, since she seems to have trouble coughing up the phlegm that develops in her lungs."

Ronald, age fourteen   The physical education teacher addresses the molecular level by noting: "Ron can thank his genetic code—the architectural guidelines in his DNA—for the impressive size of his basic musculature. Weight training and exercise can increase muscle strength, density, and tone. However, it may not do all you would like for muscle size, since size is so dependent on a person's genetic inheritance [Westcott, p. viii].

"I mentioned fast-twitch and slow-twitch muscle cells. Their separate functions result at least partly from the way they use molecular compounds. Slow-twitch muscles depend on aerobic (air) oxidation of fat and carbohydrate molecules to produce energy at a very efficient rate. Fast-twitch muscles depend more heavily on high calcium uptake and anaerobic (non-oxygen) regeneration of high energy phosphagens to produce quick power, but at the expense of fuel efficiency [Green, 1986, p. 66].

"I should note that during the few days before Ron engages in a strenuous athletic event, his diet can properly include lots of carbohydrates, such as cereals and vegetables. That will help stave off fatigue when he exercises, since such a diet helps store up glycogen in his liver and muscles before he performs. Glycogen, which consists of many sugar (saccharide) molecules linked in a long chain, controls the bloodstream's level of another form of sugar (glucose) that directly fuels muscle and brain work."

Stephanie, age seventeen   To illustrate a bit of the molecular-level condition of Stephanie's brain, the science teacher explains: "An important source of Stephanie's mental skills would be the DNA molecules she inherited from her parents. Her basic gene structure is the main determinant of the number, the arrangement, and the rate of maturation of neurons throughout her central nervous system. It is likely that the composition of Stephanie's DNA is also responsible for her myopia, since her mother says that several relatives on the mother's side of the family are also nearsighted.

"The molecular operation of Stephanie's brain at any given moment is a key determinant of how she thinks and acts at that time. For example, in her cerebral cortex, the synaptic bridges that connect neurons to each other are the conduits for electrically charged molecules that carry signals from one neuron to another. Her thoughts and actions depend on those signals.

"Scientists have already identified two dozen different chemical neurotransmitters that send messages across synaptic clefts, and several dozen more possibilities are under review. The major neurotransmitters are molecules whose signals either excite an adjacent neuron, causing it to fire, or inhibit the neuron from firing; or sometimes a neurotransmitter modifies how excitable the adjacent receiving cell will be. Without such molecules, the brain could not function. The bizarre thoughts and actions of people who have ingested certain drugs is often the result of those drugs disturbing the normal operation of neurotransmitters [Bloom & Lazerson, 1988, p. 43]."

LEVEL 5: THE ELEMENTAL/ATOMIC CHILD

The essential building materials of molecules are chemical elements. In its modern definition, an element is any substance that cannot be broken down by ordinary chemical manipulation into a simpler substance. Any substance that *can* be broken down into simpler components is not an element but, rather, a compound. The building blocks of compounds are molecules.

By the early 1990s, the number of known chemical elements was 110. Of that total, 83 occur naturally on Earth in reasonable quantities, seven occur in traces, and the remaining 20 must be manufactured in laboratory. Each element consists of its unique type of atom. This means there are 110 different types of atoms known.

Since ancient times philosophers have entertained the notion that all matter in the universe is made up of irreducible construction materials. In early Greece, Thales (640–546 B.C.) believed the single essential element was water, Anaximenes (sixth century B.C.) proposed it was air, and Heraclitus (540–470 B.C.) thought it was fire. Subsequently, Aristotle (384–322 B.C.) agreed with Empedocles (490–430 B.C.) that the basic elements numbered four (air, earth, fire, and water), a conviction that lasted well into the Middle Ages. Seven substances recognized today as elements (copper, gold, iron, lead, mercury, silver, tin) were known to ancient peoples because the seven appear in nature in rather pure form. Sixteen other elements were discovered in the latter eighteenth century as chemical analysis grew more sophisticated. Since then, quantitative analytical methods have equipped scientists to identify an additional eighty-seven, several of them within the past two decades.

The amounts and patterning of the chemical elements (atoms) that compose the molecular structure of the cells in the child's body determine whether development advances in a desired fashion or, on the contrary, is distorted or retarded. This matter of chemical balance within the human organism is the primary concern of specialists in the fields of nutrition and pathology.

How then might selected aspects of our four young subjects' development be discussed at the elemental/atomic level?

Level 5 Case Analyses

Larry, age five   The physician speculating about Larry's condition explains: "Not only does Larry's blood-system problem affect his physical activity, but he can't do mental work either if his heart can't pump enough red cells to his brain. The brain's demands for oxygen are enormous, and it's the job of the red cells to get an uninterrupted supply of oxygen to the neurons, since oxygen furnishes energy required for the brain's intense electrochemical activity. A fall in cerebral blood flow to half its normal rate is enough to cause loss of consciousness. In children during the first decade of life, the brain uses oxygen at almost twice the adult rate, so that a child's brain functions account for at least 50 percent of the body's total basal consumption of oxygen. Without oxygen, nerve cells die and, unlike other types of cells, cannot be reproduced [Sokoloff, Fitzgerald, & Kaufman, 1977, pp. 103–104]."

Charmaine, age eleven   The school nurse suggests, at the elemental/atomic level, how cigarette smoking is affecting Charmaine's development: "Among the noxious substances in tobacco, three are particularly harmful. First is nicotine, which causes addiction, so it won't be easy—and perhaps it will be impossible—to get Charmaine to give up cigarettes. Nicotine molecules are a combination of nitrogen, carbon, and hydrogen atoms.

"Second is tar, which causes chronic irritation of the girl's respiratory system— the bronchi and the alveoli sacs of the lungs. Tar is apparently damaging Charmaine's pulmonary system. The tar in tobacco is composed of carbon, hydrogen, nitrogen, oxygen, and sulfur atoms as well as a variety of other elements in small amounts.

"Third is carbon monoxide, which, as its name suggests, is a linkage of carbon

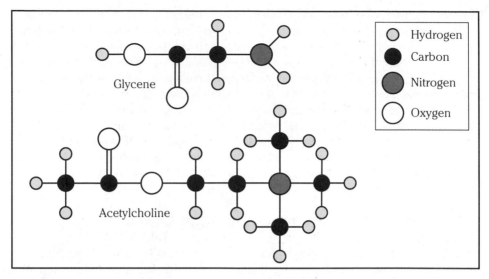

FIGURE 15.4
Atomic structure of two neurotransmitters

and oxygen atoms. It's a very poisonous gas. A few hours of inhaling it at a concentration as low as 0.05 percent can produce headaches, dizziness, and unconsciousness. A burning cigarette produces carbon monoxide, which, when inhaled, passes from the lungs into the bloodstream where it interferes with the oxygenation of tissues throughout the entire body. No wonder Charmaine fatigues easily. Persistently high levels of carbon monoxide eventually lead to hardening of the blood vessels, increasing the risk of coronary thrombosis, which is the blockage of an artery that supplies blood to the heart muscle [Clayman, 1989, p. 992]."

   Ronald, age fourteen   At the elemental/atomic level, the physical education instructor says: "I mentioned that carbohydrates in Ron's diet contribute to the creation of two types of sugar molecules (glycogen, glucose) needed for fueling muscle activity. Both types are composed of the same three kinds of atoms: carbon, hydrogen, and oxygen. So what differentiates the two types is not the kinds of elements in their construction but, rather, the number and patterning of the carbon, hydrogen, and oxygen atoms within those molecules."

   Stephanie, age seventeen   When the science teacher discusses Stephanie's brain activity in terms of elements and atoms, his explanation involves such observations as these: "If brain cells are to work properly—or, indeed, even sur-vive—they must have a constant supply of oxygen and glucose. For Stephanie, who has reached her adult stature, her brain represents only two percent of her total body weight; yet even when she's at rest her brain uses 20 percent of her body's entire oxygen consumption [Sokoloff, Fitzgerald, & Kaufman, 1977, p. 104].
   "Some neurotransmitter molecules that govern the sending of signals from one brain cell to another are rather simple in their composition, whereas others are more complex. Compare, for example, the chemical structure of the amino acid glycene with that of the monoamine transmitter acetylcholine (Figure 15.4). If these

chemicals are to be available as construction materials for Stephanie's neurotransmitters, it's important that she have in her diet and in the air she breathes a sufficient
supply of the four chemical elements—carbon, hydrogen, oxygen, and nitrogen. It
is also essential that her diet include proper quantities of potassium, sodium, and
calcium, because ions (atoms carrying an electrical charge) of these three elements
produce the electrical impulses that send signals through a neuron, causing it to
release neurotransmitter molecules into the synaptic gap and thereby pass the
signal to the adjacent neuron. Hence, Stephanie's cognitive development—
including how efficiently she learns in her science classes—depends on the
effective operation of neurotransmitters, which in turn depends on a proper supply
of chemical elements [Ackerman, 1992, pp. 31–32]."

LEVEL 6: THE SUBATOMIC-PARTICLE CHILD

The assumption that chemical elements are the most basic building blocks of
matter was dispelled with the appearance of modern-day atomic theory, which
postulates even more elemental units (electrons, protons, neutrons) from which
the atoms themselves are constructed. In terms of electrical charges, protons are
positive, electrons negative, and neutrons neutral. An atom consists of a nucleus,
containing protons and neutrons, and of electrons that circle around the nucleus
like planets around a sun. One atom (or chemical element) differs from another in
the patterning of these three types of particles.

Among the ancients who speculated that everything in the universe was built of
a single basic kind of matter, the Greek philosopher Democritus (460–370 B.C.) was
perhaps the most notable. He applied the label *atom* to this envisioned indivisible
material. However, Democritus' theory was not widely accepted, since his proposition was contrary to common sense and he was unable to support it with empirical
evidence. Although the idea of atoms was occasionally entertained by philosophers
and scientists over the following centuries, it was not until an English chemist, John
Dalton (1766–1844), published his book *New System of Chemical Philosophy* in
1808 that the modern era of atomic theory began. Dalton's success resulted from his
demonstrating that results of recent chemical experiments fit the notion of atoms.
Over the nearly two centuries since Dalton's day, scientists have continued to revise
his conception to account more accurately for the facts.

The revisionists in recent decades have proposed that protons, neutrons, and
electrons are not the most basic components of matter after all and that the nature of
these three particles is far more complex than was imagined. Hence, additional
characteristics of basic matter have been proposed and assigned such names as
leptons, positrons, neutrinos, and more. During the 1960s the American physicist
Murray Gell-Mann proposed a new arrangement of then-known subatomic particles
and demonstrated that they all could be interpreted in terms of their most fundamental constituents, which he dubbed *quarks* (Asimov, 1991). By the mid-1990s,
the elementary particles that enjoyed the greatest support among theoretical physicists were these quarks.

Hence, from the vantage point of the mid-1990s, according to a widely accepted theory called the Standard Model, all matter in the universe consists of quarks. There are only six kinds of quarks, grouped as three sets of twins: *up* and *down*, *strange* and *charm*, and *top* and *bottom*. By 1993 all but the top quark had been observed experimentally. Then in 1994 scientists employing an atom smasher managed to infer the top quark from its decay products. They were unable to observe the top quark itself since it lasts for only a hundred billionth of a trillionth of a second before decomposing into lighter particles (Begley & Holmes, 1994). But in 1995 they were able directly to confirm that they had indeed discovered the top quark (Adams et al, 1995). Only two kinds of quarks—up and down—figure in the matter we deal with in daily life, including all the matter that makes up the human body. In the composition of a human being, each proton consists of two up quarks and one down quark, whereas each neutron is built of two down quarks and one up quark (Crawford & Greiner, 1994).

Are quarks, then, really the most fundamental stuff of which the growing child is composed? So it seems—at least until theorists reduce matter to still more basic material and support their models with empirical results.

Having now arrived at the final station in this reductionism excursion, we conclude that from a bio-electrochemical perspective, the developing child is fundamentally an aggregation of quadrillions of quarks that are constantly interacting in patterns that determine the child's entire structure and all of the child's behavior. The unitary child, as an immense assortment of integrated subatomic particles, is also engaged in continual transactions with the septillions of quarks that make up the child's environment.

Then what about our four subjects—Larry, Charmaine, Ronald, and Stephanie? If we had sufficient time and expertise, we might try delineating their characteristics in terms of the electrons, protons, and neutrons that compose their atomic structures. And if the nature and operation of quarks were better understood, the four youngsters' atomic structures might further be depicted in terms of quarks. But obviously those tasks are far beyond our grasp. Furthermore, for the purpose of promoting children's development, there would be no practical use for such analysis, since attempting to manipulate the particles that compose the atoms that make up a growing child is hardly a feasible venture—at least, not at the present state of scientific knowledge.

THE BIO-ELECTROCHEMICAL MODEL: AN ASSESSMENT

For the purpose of assessment, it seems desirable to replace the term *bio-electrochemical model* with *bio-electrochemical approach*, since the paradigm adopted in this chapter does not represent a single theory but, rather, is a composite of many models that share two principal characteristics. One characteristic is the type of evidence on which such diverse models are founded and by which their validity is tested. That evidence consists entirely of descriptions and measurements of the physical construction and operation of children's bodies. The other characteristic is the set of rules or scientific canons that govern how such evidence is collected and evaluated. Hence, the bio-electrochemical approach does not depend on children's introspective reports of what they think or how they feel. The only interest investigators have in children's modes of reasoning and emotional responses is in the configuration of bio-electrochemical events that accompany such thoughts and feelings.

Keeping in mind this conception of the bio-electrochemical perspective, we now assess it in terms of our fourteen appraisal standards.

As the set of scales shows, I have rated the approach either "very well" or "moderately well" on all of the criteria. On six of the fourteen standards, the approach has been marked very high because of the particular precepts of science that guide bio-electrochemical investigation and because a large international corps of watchful scientists make sure their colleagues adhere to those precepts. The scientific community's vigilance is displayed in debates that enliven scientific meetings and fill the pages of scholarly journals. Consequently, the approach tends to enforce standards of internal consistency (item 5), economy of explanation (item 6), and falsifiability (item 7). Theorists whose proposals are weak in these regards are abruptly taken to task and required to produce publicly verifiable evidence (item 8) in support of their position.

The bio-electrochemical viewpoint earns high marks for stimulating new discoveries (item 12). A multitude of scientists throughout the world are constantly revealing new facts and then revising theories to accommodate those facts. As for novelty (item 10), the approach appears to represent a mixed bag. Over the present century, major elements of the bio-electrochemical perspective—such as the concepts of the cell, of molecules, of elements, and of electrically charged components of atoms—are no longer novel. They are well-established, durable (item 13) components of biochemical explanations. However, refinements of these basic convictions are continually being presented. Those embellishments qualify as novel contributions. It is also the case that certain new interpretations introduced in recent decades—such as those involving DNA and quarks—are sufficiently unconventional to raise the novelty level of the bio-electrochemical approach. Balancing these considerations against each other, I have rated this theoretical stance between the "very well" and "moderately well" positions. In regard to durability (item 13), I ranked the approach itself very high (the letter A) but ranked specific theories (Sp) between "moderately well" and "very poorly," because the precise models theorists offer are typically altered in view of new evidence and more carefully reasoned logic. As with other kinds of theories, it is the nature of bio-electrochemical models to be ever incomplete, to be theories in process, always subject to improvement. The canon that guides scientists' work obliges theorists to readjust their proposals to reconcile new data (item 9).

How readily a bio-electrochemical model can be understood (item 2) appears to depend on which level of the reductionism hierarchy is being considered. The lower the level, the greater the difficulty in both comprehending and accepting the theory. Anyone can understand the unitary child and the organic child, for they are easily viewed. Somewhat more difficult to conceive are the cellular child and the molecular child, since their nature is revealed only by means of a microscope or diagrams in a book. And quite contrary to common sense is the notion that a child is ultimately no more than an accumulation of subatomic particles—quadrillions of

A BIO-ELECTROCHEMICAL APPROACH

How well do I think the approach meets the standards?

Standards	Very well			Moderately well		Very poorly
1. Reflects the real world of children			X			
2. Is clearly understandable			X			
3. Explains the past and predicts the future			X			
4. Guides child rearing			X			
5. Is internally consistent	X					
6. Is economical	X					
7. Is falsifiable	X					
8. Is supported by convincing evidence	X					
9. Adapts to new data	X					
10. Is novel		X				
11. Is comprehensive				X		
12. Stimulates new discoveries	X					
13. Is durable	A				Sp	
14. Is self-satisfying		X				

infinitesimal, whirring electrical charges whose nature can be adequately grasped only by people versed in theoretical physics and advanced mathematics.

A bio-electrochemical perspective is well suited to explaining the individual child's physical development in the past, and the precision to such explanation is improving all the time as such factors as DNA, nutrition, environmental pollution, and the like are explored in increasing depth. Predictions of the child's physical future are also improving, though they continue to be considerably less precise than are explanations of the past, since scientists cannot accurately foresee what factors a given child will encounter in the years ahead to affect his or her development. Thus, the rating on item 3 reflects my balancing the more accurate explanations of the past against the less accurate predictions of the future.

Bio-electrochemical theory has much to offer in the way of advice about fostering children's optimum physical development (item 4). A host of valuable information is available about the influence on development of diet, of exercise and rest, of environmental pollution, of illness and injury, of medications, and of drugs.

But what the theory does not provide is advice about how to deal with the child's social-psychological upbringing—how to instill moral values, how to further children's academic progress, how to help them select life goals and choose suitable friends, and far more. The rating on item 4 is a compromise between the model's strength in guiding the physical aspects of child rearing and its weakness in neglecting social-psychological aspects.

On the comprehensiveness scale (item 11) I placed bio-electrochemical theory at the "moderately well" position. An important advantage of the approach is its ability to explain child development at all descending levels of physical structure from the unitary child to the subatomic child. However, humanistic psychologists, phenomenologists, and existentialists are quick to point out that theories dedicated solely to physical descriptions of the child neglect a crucial characteristic of development. That characteristic is the content of the child's thoughts and feelings as discovered by means of the child's introspection and reported in the form of testimonial and self-revelation. A "moderately well" rating has also been assigned for how well the approach reflects the real world of children (item 1). Although a bio-electrochemical perspective can furnish a realistic picture of the way the child's physical structures evolve, it cannot depict the quality of children's inner life as they experience it.

Finally, for me the model deserves a self-satisfying rating between "very well" and "moderately well" (item 14). Not only has the bio-electrochemical approach already yielded a rich harvest of knowledge about children's physical development, but it promises ever greater benefits in the future.

At any point in time, three ways of describing a child's current condition are from the perspectives of the child's bio-electrochemical composition, observed behavior, and phenomenal or existential experience. One of these perspectives does not provide the same kind of understanding as do the others, nor does one translate properly into the others. The problem here is somewhat analogous to that of describing a painting in terms of the canvas, the sizing on the canvas, the types of paints (oil, acrylic, watercolor), and the colors (their hue, value, and chroma). A description of these elements does not convey an image of a final painted portrait nor the thoughts and feelings of a person viewing the portrait. Hence, in seeking to gain a composite understanding of child development, the best we can apparently hope for is to compute correlations among the three facets: bio-electrochemical, behavioral, and experiential. This means calculating the bio-electrochemical features that parallel (1) a particular sort of behavior and (2) the child's thoughts and feelings on that occasion. Yet no matter how consistently the three facets are correlated, each still provides its own unique meaning of the developmental phenomenon being studied. All three convey valuable information required for a well-rounded understanding of child development.

I find it conceivable that advances in the sciences of biochemistry and physics will eventually permit the specification of the electrochemical correlates of every human thought and feeling as well as the identification of the processes by which these correlates change in the course of people's cognitive and affective growth. Whether this goal can ever be completely achieved for the psychic life of humans is perhaps too much to ask. Nevertheless, the pursuit of that goal may well serve as the proper ultimate mission for the field of psychobiology.

FOR FURTHER READING

Agur, A. M. R. (1991) *Grant's Atlas of Anatomy,* 9th ed. Baltimore: Williams and Wilkins. This volume is a resource for the organic level of analysis.

Asimov, I. (1991) *Atom.* New York: Truman Talley Books/Dutton. This book describes the evolution of modern-day atomic theory.

Crawford, H. J., and C. H. Greiner (1994) "The Search for Strange Matter." *Scientific American,* Vol. 270, No. 1, pp. 72–77. This article tells a tale of scientists in pursuit of quarks.

Darnell, J., H. Losish, and D. Baltimore. (1990) *Molecular Cell Biology,* 2d ed. New York: W. H. Freeman.

Gilbert, S. E. (1991) *Developmental Biology,* 3d ed. Sunderland, Mass.: Sinauer.

Singer, M., and P. Berg. (1991) *Genes and Genomes.* Mill Valley, Calif.: University Science Books.

Charting Trends of the Times

What major shifts have occurred over time in the popularity of various theories of child development?

Writing this perspective is a risky venture—like a trek through a badly lit cave, inviting slips and bumps every step of the way. The attempted trick is to trace the popularity over the past eighty-five years of the major theories reviewed in this book so as to show how enthusiastically each theory has been embraced by two sorts of groups, professionals and the concerned public.

The data base for such speculation is not very solid. It would satisfy no one's standards of adequate sampling. My three sources of information are (1) comments found in books and journal articles about the status of different theories over time; (2) published reviews of the contents of psychology textbooks, of the incidence of journal articles, and of the membership in professional organizations to reveal which theories are most in vogue at different times; and (3) my own observations during an academic career spanning the last fifty-six years of the eighty-five year period. That half century began in 1939 when, as an undergraduate, I enrolled in a psychology course entitled "The Science of Human Behavior" and was taught synapses and conditioning. In graduate school I learned of normative studies and Gesell, of Gestaltists, of Freud, and of further varieties of behaviorism (Hull, Hilgard, Tolman, Dollard, Miller). As a college instructor in 1949, I was situated in a psychology department whose personnel made the department 60 percent psychoanalytic. Since those days my work has directed me through Piaget, Vygotsky, humanistic and existential perspectives, cybernetics, Oriental religions, ecological psychology, ethology, and into the many-faceted cognitive revolution that currently dominates theorizing about child development.

My admitting to such aberrant sampling should make it clear that the intention of this perspective is not to disclose *truth* about shifts in the popularity of theories. Rather, the purpose is to estimate *trends* and thereby provoke thought and discussion. The charts throughout the perspective, and their accompanying rationales, are my guesses. Readers are invited to argue the matter and alter the trend lines in ways they believe more adequately approximate the actual state of affairs.

In each chart the pair of trend lines are labeled *professionals* and *the public*. The definition of *professionals* may vary from one theory to another, but generally it identifies people who have academic degrees in psychology, education, social work, medicine, or related disciplines. Such people are engaged in occupations that involve teaching in institutions of higher learning, conducting research, writing journal articles and books, or providing psychotherapeutic, instructional, and social services to the populace. People included under *the public* are not necessarily the entire *general public.* Instead, they are nonprofessionals who are likely to have a good chance to know about the theory under discussion. Such people might be called *the concerned* or *informed public.* As will be seen, those who qualify as members of the concerned public may differ from one theory to another.

In the charts, the word *popularity* means "acceptance of" and not just "knowledge about." A person may know a good deal about Watson's behaviorism without considering his proposal an acceptable theory of child development. Thus the trend lines in the charts identify the estimated quantity of a theory's advocates or disciples, including those partial disciples who are unwilling to endorse all features of a theory.

The unit of measurement of the vertical axis of the charts is quite inexact, ranging only from a vague "high popularity" at the top to a vague "low popularity" at the bottom. Hence the general pattern of each trend curve, not the exact height for any given year, is the important matter. The heights of the curves are certainly arguable.

So, with this multitude of caveats as a foundation, we move ahead to estimating trends of the times.

ESTIMATES OF THEORY TRENDS

The fourteen models of development reviewed below are presented in the following order: normative-descriptive studies, developmental-task theory, commonsense attribution theory, Freud's psychoanalysis, Erikson's psychosocial model, Skinner's behaviorism, social learning theory, Piaget's scheme, Soviet theory, information-processing theory, humanistic approaches, ecological psychology, ethology, and a bio-electrochemical approach.

Normative-Descriptive Studies

In Chapter Three, normative-descriptive studies were represented by the work of Gesell and his colleagues. Such studies describe the status of a group of children or adolescents on one or more dimensions or characteristics, such as height, physical agility, reading skill, aggressive versus submissive behavior, moral values, self-confidence, and hundreds more. The researchers who conduct such studies usually report the group's average performance and the amount of variability among members of the group. The performances of different age groups are often compared in order to reflect an average pace of children's development.

In the graph opposite, professionals are people who conduct research on child development or use research results in their teaching and clinical practice. The ascending slope of the professionals' line represents the rapid growth in normative-descriptive studies over the first half of the twentieth century. The descending slope for recent decades is not intended to suggest that the number of descriptive studies has declined. Rather, it is meant to show that descriptive research that is not

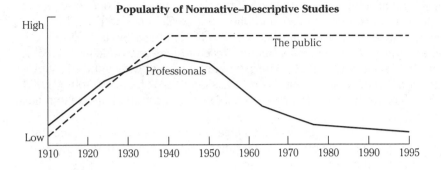

interpreted in terms of theory has been far less welcome in recent decades than it was earlier in the century. What is typically required today is a theoretical setting within which descriptive material is analyzed in terms of hypotheses tested, theoretical links explored, or new explanations generated. In other words, empirical material (description) *plus* theory is now the expectation among most professionals.

The public in this chart consists principally of concerned parents, teachers, club leaders, social workers, authors of newspaper and magazine articles, and advertisers of products that appeal to child audiences. I have drawn the public line to reflect my belief that interest in descriptive information over the first half of the century rose at the rate such material was produced and used by professionals. Subsequently, interest among this public in descriptive norms has, I believe, remained at a high level. Child development trade books, along with introductory college textbooks on development, are usually heavily laden with normative-descriptive contents.

Developmental-Task Theory

As noted in Chapter Three, the developmental-task perspective evolved chiefly from the work of leaders in the progressive education movement of the 1930s and 1940s. The rapid upsurge of interest on the part of professionals (instructors in courses on

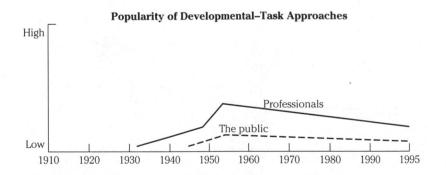

child development, curriculum developers, classroom teachers) occurred in the early 1950s as a consequence of such publications as C. Tryon and J. Lilienthal's (1950) chapter in a yearbook of the Association for Supervision and Curriculum Development and R. J. Havighurst's *Human Development and Education* (1953). Since then the developmental-task approach continues to be recognized by professionals as a useful notion, but the role assigned to it for interpreting child development has diminished. The model's usefulness in stimulating research has been minimal.

The public in this graph consists of college undergraduates who take courses in human development and members of the general public who read trade books on child rearing and education.

Commonsense Attribution Theory

The public in the graph below is meant to be the general population. The straight line across the top of the chart is intended to suggest that naive or commonsense psychology underlies most people's interpretation of child development and behavior. I am assuming that the popularity of commonsense theory remains constant over time. I am also assuming that new ideas from psychologists' theories and empirical studies that are widely disseminated and accepted within a society become incorporated into people's commonsense theory.

The line representing professionals in the chart refers to developmentalists who create theories and who write and teach about development. The line has been drawn to suggest that such professionals always accept a certain level of commonsense theory, but they differ from the general public in that they also include in their own belief systems formal theoretical notions that are not generally understood or accepted by the general public. My purpose in suggesting a rise in the level of commonsense notions among professionals after the 1950s is to suggest the influence on formal theorizing of certain commonsense ideas in recent decades. For example, the declining popularity of behaviorism after the midcentury was due in part to a reintroduction into development research of the commonsense idea that child development theory should be founded on studies of children (instead of animals) in their real-life settings (instead of in laboratories). Furthermore, the

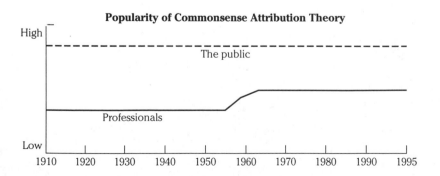

decreased popularity of Freudian theory was due in part to the commonsense belief that development theory is more validly derived from the direct study of a normal range of children than from listening to neurotic adults recalling their childhood. Social learning, contextual, ecological, and human ethology models have incorporated such commonsense ideas into their methodologies. Two recent illustrations of theorists advocating greater dependence on naive theory are V. L. Lee's (1988) and Harold H. Kelley's (1992) urging developmentalists to recognize the value of concepts found in people's ordinary talk.

Freud's Psychoanalytic Theory

By 1900, when he published his *Interpretations of Dreams,* Sigmund Freud's work was already becoming well known among psychiatrists and psychologists in Europe. But it was only after Freud accepted G. Stanley Hall's invitation to appear at the anniversary celebration of Clark University in Massachusetts in 1905 that most professionals (psychiatrists, psychologists, educators, social workers) and the general public in the United States were introduced to psychoanalytic theory. During the 1920s and 1930s, Freud's growing array of publications were translated from the original German into English, and articles reflecting Freud's revolutionary views gained a ready audience in the United States, among both professionals and members of the reading public. Freudian concepts (unconscious motives, infantile sexuality, ego, repression, regression, projection) entered the everyday parlance of informed Americans. Slips of the tongue and dreams were now considered to be disguised forms of shameful memories that slinked past the mind's censor into consciousness. By the 1940s, psychoanalytic therapy had become the dominant mode of treatment for neuroses, and advice in books about child-raising practices reflected a clear strain of psychoanalytic theory.

During the years of its greatest popularity, the psychoanalytic movement spawned alternative versions known as neo-Freudian proposals. Prominent among neo-Freudian theorists in America were Karen Horney (1885–1952), Harry Stack Sullivan (1892–1949), and Eric Fromm (1900–1980). All three agreed that Freud had failed to recognize the great influence that people's social environments exerted on their personality development. Therefore, in the place of Freud's conception that child development is dominated by biological drives, they substituted the proposal that human personality is more a product of cultural shaping than of biological determinism. Sullivan, for example, equated psychiatry with social psychology, and he described his own interpersonal theory of psychiatry as the study of people's social interactions. However, the two theorists who exerted the greatest influence on child development were Anna Freud and Erik Erikson. Such disciples helped sustain interest in psychoanalytic theory following Sigmund Freud's death in 1939 by extending their realm of investigations beyond the traditional analytic session. For example:

1. Anthropological investigations were made of the symbols, rituals, and child-rearing practices of primitive societies.

2. Laboratory experimentation was conducted, primarily animal studies of regression and fixation.
3. Tests, especially those of the projective personality variety [Rorschach ink blots, word-association lists], were used to externalize the content of the psychodynamics of the normal human [child, adolescent, and] adult. (Hillner, 1984, p. 215)

However, since the 1950s, adherents of traditional psychoanalytic theory have declined among psychotherapists, researchers, writers and teachers about child development, and early childhood educators. Social learning models and other cognitive theories founded on the study of normal children have come to dominate the field. Yet an active corps of faithful professionals continue to publish their interpretations and research in several psychoanalytically oriented journals.

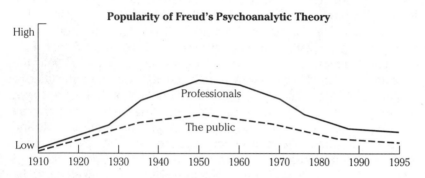

In the chart, I have drawn the line representing the public below that of the professionals throughout the eighty-five-year period to reflect my impression that the American public that became aware of Freudian theory never accepted the psychoanalytic model as willingly as had the professionals. But, as noted earlier, a variety of Freudian concepts have by now become a part of the informed public's commonsense theory. For this reason, I have indicated with the public trend line a modest but sustained Freudian influence on public thought in the mid-1990s.

Erikson's Psychosocial Theory

Although Erikson had already made significant contributions to the field of human development from the 1930s through the 1950s, a comprehensive description of his theoretical position did not appear until 1959 (Erikson, 1959). Hence, in the graph, the charting of his influence on theories of child development begins only at the close of the 1950s. Thereafter, the popularity of his psychosocial model grew rapidly, sustained by a steady flow of books elaborating on his proposal.

Theorists and practitioners who have profited from Erikson's work include those who have extended his theory, those who have sought to verify his concepts, and those who have applied his model in psychotherapy or in explaining people's behavior. Examples of extensions are Logan's "A Reconceptualization of Erikson's Theory: The Repetition of Existential and Instrumental Themes" (1986) and Franz

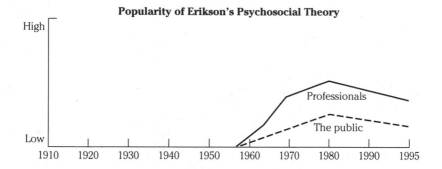

and White's "Individuation and Attachment in Personality Development: Extending Erikson's Theory" (1985). Verification studies have included Gray, Ispa, and Thornburg's "Erikson Psychosocial Stage Inventory: A Factor Analysis" (1986) and Ochse and Plug's "Cross-Cultural Investigation of the Validity of Erikson's Theory of Personality Development" (1986). Practical applications are illustrated in Hamachek's "The Self's Development and Ego Growth: Conceptual Analysis and Implications for Counselors" (1985) and Rose's "The Design of Atmosphere: Ego-Nurture and Psychic Change in Residential Treatment" (1986).

The professionals in the graph are researchers and instructors who teach child development courses as well as psychotherapists and social workers who deal with children and their parents. The public consists of college students in child development courses and members of the general public who read about development in magazines and books on child rearing. In the chart, I have suggested that the popularity of Erikson's views has diminished somewhat since the 1970s, as a variety of newer theories of children's social development have attracted the interest of both professionals and the informed public.

Skinnerian Behaviorism

In their review of American psychology from the beginning of the twentieth century, W. Kessen and E. D. Cahan (1986) pictured the years 1913 to 1930 as a doctrinaire period when behaviorism and the measurement of intelligence were the central issues. From 1930 to 1952, the versions of behaviorism provided by Clark L. Hull and B. F. Skinner were dominant. But since the mid-1950s, cognitive theories have commanded the largest following among professionals in the field.

To appraise the present-day status of behaviorism, P. A. Lamal (1989) inspected the theory's popularity in 1988, the year that marked the seventy-fifth anniversary of J. B. Watson's (1913) "Psychology as the Behaviorist Views It," the fiftieth anniversary of Skinner's (1938) *The Behavior of Organisms,* and the twentieth anniversary of the *Journal of Applied Behavioral Analysis.* Lamal reported that in 1987, when there were 95,000 members and affiliates of the American Psychological Association, only 2 percent of them were identified with the behaviorist division of the society. That same year, in a listing of 406 job openings for psychologists, less

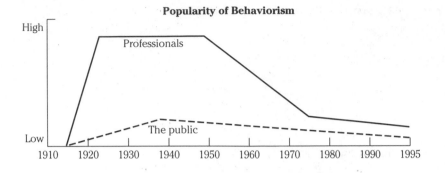

In the graph above, the term *professionals* refers to college instructors in the social sciences and education, researchers, schoolteachers, psychotherapists, and practitioners who work with the mentally handicapped.

than 7 percent called for behaviorists, and most of those were for work with the retarded and developmentally disabled. In the 1988 U.S. federal funding of research on AIDS (acquired immune deficiency syndrome), less than 2 percent was for an explicitly behavioral approach to the problem. From such data, and from more of a similar nature, Lamal (1989, pp. 530–531) concluded: "It is clear that the discipline of psychology is not influenced [at present] by behaviorism." His inspection of current books in the fields of literature and the arts led him to observe: "Here we find that if behaviorism is not ignored, it is vilified" (p. 532).

In the graph above, the term *professionals* refers to college instructors in the social sciences and education, researchers, schoolteachers, psychotherapists, and practitioners who work with the mentally handicapped. The public in this context comprises people interested in learning practical techniques for guiding their children's development in socially desirable directions. By drawing the line representing the public so far below the one representing that of the professionals, I am suggesting that even in the heyday of behaviorism in academic circles, concerned parents and teachers apparently depended on an eclectic mixture of theory to guide their child-rearing practices. The mixture would seem to contain a small portion of operant conditioning and a large measure of common sense and normative-descriptive information, as typified in the advice offered by Dr. Benjamin Spock in his books about child care, which sold more than 30 million copies between 1945 and 1985 (Spock & Rothenberg, 1985).

Social Learning Theory

Robert B. Cairns (1983, p. 334) tracked the growth of social learning models from a set of antecedents through three generations of theory evolution. The antecedents he identified during the period 1900 to 1938 include behaviorist learning theories, psychoanalysis, Baldwin's and Piaget's cognitive development schemes, and Lewin's field theory. In the first generation of social learning models (1938–1960), he placed Skinner's operant conditioning along with the proposals of four Yale University professors—John Dollard, Neal Miller, Robert Sears, and J. W. Whiting—who translated key psychoanalytic concepts into learning-theory hypotheses that could be tested experimentally. Julian B. Rotter's work also belongs in this period. A prominent characteristic of the first generation is the attention theorists directed to

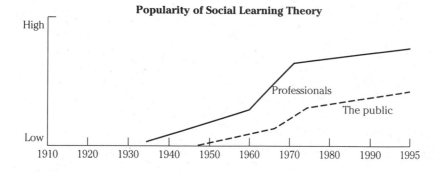

Popularity of Social Learning Theory

the way the consequences of a child's actions in a particular social setting affect the child's behavior in similar settings on future occasions. Cairns's second generation features (1) Albert Bandura, with his emphasis on the way children acquire behaviors by imitating people they observe, and (2) behavior analysts S. W. Bijou and D. M. Baer, whose concept of *reciprocal reinforcement* proposes not only that a mother's actions reinforce her child's behavior but that the child's acts also reinforce the mother's behavior. As for the third generation (the 1970s and 1980s), Cairns observed that the models he associates with this most recent period "are not as readily defined. Perhaps it is too early to expect a clear delineation of positions, or, equally likely, the trend is toward less encompassing but more precise explanations of specific phenomena" (p. 334). Within the third generation he located three sorts of theory. First is *transactional analysis,* which he identified as the study of "how the activities of the 'other' individual synchronize, facilitate, inhibit, or redirect the course" of the social interchange between two people (p. 15). Second is *social-cognitive reinterpretation,* which concerns "how the actions of others are interpreted, how children perceive the roles of other persons, how social stereotypes are formed, [and] how the cognitive stage of the child influences his social behaviors" (p. 351). Third are *social-environmental structure* models, as illustrated in the work of such theorists as Urie Bronfenbrenner. In effect, social learning schemes are a variegated lot, suggesting a diversity of directions in which future theorizing can turn.

The chart starts with Cairns's first generation and carries the social learning models well into the third generation. The term *professionals* here encompasses researchers and instructors in the field of child development as well as behavior therapists in child-guidance clinics, social agencies, and schools. The public includes college students taking courses in development and members of the general public who read about modern movements in psychology.

Piagetian Theory

In the chart, the lines representing trends in Piagetian theory refer solely to North America. If Europe were included, the popularity of Piaget's work would be shown as far higher from the 1920s through the 1950s. As R. M. Lerner (1986, pp. 22–23) noted:

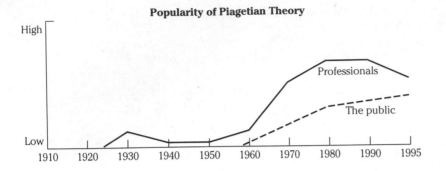

Popularity of Piagetian Theory

Piaget's theory of the development of cognition was known in America in the 1920s. Yet because of the "clinical" nature of his research methods, his nonstatistical style of data analysis, and the abstract constructs he was concerned with—all of which ran counter to predominant trends in the United States—his theory and research were not given much attention until the late 1950s. . . . [Then] the Swiss scientist Piaget was rediscovered, and it can fairly be said that concern with the abstract and conceptual ideas of his theory came to dominate developmental psychology throughout the 1960s. In fact, his influence continues . . . both as a result of further substantiation of his ideas and by promoting discussions of alternative theoretical conceptualizations.

The professionals in the chart are college instructors in the fields of development and education, child development researchers, and those educators who base curricula and instructional practices on child development theory and empirical results. The public comprises college students studying development as well as parents and members of the general public who read trade books and magazine articles on child rearing.

Soviet Theory à la Vygotsky

As in the case of Piaget, the trends in the Vygotsky chart refer to his theory's popularity in America. As I mentioned in Chapter Ten, Vygotsky's work, though received enthusiastically in the 1920s in the Soviet Union, was subsequently sup-

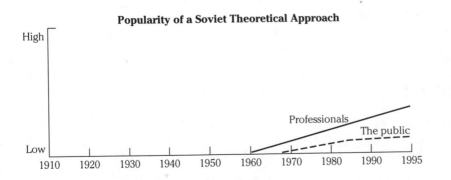

Popularity of a Soviet Theoretical Approach

pressed over the next two decades for political reasons. It did not reach audiences in Western Europe and North America until his writings were released by Soviet authorities and English translations of his work and that of his colleagues were published in the 1960s and 1970s (Luria, 1976; Vygotsky, 1962, 1963, 1978). Since then, Soviet theory has continued to rise in esteem among professionals (Americans who teach about child development, conduct research, and apply development theories to educational practice). The public in the chart is composed of college students in child development and teacher-education classes and members of the general public who read trade books and magazine articles about child development.

Information-Processing Theory

As a theory of child development, information processing traces its origins to a 1958 article by A. Newell, J. C. Shaw, and H. A. Simon entitled "Elements of a Theory of Human Problem Solving." Subsequently, as such investigators as D. Klahr and J. G. Wallace (1976) created detailed computer programs to test the elements of the theory, more members of the academic community joined the growing number of information-processing enthusiasts. At the same time, critics such as U. Neisser issued warnings about the shortcomings of the early versions of cognitive development based on computer simulations of thought and on laboratory experiments: "If cognitive psychology commits itself too thoroughly to this model, there may be trouble ahead. Lacking in ecological validity, indifferent to culture, even missing some of the main features of perception and memory as they occur in ordinary life, such a psychology could become a narrow and uninteresting specialized field" (1976, p. 7).

This recognition of the limitations in the original information-processing models led to a measure of disenchantment with their potential and stimulated theorists to integrate elements of information processing with other versions of cognitive psychology—including contextualism—to produce the more recent forms described in Chapter Eleven (Case, 1985, pp. 43–51).

The professionals in the chart are primarily psychology instructors and researchers in institutions of higher learning. The public comprises chiefly college

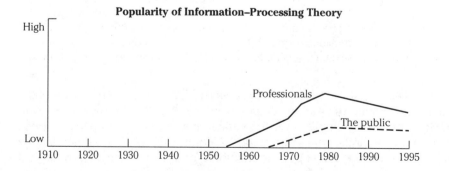

Popularity of Information–Processing Theory

students in the fields of psychology and education, and schoolteachers, therapists, and members of the general public who follow events in the realm of psychology.

Humanistic Perspectives

Humanistic conceptions of development existed in the ancient past and are likely to continue into the distant future. For centuries, the search for self and for methods of achieving higher states of personal existence have assumed prominent roles in major religions, such as Christian mysticism, Islamic Sufism, Hindu Yoga, and Zen Buddhism. In addition, many varieties of mystical practices have not been attached to traditional religions.

Recent decades have witnessed the ascension and subsequent decline of the more formal, scientifically oriented humanistic perspectives reviewed in Chapter Twelve. The leaders of this movement were already well-established academicians and therapists when, in the latter 1950s and early 1960s, they formally banded together. They were united by the belief that the true nature of humans—the experienced self and an optimistic potential for personal fulfillment—was missing from behaviorism and traditional psychoanalysis. As noted in Chapter Twelve, this group included such respected psychologists as Abraham Maslow, Carl Rogers, and Charlotte Buhler. The social climate of the 1960s, with U.S. involvement in the unpopular Vietnam War, quickly drew into the humanistic movement a host of young people searching for "more authentic" personal experience than they found in mainstream society. The humanistic movement thus attracted a mixed bag of academicians and youthful "free souls." This mixture caused certain of the academicians to distance themselves from the movement's openly displayed organizations and practices. Such was the case of Henry Murray, a Harvard professor whose landmark *Explorations in Personality* (1938) and Thematic Apperception Test had exerted so much influence on the field of personality theory. M. B. Smith, in a memorial following Murray's death in 1988, wrote:

> Murray's version of secular humanism was the worldview of a whole person, of a thoughtful, imaginative person, of a magnanimous, self-respecting person. It was the view of a psychologist who saw human potentiality and actuality in their complex multivalence, who combined a sense of the mystic and nonrational with a keen and steady eye for tough realities that contemporary culture conspires to help most people ignore or misconstrue. . . . The vaunted launching of humanistic psychology as a Third Force could hardly have been very special or newsworthy for Harry Murray. All along he had been *doing* humanistic psychology of an imaginative, solid, and well-considered kind. But he shared no common ground with the countercultural, antiscientific version of the humanistic movement that followed. (1990, p. 12)

In 1987, A. Giorgi wrote a retrospective analysis of the past three decades of the humanistic movement. His was an attempt to account for "What went wrong?" and for why "humanistic psychology, even to its adherents, has not lived up to the hopes and expectations it kindled at its beginnings" (Giorgi, 1987, p. 6). He noted that by the mid-1980s hardly 1 percent of the members of the American Psychological

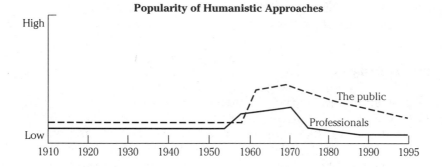

Popularity of Humanistic Approaches

Association belonged to Division 32, the humanistic subgroup. And psychologists of an openly humanistic bent were far less common in university posts than they had been a quarter century earlier. Giorgi cited several reasons for the descent of humanistic psychology: (1) it has never shed its image of being no more than a protest movement associated with the 1960s counterculture, (2) it has produced only a smattering of research that would satisfy typical canons of scientific investigation, and (3) it has failed to offer acceptable innovative research approaches for investigating the areas that humanistic psychology has properly opened for study—"values, personal growth, peace, peak-experiences, the relationship of psychology and culture, psychology and cowardice, honesty, foresight, relations with communities, creativity, play, mystic experiences and so on" (1987, p. 12). Giorgi summarized his observations by saying, "I see the crisis of humanistic psychology as being the same as that for psychology: the problem of what it means to have an authentic psychology of the human person" (p. 19).

The chart recognizes the continuation of humanistic schemes from past centuries and, at the same time, features the versions of humanistic (including existential and phenomenological) theory and practice that emerged in the 1960s. In the chart, the professionals who have made it their business to disseminate humanistic beliefs do not necessarily hold academic degrees or teach in traditional institutions of higher learning. A substantial number qualify as experts on the basis of their attendance at workshops, retreats, and training sessions conducted by proponents of their particular brand of humanistic conviction. They then assume positions within those same organizations or else set up their own programs for guiding people into elevated levels of personal experience and self-fulfillment.

The public represented in the chart is composed primarily of people between the ages of 15 and 30 during the 1960s and into the 1970s. Many were involved in the peace and free-speech movements. Many joined communes, conducted rallies protesting the actions of government and university authorities, dressed as "hippies," engaged in meditation, used psychedelic drugs to achieve extraordinary mental states, or practiced "free love." A smaller proportion of this public was composed of middle-aged aficionados attracted by the opportunities for self-expression offered by a humanistic view of life. I have estimated that the enthusiasm for humanistic practice has been greater and has lasted longer among the public (the now middle-aged who were youths in the 1960s and early 1970s) than among professionals, particularly among professionals in academic posts or those who serve as school psychologists or therapists in child-guidance clinics.

Ecological Theory

As noted in Chapter Thirteen, significant attention to the ecological settings in which children grow up was featured in Kurt Lewin's field theory and in his concept of *life space* from the latter 1920s into the 1940s. At the end of the 1940s and into the 1950s, the term *ecological psychology* was applied by a Lewin disciple, Roger Barker, to studies he and his colleagues conducted on the effect of children's environments on their behavior. These studies generated the modicum of interest in ecological forces represented by the line representing professionals in the chart between the latter 1940s and the mid-1970s. The rapid upsurge in professionals' interest in children's habitats during the 1980s can be documented by the popularity in the professional literature of the views of U. Bronfenbrenner, R. M. Lerner, K. F. Riegel, J. Valsiner, and others.

As Wozniak and Fischer observed:

> In general, behavioral and developmental scholars [in recent years] have moved toward approaches that emphasize the particularities of persons in context. Instead of expecting explanations of behavior to take the form of a few simple universal principles similar to those in Newtonian physics, researchers and theorists have moved toward approaches that are rich in description. Analyses of the ecology and the dynamics of behavior have become popular, emphasizing the particulars of people acting in specific environments and the many complex factors of human body and mind that contribute to action and thought. . . . Activities are studied as they naturally occur in everyday contexts. Children's active construction of the world around them is treated as fundamentally social in nature, occurring in families, with peers, and in cultures. Behavior is studied not as something disembodied but within a rich matrix of body, emotion, belief, value, and physical world. (1993, p. xi)

The term *professionals* in the chart refers to academicians who teach and write about child development and to such practitioners as counseling psychologists, school psychologists, the personnel of child-guidance centers, and social workers.

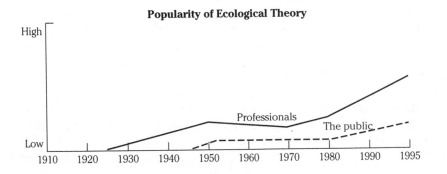

Popularity of Ecological Theory

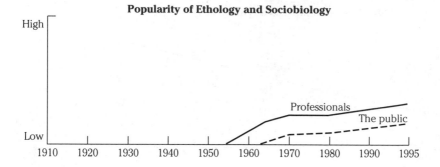

The public refers to college students in child development classes and to parents who keep abreast of books, magazine articles, and television programs that feature pioneering work in child development.

Ethology and Sociobiology

Although Darwinism has exerted a long-standing influence on theories of child development, its current presence in human ethology and sociobiology is of recent origin, in the latter 1950s with the work of J. Bowlby and his colleagues. Since that time, publications in the field have grown at an increasing pace as biologists and psychologists who traditionally focused attention on the behavior of animal species have been directly studying the manifestations of human genetic potentials within diverse habitats (Eibl-Eibesfeldt, 1989; Hinde, 1987). Although professionals (those who teach and write about child development) have begun to incorporate ethological theory into their offerings, a review of textbooks and journals in the field of child development suggests that the amount of attention to human ethology is as yet rather meager. For this reason, I have drawn the line representing professionals at a low level on the chart. And because the amount of information about ethology and sociobiology in child development publications available to parents is quite limited, I have drawn the line representing the public even lower.

Bio-Electrochemical Theory

In the accompanying graph, I cast the trends in the form of two ascending lines, a pattern intended to reflect the present century's rapid acceleration in empirical discoveries and theories bearing on children's bio-electrochemical development. A multitude of developmental phenomena that were explained by no more than poorly substantiated speculation in 1900 are today well understood in terms of their cellular, molecular, and atomic structures and functions. Consequently, professionals can now turn with growing confidence to bio-electrochemical explanations of what formerly were rather mysterious events. On the basis of sophisticated research evidence, scientists have been able to refine their theories about how

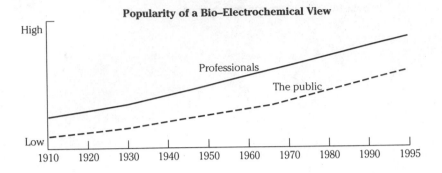

Popularity of a Bio–Electrochemical View

children's bio-electrochemical development is affected by pregnant mothers' diets and activities, and by children's genetic structures, diet, the air they breathe, injury and disease, and their social-psychological experiences. As a result, a variety of behavior disorders are now treated with medications rather than solely by verbal psychotherapy, thanks to current knowledge of the chemistry of children's central nervous systems. Progress in unraveling the structure of DNA has also enhanced the ability of genetic counselors to help expectant parents predict their unborn child's inherited characteristics, and possibilities for using genetic engineering to correct inherited disorders are in the offing. I expect that the same slope of the graph's trend lines will continue into the future.

The professionals in the graph are researchers and instructors in a variety of scientific disciplines (biology, chemistry, physics, physiological psychology, child development), pediatricians, child psychologists, and social workers. As their sources of new theories and reports of empirical studies, they employ a wide range of scholarly journals, books, and computer databases. The graph's trend line for the informed public parallels the professional line, but at a lower level. The informed public's sources of information are trade books and the news media (newspapers, magazines, television, radio) that routinely disseminate popular versions of recent scientific theories and research results.

A FINAL OBSERVATION

To summarize general trends, I would suggest that recent times have witnessed far greater attention to (1) how environmental contexts affect development, (2) how the structures and operations of the mind influence the way encounters with environments influence development, and (3) how children's genetic endowment provides a maturational foundation for development. Theorists have also been offering increasingly sophisticated versions of developmental stages in order to remedy shortcomings identified in the conceptions of stages proposed by Piaget, Vygotsky, and others.

Finally, a possible danger in tracing trends in the popularity of theories is that doing so may imply that people choose only one of the available models as their own belief system and reject all elements of the remaining options. But that is apparently more the exception than the rule. Most people—professionals and members of the public alike—seem to compound their set of convictions from elements of more than one theory. It is true that a person may emphasize one model over another, thereby appearing to be a Piagetian or Eriksonian or contextualist. But closer inspection will usually show that such people have been eclectic, adapting aspects of various models to form a convincing scheme.

THEORY CENTERED
IN VALUES:
MORAL DEVELOPMENT

A search for the ways children's and youths' moral reasoning and moral behavior evolve

All of the theories reviewed so far in this book have been broad-scale models, in the sense that all have addressed physical and mental development in general or cognitive development in general. In contrast, the two theories inspected in Part Eight concern a limited aspect of child development, that of moral reasoning and behavior. My purpose in confining this final section of the book to such a topic is twofold.

First, I wish to illustrate how a theory can be devised to focus on a restricted aspect of child life. For this purpose, I have chosen the most popular view of moral development of the past three decades, Lawrence Kohlberg's stage model of moral reasoning (Chapter Sixteen). If more general theories, such as Piaget's or Vygotsky's or Bronfenbrenner's, can be dubbed *macrotheories,* then Kohlberg's scheme can qualify as a *minitheory* because of its concentration on a restricted facet of children's lives. Other facets on which developmental minitheories have focused include play, fantasy life, creativity, skill at analyzing physical phenomena, mathematical reasoning, oral language ability, reading skill, self-esteem, and more. Minitheories have also been proposed to explain the development of different aspects of children's cognitive functions—visual perception, auditory perception, haptic perception, working memory, long-term memory, eye and hand coordination, and the like. In fact, there are dozens upon dozens of minitheories designed to account for all sorts of limited facets of human behavior. Some developmentalists believe that creating these models of restricted scope is a more profitable endeavor than are efforts to devise macrotheories intended to account for every aspect of development on the basis of a relatively few components and their interactions. Minitheories, they argue, are apt to have greater explanatory and predictive power because they are obligated to account for a narrower range of variables than are the all-encompassing macrotheories.

My second purpose in Part Eight is to demonstrate directly how a new theory can be constructed from elements of existing ones. The way new theories draw on the work of their predecessors has already been demonstrated in earlier chapters, but only incidentally. In some cases, an earlier theorist has been credited with a good idea that is now incorporated into another author's model. Piaget profited from Baldwin's ideas about parallels between linguistic and nonlinguistic development; Bandura built on Skinner's notions of reinforcing consequences; Bronfenbrenner drew on Lewin's concept of life space; and Valsiner benefited from Vygotsky's historical-cultural scheme. In other cases, a new theory represents a reaction against what its author considers to be objectionable elements of earlier models, as happened when Maslow formulated his humanistic scheme to remedy unacceptable aspects of behaviorism and psychoanalysis. Thus theorists may draw upon either positive or negative features of existing models.

This matter of the cumulative effect of successive theories is first illustrated in Part Eight with Kohlberg's work, which incorporates key concepts from such intellectual forbears as Piaget, the German philosopher Immanuel Kant (1724–1804), the American philosopher John Dewey (1859–1952), and others. But a more dramatic demonstration is the proposal described in Chapter Seventeen. To account for the contents of that chapter, I should first explain that in recent years I have been exploring the realm of moral development in some detail, motivated by a desire to synthesize a model that might clarify aspects of development that seem inadequately explained by existing proposals (Thomas, 1986, 1988, 1989a, 1989b). The results of this attempt are sketched in Chapter Seventeen under the title "An Integrated Theory of Moral Development." The word *integrated* refers to my adapting features of other theories of development in an effort to account for how children evolve their moral convictions and apply those convictions in their daily behavior.

DELINEATING THE MORAL DOMAIN

As a preparation for inspecting the contents of Chapters Sixteen and Seventeen, it will be helpful to consider ways of defining the domain on which the two theories focus—that is, the moral domain. To do this, we can begin with a more general term, *value,* of which *moral* is a subcategory.

In Chapter One, I proposed that *facts are objective information*—observations or measurements that are publicly verifiable. In contrast, *values* are opinions about the desirability or propriety or goodness of something. The "something" may be a person, an object, a place, an event, an idea, a kind of behavior, or the like. Statements of fact tell what exists, in what amount, and perhaps in what relation to other facts. Statements of value tell whether something is good or bad, well done or poorly done, suitable or unsuitable. Our focus in Part Eight is on values, not facts, although many of the values discussed will involve the use of facts.

The word *moral* as intended in the following chapters is only one subitem under the general term *value.* Many values do not qualify as moral ones. For instance, there are *aesthetic values* that involve judgments offered from an artistic viewpoint. Aesthetic values, when applied to a flower garden, a poem, a painting, or a dance performance, are reflected in such phrases as "pleasing to the eye" or "nicely turned metaphor" or "delightfully innovative." Another category is that of *technical* or *functional values.* These focus on how efficiently something operates or on how well its parts coordinate. People are applying functional values when they complain about an erratic washing machine or about government inefficiency. *Economic values* concern how much profit or loss an investment yields. *Prudential values* guide a person's social relations and her use of time and energy so as to yield the greatest benefits. A girl finds it prudent not to tell her teacher that the teacher's breath smells sour, and a boy finds it imprudent to wander away to play ball after his father asked him to mow the lawn.

What, then, are *moral values?* Although at first glance this might seem like an easy question to answer, closer inspection shows it to be a matter of considerable disagreement. For example, Piaget (1948, p. 1) wrote: "All morality consists in a system of rules, and the essence of all morality is to be sought for in the respect which the individual acquires for these rules." In contrast, Kohlberg (1976) proposed that the moral domain is one concerning issues of justice. He contended that at different age levels, children's and adolescents' moral judgments are founded on different conceptions of justice, with the highest and most worthy level based on principles of universal equal rights among all people and the overriding value of human life.

M. Siegel (1982) also sees a sense of justice, which he termed a sense of *fairness,* as the culmination of children's general moral development. This sense, he suggested, "involves an ability to consider consistently and without contradiction the interests and intentions of others, to act bearing these in mind and without the guidance of a superior authority, and to generalize fully this behavior in all relevant situations" (Siegel, 1982, p. 2). In Siegel's opinion, a sense of fairness is not simply an intuitive or emotional sense of right but, rather, is a conscious, intentional decision about how to act: "Fairness is a rational attribute not reducible to mechanistic processes. Actions taken without cognition cannot be considered moral" (Siegel, 1982, p. 5).

E. Turiel (1980) has contended that such investigations as Piaget's and Kohlberg's studies have improperly mixed moral concepts with social conventions. To Turiel (1980, pp. 71–72), moral issues are limited to ones that concern *justice,* a term he limits to acts that could cause physical or psychological harm to others, violate people's rights, or affect the general welfare. Social conventions, on the other hand, "constitute shared knowledge of uniformities in social interactions and are determined by the social system in which they are formed," with examples being conventional modes of dress, forms of greeting, and rules of games. In Turiel's view, social conventions can be changed by consent of the members of the group without seriously affecting people's welfare, whereas moral precepts cannot.

In contrast, E. Maccoby (1968, p. 229), from a social learning viewpoint, differed with Piaget, Kohlberg, and Turiel by broadly describing moral values as beliefs "shared in a social group about what is good or right." Likewise, she described moral action as "behavior a group defines as good or right and for which the social group administers social sanctions." Thus, under Maccoby's definition, Turiel's social conventions could qualify along with justice as matters of morality, so long as the members of the group agreed. The viewpoint espoused by Maccoby has been called *cultural relativism* or *social relativism* in contrast to the *universality* standard represented by Kohlberg's proposal that morality consists of equal-handed justice among all social groups, no matter what the personal notions of morality may be among the group members. A further extension of the relativistic position is *individualistic relativism,* which accords each person the right to define the moral domain in whatever ways suit his or her preferences.

A still different conception of morality is expressed by C. Gilligan (1982, 1988), who argued that males and females base their conceptions of moral matters on separate assumptions that derive from the different roles the two sexes have traditionally been assigned in their societies. She proposed that in virtually all cultures women's central activity has been in child care, whereas men have been charged with administering the society and its productive facilities. These assignments have left females in a dependent, subservient role to men. As a consequence, according to Gilligan (1982, p. 19), a woman's conception of morality that arises from caring for other people "centers around the understanding of responsibility and relationships, just as the [male's] conception of morality as fairness ties moral development to the understanding of rights and rules."

While the foregoing display of ways to define the moral domain falls short of exhausting the options, it should be sufficient to indicate that the issue of how best to portray the realm of moral development continues to be a matter of lively debate. It is therefore useful, when inspecting a theory, to know how the particular theorist has defined the realm. The definitions assumed by the theorists whose work is described in Chapters Sixteen and Seventeen are given early in those chapters.

THE LAST ISSUE

Part Eight closes with the book's final perspective, one that suggests how the essence of a theory might be expressed in the form of a concise figure of speech. This perspective has been left to the last so it might summarize the contents of the entire volume in the form of a series of metaphors, one for each prominent theory described in the book.

CHAPTER SIXTEEN

KOHLBERG'S MORAL DEVELOPMENT MODEL

Lawrence Kohlberg (1927–1987) was a Harvard University psychologist and professor of education whose research for his doctoral degree in 1958 at the University of Chicago focused on the moral reasoning skills of a group of boys aged ten to sixteen (Kohlberg, 1958). This early work formed the basis of a career that made him the most widely discussed developmentalist in the field of morality of the past three decades.

We begin our inspection of Kohlberg's model by considering the characteristics he believed distinguished moral judgments from other types of value decisions: "Unlike judgments of prudence or aesthetics, moral judgments tend to be universal, inclusive, consistent, and based on objective, impersonal, or ideal grounds" (Kohlberg, 1968b, p. 490).

Thus, according to Kohlberg, it is not a moral judgment when a girl says to her companion, "She's so sensitive about her looks that if you tell her to fix her hair differently and to wear different clothes, she'll never want to be around you again, so just don't talk about such things when you're with her." This is only a prudential judgment, for it is not universal (does not apply to all social situations), nor is it based on impersonal or ideal grounds. In contrast, it is a moral judgment when a girl says, "They should outlaw capital punishment because no one has a right to take another person's life under any circumstances." This judgment is universal, applies in all situations, and is founded on ideal convictions. Kohlberg's defining the nature of moral judgments in such a manner makes it clear that he was not a cultural relativist. He would apply his definition of moral judgments equally to all societies under all conditions.

In his theory, Kohlberg traced the steps by which children grow toward making "truly moral judgments." The steps "represent a progressive disentangling or differentiation of moral values and judgments from other types of values and judgments" (Kohlberg, 1968b, p. 410). Children who are successful in advancing to the highest stage of moral judgment by the time they become adolescents are ones who base their appraisals of moral issues on concepts of justice. In Kohlberg's view, this means that such young people ground their opinions on the *rights of the individual,* and they judge an act wrong if it violates those rights. Kohlberg further contended that a right in this sense is founded on *equality* and *reciprocity,* so that people are equal in terms of exchange (or contract) and of reward for merit. *Justice* implies that the law is impartial and applies to all equally in its maintenance of the rights of the individual (Kohlberg, 1967, pp. 173, 176).

I'll explain how Kohlberg saw children growing toward the position of basing moral judgments on concepts of justice by first describing (1) the theory's focus and (2) its research methodology. Then I'll (3) delineate the moral growth stages, (4) describe how Kohlberg saw children's natures interacting with their environments to determine their stage of moral development, (5) point out several important characteristics of the moral growth stages, (6) note what Kohlberg's beliefs imply for moral education, and (7) assess the model in terms of criteria described in Chapter One.

THE THEORY'S FOCUS

Moral development is usually viewed as one aspect of socialization, with *socialization* meaning the process by which children learn to conform to the expectations of the culture in which they grow up. In the case of moral values, children not only learn to conform, but also *internalize* these standards and thereby accept the standards as correct and as representing their own personal values. A value is considered to be internalized and not just imposed by outsiders when the child conforms in situations (1) that tempt the child to transgress and (2) that afford slight chance of the child's behavior being discovered, punished, or rewarded.

People who have sought to trace the development of morality in children have typically focused on one or more of three aspects of personality: observed behavior, feelings of guilt, or the basis for a moral judgment.

In the case of *observed behavior,* the question asked by the investigator is, Does the child display greater honesty or integrity or a sense of justice as he or she grows older? Extensive studies of honesty in children and youths have yielded either inconclusive or negative answers to this question (Hartshorne & May, 1928–1930). Rather than basing their response to temptation only on a growing internal sense of honesty, children and adolescents appear more often to base their actions on prudential judgments (How likely is it that I will be caught?) or on social pressures (Will the group disapprove?). Thus Kohlberg rejected observed behavior as a profitable criterion for moral development.

A second approach to the study of rule internalization focuses on how the *emotion of guilt* grows as the years advance. This emotion refers to the self-critical and self-punishing acts of anxiety and regret that follow transgression of a rule or cultural standard. Here the assumption is that the child obeys in order to avoid feeling guilty. Kohlberg (1968b, p. 484) said this assumption underlies the concept of conscience in psychoanalysis and in learning theories. He concluded that even though studies of children through projective techniques show a sudden upsurge in such guilt feelings in the years prior to puberty, projective techniques have not been able to predict consistently whether children really will resist temptation. Hence his own theory is not founded on charting the emotion of guilt over the years of childhood and youth. Instead, his work has centered on a third approach, that of tracing the *bases of the child's judgments of moral issues.*

In investigating the judgmental side of moral development, the question becomes, Has the child internalized a moral standard, and can the child justify that standard to himself or herself and to others? Such an approach was used in the early 1930s by Piaget and has since been refined by other scholars, with Kohlberg being the most prominent researcher in the field during the past three decades. In Kohlberg's opinion the issue is not whether the child acts honestly or whether the child feels guilty about transgressing the rules. Instead, the moral development issue is the judgmental basis the child uses for assessing moral behavior.

KOHLBERG'S RESEARCH METHODS

The studies on which Kohlberg's theoretical proposals are founded consist of describing to children a series of incidents, each involving a moral dilemma. Each child is then asked which solution would be the best or proper one for each dilemma and why that solution would be better than others. For example, here is a typical Kohlberg incident, the one known as the Heinz problem.

> Mrs. Heinz was near death from a special type of cancer. The doctors thought one kind of drug might save her. The druggist who made the medicine she needed was selling it for ten times the amount that it cost him to make it. The sick woman's husband, Heinz, did not have enough money for the medicine, so he went to borrow the money from everyone he knew, but he could collect only about half of what the druggist was charging. Heinz told the druggist his wife was dying and asked him to sell him the medicine cheaper or to let him pay later, but the druggist refused. The druggist said he discovered the drug and he was going to make money from it. So Heinz got desperate and later broke into the drugstore to steal the drug for his wife. The question then is: Should the husband have tried to steal the drug? Why or why not? (Adapted from Kohlberg, 1971, p. 156)

Responses to such moral dilemmas are then analyzed by Kohlberg and his colleagues to determine which of six developmental stages of moral judgment are reflected in the child's or youth's answers. The task of analyzing and grading children's answers does not involve simply comparing an objective answer sheet to children's responses. Rather, the grading scheme requires training and involves some measure of subjective judgment on the part of the analyst.

Kohlberg began using his moral incidents with a sample of seventy-five young American adolescents in the mid-1950s, and he subsequently tested the same subjects as they grew into adulthood in order to discover the pattern of changes in judgments that might have occurred with the passing years. Furthermore, he and his coworkers tried to discover what influence cultural factors have on the growth of moral judgments. To accomplish this, they used the test incidents with both middle-class and lower-class adolescents in the United States and with youths in such diverse locations as Mexico, Thailand, kibbutz communities in Israel, a primitive Malaysian village, Turkey, Taiwan, and others. On the basis of these studies, Kohlberg concluded that the stages of moral development he identified are universal—found in all cultures—but that the percentage of youths of different age levels who are at a given stage will vary from one society to another. The nature of these variations will be discussed after I explain the characteristics of the stages.

THE LEVELS AND STAGES OF MORAL GROWTH

In Kohlberg's system, growing up in moral judgment consists of advancing through three levels of development, from a *premoral* or *preconventional* level to one that involves conforming to *society's conventions* and finally to a top level that transcends convention and is based on personal, *self-accepted moral principles*. This top level is sometimes called *postconventional* or *autonomous*. Each level contains two stages, as defined in Table 16.1.

Besides identifying six steps or stages, Kohlberg described thirty or more aspects of life about which people make moral judgments. People reveal their dominant stage of moral judgment each time they express opinions about any of these aspects. It was Kohlberg's conviction, based on administering his moral judgment incidents to children and youths, that there is a high correlation between a person's stage in regard to one aspect and his or her stage in regard to others. For example, a young woman's judgment about the value of human life, about telling the truth, and about people's duties and obligations will all tend to reveal the same level of moral development.

The thirty or more aspects of life are divided into three varieties: (1) modes of judgment of obligation and value, (2) elements of obligation and value, and (3) issues or social institutions about which judgments are made. The principal aspects falling within each of these categories are universal, for they are found in all cultures according to Kohlberg. Here is one version of the aspects:

> *Modes of Judgment of Obligation and Value:* Judgments of (a) right, (b) having a right, (c) duty or obligation, (d) responsibility, (e) praise or blame, (f) punishment or reward, and (g) nonmoral value or goodness. Also (h) justification and explanation.
>
> *Elements of Obligation and Value:* (a) prudence (consequences desirable or undesirable to *oneself*), (b) social welfare (consequences desirable or undesirable to *others*), (c) love, (d) respect, (e) justice as liberty, (f) justice as equality, and (g) justice as reciprocity and contract.
>
> *Issues or Institutions:* (a) social norms, (b) personal conscience, (c) roles and issues of affection, (d) roles and issues of authority and democracy (division of labor between roles related to social control), (e) civil liberties (rights to liberty and equality as humans, citizens, or members of groups), (f) justice of actions apart from fixed rights (trust, reciprocity, contract in actions of one person), (g) punitive justice, (h) life, (i) property, (j) truth, and (k) sex. (1971, p. 166)

To show how one of these aspects can be interpreted in terms of the stages, consider a moral judgment incident focusing on the issue of life (item *h* in the issues list) and see how three boys reacted to the incident. The event posed to the boys involved a doctor who had to decide whether to "mercy kill" a woman requesting death because she was suffering intense pain.

T A B L E 16.1
Description of moral judgment stages

I. *Preconventional Level (Premoral Level).* A person follows society's rules of right and wrong but in terms of the physical or hedonistic consequences (punishment, reward, exchange of favors) and in view of the power of the authority who imposes the rules.

Stage 1. *Punishment and obedience orientation.* Whether an action is good or bad depends on whether it results in punishment or reward. If the individual is going to get punished for it, it's bad so he shouldn't do it. If he won't get punished, he can do it, regardless of the human meaning or value of the act.

Stage 2. *Naive instrumental orientation.* Proper action instrumentally satisfies the individual's needs and occasionally the needs of others. As in the marketplace, human relations are based on getting a fair return for one's investment. Reciprocity or fairness involves "you scratch my back and I'll scratch yours," but not out of loyalty, gratitude, or justice.

II. *Conventional Level.* A person conforms to the expectations of her family, group, or nation. She actively supports and justifies the existing social order.

Stage 3. *Good-boy, nice-girl orientation.* A person acts in ways that please or help others and are approved by them. For the first time, the individual's intention becomes important ("she means well"). Approval is earned by being "nice."

Stage 4. *Law-and-order orientation.* A person is doing the right thing when he does his duty, shows respect for authority, and maintains the existing social order for its own sake.

III. *Postconventional, Principled, or Autonomous Level.* A person tries to identify universal moral values that are valid, regardless of what authority or group subscribes to the values and despite the individual's own connection or lack of connection with such authorities or groups.

Stage 5. *Social-contract orientation.* This usually involves legalistic and utilitarian overtones. Moral behavior is defined in terms of general individual rights and according to standards that have been critically examined and to which the whole society has given its consent. This is the "official" morality of the United States Constitution and the U.S. government. There is a clear recognition that personal values and opinions are relative, and thus there are procedures for reaching consensus and for changing laws for social utility reasons (rather than freezing laws because they are inviolate, as under stage 4's law-and-order orientation).

Stage 6. *Universal ethical principle orientation.* A person's moral judgments are based on universal principles of justice, on the reciprocity and equality of human rights, and on respect for the dignity of humans as individual persons. *Right* is defined by the individual's conscience in accord with self-chosen, general ethical convictions.

Recast and simplified from Kohlberg, 1967, p. 171.

13-year-old boy: "Maybe it would be good to put her out of her pain, she'd be better off that way. But the husband wouldn't want it, it's not like an animal. If a pet dies you can get along without it—it isn't something you really need. Well, you can get a new wife, but it's not really the same." (Scored as stage 2—the value of life is instrumental to satisfying the needs of its possessor or others.)

16-year-old boy: "No, he shouldn't [kill her]. The husband loves her and wants to see her. He couldn't want her to die sooner, he loves her too much." (Scored as stage 3—the value of life is based on empathy and affection of family members toward its possessor.)

16-year-old boy: "The doctor wouldn't have the right to take a life, no human has the right. He can't create life, he shouldn't destroy it." (Scored as stage 4—life is sacred according to a categorical or religious order of rights and duties.) (Kohlberg, 1967, pp. 174–175)

To summarize, note that Kohlberg's six stages represent a movement from lower levels of moral decision, where moral decisions are entangled with other value judgments and the rules are changed as the facts in the case change, to higher levels that separate moral values (justice and reciprocity) from other sorts and that utilize universal principles that apply to anyone in any situation. To illustrate this movement from the particular to the universal rule, consider three of the stages as they relate to the value of life. At stage 1, only important people's lives are valued, at stage 3 only family members', but at stage 6 all life is valued morally equally (Kohlberg, 1971, p. 185).

THE INTERACTION OF NATURE AND NURTURE

In response to the question of which moral stages a given child will pass through and when she or he will do it, Kohlberg adopted an interactionist position. He did not believe a child's moral stages are produced entirely by genetic inheritance or entirely by factors in the environment. Rather, he proposed that four principal factors interact to determine how high in the six-stage hierarchy a person will progress and when he or she will arrive at each stage. The first factor, and the one with the greatest genetic or inherited component, is the individual's *level of logical reasoning* as identified in Piaget's cognitive growth system. The second, a personal factor that probably has both genetic and environmental elements, is the child's desire or *motivation,* sometimes referred to as the child's *needs.* The remaining two factors are entirely environmental: (1) the child's opportunities to learn *social roles* and (2) the *form of justice* in the social institutions with which the child is familiar. To understand how these factors interact, we need to inspect each in more detail.

The Level of Cognitive and Logical Development

In the realm of children's logical thinking, Kohlberg identified himself as a disciple of Piaget. First, he was convinced that it is the child's nature to pass through the cognitive development stages identified by Piaget. He further believed that the achievement of a particular cognitive level in Piaget's scheme is a necessary prerequisite of the child's achieving a particular moral reasoning stage.

To substantiate his belief, Kohlberg administered both Piagetian logical thinking tasks and his own moral-incident tests to the same group of subjects. He discovered that children who did not succeed on a given level of Piaget's tasks almost never showed the moral reasoning level that paralleled the Piagetian tasks. In contrast, children who were in the upper levels of moral reasoning could almost always complete the parallel and the lower-level Piagetian tasks. Consequently,

Kohlberg concluded that the sort of logical thinking represented by Piaget's hierarchy forms the necessary foundation for the kinds of moral reasoning measured by his own moral-decision situations. This logical thinking component, then, is the maturational or "natural growth" factor—and perhaps the most powerful of the four factors that Kohlberg believed determine a child's level of moral reasoning.

If the child's cognitive stage were the only component of moral judgment, then as soon as the child reached a given cognitive level, his or her moral judgments would likewise be at the same level. But such is not the case. There is often a gap between the two, with moral reasoning lagging behind cognitive skill in various degrees. The cause of this lag, according to Kohlberg, is the condition of the other three factors that interact with mental maturity.

The Factor of Will or Desire

While it is always in our own interests to reason at the highest level of which we are capable, it may not be in our best interests to make moral judgments at the highest level. Some people who are capable of judging morally at stage 6 may not do so because they do not wish to end up as martyrs as did Socrates, Lincoln, and Martin Luther King Jr. So a youth may have the concepts of stages 5 or 6 but not use them habitually because they do not seem worth the trouble or the risk in his particular social setting. Thus a portion of the slippage between cognitive level and moral stage may be accounted for by the operation of a girl's or boy's emotions, desires, or willpower. However, Kohlberg felt that this factor of *will* plays only a minor part in determining judgment stages. The other three factors in the quartet of influences are far more important (Kohlberg, 1971, pp. 188–190).

Social Role-Taking

Kohlberg agreed with many social psychologists that children become socialized by learning to take the roles of people around them. As children interact with others, they imagine themselves in the others' shoes and see life from others' perspectives. Children also learn to see themselves as others see them. Hence *role-taking*, or identifying and empathizing with other people, enables the child to become an effective social being.

Within the broad sphere of socialization, the development of the more specific area of moral judgment "is based on sympathy for others, as well as on the notion that the moral judge must adopt the perspective of the 'impartial spectator' or the 'generalized other' " (Kohlberg, 1971, p. 190). How well children learn to adopt others' roles depends to a great extent on the conditions of their social environment. Some environments encourage role-taking and thus hasten children's advance up the moral judgment hierarchy. Other environments limit opportunities to learn role-taking and thus slow children's advances in moral growth and may prevent them from ever reaching stages 4 or 5.

Kohlberg suggested that it is this difference in role-taking opportunities among cultures or social-class levels that apparently accounts for the marked differences in moral judgment development among societies and between middle and lower socioeconomic classes within a society.

> In four different cultures, middle-class children were found to be more advanced in moral judgment than matched lower-class children. This was not because the middle-class children heavily favored a certain type of thought which corresponded to the prevailing middle-class pattern. Instead, middle-class and working-class children seemed to move through the same sequences, but the middle-class children seemed to move faster and farther. (1971, p. 190)

Other studies by Kohlberg's group have shown that popular children who participated a great deal with their peers were far more advanced in moral judgment than unpopular or nonparticipating children. At least part of the cause of this difference seems to be differences in role-taking opportunities in the children's families. Greater role adoption was promoted by families that encouraged sharing in decisions, awarded responsibility to the child, pointed out consequences of action to others, communicated within the family group, and exhibited emotional warmth.

Some people have assumed that the most crucial of these home elements for furthering moral development is the degree to which the atmosphere is warm, loving, and identification-inducing. However, Kohlberg said this is not so. Apparently some minimum level of warmth in personal contacts with others is necessary for a child or adolescent to feel that he or she is an accepted participant in the social circle. However, what is far more important is that the environment furnish many role-taking opportunities, not that the child receive maximum affection from the group (Kohlberg, 1971, p. 191).

The Justice Structure

The fourth variable that contributes to the growth of moral judgment is the justice structure of the social groups or institutions with which the child interacts. Such social entities include the family, the neighborhood gang or play group, the school, the church, the community, the nation, and those media that provide vicarious opportunities for role-taking—television, radio, books, magazines, and the like.

At all stages of moral development, the individual has some sort of concern for the welfare of others. But only by stage 5 is this concern based on what Kohlberg regarded as principles of true justice, those of *equality* and *reciprocity*. The principle of equality means that we "treat every man's claim equally, regardless of the man" (Kohlberg, 1967, p. 169). The principle of reciprocity means equality of exchange. It means "punishment for something bad, reward for something good, and contractual exchange" or fulfilling one's bargain.

Within a given society the groups or institutions with which the growing child is intimately involved vary in their justice structures. A public school that the child is forced to attend under compulsory education laws is different from a university that the youth attends voluntarily. A neighborhood play group is different from a reformatory. A Girl Scout troop differs from a family. A family dominated by an autocratic father differs from one in which children are encouraged to make decisions, take responsibility, and be rewarded in accordance with how they carry out their self-imposed commitments.

In effect, Kohlberg proposed that children who participate in social groups that operate on a high level of equality and reciprocity will move to higher levels of moral judgment than children whose main participation is in groups that have lower sorts of justice structures.

So the dominant level of moral judgment children or youths use results from the interaction of four determinants: their level of cognitive and logical maturation, their will or desire, their opportunities for role-taking, and the dominant modes of justice in the main social groups of which they are a part.

THE THREE CHARACTERISTICS OF THE STAGES

A large proportion of modern social scientists as well as the "culturally enlightened" laity are what Kohlberg labeled *ethical relativists.* They believe that moral principles vary from one culture to another and that there is no logical way to explain or reconcile these differences among cultures. Such a line of thought can easily lead to the conviction that one culture's moral values are as good as another's, since each culture has as much right to its own value system as does any other culture. On the basis of this assumption, we would conclude that a person is morally developed or well adjusted when he abides by the dominant values of his society. But it is not necessary for an ethical relativist to stop the extension of this line of logic at the societal level. If he or she chooses, the ethical relativist can carry it on to individuals within a society. In such a case, the relativist can conclude that it is each individual's right to adopt his or her own code of ethics, since there is no logical way to judge one person's code as better than another's. (Of course, it is clear that extending ethical relativism to the individual will have important consequences for the individual's fate, because the individual who deviates markedly from the group's norms can be dubbed odd or possibly locked up by the dominant group as a criminal or lunatic.)

However, Kohlberg was not an ethical relativist. He contended that moral development does not depend on the particular society's dominant ideas of justice. Instead, he said that the developmental stages he identified are universal, integrated, and invariant.

By *universal* he meant that he believed the stages are true of all societies. Originally Kohlberg believed that in every culture there are people at all six stages. But more recently he questioned whether stage 6 is ever actually achieved (Colby, Kohlberg, Gibbs, & Lieberman, 1983, p. 5). It is true, however, that the dominant moral stage for the society as a whole, or for a given age level, differs from one culture to another. One culture may operate mostly on stage 2 reasoning, another on stage 4 reasoning. But this does not mean that the patterns of moral thought are quite different in the two cultures. Rather, the discrepancies result because the children in one society advance up the six-stage hierarchy at a different rate than the

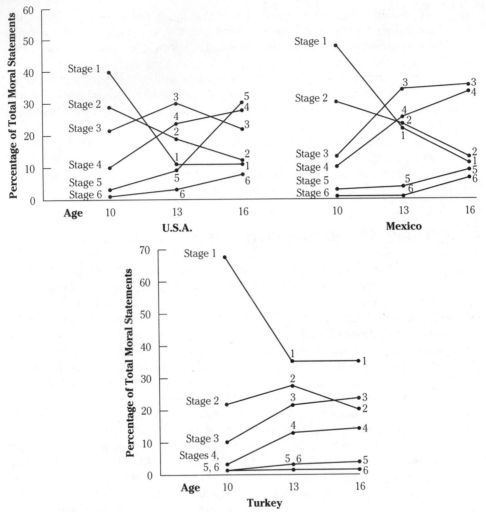

FIGURE 16.1
Boys' moral judgments in three societies (Kohlberg & Kramer, 1969, p. 104)

children in the other society. The differences in rate might be due partially to genetic differences between the two groups but more likely result from differences in the role-taking opportunities and justice structures of the two cultures. Kohlberg said that the same stages of moral reasoning are found in all societies, although the number of persons at each stage may differ, as illustrated in Figure 16.1. The graphs compare the moral judgments of boys in middle-class U.S. and Mexican communities with those in an isolated village in Turkey. The age levels charted are ten, thirteen, and sixteen. As the graphs indicate, by age sixteen some boys in each of the cultures were at each of the six levels of moral growth. However, a larger percentage of U.S. and Mexican boys than of Turkish boys were at higher stages at each age level.

By *integrated* Kohlberg meant that in various aspects of life a person's moral decisions will reflect a similar level of development. It would be rare indeed for a person to operate at stage 1 when judging honesty, at stage 3 when judging freedom, and stage 6 when judging responsibility. Rather, judgments in all realms will tend to cluster around the same level—around 1 and 2, around 3 and 4, or the like.

By *invariant* Kohlberg meant that a youth cannot skip a stage or two while advancing to a higher level. People must pass through each stage in sequence. A key reason for this invariance, in Kohlberg's opinion, is that each successive stage consists of components of the prior stage plus a new component or two.

These principles of universality, integration, and invariance, and the four proposed determinants of moral growth, have important implications for how Kohlberg's theory can be put to practical use.

PRACTICAL APPLICATIONS: FASHIONING A PROGRAM OF MORAL EDUCATION

If Kohlberg's theory is correct, what should be the form of moral education? Before applying our foregoing discussion to answering this question, we need to consider one more concept that Kohlberg adopted from Piaget's theory of cognitive development, that of *equilibration* or of seeking equilibrium. In Piaget's system, children continue to be satisfied with simplistic, unsophisticated answers to questions of relationships among things until (1) they reach a particular age of internal maturation and (2) have engaged in enough activities related to the question. At this point they begin to feel dissatisfied and a bit disordered, for they feel an incongruence between their existing schemes (or conception of reality) and a newly perceived reality. This dissonance throws them out of cognitive equilibrium and serves as a motive to "change their mind" or to accommodate in order to set things right—in order to attain equilibrium once more.

Kohlberg applied this same principle of equilibration to growth in moral judgment. When children are cognitively mature enough and have had enough role-taking experiences in relation to groups that have suitable justice structures, then they can be stimulated toward upward movement in the moral judgment stages by being confronted with problems of moral conflict. In other words, moral education properly consists of confronting the child or adolescent with moral dilemmas at the same time that the child is maturationally and socially ready to take a step ahead.

With this use of equilibration in mind, let's now review the components of a moral education system as conceived within Kohlberg's scheme. First, the goal of moral education is not to inculcate a particular set of values that are dominant or at least common in a given society. Instead, the goal is to stimulate the child's growth through the six stages that are considered universally valid for all cultures. The teacher's expectation for where the child or youth should be in moral growth at a particular time is governed by the teacher's recognition of the level of a child's cognitive development (per Piaget) and of the opportunities the child enjoys to adopt roles in social groups. The expectation is also influenced by the sorts of justice found in the groups in which the child participates and by the child's motivation—that is, will it seem worthwhile to the child to think at a higher moral level?

The methodology the teacher adopts consists primarily of posing moral decision problems for the students and having various students give their arguments to support their decisions. In this process, some students will argue from the viewpoint of a higher stage than will others. Or the teacher may argue from a higher stage. This conflict of arguments is intended to produce a feeling of disequilibrium in young people who are approaching the threshold of a new stage, so that the basis for their thinking begins to change and they are hoisted to the new level.

In summary, Kohlberg objected to a pair of commonly practiced systems of moral education: (1) the "thoughtless system of moralizing by individual teachers and principals when children deviate from minor administrative regulations" and (2) "the effort to inculcate the majority values, particularly as reflected in vague stereotypes about moral character" (Kohlberg, 1967, p. 169). In place of these he recommended a system that stimulates "the 'natural' development of the individual child's own moral judgment and of the capacities allowing him to use his own moral judgment to control his behavior." The purpose is to aid the child "to take the next step in a direction toward which he is already tending, rather than imposing an alien pattern on him" (Kohlberg, 1967, p. 169).

A further application of Kohlberg's theory takes the form of *the just community*. Kohlberg used this term to identify the practice of using the daily moral dilemmas faced in school as the subject of students' study of moral decision making. The just-community approach was tried out in an alternative school that operated under the aegis of a larger, "regular" high school. The sixty or so students enrolled in the alternative school were ones who had had difficulty meeting the academic and social behavior standards of the regular high school, so they provided a particularly good test of the just-community approach. Kohlberg's group guided the staff and students of the alternative school in establishing a system of democratic governance in which students and teachers would "overcome their reliance on traditional authority patterns" and "learn to democratically share the responsibility for decision making" (Hersh, Miller, & Fielding, 1980, p. 151). Events during the school day that involved stealing, missing classes, using drugs, and the like became discussed issues, with students and faculty members having an equal voice in how to resolve the issues. Instituting and operating such a system proved to be complex, time-consuming, and in a constant state of negotiation.

Clearly, the idea of teachers sharing power and responsibility with students for the conduct of a classroom or school is not new. It goes back at least to the early decades of this country, led by John Dewey's contention that education is not just a preparation for life but, rather, education *is* life. What is novel about Kohlberg's just community is the linking of his stages of moral development to the operation of such a system. In other words, discussions about moral issues that are faced in the conduct of the school are directed toward raising moral decisions to

> the highest level of moral reasoning available to its student members. That is not to say at a principled [stage 5 or 6] level, for no students in this school have developed

beyond stage 4, and most reason at stage 3 level. The staff's task is not to impose higher-stage reasoning but to offer the soundest reasoning students are capable of understanding and to continually encourage students to exercise the best of their moral reasoning in arriving at communal decisions. When that is achieved, and when students stand behind their decisions and enforce them, the school can be said to be operating as a just community. (Hersh, Miller, & Fielding, 1980, p. 154)

Staff members involved in this just-community project reported that it did increase students' skills in resolving moral conflicts by peaceful, reasoned means. Power's (1988) review of subsequent just-community projects in other places led him to conclude that Kohlberg's approach succeeded in establishing school cultures conducive to the development of socio-moral reasoning and action. However, Hersh, Miller, and Fielding (1980, p. 158) cautioned: "Because our schools are so oriented toward 'measurable' growth, teachers may find it frustrating to embrace a model that involves long-term learning (often up to five years) and is difficult to measure precisely."

KOHLBERG'S THEORY: AN ASSESSMENT

When Kohlberg's model of moral development is appraised according to the standards proposed in Chapter One, his theory fares well in several respects.

The theory provides both for explaining children's past moral judgment behavior and for predicting their future behavior (item 3). Not only does it permit predictions for the average child, but by proposing four interacting determinants of moral judgment development, it offers the possibility of doing so for individuals as well (if proper measures of the four variables and their interaction are made available).

The moral education scheme Kohlberg founded on his theory offers clear guidance for child rearing (item 4). Likewise, the theory appears to be internally consistent (item 5) and economical (item 6). It has also stimulated a variety of new investigations and discoveries, particularly in the way moral judgment develops in different cultures (item 12). Kohlberg has been credited with opening a number of new perspectives on moral growth and for doing "some very hard and very unfashionable thinking on moral thought" along with "producing evidence that should force psychologists to take the cognitive aspects of morality seriously as an important influence on behavior" (Alston, 1971, p. 284). In the standard psychological journal literature for 1970 to 1995, more than 770 investigations bearing on Kohlberg's theory were reported, with the total number spread rather evenly over the twenty-five-year period. Thus his work has been a source of continuing interest among researchers and educators, whose investigations in many cases have served to support and extend Kohlberg's basic model (item 8).

I have ranked the model high on novelty (item 10), in recognition of the great stir the theory has caused in the field of moral development. Few, if any, other proposals about how young people's styles of moral reasoning evolve have drawn so much attention.

In adaptability (item 9), Kohlberg's scheme appears to be moderately satis-

KOHLBERG'S THEORY

How well do I think the theory meet these standards?

Standards	Very well	Moderately well	Very poorly
1. Reflects the real world of children		X	
2. Is clearly understandable		X	
3. Explains the past and predicts the future	X		
4. Guides child rearing	X		
5. Is internally consistent	X		
6. Is economical	X		
7. Is falsifiable		X	
8. Is supported by convincing evidence	X		
9. Adapts to new data		X	
10. Is novel	X		
11. Is comprehensive			X
12. Stimulates new discoveries	X		
13. Is durable		X	
14. Is self-satisfying		X	

factory. For example, the earliest form of the model was subsequently altered to account for different average levels of moral judgment found in different cultures. Furthermore, in more recent times the results of empirical studies prompted Kohlberg to concede that the highest level of his six-stage hierarchy of reasoning was perhaps unduly idealistic and not actually found in real-life settings. In contrast to these adjustments, in certain other respects he appeared unprepared to realign his views to accommodate other criticisms.

For its durability (item 13), I have placed the theory in the "moderately well" range. Over the thirty-five years since its inception, the model has displayed noteworthy vitality. It will likely enjoy a place in the moral development literature for many years to come. But I imagine that future innovative proposals, founded on additional empirical data, will displace the Kohlberg model from its present position as the frontrunner.

On the scale of clarity (item 2), the theory deserves a mixed score. On the positive side are the many specific examples Kohlberg cited from children's answers to moral dilemmas that clarify terms and differentiate one stage from another. Such phrases as *instrumental relativist orientation* and *social-contract legalistic orientation* are illustrated with examples from children's responses. However, in the opinions of informed scholars in the field, other key terms have not been distinguished clearly. R. S. Peters (1971, pp. 246–248) took Kohlberg to task for being vague and unsophisticated in comparing *character traits* (honesty, courage, determination) unfavorably with *principles* (a sense of *justice*). A similar criticism has been directed at Kohlberg's distinctions between the *form* and *content* of moral reasoning in a given culture. Kohlberg said that the content of moral judgments may vary from culture to culture, but the more basic form of judgments does not. Yet, when these two concepts are analyzed in detail, it appears that Kohlberg failed to produce adequate criteria for differentiating between them.

To what extent is the theory falsifiable (item 7)? I judge that many aspects of the model are amenable to disconfirmation, such as the proposed sequencing of the six developmental levels, the relationship between youths' judgments and the justice structure of their society, and the ability of a moral education program to promote an individual's advancement in the hierarchy. Other features, however, do not lend themselves well to empirical testing. One is the assertion that even-handed justice is superior to other possible ultimate aims of moral development, such as obedience to God's will or compassion for people who suffer misfortune. Another is the contention that Kohlberg's scheme represents a hierarchy of absolute, universal values proper for all cultures. Balancing such considerations against each other, I have rated the theory "moderately well" on falsifiability.

On item 1, Kohlberg can be credited with basing his model on data drawn from a variety of real children. However, there is a question about how realistic he was in the scope of moral decisions that he analyzed. The theory is founded on evidence collected from having children and youths offer solutions to moral dilemma incidents posed to them. Since Kohlberg wanted to make the respondents think hard in order to test their reasoning, he necessarily posited incidents that had no obvious solutions in terms of the dominant standards of a child's culture. However, as W. P. Alston (1971, p. 284) pointed out, these represent only a minor portion of the daily moral decisions a person makes. Thus, according to Alston, Kohlberg's methodology necessarily caused him to ignore the host of judgments young people make by *habit*. Habitual judgments are easy ones because the reward and punishment system of the culture has fashioned the individual's "character" so that the solution to such moral issues is obvious and no alternative solutions can compete successfully with the habitual one. Alston believes that this lack in Kohlberg's research method distorted the theorist's view of the significance of habit or "character traits" and of emotion in determining moral thought and behavior.

This questionable representativeness of Kohlberg's moral incidents seems to have resulted from the unsystematic manner in which he selected his original dilemmas. For his doctoral research in the 1950s, he created nine moral dilemmas to which his youthful subjects were asked to respond. Since that time, these same nine incidents have been used for nearly all of the studies conducted by Kohlberg and his followers. Four of the incidents involve people taking others' property without permission, three concern people being tempted to inform on others, one involves the mercy killing of a terminal cancer patient, and one a soldier's sacrificing himself for the sake of his military unit. On the basis of respondents' reactions to these incidents (or more frequently, to only a few of the incidents), investigators have drawn conclusions about the stage of the respondents' moral reasoning. However, even a casual review of life's moral situations indicates that this selection of dilemmas is hardly representative of the decisions most people face. In effect, a sound system for choosing dilemmas has not been provided by the Kohlberg group (Thomas, 1989b). This shortcoming has caused me to mark item 1 as no higher than the "moderately well" level.

Kohlberg has also been criticized for proclaiming the principle of justice the sole occupant of the highest stage of moral thought without having sufficient cause to deem it more worthy than several other virtues that might have been selected— for example, sympathy, concern for others, courage, integrity, or autonomy. As Peters wrote, Kohlberg's findings

> are of unquestionable importance, but there is a grave danger that they may become exalted into a general theory of moral development. Any such general theory presupposes a general ethical theory, and Kohlberg himself surely would be the first to admit that he had done little to develop the details of such a general ethical theory. Yet without such a theory the notion of "moral development" is pretty unsubstantial. (1971, pp. 263–264).

The model is rated low on comprehensiveness (item 11), since it focuses solely on a narrow segment of cognitive activity, relegating to other theories the task of explaining the rest of children's intellectual life as well as all matters of children's behavior (including moral behavior) and their sense of self.

So Kohlberg's theory, like the rest we have considered, has drawn both praise and criticism. But whatever its shortcomings, it remains the most stimulating and potentially fertile model of children's moral growth in current psychological and philosophical circles. For this reason, I have rated it as moderately self-satisfying overall (item 14).

FOR FURTHER READING

Colby, A., L. Kohlberg, J. Gibbs, and M. Lieberman. (1983) *A Longitudinal Study of Moral Judgment.* Monographs of the Society for Research in Child Development, Serial No. 200, Vol. 48, Nos. 1–2. Chicago: Society for Research in Child Development.

Kohlberg, L. (1967) "Moral and Religious Education in the Public Schools: A Developmental View," in Theodore R. Sizer, *Religion and Public Education.* Boston: Houghton Mifflin.

Kohlberg, L. (1984) *The Psychology of Moral Development.* San Francisco: Harper & Row.

CHAPTER SEVENTEEN

AN INTEGRATED THEORY
OF MORAL DEVELOPMENT

Over the past few years my interest in theories has centered particularly on models of moral development (Thomas, 1986, 1988, 1989a, 1989b, 1995; Thomas & Diver-Stamnes, 1993; Diver-Stamnes & Thomas, 1995). The pursuit of this interest has prompted me to assemble components from a variety of development theories to form a composite model that I call *an integrated theory of moral development.* The view of the model offered in the following pages is a much abbreviated version of a book-length description of the theory that will appear in a forthcoming volume of the same title as this chapter.

As the contents of the chapter illustrate, the scheme offered here has been fashioned from elements of the models described earlier in the book, particularly from the role of consequences in behaviorism and social learning theory, Freud's levels of consciousness, neo-Piagetian conceptions of developmental stages, ecological psychology's concern for environments, and Kohlberg's use of moral dilemmas. The entire scheme is set within an information-processing framework. I have also added components of my own that seem necessary for explaining how children's moral values develop and are applied in moral decision situations.

The topics that compose the chapter are presented in the following order: (1) problems with existing theories, (2) foundational definitions, (3) principal features of the model, (4) foundational components, (5) long-term memory, (6) the nature of environments, (7) functions of working memory, (8) stages of moral development, and (9) an assessment of the theory.

PROBLEMS WITH EXISTING THEORIES

This scheme is designed to cope with an array of problems that seem inadequately resolved in available descriptions of moral development.

The first problem is one that A. L. Brown (1979, p. 235) claims is a shortcoming of many developmental models: "at best they provide a description of the stages or states of development but they cannot account for the transformations that lead to growth." Such is the case with Piaget's and Kohlberg's proposals. Both Piaget and Kohlberg offer some general processes (assimilation, accommodation) or conditions (neural maturation, opportunities to adopt roles) that affect moral development, but neither of them describes the way daily events effect changes in moral reasoning.

A second problem derives from the imprecise conception of moral values that existing theories provide. For instance, they fail to account for why such a principle as "thou shalt not kill" is typically applied differently in different contexts.

A third difficulty is the discrepancy between people's apparent moral values and their behavior in moral decision situations. Why do people sometimes—perhaps rather often—fail to act in keeping with their stated moral principles?

Another objection, intimately linked to all three of the foregoing difficulties, is that the analysis of environments in the development of both moral reasoning and moral behavior is inadequate in existing theories.

A fifth concern is the imprecise way that most theories depict the architecture of the mind. In particular, they fail to address the role apparently played by different levels of consciousness in people's moral thought and action.

The theory outlined in this chapter is a response to these challenges.

FOUNDATIONAL DEFINITIONS AND ASSUMPTIONS

Throughout the chapter, the term *moral development* refers to changes in the system by which people make moral decisions. The theory, in effect, intends to explain how and why the moral aspects of the mind change with the passing of time.

As noted in the introduction to Part Eight, not everyone subscribes to the same definition of the moral domain. However, the model offered in this chapter is not dependent on a particular definition of *moral*. It can accommodate nearly any popular conception of moral. It can be used with Piaget's conception of moral development as "learning the rules," Kohlberg's notion of advancing toward "contractual, even-handed justice," Gilligan's proposed "compassionate caring," or Maccoby's "cultural relativism."

One important assumption undergirding the model is that no moral values are innate. A newborn infant has not inherited a sense of right and wrong. The child does not innately know what behavior is morally good or morally bad. In other words, moral rules are learned in the process of growing up.

A second key assumption is that the child does inherit a potential for self-punishment and self-reward—that is, a capacity to feel guilty and ashamed and to feel self-satisfied and proud. This is the capacity to develop a conscience. However, the contents of the conscience—that is, exactly what events make the child feel guilty or proud—are not innate but are learned.

With these introductory ground rules in hand, we turn now to the structure of the theory.

PRINCIPAL FEATURES OF THE MODEL

Figure 17.1 offers a graphic representation of the model. Key characteristics of environments are listed on the left side and key features of the person on the right. At the bottom of the person-rectangle are foundational components that derive from the individual's genetic inheritance and current biological state. The main genetic

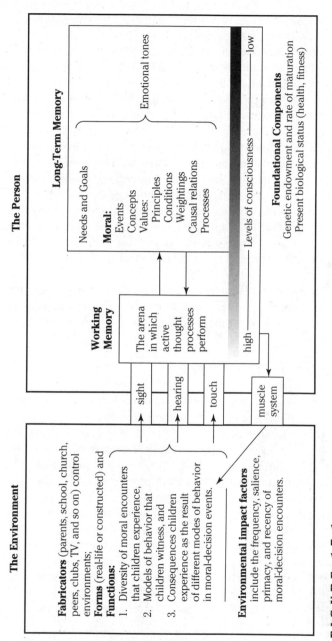

FIGURE 17.1
A moral development model

factors are (1) ability capacities, such as intellectual and physical potentials, and (2) the rate at which these capacities mature during childhood and adolescence. A person's current biological state is influenced not only by these genetic factors but also by nutrition, disease, and accident.

The foundational components support an information-processing network comprising the senses, working memory, long-term memory, and the neuromuscular system that acts on the world. Among the most important features of this network are the components of long-term memory, where the results of moral development reside. A person's current moral state is represented by the patterning of these components at any given time.

The environmental structure at the left is conceived to serve the three functions of determining (1) the opportunities a person will have to encounter moral decision situations, (2) the environmental cues that the individual believes should influence moral decisions, and (3) the kinds of consequences the person will experience from his or her actions in moral situations. The role played by these three factors in the life of a growing child is determined chiefly by the people who control the child's experiences. These people serve as fabricators of the environments the child encounters and thereby they exert a crucial influence on the child's moral development.

The following detailed description of the model begins with the foundational components, then continues with long-term memory, the nature of environments, working memory, and acting on the world.

FOUNDATIONAL COMPONENTS

Four principles of human development that seem universally accepted are that (1) genetic endowment defines a range of potential intellectual ability within which environmental influences can operate to produce the actual intellectual skills people display in their lives, (2) such genetic endowment can differ from one person to another, so that one individual's potential will differ from another's, (3) the flowering of genetic potential evolves gradually over the first two decades of life, and (4) the maturation rate of this flowering can differ from one person to another. These principles reflect basic constraints operating at any juncture of a child's life to affect how adequately the child can understand moral issues and the consequences to be expected from different responses to moral situations. In effect, these genetically seated conditions are the essential building blocks on which moral development is necessarily based. Such genetic factors are the primary determinants of the successive moral development stages postulated by both Piaget and Kohlberg. We can propose that moral education efforts that disregard such principles are bound to fail.

Another foundational factor is the physiological state of the individual as a result of nutrition, illness, or accident. The term *nutrition* in this context refers to any substance that a person ingests. I am assuming that the growing child's nutritional state can affect how adequately the child derives moral "lessons" from the environment, stores these lessons in long-term memory, and uses them in making moral decisions. An adolescent under the influence of mind-altering drugs is not likely to respond to moral decision situations in the same manner as one who is on a nutritionally balanced diet. As E. R. Hilgard (1949) once observed, the superego is soluble in alcohol. Furthermore, chemical imbalances or illnesses that influence the nervous system can affect what the child is able to learn as well as how emotions alter moral decisions, particularly such emotions as depression, rage, guilt, and fear.

THE NATURE OF LONG-TERM MEMORY

For purposes of moral development, the principal components of long-term memory are conceived to be (1) needs and goals, (2) records of events, (3) concepts, (4) moral values, (5) causal relations, and (6) processes.

Needs/Drives and Goals

I believe children are need-fulfilling organisms that use the environment to satisfy needs. In other words, the child's actions are motivated by the twofold goal of (1) identifying objects and activities in the environment that will fulfill needs and (2) developing skills and strategies for obtaining the objects and activities. From a psychoanalytic perspective, this search of the environment for objects that will satisfy needs is the function of the ego that Freud labeled the *secondary process.*

The child's need system takes the form of a hierarchy, with each higher stratum being instrumental in meeting the more basic needs on the tiers below. The all-encompassing need at the base is that of ensuring the survival and perpetuation of the human genetic line, as proposed by such sociobiologists as E. O. Wilson (1978). On the next higher stratum is the need for the individual to survive—self-preservation. On the third level are basic needs that promote such self-preservation—needs for food, drink, warmth, harm avoidance, comprehending the environment, and others. Above this level are the more specific ways that each of these third-level needs can be fulfilled. Some types of food are better than others for sustaining health and energy, some types of drink more suitable, some ways of maintaining optimum body temperature more adequate, and so on. The term *goal* in the present context refers to the types of objects or activities the child identifies as appropriate for meeting a particular need or cluster of needs.

Some people prefer to call the forces that motivate human action *drives* rather than *needs.* The two terms are like the opposite sides of a coin—two facets of the same thing. Whereas *need* suggests a lack the child is attempting to satisfy, *drive* can suggest stored-up energy the child is seeking to expend by investing it in particular objects and activities. Thus the hunger drive represents the need for food and the curiosity drive the need to comprehend the environment.

From the perspective of moral development, needs are important in at least two ways. First, in certain cultural settings, a need itself can be morally controversial. The most obvious case is the need for sexual expression, which in some religious sects has been viewed as inherently immoral, both in thought and deed. Second, and far more significant because of its all-pervasive nature, is the matter of the methods a child adopts for fulfilling a need. Some methods are considered moral and others immoral. Much of the process of socialization during childhood is directed at teaching children to become moral beings by adopting approved techniques of meeting their needs and by rejecting unacceptable techniques. Socialization in this sense is moral education.

Events

A portion of children's memories comprises past events in which they participated, as either actors or observers. These are what E. Tulving (1972) called *episodic* memories. The events of significance here are the ones interpreted as involving moral matters—a parent scolding the child for lying about who took the cookies, a Sunday school lesson about the Ten Commandments, an argument on the playground about breaking rules, a TV program in which a girl is raped, a newspaper account of an army invading a neighboring country, and the like. Memories of events are the raw materials from which the next four components of long-term memory are constructed: concepts, moral values, causal relations, and processes.

Concepts

In the present context, a *concept* is defined as a characteristic common to, and abstracted from, a variety of facts or events or other concepts, with a label attached to the concept so it can be consciously communicated in speech and writing and can be readily manipulated during thought. The label is typically a single word or a short phrase. Examples of concepts significant in moral development are cheating, honesty, exploitation, altruism, felony, fair play, injustice, philanthropy, child abuse, compassion, hard-heartedness, and kindness. The process of moral education includes teaching children meanings for such concepts so they know what sorts of behavior and values are implied when those terms are used.

Moral Values

The contents and applications of the moral values component in Figure 17.1 are characterized by four key factors: principles, conditions, weightings, and emotional tones (Thomas, 1989b; Thomas & Diver-Stamnes, 1993).

Moral principles   At the core of each value is a *moral principle* in the form of an unembellished statement of what is right or, in its reciprocal form, what is wrong. Table 17.1 illustrates several such principles. The ones selected for inclusion in the table are common to many cultures.

TABLE 17.1
A sampling of moral principles

Virtues to be encouraged	Transgressions to be avoided
Regard for human life: Everyone should protect others from harm and should seek to enhance others' physical and mental well-being.	*Disregard for human life:* No one should exploit or harm others, either physically or psychologically.
Honesty: Everyone should tell the truth.	*Deceit:* No one should try to deceive others by lying or by deviously withholding the truth.
Self-determination: All of us, within our levels of ability, should be permitted to decide on the way we will live our lives, provided that (1) we do not unduly intrude on others' rights to lead their lives and (2) we bear our fair share of responsibility in caring for our own welfare and for that of the group.	*Exploitation:* No one should be forced to yield to the demands of others in ways that decrease the individual's self-perceived welfare, provided that the individual bears a fair share of responsibility in caring for his or her own welfare and the welfare of the group.
Respect for property: Everyone should protect others' right to hold and use property to which they have proper or legal claim.	*Stealing and vandalism:* No one should take or use others' property without their permission. No one should damage others' property.
Contractual integrity: People who have freely agreed, in either written or oral form, to perform an action should faithfully carry out that commitment.	*Contractual unreliability:* People should never avoid performing actions that they have freely agreed to carry out.
Compassion, altruism: Everyone should exhibit sympathy for, and offer aid to, people who suffer misfortune.	*Disdain, coldheartedness:* No one should ignore or scorn people who suffer misfortune.

Conditions   In any moral decision, the application of a moral principle is affected by a series of *conditions.* The presumption here is that rarely if ever is any moral principle applied unconditionally to every life situation to which that principle can apply. In effect, the way a principle is used in order to arrive at a moral decision depends on certain circumstances in the particular case at hand. Here are four typical conditions:

1. *Age:* Although the age of the individuals involved in a moral situation is often a consideration in people's moral judgments, it is not really age itself but, rather, some other characteristic that is highly correlated with age (such as knowledge of right and wrong or logical reasoning ability). A three-year-old who does not tell the truth is usually judged differently than a nineteen-year-old who is not truthful.
2. *Intention:* Whether an act is deemed moral or immoral often depends on the answer to the question, "Why did he do it? What was he trying to accomplish?" Intention frequently is regarded as a defining characteristic of moral

behavior, in that intention distinguishes acts involving morality from acts that result from mistakes, accidents, and chance.

3. *Relationships among participants:* Typical relationships are those within a family (parent and child, brother and sister), between age groups (adults and adolescents), between the sexes, between ethnic or religious groups, and between social roles (police officer and thief). Perhaps the most dramatic illustration of the effect of this relationship variable appears during wartime, when moral principles applied to one's own country are distinctly different from those applied to the enemy's.

4. *Seriousness of consequences:* The severity of the consequences of a moral incident for recipients of the act as well as for the perpetrators can affect judgments about the moral status of the incident. For example, depending on the conditions, sexual intercourse may be judged in one case a mere peccadillo and in another case a mortal sin.

Other conditions that often affect people's judgments of moral incidents are the participants' degree of self-control (mental disorder, physical ability, and such), awareness of likely consequences, ethnic status, socioeconomic status, marital situation, and the legal status of an act.

In summary, conditions are contextual factors that qualify the application of moral principles in specific situations. A person discovers which conditions to apply by scanning the particular environment in which a decision is called for.

Weightings   The third distinguishing feature of moral values is a *weighting factor.* Certain principles are accorded more importance than others in people's moral judgments. For instance, in the case of a conflict between the principle of protecting human life and the principle of telling the truth, an individual can regard the value of life more highly than the value of truthfulness and therefore arrive at a decision that gives greater weight to life than to truth telling. Likewise, conditions can vary in their importance. In a decision that requires a choice between "intention" and "relationship between the participants," an individual can consider a parent-child relationship more important than intention in arriving at a moral judgment.

Emotional tone   Moral values, and their application in specific situations, are assumed to be accompanied by *affect*—that is, by feelings reflected in such terms as *guilt, pride, fear, confidence, hate, love, depression, joy,* and the like. The emotional tone of a given moral incident is often complex, involving a combination or succession of different emotions. Also, emotions can vary in intensity from weak to strong.

The emotional qualities of a moral event are significant in that they can affect a participant's willingness and ability to take particular actions. Emotions therefore have a motivating effect, inducing a person to adopt actions that will increase positive feelings and decrease negative ones. In other words, a child's *conscience* or *superego* is represented in the present theory as a linkage between moral values and positive (rewarding) or negative (punishing) emotions. These linkages are assumed to result from children's experiences with the world, so that over time children accrue a growing array of internalized rewarding and punishing emotions that influence how they feel and behave when faced with moral decisions.

Emotions can also influence how rational participants' behavior will be and how well they can foresee the consequences of their present actions. Furthermore, the emotional states of observers of moral incidents or of people who learn of past incidents (as in the case of a jury in a court trial) can also affect those individuals' moral judgments. As suggested by the diagram in Figure 17.1, an emotional tone is not only attached to moral values but to the other components of long-term memory as well.

In summary, the process of making moral decisions is assumed to involve a complex kind of mental algebra whose formulas comprise particular combinations of principles and conditions, their weightings, and accompanying emotions. The specific variables that will be manipulated in carrying out such computations during a given moral encounter is determined by (1) the current patterning of the contents of an individual's moral values (including emotions) and (2) that person's perception of which elements in the present environmental context are relevant to those contents. How such a process may operate is suggested below. But before we inspect the process, we need to understand the postulated role of causal relations.

Causal Relations

A *causal relation* is an *if-then* belief that a person holds. Such beliefs can be either *descriptive* or *prescriptive*. A descriptive or explanatory relation is an if-then conviction about what consequences actually will result in real-life situations if certain conditions obtain. For instance, "If the police catch that girl stealing jewelry from the store, she'll end up in jail." Or, "If I give money to feed hungry people and then if sometime later I need help, some kind person will also probably help me."

In contrast, a prescriptive causal relation represents a correlation that a person believes *should* obtain in life, whether or not it commonly does. For example, a prescriptive relation proposed by the Chinese philosopher Confucius is: "If there are ways that you do not wish to be treated, then do not treat others in those ways" (Waley, 1938). Or, as Jesus Christ later voiced the same basic notion in his Golden Rule: "All things whatsoever ye would that men should do to you, do ye even so to them" (Matthew 7:12), a moral principle that had appeared earlier in the works of Plato and Aristotle as well as in the writings of the Judaic scholar Hillel. Prescriptive causal relations, then, are convictions about how people should act in moral situations. Frequently, if not always, a descriptive relation (an if-then event that actually will occur) is implied in a prescriptive relation (what one should do). Thus Confucius, as a social philosopher, suggested that if his precept was followed, then individuals would be happy and their family, community, and nation would prosper. Christ, as a theologian, suggested that people who adopted his advice could expect a blissful afterlife with God in heaven: "In my Father's house are many mansions. . . . I go to prepare a place for you" (John 14:2).

Causal relations are crucial elements undergirding moral behavior, for they represent what individuals expect will result from their actions. If they think the consequences of a given act will be contrary to their welfare, they will avoid that act and choose an alternative that they expect will bring more adequate need fulfillment. Thus causal relations link behaviors to consequences. Much of moral education involves teaching children about such relations.

Processes of Moral Development

The term *processes* refers to patterns of mental operations involved in thinking about moral matters. There appear to be a number of major processes, with minor subprocesses or subroutines often embedded within them. The following example, which focuses on the function of making a moral decision, illustrates the notion of processes as intended in this theory. Other hypothesized processes that could serve equally well as examples are ones that involve (1) learning a moral concept, (2) recalling a moral event, (3) establishing a causal relation, (4) assigning a value to an event, (5) associating conditions with a moral principle, or (6) attaching an emotional tone to a moral value. I am assuming that processes are stored in long-term memory and are drawn into working memory at the time they are needed.

But before inspecting the posited decision-making process, we should recognize the significance of the *levels of consciousness* dimension in Figure 17.1. I am assuming that all of the contents of long-term memory can be at different levels of availability to consciousness. The individual, at the stage of working memory, may be quite aware of some contents and quite unaware of others; yet both the lucidly conscious and the concealed and unconscious contents are presumed to affect moral thought and behavior. Thus the process described in the following example is presumed to function at different levels of awareness when brought into working memory. I am also assuming that as children grow up, their awareness of their needs and goals, past events, concepts, values, and processes grows in amount and complexity. This awareness of how one's moral development processes operate might be dubbed *metaprocessing*. An implicit aim of moral education is to render moral components of the mind more conscious and thus more rational.

Figure 17.2 pictures a circuit or loop of eight steps representing a process of making a decision in a moral situation. Such an operation includes not only the manner of arriving at a decision but also the way the consequences of the decision affect the contents of long-term memory (Thomas, 1986, pp. 352–353).

Step 1. By means of the senses of sight and hearing, a schoolgirl's working memory encounters an event in the environment that she interprets as involving morality, because the incident fits the definition of *moral* in the moral values component of her long-term memory. (A boy has copied answers from the girl's test paper, but when the teacher accuses him of cheating, the boy denies that he copied.)

Step 2. The girl's working memory extracts events and concepts from her long-term memory that inform her of what actions she might take in this situation. (She could tell the teacher that the boy did indeed copy, she

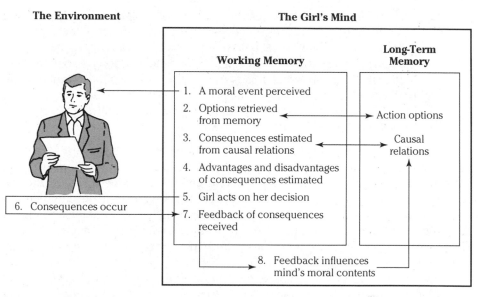

The Environment   **The Girl's Mind**

Long-Term
Working Memory   Memory

1. A moral event perceived

2. Options retrieved
   from memory   → Action options

3. Consequences estimated   Causal
   from causal relations   relations

4. Advantages and disadvantages
   of consequences estimated

6. Consequences occur   5. Girl acts on her decision

7. Feedback of consequences
   received

8. Feedback influences
   mind's moral contents

FIGURE 17.2
A decision-making process

could attack the boy physically after class, she could keep quiet about the whole affair, she could tell her classmates about the incident, she could make an anonymous phone call to the boy's parents, or she could take any of a number of other such actions that come to mind.)

Step 3. From the causal relations in her long-term memory that seem pertinent to such events and concepts, the girl predicts what consequences will likely result from the alternative actions she could take.

Step 4. Weighing (in working memory) the advantages and disadvantages of the various expected consequences, she decides how to act in order to maximize (in terms of need fulfillment) the advantages and minimize the disadvantages.

Step 5. She acts on her decision. (She does not tell the teacher, but after class she tells her classmates.)

Step 6. Following her action, consequences occur. (The classmates tease the boy on the playground, they tell pupils from other classes about the incident, and one classmate leaves an anonymous note about the matter on the teacher's desk. The boy then threatens the girl: "I'll get you for this.")

Step 7. The girl receives feedback regarding the consequences, informing her about the accuracy of her prediction of consequences at step 3. (She hears her classmates tease the boy, the teacher asks her if the accusation in the anonymous note is true, and she's threatened. In terms of her expectations at step 3, she's not surprised that her classmates tease the boy, but she is astonished that someone wrote the note the teacher asks her about. Furthermore, she did not expect the boy to threaten her.)

Step 8. The feedback influences the contents of long-term memory. To the extent that the actual consequences confirm her prediction at step 3, the feedback strengthens the patterning of the original contents—those memories of events and causal relations and the emotions associated with them. (In Piagetian terms, this is *assimilation.*) But to the extent that the prediction of consequences proves to be in error, the feedback alters the original contents by generating changes in the mind's pattern of events and causal relations (Piaget's *accommodation*).

In summary, the decision-making process, when carried through in overt action, serves moral development by strengthening the existing contents of long-term memory whenever expectations are confirmed by consequences. But whenever expectations are not confirmed, the process serves moral development by "changing the person's mind" in the sense of revising existing contents to render them more accurate, complex, and sophisticated as reflectors of reality. (Such an interpretation of development obviously draws heavily on behaviorism and social learning theory.)

It may be useful at this juncture to recall the definition of moral development intended throughout this chapter. *Moral development* refers to *changes in the system by which people make moral decisions.* That system comprises the structure and contents of long-term memory as described above. *Development* means changes in the system through interactions between internal neural maturation (determined chiefly by a genetic timing mechanism) and environmental encounters (which furnish learning opportunities that either strengthen or alter the existing contents of the mind).

Early in this chapter I mentioned Brown's (1979, p. 235) complaint that many developmental models "provide a description of the stages or states of development but they cannot account for the transformations that lead to growth." I believe that the integrated theory's conception of processes helps account for those transformations by postulating what apparently occurs as children's day-by-day encounters with moral events fashion the contents of their long-term memory.

THE NATURE OF ENVIRONMENTS

As suggested on the left side of Figure 17.1, environments can profitably be analyzed in terms of four characteristics: their fabricators, functions, forms, and impact factors. I believe that when we identify permutations of these aspects, we go a long way toward accounting for the way that children's encounters with different environments can influence those children's moral development.

Fabricators

The word *fabricators* refers to the people and institutions in the society that establish which environmental events children will experience. It seems apparent that during the early years of the child's life, the most important fabricators are parents. They determine the kinds of moral situations the young will face within the family, and they can control such outside influences as the child's companions, television programs, and storybooks. During middle childhood, while members of the family continue to be important agents for delineating the kinds of moral events children witness, the school, neighborhood, and church serve to expand the range of people and media that determine the nature of children's exposure to moral events. For instance, the incidents witnessed by boys and girls growing up in an inner-city ghetto can differ markedly from those seen by children in an affluent suburb or a small farming community.

Fabricators not only affect the kinds of moral incidents children meet but also help shape the interpretations children draw about the incidents. In particular, a fabricator influences the values children assign to incidents when the fabricator proposes answers for such questions as these: Was the behavior of the participants in that event right or wrong? Should the participants be praised or condemned, rewarded or punished? And why?

In summary, people and institutions can control the kinds of moral situations a child meets and can influence the values the child applies when interpreting those situations. Because fabricators can differ markedly in the amount of control they maintain over the sorts of encounters and values children experience, children can be expected to differ from one another in the moral contents of their minds.

Functions

For purposes of moral development, environments can be seen as serving three principal functions: they define the scope or range of moral events that children have a chance to experience; they furnish models of how people can act in moral decision situations; and they suggest the consequences that will likely follow different kinds of moral behavior.

Forms

The forms of environments in which children encounter moral matters can be divided into two general types: real-life and constructed. Real-life environments are ones met naturally in the routine of living. They have not been created by someone for either teaching or testing children. Constructed environments, on the other hand, are ones devised to promote or to assess children's moral development.

Constructed environments can vary in the degree to which they approximate real-life environments. This point can be illustrated by our aligning examples of moral instruction along a scale ranging from highly abstract at one end to highly realistic at the other. An example at the highly abstract end would be a teacher's telling pupils to be honest, loyal, just, and compassionate and then expecting the children to display such traits in daily life. In effect, exhorting the young to memorize the biblical Ten Commandments or the Boy Scout Law is a highly abstract environmental encounter.

A less abstract form is an anecdote that embodies a moral lesson. The parables of the Christian Bible and incidents from the lives of mythical or actual heroes (Sir Galahad, Joan of Arc, Abraham Lincoln, Martin Luther King Jr.) are instances of this type of constructed environment. So also are the moral dilemmas posed by Piaget and Kohlberg for assessing the stage of children's moral development. Such anecdotes, in contrast to abstract concepts of honesty and justice, are able to promote all three functions of environments listed above: they provide opportunities for children to encounter an extended range of moral issues; they offer models of behavior that children can imitate; and they suggest consequences to expect from different types of behavior in moral situations.

At a point closer to the real-life end of the scale are the more detailed accounts of moral matters found in such reading matter as novels and biographies that picture people engaged in a series of moral decisions. These extended narratives are able to depict moral matters within more complex settings than can a brief anecdote.

Reality can be approached even more closely when moral events are portrayed on the stage or in motion pictures and television programs. Unlike novels and biographies, which require considerable imagination on the part of readers, dramatic presentations can approximate the sights and sounds that real-life environments involve.

An additional aspect of reality can be achieved when children and youths engage in sociodramas that require that they interact with other players to resolve moral issues. Role playing has the advantage of obligating participants to generate spontaneous responses to other people's actions, an important characteristic of real-life events that is missing in novels and dramas. Role playing can also evoke emotions similar to those experienced in real-life environments.

Implicit throughout the foregoing discussion is the conviction that the more closely a constructed environment approximates real-life conditions, (1) the more accurately children's minds (their moral development) will represent real-life moral decisions and (2) the more accurate will be the picture of children's moral development that researchers derive from constructed environments that are used as evaluation instruments.

Impact Factors

The phrase *impact factors* refers to conditions that affect how, and to what degree, environmental encounters influence the moral contents of a child's mind. Such factors are apparently quite numerous. The ones described below have been selected for the purpose of illustration and are not a definitive list.

Perhaps the most obvious factors are those found in traditional principles of learning as proposed by educational psychologists, such as those of *frequency, salience, primacy,* and *recency.*

The *frequency principle* proposes that many repetitions of the same type of environmental encounter will exert a greater influence on moral development than will few repetitions. Witnessing forty television programs featuring sexual abuse will have a different effect on the contents of a child's mind than will two such programs, as social learning theory would suggest.

Salience refers to how intrusive, demanding, startling, or surprising something in the environment appears to be. The novelty of an environment often renders it highly salient.

In studies of certain forms of learning, the earliest items learned *(primacy)* as well as the lastest ones *(recency)* are more readily recalled than are events in between. For moral development, we can propose that environmental encounters early in a child's life can have a particularly lasting effect on the contents of the child's mind if, at the time of those encounters, the child is mature enough to assimilate the significance of the events. Likewise, we can postulate that recent events assume particular significance in affecting the moral contents because they are still likely to be "fresh in mind," undiluted by intervening events and less subject to the fading of memory that so often occurs with passing time.

With the foregoing conceptions of long-term memory and environments as a background, we turn now to working memory, which is the hypothesized place in which transactions between the mind and environment take place.

WORKING MEMORY

Working memory is considered to be the arena of active thought, the stage on which the processes of interacting with the world and of manipulating the contents of long-term memory are being performed at any given moment.

The phrase *interacting with the world* means engaging in transactions with the environment. One example would be a girl deciding whether to snitch on her teenage brother whom she has seen smoking marijuana. Another would be a student in a sociology class trying to understand the distinction between *misdemeanor* and *felony.*

The phrase *manipulating contents of long-term memory* refers to a child's thinking about matters that are drawn entirely from long-term memory rather than from the outside environment. The child already has in long-term memory all the raw materials—events, concepts, causal relations, values—required for pondering moral matters. Much of creative thought and all dreaming are of this nature. Such thinking involves rearranging materials selected from memory into new patterns. This type of manipulation takes place when a person tries to answer such questions as these: If I had to choose between saving a classmate from a fire and, in the process, getting badly burned myself, what should I do? Or, what are some of the consequences that could likely result from my writing anonymous threatening letters to the school principal?

An essential assumption made about working memory is that it can operate at more than one level of consciousness. In our earlier discussion, this matter of levels of consciousness was given only passing mention. But because degrees of consciousness play such an important role in moral development, it is appropriate at this point to inspect the matter in greater detail. The phenomenon of consciousness, as intended here, is represented as a scale ranging from highly conscious to deeply unconscious.The scale comprises one major dimension and an accompanying minor dimension. The major dimension is labeled *ease of recall,* and the minor *precision of recall.*

Ease is measured in terms of response time. The shorter the interval between the intention to recall a memory and the actual recall, the more conscious the memory, and vice versa. A person's quickly recalling a memory without the need of prompting or clues is an example from the highly conscious end of the scale. Recollection that takes more time or requires prompts to bring it about is closer to the middle. Items that cannot be retrieved at all—even with extended effort, time, and cues—are from the deeply unconscious sector.

Precision is measured in terms of detail and accuracy. The more detailed and accurate the recalled memory, the more highly conscious it is considered to be, and vice versa.

Operationally, a person is credited with *recall* whenever he or she expresses the retrieved material in verbal, graphic, or mathematical form. Although people may claim introspective recall ("I remember it now, but I can't quite put it into words"), they are not credited with retrieval unless they can express it in some public form, even if it takes the form of selecting the correct answer from a series of displayed options.

As noted earlier, I am presuming that much of the mental activity that bears on moral matters operates subliminally; that is, it occurs below the threshold of consciousness. Accepting this presumption can help explain why investigators have found the task of appraising children's moral development so troublesome. Children often cannot explain why they made a particular moral decision because they are not conscious of the factors that produced the decision.

STAGES OF MORAL DEVELOPMENT

A final aspect of the theory not portrayed in Figure 17.1 is that of development stages. Investigations of young people's moral reasoning (as tested with moral dilemma anecdotes) and of their real-life moral behavior have often revealed two sorts of inconsistency. First is the Piagetian phenomenon of *horizontal décalage:* children may reason at one level (one stage) in certain situations and at a different level (another stage) in other situations. Second, children's moral behavior may be inconsistent with what one would expect on the basis of the highest stage of moral reasoning they have displayed in their responses to hypothetical moral dilemmas.

In the present theory, the notion of stagewise development differs from traditional conceptions. A traditional view assumes that once children advance to a higher stage, they don a new set of mental spectacles that cast their world in a new light, and they henceforth abandon the previous stage's modes of interpreting life. In contrast, what I am proposing is that although children do, indeed, advance to new levels of cognitive skill, they do not abandon modes of perception held before. Instead, they retain the earlier modes in their perceptual repertoire for use on suitable occasions. Thus a *stage* in this sense means the acquisition of a significantly new ability to interpret events, but without the loss of existing tendencies or abilities. Stagewise development is therefore defined as *the progressive accumulation of options*—of adding new arrows to the cognitive quiver.

Such a view of stages enables us to make sense of apparent inconsistencies between children's "highest moral reasoning stage" and certain of their behaviors in real-life situations. We assume that when faced with real-life decisions, children (1) inspect the context to see how its characteristics match the moral values patterns (principles and their conditions) in their long-term memory and (2) select those behaviors that their causal-relations memories suggest will yield the greatest benefits in need fulfillment. Such a process of inspection and selection may lead them to choose an action based on their "highest moral reasoning stage" or it may lead them to choose a behavior from an earlier stage. Under this conception of progressive accumulation of options, the determinant of moral behavior is not the child's highest moral reasoning level but, rather, the inspection-and-selection process that guides the child's choice from the entire stockpile of interpretation-and-action options.

I believe that one of the neo-Piagetian solutions to the horizontal décalage problem is also of use in accounting for stages. Thus I would include either Case's or Fischer's proposal (see Perspective D at the end of Part Five) as an element of this integrated theory's account of development stages.

This, then, completes our tour of the integrated moral development model, and we are ready to evaluate it.

AN INTEGRATED MORAL DEVELOPMENT THEORY: AN ASSESSMENT

In view of my vested interest in this model, I can hardly claim to be objective in its assessment. But to keep the pattern of chapters consistent, I will rate this scheme on the assessment dimensions, then leave it to you to correct those ratings that seem unduly self-serving. Two symbols, *P* and *X,* have been employed in the appraisal: *P* = potential and *X* = actual. Those items whose status seems to require a history of empirical research for judging the *actual* condition have been rated here only on *potential* because the empirical evidence is not yet available. Items that can be judged on the basis of a line of logic without the need for empirical results have been given an *actual* rating.

In regard to item 1, I believe the model shows good potential for reflecting the real world of children, particularly because it provides for (1) the analysis of how different environmental conditions (fabricators, functions, forms, impact factors) help account for differences among children in their moral development and (2) the influence of nonconscious factors in moral thought and action.

My rating the model moderately well for its understandability (item 2) is based principally on the reactions of university students who have read this chapter and discussed it in class. I did not give item 2 a top rating because the students and I have both been dissatisfied with the imprecision of certain aspects of the theory. In particular, we are not at all comfortable with the lack of detail about the way working memory interacts with long-term memory, about the role of unconscious

AN INTEGRATED THEORY OF MORAL DEVELOPMENT

How well do I think the theory meets the standards?

Standards	Very well	Moderately well	Very poorly
1. Reflects the real world of children	P*		
2. Is clearly understandable		X‡	
3. Explains the past and predicts the future	P		
4. Guides child rearing	P		
5. Is internally consistent	X		
6. Is economical	X		
7. Is falsifiable	P		
8. Is supported by convincing evidence		X	
9. Adapts to new data	P		
10. Is novel		X	
11. Is comprehensive		X	
12. Stimulates new discoveries	P		
13. Is durable		?	
14. Is self-satisfying	P		

*P = potential   ‡ X = actual

factors in moral decisions, and about how different memories achieve their particular levels of consciousness. Furthermore, ways that needs or drives from long-term memory guide the child's search of the environment and ways that aspects of the environment become sufficiently salient to demand the child's attention are not explained satisfactorily. These shortcomings and similar ones prevent the theory from deserving a rating above "moderately well."

I have marked the theory potentially high on explaining the past and predicting the future (item 3) because I believe its components more adequately provide for the factors that affect children's moral developments than do existing theories. For example, such proposals as Piaget's, Kohlberg's, and Gilligan's have not been very successful (1) in accounting for why a child may make one type of moral decision in one situation and a different type in another, and (2) in explaining why children's moral behavior is often at odds with their moral reasoning. This integrated theory can, I believe, go a long way toward explaining such matters. My reasons are as follows.

First, from the perspective of the integrated theory, we would not be at all surprised to find children varying their moral principles from one situation to the next. Indeed, we would expect children to adjust their moral principles in relation to (1) how the conditions linked to their moral principles match the conditions observed in their present environmental encounter and (2) the relative weighting they give to moral principles that may be in conflict (for example, honesty versus loyalty) in that particular context. If we learn the influential conditions that a child attaches to different principles, and if we can estimate the relative importance that two principles have for the child in the present context, we are prepared to explain the child's decision and to hazard predictions about similar environmental encounters in the future.

Second, the theory has several ways to account for apparent discrepancies between children's moral reasoning and their moral behavior. First, the most popular way of evaluating children's mode of moral reasoning has been that of posing brief anecdotes about moral decision incidents—moral dilemmas—and asking the young to judge whether the decisions made by the participants in the anecdotes were morally right or wrong and why. Such anecdotes differ in several important ways from real-life moral action. They are constructed environments that fail to include many of the potential conditions that children consider when they make real-life decisions. In other words, the anecdotes have been cleaned of cues that may be significant in children's moral value systems. Then, such researchers as Piaget and Kohlberg have used a very limited number of hypothetical incidents on which to base wide-ranging generalizations. (In the case of Kohlberg, the number has been no more than nine, and usually fewer.) And there appears to be no evidence that such a selection of moral dilemmas adequately samples the broad range of moral situations children face in life (Thomas, 1989b). In addition, children who respond to hypothetical dilemmas do not need to bear the consequences of their decisions as they do in real life. In short, we should not expect accurate predictions of what behavior will occur in diverse real-life moral incidents when such predictions derive from children's answers to a few hypothetical anecdotes and when children need not suffer the consequences of their decisions. Therefore the integrated theory suggests that more adequate assessment techniques should be employed for judging the state of children's moral values and behavior. Such techniques should accommodate (1) a diversity of moral principles and their conditions that make up the moral value component of the child's long-term memory, (2) weightings given to different principles and conditions, (3) the multiple cues in different environmental contexts that can be pertinent to the conditions children link to their moral principles, and (4) the actual consequences children can experience in real-life moral situations.

On item 4—potential for guiding child rearing—I rated the integrated theory rather high because it (1) identifies four significant environmental variables that can be manipulated to influence children's moral experiences and (2) alerts adults to the complex patterns that children's moral values system can assume. I also judged the theory rather high on internal consistency (item 5) and economy (item 6). Furthermore, I believe it has the potential for generating a host of hypotheses that are testable, thereby qualifying it for being falsifiable (item 7) and fertile (item 12).

However, a major problem in terms of falsifiability is posed by the notion of levels of consciousness. The difficulty researchers have experienced over the decades in trying to fathom the nature of nonconscious mental events suggests that the task of delineating the levels-of-consciousness feature of this theory may be intractable.

The evidence supporting the scheme (item 8) is of two kinds: (1) studies from the past that bear on those portions of the model borrowed from preceding theories (psychoanalytic, behaviorist, social learning, ecological, cognitive) and (2) recent studies that have been conducted specifically to explain and substantiate certain features of the model. The first of these kinds is by far the more abundant. The second is quite meager, consisting of only the beginning steps in an intended series of investigations. The initial investigation in this series appeared as a book entitled *What Wrongdoers Deserve* (Thomas & Diver-Stamnes, 1993), a report of the opinions of 562 young people concerning the consequences that should be imposed on offenders in six cases of wrongdoing. The two aspects of long-term memory examined in the book are (1) the nature and type of moral principles and of conditions governing the application of the principles and (2) causal relations the respondents had in mind. A second book, based on interviews with 136 young people (ages nine through twenty-one), inspected the youths' expressed aims and causal relations in three cases of wrongdoing (Diver-Stamnes & Thomas, 1995). A third study, currently under way, explores how young people's moral decisions are affected by different forms of constructed environments they encounter; the effect of short moral-incident anecdotes is compared to the effect of videotaped depictions of the incidents. It seems apparent that far more such evidence illuminating specific components of the model is needed to determine the theory's accuracy and usefulness.

I believe the scheme is potentially adaptable to new data (item 9), for it is founded on the expectation that the theory is not in a final form but is still tentative, requiring revision and reinterpretation in the face of unanticipated evidence.

A relatively low rating on novelty (item 10) seems warranted since the major elements of the theory have been drawn from existing models. Whatever novelty it displays derives from the pattern in which the elements have been assembled and from such proposals as (1) the relationship of moral principles to their conditions and (2) the distinctions drawn among forms of environments.

Like Kohlberg's theory, this integrated model is very narrow in focus, explaining only one facet of cognitive development, thereby deserving no more than a low ranking on comprehensiveness (item 11). And because the model is so new, its durability (item 13) is still very much in question.

Finally, I consider this scheme fairly self-satisfying. It has helped me answer questions that I felt were not answered adequately by other theories I've studied. However, it leaves many important issues unresolved or unclear—so it's back to the drawing board and then on to more empirical investigations.

Depicting Theories in the Guise of Metaphors

What analogies are most useful for representing the central themes of theories of development?

At the most general level of analysis, authors often adopt a metaphor or simile as a poetic aid for conveying the essential nature of a theory. They typically liken the theory to some phenomenon familiar to most readers. Robbie Case (1985, pp. 57–59) illustrated this practice in reference to a number of well-known models of development. He proposed that J. M. Baldwin (1895), by drawing heavily on Darwin's views, portrayed the growing child as "an organism whose intellectual development recapitulates that of the species from which it has evolved." Piaget's child is a "young scientist, who constructs successively more powerful logico-mathematical tools." In Vygotsky's scheme, young children are social beings whose intellectual processes are tools acquired from their special historical and cultural settings. Classical information-processing theory portrays the child as a complex computer "capable of modifying the programmes with which it has been endowed, in a fashion that is responsive to the environment in which it finds itself." To characterize his own theory, Case envisioned the child as a traveler through life, a problem solver motivated by natural desires whose realization is blocked by natural barriers; fortunately, the child has the capacity to refine and recombine innate procedures so as to overcome the barriers.

In a manner similar to Case's, I now propose metaphors to represent the other theories described in earlier chapters. I begin with Gesell, who viewed the child as a genetically programmed biological oscillator that switches between good and bad phases of growth on an annual schedule.

Havighurst pictured children as laborers performing a sequence of tasks. The tasks they face at successive periods of life are assigned to them by their evolving biological nature, by their physical environment, and by the demands of their cultural settings.

From the viewpoint of commonsense theory, children are pilgrims wending their way through life. How readily they advance toward their destination depends on how well their growing array of abilities *(can do)* and the strength of their willpower *(try to)* equip them to overcome the obstacles *(task difficulty)* they meet along the way.

Freud's child is a sexually driven, hedonistic being who, when confronted with society's restrictions, reluctantly curbs his or her direct pleasure seeking by disguising his or her motives behind defense mechanisms. Erikson's child, while basically the same as Freud's, additionally faces the problem at each stage of growth of resolving the conflict between that stage's pair of dialectical tendencies.

Operant behaviorism pictures the child as a reacting robot that gradually develops habitual ways of responding to various environmental circumstances. Which actions become habitual is determined by the kinds of consequences that occur after the robot has tried acting in several different ways in a given situation. Ways of acting that produce greater reward become habits. Ways that produce less reward or result in punishment are dropped from the robot's active repertoire of responses.

Social learning theory portrays children both as actors and as members of the audience in the daily dramas that make up life's social experiences. Actors partici- pating in such dramas learn—for future reference—the consequences they can expect from playing particular roles in different social settings. Members of the audience learn these same consequences from witnessing the plays.

According to Riegel's dialectical theory, the child is an arbitrator, continually negotiating the resolution of contradictory biological, psychological, and environ- mental forces. The accumulation of experience derived from this procession of negotiations equips the child with a growing supply of skills that render the child more adept at producing future resolutions.

Valsiner's model, like Vygotsky's, depicts young children as social beings who construct their intellectual skills from the tasks they perform in their particular historical and cultural settings.

From the perspective of humanistic theory, children are explorers, with each one in search of two sorts of treasure: (1) a unique personal identity or individuality called *self* and (2) activities that promote need fulfillment, particularly activities that create an exhalted feeling of euphoria known as a *peak experience.* Although the search can yield many gems along the way, the quest is never completed but, rather, is always in a state of *becoming.*

Bronfenbrenner's ecological model depicts children as peripatetic translators who are constantly interpreting the meaning of every environmental setting they pass through. Each meaning results from a combination of (1) the interpreter's direct experiences and (2) opinions imposed by outside agencies (exosystems) and by the general culture (the macrosystem).

Ethological theory portrays the child as an organism whose species character- istics have been fashioned over eons of time by mutations in genetic structure, determining the species' ability to adjust to changing environments. The human organism's adjustment is often achieved by the organism altering the environment to make it more suitable for survival. The most important of the organism's genetic traits is its ability to profit from experience. Among all the species, humans have the greatest capacity to learn.

From a bio-electrochemical viewpoint, the child is a machine, a kind of automaton, (1) which from its inception increases in size, complexity, and func- tions with the passing of time; (2) whose structure can be analyzed at descending levels down to the most basic and simple constituents (many quadrillions of subatomic particles); and (3) whose components change according to an architectural plan embedded in identical DNA molecules that reside in nearly all of the machine's cells.

In Kohlberg's scheme, the child is a magistrate who, with the passing of time, increasingly adopts more socially oriented, rather than self-oriented, principles for distinguishing right from wrong moral behavior.

Finally, in my integrated theory of moral development, children are like architects and builders, continually reconstructing the patterns of their moral values. The process of reconstruction is governed by (1) the history of the child's cognitive and moral development up to the present time, (2) the level of maturation of the child's nervous system, and (3) the nature of the moral events that the child currently encounters in the routine of daily living.

Such, then, is one version of metaphors intended to epitomize the theories met in this book.

REFERENCES

Ackerman, S. (1992) *Discovering the Brain.* Washington, D.C.: National Academy Press.

Adams. K., Lemonick, M. D., Lofaro, L., Quinn, M., Sanders, A. L., & Urquhart, S. (1995, March 13). It's the top, *Time,* Vol. 145, No. 10, p. 39.

Adler, A. (1930) "Individual Psychology," in C. Murchinson (ed.), *Psychologies of 1930.* Worcester, Mass.: Clark University Press.

Akers, R. L., and J. K. Cochran. (1985) "Adolescent Marijuana Use: A Test of Three Theories of Deviant Behavior." *Deviant Behavior,* Vol. 6, No. 4, pp. 323–346.

Alexander, R. D., and P. W. Sherman. (1977) "Local Mate Competition and Parental Investment in Social Insects." *Science,* Vol. 196, No. 4289, pp. 494–500.

Allport, G. W. (1961) *Pattern and Growth in Personality.* New York: Holt, Rinehart & Winston.

Allport, G. W. (1968) *The Person in Psychology: Selected Essays.* Boston: Beacon.

Alston, W. P. (1971) "Comments on Kohlberg's 'From Is to Ought,' " in T. Mischel (ed.), *Cognitive Development and Epistemology.* New York: Academic Press.

Ames, L. B., and C. C. Haber. (1990) *Your Eight Year Old.* New York: Dell.

Ames, L. B., and F. L. Ilg. (1976) *Your Four Year Old.* New York: Dell.

Anastasi, A. (1958) "Heredity, Environment, and the Question 'How?' " *Psychological Review,* Vol. 65, No. 4, pp. 197–208.

Anderson, J. R. (1983) *The Architecture of Cognition.* Cambridge, Mass.: Harvard University Press.

Anthony, E. J. (1986) "The Contributions of Child Psychoanalysis to Psychoanalysis," *Psychoanalytic Study of the Child,* Vol. 41, pp. 61–87.

Archard, D. (1984) Consciousness and the Unconscious. La Salle, Ill.: Open Court.

Ashcraft, M. H. (1989) *Human Memory and Cognition.* Glenview, Ill.: Scott, Foresman.

Asimov, I. (1991) *Atom.* New York: Truman Talley Books/Dutton.

Baldwin, A. L. (1967) *Theories of Child Development.* New York: Wiley.

Baldwin, J. D., and J. I. Baldwin. (1989) "The Socialization of Homosexuality and Heterosexuality in a Non-Western Society." *Archives of Sexual Behavior,* Vol. 19, No. 1, pp. 13–29.

Baldwin, J. M. (1895) *The Development of the Child and of the Race.* New York: Macmillan. Reprint. Clifton, N.J.: Augustus M. Kelley, 1968.

Baldwin, J. M. (1906, 1908, 1911) *Thoughts and Things or Genetic Logic.* 3 vols. New York: Macmillan.

Banaji, M. R., and D. A. Prentice (1994) "The Self in Social Contexts," in L. W. Porter and M. R. Rosenzweig (eds.), *Annual Review of Psychology.* Palo Alto, Calif.: Annual Reviews.

Bandura, A. (1969) *Principles of Behavior Modification.* New York: Holt, Rinehart & Winston.

Bandura, A. (1977) *Social Learning Theory.* Englewood Cliffs, N.J.: Prentice-Hall.

Bandura, A. (1978) "The Self System in Reciprocal Determinism." *American Psychologist,* Vol. 33, pp. 344–358.

Bandura, A. (1986) *Social Foundations of Thought and Action: A Social Cognitive Theory.* Englewood Cliffs, N.J.: Prentice-Hall.

Bandura, A. (1990a) "Perceived Self-Efficacy in the Exercise of Control Over AIDS Infection." *Evaluation and Program Planning,* Vol. 13, No. 1, pp. 9–17.

Bandura, A. (1990b) "Perceived Self-Efficacy in the Exercise of Personal Agency." *Journal of Applied Sport Psychology,* Vol. 2, No. 2, pp. 128–163.

Bandura, A. (1990c) "Selective Activation and Disengagement of Moral Control." *Journal of Social Issues,* Vol. 46, No. 1, pp. 27–46.

Bandura, A. (1991) "Social Cognitive Theory of Self-Regulation." *Organizational Behavior and Human Decision Processes,* Vol. 50, No. 2, pp. 248–287.

Bandura, A., and F. J. Jourden. (1991) "Self-Regulatory Mechanisms Governing the Impact of Social Comparison on Complex Decision Making." *Journal of Personality and Social Psychology,* Vol. 60, No. 6, pp. 941–951.

Bandura, A., and R. H. Walters. (1963) *Social Learning and Personality Development.* New York: Holt, Rinehart & Winston.

Barker, R. G. (1968) *Ecological Psychology: Concepts and Methods for Studying the Environment of Human Behavior.* Stanford, Calif.: Stanford University Press.

Barker, R. G. (ed.). (1978) *Habitats, Environments, and Human Behavior.* San Francisco: Jossey-Bass.

Barker, R. G., T. Dembo, and K. Lewin. (1943) "Frustration and Regression," in R. G. Barker, J. S. Kounin, and H. F. Wright (eds.), *Child Behavior and Development.* New York: McGraw-Hill.

Barker, R. G., and P. V. Gump. (1964) *Big School, Small School.* Stanford, Calif.: Stanford University Press.

Barker, R. G., et al. (1970) "The Ecological Environment: Student Participation in Non-Class Settings," in M. B. Miles and W. W. Charters, Jr. (eds.), *Learning in Social Settings.* Boston: Allyn & Bacon.

Battro, A. M. (1973) *Piaget: Dictionary of Terms.* New York: Pergamon Press.

Batson, C. D., J. Fultz, P. A. Schoenrade, and A. Paduano. (1987) "Critical Self-Reflection and Self-Perceived Altruism: When Self-Reward Fails." *Journal of Personality and Social Psychology,* Vol. 53, No. 3, pp. 594–602.

Begley, S., and S. Holmes. (1994, May 9) "How Many Scientists Does It Take to Screw in a Quark?" *Newsweek,* pp. 54–55.

Bell, R. W., and W. P. Smotherman (eds.). (1980) *Maternal Influences and Early Behavior.* New York: Spectrum.

Bernard, H. W. (1970) *Human Development in Western Culture.* Boston: Allyn & Bacon.

Berne, E. (1967) *Games People Play.* New York: Grove Press.

Berne, E. (1972) *What Do You Say after You Say Hello?* New York: Grove Press.

Bernsen, N. O. (1989) "General Introduction: A European Perspective on Cognitive Science," in A. Baddeley and N. O. Bernsen, *Cognitive Psychology—Research Directions in Cognitive Science: European Perspectives,* Vol. 1. Hillsdale, N.J.: Erlbaum.

Biggs, J. B. (1976) "Schooling and Moral Development," in V. P. Varma and P. Williams (eds.), *Piaget, Psychology, and Education.* Itasca, Ill.: F. E. Peacock.

Bijou, S. W. (1976) *Child Development: The Basic Stage of Early Childhood.* Englewood Cliffs, N.J.: Prentice-Hall.

Bijou, S. W. (1979) "Some Clarifications on the Meaning of a Behavior Analysis of Child Development." *Psychological Record,* Vol. 29, No. 1, pp. 3–13.

Bijou, S. W. (1985) "Behaviorism: History and Educational Applications," in T. Husén and T. N. Postlethwaite (eds.), *International Encyclopedia of Education,* Vol. 1. Oxford, England: Pergamon Press, pp. 444–451.

Bijou, S. W., and D. M. Baer. (1961) *Child Development.* Vol. I: *A Systematic and Empirical Theory.* New York: Appleton-Century-Crofts.

Bijou, S. W., and D. M. Baer. (1965) *Child Development.* Vol. II: *Universal Stage of Infancy.* New York: Appleton-Century-Crofts.

Bijou, S. W., and D. M. Baer. (1967) "Operant Methods in Child Behavior and Development," in S. W. Bijou and D. M. Baer (eds.), *Child Development: Readings in Experimental Analysis.* New York: Appleton-Century-Crofts.

Block, J. H., and L. W. Anderson. (1975) *Mastery Learning in Classroom Instruction.* New York: Macmillan.

Bloom, F. E., and A. Lazerson. (1988) *Brain, Mind, and Behavior,* 2d ed. New York: Freeman.

Blurton Jones, N. G. (ed.). (1972) *Ethological Studies of Child Behaviour.* Cambridge, England: Cambridge University Press.

Boring, E. G. (1963) *The Physical Dimensions of Consciousness.* New York: Dover.

Bowie, M. (1994) *Psychoanalysis and the Future of Theory.* Cambridge, Mass.: Blackwell.

Bowlby, J. (1951) *Maternal Care and Mental Health.* London: HMSO.

Bowlby, J. (1969) *Attachment and Loss.* Vol. 1. *Attachment.* New York: Basic Books.

Bowlby, J. (1973) *Attachment and Loss.* Vol. 2. *Separation: Anxiety and Anger.* New York: Basic Books.

Bowlby, J. (1980) *Attachment and Loss.* Vol. 3. *Loss.* New York: Basic Books.

Brainerd, C. J. (ed.). (1983) *Recent Advances in Cognitive-Developmental Theory.* New York: Springer-Verlag.

Bretherton, I. (1985) "Attachment Theory: Retrospect and Prospect," in I. Bretherton and W. Waters (eds.), *Growing Points of Attachment Theory and Research* (Monographs of the Society for Research in Child Development, Serial No. 209, Vol. 50, Nos. 1–2). Chicago: University of Chicago Press, pp. 3–35.

Bricker, D. D. (1986) *Early Education of At-risk and Handicapped Infants, Toddlers, and Preschool Children.* Glenview, Ill.: Scott, Foresman.

Broadbent, D. E. (1958) *Perception and Communication.* New York: Macmillan.

Broadbent, D. E. (1970) "Psychological Aspects of Short-Term and Long-Term Memory." *Proceedings of the Royal Society* (London), Series B, Vol. 175, pp. 333–350.

Bronfenbrenner, U. (1979) *The Ecology of Human Development.* Cambridge, Mass.: Harvard University Press.

Bronfenbrenner, U. (1993) "The Ecology of Cognitive Development: Research Models and Fugitive Findings" in R. H. Wozniak and K. W. Fischer (eds.), *Development in Context: Acting and Thinking in Specific Environments.* Hillsdale, N.J.: Erlbaum.

Brook, D. W., and J. S. Brook. (1985) "Adolescent Alcohol Use." *Alcohol and Alcoholism,* Vol. 20, No. 3, pp. 259–262.

Brown, A. L. (1979) "Theories of Memory and the Problems of Development: Activity, Growth, and Knowledge," in L. S. Cermak and F. I. M. Craik (eds.), *Levels of Processing in Human Memory.* Hillsdale, N.J.: Erlbaum, pp. 225–258.

Brown, A. L., and J. S. DeLoache. (1978) "Skills, Plans, and Self-Regulation," in R. Siegler (ed.), *Children's Thinking: What Develops.* New York: Wiley.

Brown, G. I. (1971) *Human Teaching for Human Learning: An Introduction to Confluent Education.* New York: Viking Press.

Bruner, J. S. (1964) "The Course of Cognitive Growth." *American Psychologist,* Vol. 19, No. 1, pp. 1–15.

Buhler, C., and M. Allen. (1972) *Introduction to Humanistic Psychology.* Pacific Grove, Calif.: Brooks/Cole.

Buhler, C., and F. Massarik (eds.). (1968) *The Course of Human Life.* New York: Springer.

Bullough, V. I. (1981) "Age at Menarche: A Misunderstanding." *Science,* Vol. 213, No. 4505, pp. 365–366.

Burke, J. P. (1983) "Rapprochement of Rotter's Social Learning Theory with Self-Esteem Constructs." *Social Behavior and Personality,* Vol. 11, No. 1, pp. 81–91.

Burks, B. S. (1928) "The Relative Influence of Nature and Nurture upon Mental Development," in *Nature and Nurture.* Part I: *Their Influence upon Intelligence.* 27th Yearbook of the National Society for the Study of Education. Bloomington, Ill.: Public School Publishing.

Bush, P. J., and R. J. Iannotti. (1985) "The Development of Children's Health Orientations and Behaviors: Lessons for Substance Use Prevention." *National Institute on Drug Abuse Research Monograph Series,* No. 56, pp. 45–74.

Buss, A. R. (1976) "Development of Dialectics and Development of Humanistic Psychology." *Human Development,* Vol. 19, No. 4, pp. 248–260.

Cairns, R. B. (1977) "Sociobiology: A New Synthesis or an Old Cleavage?" *Contemporary Psychology,* Vol. 22, No. 1, pp. 1–3.

Cairns, R. B. (1983) *Social Development: The Origins and Plasticity of Interchanges.* San Francisco: W. H. Freeman.

California State Penal Code. (1975) Sacramento: State of California, Title I, Sec. 26.

Campbell, S. F. (1976) *Piaget Sampler.* New York: Wiley.

Captain, P. A. (1984) *Eight Stages of Christian Growth.* Englewood Cliffs, N.J.: Prentice-Hall.

Case, R. (1985) *Intellectual Development, Birth to Adulthood.* Orlando, Fla.: Academic Press.

Case, R. (1986) "The New Stage Theories in Intellectual Development: Why We Need Them; What They Assert," in M. Perlmutter (ed.), *Perspectives for Intellectual Development.* Hillsdale, N.J.: Erlbaum, pp. 57–96.

Case, R. (1992) *The Mind's Staircase.* Hillsdale, N.J.: Erlbaum.

Catania, A. C., and S. Harnad (eds.). (1988) *The Selection of Behavior: The Operant Behaviorism of B. F. Skinner: Comments and Consequences.* New York: Cambridge University Press.

Chaplin, W. F. (1987) "On the Thoughtfulness of Cognitive Psychologists." *Journal of Mind and Behavior,* Vol. 8, No. 2, pp. 269–279.

Chapman, A. J., and H. C. Foot (eds.). (1976) *Humour and Laughter: Research and Applications.* London: Wiley.

Chi, M. T. H. (1976) "Short-Term Memory Limitations in Children: Capacity or Processing Deficits?" *Memory and Cognition,* Vol. 4, No. 5, pp. 559–572.

Chilman, C. S. (1983) *Adolescent Sexuality in a Changing American Society,* 2d ed. New York: Wiley.

Chomsky, N. (1967). "Review of Skinner's Verbal Behavior," In L. A. Jakobovits and M. S. Morn (eds.), *Readings in the Philosophy of Language.* Englewood Cliffs, N.J.: Prentice-Hall.

Clayman, C. B. (1989) *The American Medical Association Encyclopedia of Medicine.* New York: Random House.

Colby, A., L. Kohlberg, J. Gibbs, and M. Lieberman. (1983) *A Longitudinal Study of Moral Development.* Monographs of the Society for Research in Child Development, Serial No. 200, Vol. 48, Nos. 1–2.

Cole, J. E., and C. Levine. (1987) "A Formulation of Cole's Theory of Ego Identity Formation." *Developmental Review,* Vol. 7, No. 4, pp. 273–325.

Cole, M. (ed.). (1977) *Soviet Developmental Psychology.* White Plains, N.Y.: Sharpe.

Coles, R. (1970) *Erik H. Erikson: The Growth of His Work.* Boston: Little, Brown.

Combs, A. W. (1962) "A Perceptual View of the Adequate Personality," in A. W. Combs, E. C. Kelley, A. H. Maslow, and C. R. Rogers (eds.), *Perceiving, Behaving, Becoming.* Washington, D.C.: Association for Supervision and Curriculum Development.

Combs, A. W. (1975) "Humanistic Goals of Education," in D. A. Read and S. B. Simon (eds.), *Humanistic Education Sourcebook.* Englewood Cliffs, N.J.: Prentice-Hall.

Combs, A. W., and D. Snygg. (1959) *Individual Behavior.* New York: Harper & Row.

Craik, F. I. M., and R. S. Lockhart. (1972) "Levels of Processing: A Framework for Memory Research." *Journal of Verbal Learning and Verbal Behavior,* Vol. 11, pp. 671–684.

Crawford, H. J., and C. H. Greiner. (1994) "The Search for Strange Matter." *Scientific American,* Vol. 270, No. 1, pp. 72–77.

Crews, F. (1993) "The Unknown Freud." *New York Review of Books,* Vol. 48, No. 19, pp. 55–66.

Damon, W., and D. Hart. (1988) *Self-Understanding in Childhood and Adolescence.* New York: Cambridge University Press.

Dangelo, D. A. (1989) "Developmental Tasks in Literature for Adolescents: Has the Adolescent Female Protagonist Changed?" *Child Study Journal,* Vol. 19, No. 3, pp. 219–238.

Dason, P. R. (ed.). (1977) *Piagetian Psychology, Cross-Cultural Contributions.* New York: Gardner.

Davidov, V. V. (1985) "Soviet Theories of Human Development," in T. Husén and T. N. Postlethwaite (eds.), *International Encyclopedia of Education,* Vol. 8. Oxford, England: Pergamon, pp. 4721–4727.

Deutsch, J. M. (1943) "The Development of Children's Concepts of Causal Relations," in R. G. Barker, J. S. Kounin, and H. F. Wright (eds.), *Child Behavior and Development.* New York: McGraw-Hill.

de Vries, H., M. Dijkstra, and P. Kuhlman. (1988) "Self-Efficacy: The Third Factor Besides Attitude and Subjective Norm as a Predictor of Behavioural Intentions." *Health Education Research,* Vol. 3, No. 3, pp. 273–282.

DiBlasio, F. A. (1988) "Predriving Riders and Drinking Drivers." *Journal of Studies on Alcohol,* Vol. 49, No. 1, pp. 11–15.

Distler, W., and L. Beck (eds.). (1990) *Endorphins in Human Reproduction and Stress Response.* New York: Springer-Verlag.

Divers-Stamnes, A. C., and R. M. Thomas. (1995) *Prevent, Repent, Reform, Revenge—Adolescents' Aims of Sanctions for Crimes and Misdeeds.* Westport, Conn.: Greenwood.

Dollard, J., and N. E. Miller. (1950) *Personality and Psychotherapy.* New York: McGraw-Hill.

Dooling, D. J., and R. E. Christiaansen. (1977) "Episodic and Semantic Aspects of Memory for Prose." *Journal of Experimental Psychology: Human Learning and Memory,* Vol. 3, No. 4, pp. 428–436.

Dreikurs, R. R. (1950) *Fundamentals of Adlerian Psychology.* New York: Greenberg.

Drum, P. A. (1990) "Language Acquisition and Human Development," in R. M. Thomas (ed.), *The Encyclopedia of Human Development and Education.* Oxford, England: Pergamon, pp. 269–275.

Dunstan, J. I. (1961) *Protestantism.* New York: Braziller.

Durkin, D. (1976) *Teaching Young Children to Read,* 2d ed. Boston: Allyn & Bacon.

Dusek, J., O. B. Carter, and G. Levy. (1986) "The Relationship Between Identity Development and Self-Esteem during the Late Adolescent Years: Sex Differences." *Journal of Adolescent Research,* Vol. 1, No. 3, pp. 251–265.

Duvall, E. M. (1971) *Family Development.* Philadelphia: Lippincott.

Eibl-Eibesfeldt, I. (1975) *Ethology: The Biology of Behavior,* 2d ed. New York: Holt, Rinehart & Winston.

Eibl-Eibesfeldt, I. (1989) *Human Ethology.* New York: Aldine de Gruyter.

Elkind, D. (1971) *Children and Adolescents: Interpretive Essays on Piaget.* New York: Oxford University Press.

Elkind, D. (1976) *Child Development and Education.* New York: Oxford University Press.

Elkington, J. (1986) *The Poisoned Womb: Human Reproduction in a Polluted World.* Harmondsworth, England: Penguin.

Ellenberger, H. (1970) *The Discovery of the Unconscious.* New York: Basic Books.

Elley, W. B. (ed.). (1994) *The IEA Study of Reading Literacy: Achievement and Instruction in Thirty-Two School Systems.* Oxford, England: Pergamon.

Emde, R. N. (1992) "Individual Meaning and Increasing Complexity: Contributions of Sigmund Freud and Rene Spitz to Developmental Psychology." *Developmental Psychology,* Vol. 28, No. 3, pp. 347–359.

Erikson, E. H. (1958) *Young Man Luther: A Study in Psychoanalysis and History.* New York: Norton.

Erikson, E. H. (1959) *Identity and the Life Cycle in Psychological Issues* (monograph). Vol. 1, No. 1. New York: International Universities Press.

Erikson, E. H. (1963) *Childhood and Society,* 2d ed. New York: Norton.

Erikson, E. H. (1964) *Insight and Responsibility.* New York: Norton.

Erikson, E. H. (1968) *Identity: Youth and Crisis.* New York: Norton.

Erikson, E. H. (1969) *Gandhi's Truth.* New York: Norton.

Erikson, E. H. (1975) *Life History and the Historical Movement.* New York: Norton.

Erikson, E. H. (1977) *Toys and Reasons.* New York: Norton.

Erikson, E. H. (1982) *The Life Cycle Completed.* New York: Norton.

Fantini, M., and G. Weinstein. (1968) *Toward a Contact Curriculum.* New York: Anti-Defamation League of B'nai B'rith.

Farnham-Diggory, S. (1972) *Information Processing in Children.* New York: Academic Press.

Faulkner, J. A., D. R. Claflin, and K. K. McCully. (1986) "Power Output of Fast and Slow Fibers from Human Skeletal Muscles," in N. L. Jones, N. McCartney, and A. J. McComas (eds.), *Human Muscle Power.* Champaign, Ill.: Human Kinetics.

Fischer, K. W. (1980) "A Theory of Cognitive Development: The Control and Construction of Hierarchies of Skills." *Psychological Review,* Vol. 87, No. 6, pp. 477–531.

Fischer, K. W., and R. L. Canfield. (1986) "The Ambiguity of Stage and Structure in Behavior: Person and Environment in the Development of Psychological Structures," in I. Levin (ed.), *Stage and Structure: Reopening the Debate.* Norwood, N.J.: Ablex.

Fisher, J. D., P. A. Bell, and A. Baum. (1984) *Environmental Psychology,* 2d ed. New York: Holt, Rinehart & Winston.

Fisher, S. (1985) *The Scientific Credibility of Freud's Theories and Therapy.* New York:

Flavell, J. H. (1977) *Cognitive Development.* Englewood Cliffs, N.J.: Prentice-Hall.

Flexner, S. B., and L. C. Hauck. (1987) *The Random House Dictionary of the English Language,* 2d ed. New York: Random House.

Flora, J. A., and C. E. Thoresen. (1988) "Reducing the Risk of AIDS in Adolescents." *American Psychologist,* Vol. 43, No. 11, pp. 965–970.

Fodor, J. A. (1983) *The Modularity of Mind.* Cambridge, Mass.: MIT Press.

Forbes, M., and F. Bloch. (1990) *What Happened to Their Kids? Children of the Rich and Famous.* New York: Simon and Schuster.

Franz, C. E., and K. M. White. (1985) "Individuation and Attachment in Personality Development: Extending Erikson's Theory." *Journal of Personality,* Vol. 53, No. 2, pp. 224–256.

Freeman, D. (1983) *Margaret Mead and Samoa: The Making and Unmaking of an Anthropological Myth.* Cambridge, Mass.: Harvard University Press.

Frenkel-Brunswik, E. (1954) *Psychoanalysis and the Unity of Science. Proceedings of the Academy of Arts and Sciences,* Vol. 80.

Freud, A. (1974) *The Writings of Anna Freud.* 5 vols. New York: International Universities Press.

Freud, S. (1900) "The Interpretation of Dreams," in J. Strachey (ed.), *The Standard Edition of* the Complete Psychological Works of Sigmund Freud. Vol. 4. London: Hogarth, 1953, pp. 1–338.

Freud, S. (1910) "Five Lectures on Psychoanalysis," in J. Strachey (ed.), *The Standard Edition of the Complete Psychological Works of Sigmund Freud.* Vol. 11. London: Hogarth, 1957, pp. 3–56.

Freud, S. (1915a) "Repression," in J. Strachey (ed.), *The Standard Edition of the Complete Psychological Works of Sigmund Freud.* Vol. 14. London: Hogarth, 1957, pp. 141–185.

Freud, S. (1915b) "The Unconscious," in J. Strachey (ed.), *The Standard Edition of the Complete Psychological Works of Sigmund Freud.* Vol. 14. London: Hogarth, 1957, pp. 159–215.

Freud, S. (1917) "Introductory Lectures on Psychoanalysis, Part III," in J. Strachey (ed.), *The Standard Edition of the Complete Psychological Works of Sigmund Freud.* Vol. 16. London: Hogarth, 1957, pp. 243–482.

Freud, S. (1920) "Beyond the Pleasure Principle," in J. Rickman (ed.), *A General Selection from the Works of Sigmund Freud.* New York: Liveright, 1957, pp. 141–168.

Freud, S. (1923) *The Ego and the Id.* London: Hogarth, 1974.

Freud, S. (1933) *New Introductory Lectures on Psychoanalysis.* New York: Norton.

Freud, S. (1938) *An Outline of Psychoanalysis.* London: Hogarth, 1973.

Freud, S. (1964) *The Standard Edition of the Complete Psychological Works of Sigmund Freud.* 30 vols. James Strachey (trans. and ed.). London: Hogarth.

Freud, S. (1992) *The Diary of Sigmund Freud 1929–1939: A Record of the Final Decade* (trans. M. Molnar). New York: Charles Scribner's Sons.

Fry, D. P. (1988) "Intercommunity Differences in Aggression among Zapotec Children." *Child Development,* Vol. 59, No. 4, pp. 1008–1019.

Fuller, R. C. (1986) *Americans and the Unconscious.* New York: Oxford University Press.

Furstenburg, F. (1981) "Implicating the Family: Teenage Parenthood and Kinship Involvement," in T. Ooms (ed.), *Teenage Pregnancy in Family Context.* Philadelphia: Temple University Press, pp. 131–164.

Furth, H. G., and W. Wachs. (1975) *Thinking Goes to School.* New York: Oxford University Press.

Gardner, A. (1983) *Frames of Mind.* New York: Basic Books.

Gelman, R. (1969) "Conservation Acquisition: A Problem of Learning to Attend to Relevant Attributes." *Journal of Experimental Child Psychology,* Vol. 7, pp. 167–187.

Gesell, A., and F. L. Ilg. (1949) *Child Development: An Introduction to the Study of Human Growth.* New York: Harper & Row.

Gesell, A., F. L. Ilg, L. B. Ames, and G. E. Bullis. (1977) *The Child from Five to Ten.* New York: Harper & Row.

Gilligan, C. (1982) *In a Different Voice.* Cambridge, Mass.: Harvard University Press.

Gilligan, C., J. V. Ward, and J. M. Taylor (eds.). (1988) *Mapping the Moral Domain.* Cambridge, Mass.: Harvard University Press.

Giorgi, A. (1987) "The Crisis of Humanistic Psychology." *The Humanistic Psychologist,* Vol. 15, No. 1, pp. 5–20.

Godin, A. (1971) "Some Developmental Tasks in Christian Education," in M. P. Strommen (ed.), *Research in Religious Development.* New York: Hawthorne Books.

Grams, M. (1988) *Breast Feeding Sourcebook.* Sheridan, Wyo.: Achievement Press.

Gray, M. M., J. M. Ispa, and K. R. Thornburg. (1986) "Erikson Psychosocial Stage Inventory: A Factor Analysis." *Educational and Psychological Measurement,* Vol. 46, No. 4, pp. 979–983.

Green, H. J. (1986) "Muscle Power: Fibre Type Recruitment, Metabolism, and Fatigue," in N.

L. Jones, N. McCartney, and A. J. McComas (eds.), *Human Muscle Power*. Champaign, Ill.: Human Kinetics.

Gresham, F. M., and S. N. Elliott. (1989) "Social Skills Deficits as a Primary Learning Disability." *Journal of Learning Disabilities,* Vol. 22, No. 2, pp. 120–124.

Guilford, J. P. (1967) *The Nature of Human Intelligence.* New York: McGraw-Hill.

Hagen, J. W., R. H. Jongeward, Jr., and R. V. Kail, Jr. (1975) "Cognitive Perspectives on the Development of Memory," in H. W. Reese and L. P. Lipsitt (eds.), *Advances in Child Development and Behavior.* Vol. 10. New York: Academic Press.

Hagenhoff, C., A. Lowe, M. F. Hovell, and D. Rugg. (1987) "Prevention of the Teenage Pregnancy Epidemic: A Social Learning Theory Approach." *Education and Treatment of Children,* Vol. 10, No. 1, pp. 67–83.

Halford, G. S. (1982) *The Development of Thought.* Hillsdale, N.J.: Erlbaum.

Hall, C. S. (1954) *A Primer of Freudian Psychology.* Yonkers, N.Y.: World Book.

Hall, C. S., and G. Lindzey. (1970, 1978) *Theories of Personality,* 2d, 3d eds. New York: Wiley.

Hall, G. S. (1891) "The Contents of Children's Minds on Entering School." *Pedagogical Seminar,* Vol. 1, No. 2, pp. 139–173.

Hall, G. S. (1904) *Adolescence.* 2 vols. New York: Appleton-Century-Crofts.

Hamachek, D. E. (1985) "The Self's Development and Ego Growth: Conceptual Analysis and Implications for Counselors." *Journal of Counseling and Development,* Vol. 64, No. 2, pp. 136–142.

Hamill, P. V. V. (1977) *NCHS Growth Curves for Children.* (Vital and Health Statistics, Series 11, No. 165. Data from the National Health Survey). Washington, D.C.: U.S. Government Printing Office.

Hamilton, W. D. (1964) "The Genetical Evolution of Social Behavior." *Journal of Theoretical Biology,* Vol. 7, No. 1, pp. 1–52.

Harris, M. L., and C. H. Harris. (1971) "A Factor Analytic Interpretation Strategy." *Educational and Psychological Measurement,* Vol. 31, No. 3, pp. 589–606.

Hartman, D. (1990) "Jewish Theory of Human Development," in R. M. Thomas (ed.), *The Encyclopedia of Human Development and Education* (pp. 125–131). Oxford: Pergamon.

Hartmann, H. (1959) "Psychoanalysis as a Scientific Theory," in S. Hook (ed.), *Psychoanalysis, Scientific Method, and Philosophy.* New York: New York University Press.

Hartshorne, H., and M. A. May. (1928–1930) *Studies in the Nature of Character.* 3 Vols. New York: Macmillan.

Hattie, J. (1992) *Self-Concept.* Hillsdale, N.J.: Erlbaum.

Hausfater, G., and S. B. Hrdy (eds.). (1984) *Infanticide.* New York: Aldine.

Havighurst, R. J. (1953) *Human Development and Education.* New York: Longmans, Green.

Hawkins, J. D., and J. G. Weis. (1985) "The Social Development Model: An Integrated Approach to Delinquency Prevention." *Journal of Primary Prevention,* Vol. 6, No. 2, pp. 73–97.

Hebb, D. O. (1970) "A Return to Jensen and His Social Critics." *American Psychologist,* Vol. 25, No. 6, p. 568.

Heider, F. (1958) *The Psychology of Interpersonal Relations.* New York: Wiley.

Hersh, R. H., J. P. Miller, and G. D. Fielding. (1980) *Models of Moral Education.* New York: Longman.

Hilgard, E. R. (1949) "Human Motives and the Concept of the Self." *American Psychologist,* Vol. 4, No. 9, pp. 374–382.

Hilgard, E. R. (1952) "Experimental Approaches to Psychoanalysis," in E. Pumpian-Mindlin (ed.), *Psychoanalysis as a Science.* Stanford, Calif.: Stanford University Press.

Hilgard, E. R., and G. H. Bower. (1975) *Theories of Learning,* 4th ed. Englewood Cliffs, N.J.: Prentice-Hall.

Hillner, K. P. (1984) *History and Systems of Modern Psychology.* New York: Gardner.

Hinde, R. A. (1974) *Biological Bases of Human Social Behavior.* New York: McGraw-Hill.

Hinde, R. A. (1983) "Ethology and Child Development," in M. M. Haith and J. J. Campos (eds.), *Handbook of Child Psychology.* Vol. II: *Infancy and Developmental Psychobiology.* New York: Wiley, pp. 27–93.

Hinde, R. A. (1987) *Individuals, Relationships, and Culture: Links between Ethology and the Social Sciences.* New York: Cambridge University Press.

Hinde, R. A., and L. McGinnis. (1977) "Some Factors Influencing the Effects of Temporary Mother-Infant Separation: Some Experiments with Rhesus Monkeys." *Psychological Medicine,* Vol. 7, No. 2, pp. 197–212.

Hirsch, J. (1970) "Behaviour-Genetic Analysis and Its Biosocial Consequences." *Seminars in Psychiatry,* Vol. 2, pp. 89–105.

Hogan, J. D., and M. A. Vahey. (1984) "Modern Classics in Child Development: Authors and Publications." *Journal of Psychology,* Vol. 116, No. 1, pp. 35–38.

Holt, R. F. (1989) *Freud Reappraised: A Fresh Look at Psychoanalytic Theory.* New York: Guilford.

Hook, S. (1959) "Science and Mythology in Psychoanalysis," in S. Hook (ed.), *Psychoanalysis, Scientific Method, and Philosophy.* New York: New York University Press.

Horton, D. L., and T. W. Turnage. (1976) *Human Learning.* Englewood Cliffs, N.J.: Prentice-Hall.

Hurlock, E. G. (1968) *Developmental Psychology,* 3d ed. New York: McGraw-Hill.

Ilg, F. L., and L. B. Ames. (1955) *The Gesell Institute's Child Behavior.* New York: Dell.

Ilg, F. L., L. B. Ames, and M. D. Baker. (1981) *Child Behavior.* New York: Harper & Row.

Inhelder, B. (1968) "Foreword," in I. E. Sigel and F. H. Hooper (eds.), *Logical Thinking in Children.* New York: Holt, Rinehart & Winston.

Inhelder, B., and J. Piaget. (1958) *The Growth of Logical Thinking from Childhood to Adolescence.* New York: Basic Books.

Inhelder, B., and J. Piaget. (1964) *The Early Growth of Logic in the Child.* London: Routledge & Kegan Paul.

Ittyerah, M., and A. Samarapungavan. (1989) "The Performance of Congenitally Blind Children in Cognitive Developmental Tasks." *British Journal of Developmental Psychology,* Vol. 7, No. 2, pp. 129–139.

James, W. (1890) *The Principles of Psychology.* New York: Holt, Rinehart & Winston.

James, W. (1892/1961) *Psychology: The Briefer Course.* New York: Harper & Row.

Jensen, A. R. (1969) "How Much Can We Boost IQ and Scholastic Achievement?" *Harvard Educational Review,* Vol. 39, No. 1, pp. 1–123.

Jensen, A. R. (1973) *Educability and Group Differences.* New York: Harper & Row.

Jersild, A. T. (1952) *In Search of Self.* New York: Columbia University Teachers College.

Johnston, L. D., P. M. O'Malley, and J. G. Bachman. (1986) *Drug Use among American High School Students, College Students, and Other Young Adults: National Trends through 1985.* Rockville, Md.: U.S. National Institute on Drug Abuse.

Jones, E. (1961) *The Life and Works of Sigmund Freud.* New York: Basic Books.

Jones, E. E., and K. E. Davis. (1965) "From Acts to Dispositions: The Attribution Process in Person Perception," in L. Berkowitz (ed.), *Advances in Experimental Social Psychology.* Vol. 2. New York: Academic Press.

Jones, E. E., D. E. Kanouse, H. H. Kelley, R. E. Nisbett, S. Valins, and B. Weiner. (1971) *Attribution: Perceiving the Causes of Behavior.* Morristown, N.J.: General Learning Press.

Jones, E. E., and R. E. Nisbett. (1971) *The Actor and the Observer: Divergent Perceptions of the Causes of Behavior.* Morristown, N.J.: General Learning Press.

Jung, C. G. (1953) "On Psychical Energy," in *Collected Works.* Vol. VIII. New York: Pantheon.

Kail, R., and J. Bisanz. (1982) "Information Processing and Cognitive Development," in H. W. Reese and L. P. Lipsitt (eds.), *Advances in Child Development and Behavior.* Vol. 17. New York: Academic Press.

Kail, R., and J. W. Pellegrino. (1985) *Human Intelligence: Perspectives and Prospects.* New York: W. H. Freeman.

Kantor, J. R. (1959) *Interbehavioral Psychology,* 2d rev. ed. Bloomington, Ind.: Principia.

Karp, L. E. (1976) *Genetic Engineering: Threat or Promise?* Chicago: Nelson-Hall.

Kaufman, L. (1974) *Sight and Mind.* New York: Oxford University Press.

Kazdin, A. E. (1978) *History of Behavior Modification: Experimental Foundations of Contemporary Research.* Baltimore, Md.: University Park Press.

Kazdin, A. E. (1981) "Behavior Modification in Education: Contributions and Limitations." *Developmental Review,* Vol. 1, No. 1, pp. 34–57.

Keller, F. S., and W. N. Schoenfeld. (1950) *Principles of Psychology.* New York: Appleton-Century-Crofts.

Keller, F. S., and J. G. Sherman. (1974) *The Keller Plan Handbook.* Menlo Park, Calif.: Benjamin Cummings.

Kelley, E. C. (1962) "The Fully Functioning Self," in A. W. Combs, E. C. Kelley, A. H. Maslow, and C. R. Rogers (eds.), *Perceiving, Behaving, Becoming.* Washington, D.C.: Association for Supervision and Curriculum Development.

Kelley, H. H. (1967) "Attribution Theory in Social Psychology," in D. Levine (ed.), *Nebraska Symposium on Motivation, 1967.* Vol. 15. Lincoln: University of Nebraska Press.

Kelley, H. H. (1971) *Attribution in Social Interaction.* Morristown, N.J.: General Learning Press.

Kelley, H. H. (1972) *Causal Schemata and the Attribution Process.* Morristown, N.J.: General Learning Press.

Kelley, H. H. (1973) "The Process of Causal Attribution." *American Psychologist,* Vol. 28, No. 2, pp. 107–128.

Kelley, H. H. (1992) "Common-Sense Psychology and Scientific Psychology," in M. R. Rosenzweig and L. W. Porter (eds.), *Annual Review of Psychology,* Vol. 43. Palo Alto, Calif.: Annual Reviews, pp. 1–23.

Kessen, W., and E. D. Cahan. (1986) "A Century of Psychology: From Subject to Object to Agent." *American Scientist,* Vol. 74, No. 6, pp. 640–649.

Kevles, D. J. (1985) *In the Name of Eugenics: Genetics and the Uses of Human Heredity.* New York: Knopf.

Kihlstrom, J. F. (1987) "The Cognitive Unconscious." *Science,* Vol. 237, No. 4821, pp. 1445–1452.

Kindermann, T. A. (1993) "Fostering Independence, in Mother-Child Interactions." *International Journal of Behavioral Development,* Vol. 16, No. 4, pp. 513–535.

Kirsch, M. M. (1987) *57 Reasons Not to Light Up.* Minneapolis, Minn.: CompCare.

Klahr, D., and J. G. Wallace. (1976) *Cognitive Development: An Information-Processing View.* Hillsdale, N.J.: Erlbaum.

Klaus, M. H., and J. H. Kennell. (1976) *Maternal-Infant Binding.* St. Louis: Mosby.

Klatzky, R. L. (1980) *Human Memory: Structures and Process.* San Francisco: W. H. Freeman.

Klein, D. B. (1977) *The Unconscious: Invention or Discovery.* Santa Monica, Calif.: Goodyear.

Kleinginna, P. R., and A. M. Kleinginna. (1988) "Current Trends Toward Convergence of the Behavioristic, Functional, and Cognitive Perspectives in Experimental Psychology." *Psychological Record,* Vol. 38, No. 3, pp. 368–397.

Knapp, T. J. (1985) "Who's Who in American Introductory Psychology Textbooks: A Citation Study." *Teaching of Psychology,* Vol. 12, No. 1, pp. 15–17.

Kohlberg, L. (1958) "The Development of Modes of Thinking and Choices in Years 10 to 16." Ph.D. diss., University of Chicago.

Kohlberg, L. (1967) "Moral and Religious Education in the Public Schools: A Developmental View," in T. R. Sizer (ed.), *Religion and Public Education.* Boston: Houghton-Mifflin.

Kohlberg, L. (1968a) "The Child as a Moral Philosopher." *Psychology Today,* Vol. 2, No. 4, pp. 25–30.

Kohlberg, L. (1968b) "Moral Development," in *International Encyclopedia of the Social Sciences.* New York: Macmillan.

Kohlberg, L. (1971) "From Is to Ought," in T. Mischel (ed.), *Cognitive Development and Epistemology.* New York: Academic Press.

Kohlberg, L. (1976) "Moral States and Moralization: The Cognitive-Developmental Approach," in T. Likona (ed.). *Moral Development and Behavior.* New York: Holt, Rinehart & Winston.

Kohlberg, L. (1984) *The Psychology of Moral Development.* San Francisco: Harper & Row.

Kohlberg, L., and R. Kramer. (1969) "Continuities in Childhood and Adult Moral Development." *Human Development,* Vol. 12, No. 2, pp. 93–120.

Kolominskly, Y. L., and M. H. Meltsas. (1985) "Sex-Role Differentiation in Preschool Children" (in Russian). *Voprosy-Psikhologii,* No. 3, pp. 165–171.

Kozulin, A. (1990) *Vygotsky's Psychology: A Biography of Ideas.* Cambridge, Mass.: Harvard University Press.

Kris, E. (1947) "The Nature of Psychoanalytic Propositions and Their Validation," in S. Hook and M. R. Konvitz (eds.), *Freedom and Experience.* Ithaca, N.Y.: Cornell University Press, pp. 239–259.

Krohn, M. D., W. F. Skinner, J. L. Massey, and R. L. Akers. (1985) "Social Learning Theory and Adolescent Cigarette Smoking: A Longitudinal Study." *Social Problems,* Vol. 32, No. 5, pp. 455–473.

Kuhn, T. S. (1962) *The Structure of Scientific Revolutions.* Chicago: University of Chicago Press.

Lamal, P. A. (1989) "The Impact of Behaviorism on Our Culture: Some Evidence and Conjectures." *Psychological Record,* Vol. 39, pp. 529–535.

Layzer, D. (1974) "Heritability Analyses of IQ Scores: Science or Numerology?" *Science,* Vol. 183, No. 4131, pp. 1259–1266.

Leahy, A. M. (1935) "Nature-Nurture and Intelligence." *Genetic Psychology Monographs,* Vol. 17, pp. 236–308.

Lee, V. L. (1988) *Beyond Behaviorism.* Hillsdale, N.J.: Erlbaum.

Leff, H. L. (1978) *Experience, Environment, and Human Potentials.* New York: Oxford University Press.

Lenhoff, H. M. (1989) *Conceptions to Birth: Human Reproduction, Genetics, and Development.* Dubuque, Iowa: Kendall/Hunt.

Lerner, D. (1965) "Introduction," in D. Lerner (ed.), *Cause and Effect.* New York: Free Press, pp. 1–10.

Lerner, R. M. (1976) *Concepts and Theories of Human Development.* Reading, Mass.: Addison-Wesley.

Lerner, R. M. (1986) *Concepts and Theories of Human Development,* 2d ed. New York: Random House.

Levin, I. (ed.). (1986) *Stage and Structure: Reopening the Debate.* Norwood, N.J.: Ablex, pp. 40–58.

Lewin, K. (1942) "Field Theory and Learning," in *Forty-First Yearbook, National Society for the Study of Education.* Part II. Bloomington, Ill.: Public School Publishing.

Lewis, M. (1990) "Self Knowledge and Social Development in Early Life," in L. A. Previn (ed.), *Handbook of Personality.* New York: Guilford.

Loftus, E. F. (1975) "Leading Questions and Eyewitness Report." *Cognitive Psychology,* Vol. 7, No. 4, pp. 560–572.

Logan, R. D. (1986) "A Reconceptualization of Erikson's Theory: The Repetition of Existential and Instrumental Themes." *Human Development,* Vol. 29, No. 3, pp. 125–136.

Logue, A. W. (1985) "The Growth of Behaviorism: Controversy and Diversity," in C. E. Buxton (ed.), *Points of View in the Modern History of Psychology.* Orlando, Fla.: Academic Press, pp. 169–196.

Lorenz, K. Z. (1977) *Behind the Mirror: A Search for a National History of Human Knowledge.* New York: Harcourt Brace Jovanovich.

Love, S. Q., T. H. Ollendick, C. Johnson, and S. E. Schlesinger. (1985) "A Preliminary Report of the Prediction of Bulimic Behaviors: A Social Learning Analysis." *Bulletin of the Society of Psychologists in Addictive Behaviors,* Vol. 4, No. 2, pp. 93–101.

Lowrey, G. H. (1978) *Growth and Development in Children,* 7th ed. Chicago: Year Book Medical Publications.

Luria, A. R. (1976) *Cognitive Development: Its Cultural and Social Foundations.* Cambridge, Mass.: Harvard University Press.

Luria, A. R., and R. Yudovich. (1971) *Speech and the Development of Mental Processes in the Child.* Harmondsworth, England: Penguin.

Maccoby, E. (1968) "The Development of Moral Values and Behavior in Childhood," in J. A. Clausen (ed.), *Socialization and Society.* Boston: Little, Brown.

Mackworth, J. F. (1976) "Development of Attention," in V. Hamilton and M. D. Vernon (eds.), *The Development of Cognitive Processes.* New York: Academic Press.

Magary, J. F., M. K. Poulsen, P. J. Levinson, and P. A. Taylor (eds.). (1977) *Piagetian Theory and Its Implications for the Helping Professions.* Los Angeles: University of Southern California.

Mahoney, M. J. (1989) "Scientific Psychology and Radical Behaviorism." *American Psychologist,* Vol. 44, No. 11, pp. 1372–1377.

Mahrer, A. R. (1978) *Experiencing: A Humanistic Theory of Psychology and Psychiatry.* New York: Brunner/Mazel.

Mahrer, A. R. (1989) *Experiencing: A Humanistic Theory of Psychology and Psychiatry.* Ottawa: University of Ottawa Press.

Malina, R. M., and A. F. Roche. (1983) *Manual of Physical Status and Performance in Childhood.* Vols. 1 & 2: *Human Growth: A Comprehensive Treatise.* New York: Plenum.

Malinowski, B. (1948) *Magic, Science, and Religion and Other Essays.* Garden City, N.Y.: Doubleday.

Marek, J. C. (1988) "A Buddhist Theory of Human Development," in R. M. Thomas (ed.), *Oriental Theories of Human Development.* New York: Peter Lang, pp. 76–115.

Martindale, C. (1987) "Can We Construct Kantian Mental Machines?" *Journal of Mind and Behavior,* Vol. 8, No. 2, pp. 261–268.

Marx, K. (1847) "The Communist Manifesto," in D. McLellan (ed.), *Karl Marx, Selected Writings.* Oxford, England: Oxford University Press, 1977.

Marx, K. (1859) "Preface to A Critique of Political Economy," in D. McLellan (ed.), *Karl Marx, Selected Writings.* Oxford, England: Oxford University Press, 1977.

Marx, M. H., and F. E. Goodson (eds.). (1976) *Theories in Contemporary Psychology.* New York: Macmillan.

Maslow, A. H. (1968) *Toward a Psychology of Being.* Princeton, N.J.: Van Nostrand Reinhold.

Maslow, A. H. (1970) *Motivation and Personality,* 2d ed. New York: Harper & Row.

Maslow, A. H. (1971) *The Farther Reaches of Human Nature.* New York: Viking Press.

May, K. M., and C. R. Logan. (1993) "Family Type and the Accomplishment of Developmental Tasks Among College Students." *Journal of College Student Development*, Vol. 34, No. 6, pp. 387–400.

Mead, G. H. (1934) *Mind, Self, and Society*. Chicago: University of Chicago Press.

Mead, M. (1968) *Coming of Age in Samoa*. New York: Dell.

Miller, G. A. (1956) "The Magical Number Seven, Plus or Minus Two: Some Limits on Our Capacity for Processing Information." *Psychological Review*, Vol. 63, No. 2, pp. 81–97.

Miller, L. (1988) "Behaviorism and the New Science of Cognition." *Psychological Record*, Vol. 28, No. 1, pp. 3–18.

Miller, P. H. (1983) *Theories of Developmental Psychology*. San Francisco: W. H. Freeman.

Mishkin, M., and T. Appenzeller. (1987) "The Anatomy of Memory." *Scientific American*, Vol. 256, No. 6, pp. 80–89.

Moll, L. C. (ed.). (1990) *Vygotsky and Education: Instructional Implications and Applications of Sociohistorical Psychology*. New York: Cambridge University Press.

Montagu, A. (1959) *Human Heredity*. New York: Harcourt Brace Jovanovich.

Montemayor, R., and M. Eisen. (1977) "The Development of Self-Conception from Childhood to Adolescence," *Developmental Psychology*, Vol. 48, pp. 121–132.

Moore, J. (1990) "On Mentalism, Privacy, and Behaviorism." *The Journal of Mind and Behavior*, Vol. 11, No. 1, pp. 19–36.

Mounoud, P. (1986) "Similarities between Developmental Sequences at Different Age Periods," in I. Levin (ed.), *Stage and Structure: Reopening the Debate*. Norwood, N.J.: Ablex, pp. 40–58.

Mueller-Schwarze, D. (ed.), (1978) *Evolution of Play Behavior*. Stroudsburg, Penn.: Dowden, Hutchinson, & Ross.

Muller, P. (1969) *The Tasks of Childhood*. New York: McGraw-Hill.

Munro, D. J. (1977) *The Concept of Man in Contemporary China*. Ann Arbor: University of Michigan Press.

Murray, H. A. (1938) *Explorations in Personality*. New York: Oxford University Press.

Muzika, E. G. (1990) "Evolution, Emptiness, and the Fantasy Self." *Journal of Humanistic Psychology*, Vol. 30, No. 2, pp. 89–108.

Nagel, E. (1959) "Methodological Issues in Psychoanalytic Theory," in S. Hook (ed.), *Psychoanalysis, Scientific Method, and Philosophy*. New York: New York University Press.

Nagel, E. (1965) "Types of Causal Explanation in Science," in D. Lerner (ed.), *Cause and Effect*. New York: Free Press, pp. 11–32.

Nagel, T. (1994) "Freud's Permanent Revolution," *New York Review of Books*, Vol. 41, No. 9, pp. 34–38.

Neisser, U. (1976) *Cognition and Reality*. San Francisco: W. H. Freeman.

New England Primer: Or an Easy and Pleasant Guide to the Art of Reading. (1836) Boston: Massachusetts Sabbath School Society.

Newell, A., J. C. Shaw, and H. A. Simon. (1958) "Elements of a Theory of Human Problem Solving." *Psychological Review*, Vol. 65, No. 3, pp. 151–166.

Newell, A., and H. A. Simon. (1972) *Human Problem Solving*. Englewood Cliffs, N.J.: Prentice-Hall.

Newman, F., and L. Holzman. (1993) *Lev Vygotsky: Revolutionary Scientist*. New York: Routledge & Kegan Paul.

Nimmons, D. (1994) "Sex and the Brain." *Discover*, Vol. 15, No. 3, pp. 64–71.

Obeid, R. A. (1990) "Islamic Theory of Human Development," in R. M. Thomas (ed.), *The Encyclopedia of Human Development and Education* (pp. 137–140). Oxford: Pergamon.

Ochse, R., and C. Plug. (1986) "Cross-Culture Investigation of the Validity of Erikson's Theory of Personality Development." *Journal of Personality and Social Psychology*, Vol. 50, No. 6, pp. 1240–1252.

Ornstein, P. A., and M. J. Naus. (1978) "Rehearsal Processes in Children's Memory," in P. A. Ornstein, *Memory Development in Children*. Hillsdale, N.J.: Erlbaum.

Oswalt, W. H. (1972) *Other Peoples, Other Customs*. New York: Holt, Rinehart, & Winston.

Ouspensky, P. D. (1957) *The Fourth Way*. London: Routledge & Kegan Paul.

Palmonari, A., M. L. Pombeni, and E. Kirchler. (1990) "Adolescents and Their Peer Groups: A Study of the Significance of Peers, Social Categorization Processes, and Coping with Developmental Tasks." *Social Behaviour*, Vol. 5, No. 1, pp. 33–48.

Paniagua, F. A. (1986) "Synthetic Behaviorism: Remarks on Function and Structure." *Psychological Record*, Vol. 36, No. 2, pp. 179–184.

Paris, S. G. (1978) "The Development of Inference and Transformation as Memory Operations," in P. A. Ornstein, *Memory Development in Children*. Hillsdale, N.J.: Erlbaum.

Pascual-Leone, J. (1976) "A View of Cognition from a Formalist's Perspective," in K. F. Riegel and J. Meacham (eds.), *The Developing Individual in a Changing World*. The Hague: Mouton, pp. 89–100.

Peel, E. A. (1976) "The Thinking and Education of the Adolescent," in V. P. Varma and P. Williams (eds.), *Piaget, Psychology, and Education*. Itasca, Ill.: F. E. Peacock.

Pellegrino, J. W., and C. K. Varnhagan. (1985) "Abilities and Aptitudes," in T. Husén and T. N. Postlethwaite, *International Encyclopedia of Education*. Vol. 1. Oxford, England: Pergamon Press, pp. 1–8.

Pepler, D., and K. Rubin. (1982) *Play of Children: Current Theory and Research*. New York: Karger.

Pepper, S. C. (1942) *World Hypotheses: A Study in Evidence*. Berkeley: University of California Press.

Perls, F. S., R. F. Hefferline, and P. Goodman. (1951) *Gestalt Therapy*. New York: Julian Press.

Petermann, F. (1987) "Behavioral Assessment and Reduction of Children's Aggression." *Journal of Human Behavior and Learning*, Vol. 4, No. 1, pp. 48–54.

Peters, R. S. (1971) "Moral Development: A Plea for Pluralism," in T. Mischel, *Cognitive Development and Epistemology*. New York: Academic Press.

Phillips, D. C., and M. E. Kelley. (1975) "Hierarchical Theories of Development in Education and Psychology." *Harvard Educational Review*, Vol. 45, No. 3, pp. 351–375.

Phillips, J. L., Jr. (1975) *The Origins of Intellect: Piaget's Theory*, 2d ed. San Francisco: W. H. Freeman.

Piaget, J. (1930) *The Child's Conception of Physical Causality*. London: Routledge & Kegan Paul.

Piaget, J. (1946) *Le Développement de la Notion de Temps chez l'Enfant*. Paris: Presses Universitaires de France.

Piaget, J. (1948) *The Moral Judgment of the Child*. Glencoe, Ill.: Free Press.

Piaget, J. (1950) *The Psychology of Intelligence*. London: Routledge & Kegan Paul.

Piaget, J. (1951) *Play, Dreams, and Imitation in Childhood*. New York: Norton.

Piaget, J. (1952) *The Child's Conception of Number*. London: Routledge & Kegan Paul.

Piaget, J. (1953) *Logic and Psychology*. Manchester, England: Manchester University Press.

Piaget, J. (1963) *The Origins of Intelligence in Children*, 2d ed. New York: Norton.

Piaget, J. (1969) *The Child's Conception of Movement and Speed*. New York: Basic Books.

Piaget, J. (1970a) *Genetic Epistemology*. New York: Columbia University Press.

Piaget, J. (1970b) *Science of Education and the Psychology of the Child*. New York: Viking Press.

Piaget, J. (1972) *Psychology and Epistemology*. London: Penguin.

Piaget, J. (1973) *The Child and Reality.* New York: Viking Press.

Piaget, J., L. Apostel, and B. Mandelbrot. (1957) *Logique et Equilibre.* Paris: Presses Universitaires de France.

Piaget, J., and B. Inhelder. (1956) *The Child's Conception of Space.* London: Routledge & Kegan Paul.

Piaget, J., and B. Inhelder. (1969) *The Psychology of the Child.* New York: Basic Books.

Piaget, J., A. Jonckheere, and B Mandelbrot. (1958) *La Lecture de l'Expérience.* Etudes d'Epistémologie Génétique V. Paris: Presses Universitaires de France.

Piaget, J., and A. Szeminska. (1952) *The Child's Conception of Number.* Atlantic Highlands, N.J.: Humanities Press.

Pickar, D. B., and C. D. Turi. (1986) "The Learning Disabled Adolescent: Eriksonian Psychosocial Development, Self-Concept, and Delinquent Behavior." *Journal of Youth and Adolescence,* Vol. 15, No. 5, pp. 429–440.

Posner, M. I. (ed.). (1989) *Foundations of Cognitive Science.* Cambridge, Mass.: MIT Press.

Poulsen, M. K., and G. I. Luben. (1979) *Piagetian Theory and Its Implications for the Helping Professions.* Los Angeles: University of Southern California.

Power, C. (1988) "The Just Community Approach to Moral Education." *Journal of Moral Education,* Vol. 17, No. 3, pp. 195–208.

Price, R. W. (1979) *Basic Molecular Biology.* New York: Wiley.

Pylyshyn, Z. W. (1989) "Computing in Cognitive Science," in M. I. Posner (ed.), *Foundations of Cognitive Science.* Cambridge, Mass.: M.I.T. Press, p. 52–91.

Reese, H. W., and W. F. Overton. (1970) "Models for Development and Theories of Development," in L. R. Goulet and Paul B. Baltes (eds.), *Life-Span Developmental Psychology.* New York: Academic Press.

Reeves, C. (1977) *The Psychology of Rollo May.* San Francisco: Jossey-Bass.

Reyna, V. F. (1992) "Reasoning, Remembering, and Their Relationship: Social, Cognitive, and Developmental Issues" in M. L. Howe, C. J. Brainerd, and V. F. Reyna (eds.), *Development of Long-Term Retention.* New York: Springer-Verlag.

Rieber, R. W., and A. S. Carton. (1987, 1993) *The Collected Works of L. S. Vygotsky.* New York: Plenum.

Riegel, K. F. (1972) "Time and Change in the Development of the Individual and Society," in H. W. Reese (ed.), *Advances in Child Development and Behavior.* Vol. 7. New York: Academic Press, pp. 91–113.

Riegel, K. F. (1973) "Dialectical Operations: The Final Period of Cognitive Development." *Human Development,* Vol. 16, No. 5, pp. 346–370.

Riegel, K. F. (1975) "Toward a Dialectical Theory of Development." *Human Development,* Vol. 18, No. 1–2, pp. 50–64.

Riegel, K. F. (1976) "From Traits and Equilibrium toward Developmental Dialectics," in W. J. Arnold (ed.), *Conceptual Foundations of Psychology.* Nebraska Symposium on Motivation, 1975, Vol. 23. Lincoln: University of Nebraska Press, pp. 349–497.

Riegel, K. F. (1979) *Foundations of Dialectical Psychology.* New York: Academic Press.

Rifkin, J. (1985) *Declaration of a Heretic.* Boston: Routledge & Kegan Paul.

Roback, A. A. (1964) *History of American Psychology.* New York: Collier Books.

Rogers, C. F. (1961) *On Becoming a Person.* Boston: Houghton Mifflin.

Rogers, C. F. (1973) "My Philosophy of Interpersonal Relationships and How It Grew." *Journal of Humanistic Psychology,* Vol. 13, No. 2, pp. 13–15.

Romig, C. A., and J. G. Thompson. (1988) "Teen-age Pregnancy: A Family Systems Approach." *American Journal of Family Therapy,* Vol. 16, No. 1, pp. 133–143.

Rose, M. (1986) "The Design of Atmosphere: Ego-Nurture and Psychic Change in Residential Treatment." *Journal of Adolescence,* Vol. 9, No. 1, pp. 49–62.

Rose, S. R. (1987) "Social Skills Training in Middle Childhood: A Structured Group Approach." *Journal for Specialists in Group Work*, Vol. 12, No. 4, pp. 144–149.

Rosenthal, D. A., S. M. Moore, and M. J. Taylor. (1983) "A Study of the Self-Image of Anglo-, Greek-, and Italian-Austrian Working Class Adolescents." *Journal of Youth and Adolescence*, Vol. 12, No. 2, pp. 117–135.

Ross, R. P. (1985) "Ecological Theory of Human Development," In T. Husén and T. N. Postlethwaite (eds.), *International Encyclopedia of Education*, Vol. 3. Oxford, England: Pergamon Press, pp. 1513–1517.

Rotter, J. B. (1954) *Social Learning and Clinical Psychology*. New York: Johnson Reprint Company, 1980.

Rotter, J. B. (1982) *The Development and Application of Social Learning Theory*. New York: Praeger.

Rousseau, J. J. (1773) *Emilius; or, A Treatise of Education*. 3 vols. Edinburgh: W. Coke.

Sandor, D., and D. A. Rosenthal. (1986) "Youths' Outlooks on Love: Is It Just a State or Two?" *Journal of Adolescent Research*, Vol. 1, No. 2, pp. 199–212.

Savin-Williams, R. C. (1976) "An Ethological Study of Dominance Formation and Maintenance in a Group of Human Adolescents." *Child Development*, Vol. 47, No. 4, pp. 972–979.

Schnaitier, R. (1987) "Behavior Is Not Cognitive and Cognitivism Is Not Behavioral." *Behaviorism*, Vol. 15, No. 1, pp. 1–11.

Schneider, W., and M. Pressley. (1989) *Memory Development Between 2 and 20*. New York: Springer-Verlag.

Schneirla, T. C. (1957) "The Concept of Development in Comparative Psychology," in D. B. Harris (ed.), *The Concept of Development*. Minneapolis: University of Minnesota Press.

Schneirla, T. C. (1972) in L. R. Aronson, E. Tobach, J. S. Rosenblatt, and D. S. Lehrman (eds.), *Selected Writings of T. C. Schneirla*. San Francisco: W. H. Freeman.

Schoggen, P. (1989) *Behavior Settings*. Stanford, Calif.: Stanford University Press.

Scholnick, E. K. (ed.). (1983) *New Trends in Conceptual Representation: Challenges to Piaget's Theory?* Hillsdale, N.J.: Erlbaum.

Scriven, M. (1959) "The Experimental Investigation of Psychoanalysis," in S. Hook (ed.), *Psychoanalysis, Scientific Method, and Philosophy*. New York: New York University Press.

Sears, R. R., L. Rau, and R. Alpert. (1965) *Identification and Child Rearing*. New York: Harper & Row.

Seppala, M., and L. Hamberger (eds.). (1991) *Frontiers in Human Reproduction*. New York: New York Academy of Sciences.

Shapiro, L., M. Hager, P. Wingert, and K. Springen. (1994) "A Tomato with a Body That Just Won't Quit," *Newsweek*, June 6, pp. 80–82.

Shavelson, R. J., R. Bolus, and J. W. Keesling. (1983) "Self-Concept: Recent Developments in Theory and Method," *New Directions for Testing and Measurement*, Vol. 7, pp. 25–43.

Shaver, K. G. (1975) *An Introduction to Attribution Processes*. Cambridge, Mass.: Winthrop.

Sherif, M. (1966) *In Common Predicament: Social Psychology of Intergroup Conflict and Cooperation*. Boston: Houghton Mifflin.

Shuttleworth, F. K. (1935) "The Nature versus Nurture Problem: II. The Contributions of Nature and Nurture to Individual Differences in Intelligence." *Journal of Educational Psychology*, Vol. 26, No. 9, pp. 655–681.

Sidman, M. (1986) "Functional Analysis of Emergent Verbal Classes," in T. Thompson and M. D. Zeiler (eds.), *Analysis and Integration of Behavioral Units*. Hillsdale, N.J.: Erlbaum, pp. 213–245.

Siegel, M. (1982) *Fairness in Children*. London: Academic Press.

Siegler, R. S. (1976) "Three Aspects of Cognitive Development." *Cognitive Psychology*, Vol. 4, pp. 481–520.

Sigel, I. E., and R. C. Cocking. (1977) *Cognitive Development from Childhood to Adolescence: A Constructivist Perspective*. New York: Holt, Rinehart & Winston.

Sigel, I. E., and F. H. Hooper. (1968) *Logical Thinking in Children*. New York: Holt, Rinehart & Winston.

Singer, M., and P. Berg. (1991) *Genes and Genomes*. Mill Valley, Calif.: University Science Books.

Skeels, H. M. (1940) "Some Iowa Studies of the Mental Growth of Children in Relation to Differentials of the Environment: A Summary," in *Intelligence: Its Nature and Nurture*. 39th Yearbook of the National Society for the Study of Education. Bloomington, Ill.: Public School Publishing.

Skinner, B. F. (1938) *The Behavior of Organisms: An Experimental Analysis*. New York: Appleton-Century-Crofts.

Skinner, B. F. (1945) "Baby in a Box," in B. F. Skinner (ed.), *Cumulative Record: A Selection of Papers*, 3d ed. New York: Appleton-Century-Crofts, 1972.

Skinner, B. F. (1948) *Walden Two*. New York: Macmillan.

Skinner, B. F. (1950) "Are Theories of Learning Necessary?" *Psychological Review*, Vol. 57, No. 4, pp. 193–216.

Skinner, B. F. (1969) *Contingencies of Reinforcement: A Theoretical Analysis*. Englewood Cliffs, N.J.: Prentice-Hall.

Skinner, B. F. (1971) *Beyond Freedom and Dignity*. New York: Knopf.

Skinner, B. F. (1972) *Cumulative Record: A Selection of Papers*, 3d ed. New York: Appleton-Century-Crofts.

Skinner, B. F. (1974) *About Behaviorism*. New York: Knopf.

Skinner, B. F. (1984) "The Shame of American Education." *American Psychologist*, Vol. 39, No. 9, pp. 947–954.

Skinner, B. F. (1985) "Cognitive Science and Behaviourism." *British Journal of Psychology*, Vol. 76, No. 3, pp. 291–301.

Skinner, B. F. (1987) *Upon Further Reflection*. Englewood Cliffs, N.J.: Prentice-Hall.

Skodak, M. (1939) "Children in Foster Homes: A Study of Mental Development." *University of Iowa Studies in Child Welfare*, Vol. 16, No. 1 (entire issue).

Smith, M. B. (1990) "Henry A. Murray (1893–1988): Humanistic Psychologist." *Journal of Humanistic Psychology*, Vol. 30, No. 1, pp. 6–13.

Smith, P. K., and K. J. Connolly. (1980) *The Ecology of Preschool Behaviour*. Cambridge, England: Cambridge University Press.

Sober, E. (1989) "What Is Psychological Egoism?" *Behaviorism*, Vol. 17, No. 2, pp. 89–131.

Sokoloff, L., G. G. Fitzgerald, and E. E. Kaufman. (1977) "Cerebral Nutrition and Energy Metabolism," in R. J. Wurtman and J. J. Wurtman (eds.), *Nutrition and the Brain*, Vol. 1. New York: Raven Press.

Spitz, R. A. (1950) "Anxiety in Infancy; A Study of Its Manifestations in the First Year of Life." *International Journal of Psychoanalysis*, Vol. 31, pp. 138–143.

Spock, B., and M. B. Rothenberg. (1985) *Dr. Spock's Baby and Child Care*. New York: Pocket Books.

Stafford-Clark, D. (1967) *What Freud Really Said*. London: Penguin.

Stemmer, N. (1989) "The Acquisition of the Ostensive Lexicon: The Superiority of Empiricist over Cognitive Theories." *Behaviorism*, Vol. 17, No. 1, pp. 41–59.

Stephansky, P. E. (1986) *Freud, Appraisals and Reappraisals*. Hillsdale, N.J.: Analytic Press.

Sternberg, S. (1969) "Memory-Scanning: Mental Processes Revealed by Reaction-Time Experiments." *American Scientist*, Vol. 57, No. 4, pp. 421–457.

Stevenson, H., H. Azuma, and K. Hakuta (eds.). (1986) *Child Development and Education in Japan.* New York: W. H. Freeman.

Stevick, D. B. (1968) *B. F. Skinner's Walden Two.* New York: Seabury Press.

Strayer, F. F., and J. Strayer. (1976) "An Ethological Analysis of Social Agonism and Dominance Relations among Pre-School Children." *Child Development,* Vol. 47, pp. 980–999.

Strazicich, M. (ed.). (1988) *Moral and Civic Education and Teaching about Religion.* Sacramento: California State Department of Education.

Suppes, P. C. (1969) *Studies in the Methodology and Foundations of Science.* Dordrecht, Holland: R. Reidel.

Tart, C. T. (1990) "Extending Mindfulness to Everyday Life." *Journal of Humanistic Psychology,* Vol. 30, No. 1, pp. 81–106.

Terman, L. M., and M. A. Merrill. (1960) *Stanford-Binet Intelligence Scale: Manual for the Third Revision, Form L-M.* Boston: Houghton Mifflin.

Thagard, P. R. (1978) "The Best Explanation: Criteria for Theory Choice." *Journal of Philosophy,* Vol. 75, No. 1, pp. 76–92.

Thomas, R. M. (1960) *Judging Student Progress.* New York: Longmans, Green.

Thomas, R. M. (1985) "Christian Theory of Human Development" in T. Husén and T. N. Postlethwaite (eds.), *International Encyclopedia of Education.* Vol. 1. Oxford, England: Pergamon Press, pp. 715–721.

Thomas, R. M. (1986) "Assessing Moral Development." *International Journal of Educational Research,* Vol. 10, No. 4, pp. 349–476.

Thomas, R. M. (ed.). (1988) *Oriental Theories of Human Development.* New York: Peter Lang.

Thomas, R. M. (1989a) "Moral and Ethnic Identity." *International Journal on the Unity of the Sciences,* Vol. 2, No. 4, pp. 381–403.

Thomas, R. M. (1989b) "A Proposed Taxonomy of Moral Values." *The Journal of Moral Education,* Vol. 18, No. 1, pp. 60–75.

Thomas, R. M. (1989c) *The Puzzle of Learning Difficulties—Applying a Diagnosis and Treatment Model.* Springfield, Ill.: Charles C Thomas.

Thomas, R. M. (1990a) "Christian Theory of Human Development," in R. M. Thomas (ed.), *The Encyclopedia of Human Development and Education* (pp. 131–137). Oxford: Pergamon.

Thomas, R. M. (1990b) *Counseling and Life-Span Development.* Newbury Park, Calif.: Sage.

Thomas, R. M. (1995) *Classifying Reactions to Wrongdoing: Taxonomies of Misdeeds, Sanctions, and Aims of Sanctions.* Westport, Conn.: Greenwood.

Thomas, R. M., and D. L. Brubaker. (1971) *Curriculum Patterns in Elementary Social Studies.* Belmont, Calif.: Wadsworth.

Thomas, R. M., and A. Diver-Stamnes. (1993) *What Wrongdoers Deserve: The Moral Reasoning Behind Responses to Midconduct.* Westport, Conn.: Greenwood.

Thomas, R. M., and S. M. Thomas. (1965) *Individual Differences in the Classroom.* New York: David McKay.

Tinbergen, N. (1951) *The Study of Instinct.* Oxford, England: Oxford University Press.

Tinbergen, N. (1973) *The Animal in Its World: Explorations of an Ethologist 1932–1972.* Cambridge, Mass.: Harvard University Press.

Tomlinson, S. (1982) *A Sociology of Special Education.* London: Routledge & Kegan Paul.

Travers, J. F. (1977) *The Growing Child.* New York: Wiley.

Trivers, R. L., and H. Hare. (1976) "Haplodipoidy and the Evolution of the Social Insects." *Science,* Vol. 191, No. 4224, pp. 249–263.

Tronick, E., and P. M. Greenfield. (1973) *Infant Curriculum: The Bromley-Heath Guide to the Care of Infants in Groups.* New York: Media Projects.

Tryon, C., and J. Lilienthal. (1950) "Development Tasks: I. The Concept and Its Importance," in *Fostering Mental Health in Our Schools.* Washington, D.C.: Association of Supervision and Curriculum Development, National Education Association.

Tulving, E. (1972) "Episodic and Semantic Memory," in E. Tulving and W. Donaldson (eds.), *Organization and Memory.* New York: Academic Press.

Turiel, E. (1980) "The Development of Social-Conventional and Moral Concepts," in M. Windmiller, N. Lambert, and E. Turiel (eds.), *Moral Development and Socialization.* Boston: Allyn & Bacon, pp. 69–106.

Tuttman, S. (1988) "Psychoanalytic Concepts of 'the Self.' " *Journal of the American Academy of Psychoanalysis,* Vol. 16, No. 2, pp. 209–219.

Tyler, L. (1986) "Meaning and Schooling." *Theory into Practice,* Vol. 25, No. 1, pp. 53–57.

Uttal, W. R. (1981) *A Taxonomy of Visual Processes.* Hillsdale, N.J.: Erlbaum.

Valsiner, J. (1987). *Culture and the Development of Children's Action.* Chicester, England: Wiley.

Valsiner, J. (ed.). (1988a) *Child Development within Culturally Structured Environments.* Vols. 1 & 2. Norwood, N.J.: Ablex.

Valsiner, J. (1988b) *Developmental Psychology in the Soviet Union.* Bloomington: Indiana University Press.

van der Veer, R., and J. Valsiner. (eds.). (1994) *The Vygotsky Reader.* Cambridge, Mass.: Blackwell.

van Vliet, W. (1985) "The Role of Housing Type, Household Density, and Neighborhood Density in Peer Interaction and Social Adjustment," in J. F. Wohlwill and W. van Vliet (eds.), *Habitats for Children.* Hillsdale, N.J.: Erlbaum, pp. 165–200.

Vawkey, T., and A. Pellegrini. (1984) *Child's Play: Developmental and Applied.* Hillsdale, N.J.: Erlbaum.

Vonéche, J. J. (1985) "Genetic Epistemology: Piaget's Theory," in T. Husén and T. N. Postelthwaite (eds.), *International Encyclopedia of Education.* Vol. 4. Oxford, England: Pergamon Press, pp. 1997–2007.

Vurpillot, E. (1976) "Development of Identification of Objects," in V. Hamilton and M. D. Vernon (eds.), *The Development of Cognitive Processes.* New York: Academic Press.

Vygotsky, L. S. (1962) *Thought and Language.* Cambridge, Mass.: M.I.T. Press.

Vygotsky, L. S. (1963) "Learning and Mental Development at School Age," in B. Simon and J. Simon (eds.), *Educational Psychology in the USSR.* London: Routledge & Kegan Paul, pp. 21–34.

Vygotsky, L. S. (1971) *Psychology of Art.* Cambridge, Mass.: M.I.T. Press.

Vygotsky, L. S. (1978) in M. Cole, V. John-Steiner, S. Scribner, and E. Souberman (eds.), *Mind in Society.* Cambridge, Mass.: Harvard University Press.

Wadsworth, B. J. (1971) *Piaget's Theory of Cognitive Development.* New York: David McKay.

Waley, A. (1938) *The Analects of Confucius.* New York: Knopf.

Watson, J. B. (1913) "Psychology as a Behaviorist Views It." *Psychological Review,* Vol. 20, No. 2, pp. 158–177.

Weiner, B. (1974) *Achievement Motivation and Attribution Theory.* Morristown, N.J.: General Learning Press.

Weiner, B. (1980) "Dedication to Professor Heider," in D. Gorlitz (ed.), *Perspectives on Attribution Research and Theory.* Cambridge, Mass.: Ballinger.

Werner, H. (1961) *Comparative Psychology of Mental Development.* New York: Science Editions.

Wertsch, J. V. (1985) *Vygotsky and the Social Formation of Mind.* Cambridge, Mass.: Harvard University Press.

Westcott, W. L. (1987) *Strength Fitness: Physiological Principles and Training Techniques.* Boston: Allyn & Bacon.

White, B. L. (1971) *Human Infants: Experience and Psychological Development.* Englewood Cliffs, N.J.: Prentice-Hall.

Whyte, L. L. (1960) *The Unconscious before Freud.* New York: Basic Books.

Wilson, E. O. (1975) *Sociobiology: The New Synthesis.* Cambridge, Mass.: Harvard University Press.

Wilson, E. O. (1978) *On Human Nature.* Cambridge, Mass.: Harvard University Press.

Winitz, H. (1969) *Articulation Acquisition and Behavior.* New York: Appleton-Century-Crofts.

Wohlwill, J. F. (1976) "The Age Variable in Psychological Research," in N. W. Endler, L. R. Boulter, and H. Osser (eds.), *Contemporary Issues in Developmental Psychology.* New York: Holt, Rinehart & Winston.

Wohlwill, J. F., and W. van Vliet. (1985) *Habitats for Children.* Hillsdale, N.J.: Erlbaum.

Woodworth, R. S. (1929) *Psychology.* New York: Holt, Rinehart & Winston.

Worchel, S., and J. Cooper. (1979) *Understanding Social Psychology.* Homewood, Ill.: Dorsey Press.

Wozniak, R. H., and K. W. Fischer. (1993) "Development in Context: An Introduction," in Wozniak, R. H., and K. W. Fischer (eds.), *Development in Context: Acting and Thinking in Specific Environments.* Hillsdale, N.J.: Erlbaum.

Wright, C. (1988) "Home School Research: Critique and Suggestions for the Future." *Educational and Urban Society,* Vol. 21, No. 1, pp. 96–113.

Wuthnow, R. (1978) "Peak Experiences: Some Empirical Tests." *Journal of Humanistic Psychology,* Vol. 18, No. 3, pp. 57–75.

Zigler, E. (1963) "Metatheoretical Issues in Development Psychology," in M. H. Marx (ed.), *Theories in Contemporary Psychology.* New York: Macmillan.

Zimmerman, B. J. (1983) "Social Learning: A Contextualist Account of Cognitive Functioning," in C. J. Brainerd (ed.), *Recent Advances in Cognitive-Developmental Theory.* New York: Springer-Verlag, pp. 1–50.

Name Index

This index contains two types of names: (1) those of people whose specific publications are cited in the text and (2) those of people whose ideas are cited but whose specific publications are not.

Ackerman, S., 425–426, 432
Adler, A., 43–44, 166, 210
Agur, A. M. R., 437
Akers, R. L., 208
Alexander, R. D., 400
Allen, M., 344, 347, 366
Allport, G. W., 342–343
Alpert, R., 129
Alston, W. P., 473, 475
Ames, L. B., 42, 55–56, 71
Amsel, A., 194
Anastasi, A., 31, 33, 35–36
Anaximenes, 430
Anderson, J. R., 315, 320
Anderson, L. W., 190
Anthony, E. J., 134
Apostel, L., 234
Appenzeller, T., 190
Archard, D., 160
Aristotle, 49, 430, 485
Ashcraft, M. H., 325–329, 338, 341
Azimov, I., 432, 437
Azuma, H., 72, 84

Baer, D. M., 167, 171, 184–185, 195, 447
Baldwin, A. L., 51, 89–91
Baldwin, J. D., 208
Baldwin, J. I., 208
Baldwin, J. M., 219, 253, 297, 446, 458, 497
Baltimore, D., 437
Bandura, A., 5, 8–9, 22–23, 69, 151, 196–209, 212, 219, 447, 458

Barker, R. G., 23, 196, 295, 375, 380–381, 393, 452
Batson, C. D., 208
Battro, A. M., 257, 267, 269
Baum, A., 381
Beck, L., 70
Bee, H. L., 48
Begley, S., 433
Bell, P. A., 381
Bell, R. W., 403
Berg, P., 422, 426, 437
Bernard, H. W., 58
Berne, E., 349
Bernsen, N., 329
Biggs, J. B., 259
Bijou, S. W., 167, 171, 184–187, 191, 195, 447
Binet, A., 274, 402
Bisanz, J., 314–315, 318, 321
Bjork, D. W., 194
Block, F., 191
Block, J. H., 190
Bloom, F. E., 429
Blurton Jones, N. G., 410
Bolus, R., 361
Boring, E. G., 155–156
Bower, G. H., 174–175, 197–198, 265
Bowie, M., 134
Bowlby, J., 394, 398–399, 410, 452
Brainerd, C. J., 264, 266–267
Bretherton, I., 398
Broadbent, D. E., 315
Bronfenbrenner, U., 71, 375, 379, 382–393, 452, 457–458, 498

Brook, D. W., 208
Brook, J. S., 208
Broughton, J. M., 48
Brown, A. L., 224, 338, 477, 488
Brown, G. I., 356, 359
Brubaker, D. L., 355
Bruner, J. S., 266, 281, 297, 308
Buckley, K. W., 194
Buddha, 56
Buhler, C., 344–345, 347–348, 350–351, 366, 450
Burke, J. P., 211
Burks, B. S., 32
Bush, P. J., 208
Buss, A. R., 357

Cahan, E. D., 445
Cairns, R. B., 446–447
Campbell, S. F., 269
Canfield, R. L., 296, 309
Captain, P. A., 47
Carter, O. B., 152
Carton, A. S., 293
Carus, F. A., 53–54
Case, R., 71, 264, 266, 296–302, 308, 449, 493, 497
Catania, A. C., 169, 190
Chaplin, W. F., 190
Charcot, J., 104
Chi, M. T. H., 338
Cirillo, W., 26
Chomsky, N., 192–193
Christiaansen, R. E., 321
Clayman, C. B., 11, 423, 426–427
Cochran, J. K., 208
Cocking, R. R., 269
Colby, A. L., 469, 476
Cole, J. E., 152
Cole, M., 48, 294
Cole, S. R., 48
Coles, R., 153
Columbus, C., 49
Combs, A. W., 342–344, 354
Confucious, 56, 485
Conger, J. J., 48
Connolly, K. J., 410
Cooper, J., 89
Copernicus, N., 103
Craik, F. I. M., 322
Crawford, H. J., 433, 437

Crews, F., 135
Crick, F., 427
Cronan-Hillix, H. A., 27

Dalton, J., 432
Damon, W., 48, 361–363, 366
Dangelo, D. A., 58
Darnell, J., 437
Darwin, C., 54, 69, 103, 179, 264, 372, 376, 394–396, 410
Dason, P. R., 266–267
Davidov, V. V., 288–289
Davis, K. E., 74
DeLoache, J. S., 338
Dembo, T., 23, 295
Democritus, 432
de Vries, H. M., 208
Dewey, J., 458, 472
DiBlasio, F. A., 208
Dijkstra, M., 208
Distler, W., 70
Diver-Stamnes, A. C., 64, 477, 482, 496
Dollard, J., 28, 129, 439, 446
Dooling, D. J., 321
Dreikurs, R. R., 156, 210
Drum, P. A., 164
Dunstan, J. I., 42
Durkin, D., 90
Dusek, J., 152

Edwards, J., 162, 367
Eibl-Eibesfeldt, I., 375–376, 403–404, 407, 410–411, 452
Eisen, M., 361
Elkind, D., 260–261, 263, 364
Elkington, J., 70
Elkonin, D. G., 71, 370
Ellenberger, H., 158
Elley, W. B., 67, 69
Elliott, S. N., 207
Emde, R., 130
Emerson, R. W., 162
Empedocles, 430
Engells, F., 272
Erikson, E. H., 40, 46, 71, 103–104, 136–153, 296, 370, 372, 443–445, 497–498

Fantini, M., 359
Farnham-Diggory, S., 333
Fielding, G. D., 472–473

Fischer, K. W., 296, 302–306, 308–309, 452, 493
Fisher, C. B., 48
Fisher, J. D., 381
Fisher, S., 135
Flavell, J. H., 335, 341
Flexner, S. B., 155
Flora, J. A., 207
Fodor, J. A., 164
Forbes, M., 191
Franz, C. E., 152, 444
Freeman, D., 388
Frenkel-Brunswik, E., 129
Freud, A., 103, 106, 126–128, 135, 443
Freud, S., 5, 7–8, 21–23, 25, 29–30, 39–44, 46, 65–67, 69, 74, 103–135, 151, 157– 162, 165, 178, 205, 210, 224, 264, 274, 296, 375, 439, 443–444, 497–498
Froebel, F. W. A., 53
Fromm, E., 443
Fry, D. P., 208
Fuller, R. C., 158, 162
Furth, H. G., 262–263, 267

Galahad, S., 490
Galen, C., 418
Gandhi, M., 151
Gardner, A., 65, 78, 90
Gautama Siddhartha, 56
Gell-Mann, M., 432
Gelman, R., 296
Gesell, A., 17, 30, 39–41, 43, 45, 54–56, 59, 66–67, 71, 96, 296, 369, 372, 439– 441, 497
Gibbs, J., 469, 476
Gilbert, S. E., 437
Gilligan, C, 460, 478, 494
Giorgi, A., 450–451
Goodman, P., 343
Gray, M. M., 151, 445
Green, M., 26
Greenfield, P. M., 267
Greiner, C. H., 433, 437
Gresham, F. M., 207
Guilford, J. P., 65
Gump, P. V., 381

Hagen, J. W., 335, 338
Hagenhoff, C., 207
Hakutra, K., 72, 84

Halford, G. S., 308
Hall, C. S., 13, 43, 134
Hall, G. S., 54, 443
Hamachek, D. E., 152, 445
Hamberger, L., 70
Hamilton, W. D., 400
Hare, H., 400–401
Harnad, S., 169
Harris, C. H., 90
Harris, M. L., 90
Hart, D., 361–363, 366
Hartman, D., 71, 292
Hartmann, H., 103
Hartshorne, H., 462
Hattie, J., 361, 363–366
Hauck, L. C., 155
Hausfater, G., 403
Havighurst, R. J., 15, 19, 30–31, 40, 57–58, 72, 96, 296, 369, 442, 497
Hawkins, J. D., 207
Hebb, D. O., 36
Hefferline, R. F., 343
Hegel, G. W. F., 56, 212–213
Heider, F., 49–52, 73–93, 221, 380
Heraclitus, 430
Hersh, P. H., 472–473
Hetherington, E. M., 48
Hilgard, E. R., 129, 131, 174–175, 197–198, 265, 439, 481
Hillel, 485
Hillner, K. P., 226, 311
Hinde, R. A., 394–397, 399, 403, 405, 410– 412, 452
Hirsch, J., 36
Hitler, A., 152
Hogan, J. D., 151
Holt, R. F., 129, 135
Holmes, S., 433
Holzman, L., 293
Hook, S., 134
Hooper, F. H., 267
Horney, K., 443
Horton, D. L., 322, 332
Hrdy, S. B., 403
Hull, C., 210, 439, 445
Hurlock, E. G., 58

Iannotti, R. J., 208
Ilg, F. L., 42, 55–56
Inhelder, B., 235, 241, 246, 261

Ispa, J. M., 151, 445
Ittyjerah, M., 58

Jahoda, G., 48
Jahoda, M., 137
James, W., 162, 322, 361–362
Jenet, P., 275
Jensen, A. R., 36
Jersild, A., 361
Jesus, 56, 485
Joan of Arc, 490
Johannsen, W., 426
Jonckheere, A., 237
Jones, E. E., 73–74
Jongeward, R. H., 335, 338
Jung, C. G., 25, 158–158, 161, 166

Kagan, J., 48
Kail, R., 78, 314–315, 318, 321, 335, 338
Kant, I., 458
Kantor, J. R., 178, 184
Karp, L. E., 428
Kaufman, L., 336
Kazdin, A. E., 190
Keesling, J. W., 361
Keller, F. S., 175–176, 190
Kelley, E. C., 343, 354
Kelley, H. H., 72, 74
Kelly, M. E., 40
Kennell, J. H., 398
Kessen, W., 445
Kevles, D. J., 428
Kihlstrom, J. F., 157, 163–164
King, M. L., 467, 490
Kindermann, T. A., 59
Kirchler, E., 58
Kirsch, M. M., 93
Klahr, D., 296–297, 308, 315, 324, 341
Klatzky, R. L., 317, 321
Klaus, M. H., 398
Klein, D. B., 158–160, 165
Kleinginna, A. M., 190
Kleinginna, P. R., 190
Knapp, T. J., 151
Koffka, K., 73, 380
Kohlberg, L., 30, 40, 43, 457–459, 461–478, 494–496, 499
Köhler, W., 275
Kolominsky, Y. L., 208
Kozulin, A., 293

Kreppner, K., 48
Kris, E., 129
Krohn, M. D., 208
Kuhlman, P., 208
Kuhn, T. S., 12–13

Lamal, P. A., 445–446
Lao-tzu, 56
Laurendreau, M., 262
Layzer, D., 36
Lazerson, A., 429
Leahy, A. M., 32
Lee, V. L., 52, 169, 187–188
Leff, H. L., 359
Lenhoff, H. M., 70
Lenin, V. I., 289
Lerner, D., 367–368
Lerner, R. M., 27, 48, 186, 196, 447, 452
Levin, I., 297, 309
Levine, C., 152
Levinson, P. J., 267
Levy, G., 152
Lewin, K., 23–24, 73, 210, 219, 295, 372, 375, 380, 446, 452, 458
Lewis, I. M., 343
Lieberman, M., 469, 476
Lilienthal, J., 58, 60–63, 442
Lin, H. Y., 72
Lincoln, A., 320, 467, 490
Lindzey, G., 13, 43
Locke, J., 31, 56
Lockhart, R. S., 322
Loftus, E. F., 321
Logan, C. R., 59
Logan, R. D., 152, 444
Logue, A. W., 168–169
Lorenz, K. Z., 394, 399, 410
Losish, H., 437
Love, S. Q., 208, 211
Luben, G. I., 267
Lundin, R. W., 27
Luria, A. R., 270–271, 287, 289, 292, 294, 449
Luther, M., 152

Maccoby, E., 459, 478
Mackworth, J. F., 332
Magary, K. F., 267
Mahoney, M. J., 194

Mahrer, A. R., 345–347, 349, 350–351, 355, 366
Maier, H. W., 27
Malinowski, B., 70
Mandelbrot, B., 234, 237
Martindale, C., 190
Marx, K., 56, 213, 271–273, 289, 292–293
Marx, M. H., 27
Maslow, A. H., 42–44, 46, 71, 344–355, 357–360, 366, 370, 450, 458
Massarik, F., 348, 350–351
May, K. M., 59
May, M. A., 462
May, R., 342–343
McDougall, W., 168
McGinnis, L., 399
Mead, G. H., 81
Mead, M., 388
Meltsas, M. H., 208
Mendel, G., 426
Merrill, M., 65
Meyer, M., 177
Miller, G. A., 318
Miller, J. P., 472–473
Miller, L., 189
Miller, N. E., 28, 129, 439, 446
Miller, P. H., 27, 257
Mishkin, M., 190
Modgil, C., 194
Modgil, S., 194
Moll, L. C., 289, 293
Montegue, A., 33
Montemayor, R., 361
Moore, J., 189
Moore, S. M., 151–152
Morgan, L., 20, 91
Moses, 56
Mounoud, P., 223, 306–308
Mueller-Schwarze, D., 403
Muhammad, 56
Muller, P., 58
Munro, D. J., 84
Murray, H. A., 450
Mussen, P. H., 48
Muzika, E. G., 360

Nagel, E., 131–132, 165, 371
Nagel, T., 130
Naus, M. J., 335
Neisser, U., 325, 449

Newman, F., 293
Newell, A., 315, 449

Obeid, R. A., 72, 292
Occam, W., 20
Ochse, R., 152, 445
Ornstein, P. A., 335
Ouspensky, P. D., 348–349
Overton, W. F., 12

Palmonari, A., 58
Paniagua, F. A., 190
Paris, S. G., 335
Parke, R. D., 48
Pascual-Leone, J., 266, 297, 308
Pavlov, I. P., 171–172, 409
Peel, E. A., 261
Pellegrino, J. W., 78
Pepper, S. C., 12
Perls, F. S., 343
Petermann, F., 208
Peters, R. S., 475
Phillips, D. C., 40
Phillips, J. L., 260, 262, 269
Piaget, J., 5–7, 19, 23–24, 30, 38–41, 44, 59, 65–68, 71, 151, 157, 178, 186, 214, 219, 225, 229–269, 274, 290, 294, 296–297, 302, 306–308, 324, 359, 369, 372, 375, 402, 439, 446, 447–448, 457–459, 463, 466–467, 471, 477–478, 492, 494, 497
Pickar, D. B., 151
Pinard, A., 262
Plato, 56, 485
Plug, C., 152, 445
Pombeni, M. L., 58
Posner, M. I., 341
Poulsen, M. K., 267
Power, C., 473
Pressley, M., 338
Price, F. W., 422
Pylyshyn, Z. W., 314

Quételet, L. A., 54

Rau, L., 129
Reese, H. W., 12
Reeves, C., 342
Reyna, V. F., 335–336
Rieber, R. W., 293

Riegel, K. F., 196, 212–215, 219, 266, 452, 498
Rifkin, J., 428
Roback, A. A., 156, 168
Rogers, C. F., 343, 353, 450
Rose, M., 151, 445
Rose, S. R., 208
Rosenthal, D. A., 151–152
Ross, R. P., 381
Rothenberg, M. B., 446
Rotter, J. B., 196, 210–212, 219, 446
Rousseau, J. J., 17, 31, 42, 53
Russell, B., 367

Salkind, N. J., 27
Samarapungavan, A., 58
Sandor, D., 151
Savin-Williams, R. C., 403
Schnaitier, R., 189
Schneider, W., 338
Schneirla, T. C., 37
Schoenfeld, W. N., 175–176
Schoggen, P., 382, 393
Scholnick, E. K., 266
Scriven, M., 131
Sears, R. R., 129, 446
Seppala, M., 70
Shapiro, L., 427
Shavelson, R. J., 361
Shaver, K. G., 74, 78, 81, 93
Shaw, J. C., 449
Sherif, M., 403
Sherman, J. G., 190
Sherman, P. W., 190, 400
Shuttleworth, F. K., 32
Sidman, M., 188
Siegal, M., 459
Siegler, R. S., 300
Sigel, I. E., 267, 269
Simon, H. A., 315, 449
Singer, M., 422, 426, 437
Skeels, H. M., 32
Skinner, B. F., 12, 27, 30, 38–39, 44, 46, 69, 151, 167–184, 189, 191–197, 200, 203, 208, 221, 302, 355, 369, 445, 458
Skodak, M., 33
Smith, M. B., 450
Smith, P. K., 410
Smotherman, W. P., 403
Snygg, D., 342–344

Sober, E., 189
Socrates, 467
Spinoza, B., 367
Spitz, R. A., 399
Spock, B., 446
Stafford-Clark, D., 134
Stemmer, N., 189
Stephansy, P. E., 135
Sternberg, S., 318
Stevenson, H. W., 72, 84
Stevick, D. B., 193
Strayer, F. F., 403
Strayer, J., 403
Strazicch, M., 228
Sullivan, H. S., 443
Suppes, P. C., 13

Tart, C. T., 360
Taylor, M. J., 151–152
Taylor, P. A., 267
Terman, L., 65
Thagard, P. R., 23
Thales, 430
Thomas, R. M., 27, 38, 64, 69, 72, 84, 161, 292, 338, 355, 458, 475, 477–496
Thomas, S. M., 69
Thorensen, C. E., 207
Thornburg, K. R., 151
Thorndike, E. L., 210
Tiedemann, D., 53, 394
Tinbergen, N., 394
Titchener, E. B., 156
Tolman, E. C., 210, 439
Tomlinson, S., 64
Travers, J. F., 58
Trivers, R. L., 400–401
Tronick, E., 267
Tryon, C., 58, 60–63, 442
Tulving, E., 319, 482
Turi, C. D., 151
Turiel, E., 459
Turnage, T. W., 322, 332
Tuttman, S., 152
Tyler, L., 151

Uttal, W. R., 315, 322

Vahey, M. A., 151
Valsiner, J., 20–21, 215–219, 266, 274–275, 293–294, 375, 452, 458, 498

van der Veer, R., 293
van Vliet, W., 382
Varnhagen, C. K., 78
Versalius, A., 418
Vonéche, J., 253
Vurpillot, E., 333
Vygotsky, L. S., 71, 217, 219, 225, 229–230,
    270–294, 369–370, 372, 439, 448–449,
    457–458, 497–498

Wachs, W., 262–263, 267
Waley, A., 485
Wallace, J. G., 296–297, 308, 315, 324, 341
Walters, R. H., 202, 206–207
Wapner, S., 26
Watson, J., 427
Watson, J. B., 71, 156, 167–168, 177–178,
    186, 189, 193–194, 445
Washington, G., 320
Weiner, B., 74, 85
Weinstein, G., 359

Weis, J. G., 207
Werner, H., 38, 295, 380
Wertsch, J. V., 293
White, K. M., 152, 445
Whiting, J. W., 446
Whyte, L. L., 157
Wilkins, M. H. F., 427
Wilson, E. O., 68, 395, 400, 403–404, 407–
    410, 481
Winitz, H., 96
Wohlwill, J. R., 382
Woodworth, R. S., 156, 168
Worchel, S., 89
Wozniak, R. H., 452
Wright, H. F., 380
Wundt, W., 156
Wuthnow, R., 350

Yudovich, R., 294

Zimmerman, B. J., 196, 212, 266, 325

SUBJECT INDEX

Abilities, 4, 32, 75, 77–79, 88, 100, 222, 329, 363
Abnormal, 45–46, 95–101, 353–354
Accommodation, 42, 236–238, 243, 256, 266, 477, 488
Activities, 288–289, 393
Adaptability, 92–93, 192, 194, 209, 238, 265, 268, 291, 293, 339–340, 357, 360, 391, 393, 409, 411, 434–435, 473–474, 494, 496
   defined, 22
Adjustment mechanisms, 133, 160. *See also* Defense mechanisms.
Affect, affection, 123, 160, 181, 186, 207, 236, 274, 302, 319, 462, 479, 484–485
Age, chronological, 19, 30, 39–40, 55, 483
Aggression, 133, 208, 407–408
AIDS, 207, 446
Alcohol, 11, 208
Allocentric stage, 259
Altruism, 189, 400–401
Ambivalence, 115
Amoral, 42
Anabolic steroids, 11
Anal-urethral period, 113, 116–117, 123, 127–128, 139, 141–142, 370
Analogy defined, 13
Animism, 70
Anthropology, 46
Anticathexis, 116
Antithesis, 212–213
Anxiety, 107, 128, 182
   free-floating, 22, 124
Applications, practical. *See* Child-rearing applications.
Apprehension span, 333

Assimilation, 42, 236–238, 243, 256, 266, 477, 488
Associations, 110, 222–223, 335, 337
Assumptions, 18, 29, 46, 88
   defined, 14–15
Atomic level, 413, 429–432, 434, 453
Attachment theory, 398–399
Attention, attention span, 155, 158, 199, 295, 321–322, 325, 333
Attitudes, 78, 99–100, 160
Attribution theory, 51–52, 73–93, 440, 442–443
Authority, 21
Autonomous morality, 6, 59, 464–465
Autonomy, 139, 141–142, 153, 353
Axiom defined, 14–15

Behavior
   complex, 202–203
   management, 187
   modification, 187, 191, 203–204, 207
   moral, 118, 207
   observed, 462
   settings, 381, 383, 387
Behavior-constraint model, 382
Behavioral engineering, 181, 183
Behaviorism, 22, 26, 38–39, 44, 46, 69, 71, 156, 166–196, 208, 210, 223, 225–226, 344, 358–360, 440, 442, 445–446, 458, 477, 496
Bifocal coordination, 298–300
Bio-electrochemical perspective, 5, 9–11, 23, 360, 413–437, 440, 453–454, 498–499
Birth, 165, 182, 241
Birth trauma, 114
Biting stage, 115

Bonding, 397–398
Brain, 10, 70, 424–245
  cells, 10, 425
Bronchitis, 420
Buddhist theory, 70, 360, 450

Cancer, 423
Cathexis, 114, 116, 119
Causal relations, 4–5, 479, 485–487
Cause, causality, causation, 4–5, 10, 31–
  38, 74–83, 90, 188, 204–206, 222, 238–
  240, 250–251, 312, 365, 367–375
  final, ultimate, 371–372
Cellular level, 413, 422–426, 434, 453
Centration, 65
Chaining, 47, 176–177, 295
Character traits, 77
Chemical elements, 429–432, 434
Child-rearing applications, 19, 87–91, 130–
  131, 166, 191–192, 208–209, 218, 265,
  267–268, 289–292, 337–338, 339, 354–
  358, 390–392, 435–436, 471–474, 494–
  496
Christian theory, 37, 42, 47, 70–72, 86,
  193, 376, 409–411, 450
Chunk, 318, 324, 333
Circular reactions, 242–243
Circulatory system, 419
Clarity criterion, 18, 88–89, 130–131, 191–
  192, 208–209, 265–267, 291, 338–339,
  357–358, 390–392, 409–410, 434–435,
  474–475, 493–494
Classification
  abilities, 235
  schemes, 4–5, 59, 64–65
Clinical method, 231–233, 274, 448
Coding, 199–200, 295, 321
Cognitive psychology, cognitivism, 166,
  190–191, 197, 449, 496
Collective monologue, 246
Color-blindness, 418, 424
Common sense, 37, 49–93, 221, 233, 371,
  381, 416–417, 440, 442–443, 497
Compensation, 113, 246
Complexes, thinking in, 284–285
Comprehensiveness criterion, 89, 93, 130–
  131, 192–193, 208–209, 265, 268, 291,
  293, 339–340, 357, 360, 391–393, 409,
  411, 435–436, 474, 476, 494, 496
  defined, 23–24

Compulsion, 197
Computers, 311, 313, 324–325, 329–331,
  419
Concepts, 285–286, 319, 333, 479, 482
Conceptually driven, 325–328
Conceptuomotor, 307
Conditioning, 197
  classical, 159, 171–172, 197
  instrumental, 172–173
  operant, 171–173, 191, 193, 200–201,
  207, 295, 369, 498
  respondent, 171–172
Conditions, moral, 483–484, 496
Confluent education, 356
Confucian theory, 37, 70, 72
Congeries, thinking in, 283–284
Conscience, 75, 77, 80, 111, 128, 191,
  206–207
Conscious, consciousness, 106–108,
  120–124, 133, 155–166, 318, 325,
  327–328, 343, 348, 354–355, 477–479,
  491
Consequences, role of, 173–175, 188, 200–
  202, 458, 484, 487, 498
Conservation, 5, 235, 247, 249, 266, 304
Consilience criterion, 13
Contextualism, 47, 167–168, 196–219, 223,
  225, 325–326, 372
Contingencies, 188–189
Continuity-discontinuity issue, 38–39, 42
Control, experimental, 222–223
Conventional morality, 464–465
Conversion hysteria, 65, 106–107
Countercathexis, 116
Creativity, 193, 199
Crises, psychosocial, 138–144, 370
Critical periods, 399–400
Cross-sectional research, 227
Cultural-historical theory, 215–219, 273,
  287–288, 458
Cultural
  conceptions, 53–72
  influences, 40, 57, 148, 150, 287–288,
  365, 449, 468
  milieu, 30–31, 50, 65–66, 125, 381, 387,
  481
  relativism, 459
  values, 481–482
Culture, folk, 416–417
Curriculum sequencing, 259–260

Cybernetic, 325, 329
Cystic fibrosis, 3, 11

Darwinism. *See* Neo-Darwinism.
Data-driven, 325, 327–328
Death, 71
   instinct, 8, 108, 133
Décalage, 255–256, 266, 301, 492–493
Decentration, 246, 248
Defense mechanisms, 111–113, 119, 497
Descriptions, self, 363
Descriptive studies, 46, 53–56, 100–101,
   312, 373, 440–441
Determinism, 90–91
Development
   abnormal, 29, 45–46, 353–354
   cognitive (mental), 5–7, 18, 23, 30, 32–
      35, 38, 71, 239–240, 252, 466–467, 499
   continuous, 28, 38
   defined, 38
   direction of, 18
   desirable, 29, 45–46, 52, 95–101, 353–
      354, 415
   emotional, 18, 23, 30, 34–35, 55
   healthy, 352–354
   language, 39, 229–294
   moral, ethical, 29–30, 42, 55, 118, 457–
      496, 499
   natural, 45–46, 52, 95–101
   normal, 29, 40, 45–46, 52, 95–101, 127,
      353–354
   physical, 10–11, 18, 23, 30, 33, 38–39
   processes, 479, 486–488
   psychological, 259
   psychosexual, 7, 69, 106, 108
   psychosocial, 136–153, 259
   recognitive, 364–365
   sexual, 39, 43, 55
   social, 18, 23, 30, 38–39
   speech, 281–282
   spontaneous, 259
   stepwise, 38
   typical, 56
   unhealthy, 45–46, 95–101
Developmental tasks, 15, 19, 31, 44, 57–
   63, 72, 96, 100, 440–442, 497
Deviance, 203–206
Dialectical theory, 212–215, 266, 272, 498
Dimensional stage, 297–299, 301
Disconfirmability. *See* falsifiability.

Discrepancy resolution, 25
Dispositions, emotional, 75, 77, 80–81
Distantiation, 144
DNA (deoxyribonucleic acid), 10, 423,
   426–429, 434–435, 454
Domains of functioning, 301
Dominance, 402–404
Double-stimulation method, 275–277
Doubt, 140–142
Dramatic element, 148–150
Dreams, 7, 46, 55, 107, 113, 122, 131, 134,
   162, 224–225
Drives, 8, 43, 126, 160, 165, 178, 347, 481–
   482
Drugs, 208
Durability criterion, 89, 93, 130, 133, 192,
   194, 209–210, 265, 268, 291–293, 339–
   340, 357, 360, 391, 393, 409, 411,
   434–435, 474, 494, 496
   defined, 25

Ecological
   psychology, 71, 209, 223, 225, 295, 375–
      393, 440, 452–453, 477, 496, 498
   transition, 387
   validity, 388, 449
Economy criterion, 89, 91, 130, 133, 192,
   208–209, 218, 265–266, 291–292, 339–
   340, 357, 359, 391–392, 434–435, 473–
   474, 494–495
Educational implications, 258–264, 289–
   290, 337–338, 354–356, 471–473
Effectance-promoting objects, 355
Effort, 85
Ego, 42, 46, 108, 110–112, 116, 119,
   120–124, 126, 128, 132, 152, 166–167,
   191
   ideal, 111
   identity, 136–137, 140
   strength, 106, 120, 124–126
Egocentrism, 65, 119, 235, 252
Elaborated coordination, 298–301
Electra complex, 117–118
Elemental level, 9, 413, 429–432, 434
Emotions. *See* Affect.
Empathic attitude, 75, 77, 81
Emphysema, 420, 428
Empiricists, 325–326
Encoding, 316, 318–319, 323, 336
Endorphins, 70

Environment, 5, 35, 41, 44, 77, 79, 81–82, 99, 110, 124, 145, 163–165, 167–168, 178–180, 186, 196, 222, 236, 287, 305–306, 313, 316, 323, 327, 332, 334, 342, 369, 375–393, 435, 447, 477–480, 487–491, 498
  constructed, 489–490
  fabricators, 488–489
  forms, 489–490
  impact factors, 490–491
  real-life, 489. *See also* Nature-nurture issue.
Environmental coercion, 75, 77, 82
Environmental psychology. *See* Ecological theory.
Environmentalists, 31–32, 36, 180–181
Epigenetic principle, 47, 136–138, 145, 167, 372
Equilibration, equilibrium, 42, 238, 240, 255–258, 266–267, 471
Erogenous zones, 113, 116
Eros, 43
Escape, 113
Ethical principles, 465
Ethology, ethological theory, 223, 225, 295, 372, 440, 453, 498
Events, 319
  moral-related, 479, 481
Evidence, 21, 89, 92, 130–132, 192–193, 209, 265–266, 291, 293, 339–340, 357, 360, 391, 393, 409, 411, 434–435, 473–474, 494, 496
  defined, 16
Evolution, 69. *See also* Darwinism.
Exercise, 10, 78
Existentialism, 344, 436
Exosystem, 384, 386–389
Experience, 238–240, 345
Experiential psychotherapy, 346
Experimental evidence, 26, 47
Explanation, 4–5, 373
Expulsion stage, 116
Extinction, 174

Fabricators of environments, 479, 488–489
Facts, 1, 3–4, 17, 69, 85, 327, 458
Faculty psychology, 274
Falsifiability, 89, 92, 132–133, 192, 208–209, 265, 268, 291–292, 339–340, 357–359, 391–392, 409–410, 434–435, 474–475, 494–496
  defined, 20–21
Fear, 55, 81
Feasibility criterion, 222, 227–228
Feelings. *See* Affect.
Fertility criterion, 89, 93, 129–130, 192, 208–209, 265–266, 291–292, 339–340, 357, 359–360, 391–392, 409, 411, 434–435, 473–474, 494–496
  defined, 24–25
Field theory, 210, 380
Fixation, 41–42, 115–116, 119, 126
Free association, 107, 127, 134, 224
Free will, 90–92
Freudian theory, 7–8, 22, 46–47, 103–135, 165–166, 204–205, 225, 227, 359–360, 370, 440, 443–444, 458, 477, 496–497
Functional invariants, 238, 247, 256–257
Functional relationships, 235, 368
Functionalists, 295
Functions, 286, 331
Fuzzy-trace theory, 335–336

Gang age, 118
Gay community, 9–10
Gastrointestinal system, 419
Gene pool, 402
Generational sanction, 149–150
Generativity, 139, 144
Genes, 10, 11, 147, 426–428
Genetic
  causes, 179
  clock, 180
  code, 428
  counseling, 427
  endowment, 11, 34–35, 41, 180, 209, 222, 408, 478–480
  engineering, 11, 427–428
  epistemology, 231, 253–254
  explanation, 371
  plan, 10, 97, 375–377, 395–396
  relatedness, 400–401
  structure, 498
Genetics, influence of, 31, *See also* Heredity; Nature-nurture issue.
Genital periods, 113–114, 117–119, 127, 139, 370
Gestalt psychology, 73, 273, 393
Goals, 163, 210–211, 319, 479, 481–482

Gradualism, 9
Growth, 353–354
  defined, 38
  directions, 352
  gradients, 47, 54–56, 96
Guilt, 124, 139, 142, 150, 348, 462

Habit, 175, 177, 190, 475
Hereditarians, 32, 36, 180
Heredity, 5, 35, 79, 145, 209, 238–239, 369.
  See also Nature-nurture issue.
Heteronomous morality, 6, 59
Heterosexuality, 10, 119, 208
Hindu theory, 37, 70, 72, 360, 450
Historical significance, 25
Holistic psychology, 380
Homosexuality, 6, 10, 118, 208
Hope, development of, 144–145
Human nature, 376
Humanistic theory, 21, 26, 46, 71, 92, 157,
  162, 166, 186, 221, 225–226, 311–312,
  342–360, 372, 436, 440, 450–452, 498
Hypnosis, 105, 107
Hypothesis, 20, 57, 106
  defined, 15–16

Id, 42, 46–47, 108–111, 114, 120–124, 132
Identification, 8, 118, 362
Identity, 139, 143, 343, 361
  crisis, 136, 139, 143–144
  diffusion, 139, 143–144
Imaging, visual, 222–223
Imitation, 8, 197
Imprinting, 594
Individual differences, 29, 45, 69–69, 329
Individual psychology, 210
Industry, 142–143
Infantile amnesia, 118
Infantile sexuality, 103, 113, 117–118, 127
Inference, strong, 410
Inferiority, 85, 139, 142–143
Information-overload model, 381
Information-processing theory, 71, 157,
  163–165, 168, 225–226, 295, 311–341,
  449–450, 477, 480, 497
  classical, 314–324, 325–326
  modified, 324–331
Intuition, 359–360
Innate characteristics, 31, 163
Instigative characteristics, 385–386

Instinct, 8, 108, 122, 126, 160, 165
Integrated theory, 458, 477–496, 499
Integrity, 139, 144
Intelligence, 65, 77–78, 90, 165, 234, 252,
  401
  artificial, 324, 329
  practical, 245
  reflective, 263
  social, 401
  tests, 401–402, 445. *See also* Develop-
    ment, cognitive.
Intention, 75–77, 79–80, 483–484
Interactionists, 33–36
Interactive distance, 355
Internal consistency, 88–89, 130, 133, 192,
  208–209, 218, 265–266, 291–292, 339–
  340, 357, 359, 391–392, 409–410, 434–
  435, 473–474, 494–495
  defined, 19
Internalization of action, 235, 249
Interpersonal relations, 383
Intervening variables, 42, 168
Intervention, 97
  supernatural, 37–38
Intimacy, 144
Introspection, 26, 46, 99, 168, 225, 274,
  313, 358, 434
Investigative methods. *See* Research
  methods.
Islamic theory, 37, 70–72, 376, 450

Jain theory, 70
Judaic theory, 37, 70–71, 376
Judgment, moral, 118, 461–476
Just community, 472–473
Justice, 459, 461–462, 464, 468–469, 475,
  478

Knowledge, 233–235
  base, 317
  declarative, 163, 302
  episodic, 163
  nature of, 233–235
  procedural, 163–164, 302, 319
  semantic, 163, 319
  system, 326
  tacit, 326–328

Language development. *See* Development,
  language, speech.

Latency period, 114, 116–119
Law, 92
  defined, 14–16
  of effect, 211
Leading activity, 288–289, 370
Learning, 29, 31, 43–45, 174–175, 190
  activity, 288–289
  connotative, 263
  disabilities, 207
  figurative, 263
  incidental, 198
  observational, 197, 199
  operative, 263
  transfer of, 186
  vicarious, 197
Libido, 43, 108, 110, 113, 115, 119, 125,
    132
Life
  instinct, 8, 108
  space, 372, 380, 452, 458
Locus of control, 211
Longitudinal research, 227
Luck, 75–76, 83

Macrosystem, 384, 387–389
Macrotheory, macromodel, 24, 57
Masculinity, 7
Mastery learning, 190
Maturation, 31, 77, 85, 97, 99, 123, 163,
    165, 209, 234, 477
Maturity, 54
Memory, 207, 234, 274, 286–287, 295, 321–
    322, 329–330, 341
  abstract, 287
  active, 234, 317
  auditory, 316–317
  episodic, 482
  haptic, 316–317, 479
  iconic, 316–317
  long-term, 42, 163–164, 314, 316, 318–
    321, 323–324, 327–329, 332, 334–336,
    477, 479–480, 487–488, 491
  natural, 286–287
  permanence, 200
  primary, 317
  semantic, 316, 318–319, 323, 327
  sensory, 316–317
  short-term, 42, 302, 314, 316–318,
    320–321, 323–324, 327, 332–334, 336,
    479

  working, 163, 314, 316–318, 327, 479–
    480, 486–487, 491–492
Menstruation, 417, 420, 424
Mental development. See Development,
    cognitive.
Mental images, 122, 199
Mentalism, 71, 177–178, 191, 197
Mesosystem, 384, 396–389
Metaanalysis, 13
Metacognition, 13, 326, 328
Metalearning, 13
Metamemory, 13
Metaperception, 13
Metaphors, 497–499
Metaprinciples, 13
Metaprocessing, 486
Metatheory, 13–14
Microtheory, micromodel, 23, 57, 457
Microsystem, 382–385, 387–390
Mind, 42, 46, 167, 313, 348–349
Minitheory, minimodel, 57, 457
Mnemonic techniques, 334–335, 337
Model defined, 12–13
Models, learning from (modeling), 8–9,
    150, 197, 200, 202, 204, 206, 295
Molecular level, 9, 413, 426–429, 434,
    453
Morality, 118
  behavior, 495
  defined, 42
  dilemmas, 463, 477, 495
  education, 471–473
  condition of child, 28, 42
  principles, 475, 482–483, 496
  processes, 486–488
  reasoning, 461–496
  development theories, 457–496.
Morgan's canon, 20, 91
Motivation, 29, 43–45, 65, 75–77, 79–80,
    183, 191, 199–201, 207, 350–351, 359
  unconscious, 128, 133
Muscle systems, 10–11, 314, 421, 424,
    428–429, 479–480
Myopia, 418, 421–422
Mysticism, 344

Naive psychology, 37, 50–52, 73–93, 281
National character, 372
Nativism, 31
Natural selection, 396

Nature-nurture issue, 28, 31–38, 179, 308, 354, 409–410, 466. *See also* Environment; Heredity.
Nature's plan, 372–373
Nearsightedness. *See* Myopia.
Needs, 43–44, 57, 98–100, 109–110, 112, 114, 122, 167, 183, 347–348, 370, 479, 481–482
  deficiency, 347
  defined, 347–348
  learned, 211
  physiological, 173
  self-actualization, 347, 357
Neobehaviorists, 168
Neo-Darwinism, 69, 264, 372, 395–396, 410, 497
Neo-Pigetian, 296, 477, 493
Neuron, 425–426
Neurotransmitter, 425, 429, 431–432
Nervous system, 10, 419, 421, 424–426, 499
Neuroses, 107, 113, 115, 120, 123, 125–126, 206
Normality, 95–101, 127, 203–206, 353
Normative studies, 54–56, 101, 312, 440–441
Norms, 54–56, 203
Novelty criterion, 23, 89, 93, 129–130, 192–194, 209, 265, 291–292, 332, 339–340, 357, 360, 391, 393, 409, 411, 434–435, 473–474
Numinous element, 148–150
Nurturance, 44
Nutrition, 33, 78, 92–93, 435, 480

Object
  permanence, 235
  relations, 245–246
Observation techniques, 26, 127, 131, 404–407
Obsession, 107
Occam's razor, 20
Oedipus complex, conflict, 117–119, 123–124, 132–133, 142, 166
Ontogeny, 376
Operational
  definitions, 65
  consolidation, 298–299
Operations
  concrete, 6, 245, 248–251, 297, 307

  defined, 245, 249–250
  formal, 6, 47, 186, 245, 249, 251–252, 297, 307
Oral period, 113–116, 123, 127–128, 139–141, 370
Organic level, 9, 413, 428–422
Originality. *See* Novelty criterion.
Ought forces, 80, 86

Paradigm, defined, 13
Parsimony, law of, 20
Participant-observers, 407
Peak experience, 350, 498
Perception, 200, 234, 274, 287–288, 321–322, 363
Perceptual recognition, 318
Perceptuomotor, 307
Permissive regime, 355
Personal power, 77–78
Personality, 113, 115, 117, 133, 150, 162, 165, 179, 222, 342, 346, 351
  healthy, 136–137, 313, 359
  primitive, 346, 351
  structure, 29, 42, 105
Phallic stage, 117
Phenomenological perceptions, 388
Phenomenology, 344, 436
Philosophical foundations, 46
Phobia, 107
Phylogeny, phylogentic adaptation, 376
Piagetian theory, 5–7, 231–269, 290, 359, 440, 447–448, 497
Pitch discrimination, 11
Play, games, 55, 129, 142, 145, 147, 150, 288
Pleasure principle, 43, 109, 160, 165
Population, 395
Postconventional morality, 464–465
Positivism, 358
Postulate defined, 14–15
Precision criterion, 224–225
Preconscious, 108, 120–124, 158, 165, 167
Preconventional morality, 464–465
Predeterminists, 31–32, 36, 41
Predicting development, 18–19, 89–90, 192, 208–209, 218–219, 265, 267, 291–292, 338–339, 356–357, 391–392, 409–410, 435, 473–474, 494–495
Preformationists, 31–32, 36

Preoperational period, 244–248, 250, 297, 307
Prescriptions, 373
Primacy, 490–491
Primary process, 109–110, 160, 165
Primitive speech stage, 281–282
Principle defined, 14–16
Privilege, 85–87
Process, 320, 479
Process-person-context model, 386
Processing
  parallel, 325, 327–328
  serial, 325, 327–328
Programmed instruction, 171, 190–191
Projection, 112, 162
Proof, defined, 16
Pseudoconcept complexes, 284–285
Pseudo-species, 148
Psychic energy, 43, 122, 160–162
Psychoanalysis. *See* Freudian theory.
Psychohistory, 152
Psychosocial theory, Erikson's, 136–150, 440, 444–445, 497–498
Puberty, pubescence, 114, 138–139, 143
Pulmonary system, 419
Punishment, 111, 174, 193, 197, 202, 204–205, 207, 209, 484–485
Purpose, development of, 144–145

Qualitative research, 224–225
Quantitative research, 66–68, 224–225
Quarks, 413, 432–434

Rationalization, 65, 113, 128
Reaction formation, 112–113, 132–133
Readiness, 165, 290, 400
Reality criterion, 17–18, 89–90, 130–132, 192–193, 208–209, 222–224, 265–266, 291, 338–339, 352, 356–357, 391–392, 408–410, 435–436, 474–475, 493–494
Reality principle, 110, 119, 252
Recency, 490–491
Receptive stage, 115
Reductionism, 186, 413, 433–434
Reference group, 205–206, 365
Regression, 41–42, 112
  infinite, 371
Rehearsal, 222–223, 334–335, 337
Reinforcement, 8–9, 173–176, 179, 190, 193, 197–198, 204–207, 211, 295, 447, 458

Reinterpretation, 22
  social-cognitive, 447
Relational stage, 298
Relationships, 319
  causal, 4–5, 319, 485–486
  structural, 4
Relativism
  cultural, 31, 459
  ethical, 469
  individualistic, 460
  social, 459
Replication studies, 25
Representations, 306, 320
Repression, 106–107, 112, 117–118, 122, 132, 160–162, 165–166
Reproducibility criterion, 225–226
Research methods, 29, 46, 186, 214, 218, 221–228, 274–277, 313, 323–324, 359, 360, 394, 404–407, 418–420, 433–434, 448–449, 463–464
Responsibility, 85–87, 99–100
Responsivity, selective, 385
Retardation, 41, 59
Rate of growth, 30
Retention stage, 117
Reversibility, 249–250
Revision, theory, 22
Reward, 8–9, 111, 173, 197, 202–203, 204, 209, 484–485. *See also* Reinforcement.
Rights, 99–100, 461, 465
Rites, ritualization, 147–150
Role
  confusion, 143
  prescription, 75, 77, 82
  taking, 467–469, 490
Roles, 390–391, 477

Salient stimulus, 490–491
Sampling, 66, 405–406
Schema, schemata, scheme, 236
Scientific
  knowledge, 52
  method, 50, 90–91, 360
  theories, 49, 49–72
Scope of theories, 28–32, 177
Secondary process, 110, 160
Self, 26, 30, 55, 77–81, 83, 100, 152, 311, 313, 342–366
  absorption, 139

Self (*continued*)
  acceptance, 353
  actualization, 44, 346, 352–353
  affirmation, 26
  awareness, 356
  concept, 36, 85, 225, 363–366
  confirmation, 365
  control, 142, 206–207, 484
  definition, 143
  disconfirmation, 365–366
  efficacy, 85, 207
  enhancement, 162
  esteem, 85, 142, 152, 347
  experiencing, 360
  fulfillment, 451
  interest, 361
  management, 186
  perception, 100
  preservation, 43
  realization, 345, 358
  reports, 46, 225, 359
  respect, 347
  transcendence, 162
  understanding, 361–363
Semioticomotor, 307
Senses, 42, 49, 163, 314–316, 327, 332, 479–480
Sensitive periods, 399–400
Sensorimotor development, 55, 241–244, 297–299, 303–304, 307, 329
Separation, mother-child, 398–399
Sexual
  behavior, 112
  drives, 103, 126, 184, 481–482
  expression, 44, 184
  roles, 208
Shame, 124, 140–142
Shaping, 176, 197, 295
Shinto theory, 37, 70, 72
Significance criterion, 226–227
Skill theory, Fischer's, 302–306
Skinner's baby box, 181–182, 191
Slips of tongue, 162
Social
  communication, 246
  controls, 31
  conventions, 459
  status, 78
  stereotypes, 26
  transmission, 238–240

Social cognitive theory, 207–210
Socialization, 82, 138, 482
Social learning theory, 8–9, 19, 44, 69, 167–168, 196–219, 225–226, 440, 446–447, 477, 496, 498
Sociobiology, 66, 372, 375–377, 394–412, 453
Sociometric charting, 405
S-O-R behaviorists, 168
Soul, 70, 167
Soviet psychology, 157, 229–230, 270–294, 440, 448–449, 497–498
Species, 395–396
  defined, 395
  reproduction, 395
Speech. *See* Development, speech.
Speech, egocentric, 245–246, 281–282
Stage theory, intra-individual, 375
Stages of development, 28, 38–42, 180, 230, 295–309, 477, 492–493
  Baer & Bijou's, 184–185
  Buhler's, 349–350
  Case's, 297–302
  developmental task, 60–63
  Erikson's, 136, 138–150
  Fischer's, 303
  Freud's, 7, 29, 106, 113–120, 126, 133, 139, 146, 204
  Kohlberg's, 464–466, 469–471
  Mahrer's, 349, 351–353
  Maslow's, 349–350
  Mounoud's, 307
  Piaget's, 6, 71, 240–257
  Skinner's, 180–184
  Vygotsky's, 71, 281–286
Stimulation, subliminal, 158
Stimulus-response (S-R), 159, 168, 172, 197
Stream of consciousness, 122
Structuralists, structuralism, 156, 180, 286, 325–326
Structure, 306, 319–320, 330
  defined, 13
Structuring proclivity, 385
Subatomic level, 413, 432–433
Sublimation, 8, 112, 119, 125
Submission, 402–404
Superego, 42, 46, 108, 110–111, 118–119, 121–124, 127, 132–133, 160, 166, 348

Supernatural intervention, 37–38, 70, 75, 77, 82–83
Survival, 66, 178–179
Symbolic functioning, 116, 161–162, 235
Symbols, 9, 234
    Freudian, 7–8, 122, 131–133
Symptom substitution, 205
Synthesis, 212–213, 285–287
System, 303
    defined, 13
System perceptual conscious, 122

Tabula rasa, 31
Task difficulty, 75, 77–79, 83, 88
Taxonomies, 4, 59, 64
Teaching machines, 171
Teaching methods, 262–264, 471–473
Teleology, 91–92, 372
Thanatos, 43
Theory defined, 3–4, 12, 17
Therapy, psychoanalytic, 120
Thesis, 212–213
Thought, 229–294
    conceptual, 283–286
    intuitive, 246–248, 359
    processes, 123, 486–488
Time boundaries, 381
Time sampling, 406
Tobacco, 45, 93, 208, 428, 430–431
Topological psychology, 380
Transactional analysis, 447

Transitivity, 251–252
Trust-mistrust, 140–141
Typologies, 4, 59, 64

Unconscious, 8, 103, 108–109, 120–124, 132–133, 155–167, 343, 348, 486
    collective, 159
    racial, 158
Understimulation theory, 381–382
Unifocal coordination, 298–299
Unitary child, 413, 415–418

Validity, 47
    developmental, 389
    ecological, 388
Vectorial stage, 298–299
Values, 100, 160, 206, 350, 365, 457–460, 478–479, 482–485
Verbal loop, 336–337
Verification studies, 25
Virtues, development of, 144–146
Vygotsky blocks, 282–283

Walden Two, 179–184, 191, 193, 355
Will, 37, 43, 144–145, 467, 469

Zone
    of free movement, 216–218
    of promoted action, 216–217
    of proximal development, 47, 217, 290

CREDITS

Chapter 3: 60: Table 3.1 adapted from "Developmental Tasks: I. The Concept and Its Importance," by C. Tryon and J. Lilienthal, in *Fostering Mental Health in Our Schools,* pp. 77–89. Reprinted with permission of the Association for Supervision and Curriculum Development. Copyright © 1950 by the Association for Supervision and Curriculum Development. All rights reserved.

Chapter 9: 232: Excerpt adapted from *The Early Growth of Logic in the Child,* by B.Inhelder and J. Piaget, p. 107. Copyright © 1964 Routledge & Kegan Paul. Used by permission of Harper & Row, Publishers, Inc. and Routledge & Kegan Paul Ltd.

Chapter 10: 298: Figure D.1 adapted from *Intellectual Development, Birth to Adulthood,* by R. Case, p. 413. Copyright © 1985 Academic Press. Reprinted by permission.

300: Figure D.2 adapted from *Intellectual Development, Birth to Adulthood,* by R. Case, p. 104. Copyright © 1958 Academic Press. Originally appeared in "Three Aspects of Cognitive Development," by R. S. Siegler, in *Cognitive Psychology,* Vol. 4, pp. 481–520 (1976). Reprinted by permission.

307: Table D.2 adapted from "Similarities between Developmental Sequences at Different Age Periods," by P. Mounoud, p. 52. In I. Levin (ed.), *Stage and Structure: Reopening the Debate,* p. 52. Copyright 1986 Ablex Publishing Corporation. Reprinted by permission.

Chapter 16: 465: Table 16.1 adapted from "Moral and Religious Education in the Public Schools: A Developmental View," by L. Kohlberg. In T. R. Sizer, *Religion and Public Education,* p. 171. Copyright © 1967 Houghton Mifflin Company. Reprinted by permission.

470: Figure 16.1 from "Continuities in Childhood and Adult Moral Development," by L. Kohlberg and R. Kramer, 1969, *Human Development, 12,* pp. 93–120. Copyright © 1969 S. Karger AG. Reprinted by permission.